3

Power, Purpose, and
Collective Choice

Power, Purpose, and Collective Choice

ECONOMIC STRATEGY IN SOCIALIST STATES

EDITED BY

ELLEN COMISSO and
LAURA D'ANDREA TYSON

Cornell University Press

ITHACA AND LONDON

This book first published 1986 by Cornell University Press.

© 1986 by the World Peace Foundation and the Massachusetts Institute of Technology.

Most of the contents of this book first appeared in volume 40, number 2, of the journal *International Organization*.

International Standard Book Number (cloth) 0-8014-1981-6
International Standard Book Number (paper) 0-8014-9435-4
Library of Congress Catalog Card Number 86-47639

Printed in the United States of America

The paper in this book is acid-free and meets the guidelines for permanence and durability of the Committee on Production Guidelines for Book Longevity of the Council on Library Resources.

Contents

4. Responding to International Economic Change outside the CMEA

Contributors

Thomas Baylis is Associate Professor of Political Science at the University of Texas, San Antonio.

Iván T. Berend is President of the Hungarian Academy of Sciences, Budapest.

Ellen Comisso is Associate Professor of Political Science at the University of California, San Diego.

P. Nikiforos Diamandouros is Staff Associate for Western Europe and the Near and Middle East at the Social Science Research Council, New York City.

Albert Fishlow is Professor of Economics at the University of California, Berkeley.

Jerry F. Hough is Professor of Political Science at Duke University, Durham, North Carolina, and a Fellow at the Brookings Institution, Washington, D.C.

Chalmers Johnson is the Walter and Elise Haas Professor of Asian Studies at the University of California, Berkeley.

Ronald H. Linden is Associate Professor of Political Science and Director of the Center for Russian and East European Studies at the University of Pittsburgh, Pennsylvania.

Paul Marer is Professor of International Business at the School of Business, Indiana University, Bloomington.

Michael Marrese is Associate Professor of Economics at Northwestern University, Evanston, Illinois.

Kazimierz Poznański is Associate Professor of Economics at Rensselaer Polytechnic Institute, New York.

Laura D'Andrea Tyson is Associate Professor of Economics at the University of California, Berkeley.

Susan L. Woodward is Associate Professor of Political Science at Yale University, New Haven, Connecticut.

To Elliot and Juliana

Preface

. . . Fortune is the ruler of half our actions, but . . . she allows the other half or thereabouts to be governed by us.

Machiavelli, The Prince

Changes in the international order present both challenges and opportunities to political actors at all levels. Traditionally the individual state has been responsible for mediating the impact of often unpredictable and frequently uncontrollable international forces on the domestic political and economic system. Yet its ability to do so at any given time has been conditioned as much by its position in a world order characterized by grave disparities in power and wealth as by internal political and economic factors shaping its reaction to the international environment.

Responses to the oil-price shocks of the 1970s were a case in point, indicating very different modes of seizing that ever-elusive lady, *fortuna*. Whereas the advanced capitalist countries, the North so to speak, in many cases responded to the shocks with deflationary measures, less developed countries—including the East European socialist states—reacted by taking advantage of the sudden surge of capital created by excess petrodollars and Western recession to pursue expansionary policies.[1] Conflicts over the implementation of austerity programs in the West created a boom industry on the "crisis of governability";[2] it was countered in the East by rosy discus-

1. For an overview, see Laura D'Andrea Tyson, *Economic Adjustment in Eastern Europe* (Santa Monica: Rand, 1984); on Eastern Europe see Paul Marer, "East European Economies: Achievements, Problems, Prospects," in Teresa Rakowska-Harmstone and Andrew Gyorgy, eds., *Communism in Eastern Europe* (Bloomington: Indiana University Press, 1981), pp. 244–90.

2. See Michel Crozier, Samuel Huntington, and Joji Watanuki, *The Crisis of Democracy* (New York: New York University Press, 1975); Anthony King, "Overload: Problems of Governing in the 1970s," *Political Studies* 23 (1975), pp. 162–74; J. Logue, "The Welfare State—Victim of Its Success?" *Daedalus* 108, no. 4 (1979), pp. 69–87; Claus Offe, "Competitive Party Democracy and the Keynesian Welfare State: Factors of Stability and Disor-

International Organization 40, 2, Spring 1986   0020-8183 $5.00
© 1986 by the Massachusetts Institute of Technology and the World Peace Foundation

sions of "integration into the international division of labor,"[3] and in the South by growing attention to politics and economics in a new category of states, the newly industrializing countries (NICs).[4]

Meanwhile, the specific adjustment strategies pursued in the advanced North varied significantly from state to state, as did their consequences for the domestic distribution of income and their subsequent impact on the ability of individual nations to maintain or advance their position in the international politico-economic order. Outside the states in the Organization for Economic Cooperation and Development (OECD), too, borrowing and growth strategies varied considerably, both within regions and among them. As a result, even states starting at roughly similar levels of development could find themselves in very different positions when the moment to repay past debts arrived in the 1980s. Likewise, although the measures debtor states were forced to take can all be broadly described as austerity, their specific contours and domestic sociopolitical consequences were often quite different, even in states with roughly similar political structures. The causes and consequences—both domestic and international—of these regional and national differences emerge quite clearly in a comparison of the adjustment responses of states outside the OECD to the energy shocks of the 1970s and the debt crises of the 1980s.

Both abroad and at home, political factors clearly played central roles in the different adjustments made by various states. Explaining why the advanced capitalist states of the North adopted very different economic strategies to cope with a common international challenge formed the focus of inquiry for Peter Katzenstein's *Between Power and Plenty*. In that intellectual predecessor to the current volume Katzenstein makes a powerful argument for the importance of domestic factors in determining a state's international position; he attributes differences in both the objectives of foreign economic strategies chosen by the OECD states and the instruments

ganization," in Thomas Ferguson and Joel Rogers, eds., *The Political Economy* (Armonk, N.Y.: Sharpe, 1984), pp. 349–69. Essays in Fred Hirsch and John Goldthorpe, *The Political Economy of Inflation* (Cambridge: Harvard University Press, 1978), and Suzanne Berger, ed., *Organizing Interests in Western Europe* (New York: Cambridge University Press, 1981), are also preoccupied with the theme of governability.

3. See József Biró, "Hungarian Foreign Trade in the Seventies," in Denis Simon, ed., *Modern Hungary* (Bloomington: Indiana University Press, 1973), pp. 164–85.

4. For examples, see Peter Evans, *Dependent Development: The Alliance of Multinational, State and Local Capital in Brazil* (Princeton: Princeton University Press, 1979); Joseph Grunwald, ed., *Latin America and the World Economy* (Beverly Hills: Sage, 1978); Charles W. McMillion, "International Integration and Intra-national Disintegration: The Case of Spain," *Comparative Politics* 13 (April 1981), pp. 291–313; G. S. Fields, "Who Benefits from Economic Development?—A Reexamination of Brazilian Growth in the 1960s," *American Economic Review* 67 (September 1977), pp. 570–82; D. L. Chinn, "Distributional Equality and Economic Growth: The Case of Taiwan," *Economic Development and Cultural Change* 26 (October 1977), pp. 65–79; and Bruce Cumings, "The Northeast Asian Political Economy," *International Organization* 38 (Winter 1984), pp. 1–41.

with which they were implemented to a set of variables subsumed by the concept of domestic structure. The concept's key elements, according to Katzenstein, are the nature of the coalition between business and the state, and the degree of fragmentation and/or integration in the policy networks between the two. Moreover, these elements are themselves only reflections of deeper sociopolitical relations, namely the degree of centralization in the state and society on the one hand, and the degree of differentiation between them on the other.[5]

This book takes its inspiration from *Between Power and Plenty* and addresses itself to an analysis of the foreign economic strategies of the European members of the Council for Mutual Economic Assistance (CMEA). Clearly, there are vast differences between the East European states and OECD members, but these striking contrasts are precisely what make the CMEA cases such an interesting testing ground for the approach and hypotheses elaborated in *Between Power and Plenty*. As editors we initially intended to compile a socialist sequel that would complement the Katzenstein volume; we hoped that application of a structural approach would yield equally persuasive explanations in the CMEA cases.

As the book took shape, however, that hope was disappointed for several reasons. For one thing, in small, resource- and/or capital-poor countries far from the "core" of the international economy—and in Eastern Europe in particular—even domestic economic policy choices proved impossible to explain without reference to the way in which international events, external powers, treaty obligations, and trade arrangements shape both the cost-benefit tradeoffs that political actors confront on the domestic stage and the distribution of power among them. In addition, partly because of these exogenous factors, domestic structure in the states that comprise Eastern Europe is so similar that it did not prove to be a determining variable in accounting for the rather different economic strategies these states selected in the 1970s and 1980s. Consequently, instead of asking how domestic structure affected economic strategy, this book focuses on the connection between economic policy choices and the way in which political elites making them stay in power.

In its entirety, *Power, Purpose, and Collective Choice* represents a genuinely interdisciplinary effort by political scientists and economists. As individuals we use approaches to the problem which are far from uniform, but as a group we shared several common concerns.

First, we were all anxious to rescue the study of socialist political and economic systems from the ghettos where they currently lie in their re-

5. See Peter Katzenstein, *Between Power and Plenty: Foreign Economic Policies of Advanced Industrial States* (Madison: University of Wisconsin Press, 1978); Katzenstein, "Introduction: Domestic and International Forces and Strategies of Foreign Economic Policy," and his "Conclusion: Domestic Structures and Strategies of Foreign Policy," *International Organization* 31 (Autumn 1977), pp. 587–607, 879–920.

spective disciplines. In this respect, if our choice of the states examined was limited by spatial considerations, access to information, and the availability of scholars familiar with an area-specific yet interdisciplinary subject matter, it was also guided by a desire to focus on cases with broad intellectual appeal. For these reasons we decided to omit Albania, and Czechoslovakia and Bulgaria—perhaps unfortunately—are treated only in the general essays. However, the states that did react to a changed international environment in a more innovative style—Romania, Hungary, East Germany, and Poland—are the subjects of full-length country studies.

Second, we are all quite conscious of the unique historical and institutional features of Eastern Europe, yet we felt these could be best appreciated within a broader comparative context. Thus we sought to take advantage of the fact that in the last analysis the CMEA states are late developers and far weaker economically than their Western counterparts by comparing the adjustment strategies of the smaller socialist states with those of other NICs outside the socialist bloc. Yugoslavia, a socialist country though not a member of the CMEA, represented an ideal bridge in this respect and so is given fuller treatment than other NICs.

On the one hand, a comparison of CMEA members and other late developers outside the OECD allowed us to clarify the significance of domestic factors and international alignments in shaping foreign economic strategy in states that are neither economically nor politically the makers and shakers of the international order. To this end brief comments compare the adjustment responses to international economic disturbances of East Asian, Latin American, and Mediterranean Basin NICs with the reactions of their East European counterparts.

On the other hand, such a comparison serves to highlight the unique historical evolution, international position, and structural features of CMEA states as explanatory factors in their responses to a set of economic pressures they shared with one another and with the Third World. A peculiar economic, political, and historical background distinguishes the position of Eastern Europe in the international system.

Third, all of the essays in this volume acknowledge a great debt to the many rich and high-quality economic analyses of individual East European states and the CMEA as a whole which have appeared both in the United States and elsewhere. Detailing the economic logic (or lack of it) behind the various options the countries have chosen, such work goes far to illuminate the obstacles and constraints policy makers confront when selecting an economic strategy.

Nevertheless, the economic choices that CMEA states made are also the product of political factors, and the ability of purely economic analyses to account for the varying weights of interest groups, political factions, ideology, and the like is necessarily weak. Similarly, economic studies have made a major contribution to highlighting the objectives of economic policy and describing the degree to which these have been achieved. Yet by themselves such studies cannot fully explain why some goals are attained while others remain empty phrases. Hence, regardless of their disciplinary loyalties, authors in this volume have chosen to build on the economic literature by concentrating on the political factors that have played such an important role in producing the outcomes that economic analyses describe.

In examining the connection between holding domestic power and formulating economic policy, authors took a rather eclectic approach, focusing on those factors which seemed most persuasive in each case. Such an approach allowed us to avoid the eternal is-the-glass-half-full-or-half-empty dilemma of "how much" behavior is explained by international and domestic factors respectively. Instead we viewed the interplay of international changes and external forces as responsible for creating both opportunities and constraints for domestic actors by altering the availability of domestic political resources to contending elites and groups. Political entrepreneurs can thus creatively use (or abuse) opportunities that external occurrences afford in order to pursue their own programs, preferences, and ambitions; occasionally they may even alter elements of domestic structure to solidify their positions within it and undercut the claims of domestic and external rivals to share power.[6]

In such a scenario the international environment plays the role of Machiavelli's *fortuna*. Always impetuous, she smiles on the advances of some suitors and scorns the offers of others, as the ups and downs of Hungarian reform efforts—and the political fortunes associated with them—illustrate. Although she yielded to the bold in Romania, Poland's Edward Gierek learned to his dismay that a "prince who bases himself entirely on fortune is ruined when fortune changes." And as Walter Ulbricht's initially effective but ultimately futile resistance to West German *Ostpolitik* indicates, "he is unfortunate whose mode of procedure is opposed to the times."[7]

Although the distinct strategies adopted by East European states support a view of *fortuna* as a force against which barriers can be built, she is also a force that can never be conquered by small states lacking the resources and force to overcome her. Major powers, however, do have the possibility of redirecting her currents in the course of building barriers and banks designed to contain her. Such is the situation facing the Soviet Union in the 1980s, and the choices political elites there make in the course of confronting new international and domestic developments will both be influenced by and have major consequences for the policy options emerging in East Europe.

6. Peter Gourevitch suggests such possibilities in "The Second Image Reversed: The International Sources of Domestic Politics," *International Organization* 32 (Autumn 1978), pp. 881–913; Albert Hirschman, in "Beyond Asymmetry: Critical Notes on Myself as a Young Man and on Some Other Old Friends," ibid. 32 (Winter 1978), pp. 45–51.
7. Niccolo Machiavelli, *The Prince and the Discourses* (New York: Random, 1950), p. 92.

Finally, seeking to illuminate the connection between economic strategy choices and the way in which leaders attain and maintain positions of political power forced us to examine more closely both "political" variables (namely, how leaders gain access to power and what they wish to do with it) and larger structural ones, for only by understanding the dynamic interaction between the two can the factors involved in economic strategy choices be elucidated. Consequently, although "structure" is central in our analyses, "politics" plays a far more important role than a purely structural model suggests. Political leaders emerge as an active and creative factor defining a changing relationship between state and society rather than passively reflecting it. Moreover, when state structures are relatively uniform, as they are in the CMEA, differentiated political processes—the "regularized practices" through which political elites advocate alternative visions of collective order and strategically interact to attain positions of power from which to accomplish them—bear a relatively systematic and organic connection to concrete and specific policy choices. Accordingly, state structures certainly provided elites with tools with which to make and to implement policy choices; yet how political elites used those tools was also a function of the terms on which they could capture them, the particular materials international opportunities and domestic societies provided, and what leaders sought to accomplish. The relationship between state structures, political processes, and strategy choices is examined more fully in Ellen Comisso's introductory essay, which seeks to derive a model of politics in socialism different from but with implications for models of the policy-making process in nonsocialist systems.

Paradoxically, then, although this volume began with the expectation that employing models of the policy process in Western states would serve to illuminate decision making in Eastern Europe, its evolution revealed that an analysis of strategic political choice grounded in the experience of the socialist states may well have wider application elsewhere. As Comisso's concluding essay observes, state structures in Eastern Europe were indeed different in kind as well as degree from those prevailing in non-CMEA NICs. As a result, the problems, possibilities, and incentive structures their respective elites confronted were quite distinctive. Nevertheless, if the substance of state structures were different, the relationship between structural parameters and strategy choices proved quite similar, and the former hardly determined the latter in either CMEA or the NICs. In both cases, political elites were able to modify state structures when the exigencies of power and the requirements of purpose motivated them to do so. Hence, to understand policy choices, it is not enough simply to analyze the state; we must examine the "government" and "opposition" as well, for it is these which breathe life into political structures.

Integrating this set of essays was a long and complex undertaking, involving both a workshop held in June 1984 at the Harriman Institute at Columbia University and the Conference on Foreign Economic Strategies of Eastern Europe, held in February 1985 at the Institute of International Studies at the University of California, Berkeley. The project received funds and assistance from the Ford Foundation, the International Research and Exchange Board, the Berkeley-Stanford Program on Soviet International Behavior, the Harriman Institute, the Joint Committee on Eastern Europe and both the Center for Slavic and East European Studies and the Institute of International Studies at the University of California, Berkeley. As co-editors, we express our great appreciation for such support. In addition, we thank James Caporaso, Benjamin Cohen, and Peter Gourevitch, who carefully read and commented on numerous drafts. Peter Katzenstein, the editor of *International Organization,* nurtured the project from its inception, devoting many hours to reviewing the essays and coordinating and guiding the project to fruition. The quality of the volume was greatly improved by the efforts of these individuals. Last, but hardly least, Emily Wheeler's careful editing helped turn interesting and thought-provoking essays into eminently readable ones.

ELLEN COMISSO
LAURA D'ANDREA TYSON

La Jolla and Berkeley, California

Power, Purpose, and
Collective Choice

Eastern Europe

Introduction: state structures, political processes, and collective choice in CMEA states Ellen Comisso

The interplay between power and purpose is at the heart of political life, and it is fundamental to the way states select an economic strategy. In any state, economic policy is simultaneously a choice among competing social visions and an outcome of the struggle for the positions of power from which such choices can be made. On the one hand, a vision of collective order can be implemented only if its protagonists have access to the political power required for its realization. On the other, insofar as political power itself derives from the creation of a community capable of collective action, a critical component in its generation is precisely the social vision on whose behalf it is exercised.[1] Accordingly, a state's economic strategy will reflect the purposes that political elites within it advocate as well as their ability to capture and hold onto the power required to realize them.

Certainly, the connection between power and purpose in the small socialist states of Eastern Europe is rather different from that in either the advanced capitalist nations of the Organization for Economic Cooperation and Development (OECD) or the newly industrializing countries (NICs) of the Third World. In part, the difference stems from the unique political and economic structure of members of the socialist bloc. Its elements include a highly

The fieldwork on which this essay is based was generously funded during 1981–82 by the International Research and Exchange Board and the German Marshall Fund. I completed the essay during 1984–85 while a fellow at the Center for Advanced Study in the Behavioral Sciences, Stanford, California. I am grateful for the financial support provided by the Exxon Educational Foundation during my stay there. I also thank the referees, the contributors to the volume, and Peter Katzenstein and Laura Tyson for their helpful comments and criticisms.

1. This view of politics reflects the classical use of the term. See *The Politics of Aristotle*, ed. and trans. by Ernest Barker (New York: Oxford University Press, 1962), bk. 1, pp. 1–8; Hannah Arendt, *On Violence* (New York: Harcourt, Brace & World, 1969), pp. 40–56; Sheldon Wolin, *Politics and Vision* (Boston: Little, Brown, 1960), pp. 1–28; Max Weber, "Politics as a Vocation," in H. Gerth and C. W. Mills, eds., *From Max Weber* (New York: Oxford University Press, 1958), pp. 77–129. It differs from the behaviorist view, which sees politics as being concerned purely with questions of power. See Robert Dahl, *Modern Political Analysis*, 4th ed. (Englewood Cliffs, N.J.: Prentice-Hall, 1984), pp. 8–19.

International Organization 40, 2, Spring 1986   0020-8183 $5.00

centralized, hierarchically organized state and economy; a lack of differentiation between state-governmental and economic-productive institutions; a single Marxist-Leninist party with a monopoly on political power; and a politically penetrated form of sovereignty in which party interests rather than national or economic interests govern foreign policy, and politically determined shortages rather than comparative advantage are the motor of international trade.

Such structural features mean that physical shortages and bottlenecks rather than prices guide both micro- and macroeconomic decisions in CMEA states.[2] Moreover, both the creation and the management of shortages reflect the political priorities of the ruling party rather than the autonomous responses of producers and consumers. Section 1 of this essay shows how the role of politically created and controlled shortages in resource allocation explains why East European reactions to the international economic disturbances of the past decade look so similar to each other and differ so significantly from those of states with price-sensitive economies.

Section 1 also describes rather significant differences in the strategies CMEA states selected to deal with shortages in the 1970s and 1980s, suggesting that the link between state structures and policy choices is loose and ambiguous. Nor do existing models of politics in Eastern Europe adequately explain such differences—often because such models draw directly from Western political systems without accounting for Eastern Europe's peculiar structural features. Although policy choices are not explained by state structures, they cannot be explained without them, either.

Section 2 presents a synthetic approach to explaining economic strategy in which the role of state structure is to define problems political elites must solve, possibilities among which they may choose, and political resources and allies upon which they may draw in the course of choosing among alternative possibilities and resolving concrete problems. The choices that they make, however, are outcomes of a political process, in which leaders mobilize resources and allies to capture positions of power from which they can pursue the purposes they advocate, including purposes that may modify state structure itself.

When state structure remains constant—as has been the case in Eastern Europe since 1948—a symbiotic and organic association between economic strategy and political process occurs. Sections 3 and 4 of this essay describe the two rather distinctive political processes that have emerged in Eastern Europe in the postwar period; each is associated with a particular type of development strategy. On the one hand, political processes dominated by a single leader have either given rise to or been the product of economic strategies seeking rapid and extensive social and economic transformation.

2. See János Kornai, *Economics of Shortage*, 2 vols. (Amsterdam: North Holland, 1980).

On the other hand, political processes characterized by collective leadership are accompanied by far more incrementalist development strategies.

If the type of strategy a state selects is consistent with the form of its political process, the components of strategy are tied to the content that enters it. In this way, the national characteristics (from natural endowments and demographic structure to previous historical traumas) of the state in question can inform its policy choices. In systems with a single leader, the personal vision and power requirements of the driving figure embody national peculiarities; in collegial politics, the historically evolving sources of cohesion and conflict among contending factions reflect these peculiarities.

Political processes thus allow political subjectivity to govern and modify objective structures of rule. As such, political processes describe how leaders act without prescribing what leaders want, indicate the bases for collective choice without dictating choices themselves. If strategy is selected in a political process, it is not determined by it, and choice itself remains open-ended. Dominant individual leaders may well opt for decelerating socioeconomic change, just as rival factions can unite behind strategies of pressurized economic transformation. In such cases, political processes themselves are likely to be altered to better fit policy choices: if the pace of change slows, collective leadership is likely to replace individual rule; when incrementalism is abandoned for a strategy seeking a major breakthrough, collegial politics breaks down and/or is transformed into one-person rule.

While the interaction of state structures and changing empirical conditions establish an agenda and an arena for collective choice, then what choices are made are the product of how leaders capture power and what they wish to do with it. As section 5 of this essay suggests, if the structural features of a state constitute the tools and societies supply the materials with which policy is constructed, how tools come to shape materials may vary depending on both how alternative models are selected and what concrete alternatives potential policy architects propose. Analogously, the dynamic interaction of the form and content of political processes has allowed economic strategy among CMEA states to vary by time and place despite rather uniform domestic structures.

1. CMEA responses to international change in comparative perspective: the dependent variable[3]

In OECD states the sudden rise in the cost of imported fuel in 1973 was transmitted as higher prices at home. Many states responded with deflationary

3. The description of CMEA adjustment strategies is drawn from many sources, including László Csaba, "Adjustment to the World Economy in Eastern Europe," *Acta Oeconomica* 30, no. 1 (1983), pp. 53–75; Csaba, "Some Problems of the International Socialist Monetary System," *Acta Oeconomica* 23, nos. 1–2 (1979), pp. 17–37; Marie Lavigne, "The Soviet Union inside Comecon," *Soviet Studies* 35 (April 1983), pp. 135–53; Philip Hanson, "Soviet Trade with

policies, and nearly all experienced significant recessions. Consequently, Western banks found themselves with large sums of petrodollars and few domestic outlets for them. As interest rates dropped, they sought to export capital outside the advanced capitalist world, complementing efforts of Western producers to find new markets abroad.

As Laura Tyson's essay indicates, Third World NICs also experienced the higher prices and inflation of the energy crisis, but many were able to accelerate out of it by borrowing on suddenly generous international capital markets at favorable rates.

The content of the ensuing expansion and the state's role and techniques in engineering it varied widely among the NICs, as did its internal consequences for the distribution of income and productive resources. Yet if expansionary fiscal and monetary policies on the part of states stimulated robust economic growth, expansion was accomplished through relatively autonomous responses of consumers and producers to domestic and international prices, even where prices were politically shaped and enterprises owned by the state.

Expansion in developing areas also saw a rapid—if unequally distributed—rise in both the absolute and relative share of world trade these areas enjoyed. Yet precisely because participation in international trade grew, the vulnerability of both macro- and microeconomic actors in the NICs to its fluctuations increased as well.

That vulnerability became highly transparent by 1982, after the second oil-price rise of 1979 and the jump in interest rates that began at the start of the new decade. This time austerity measures, whose severity depended heavily on whether the previous expansion had been export-led or a response to the stimulation of domestic demand, aggravated inflation in debtor NICs. In the latter cases, devaluations put some sectors in a better position to export but simultaneously prompted a wave of bankruptcies, a dramatic deterioration of real incomes, and heavy inflation. Cuts in domestic spending by heavily indebted governments impaired their ability to take countercyclical measures; recessions were sharp and severe, output losses substantial, and unemployment high. The response of domestic capital to suddenly changed prices—to seek more profitable outlets abroad—hardly improved the situation. Indeed, in many NICs where military governments had maintained themselves in power on the wave of expansion, serious economic difficulties formed the background to a transition to civilian rule.

In CMEA states, money and prices do not play active roles in resource allocation. Hence higher world energy prices were not transmitted as domestic

Eastern Europe," in Karen Dawisha and Hanson, eds., *Soviet-East European Dilemmas* (New York: Holmes & Meier, 1981), pp. 90–108; Laura D'Andrea Tyson and Egon Neuberger, eds., *The Impact of International Economic Disturbances on the Soviet Union and Eastern Europe* (Elmsford, N.Y.: Pergamon, 1980); and Michael Marrese and Jan Vaňous, *Soviet Subsidization of Trade with Eastern Europe* (Berkeley: Institute of International Studies, University of California, 1983).

inflation. Rather, they were felt as a shortage in energy supplies. Nor was the CMEA's response to cut back on energy consumption. On the contrary, the CMEA attempted to overcome shortages by expanding supply sources and access to them. Thus, far more than favorable conditions on international capital markets, shortages prompted expansionary policies in the CMEA; in contrast to Third World NICs, borrowing was more a consequence than a cause of decisions to expand and modernize output, decisions that had actually been made much earlier and on the basis of pre-1973 prices.

Borrowing capital on private Western financial markets for purposes of technology transfer was a relatively new phenomenon in East-West trade, but it picked up considerable steam after 1973. Several factors, one of which was, of course, the simple availability of such funds, lay behind this development. First, pressure on Soviet supplies precipitated a change in CMEA pricing mechanisms, such that after 1975 intrabloc energy prices were based on an annually changing five-year world price. As in the past, simple increases in CMEA prices did not suppress demand for Soviet raw materials and fuel, because demand for goods in East European economies arises relatively independently of price considerations: in large part, it is a response to politically determined plan priorities. In fact, it was only later in the decade and especially in 1982, when further Soviet supplies simply became physically unavailable, that serious attempts to conserve energy began in Eastern Europe.

The new price mechanism did, however, signify the need for a larger volume of East European exports to cover planned levels of Soviet imports. Producing sufficient goods of satisfactory quality entailed both expanding current output and considerable new investment. Both courses called for extensive imports of Western technology, paid for primarily by borrowing from Western sources.

Second, expansionary policies exacerbated existing fuel shortages. One response was to resume importing Middle Eastern oil after 1977; another was to utilize alternative fuels and initiate conservation measures. Most important, however, were CMEA joint-investment programs (e.g., the Orenburg pipeline) aimed at expanding the supply of Soviet energy in Eastern Europe. Their effect, however, was to drain off investment needed for domestic purposes; again, borrowing made up the difference.

Precisely because growth was geared to diminishing domestic shortages, it did not serve to enhance export competitiveness on world markets. Firms experienced the expansion as higher output targets and responded by disproportionately increasing requests for inputs whose cost they themselves did not bear. Shortages thus intensified, and imports grew at the same time that the volume of goods available for export diminished. Thus, Eastern Europe's share of world trade stagnated in the 1970s, in direct contrast to the experience of the Third World.

For reasons that Michael Marrese describes in his essay on the CMEA, intrabloc trade arrangements hardly helped. Designed to reallocate and minimize tensions arising from shortages among member states, they prescribe bilateral bargaining among governments seeking to balance goods in short supply ("hard" goods) against commodities in surplus ("soft" goods), where "hardness" and "softness" reflect priorities of domestic plans rather than prices. When states have only "soft" goods to exchange with each other, their interest in trade understandably declines. This was precisely the situation within Eastern Europe in the 1970s: sophisticated technology and raw materials were what all states wanted, and they were, for the most part, commodities no state produced for trade purposes. Expansion thus relied on increased imports from Western states and the Soviet Union, which brought about a relative decline in intraregional exchange.

Thus, the result of expansionary policies in the 1970s for Eastern Europe was increased indebtedness to both Western lenders and the Soviet Union. By the 1980s, the situation was one in which the Soviet Union was willing (with increasing reluctance) to provide credits but not the necessary raw materials; hard-currency states, in contrast, were quite happy to sell oil and technology (also with increasing reluctance) but were no longer willing to extend the credit with which to purchase them.

The 1980s thus witnessed the convergence of two sets of shortages in Eastern Europe: supplies and liquidity. Although adjustment took the same form of austerity in Eastern Europe as it took in the price-governed economies of the Third World, its content was distinctly different.

In Eastern Europe reduced growth rates and investment diminished supply tensions, allowing authorities to impose strict import controls. Such actions freed up more goods for export, especially once authorities began to reward producers on the basis of (planned) export performance. Monetary and fiscal measures played as marginal a role in contraction as they had played in expansion, reflecting the passive role of prices in Eastern Europe, in distinct contrast to Third World economic policy.

Employment levels remained high, dramatic currency devaluations were avoided, and—outside Romania and Poland—precipitous drops in the standard of living did not occur. Bridge financing was sought from the West, and interest in CMEA integration revived, as regional trade was forced to resume its traditional role as a substitute for participation in the larger international economy. Although the economic structure of CMEA states hurt their ability to compete on the international marketplace, the socialist safety net such structures created also protected them from the worst of its fluctuations.

The role of shortages in resource allocation at micro-, macro-, and supranational-CMEA levels thus gave CMEA states a unique perspective and role in international trade. For them a "gain" in trade consisted of reducing the shortages constraining the ability of the economy to achieve the politically determined objectives of central authorities and not in increasing efficiency or international competitiveness per se. Not surprisingly, the impact of international economic disturbances in Eastern Europe was quite different from the effect of such disturbances on economies governed by price considerations, be they in OECD or in developing countries.

Nevertheless, if economic structure in CMEA states describes an allocation process in which political decisions both create and manage shortages, it does not offer prescriptions for how to deal with them. In fact strategies for handling shortages differed considerably within the CMEA. Poland and Romania selected strategies of accelerated economic transformation; Hungary, East Germany, Czechoslovakia, and Bulgaria, in contrast, opted for far more incrementalist methods of economic management.

In Poland expansion took an exaggerated form. As Kazimierz Poznański describes, the political exigencies of the Gierek leadership simultaneously produced a strategy of accelerated, "import-led" growth while preventing it from implementing the very policies that might have given that strategy a chance of success. Instead, rapid growth in investment and wages quickly exhausted available resources and enjoined against viable economic reform and even an economically coherent rationale for allocating goods in short supply. Like many NICs, Poland required a change in government to implement austerity in the 1980s. Whereas outside the CMEA, the transition was from military rule to civilian government, in Poland it was the reverse. Neither was the result of a drive to penetrate Western markets; instead, it was a net reorientation of trade eastward.

Like Poland, Romania also pursued a strategy of highly accelerated growth in the 1970s. Yet whereas Poland sought to expand on the basis of imports, Romania aspired to economic autarchy; unlike all other states in the CMEA, Romania's trade turnover actually declined in the 1970s.[4] If such an attempt did not in the end succeed economically, it brought considerable political benefits to its promulgator. As Ronald Linden shows in his essay, the development strategy that had created so many difficulties in the rest of Eastern Europe in the 1950s worked in Romania to consolidate Nicolae Ceauşescu's monopoly of power and political initiative. Consequently, he was able to use his control of government and party alike to enforce an austerity program far more severe than anywhere else in the CMEA. If Romania resembles Poland in its nonincrementalist dash for growth and sudden interest in CMEA integration in the 1980s, the political repercussion of such policies are very different indeed.

Hungary and East Germany followed far more incrementalist strategies, avoiding both Poland's spectacular political denouement and Romania's campaign-style austerity. Both found their terms of trade with the West deteriorating sharply after 1973, and both incurred large hard-currency debts to cover the deficits created by expanded East-West trade. Neither used the occasion to pursue domestic economic reform; indeed, in the 1970s both

---

4. See Csaba, "Adjustment to the World Economy," p. 61.

countries turned away from earlier experiments that enlarge the enterprise autonomy. However, Paul Marer and I argue that in Hungary the particular complexion of political cleavages within the leadership kept the principle of economic reform alive and allowed the combined energy and debt crisis at the end of the decade to serve as a political springboard for those favoring a return to economic reform in practice.

In East Germany the reformist impulse had always been much weaker, because an emphasis on technical rather than economic efficiency had long been a source of unity and advancement within the political elite. Precisely because rapid growth creates shortages and hence tensions inimical to smooth technical operations, East German leaders showed little interest in sudden accelerated expansion, and growth rates—both planned and actual—were modest and regular in the 1970s. Such a strategy also helped the elite to make good on its promise to provide higher private and especially social standards of living, an important basis for differentiating itself from potential competitors in Bonn. As Thomas Baylis indicates in his essay, foreign-policy ambivalences over relations with West Germany and the Soviet Union had long been the key framework within which East Germany settled domestic issues. East Germany's economic strategy in the 1980s reflected these divisions, providing for stepped-up integration within the CMEA, greater exploitation of a unique relationship with West Germany, and an affirmation of the social welfare policies critical to East Germany's sense of identity.

Bulgaria and Czechoslovakia provide variants on the Hungarian and East German themes.[5] Yet whereas the political dynamics of incrementalism in Hungary and East Germany worked in favor of expanding trade—and particularly exports—with the West in the 1980s, in Bulgaria and Czechoslovakia they led to further integration with the East. Bulgaria, too, was a heavy borrower in the early 1970s, yet it began to reduce its hard-currency debts and scale down import levels much earlier than did others in the CMEA. Although in the 1980s Bulgaria has moved to bring domestic and foreign prices into line while pushing enterprises to become financially self-supporting units, it has left the machinery of central planning intact. At the same time, its hard-currency debts were manageable, and its decision to "specialize" in agriculture in the 1970s put Bulgaria in a relatively strong position within the CMEA, given Soviet hopes for increased food imports from Eastern Europe in the 1980s. It was not surprising then that Bulgaria looked to the East in its trade relations.

In Czechoslovakia the option of economic reform remained a dead one following the expulsion of reformists from the Czech party in the early 1970s.

---

5. On Czechoslovakia and Bulgaria, see Lászlo Csaba, *Economic Mechanism in the GDR and in Czechoslovakia* (Budapest: Hungarian Scientific Council for World Economy, 1983); Adam Zwass, "The Economies of Eastern Europe," *International Journal of Politics* 13 (Winter 1983–84), pp. 23–81; H. Hohmann, Michael Kaser, and Karl Thalheim, eds., *The New Economic Systems of Eastern Europe* (London: C. Hurst, 1983).

Its borrowing activities on Western capital markets were far more restrained than those of its socialist allies, and Czechoslovakia's reduced growth rates in the 1980s were more a response to the general slowdown in the CMEA than to an imminent liquidity crisis. Strident warnings to its socialist allies of the dangers of further involvement with capitalist economies accompanied Czechoslovakia's reduced growth. Because the country continued to rely heavily on CMEA integration to meet its trade needs and shape its economy, it showed some interest in reforming intrabloc crediting arrangements at the same time that it appeared to be bidding for Walter Ulbricht's role as the strongest enemy of Western imperialism in Eastern Europe.

2. Explaining economic strategy: a theoretical framework

Although the role of shortages in resource allocation explains many of the underlying similarities among the responses of East European states to international economic disturbances, it does not explain the rather significant differences in the way states in the region managed them.

Contending paradigms

Economic analyses certainly provide the raw material for such an explanation: for example, the fact that Poland's terms of trade improved in the 1970s certainly facilitated growth of the enormous debt it confronted in the 1980s. Yet reserves of hard coal did not produce import-led development any more than the deterioration of Hungary's terms of trade produced recentralization and borrowing. Rather, such responses were political choices, and it is in this context that they need to be explained.

On the political side, there are a number of paradigms. All explain certain aspects of policy making in Eastern Europe, but none of them seems to capture fully the complexity of the policy-making process as a whole. Ruling-class paradigms,[6] for example, draw attention to the limits to potential economic and political change in CMEA states and to rather striking and well-institutionalized inequalities in the distribution of political power there. However, they are not very useful in accounting for or predicting the degree of change that has occurred and does occur (including changes in economic

---

6. See Milovan Djilas, *The New Class* (New York: Praeger, 1958); C. Castonadis, *La Société bureaucratique* (Paris, 1973); Serge Mallet, *Bureaucracy and Technocracy in the Socialist Countries* (Nottingham: Spokesman, 1974); Charles Bettelheim, *The Transition to Socialist Economy* (Sussex: Harvester, 1975); Rudolf Bahro, *The Alternative in Eastern Europe* (London: NLB, 1977); György Konrad and Iván Szelényi, *La marché au pouvoir des intellectuels* (Paris: Editions du Seuil, 1979). Critiques of these theories appear in Anthony Giddens, *The Class Structure of the Advanced Societies* (New York: Harper & Row, 1973), pp. 238–54; Alec Nove, "Is There a Ruling Class in the USSR?" *Soviet Studies* 27, no. 4 (1975), pp. 615–35; and Jadwiga Staniszkis, "Martial Law in Poland," *Telos* 16 (Winter 1982–83), pp. 87–89.

strategy) or why different states with presumably similar class structures (e.g., Hungary and Poland) follow different strategies.

Furthermore, class analyses typically posit the political leadership as a class but either fail to specify a class mission, leaving us in the dark as to what leaders will do, or define a class mission in ways that the actions of the ruling class patently contradict. If the first problem is most apparent in Milovan Djilas's analysis, "state capitalist" theories fail to explain why rulers bent on maximizing accumulation or surplus routinely select such highly inefficient economic policies.

Finally, if East European political elites constitute a class by virtue of their position in the social structure, it is unclear why political leaders in any country would not also form at least a "potential" class by the same criterion. Certainly, political leaders everywhere try to stay in power and maintain and reinforce the state as they do so; and in performing such activities, leaders act to preserve the state regardless of whether it is pluralist, authoritarian, corporatist, praetorian, or socialist. Thus whether the appellation "class"—which, at least in its Marxist sense, implies a class mission, interest, and regime-type affinity—can be applied anywhere to describe political elites is questionable.

Explanations of East European strategy choices based on Soviet hegemony remind us that in formulating both foreign and domestic economic policies,[7] East European states must take account of their neighboring superpower. They are much less helpful, however, in explaining *how* East European leaders take account of Soviet interests. That is, Soviet hegemony theories simply assume that the bargaining power of the small country is fixed and unilaterally determined by its larger neighbor; whereas in fact, bargaining power may well be a variable, influenced as much by the degree of strength and independence political leaders in the small country want as by what the Soviet Union is prepared to give.

Much evidence in this volume suggests that if East European leaderships have occasionally sought to maintain some distance from Moscow (Edward Gierek's "opening to the West," for example), it is much more typically in their interests to maintain close ties with the Soviet Union. If so, it may well

7. See Walker Clemens, Jr., "The European Alliance Systems: Exploitation or Mutual Aid?" in Charles Gati, ed., *The International Politics of Eastern Europe* (New York: Praeger, 1976), pp. 217–37; Andrzej Korbonski, "The Warsaw Treaty after Twenty-Five Years: An Entangling Alliance or an Empty Shell?" in Robert Clawson and Lawrence Kaplan, eds., *The Warsaw Pact: Political Purpose and Military Means* (Wilmington: Scholarly Resources, 1982), pp. 3–27; R. Barry Farrell, "Top Political Leadership in Eastern Europe," in Farrell, ed., *Political Leadership in Eastern Europe and the Soviet Union* (Chicago: Aldine, 1970), pp. 88–108; William Zimmerman, "The Energy Crisis, Western 'Stagflation,' and the Evolution of Soviet-East European Relations: An Initial Assessment," in Neuberger and Tyson, eds., *International Economic Disturbances*, pp. 409–44. Zimmerman's earlier work gives far more play to the complementarity of interests and interpenetration of decision making in Eastern Europe and the Soviet Union, in contrast. See his "Hierarchical Regional Systems and the Politics of System Boundaries," *International Organization* 24 (Spring 1972), pp. 18–36.

be erroneous to regard the policy choices of Eastern-bloc countries as reflecting only "what they can get away with." Rather, such choices may mirror ambivalences within each national leadership over the degree of political and economic independence it desires.

Theories based on group politics call attention to the cleavages and conflicts within the various political elites of socialist states,[8] suggesting that these conflicts are related in some way to social differentiation in the society that elites govern. Group conflict theories, however, suffer from a serious lack of empirical support for their key assumption, namely, that social groups in CMEA states have either the autonomy or the political resources they would require to press their claims on political leaders effectively.

Certainly, both the Hungarian and East German cases indicate that individual actions taken on a broad enough scale can influence policy choices: high labor turnover can affect wage regulation, declines in farm output can produce changes in tax and price policy, requests for exit visas may influence emigration policy, consumer rejection of a product can cause its production to be discontinued. Yet even a large number of individuals using an "exit" option is not equivalent to establishing the common "voice" that is a fundamental requirement for the exercise of genuine political power by groups.[9]

The organizational-bureaucratic politics paradigm highlights the role of established organizations as political actors,[10] viewing conflicts among institutional interests for survival and expansion and among organizational elites representing these interests as central factors in policy choices.

The problem with the organizational politics model is not empirical. Bargaining and haggling are clearly endemic to socialist systems; indeed, the

8. The pathbreaking essay here is H. Gordon Skilling's "Interest Groups and Communist Politics," *World Politics* 18 (1966), pp. 435–61. See also Joel Schwartz and William Keech, "Group Influence on the Policy Process in the Soviet Union," *American Political Science Review* 62 (September 1968), pp. 840–85; Roger Kanet, "Political Groupings and Their Role in the Process of Change in Eastern Europe," in Andrew Gyorgy and James Kuhlmann, eds., *Innovation in Communist Societies* (Boulder: Westview, 1978), pp. 41–58. This type of theorizing has been revived in theories positing a "social compact" between state and society in Eastern Europe. See Alex Pravda, "East-West Interdependence and the Social Compact in Eastern Europe," in M. Bornstein, Z. Gitelman, and W. Zimmerman, eds., *East-West Relations and the Future of Eastern Europe* (London: Allen & Unwin, 1981), pp. 162–91. The best critique of this view is by Andrew Janos, "Group Politics in Communist Society: A Second Look at the Pluralist Model," in S. Huntington and C. Moore, eds., *Authoritarian Politics in Modern Society: The Dynamics of One-Party Systems* (New York: Basic, 1970).

9. See Albert O. Hirschman, *Exit, Voice, and Loyalty* (Cambridge: Harvard University Press, 1970).

10. See Jiri Valenta, *Soviet Intervention in Czechoslovakia 1968: Anatomy of a Decision* (Baltimore: Johns Hopkins University Press, 1979); T. H. Rigby, "Politics in the Mono-organizational Society," in Andrew Janos, ed., *Authoritarian Politics in Communist Europe* (Berkeley: Institute of International Studies, University of California, 1976), pp. 31–81; Teréz Laky, "Enterprises in Bargaining Position," *Acta Oeconomica* 22, nos. 3–4 (1979), pp. 227–46; Laky, "The Hidden Mechanisms of Recentralization in Hungary," *Acta Oeconomica* 24, nos. 1–2 (1980), pp. 95–109. Karen Dawisha provides strong criticism of the approach in "The Limits of the Bureaucratic Politics Model: Observations on the Soviet Case," *Studies in Comparative Communism* 13 (Winter 1980), pp. 300–327.

lack of an active price mechanism means they are the only techniques available for allocating resources at the microeconomic level. Yet focusing on the bargaining process alone ignores the fact that the arenas within which bargaining occurs are strictly limited and the issues up for bureaucratic negotiation are tightly restricted.[11] Further, the bargaining partners themselves (e.g., enterprises and ministries) do not determine these limits and restrictions; rather, the political leaders outside them do. Thus, not only may the same organization pursue entirely different goals at different times, but, far from "representing" organizational interests, leaders are typically appointed to their posts in order to forward the interests of political bodies external to it.

Finally, it is difficult to explain how "strong" ministries, industries, and mass organizations ever "lose" if policy changes are simply the product of organizational competition. Yet enterprise associations (VVBs) did lose their autonomy in East Germany, the Ministry of Industry was cut back and reorganized in Hungary, and the Polish Union Workers' party (PUWP) was streamlined and its apparatus reduced in Poland.

It follows, then, that the organizational politics model is not invalid but merely insufficient, and an understanding of organizational behavior and policy decisions must derive from a theory explaining conflict and consensus in the political leadership itself, for it is here where organizational interests originate, appointments are made, and strategies are selected.

Although none of the preceding paradigms fully captures the policy-making process, each highlights different factors entering into it. The desires of political leaders to stay in power and their commitment to the political forms of state socialism; the influence external actors and the Soviet Union in particular exert on domestic preferences; the impact policy measures are likely to have on social groups; the ability of formal organizations to carry out tasks assigned to them and their methods for supplying decision makers with advice and information are all clearly essential components in policy choices. The question remains, however: how do political elites making these choices weigh these factors against each other and their own policy preferences?

Structure in CMEA states

By itself, the notion of "state structure" cannot answer this question, insofar as it excludes precisely the political process by which tradeoffs are made and alternatives created and synthesized. Yet, in Lenin's memorable terminology, although the political process decides "what is to be done," state structure specifies "*kto/kovo*" (who can do what to whom) in both the state and economy. Hence this analysis will begin by translating the concept

11. James March and Herbert Simon make this distinction: "Politics is a process in which the situation is the same as in bargaining—there is intergroup conflict of interest—but the arena of bargaining is not taken as fixed by participants." See March and Simon, *Organizations* (New York: Wiley & Sons, 1958), p. 130.

of state structure that Peter Katzenstein develops in *Between Power and Plenty* into a socialist context and specifying its elements in Eastern Europe.[12]

The first component of Katzenstein's structure is the *degree of centralization in the state and economy*, which is extremely high throughout Eastern Europe. Whether we speak of the relationship between local and national governments or between enterprise and central planning agencies, authority over resource allocation in socialist states is hierarchically distributed, and subordinate units typically require the approval, financial support, or—outside Hungary— even instructions from higher authorities to engage in activities of their own choosing.

In the economy, centralization creates a highly concentrated and monopolistic industrial structure. In such a context, because prices cannot govern the decisions of enterprises or allocate scarce resources, administrative and political controls must replace or supplement them. Moreover, such controls must be exerted from above, since low-level units lack the knowledge and perspective from which to make decisions consistent with those of other producers and consumers or with national economic priorities. As a result, subordinate units are unable to react autonomously to horizontal stimuli— be they economic cues from buyers and sellers or political pressures of local leaders and groups whose demands conflict with central priorities.

Politically, a high degree of centralization deters independent political initiative at subnational levels, as there are few autonomous constituencies available to mobilize. Because political discretion and power are concentrated at the top reaches of the system, local leaders anxious to realize their own ambitions in their area look upward rather than outward and downward for support.

A highly centralized state and economy only creates a possibility for the hierarchical allocation of resources and coordination of economic life. It neither guarantees the opportunity will be exploited to the fullest nor prescribes the purposes that the hierarchy will serve. Political elites may choose to ration goods among consumers, or they may allow consumers to select their own goods based on their income, prices, and/or willingness to stand in queues, as Poland has done at various times. Likewise, if high centralization makes economic actors strive to meet the politically determined standards of state authorities, the standards themselves may reflect market cues ("economic parameters") rather than commands designed to counteract market processes; Hungary's New Economic Mechanism (NEM) is a case in point.

The objectives control serves may also differ. Romania used central control

12. See Peter Katzenstein, "Introduction: Domestic and International Forces and Strategies of Foreign Economic Policy," and Katzenstein, "Conclusion: Domestic Structures and Strategies of Foreign Policy," *International Organization* 31 (Autumn 1977), pp. 587–607; 879–920. What Katzenstein referred to as "society" in those essays on the OECD states I call "economy" here, partly because it simplifies the language of the analysis and partly because even in his essays, "society" is more or less a stand-in term for the economy.

to pursue "extensive" development and autarchy, Czechoslovakia to specialize within the CMEA, Hungary and Poland to open their economies to world-market influences. Moreover, political leaders may and frequently do embrace contradictory goals; thus, under a system of central control the degree of correspondence between results and initial objectives may be considerably less than the structural possibility for it implies.

The degree of differentiation between the state and the economy is the second component of structure in CMEA states. In a narrow sense, the degree of differentiation is coterminous with the extent to which assets are state-owned. In a broad sense, it measures the degree to which activities of producers, consumers, and labor suppliers depend on the decisions of (by and large, central) state authorities. If centralization in CMEA states is high, differentiation is correspondingly low, especially for producers.

Low differentiation between state and economy means producing units bear neither the costs nor the risks of their activities. Rather, budget constraints are "soft," and adjustment costs, benefits, and strategies of individual economic units can—and in cases such as Czechoslovakia or Romania, must—be shifted to the higher-level authorities whose decisions determine them. Yet precisely because producers are insensitive to costs, their demand for inputs is "insatiable," creating continual shortages.[13]

The result is a perpetual sellers' market in the domestic economy along with a tendency to "suck" in all imports authorities will permit. For such reasons, "protectionism" in CMEA economies cannot take the form of tariffs or manipulated exchange rates; rather, it consists of administrative decisions of what products to import.

Low differentiation makes political clout the foundation for economic control, in distinct contrast to economies based on private ownership. In the latter, accumulation of economic resources may occur independently, outside the state, and translate into political influence within it. In Eastern Europe, however, it is the accumulation of political support which allows one to influence the allocation of economic resources. Thus, the village plumber may well be the envy of his friends thanks to the fine house he possesses and his frequent trips abroad, but his influence on plans for a new local sewage system is likely to be nonexistent.

Again, low differentiation between state and economy merely provides a possibility for political and administrative control of economic life; whether such potential for control is used effectively depends both on the purposes to which it is put and the level of unity among the elite employing it. For example, a relatively unified leadership in Hungary employed political control of the economy to reduce administrative centralization and industrial concentration in the economy in the late 1970s. In East Germany, however, an equally cohesive leadership used its power to recentralize and deprive eco-

---

13. See Kornai, *Shortages,* vol. 1.

nomic conglomerates of autonomy in the late 1960s. In Poland, however, serious political cleavages have prevented the center from carrying out its decisions consistently, indicating a serious absence of effective central control despite the "structural" possibility for exerting it.

Centralization and differentiation are sufficient to describe "structure" in the OECD cases that Katzenstein analyzes, but two additional components are needed to accommodate the East European states. The third component of structure is *politically penetrated sovereignty*: party interests rather than national or economic interests are the basis for interaction within the bloc and between it and outside actors.

Economically, membership in the CMEA facilitates the ability of each Communist party to achieve its domestic objectives. Arrangements in the CMEA work to minimize and reallocate the tensions arising from shortages that member states create in the course of realizing their domestic goals. At the same time that it insulates political elites from having to take prices into account when selecting objectives, it encourages them to take the plans of socialist trade partners—especially their major supplier and consumer, the Sovier Union—into consideration.

As a consequence, however, benefits from trade within the CMEA often preclude gains from trade with the larger international economy and perpetuate patterns of production which are inefficient by international standards. For example, unlike West European states, CMEA members did not take advantage of favorable international prices and considerations of efficiency to switch their economies to oil and gas in the 1950s and 1960s. Instead, they relied on the plentiful coal supplies available within the bloc and followed a highly energy-intensive pattern of industrialization. In the 1970s, the exhaustion of coal supplies and the greater availability of Soviet nonsolid fuels increased the share of oil and gas in East European energy consumption, despite higher prices inside and outside of the CMEA.

Members of the socialist alliance may not take political actions that jeopardize existing treaty arrangements, the domestic position of neighboring Communist parties, or the solidarity of the bloc as a whole. Hence, if expanded East-West trade increased the vulnerability of CMEA members to the world economy in the 1970s, it was carefully orchestrated to avoid a parallel increase in political vulnerability to non-CMEA actors. In fact, East Germany and Bulgaria increased defense expenditures in the 1980s despite their hard-currency debts;[14] human rights deteriorated in Poland and Romania not only despite but also because of increased vulnerability to the world economy. Likewise, the flurry of industrial cooperation agreements of the 1970s may have been profitable for Western investors in Eastern Europe, but it scarcely gave them political influence there.

14. See Condolezza Rice, "Defense Burden Sharing," in David Holloway and Jane Sharp, eds., *The Warsaw Pact: Alliance in Transition?* (Ithaca: Cornell University Press, 1984), pp. 59–87.

Penetrated sovereignty has also entailed a unique pattern of interaction within the bloc, in which the tensions of asymmetric power relations among allied Communist parties must be mitigated by making power into a sum-positive game for alliance members.[15] Reproducing such power relations has caused the Soviet Union to develop quite differentiated relations with its East European allies at the same time that it has allowed Communist parties to interpenetrate each other even when purely domestic decisions are at stake. Thus, while the radial pattern of CMEA trade as well as the domestic political position of the East European parties give them a strong incentive to take Soviet preferences into account when making their own decisions, how Soviet preferences affect domestic decisions varies widely, and the result is hardly a 1:1 correlation between what the Soviet Union "wants" and what, say, Poland does.[16] Furthermore, interpenetration is a two-way street, and Soviet preferences themselves are generated through a political process in the Soviet Union on which East European "lobbies" can have a substantial impact, as Polish and German pressures for strong action in Czechoslovakia in 1968 revealed.

For domestic political actors, party interpenetration means that political resources can be generated abroad as well as at home.[17] The support that factions in individual East European policy-making bodies receive from other CMEA parties and the Soviet party in particular for positions they advocate is thus a source of significant influence on domestic decisions.

Again, penetrated sovereignty describes a set of possibilities rather than presenting a course of action. Although political leaders may choose to ignore economic advantages or national interest in formulating policy, they may also choose to make one or both a top priority: witness Romania's embrace of explicitly nationalist goals. Likewise, if all states must trade with each other by CMEA rules, those rules may change to reflect the political exigencies of bloc members, as the evolution of price mechanisms and complex development programs suggests. Moreover, the volume and relative proportion of trade conducted within the CMEA may vary substantially, as a comparison of Hungarian and Bulgarian choices illustrates. And finally, although each Communist party has a voice in the decisions of others, it is not obligated

15. See Ellen Comisso, "Soviet-East European Relations: Unconventional Gains from Trade or a Positive-Sum Power Game?" (Paper presented to the Institute of International Studies, University of California, Berkeley, 6 December 1984).

16. For example, the former Yugoslav ambassador to Moscow reports a 1957 meeting: "After the Polish ambassador arrived . . . Khrushchev became much more reserved. He no longer mentioned political problems. He didn't criticize the Poles, even once, a sure sign of coldness and distance in their relation." Veljko Mićunović, *Journées de moscou, 1956–1958* (Paris: Laffont, 1977), p. 234 (my translation). More recently, neither Czechoslovakia nor Hungary has responded to Soviet requests to increase defense expenditures. See Rice, "Defense," pp. 61–64.

17. See Kent Brown, "Coalition Politics and Soviet Influence in Eastern Europe," in Jan Triska and Paul Cocks, eds., *Political Development in Eastern Europe* (New York: Praeger, 1977), pp. 241–56; Erwin Weit, *At the Red Summit* (New York: Macmillan, 1970).

to exercise this voice, and whether that voice will prove a determining one is hardly a preordained fact. Hence neither strident Czech criticism nor Soviet disapproval prevented Hungary from joining the International Monetary Fund (IMF) in 1982.

Finally, the fourth component of structure in CMEA states is the presence of *a single, hegemonic party organized on Leninist lines* that faces no electoral constraint, operates according to democratic centralism, and has an exclusive right to monopolize the means of collective action.[18] Hence the party, not the state, exercises political power and controls the allocation of political resources. Such a party is distinguished from parties in other states (including other single-party states) in that its task is not only to formulate the policy priorities and directives the state administration carries out but also to supervise their implementation, intervening if necessary in the formal and legal chain of command in the state apparatus to ensure respect for the spirit as well as the letter of central directives.[19]

Although the hierarchical state administration is delegated authority to allocate economic resources according to politically prescribed plans, responsible party officials have the power to cut through bureaucratic red tape to see that "the job gets done." Economic shortages enhance the strategic role of the party and/or of whomever controls it: when resources are overcommitted, it is the party's task to ensure that projects with political priority get their necessary share. Hence suppliers of strategic commodities—be they enterprises or workers—*lose* discretion over their allocation when shortages are severe, in direct contrast to the impact of scarcity on the distribution of economic power in economies with active price mechanisms. For example, tight labor markets in Hungary have not acted to give workers more power or raise wages; rather, they have given local party officials more discretion over regional employment practices.

Insofar as a single Leninist party monopolizes the means of collective action, genuine political life can occur only within the party itself. Even state and mass organizations do not possess independent political power, for they derive their activities and functions from party directives. As a result, if coalitions form, they tend to be within the party rather than between party groups and social forces or institutions outside it. Certainly, leaders of nonparty organizations who are simultaneously members of party decision-making

18. Certainly, a Leninist party is not an element of "structure" the way the state and economy are. Whereas any individual residing in a territory is "necessarily" a part of the state insofar as she or he is a citizen, and anyone residing in the territory "necessarily" participates in the economy (even if only to consume goods), the party is a voluntary association and has no direct authority over anyone who is not a party member. Nevertheless, insofar as neither the state nor the economy could operate without the party, it should stand as an element of structure in its own right.

19. The best work on the role of the party as a "check" on the implementation of policy by the state administration remains Jerry F. Hough's *The Soviet Prefects* (Cambridge: Harvard University Press, 1966).

bodies or who possess information vital for party decisions may participate in the exercise of power. But they do so in the context of their party roles rather than in their official, paid capacities. Consequently, control over appointments and access to information are important political resources within the party itself.

Finally, since democratic centralism concentrates power at the party's highest levels, lower-level leaders can exercise it only according to conditions and purposes prescribed at the top. Hence the strength of coalitions depends far more on the "quality" of members (i.e., the positions they occupy) than on their quantity.

The presence of such a party in Eastern Europe only makes hegemonic rule possible; it neither guarantees hegemonic rule nor predicts what actions such a party will take. In fact, the establishment and maintenance of hegemonic rule depend heavily on the commitment of party elites to preserving it as well as on the specific actions they take and institutional procedures they create for this purpose. The very different "lessons" political elites in Poland and Hungary derived from the disturbances of 1956 are illustrative.

Even the reality of hegemonic rule does not necessarily mean it will be directed against society (i.e., the mass of the population). Indeed, "society"— its welfare, its characteristics, its organization, its development—is a very central concern of Leninist elites; it is simply not an autonomous political actor when party hegemony prevails. The result is not that political leaders do not seek what they judge to be in society's best interest or that they refuse to do what is in society's interest and even what society might very well want them to do. Lack of autonomy merely means that society lacks the political mechanisms to make these judgments for itself. If it is the object of all decisions, it is typically the subject of none.

State structure thus creates a series of possibilities and defines a set of political resources that domestic contenders for power can exploit for their own purposes and aspirations. "Political resources" can be thought of as sources of support which allow their holders to make a claim on collective choice. "Possibilities" show up on the political agenda as problems political leaders must solve, while a solution constitutes a specific choice among alternatives.

Political leaders may be of one mind on current issues or they may be sharply divided; the solutions they prefer in one case may be utterly inconsistent with their preferences in others, or the fit may be reasonably close and consistent. Elites may differ on how they define problems as well as on how they envision solutions. Yet no matter how broadly or narrowly a problem is defined and regardless of the level of controversy it generates, political leaders must reach some solution, simply because the structure of the state and economy in CMEA states does not permit anyone else to do so.

The political process

Structure may make decisions possible and even necessary, but it neither makes the decisions themselves nor makes any particular decision necessary. Rather, collective choices emerge out of a political process, "an arena of bargaining" whose limits "are not taken as fixed by participants."[20] In that arena actors make strategic calculations, articulating and selecting among alternative possibilities (e.g., high or low growth), debating the importance and urgency of various problems (e.g., equality versus efficiency), and mobilizing political resources to attain positions of power from which they can accomplish preferred purposes.

A political process is but a historically contingent pattern of strategic interaction among its participants.[21] It consists of political practices—from forming coalitions to writing articles and checking on state officials—that are simultaneously regularized (i.e., they follow a certain logic) and improvised (i.e., they embody creative and unanticipated responses to new conditions and challenges). The regularities of political processes constitute their *form* and describe the way in which political actors interact with and control each other. The improvisations elites express in political processes constitute their *content* and delineate the specific alternatives political actors propose for collective action.

In postwar Eastern Europe, politics has taken two basic forms: patrimonialism and collegiality. Comparable to Aristotle's distinction between "rule by One" and "rule by the Few," respectively, each form has had an ideal and a degenerate manifestation: ". . . when One or the Few . . . rule with a view to the common interest, the constitutions are right constitutions. On the other hand, the constitutions directed to the personal interest of the One or the Few . . . must necessarily be perverse."[22]

Patrimonialism has thus appeared as charismatic leadership (analogous to Aristotle's "kingship") or as a personality cult ("tyranny"). Collegiality, in turn, has occurred as collective leadership ("aristocracy") or factionalism ("oligarchy").

Significantly, "rule by the Many" is a third form of politics which has yet to enter the realm of historical possibility in CMEA states. Only when patrimonialism and collegiality have assumed perverse manifestations has society played an active role in political outcomes. For example, although the collectivization drives of the 1950s were accomplished under "tyranny," they did settle numerous petty jealousies and local rivalries that arose quite independently of leadership goals. Likewise, the degeneration of collegiality

---

20. March and Simon, *Organizations*, p. 130.
21. My notion of "political process" and its relationship to "state structure" is closely akin to Pierre Bourdieu's concept of "habitus" and its relationship to the "structure" of social life. See his *Outline of a Theory of Practice* (New York: Cambridge University Press, 1977), p. 78.
22. Aristotle, *Politics*, bk. 3, p. 144.

into "oligarchy" in Poland saw repeated attempts by individual leaders to mobilize and inflate the claims of social groups to use as weapons in personalistic struggles against each other.

In their ideal manifestations, however, the party monopolizes the means of collective action in both collegiality and patrimonialism, and leaders determine needs and preferences based on their ideologically informed social visions and their subjective assessments of social needs and actual possibilities for meeting them. To paraphrase a Hungarian observer, in "ideal" collegiality or patrimonialism, leaders find out what workers want by reading Marx and Lenin; in this sense, rule by the One is distinguishable from rule by the Few only according to the rules for determining whose reading of Marx and Lenin will be definitive.

The form the political process takes thus describes whether leaders pursue personal or common interests and how they determine what those interests are. As such, it is systematically connected with the type of economic strategy they select. Whereas patrimonialism has an "elective affinity" with strategies calling for major socioeconomic changes and accelerated breakthroughs, collegiality is associated with far more incrementalist forms of adaptation to change.

Choice, however, is open-ended, insofar as it is governed by the specific goals elites embrace as well as by the exigencies of acquiring power to achieve them. If the form of political process describes how common or personal interests of leaders are arrived at and pursued, its content delineates what such interests are. Content is thus a product of noninstitutional factors and reflects how leaders react to particular national and international conjunctures, even when the form of the political process is held constant. Hence patrimonial leaders may advocate pursuing accelerated growth strategies in total isolation from the world economy by relying heavily on Western imports or as part of an export drive to either convertible-currency or CMEA markets. Likewise, incrementalism may reflect the desire to integrate into the international economy; to draw closer to the CMEA; or to straddle the fence, depending on historically conditioned bases of cleavage and conflict among elites.

Moreover, depending on how elites construe domestic and international opportunities, patrimonial leaders may decide to slow down or reorient the pace of change, just as rival factions may find they can unite around a strategy by calling for a sudden breakthrough. In such cases the form of the political process itself is likely to break down or be transformed in order to accommodate a very different content.

The outcomes of political processes adapt, reproduce, or change domestic structures in the face of new and unanticipated historical conditions. Although political processes have a certain logic and content, no particular form or content is "necessary" to the survival of the overall structure within which it takes place. If the political process in Eastern Europe has historically taken two forms or "logics," its content has been even less uniform, while remaining as a whole consistent with the elements of structure noted above. At the same time, that the political process has taken only two forms and relatively stable contextual variations to date need not imply that other forms and contents are not possible at some future time, depending on the exigencies of power and purpose its participants embrace and the opportunities historical conjunctures present.

With this in mind, let us now consider the relationship between political process and economic policy choices in patrimonial and collegial systems.

3. Patrimonialism

In both patrimonial and collegial systems the party enjoys a monopoly on the means of collective action, and power within it flows from top to bottom. In patrimonial systems, however, the power of the party as a whole essentially depends on and reflects a single individual. Other members of the political elite maintain their positions thanks to the patronage of the main leader, who personally controls the allocation of political resources to reward loyal followers. In patrimonialism, then, "what is to be done" is the personal decision of an individual, reflecting his particular vision of what socialist reality should be as well as his need to eliminate internal and external challenges to the patrimonial rule and state structure deemed necessary to create that reality.

Regardless of whether patrimonialism assumes its ideal or degenerate version, the ruler always "governs at his own discretion in all affairs."[23] Specific policy objectives reflect the ruler's individual programmatic commitments, and whether the ruler rules in the common interest or for his own advantage is quite literally a personal decision. The limited applicability of law is thus a vital condition for the survival of patrimonialism and explains the "elective affinity" between this type of political process and an economic development strategy of rapid, extensive growth. Hence it is hardly accidental that patrimonial rule was the norm in Eastern Europe from 1948 to 1953 and that it survives today only in Romania.

The mechanisms linking patrimonial rule and accelerated industrialization are several. First of all, when economic growth is rapid and extensive, plans are extremely taut; material shortages and bottlenecks are endemic and unpredictable, enjoining against the application of regulations governing the allocation of resources. As a result, the empirical conditions for obedience to the "rule of law" are absent at all levels of the state administration: enterprises cannot meet unrealistically high output targets, local housing agencies cannot accommodate sudden inflows of labor to urban areas, ministries cannot allocate resources that have not been produced—yet all are

23. Ibid., bk. 5, p. 244.

legally bound to accomplish just these tasks. Not only is political intervention endemic in such conditions, but it must be strictly monitored and controlled from above, since only the political center has sufficient information and breadth of view to make coherent judgments over competing priorities.

In addition, the central leadership itself must be highly united in choosing and implementing its priorities: if the national plan merely aggregates the pet projects of equally powerful regional barons, it can easily become impossible to make choices when authorized projects compete for overcommitted resources, as occurred in Poland in the 1970s. In effect, those with power over the economy must act "as one man," a situation highly conducive to the emergence of a single leader able to discipline the others.

Second, rapid and extensive development creates manifold opportunities for patronage which a clever leader can easily exploit to create a following loyal to both the development strategy and the leader making it possible. The support of upwardly mobile cadres is particularly useful should opposition arise to either individual rule or the policy choices it entails, as the victory of Romania's Gheorghe Gheorghiu-Dej over Pauker and Luca in 1952 demonstrated. In addition, the need continually to generate rewards for loyal supporters reinforces the ruler's commitment to extensive development.

Third, the very pace and scope of change create continual emergencies, unanticipated shortages, and constant shifts in priorities which must be managed politically.[24] Leaders at lower levels thus have an incentive to be committed to the overall strategy and the leader promulgating it rather than to the specific projects with which they are entrusted. Commitment, in effect, is to "building socialism" rather than to building a factory, a school, or even a local party organization. Yet it is only the latter type of commitment which permits leaders at any level to evaluate the viability of specific policies and assess alternatives to them.

Accordingly, political cleavages in patrimonial systems usually take the form of personal intrigues rather than debates among informal coalitions over genuine policy alternatives. In such a context, information is an important strategic resource; but it consists of knowledge about the potentially suspect personal activities of one's rivals (a factor obviously strengthening those with ties to the secret police) rather than concrete facts and data concerning the actual operation and impact of policies and institutions. Indeed, the commitment of patrimonial rule to "teleological" planning not only makes the latter type of information relatively irrelevant to currying favor with the ruler but may make its possession dangerous should it call the central leader's priorities into question.[25]

24. The rather short lives slogans enjoy is but one indicator. A good picture of the varied tasks Czech leaders faced after 1948 appears in Ladislav Mnacko, *A Taste of Power* (New York: Praeger, 1966).
25. For the distinction between "teleological" and "genetic" planning, see Alec Nove, *An Economic History of the USSR* (New York: Penguin, 1980).

When informal coalitions that support policy alternatives arise—as they did wherever the "new course" appeared on party agendas in 1953–54—it is a sign that patrimonial rule is in crisis. Meanwhile, a number of features of patrimonial rule militate against the formation of such coalitions.

Since highly accelerated socioeconomic change abridges the rule of law, bureaucratization in the state is necessarily incomplete under patrimonialism. Rather than a clear separation between party and political responsibilities and state and administrative authority, there is a fusion between power and authority. Party functionaries often find themselves assuming tasks and roles that belong legally to state officials, and state officials (e.g., the police) may wind up usurping party functions. On the one hand, such a fusion of party and state roles prevents party institutionalization, making the fortunes of both the organization and the individuals within it dependent solely on their loyalty to the patrimonial ruler, who himself frequently violates party rules and procedures to pursue his own mission.

On the other hand, the absence of horizontal controls between the party and the state allows individuals to create "private" power bases and personal fiefs that can be employed for purposes that conflict with those of the patrimonial ruler. To prevent this, an elaborate network of vertical controls operates, most obviously through the police, and purges and screening of cadres in the party. Such controls from the top may be supplemented by controls from the bottom, as the leader calls on "the masses" to inform on cases of arbitrary decisions, corruption, and the like; initiates periodic campaigns against "bureaucracy"; and so on. Coordinating these vertical controls provides a rationale for the patrimonial ruler's own assumption of top positions in both the state and the party.

Given such conditions, potential political entrepreneurs who wish to organize policy coalitions obviously face stiff barriers. Moreover, since rewards flow to loyalty rather than to good advice, there is scant incentive to surmount them. Nevertheless, opportunities can and do arise, and leaders committed to purposes different from those of the patrimonial ruler can exploit them to arrive at positions of power. The promise of external support from other Communist parties provides one such opportunity: changes in the Soviet party after Stalin's death played a critical role in the emergence of alternatives to patrimonial rule in Eastern Europe, Imre Nagy's sudden rise to power in Hungary being perhaps the most outstanding case.

Other opportunities arise when beneficiaries of the leader's confidence and policies themselves become disenchanted with either the leader's rule or program, be it because they develop institutional loyalties that continued patrimonial rule threatens, or because they find economic crisis has eliminated opportunities for promotion, or for purely idiosyncratic reasons. Such motives were important in Poland's de-Stalinization in 1956, as was the occasion to act on these dissatisfactions which spontaneous revolt from below provided.

Finally, patrimonial leaders themselves may for their own reasons decide that "extensive development" is no longer appropriate, as Walter Ulbricht apparently did in East Germany. Edward Ochab's resignation in favor of Władysław Gomułka in 1956 in Poland was a variant of this pattern; another far more dramatic version occurred in Yugoslavia following its expulsion from the Cominform in 1948. In all these cases, individual leaders themselves took the initiative in altering both the development strategy and the underlying pattern of elite interaction to provide a better fit of power to purpose. Interestingly, Ceauşescu's accession to power was also accompanied by moves to create a more collegial political process but without changing the development strategy—indeed, the emphasis on forced growth of heavy industry and economic autarchy increased in the late 1960s and the 1970s. The political difficulties of accommodating both goals were a primary factor in the abandonment of the "collegial norms" Ceauşescu initially espoused.

"Rule by the One" may occur as kingship or tyranny; one indicator is that "kings are guarded by the arms of their subjects; tyrants by a foreign force."[26] In this sense, all cases of patrimonialism in Eastern Europe since the war are tyrannies. The arbitrary power exercised by Mátyás Rakosi in Hungary, Bolesław Bierut in Poland, or Gheorghiu-Dej in Romania was closely linked to their privileged personal relations with Stalin, who supplied the foreign forces and support they used to build a socialist state, eliminate potential (or imagined) rivals, and create a following of cadres loyal to them and their policies. The content of the accelerated industrialization drives that they launched was consistent with such a power base: if economic growth and social transformation were extensive and rapid, they were also geared to enhancing the international strength of the Soviet Union, and a net transfer of resources out of Eastern Europe and into the Soviet Union accompanied industrialization.

As is well known, the tyrants of Eastern Europe in the 1950s governed for the most part with the "traditional methods of repression."[27] Yet depending on their purposes, patrimonial rulers can also "turn tyranny into the nature of a kingship—subject to the one safeguard that the reformed tyrant still retains power, and is still in a position to govern his subjects with or without their consent."[28] Such a choice constitutes Nicolae Ceauşescu's unique contribution to the art of socialist politics.[29]

26. Aristotle, *Politics*, bk. 3, p. 138.
27. Aristotle lists them as "the 'lopping off' of outstanding men . . . , the adoption of every means for making every subject as much of a stranger as is possible to every other . . . , [requiring] every resident . . . to be constantly appearing in public. . . , endeavoring to get regular information about every man's saying and doings. . . , impoverishing [the] subjects. . . ," and so forth. *Politics*, bk. 5, p. 244.
28. Ibid., p. 247.
29. See Linden's essay in this volume. In addition, see Kenneth Jowitt, *Revolutionary Breakthroughs and National Development* (Berkeley: University of California Press, 1971); Jowitt, "Inclusion and Mobilization in European Leninist Regimes," in Triska and Cocks, *Political Development*, pp. 119–47; Trond Gilbert, "The Communist Party of Romania," in Stephen Fischer-Galati, ed., *The Communist Parties of Eastern Europe* (New York: Columbia University Press, 1979), pp. 281–327.

Reflecting the fact that Romania's level of development had traditionally lagged behind that of other states in Eastern Europe, Romanian leaders had long been committed to rapid domestic industrialization in order to catch up. By the late 1950s such commitments ran directly counter to CMEA plans for intrabloc specialization; moreover, Romania's socialist partners—mainly the Soviet Union—proved unwilling to provide the extensive material support needed to satisfy such ambitions. Such an international challenge provided Ceauşescu with the opportunity to become the architect of a strategy that would permit rapid national development independent of the CMEA. Hence, whereas East European patrimonialism of the 1950s geared rapid industrialization to the military and political needs of the socialist alliance and the Soviet Union in particular, Ceauşescu oriented accelerated growth in Romania to the achievement of self-sufficiency, in effect modifying the political and economic constraints that penetrated sovereignty prescribed. Rather than national interest being only one interest among the many a hegemonic party must accommodate, in Romania the national, party, and especially personal interests of Ceauşescu became identical.

Military policy reflected the new priorities. Although coverage by the Warsaw Treaty Organization (WTO) defense umbrella remains an important factor for Romanian security in the international system—and consequently, for the security of the regime in the domestic system—the Romanian army itself, with Ceauşescu its commander-in-chief, is geared primarily to "national defense" rather than to bloc commitments. Ceauşescu's decision to rely on "the arms of the subjects" became a critical factor increasing both his own sphere of discretion in the foreign-policy arena and his personal popularity and hold on the Romanian state and party.

Commitment to autarchic policies of rapid and extensive development maintained patrimonial rule but caused Ceauşescu to convert it more to the "nature of a kingship." Aristotle's observations are again apropos:

> Kingships have grown from the purpose of helping the better
> classes . . . and it is from these classes that kings have been drawn. . . .
> Kings are maintained and secured by their friends; tyrants, going on the
> principle, "All men want my overthrow, but my friends have most
> power to effect it," distrust them above all others.[30]

As a party secretary in charge of cadres (clearly, "the better classes"), Ceauşescu relied on "friends"—as opposed, for example, to support from abroad—a critical factor in his succession to party leadership upon Gheorghiu-Dej's death. If his commitment to Romanian national development mobilized such support, it was reciprocated with patronage and opportunities for greater participation in decision making. Ceauşescu's continued reliance on a small coterie of friends and family, linked more by clientelistic relations than by

---

30. Aristotle, *Politics*, bk. 5, pp. 235, 245.

formal and hierarchical subordination, remains a distinctive characteristic of his rule. And as the substantial material and political benefits such individuals (and their clients) enjoy are contingent upon maintaining his leadership, the temptation to replace him or his policies even in the current economic crisis is greatly diminished.

In social policy, too, Ceausescu has preserved patrimonialism by carefully heeding Aristotle's advice to induce both "the poor and the rich . . . to think that it is the tyrant's power that . . . prevents either from suffering injury at the hands of the other."[31] If the personal patronage and support of Ceauşescu have allowed his lieutenants to take unpopular actions, the fact that he himself does not take them has prevented (at least until recently) his image from becoming tarnished among the wider population. At the same time, his "flying visits" to factories and local party headquarters, his antibureaucratic campaigns, and his insistence on "rotating cadres" out of central administrative posts and into regional positions and points of contact with "direct production," not to mention his stress on the continuity of the Romanian national tradition (especially its tradition of kingship!) have helped him to "appear to his subjects not as a despot but as a steward and king of his people."[32]

Maintaining such a political process and Ceauşescu's patrimonial position within it has been part and parcel of the "multilaterally developed society" Ronald Linden describes. The rejection of incrementalism and the pursuit of rapid growth in an autarchic economic framework have both produced patrimonial rule and provided Ceauşescu with the political resources required to maintain it.

Not surprisingly, Romania's response to the sudden rise in petroleum prices was not only accelerated expansion and heavy borrowing but also the elimination of the "economic line" and its protagonists from the leadership coterie in 1974. The reaction to the debt burden was also consistent with this pattern, involving an initial mobilization to resist IMF conditionality and subsequently an equally "multilateral" austerity campaign designed to eliminate the financial constraints on Ceauşescu's sphere of discretion and policy preferences as rapidly as possible. Forced to allocate the costs of such austerity, Ceauşescu respected the obligations of kingship to "help the better classes," and investment—important for maintaining the support of "friends" in key posts of economic administration—suffered significantly less than did consumption. The distinctive characteristic of Romanian adjustment in the 1980s was a sudden drop in the standard of living; it was a strategy with far less appeal to elites in collegial systems, as we shall see.

31. Ibid. p. 249.
32. Ibid.

4. Collegiality

Rather different political dynamics characterize collegial politics. Where "rule by the Few" is the norm, the power of the party does not depend on a single individual. Rather, political power is a collective monopoly of the party as a whole, and any individual's power—including that of the proverbial *primus inter pares*—depends on the ability of the organization to act as a coherent body.[33]

Indeed, individuals who attempt to replace "rule by the Few" with personal command—as did Gomułka with his "failure to consult" in 1970—jeopardize the integrity of the party organization. Hence, they constitute a threat to their peers, each of whose own access to power rests on maintaining existing political procedures. Accordingly, where the patrimonial ruler individually controls the allocation of political resources and disciplines colleagues through a vertical network of police, party, and popular controls, collegial systems can employ horizontal controls on political actors, and rival factions compete for access to the political resources that the party as a whole allocates.

The result is a "politics of notables": neither bureaucratic organizations, the masses, the Soviet Union, nor the police directly controls political leaders. Instead, *they control each other*, and the degree of reciprocal control leaders exert on each other corresponds to their ability to establish a set of common interests (and prevent individual notables from pursuing personal causes) as well as to collegiality's "elective affinity" with incremental types of policy changes. At the same time, the mechanisms through which leaders control and check each other are precisely what produce inflexibility and inefficiency in the economy.

Collegial rule came to East Germany, Poland, Czechoslovakia, Hungary, and Bulgaria in the late 1950s. In part, its arrival was a response of political elites who favored a reformed political process to new opportunities created by changed international conditions: Stalin's death, the rise of collective leadership in the Soviet Union, the "thaw" in East-West relations, and changes in the mechanisms governing the socialist alliance. Equally important, especially in Poland and Hungary, collegial rule was a response to the domestic political tensions and arbitrary excesses against the population and the political elite alike generated under patrimonial rule. The experiences of the previous decade thus informed collective leadership; although its introduction entailed no changes in the domestic structure, it was accompanied by a strong com-

33. For example, Kádár's first moves in Hungary in 1956 were designed not to build up a personal following but to rebuild the party organization, a process that entailed including many cadres who were less than enthusiastic about his leadership. For them, however, accepting Kádár's leadership represented their only hope of reentering political life, while for Kádár, the reestablishment of party rule was the only condition under which he himself could affect the course of development in Hungary. See the essay by Ellen Comisso and Paul Marer in this volume.

mitment on the part of political elites to altering relationships between domestic structures and between the party and the state in particular.

Patrimonial rule fused power and authority in the hands of individuals who enjoyed the confidence of the leader, permitting them to exercise great power subject to no controls other than those of the top leader himself. Collegiality, in contrast, separates power and authority.[34] Although power is the collective monopoly of the party, authority is delegated to the state administration; each acts to check and balance the other, severely constraining the exercise of individual discretion within each.

The law specifies the organizational hierarchies and divisions of competencies within the state, establishing a legal and bureaucratic chain of command. As a result, state officials may exercise discretion only within juridically defined limits and are legally responsible to administrative superiors within the state itself. Hence the "interests" of state functionaries—not to mention their opportunities for promotion—consist of satisfying the expectations of superiors in the state hierarchy itself. Yet such expectations do not originate within the state but are determined politically, by the hierarchically organized party acting as a collective whole through its highest bodies.

Consequently, state organizations—from local government and police agencies to enterprises and hospitals—are no longer "available" to take on tasks and projects an individual party leader favors unless such projects are legally authorized and fall within the competence of the organization. For example, although it may be politically desirable for all preschoolers in Dresden to enroll in daycare centers, if this involves a level of overcrowding contrary to national regulations, center directors have the right and the legal obligation to resist local party demands to this effect. In such ways the bureaucratization of a highly centralized state apparatus reinforces orderly hierarchy in the party itself.

Likewise, state officials can no longer assume or invent political tasks not authorized by their formal mandates: our Dresden daycare center director cannot pressure a local enterprise to set up a nursery for the infants of employees. State officials may sit on party committees and propose political

---

34. "*Power* corresponds to the human ability not just to act but to act in concert. Power . . . belongs to a group and remains in existence only so long as the group keeps together . . . *Authority* can be vested in persons . . . or . . . in offices . . . . Its hallmark is unquestioning recognition by those asked to obey; neither coercion nor persuasion is needed. To remain in authority requires respect for the person in office." Arendt, *On Violence*, pp. 44–45. To use Rosabeth Kantor's formulation, "Power is the ability to get things done . . . to get and use whatever it is that a person needs for the goals he or she is attempting to meet . . . and thus it means having access to what is needed for the doing." Kantor, *Men and Women in the Corporation* (New York: Harper & Row, 1977), p. 166. Authority, in contrast, is "the established *right* . . . to determine policies, to pronounce judgments on relative issues, and to settle controversies." Robert MacIver, *The Web of Government* (New York: Macmillan, 1963). Authority thus needs to be backed by power to be effective, whereas power must be exercised through authorized agents to command automatic obedience. Hence the possibility for checks and balances if the agents exercising each are separate and distinct.

tasks (from building daycare centers to calling for "voluntary" work on Sundays), but only the party itself can take such actions. Even then, lower party organizations cannot act counter to directives taken at higher party levels.

Hence neither state organizations nor their leaders can articulate or mobilize interests independently of the party. They are bureaucracies and may bargain with their administrative superiors within a politically predetermined arena, but they are not political communities capable of generating an autonomous collective interest outside that arena. Indeed, when organizations do assert autonomous interests and pursue them independently, as they did in Poland in the 1970s, the system of checks and balances upon which collective leadership rests is greatly endangered.

If the rule of law reigns in the state administration, maintaining a monopoly on power requires the party to shoulder its political consequences. Party functionaries can indeed intervene in the bureaucratic chain of command to make sure that following the letter of the law does not abridge its spirit as defined by central party priorities. When ordered to cut costs factory directors cannot lay off workers without the local party's approval, nor can monopolistic suppliers fill orders from low-priority firms if it means delaying deliveries to high-priority projects—even when enterprise plans prescribe the former.

Not only does the party act to check the bureaucratic implementation of policies it formulates, but the party must also approve appointments to leading positions within the state and the party apparatus. Similar relationships of policy and personnel prevail between the party and mass organizations (from the trade unions and the Popular Front to pensioners' clubs and boy scouts), who are equally incapable of articulating or mobilizing interests independently of the party. Yet although reciprocal institutional controls act to prevent political and bureaucratic arbitrariness in the execution of policy, protect leaders from becoming the victims of personal intrigues, and concentrate political discretion at the top levels of the party, they do not guarantee that either policy or personnel decisions will reflect a "common interest" to start with. For this the party must develop internal controls; political checks and balances, "ambition counteracting ambition," in the party itself must complement the institutional checks and balances of party-state relations.

Bureaucratization of the state permits far more party institutionalization and respect for procedures in policy and personnel choices than under patrimonial rule. In collegiality, committees that stand in hierarchical relationship to one another make such choices. Individuals thus have an opportunity to influence the exercise of power, but power itself belongs to the collective body in whose deliberations they participate and whose decisions they must carry out regardless of their personal preferences.

Access to positions that provide opportunities to participate in collective decision making is based on demonstrated loyalty to the organization and its decisions as measured by performance in roles assigned by the party and the quality of previous participation in party life. As befits a politics of notables, "merit"—one's ability to carry out the directives adopted in collective party bodies—is judged politically by the bodies initially formulating the directives.[35]

Since merit reflects subjective political considerations, personal loyalties and friendships necessarily play a major role in appointments; in this sense, patrimonialism has no monopoly on patron-client relationships. Yet because power is an organizational rather than an individual attribute, clientelism has rather different consequences under collective leadership. First, there are multiple "patrons," each of whom must justify his or her candidates to the others. Second, "clients" are well aware that although their patron may offer them some protection against attack from rivals, ultimately their opportunities for advancement rest on serving the organization. Hence, sponsorship may ensure individual cooperation, but it is hardly a guarantee of personal fealty.

Because the ability to implement party directives is so important for promotion and access to power itself, leaders at all levels have an incentive carefully to evaluate alternative and specific policy lines; in, say, Hungary, Czechoslovakia, or East Germany, elites build factories or schools rather than an undifferentiated "socialism" whose components vary with the will of a single ruler. Since the probability of being able to accomplish an objective is as important a consideration as is its abstract desirability, collegial politics misleadingly appears "de-ideologized." In fact, collegiality is precisely what permits decisions to be politicized.

Since individual members of collective bodies differ in their policy preferences and personnel favorites, debate over "what to do" is possible and coalitions ranged around alternatives may form. Such policy cleavages are highly desirable in collegial systems, as they supply leaders with incentives to control their peers without reducing politics to a purely individual power struggle.

Significantly, "losers" in policy conflicts retain strong incentives to abide by decisions they oppose, since influence on future choice depends heavily on the "virtue" losers show in the implementation process. For this reason, they are often put in charge of the very policies they oppose, as was Lajos Feher in the management of Hungarian collectivization or Erich Honecker

---

35. "Performance" and "merit" thus reflect *political* considerations. Hence an enterprise director whose firm produces goods at a loss may be far more "meritous" than one whose firm runs a profit, if, say, the former is satisfying a supply constraint for items to which political leaders accord national economic importance.

Readers unfamiliar with Eastern Europe should bear in mind that a position allowing one to be a member of a party committee need not be a party position itself. The mayor of a town, for example, will normally be a member of the town party committee, but he or she is a full-time state office-holder.

in the stabilization of German relations. Not only does this technique deter strong opposition, but co-optation of the leadership prevents its persistence.

If political debate and factional cleavages are both possible and desirable in collegiality, on what bases do factions and coalitions form? Insofar as the preferences leaders advocate have differential consequences for nonparty groups and institutions (e.g., raising food prices may help peasants at the expense of urban consumers), it is tempting to view leaders as "representing" identifiable social groups or institutions. Nevertheless, as indicated above and amply documented in the Hungarian and East German country studies in this volume, there are no mechanisms by which such interests can keep representatives accountable or shift their support from one leader to another. On the contrary, organizational leaders are accountable to the party committees and state authorities who "elect" them to their positions; they do not vie for the support of organization members in competitive contests.

Nevertheless, much evidence also suggests that leaders and factions do pursue programs and purposes they are associated with and that their influence on collective decisions tends to be greater on issues and appointments directly affecting the organizations they manage. The "lobbying" of the Borsod County steel and chemicals complex or the influence of a Béla Csikos-Nagy on price policy in Hungary and the frequent advice solicited from the defense-security nexus in East Germany are illustrative.[36] Hence it is possible to speak of representation in collegial socialism, but it does not take the form of a "mandate" from a defined constituency as occurs in systems based on mass politics. Collegiality offers instead a socialist variant of the "virtual" representation Edmund Burke prescribed for 18-century Britain—a form of representation ideally suited for assemblies of notables in a system of highly limited suffrage, without major ideological cleavage among contestants for rule, and where members of the "legislature" (i.e., the party committee) are also the backbone of the nation's administrative and economic system.[37]

In such a polity, leaders are accountable to their peers, not their constituents. They make political "judgments" based on their conception of the "public" interest rather than expressing the mere "opinions" of the actual public itself.[38] Hence leaders may "embody" interests but they do not represent them.

For example, workers may find their preferences articulated at the highest party levels—but not necessarily by the trade union delegate who is nominally

36. Csikos-Nagy was head of the Materials and Price Commission.

37. Burke's views on representation are scattered through his writings and parliamentary speeches. See Peter J. Stanlis, ed., *Selected Writings and Speeches* (Chicago: Gateway, 1964); Edmund Burke, *Reflection on the Revolution in France* (Indianapolis: Bobbs-Merrill, 1955); Ross Hoffman and Paul Levack, eds., *Burke's Politics* (New York: Knopf, 1949). See also Hanna Pitkin, *The Concept of Representation* (Berkeley: University of California Press, 1967).

38. As Burke told the electors of Bristol, "Your representative owes you, not his industry but his judgment; and he betrays you, instead of serving you, if he sacrifices it to your opinion." Cited by Stanlis, *Writings*, p. 187.

their representative. Women anxious for contraceptive devices may find that demand voiced not by the head of the women's association or the Ministry of Social Welfare but by the party secretary of a firm negotiating for a license to manufacture them. At the same time, their desires for adequate nursery schools or better employment opportunities may not be articulated at all.

A constituency's interest thus exists only insofar as it is part of the larger "social" interest, and coalitions must justify their choices by criteria and standards that their opponents endorse as well. As Burke noted:

> Parliament is not a congress of ambassadors from different and hostile interests, which interests each must maintain, as agent and advocate, against other agents and advocates; but Parliament is a *deliberative* assembly of *one* nation, with *one* interest, that of the whole—where not local purposes, not local prejudices, ought to guide, but the general good, resulting from the general reason of the whole.[39]

Like the early British Parliament, leaders in collegial socialism join "parties" (i.e., enter coalitions) in the legislature, not before. "Elections" are not competitive, except in a personal sense, so party/factional labels are unnecessary: the electorate (i.e., the party committee approving the appointment) is so small the candidate is already well known to the voters. Likewise, the composition of legislative coalitions is fluid and shifting: just as no crude party discipline prevails at an assembly of notables, the ban on factionalism in Leninist parties deprives coalitions of any means to discipline their members. Hence the displacement of opponents on one issue is not equivalent to eliminating opposition.

The "strength" of a faction in a Burkean Parliament is not measured by the number of votes it can muster outside Parliament (which would make virtue a slave of popularity) but by the number of votes it controls inside the legislature. Thus, leaders have no incentive to mobilize "spontaneous" social forces or nonparty groups on behalf of the causes they espouse, although they are able and willing to use their influence to garner favors for their "district."[40] Popular support is not a potent political resource in a politics

39. Ibid., p. 22.
40. See below, p. 230. Burke presents a highly idealized picture of 18-century British politics. In fact, according to Sir Lewis Namier, even in secure pocket boroughs or where the Crown covered a candidate's campaign expenses, "power was used . . . to satisfy local or even personal needs." See Namier's *The Structure of Politics at the Accession of George III*, vol. 1 (London: Macmillan, 1929), p. 163. The same is true in the real world of collegial socialism and for the same reasons: "At all times a system of spoils and benefits necessarily obtains in governing representative bodies where sharp contrasts of ideas and interests or strong party organizations do not pre-determine the vote of the individual Member, and do not reduce him to a mere pawn in the Parliamentary game. If personal disinterestedness is expected from independent members, they have at least to secure benefits and advantages for their constituents; and where the constituents are too numerous to be benefitted individually, it becomes a question of a commercial treaty, a tariff or a bounty favouring some local industry or public works in the district, etc." Ibid., p. 22. As we shall see below for the socialist analogue to the politics of notables, Burke and Namier do not present mutually exclusive descriptions of a single reality but rather two sides of the same coin.

of notables (although claiming to speak for "the people" is every bit as important for Honecker and János Kádár as it was for Burke),[41] and the Polish experience illustrates how attempts by individual leaders to mobilize nonparty groups in factional struggles can prove as destructive to collective leadership as they proved to a Parliament limited to aristocrats in Britain.

Instead, the influence of a faction depends on other factors, from the "quality" of its members (the director of a major enterprise whose appointment is approved by the Central Committee will carry more weight than the head of a local collective farm) to the "virtue" they show in carrying out their tasks (an enterprise director who successfully implements various policy changes will be heeded more than one who is widely regarded as incompetent). The nature of the particular problem at hand is another consideration; for example, trade union officials are more influential on issues of labor regulation than on balance-of-payments questions.[42] Finally, personal characteristics and ties are equally critical components of influence. Individuals with strong connections in central party bodies carry more political clout than do purely local figures and, to quote Sir Lewis Namier in the British case, "personality, eloquence, debating power, prestige counted for more in the eighteenth century House of Commons . . . than it [*sic*] does now."[43]

Since quality rather than quantity of support is vital to the exercise of influence, leaders of all policy orientations have an incentive to promote virtue in the ranks: supporting a candidate for a local position who seems destined to rise to bigger and better things not only creates a potentially important ally but also indicates good judgment on personnel questions, a source of political credit that can be cashed in at a future time. Thus, the "professionalization" of party and state cadres has not occurred against the will of political leaders in collegial systems but because of it. As Baylis has shown in the East German case, the rise of technocrats did not signify the rise of a counterelite to the party leadership but rather an expansion of the political resources available to it.[44]

The goal, in effect, is to recruit the nation's "superior elements" to political service, much as Burke would have it, not to guarantee a vulgar unanimity of opinion. If this strategy is successful, opportunities for notables to exercise individual judgment can be enhanced and pluralism of opinions encouraged. Peers can be counted upon to control one another, and virtue is its own restraint.

41. "I reverentially look up to the opinion of the people, and with an awe that is almost superstitious. I should be ashamed to show my face before them, if I changed my ground as they cried up or cried down men or things or opinion." In Stanlis, *Writings*, p. 322.
42. Hence power to control the agenda is a strategic political resource of considerable value, as is access to information. Interestingly, Namier also draws attention to the "remarkable level" on which naval debates were conducted in the House of Commons thanks to the heavy population of admirals among its members. See *Structure of Politics*, p. 41.
43. Ibid., p. 11.
44. See Baylis's essay in this volume.

"The spirit of moderation is what we call virtue in an aristocracy," says Montesquieu,[45] and in collective leadership, moderation shows up as incrementalism in policy making. The responses of Hungary, East Germany, Czechoslovakia, and Bulgaria to relatively dramatic changes in the international economy are illustrative. Incremental change is vital to preserving the rule of law in the state and respect for procedures in the party. In the economy, such change permits shortages to be foreseen and managed through institutionalized procedures rather than becoming opportunities for arbitrary individual solutions and sudden campaigns. Incrementalism characterizes policy making in collegial systems, however, not because of any abstract "functional necessity" but because political checks and balances among rival, fluid factions competing for both purposes and power give leaders built-in incentives to find solutions with which all can live.

The role of the *primus inter pares* is critical in this regard, especially at the national level where power is concentrated. What distinguishes him from the patrimonial leader is not so much the extent of his influence but the techniques by which and the purposes for which it is exercised. Whereas the patrimonial leader is above all an executive, committed to a highly specific program and able to order his subordinates to achieve it, a *primus inter pares* is a legislative leader. If no "legislation" passes without his approval, his preferences are normally quite flexible; indeed, his flexibility is precisely what enables him to maintain his position.[46]

Such individuals "manage the coalitions" that arise in the decision-making process, acting as "agent[s] for multiple principals." They exert leadership not by keeping a distance from all sides but by fostering an image that leads each faction to believe that the *primus inter pares* is "really" one of their own. Kádár, for example, is as widely believed by reformists to be sympathetic to their goals as he is held by conservatives to be a bastion of support.

To maintain his leadership, a *primus inter pares* searches for "solutions" to problems which reinforce this image and indeed focuses attention on problems capable of being solved this way. Not surprisingly, radical changes that might "partisanize" the image of the *primus inter pares* are unlikely to receive his support. As a result, only changes that appear to be in the interest of all sides in a controversy (the "common interest") are likely to occur.

Rule by the Few may well have an "elective affinity" with incremental change, but the substance of what constitutes an "increment" varies considerably by country, reflecting particular national circumstances and the

45. Montesquieu, *The Spirit of the Laws*, trans. by Thomas Nugent (New York: Hafner, 1966), p. 49.

46. On the techniques of legislative leaders in assemblies with weak party discipline, see Kenneth Shepsle and Brian Humes, "Legislative Leadership: Organizational Entrepreneurs as Agents" (Paper presented at the Conference on Adaptive Institutions, Stanford University, 8–9 November 1984); and Morris Fiorina, *Representatives, Roll Calls and Constituencies* (Lexington, Mass.: Lexington Books, 1974).

policy orientations around which factions in each national party have crystalized. Thus, policy outcomes reflect a nation-specific content—what the "common interest" is—as well as the general form of the political process in which they are selected. It is thus the *content* of the policy process that explains why, say, Czechoslovakia did not avail itself of borrowing opportunities in the 1970s or why Hungary and East Germany responded to the need to pay back hard-currency debts by expanding capacities for export to non-CMEA markets.

In East Germany, Hungary, Czechoslovakia, and Poland, the sources of political cleavage are rooted in national history, and national party history in particular. In questions of economic policy—as well as other matters—the patterns of cleavages in each party are consistent and continuous, and although the individuals sitting on each side of the fence vary, the fence itself is rather stable. If the nature of state structure makes shortages a problem with which all must deal and if the form of the political process suggests the solution will be an incremental one, then which shortages (e.g., energy, consumer goods, convertible currency) dominate the political agenda, and how they are managed (e.g., increased exports to the West, higher agricultural procurement prices, further integration within the CMEA) will vary, depending on the goals and priorities political actors advance in each state.

In Hungary, the great divide centers on altering the economic mechanism and manifests itself in regard to issues of how to allocate investment, regulate wages, organize banking, determine prices, and so forth. This cleavage dates back to the party's ambiguous interpretation of the revolt of 1956, its willingness to accept reformists and conservatives alike into its ranks, and the presence of both at the top levels of the post-1956 elite. In Czechoslovakia, in contrast, the trauma and purges following the 1968 invasion closed off political life to leaders who advocated the use of market mechanisms and opening the economy to Western influence. The range of policy positions narrowed, as economic reform was pushed off the political agenda. Incrementalism thus takes the form of debating quantitative rather than qualitative economic adjustments, of technical and administrative changes rather than economic or political ones. East Germany presents a third variant, in which increments are approached in terms of their contribution to preserving cohesion within a highly technocratic elite and maintaining the distinctive identity of the German Democratic state. There economic reforms have not so much been pushed off the agenda as they have been substituted for by a "scientific and technical revolution"; a relatively satisfactory economic performance and strong ties to the CMEA give leaders few incentives to advocate systemic economic change. At the same time, since Western states are the source of much of the technology that elites are committed to acquiring, they were understandably unwilling to cut themselves off from it in the 1980s, despite Czech advice to do just that.

Incremental change is not necessarily insignificant change and can indeed lead to modifications in state structure, as did some aspects of the Hungarian reform. Moreover, any change alters the political weights of contending factions; if this can work to reverse change, it can also allow changes to cumulate, ultimately repositioning the fence altogether, as has apparently occurred in Hungarian agricultural policy and inter-German relations.

Nevertheless, the same political and institutional checks and balances that produce incremental change and political stability are also responsible for much of the economic inefficiency and inflexibility that distinguish CMEA states. Enterprise directors wring their hands over the number of inspections, audits, and approvals which must accompany even the most minor changes; party secretaries lose sleep over how to replace an executive in a local firm whose friends on the local party committee insist on rewarding his years of loyal service; foreign-trade officials find their schemes to increase exports by betting on the winners thwarted by other party and state officials who point to "supply constraints" while pressing the claims of their own favorites.

The politics of notables hurts economic efficiency in other ways as well. Like the peers of 18-century Britain, socialist elites have quite concrete, material interests at stake in the abstract, public-minded judgments they make. Obviously they are not the interests of a propertied aristocracy or commercial class out to tap the state for the sake of protecting or amassing personal wealth. Socialist elites may have privileges, but they do not own income-generating property, so their concrete material interests hardly lie in protecting and accumulating it. Socialist elites do, however, have a strong interest in preserving and enlarging their *political* base, which is accomplished not by increasing their share of individual goods but rather by enlarging the stock of *collective* goods (i.e., the socialist sector) in their area of responsibility.

Collective goods—factories, schools, hospitals—provide leaders with both appointment possibilities and opportunities to participate in decisions affecting the fate of the collective goods themselves. Moreover, insofar as power to define and allocate socialized resources is so concentrated at top party levels, all leaders strive to acquire responsibility for economic activities of national importance. Hence local leaders are anxious for "their" enterprises to achieve supply monopolies on domestic markets, hook regional economic activities into centrally sponsored projects, locate large plants in their region, and so on. Such intraelite competition for political resources not only pushes toward monopoly and centralization in the economy but is the prime cause of the "expansion drive" so characteristic in CMEA states. Ironically, even leaders who in principle favor more competition and decentralization must behave this way if they are to acquire the influence necessary to introduce a change. In effect, responsibility for a chemicals plant so large it drags down the entire national balance of payments would give one a far more important voice in the formulation of economic policy than would answering for a small but highly profitable collective farm serving the local market.

State structure itself aggravates the problem. Political leaders everywhere are rarely interested in economic efficiency or terribly skilled at inducing it. But in socialist states "politics is in command": if political elites take no interest in economic rationality, no one else can. Further, there are few inducements for them to take such an interest. In, say, OECD states, leaders face an electoral constraint in polities where a large private sector wields substantial political clout; in addition, their states must compete with others in an open and competitive international economy. For these reasons, political elites in Western states are literally forced to take an interest in rational economizing even when they would not if left to their own devices.

In socialism, however, political resources are a party monopoly. Far from increasing responsiveness to the private sector, intraelite competition produces the expansionistic economic policies that cause economically dysfunctional shortage tensions. These, in turn, simply enhance the autonomy of the party. Nor are CMEA states in a competitive relationship with one another. Not only is it less necessary for elites to be concerned with microeconomic efficiency, but CMEA trade arrangements often penalize attempts to foster it.

The bias that state structure and the politics of notables give political elites to expand the socialist sector is complemented by an equally strong prejudice against the private sector. Nor is that bias entirely unreasonable: even when private activities help to improve the performance of the all-important socialist sector, the latter's insensitivity to costs creates opportunities for windfall private profits that are neither economically nor politically justifiable. Precisely for this reason, private activities in CMEA states have generally been limited to spheres where entrepreneurs deal directly with cost-conscious private consumers.

Moreover, a prosperous and extensive private sector not only allows wealth to rival virtue in the allocation of status but distributes it independently of political control. It reduces opportunities to recruit talent into the party and state while greatly increasing incentives to engage in corruption for those who remain within the socialist sector. Finally, it may create an economic base for collective action independent of party control—especially if the socialist sector comes to depend on it for supplies.

Nevertheless, the exigencies of power and purpose can alter political biases against the private sector. First, purpose as well as power motivates leaders, who may well support a vision of social order (including an economic check on party hegemony and disciplining the state sector to compete for its advantages) that an extension of private activities would entail; the simple fact that such elites rise to power within an existing state structure does not necessarily entail reproducing it in unaltered form, as recent changes in Hungary suggest. Second, if a semilegal second economy is booming while the socialist sector stagnates, its "corrupting" effects are likely to be felt in any case; the economic and political impacts of widespread circulation of the deutsche mark in East Germany are an example. In such circumstances, legalizing the private sector (and/or taking formal measures regulating the use of hard currency) benefits even elites who are averse to private activities by allowing the latter to be more openly controlled. Such logic undoubtedly underlies the recent liberalization of rules governing the private sector in East Germany.

Moreover, the same structure and processes that produce the "expansion drive" in the socialist sector also provide political elites with instruments for cutting it back and/or making it more competitive, decentralized, and efficient if they choose. As the periodic downturns in investment cycles indicate, when the central leadership comes down decisively in favor of austerity and cutbacks, it is in the political interest of elites at all levels to demonstrate their "virtue" in managing the austerity process. Likewise, exogenous shocks or internal changes in the composition of the top leadership can make microeconomic efficiency and managing limited resources as desirable to a center facing "hard" budget constraints vis-à-vis the international economy as growth and creating new resources are to subelites.

Rule by the Few can take both "good" and "perverse" forms. It can appear as collective leadership and the politics of notables, as in Hungary, East Germany, Czechoslovakia, and Bulgaria. There, power and authority check and balance each other, ambition constrains ambition, and political leaders are forced to find solutions to problems in the "common interest" of the leadership as a whole.

But rule by the Few can also appear as oligarchy: leaders pursue only their individual interests, and the "common interest" evaporates under the pressures of internecine factionalism. In oligarchy, power does not restrain power; authority and power do not counterbalance each other. Instead, individual leaders divide up power and authority among themselves so that each is free to act "at will." Such was the case in Poland.[47]

Political and party life in Poland evolved differently than in other CMEA states. The lessons Poland learned from 1956 were unique. The Hungarian party discovered the dangers of spontaneous protest and institutionalized measures that deterred political leaders from advancing their own cause by appealing to extraparty social forces or organizations. In Poland, however, popular protests and the support of nonparty groups (including the Catholic church) became valuable resources for discrediting opponents and forcing through desired policy changes within the party itself. If liberals used workers' councils in 1956 to push for reforms, the faction organized around Mieczusław

47. See Kazimierz Poznański's article in this volume. See also M. K. Dziewanowski, *The Communist Party of Poland*, 2d ed. (Cambridge: Harvard University Press, 1976); Jadwiga Staniszkis, *Poland's Self-Limiting Revolution* (Princeton: Princeton University Press, 1983); Jean Woodall, ed., *Policy and Politics in Contemporary Poland* (London: Frances Pinter, 1982); Andrzej Korbonski, "Leadership Succession and Political Change in Eastern Europe," *Studies in Comparative Communism* 9 (Spring 1976), pp. 3–23; and Neal Ascherson, *The Polish August* (New York: Penguin, 1981).

Moczar utilized student demonstrations in 1968 for more repressive purposes. Taking advantage of the 1970 protests to oust Gomułka was thus scarcely a new departure in Poland.

That leaders could employ extraparty political resources to forward their own ambitions proved disastrous to the maintenance of collective leadership. On the one hand, party leaders had a much weaker incentive to accommodate each other, since in a dispute the availability of external political resources not subject to reciprocal factional control encouraged each side to seek a total victory over opponents. On the other, each faction had an incentive to exaggerate the claims or the dangers that extraparty forces posed in order to force its preferences on the others.

Furthermore, as control over organizations—be they enterprises, the police, union branches, or local party organizations—was critical for wielding clout in the party and protecting oneself from rivals, overall party control over subordinate organizations declined as individual control increased. Hence, even when a collective decision was made, it could easily remain a dead letter if opponents of the decision controlled the organization that had to implement it. Whereas in Hungary, then, "virtue" in carrying out a decision one opposed could be rewarded with increased influence, in Poland precisely the opposite was the case: individual leaders and rival factions had far more incentives either to stonewall decisions or to provoke protests against them than to carry them out. Rather than a checks-and-balances relationship between the state and party, a relationship developed that was based on veto power of one against the other. Not surprisingly, even moderate economic reform was impossible in such conditions.

Factional warfare remained covert in the 1960s largely because Gomułka made no significant domestic policy innovations. And when in 1970 he introduced relatively mundane changes—without the "consultation" that would surely have blocked even such minor alterations—Gomułka was ousted.

It was in this situation that Gierek took over the party's helm. Conceivably, he could have simply restored the status quo ante while permitting a moderate rise in wages to quiet the situation in the factories. If he had done so, he would have remained—as Gomułka had become—a prisoner of the feuding party factions, an ineffectual leader, and a sitting duck for the Moczar group should it decide to move against him.

Such passivity hardly suited Gierek, who chose to interpret his mandate as a call to end the party's isolation from the larger society. Hence, rather than reducing the role of social groups in party decisions, Gierek sought to increase it in order to buttress his own position in the party leadership.

Initially, the strategy was highly successful; "renewal" was popular in party and society alike, and by December 1971 Gierek was able to demote or eliminate the party's old guard and replace it with leaders loyal to himself and to socialist renewal.

It was a costly victory. The promises made to groups and party elites in return for their support forced Gierek to adopt a distinctly nonincremental economic strategy, with disastrous repercussions for maintaining the already weak "rule of law" within the state apparatus. Procedures and rules no longer applied, and targets became irrelevant to real economic capacities. Makeshift solutions became the mode, while economic and administrative actors could literally purchase permission to do as they wish or use the threat of spontaneous group protest to claim the resources they wanted—often for purposes quite unconnected with group demands. On lower levels the attenuation of rules was reflected in wage drift; on higher levels it materialized as bribery and corruption. The 1973 reform granting large enterprises autonomy was thus part of the disease rather than a cure: the reform simply legally emancipated the firms to pursue whatever the individuals controlling them wanted.

Had Gierek been able to transform the political process into patrimonial rule à la Ceauşescu, he might have avoided the political consequences this strategy produced even as the economy deteriorated. To give him credit, Gierek did move in this direction with the 1973 reorganization of regional party and state administrations. Not only were party secretaries given direct authority in the state, but Gierek was able to promote his own followers to the now extremely powerful provincial leadership positions.

Nevertheless, in part because of the "renewal" program to which he was committed, Gierek did not capitalize on the political debt his followers now owed him to create a vertical network of police and party controls to discipline their newly expanded powers. Rather, he reciprocated their loyalty by liberating them from top-down controls, leaving "society" the task of preventing abuses in the provinces.

The failure to combine the stick with the carrot created additional pressures for rapid economic expansion. Loyalty had to be retained by supplying provincial barons with resources to do as they wanted, leaving them to deal with the claims of local groups as best they could. When resources were plentiful, groups could be bought off, but as resources became scarce (or when provincial leaders had plans of their own for them), the police served as a viable substitute for resources. In effect, once Gierek opted not to use the police to control political elites, they could be used by those elites to control recalcitrant social groups.

Consequently, the use of repression ceased to be a national monopoly but was available to local leaders for their own purposes. Moreover, the police could easily exploit the Balkanization of political power to act independently of both regional and national elites. And such a situation pervaded the state administration (be it the police, the press, the censors, even the offices issuing building permits for new churches). The upshot was that those who were in principle politically responsible for state actions in practice found themselves unable to control them. As a result, while the party retained the right and remained the only political organization with the ability to make collective choices, its failure to monopolize the means of collective action meant it lacked the ability to carry out its own decisions.

Not surprisingly, when political leaders made concessions and agreements with groups—both before and after 1980—they found themselves unable to enforce them on either their own following or the state administration they theoretically controlled. Not only were promises violated, but it became impossible to determine who was responsible for the violations. Equally predictably, this merely encouraged social groups to up their demands, strengthen their own organizations, and deny legitimacy to the political leadership. The result was a classic praetorian situation, in which only a military coup could relieve political tensions.[48]

The Polish crisis is thus strongly reminiscent of the experience of many Latin American states, which indicates that military elites can indeed impose order, enforce austerity, and even restructure economies. Wojciech Jaruzelski appears to be conforming with such a pattern, although his "restructuring" is along the lines of orienting the economy eastward, toward the CMEA, rather than preparing for a jump into the larger international system.

Military elites, however, are much less skilled at creating viable political institutions, which is the heart of the problem in Poland. The difficulty is not so much one of reviving or restraining social groups but of reorganizing the party into a genuine political institution in its own right, able and willing to negotiate with other groups without its membership subverting agreements it is bound to observe. If there are elements in the Polish situation that would permit such an evolution, there are also many factors militating against it.

5. Conclusion

The political dynamics that led to the Polish crisis are a graphic reminder of the variety of collective choices and policy outcomes which is possible within relatively uniform structures and of the creative (and destructive) roles political elites play in fashioning these. To describe the relationship between state structures, political processes, and strategy choices, the metaphor of building a house is instructive.

Like an economic strategy, a house is the outcome of a building process, and it may be well or poorly constructed for the purposes it is to serve. If one imagines (historically changing) societies and territories as the materials

48. "The absence of effective political institutions capable of mediating, refining, and moderating group action" led to a situation in which "each group employs means which reflect its peculiar nature and capabilities. The wealthy bribe; the students riot; workers strike; mobs demonstrate; and the military coup." Samuel Huntington, *Political Order in Changing Societies* (New Haven: Yale University Press, 1968), p. 196. The parallels between the Polish crisis and the economic background to military takeovers in Latin America are striking. See Guillermo O'Donnell, *Modernization and Bureaucratic Authoritarianism* (Berkeley: Institute of International Studies, University of California, 1979).

out of which the "house of policy," so to speak, is built, state structures constitute the tools available for erecting it. Accordingly, the architectural problems with which environmental obstacles and changes present potential builders are at least in part a product of the tools and materials they have at their disposal.

Analogously, the conjuncture of state structure and particular economic capacities in CMEA states made international economic disturbances appear to policy makers as a problem of physical shortages, in contrast to the problem of price adjustments they posed outside Eastern Europe. Likewise, if state structures provided East European elites with the means for resolving shortage tensions which even socialist NICs did not possess (such as an administrative and political machinery for rationing goods in short supply or the possibility of politically negotiated resource transfers from CMEA partners), they also deprived them of tools that proved critical in adjustment efforts outside the bloc—from an active price mechanism to a network of small and competitive enterprises. Finally, the nature of the tools available in the CMEA was such that they were available only to professional builders, so to speak: faced with an exceptionally cold winter, residents of the building under construction could not go out and buy their own space heaters. Thus, in Eastern Europe adjustment to external change did not occur through the autonomous responses of microeconomic actors but on the basis of explicit decisions made by central political leaders.

Continuing the metaphor, the tools and materials with which builders work are clearly critical factors in both the design they select and the way in which they select it. Correspondingly, state structures have an equally strong impact on the policy alternatives elites propose and on the way in which they capture power to implement these alternatives. Among CMEA states, tools follow a rather standardized pattern; they are quite different from those available to construction engineers outside Eastern Europe. Not surprisingly, the buildings that result and the dynamics of their selection vary as well—even where similar selection processes or policy objectives are adopted.

For example, "rule by the One" in Romania may have shared the "pomp and splendour" Montesquieu found appropriate to kings everywhere with equally monocratic rulers in the Philippines or pre-Sandinista Nicaragua. Its "elective affinity" with accelerated industrialization through a command economy, however, is difficult to imagine in states whose domestic structures describe large private sectors. Likewise, if "collective leadership" in cabinet governments of Western parliamentary systems gives rise to the incrementalism and "muddling through" in policy making that appear in Hungary, its dynamics work to encourage leaders to strengthen their ties to distinct social constituencies rather than to deter their formation. Finally, where leaders of differently structured states opt for similar priorities, the consequences are likely to diverge. Hence, high growth rates in the shortage economies of the CMEA provoked a stagnation or decline in participation in international trade where state and economic structure in South Korea allowed political elites to use high growth to expand their share of world markets.

By filtering problems, creating possibilities, and weighing political resources, state structures may well shape both the agenda and the arena for collective choices. Nevertheless, they do not make the choices themselves. To return to our metaphor, the conjuncture of tools and materials may make construction possible, but it hardly prescribes a specific project design. Likewise, although the stock of available tools and materials limits feasible designs, it does not prevent builders from choosing a model that cannot, in practice, be constructed with them. Finally, neither tools nor materials alone are capable of designing and building a house. Rather, construction proceeds from the actions and practices of builders, who propose alternative designs and architectural visions while seeking to capture control of the tools and materials required to build them.

Consequently, the fact that several groups of builders each confronts a uniform set of tools does not by any means imply that they will build the same house or reach a decision about which house to build in the same way. As we saw in the CMEA cases, the vision of a single master builder such as Romania's Ceaușescu may prove so compelling that he is able to control tools and materials unilaterally, putting him in a position to order the others to conform to his design. Alternatively, builders may find reciprocal cooperation advantageous and not allow any single builder access to tools or materials without the consent of his peers. In such a case, the design will reflect a synthesis of the different models each proposes, as in Hungary and East Germany. In a third arrangement, builders may disagree so sharply as to the nature of the edifice that they simply parcel up the tools and materials among each other. While those controlling strategic pieces of equipment may find themselves in a position to block the projects of others, they may also find they lack the tools required to complete edifices of their own. Poland's experience is a case in point. Moreover, designs may change in the course of construction for reasons of exogenous change, because the materials prove unmalleable, or other causes. As a result, the negotiating process may be reopened and reshaped to correspond to new construction needs.

In addition, even where tools are uniform and builders employ similar methods for disposing of them and selecting appropriate designs, the materials with which they must work may vary considerably. Not surprisingly, designs will reflect these differences, as the content of the political process in East European states reflects distinct national characteristics and endowments. Significantly, too, the fit between tools and materials may not be a very close one, a possibility particularly apropos in the East European cases. Builders with highly sophisticated equipment may find themselves lacking skilled labor to operate it; the tools for installing oil heating may be plentiful, but petroleum lacking. In such conditions, finding an appropriate design is far from an easy task. Builders may opt for designs more closely tailored to the specificity of the materials available, perhaps modifying the tools they employ for this purpose—as was the case with Hungarian agriculture. Alternatively, leaders may be committed to a fixed design and set of tools and turn their efforts to changing the available materials—as was the case in Eastern Europe in the 1950s. Likewise, if materials prove inadequate, builders may choose to expand them through purchases from external agents, a factor that may force a revision of the design if it fails to generate resources to cover the materials its construction absorbs.

Despite uniform state structures, then, political elites in CMEA states varied considerably in the visions of social order they espoused and in their abilities to capture power to pursue them. If domestic structure shaped the strategies they proposed and the political resources they mobilized to pursue them, "divergencies in foreign economic strategies" among CMEA states nonetheless were not "due principally to divergencies in their domestic structures."[49] Rather, those differences reflected the dynamic interaction of the form and the content of political processes which occurs within common state structures. While the conjuncture of tools and materials thus makes the construction of policy possible, in the absence of builders nothing happens, and tools and materials alike decay under the wear and tear of environmental change. Hence, if understanding state structures is a necessary condition for explaining policy choices and consequences, the survival, reproduction, and adaptation of those structures themselves depend on the strategic interaction of policy makers and the choices they make in political processes.

49. As Katzenstein found in the OECD cases. See Katzenstein, "Conclusion," p. 920.

The debt crisis and adjustment responses in Eastern Europe: a comparative perspective Laura D'Andrea Tyson

In retrospect, the first major increase in oil prices in 1973–74 marked a turning point in the world economy. Before then, the postwar economy had undergone several decades of economic recovery and expansion, fueled by growing trade and capital flows that had tied economies together in an increasingly interdependent web. Such interdependence brought many of the expected benefits of liberalization in trade and capital movements, as both developed and developing countries shared in the impetus to growth that expanding world markets generated. Despite these benefits, interdependence had its dangers, dangers that were suggested by the recurrent balance-of-payments crises of individual countries and the constraints on domestic economic policy choices which such crises inevitably produced. The negative implications of interdependence, however, did not become fully apparent until the economic shocks of the 1973–84 period. The magnitude of these shocks and the interdependence of the world's economies made external economic events a major determinant of economic performance and a major constraint on economic policy in both the developed and developing world and in both the East and the West.[1]

Although their repercussions were felt worldwide, the external economic shocks of the 1970s created different economic constraints and opportunities

Earlier drafts of this essay have benefited from the comments, criticisms, and suggestions of Ellen Comisso, Peter Katzenstein, Benjamin Cohen, Jim Caporaso, Peter Gourevitch, Peter Hardi, Albert Fishlow, and the other authors contributing to this volume. The research was sponsored in part by a grant from the Berkeley-Stanford Program in Soviet International Behavior funded by the Rockefeller Foundation. I am deeply grateful to Leyla Woods for invaluable research assistance and comments.

1. I shall use the terms *East* and *West* to distinguish between the East European countries of the Soviet bloc and the rest of the world. Although this is a rough distinction, I shall use it mainly to differentiate between the East European countries that are members of the Council for Mutual Economic Assistance (CMEA) and the Warsaw Pact, and newly industrializing countries (NICs) in the rest of the world. Accordingly, Yugoslavia is not in the East but in the West.

International Organization 40, 2, Spring 1986   0020-8183 $5.00

for individual countries. Countries varied significantly in their sensitivity to external shocks according to their size, their level of development, and their natural resource endowment. There were major differences between oil-exporting and oil-importing countries and, within the group of oil-importing countries, between developed and developing countries. Because of significant differences in regional trading and policy relationships, there were also major differences between Eastern-bloc countries and the developed and developing countries of the West.

Differences in the constraints and opportunities occasioned by external shocks produced diverse policy responses among countries. To a large extent, such responses reflected the different underlying structures of political and economic institutions in place at the time the shocks occurred. Differences in structure, however, are not by themselves sufficient to explain the styles of reactions that developed. Differences in the objectives of political leaders— in their purposes—and in their power to realize these objectives are also important explanatory variables.

This essay illustrates the links between structure and purpose, on the one hand, and policy reactions to external shocks and their consequences for economic performance, on the other, by comparing the experiences of the East European countries with a group of newly industrializing countries (NICs) in East Asia and Latin America. The Latin American countries include Brazil and Mexico, and the East Asian countries include Korea, Taiwan, and Singapore. Yugoslavia is also included in the NICs, although it differs in many important economic, political, and geopolitical respects from both the countries of Eastern Europe and other NICs. The countries sampled provide a telling basis of comparison because they have roughly similar levels of development;[2] they all suffered from adverse changes in world trade; and they all stood to gain from the availability of cheap foreign capital in the 1973–79 period and to lose from its dramatic contraction thereafter. These broad similarities notwithstanding, responses to external shocks and economic performance varied widely, according to underlying differences in basic economic characteristics and differences in both structure and purpose.

The first section of this essay provides a brief overview of the shocks in world trade and capital markets in the 1970s. The second section examines

---

2. The World Bank classifies all of the NICs examined here as "upper-middle-income" countries. In 1982 dollars, gross national product (GNP) per capita ranged from a low of $1,910 in Korea to a high of $5,910 in Singapore. Because of significant differences in accounting conventions for determining national income and suspected biases in statistical reporting in the East, precise comparisons of income levels between the NICs and the countries of Eastern Europe are impossible. Using CIA figures, Jan Vaňous estimates that within Eastern Europe 1983 GNP per capita ranged from a low of $4,742 in Romania to a high of $9,070 in the GDR. These estimates suggest that in terms of the level of GNP per capita, the GDR, Czechoslovakia, and possibly Hungary may be more comparable to the industrial market economies of the West than to the NICs. See Vaňous, "Diverging Trends in CMEA Economies in 1984: Recovery in Eastern Europe and Downturn in the Soviet Union," Wharton Econometric Forecasting Associates, *Centrally Planned Economies: Current Analysis*, 27 March 1985.

the role of both external shocks and internal policy choices in the evolution of balance-of-payments difficulties. The third section describes policy reactions to the first round of trade and capital-market shocks during the 1973–79 period and identifies their implications for future economic performance. The fourth and fifth sections describe policy reactions and economic performance during the second round of trade and capital-market shocks of the 1979–84 period. The argument focuses on the ensuing debt crisis and on the austerity programs that either were voluntarily adopted or were necessitated by external financing constraints. The economic costs of austerity, in terms of forgone output, the distribution of these costs across different spending categories and spending groups, and the effects of austerity on external economic performance and debt are considered. Finally, the last section draws some conclusions about the long-run effects of external shocks on both structure and purpose.

1. External economic shocks and their implications for economic performance

During the 1973–84 period, there were a series of major economic shocks in international markets for traded goods and in international capital markets. The oil-price rises of 1973–74 and 1979–80 touched off major changes in the terms of trade between manufactured goods and raw materials. These price shifts were accompanied by slowdowns in world trade in 1974–75 and again in 1979–83, largely because of recessionary conditions in the advanced industrial countries whose markets had been the source of dynamism of world trade in the 1960s. The ensuing world recession during 1979–83 was the longest in postwar history and affected both developed and developing countries in both the East and the West.

The first major change in world capital-market conditions occurred in 1974–79, in the wake of the first oil-price shock of 1973–74. Previously, most of the external funding available to the developing countries had come from the savings of the industrial economies, and much of this had been distributed through official government channels or through multilateral institutions, such as the International Monetary Fund (IMF) or the World Bank. After 1973–74 the oil-exporting countries began to provide substantial savings to be recycled by the commercial banks. The dramatic growth in the supply of loanable funds from this savings and the resulting competition among commercial banks pushed down the real rate of interest on commercial bank loans. The low and sometimes negative real interest rates resulting from such conditions enhanced the attractiveness of external borrowing as a way to finance continued growth, despite adverse shifts in the terms of trade and temporarily reduced export prospects for many countries.

Most of the NICs and most of the East European countries took advantage of the improved credit-market conditions by building up their international indebtedness.[3] In 1979, however, world credit-market conditions began to tighten as a result of the simultaneous introduction of restrictive monetary policies in several industrial economies, most significant, the United States. These policies drove real interest rates sharply upward and began to attract capital flows from the developing to the developed economies. The sharp contraction in the amount of credit available and the steep increase in interest rates on outstanding debt for both the countries of Eastern Europe and the NICs were major external shocks that posed serious constraints on policy choice during the 1980–84 period. In contrast to the 1974–78 period, when lax credit-market conditions broadened policy choices, in the later period capital-market conditions sharply curtailed them. Significantly, it is correct to characterize credit-market conditions during both periods as deviating from a sustainable long-run position: during the early period, because real interest rates were excessively low, and during the later period, because they were excessively high relative to historically realistic levels. In both periods, credit-market conditions provided a distorted signal for long-run policy choice.

For the countries of Eastern Europe, membership in the Council for Mutual Economic Assistance (CMEA) and general political trends in East-West relations influenced both the timing and the extent of the impact of adverse developments in the world economy. Within the CMEA, relative prices adjusted only gradually to world-market changes over the 1974–83 period and worked to the benefit of the Soviet Union, the major net exporter of energy and raw materials in the bloc, and to the detriment of the East European states, all of which were net energy importers in this market by the end of the 1970s.[4] In addition to terms-of-trade losses in CMEA trade, the East European countries also suffered considerable terms-of-trade losses in their trade with nonbloc partners during the 1974–83 period.

Within the Eastern bloc, Soviet sales of oil and other energy products at prices below world-market levels at least through the end of 1982 meant an implicit price subsidy of significant magnitude to its East European trading partners.[5] The Soviet Union also provided direct credit to its East European trading partners (except Romania) by financing large ruble deficits. (For more on the extent of these subsidies and details of the deficit financing see Michael

3. Between 1973 and 1978 the gross medium- and long-term debt of the developing countries increased by 200%, with debt from private creditors increasing fourfold.

4. For example, compared to 1980, East European terms of trade with the Soviet Union declined by about 7% annually between 1981 and 1982, mainly as a result of the rapid growth in the prices of Soviet energy exports compared to the prices of East European machinery and industrial goods exports. These shifts in CMEA prices reflected similar shifts in energy and industrial prices which occurred in world markets in 1979 and 1980.

5. The ruble price of oil, which was still about 25% below the world-market price in 1982, appeared to have pulled even with the falling world-market price by 1983. United Nations, Economic Commission for Europe, *Economic Survey of Europe in 1983*, Section 4.3 (New York: United Nations, 1984), p. 219.

Marrese's essay in this volume.) On the other hand, the increased attractiveness of energy and raw material sales on world markets, stemming from developments in world prices, encouraged the Soviet Union to divert these "hard" exports to nonbloc markets, thereby gradually tightening supply constraints on intrabloc trade in nonfood raw materials and fuels. These supply constraints were the result not only of the diversion of such trade to more profitable world markets but also of a longer-term Soviet strategy to reduce East European dependence on Soviet exports of such products. After 1979, as debt-repayment problems worsened throughout Eastern Europe, supply constraints on bloc markets tightened, because a number of East European countries sought to divert a portion of their exports of hard goods from bloc markets to Western ones.[6]

Bloc membership also influenced the impact of capital-market shocks on the countries of Eastern Europe. During the 1974–79 period, East European borrowers were especially attractive to Western lenders for a variety of reasons, not the least important of which was the common perception of a Soviet umbrella guaranteeing the creditworthiness of its Eastern-bloc allies. As a result of this perception and of a general tendency on the part of Western commercial lenders to prefer more developed countries to less developed ones, and state-sponsored projects and credit initiatives to private ones, the East European countries found themselves in a favorable borrowing climate.[7] The emphasis on detente during this period also stimulated the growth of private credit flows to Eastern Europe, often under the guarantee of state agencies.

The situation began to change in 1979 when credit-market conditions confronting Eastern Europe began to tighten even more than worldwide credit-market conditions. The Afghan crisis and deteriorating U.S.–Soviet relations caused Western bankers to reevaluate their positions in Eastern Europe and to take more defensive postures. Incipient debt-repayment difficulties in Poland as early as 1978 and subsequent reverberations throughout the Eastern bloc influenced their behavior. By the first half of 1981, Western bankers, governments, and suppliers had imposed a credit squeeze on Eastern Europe. This occurred about one year earlier than the credit squeeze on most of the NICs which did not start in earnest until the second half of 1982. In

---

6. Within CMEA trade, "hard" goods are those for which there is generalized excess demand and which can usually be sold without significant price reductions on Western markets. "Soft" goods are those for which there is excess supply and which face more limited sales prospects on Western markets because of quality problems or because they are made to fit the specifications of a bloc purchaser.

7. For a comparison of interest rates and credit availability between the East European countries and other developing countries during this period, see Richard Portes, "East Europe's Debt to the West: Interdependence Is a Two-Way Street," *Foreign Affairs*, no. 2 (July 1977), pp. 751–82. East European borrowers were especially attractive among the West European banks, which continued to expand their lending to such borrowers even as the willingness of U.S. banks to lend to them began to wane after the mid-1970s.

this sense, the debt crisis in Eastern Europe was precipitated by economic conditions within the bloc and by interbloc relations, and was distinct from and a precursor to the debt crisis of the NICs in 1982 and 1983. In any event, the earlier cutback in credit available to Eastern Europe forced the enactment of measures to reduce trade and current account deficits, and precluded the continued rapid buildup of short-term, high-interest debt, which proved to be a momentous policy error for several NICs in 1981 and the first half of 1982. In short, the credit market refused to provide Eastern Europe with the credit rope on which many other NIC borrowers, particularly those in Latin America, were to find themselves hanging by the end of 1982.

2. External shocks and economic performance: the role of internal structure and policy choice

The trade deficits that spawned the large accumulation of debt in Eastern Europe and many NICs during the 1970s were the product of both internal and external factors. Adverse trade shocks aggravated long-term balance-of-trade difficulties traceable to internal economic structure and policy choice. To understand the role of these internal factors in the evolution of the debt crisis and subsequent policy responses, it is necessary to understand some important distinctions between the countries of Eastern Europe and the other countries examined here.

The East European countries share a common economic structure, the basic features of which include state ownership of the means of production and hierarchical, bureaucratic control over all major economic decisions. In these systems, the state is highly centralized and there is little differentiation between it and the economy: the state has the right and responsibility to make all major economic decisions. The high degree of centralization and the low degree of differentiation between state and economy provide for political and administrative control over economic life to an extent not possible in economic systems based on private ownership and decentralized decision making by private actors in response to market signals. Finally, all of the economies of Eastern Europe have a single hegemonic party, organized along Leninist lines and guided by certain socialist objectives. In her introductory essay, Ellen Comisso considers some of the political ramifications of this organizational and ideological tradition. For my purposes it is sufficient to note that this tradition is often the critical determinant of economic policy. For example, the commitment to rapid growth and industrialization and to certain indicators of "socialist social welfare," such as job security and "fairness" in the distribution of economic rewards, are important outgrowths of socialist ideology.

It is also important to note that in this organizational setup, the party rather than the state makes policy. In the countries of East Asia and Latin

America, the state-party distinction can be a much more important one, with the state frequently the ruling force in policy and the party or parties in power often reigning de jure rather than ruling de facto. For the purposes of simplifying my discussion, I will use the term *state* when comparing how the responses to economic difficulties in different countries varied among government actors with real decision-making power, but the underlying state-party distinction should not be forgotten.

A key feature of economic structure in Eastern Europe is central planning.[8] Plan indicators, usually specified in quantitative terms, determine production decisions for enterprises, assisted by success indicators that link rewards for managers and sometimes workers to fulfillment of these targets. Prices are set centrally and are frequently constant for long periods of time, despite imbalances between demand and supply and despite changes in world-market prices. Changes in quantitative planning, formal or informal rationing, or a combination of all three act to adjust such imbalances.

Success indicators emphasizing output performance and a legacy of rapid industrialization have created a unique set of incentives guiding economic decisions. The overwhelming incentive behind economic behavior is what János Kornai calls "the expansion drive"—the desire to produce as much as possible and to worry considerably less about the cost, quality, and salability of goods produced.[9] The expansion drive percolates through the bureaucratic-hierarchical structure, from the top leadership through the planning and ministerial apparatus and down to the enterprises. Even in Hungary and Yugoslavia, where quantitative planning has been abolished and where profitability is theoretically the major indicator of the success of an enterprise, the expansion drive persists in large part because enterprises continue to face a protected sellers' market—buoyant domestic demand and limited external competition—that reduces incentives to worry about cost, quality, and marketing.

A corollary of the expansion drive is the phenomenon of shortage. In contrast to market economies, in which demand constrains output levels, in the economies of Eastern Europe the availability of resources constrains output levels. The drive to realize ambitious output plans generates constant pressure on resources and a widespread perception of shortages of resources as a barrier to plan fulfillment. Seen in this light, it is clear why adverse

8. As I note later in the essay, the 1968 economic reforms in Hungary abolished quantitative central planning and gave enterprises the right to decide on output levels and input use. In practice, a variety of state policies that shaped enterprise decisions continued to strongly influence enterprise choices. For more detail on the structure and functioning of the Hungarian economy during the 1970s, see Ed Hewett, "The Hungarian Economy: Lessons of the 1970s and Prospects for the 1980s," in Joint Economic Committee, *East European Economic Assessment*, pt. 1 (Washington, D.C.: GPO, 1981), and the Comisso-Marer essay in this volume.

9. For a complete discussion of the expansion drive and the general theory of the shortage economy under central planning, see János Kornai, *The Economics of Shortage* (Amsterdam: North Holland, 1981).

changes in oil prices and availability in the 1970s were widely perceived as shortage constraints, thus limiting output, while both enterprises and planners largely discounted the potential demand constraints stemming from recession in Western markets.

On a microeconomic level a fundamental reason for the expansion drive is the existence of "soft" budget constraints.[10] Because they are ultimately owned by the state and because the state is ultimately responsible for their welfare and performance, enterprises act in the correct expectation that if they run into financial difficulties, the state will bail them out. In the traditional centrally planned economies (CPEs), including Romania, East Germany (the GDR), Bulgaria, Czechoslovakia, and Poland, this expectation is based on the fact that given artificially controlled and distorted domestic prices and quantitative planning, enterprises have essentially no control over whether they operate at a profit or a loss. In Yugoslavia and Hungary there is considerably more price flexibility in response to market conditions, enterprises make their own output and input choices, and both managers and workers stand to share in enterprise profits. Nonetheless, even in these countries the expectation of preferential state policy should an enterprise's choices generate persistent losses has an important effect on behavior. In particular, the resulting softness of budget constraints considerably weakens incentives to respond to changing prices. Consequently, even in these economies, if the state wishes to change the behavior of enterprises, it must do more than simply "get the prices right"—and as we shall see in later sections, even getting the prices right often proves very difficult for state officials unaccustomed to interpreting and responding to changing world-market conditions.

Taken together, the expansion drive and the soft budget constraints provide a set of incentives that differ fundamentally from those that guide decisions in economies based on private ownership and pursuit of private financial gain. In such economies—which characterize all of the NICs I examine—decision making is guided primarily by considerations of profitability and is sensitive to price, quality, and marketing issues. The state influences these decisions by a variety of policies that change market indicators. For example, the state may pursue an expansionary macroeconomic strategy and erect tariff and quota barriers, all of which will tend to create a protected domestic market. Even within this sheltered environment, however, enterprises will remain responsive to market signals as long as their budget constraints are hard, meaning the state is unlikely to bail them out of financial difficulties.

Clearly, the hardness or softness of budget constraints both within and across economies is a matter of degree. State-owned enterprises in the NICs are likely to have soft budget constraints similar to those in Eastern Europe, and large privately owned enterprises that serve employment and output

10. For a discussion of soft budget constraints see Kornai, ibid., and his " 'Hard' and 'Soft' Budget Constraints," *Acta Oeconomica* 25, nos. 3–4 (1980).

objectives critical to the state's political interests are likely to have softer budget constraints than do small privately owned enterprises whose financial difficulties do not pose political problems. Nonetheless, as a simple principle of classification, it seems reasonable to distinguish clearly between incentives for enterprises stemming from the expansion drive and soft budget constraints in Eastern Europe and Yugoslavia, and incentives for enterprises—at least within the private sector—stemming from the profit drive and hard budget constraints in the other NICs.

The system of quantitative planning and the unique incentives for enterprises which it creates are important internal factors behind the recurrent balance-of-trade difficulties of the East European economies in East-West trade. In traditional CPEs, decisions about what to import and what to export are based on a quantitative assessment of domestic shortfalls and surpluses, given plan targets. Trade decisions are residuals of plans for domestic supply and domestic demand, and in this sense neither the state nor the enterprise formulates an independent trade strategy based on external market opportunities and considerations of comparative advantage. Enterprises face the same domestic price regardless of whether they sell their output to a domestic or foreign buyer or whether they purchase a domestic or a foreign input. Under these circumstances, enterprises have no incentive to economize on imports whose world price has increased or to engage actively in searching out export opportunities. Indeed, given their underlying drive to expand, they are also motivated by a corresponding import hunger: the desire to obtain the largest possible quantity of imports necessary to realize their production targets. On the export side, they lack the incentive to search out foreign buyers since the domestic economy offers more certain, sellers'-market conditions. Clearly, under these conditions, active policy responses by central authorities to enforce import reductions or to mobilize additional exports predicated effective adjustment to adverse external shocks in the 1970s.

The economic reforms in Hungary and Yugoslavia were designed to improve foreign-trade incentives by linking domestic prices to world prices, by replacing the expansion drive with a profitability drive, and by allowing enterprises to make their own import and export decisions. In practice, the effects of the reforms were blunted by a number of factors, the most important of which were state policies that weakened the links between domestic and world prices and soft budget constraints that weakened the sensitivity of enterprises to price indicators, however distorted.

A country's choice of development strategy, like its economic structure, proved to be an important internal factor causing balance-of-trade difficulties in the 1970s. In development strategy as in economic structure, the East European countries differed in important ways from the NICs. A starting point for understanding these differences is the distinction between inward-

and outward-oriented development strategies.[11] Inward-oriented strategies focus on developing an economic base to satisfy the domestic market, while outward-oriented strategies focus on developing a base that conforms to world-market opportunities. Inward-oriented strategies foster industrialization based on the principle of import substitution, while outward-oriented strategies foster industrialization based on the principle of export promotion. Both strategies are consistent with a high degree of centralization and state intervention in the economy; indeed, from a long-term perspective, a successful export-promotion strategy usually rests upon an initial period of import substitution during which infant industries are actively sheltered from foreign competitors. Thus, in practice it is often difficult to distinguish an inward-oriented strategy from an outward-oriented one. Neither the extent of state intervention nor the degree of protection of the domestic market will do, as the case of Japan indicates.

The fundamental distinction seems to lie in the objectives or purposes of the state. In the East Asian NICs development strategy has been driven by a sense of dependence on world markets, especially for imported raw materials, and by the decision to develop a broad industrial export base from which to finance import needs.[12] World-market opportunities and constraints have been a critical factor shaping decisions about the domestic industrial base, and a peculiar mix of openness and dependence, on the one hand, and the drive for greater national economic autonomy, on the other, has informed policy in these countries. State intervention has been extensive, relying on a variety of policies to steer private investment and trade decisions toward the pursuit of the state's development objectives.

In the Latin American NICs domestic economic objectives have been the fundamental determinant of development strategy.[13] In part, the larger size of these countries and their superior resource endowments explain this choice: the costs of import substitution are lower and the perception of dependence on world markets is weaker than in East Asia. The focus on domestic economic conditions, however, does not mean that development strategy in Latin America has been unaffected by world-market conditions. Production for the home market, not for export, has been the primary objective, but considerations of comparative costs and a long-term desire to create domestic

11. For more on the distinction between inward- and outward-oriented development strategies, see Bela Balassa, "Structural Adjustment Policies in Developing Countries," *World Development* (January 1982), pp. 23–38.

12. For reasons of stylistic convenience, I shall frequently use the term *East Asian NICs* to generalize from the experiences of Taiwan, Korea, and Singapore and the term *Latin American NICs* to generalize from the experiences of Brazil and Mexico. In reality, of course, there are many differences among the countries of East Asia and among those of Latin America; thus the generalizations drawn from the sample of countries I examine are not always representative of other countries in the two regions.

13. For a brief comparison of development strategies in Brazil and Mexico, see the comment by Albert Fishlow in this volume.

industries that are competitive by world-market standards have influenced the state's production, investment, and trade objectives.

As in East Asia, the state has used a variety of policies to encourage private behavior to conform to its development objectives. Moreover, on occasion, export prospects have become a more significant determinant of development strategy, particularly in Brazil in the late 1960s and early 1970s in response to buoyant world-market conditions. After the first oil shock, dwindling export prospects and the drive for import substitution in energy encouraged a return to its more traditional inward orientation.

The difference between the development strategies of the Latin American NICs and the East European countries is more a difference of degree than of kind. Like those of the Latin American NICs, the development strategies of Eastern Europe have been inward-oriented, with domestic or intrabloc considerations primarily guiding industrialization targets. East European countries, however, have pursued these strategies in a structure of central planning in which imports and exports have been residuals from a quantitative assessment of domestic supply and demand. In this structure, the influence of external market conditions on industrialization objectives has been considerably weaker than in Latin America.

Throughout the 1950s and well into the 1960s, the East European countries pursued extensive first- and second-stage import substitution with the objective of reducing import dependence and enhancing national autonomy.[14] Economic conditions within the bloc—the availability of raw materials in the Soviet Union and its need for reliable sources of supply for machinery imports—initially shaped these strategies. Thus to this extent, external considerations, albeit limited to bloc rather than to world markets, obviously played a role in Eastern Europe's development strategy. Even intrabloc considerations, however, increasingly took second place behind the efforts of individual East European states to achieve internal economic development based on industrialization. How else can one explain the similarity in industrialization patterns among the East European countries and the resulting duplication of capacity within the bloc, resulting in small high-cost facilities within each country and a growing surplus of soft goods in bloc trade?

Predictably, the extreme variant of inward orientation peculiar to the East European economies produced a structure of import needs and export limitations that created balance-of-payments difficulties vis-à-vis Western markets. Import hunger and the lack of incentives for exports aggravated these difficulties, since enterprises often overlooked even real opportunities for

14. First-stage import substitution involves import substitution in consumer goods industries, while second-stage import substitution involves import substitution in intermediate and capital goods industries. The former is generally thought to be easier to accomplish than the latter and usually occurs first in developing countries. In Eastern Europe the objectives of the central planners for heavy industry tended to place special priority on second-stage import-substitution projects.

import savings and export earnings within the existing industrial structures for want of appropriate reward. By the mid- to late 1960s, concerns about foreign-trade performance were a primary motivating force behind economic reform. Only in Hungary, however, did these pressures ultimately lead to reform.

By the beginning of the 1970s, mounting concern over competitive difficulties in Western markets led the East European economies to accelerate imports of capital goods and technology from the West in an attempt to increase export prospects over the longer run. This decision reflected a new strategy of increased linkage to the world economy—a strategy that was similar to the more open variant of import substitution in the Latin American NICs. Growth was to be led by imports and fueled by modernization based on Western technology and by the development of domestic industries that could both satisfy internal needs and compete on world markets. Unfortunately, because of the lack of a radical change in structure, the hoped-for gains in growth and efficiency anticipated from this new strategy failed to materialize.

From the perspective of the resilience of their development strategy to the adverse trade shocks of the 1973–84 period, the East Asian NICs clearly outperformed East European countries. Because of their openness, their dependence on raw material and energy imports, and their size, these countries were especially vulnerable to trade disturbances. On the other hand, the existence of a domestic industrial base capable of generating competitve products and the incentives and marketing experience needed to sell them allowed the East Asian NICs to capture growing shares of dwindling world markets, thereby earning revenues to finance higher import bills and/or to service debt. In contrast, the East European countries and the Latin American countries were saddled with a structural dependence on imports, a domestic industrial base that was largely noncompetitive on world markets, and a lack of expertise in world marketing. The situation was clearly worse in Eastern Europe than in Latin America, as indicated by the fact that between 1970 and 1980, Eastern Europe (excluding Yugoslavia) lost export-market share, while the Latin American NICs gained share slightly in the countries of the Organization for Economic Cooperation and Development (OECD). Even more impressive, during this period the Latin American NICS managed to more than double their share in OECD imports of manufactured goods, while the East European share rose only marginally.[15]

So far the discussion has focused on economic structure and development strategy as internal factors underlying balance-of-payments difficulties in

15. These findings are reported by Kazimierz Poznański, "Competition between Eastern Europe and Developing Countries in the Western Markets for Manufactured Goods," Joint Economic Committee, *East European Economies: Slow Growth in the 1980's* (Washington, D.C.: GPO, 1986). His findings for Latin America are based on the export performance of Mexico, Brazil, and Argentina.

Eastern Europe and in the NICs. A final internal factor is lax macroeconomic control. In Eastern Europe, the cases of Poland and Romania, and among the NICs, the cases of Yugoslavia and Mexico come to mind. In each of these cases, at different times during the 1973–84 period, internal policies produced a rapid expansion of demand which outpaced the economy's supply potential. The predictable consequences of these policies were rapid growth in import demands; a diversion of resources to production for the home market; and an intensification of inflationary pressure which showed up either openly in rapidly rising prices or covertly in shortages, black markets, and the like. Because such policies were not a necessary outgrowth of the underlying economic structure or development strategy, we can interpret them as an independent internal factor contributing to balance-of-payments difficulties.

Two important but largely unanswerable questions concern the relative importance of internal factors and adverse trade shocks on mounting trade deficits in different countries in the 1970s. To what extent were these deficits and the borrowing they generated the result of internal causes rooted in structure, development strategy, and macroeconomic policy, and to what extent were they the result of adverse trade shocks? Behind these questions lies a more fundamental question that has intrigued both scholars and policy makers about the ultimate responsibility for the debt crises that developed in the early 1980s. Would these crises have occurred in the absence of external trade shocks, in which case the ultimate responsibility rests with internal policy choices, or in the absence of such shocks would these crises have failed to develop, in which case the ultimate responsibility rests with external factors?

It is impossible to provide a precise counterfactual history in answer to this question. A series of studies by Bela Balassa, using a methodology that is revealing but necessarily simplistic in its underlying assumptions, yields some suggestive and not surprising conclusions.[16] His findings indicate that the balance-of-payments effects of external trade shocks in the mid-1970s measured relative to GNP were largest in small open economies, such as Singapore's; of intermediate importance in larger or less open economies, such as Yugoslavia's, Hungary's, Korea's, and Taiwan's; and smallest in large, less open economies, such as Brazil's and Mexico's. Although his research does not extend to the other countries of Eastern Europe, it seems reasonable to speculate that their experience was not dissimilar to that of

16. Balassa's methodology rests on the assumptions that in the absence of external trade shocks each country's terms of trade would have remained at its average 1971–73 levels throughout the 1974–78 period and that the world demand for exports from developing countries would have increased during this period at the same rate as in the 1963–73 period. For a complete description of this methodology, see Bela Balassa, "Adjusting to External Shocks: The Newly-Industrializing Developing Countries in 1974–76 and 1979–81," *Weltwirtschaftliches Archiv* 121, no. 1 (1985).

Hungary, which they roughly resemble in size and openness.[17] Two conclusions emerge from these findings: first, internal policy choices were more important to the genesis of the debt crisis in Latin America than in Eastern Europe; and second, differences in the severity of the debt crises among East European countries are attributable mainly to differences in their internal policy choices rather than to differences in their sensitivity to external shocks.

Although provocative, questions about the contribution of internal and external factors to the evolution of the debt crisis in individual countries are ultimately misguided because they overlook the fact that internal choices everywhere were affected by a unique external condition—the availability of cheap credit to finance trade deficits of unprecedented magnitudes in the mid-1970s. Debt became an instrument that countries could use to pursue very different objectives. Attractive capital-market conditions meant that countries could use cheap capital to finance internal policies that were not sustainable over the longer run. Alternatively, cheap capital could be used to cover temporary terms-of-trade losses and export shortfalls while maintaining domestic living standards and gradually adjusting economic policies to conform to new international conditions. Individual countries built up debt for a particular constellation of internal and external reasons, but the common precondition for the debt crises was the availability of cheap capital in the mid-1970s and its dramatic contraction by the decade's end.[18]

3. Balance-of-payments problems and adjustment responses, 1973–79

Because the adverse trade shocks of the mid-1970s were both unanticipated and widely regarded as temporary, it is not surprising that policy responses to them did not involve changes in structure in any of the countries considered here.[19] External events at the time did not seem to warrant any fundamental, politically sensitive, risky changes. Even within the context of a given structure, however, policy makers faced a choice between adjustment in development

17. Undoubtedly, there were some important differences in the magnitude of the effects of external shocks within Eastern Europe. For example, in the mid-1970s these effects were smaller in Poland and Romania than in the other East European countries because the former two were net exporters of energy at that time, so their terms-of-trade losses were smaller. Indeed, Poland's overall terms of trade actually improved between 1974 and 1976 when the terms of trade of the other East European countries declined sharply. See Laura D'Andrea Tyson, *Economic Adjustment in Eastern Europe* (Santa Monica: Rand, 1984).

18. Indeed, some observers have argued that the irresponsibility of the banks was the real cause of the worldwide debt crisis. See, for example, William Darity, "Loan Pushing: Doctrine and Theory," *International Finance Discussion Paper 253* (Washington, D.C.: Federal Reserve, 1984).

19. One could argue that the slowdown and partial reversal of economic reform in Hungary in the mid-1970s was a structural change in response to external shocks. Most observers, however, believe that this reversal was already underway before these shocks occurred as a result of internal opposition to the reform and its effects on income differentials. Economic difficulties caused by external events simply strengthened this process.

strategy, adjustment in macroeconomic policy, and reliance on external finance. To some extent, development strategy was modified in Brazil, Yugoslavia, and Mexico. In Brazil and Yugoslavia, policies introduced in the late 1960s to promote exports were partially reversed; exchange rates became overvalued, further depressing export incentives; and traditional import-substitution objectives were reaffirmed in investment allocation. The net result was a more inward-oriented development strategy, reflected in aggressive investment programs to substitute domestic energy and raw materials for high-priced imports. In Mexico the discovery of large oil reserves in 1977–78 also altered that country's development strategy, and it undertook a major investment effort to promote oil development as a future export base. Mexico's development strategy thus became more outward-oriented, although the overvaluation of the peso discouraged exports of manufactured goods.

In addition to adjusting overall developmental priorities, policy makers could act to control the trade deficit by deflating domestic demand, thereby reducing import demand and freeing up goods and services for export. The adverse trade shocks worked automatically to deflate domestic demand in market economies through two channels. First, an adverse shift in the terms of trade was equivalent to an excise tax that had to be paid to the rest of the world. The tax reduced real resources available for domestic use, and real income fell. This was true for all economies in which the terms of trade deteriorated, regardless of structure or strategy. Structure, however, played a key role in how the fall in real income affected behavior. In market economies, in which output was constrained by demand and consumption depended on income, an adverse shift in the terms of trade tended to produce both a decline in real income *and* an automatic contraction in domestic demand and output, in the absence of offsetting policy. The decline in export demand stemming from recession in Western market economies was the second channel through which deflationary pressure on market economies emanated automatically. The policy issue under such circumstances was whether and by how much to reinforce or to counteract these automatic deflationary tendencies.

The situation in the economies of Eastern Europe was quite different. Because incentives offered to individual producers and consumers were effectively insulated from changes in world economic conditions, and because given these incentives, output was constrained by the availability of resources rather than by demand, there were no *automatic* deflationary effects of adverse trade shocks. Even the decline of real national income as a result of a deterioration in the terms of trade had an effect on domestic demand and output only insofar as the state actively adjusted spending and output targets. In short, deflationary adjustment to the balance-of-payments difficulties of the mid-1970s required active policy responses in Eastern Europe, while such an adjustment was to some degree automatic in the market economies of East Asia and Latin America.

In the area of macroeconomic policy response, continuity rather than change was the best predictor of actual events in East Asia and Latin America. In Singapore and Taiwan active deflationary measures enhanced the automatic contractionary effects of external shocks. Deflation was especially severe and dramatic in Taiwan, a country with a tradition of fiscal conservatism in which the fight against the inflationary implications of higher prices for oil and raw materials was the primary policy objective. In both Taiwan and Singapore the sense of vulnerability to shifts in world-market conditions, the recognition that continued prosperity required rapid adjustment given this vulnerability, and the perception of relative domestic income equality made a temporary dose of deflation politically acceptable.

Short-run macroeconomic austerity, combined with the continued long-run success of their outward-oriented development strategies, obviated the need for external debt financing in these countries. Indeed, by 1976 Taiwan actually began to run a trade surplus that allowed it to build up its reserves and pay off its outstanding debt. In contrast, Singapore continued to run a trade deficit but eschewed debt financing in favor of equity financing in the form of direct foreign investment.[20] Given the prevailing interest rates, the decisions of Taiwan and Singapore to forgo debt financing seemed at the time to conflict with market signals and to represent a kind of artificial closure to world-capital markets. Taiwan's decision to guard its autonomy by forgoing both debt and equity finance despite its low level of development seemed especially perverse. In retrospect, however, it is the capital-market signals rather than the decisions to override them which seem distorted. By forgoing artificially cheap debt finance in the mid-1970s, both countries avoided the ensuing policy constraints that resulted from adverse shifts in world capital markets at the end of the decade.

All of the East European countries, with the exception of Romania, and Mexico, Brazil, Korea, and Yugoslavia chose a growth-cum-debt response to balance-of-payments difficulties in the 1973–78 period. Active policies to deflate domestic demand were insufficiently strong or long-lived to prevent a dramatic increase in reliance on external debt financing. For the countries of Eastern Europe, the decision to borrow extensively from international capital markets was a significant departure from past behavior. The new import-led growth strategies adopted throughout Eastern Europe at the beginning of the 1970s partially explain this departure. Even in the absence

20. Ironically, although much of the developing world viewed direct foreign investment with suspicion because of its perceived threat to national autonomy, in one important respect it was a smaller threat than borrowing at variable interest rates because its risk was shared by both borrower and lender. This was to become painfully apparent when the need to impose austerity measures to deal with the debt crisis during the 1979–84 period became a major constraint on national autonomy.

of external shocks, the pursuit of such strategies probably would have led to greater reliance on international credit flows. The external shocks meant that the balance-of-payments deficits and borrowing requirements associated with such strategies were much larger than anticipated. On the supply side, credit to Eastern Europe was readily available and at attractive interest rates in part because of the effect of detente on the willingness of Western governments and banks to lend in order to stimulate East-West trade.

For Korea, Yugoslavia, Brazil, and Mexico, the decision to accumulate debt to finance balance-of-payments deficits did not represent a radical break with the past. All of these countries had been open to international credit flows earlier.[21] Yugoslavia, Brazil, and Mexico had histories of recurrent balance-of-payments deficits financed by foreign borrowing and usually culminating in stabilization crises and IMF intervention. In Korea debt had become an increasingly important source of finance for balance-of-payments deficits after the flow of subsidized aid began to dwindle in the late 1960s.

Ultimately, the growth-cum-debt response pattern characterizing both these countries and the East European countries, except Romania, can be explained in one of two ways. First, under the reasonable assumption that the shocks to world trade flows were temporary and given the low cost of external finance, the decision not to change domestic policy and growth targets was a reasonable one. From this perspective, it is the deflation-without-debt response rather than the growth-cum-debt response that seems to contradict market signals, although the former strategy was certainly considerably less risky than the latter. Alternatively, even when it became apparent that balance-of-payments difficulties were not temporary and that debt levels were growing rapidly, concerns about distribution—both among income groups and between consumption, investment, and government—made the deflationary policies that were necessary to reduce domestic demand politically risky and militated in favor of continued growth to accommodate competing social groups and objectives. Under these circumstances, the perceived political gains from continued borrowing to protect domestic living standards remained high, while the expected borrowing costs remained low.

Ironically, in light of recent history, the growth-cum-debt strategy of the mid-1970s appeared prudent at the time not only from a political perspective but also from an economic one. Increases in the inflow of foreign capital were associated with increases in investment rates, which in turn were taken as evidence by both borrowers and lenders that foreign borrowing rather than being "wasted" was supporting future development. In Eastern Europe

---

21. By openness to international capital flows, I do not mean that there were no state controls over such flows. To different degrees, the state played an active role in controlling the magnitude, composition, and objectives of foreign borrowing in all of these countries. Control was strongest in the East European countries where state agencies made or approved all decisions regarding foreign borrowing. Control was weakest in Mexico because of the difficulties of enforcing exchange controls and capital movements over a relatively open border with the United States.

higher investment rates were an outgrowth of the 1971–75 plans calling for modernization and greater integration into the world economy linked to imports of Western technology and capital. Bankers and firms in Western Europe, buoyed by detente and by the prospects of growing demand in Eastern Europe to substitute for stagnant demand in the West, were enthusiastic about supporting these plans and were encouraged by public loan guarantee programs to do so. In Eastern Europe, as in the other NICs pursuing a growth-cum-debt strategy, ambitious investment rates led both borrowers and lenders mistakenly to conclude that on an aggregate level debt could be repaid out of the returns to investment without necessitating a slowdown in future consumption. No one foresaw that changing external circumstances at the end of the decade would dramatically worsen repayment burdens.

Within the group of countries accumulating debt, however, by 1978 — prior to these external changes — there were already signs of future repayment difficulties. Among the NICs, debt-service ratios increased sharply between 1974 and 1978, rising to dangerously high levels in both Brazil and Mexico (see Table 1). In Yugoslavia, although the debt-service ratio increased only slightly, large trade and current account deficits in 1977 and 1978 foreshadowed future difficulties. In Eastern Europe, despite the downward adjustment of the 1976–80 plans and the more restrained macroeconomic policies this entailed, the slowdown in growth rates over the 1976–77 period produced only modest improvements in trade deficits with the West, except in Bulgaria, which realized a trade surplus in 1978.[22] In contrast, by 1978 growth rates in Mexico and Korea were accelerating, while trade deficits remained sharply below their 1974–75 levels, mainly as a result of a dramatic expansion in exports. Export revenues throughout Eastern Europe, with the exception of Bulgaria, grew comparatively slowly during the 1975–78 period. In this respect, the East European experience was similar to that of Yugoslavia and Brazil and reflected long-term weaknesses in structure and development strategy which boded ill for the ease of future debt repayment. Future debt-repayment difficulties in Eastern Europe were also suggested by sharp increases in debt-service ratios, particularly pronounced in Poland, Hungary, and East Germany.[23]

Finally, it is interesting to note that during the 1974–78 period, the Romanian experience differed from the experiences of East European countries and the NICs. According to Romanian statistics, Romania performed

22. Poland's hard-currency trade deficit declined by 30% between 1975 and 1978 but remained very large by pre-1975 standards. Hard-currency trade deficits actually increased during this period in Czechoslovakia, the GDR, and Hungary. In contrast, Brazil's trade deficit declined by 42%, Mexico's by 76%, and Korea's by 48% during the same period.

23. Became my focus is Eastern Europe's balance-of-payments problems and debt problems with the West, the debt-service ratios in question are measured relative to debt-repayment requirements and export revenues in convertible currencies, and exclude debt and export revenues in nonconvertible bloc currencies. See the notes to Table 1 for more detail.

TABLE 1. *Debt-service and debt-export ratios*

	Debt-Service Ratios (%)[a]			
	1975	*1978*	*1981*	*1984*
Newly Industrializing Countries[b]				
Mexico	35	74	45	38 (1983)
Brazil	37	54	57	54 (1983)
Korea	14	14	21	14 (1983)
Yugoslavia[c]	30	32	33	25 (1983)
East European Countries[d]				
Bulgaria	33	47	23	13
Czechoslovakia	14	20	26	23
GDR	25	49	44	38
Hungary	19	36	45	43
Poland	30	79	102	92
Romania	23	21	35	21

	Debt-Export Ratio in 1984[a]
Newly Industrializing Countries[e]	
Mexico[e]	293
Brazil[e]	331
Korea[e]	120
Yugoslavia[f]	215
East European Countries[g]	
Bulgaria	22
Czechoslovakia	46
GDR	95
Hungary	90
Poland	399
Romania	49

a. The ratios shown here are not comparable across country groups but are representative of differences within these two groups. Yugoslavia is probably best compared with the other East European countries. For this group, the ratios refer only to debt and exports in convertible currency and thus leave out the significant fraction of export revenues earned on bloc markets. Such revenues cannot be used to service convertible-currency debt. For Korea, Brazil, and Mexico, the ratios encompass total debt and total export revenues, although some fraction of such revenues may derive from countertrade, barter, or other arrangements and may therefore not be used for debt repayment.

b. Debt-service ratios are measured as estimated debt-service payments expressed as a percentage of merchandise and nonfactor service exports. Figures for 1975–81 are taken from Bela Balassa, *Adjusting to External Shocks: The Newly Industrializing Economies in 1974–76 and 1978–81*, Development Research Department Working Paper Report no. DRD89 (Washington, D.C.: World Bank, 1984). I derived figures for 1983 from statistics on

TABLE 1. *Debt-service and debt-export ratios (cont.)*

debt service in OECD, *External Debt of Developing Countries, 1983 Survey* (Paris: OECD, 1984), Table 22, and from statistics on exports of goods and nonfactor services provided to me in an update to World Bank, *World Tables*, 3d ed. (Baltimore: Johns Hopkins University Press, 1983).

c. Debt-service ratios are measured as estimated convertible currency, debt-service payments expressed as a share of convertible-currency merchandise and nonfactor service exports. Figures for 1975–81 are from Balassa, ibid. I derived the 1983 figure from statistics on debt service in OECD, *External Debt of Developing Countries*, Table 22, and statistics on exports from official Yugoslav sources.

d. For the East European countries, debt-service ratios are measured as estimated debt-service payments in convertible currency expressed as a percentage of convertible-currency merchandise exports. Figures are taken from Wharton Econometric Forecasting Associates, *Centrally Planned Economies: Current Analysis*, April 1982 and April 1985.

e. For these countries the debt-export ratio is measured as the average of gross external debt at beginning and end of year as a percentage of exports of goods and nonfactor services. Figures are taken from Morgan Guaranty Trust Company of New York, *World Financial Markets*, October–November 1984.

f. For Yugoslavia, the debt-export ratio is measured by gross convertible-currency debt as a percentage of convertible-currency exports of goods and nonfactor services. The gross debt estimate is $20.6 billion and is taken from the United Nations Economic Commission for Europe, *Economic Survey of Europe in 1984–85* (New York: United Nations, 1985), and the export estimate is taken from official Yugoslav sources.

g. Net debt in convertible currency as a percentage of convertible-currency exports. Figures are taken from sources in note d above.

remarkably well during the 1974–78 period.[24] Domestic growth rates stayed at high levels, and after a temporary increase in 1974, Romania's trade deficit with the West declined to levels that were low by standards set before the shocks. Both export-promotion and import-substitution investment projects activated during this period were responsible for improved trade performance.[25] The turning point in Romanian economic performance came in 1978, when industrial growth began to fall. The economic downturn predated the second round of external trade and capital shocks and was the consequence of growing supply constraints and excess demand attributable to the investment boom launched in the early 1970s. In 1978 Romania began the dramatic accumulation of debt which was to lead to its repayment difficulties by 1981.

4. The second wave of external shocks and the emerging debt crisis

The economic shocks that began in 1978 were dramatic, unexpected, and greater in magnitude than those that occurred in the mid-1970s. For the

24. Romanian statistics must be viewed with great skepticism. They often contain large inconsistencies and gaps that make any definite conclusions impossible. They are widely believed to overstate growth in overall output and improvements in the standard of living.

25. For a detailed discussion of the success of export promotion and import substitution in Romania in the mid-1970s see Tyson, *Economic Adjustment in Eastern Europe*, chap. 3.

countries that opted for a growth-cum-debt strategy in the mid-1970s, these shocks were particularly disastrous because of their dramatic effects on the interest burden on outstanding debt. Whereas in the earlier period lax capital-market conditions broadened the policy choices available, in the later period tight capital-market conditions narrowed them. Under the new capital-market conditions, reliance on external finance to cover the growing trade imbalances that resulted from more adverse world trade conditions became infeasible. Instead, by 1980–81 in Eastern Europe and Yugoslavia and by 1982 in Brazil and Mexico, capital-market constraints limited the sustainable size of trade deficits and required austerity policies to pare trade deficits down to financing capabilities.

Because of their earlier decision to forgo external debt, Taiwan and Singapore found themselves in relatively favorable positions during the second round of shocks. They did not confront the burden of rising interest rates on existing debt, and international lenders continued to view them with favor while gradually cutting back on the amount of credit they were willing to extend to countries with high outstanding debts. As a consequence, Taiwan and Singapore had the same option of using external finance to maintain growth under more adverse trade conditions that they had had during the earlier period. As in this earlier period and for the same reasons, however, they chose not to exercise this option, once again falling back on a temporary deflation to control their trade balances in the short run and on export-promotion efforts to improve their world-market shares in the long run.

Korea pursued a similar strategy. Following the assassination of President Park in October 1979, Korea's outward development strategy was reaffirmed, and a devaluation, along with the strengthening of export-incentive schemes, led to new gains in export-market shares. In addition, a temporary sharp deflation of domestic demand in 1980 led to reduced import demand, which also helped to keep the trade imbalance under control.[26] Thus, despite its high initial level of indebtedness, Korea suffered no debt crisis. As the figures in Table 1 indicate, Korea's debt-service ratio remained dramatically lower than the ratios of the other large debtor countries because of its large and growing export revenues. After a temporary slowdown, Korea's rapid economic growth resumed, and its debt-service and debt-export ratios began to decline. At no point did Korea confront either temporary difficulties in debt repayment or a liquidity crisis resulting from a sharp, unexpected drop in its access to external finance. As a consequence, at no point did it have to impose the kind of sharp cuts in imports that so disrupted production in Latin America, Yugoslavia, and Eastern Europe.

In the East Asian economies adjustment to the second wave of external shocks was voluntary and occurred at a pace and magnitude reflective of

26. That output in Korea actually declined by 3.5% in 1980, after rising at an average rate of nearly 11% between 1976 and 1979, indicates the severity of the deflation.

internal policy responses to changed world trade and capital-market conditions rather than of enforced reactions to external capital-market constraints. The situation was different in Eastern Europe, Yugoslavia, and Latin America. At different times during the 1979–84 period, unexpectedly large debt-service burdens attributable to higher interest rates and unexpected contractions in the availability of credit set a limit on sustainable trade deficits. Under these circumstances, the pace of adjustment was a forced reaction to borrowing constraints rather than a voluntary response to borrowing opportunities. Elements of forced adjustment were certainly at work in Poland by 1979, in Romania and Yugoslavia by 1981, and throughout the rest of Eastern Europe, with the possible exception of Czechoslovakia and Bulgaria, between mid-1981 and the end of 1982. In Brazil and Mexico forced adjustment began only in 1982.

Capital-market pressure on Eastern Europe reached a high point in 1981–82. In 1981 both Poland and Romania were forced to reschedule, and this development, along with the general deterioration in East-West relations, led to a virtual drying up of new credits to Eastern Europe and, as a result of spillover effects, to Yugoslavia as well. Under these circumstances, existing efforts to reduce borrowing needs by slowing the growth of domestic demand proved inadequate; more severe austerity was required. The only alternative was additional rescheduling, an option formally necessary in Poland and Romania in 1982. Yugoslavia was the recipient of an emergency credit package in 1982, put together under the auspices of the IMF and actively promoted by the U.S. government, which also entailed a rescheduling of debt. Hungary avoided a formal rescheduling, but not without a sharp loss in liquidity and not without emergency bridge financing provided by the Western central banks and the provision of an IMF standby agreement at the end of the year. Hungary's decision to join the IMF and both Soviet and U.S. willingness to allow it to do so were critical to the resolution of its liquidity crisis in 1982 and to its adjustment process thereafter.[27] In East Germany the financial situation never became as precarious as it did in the other big debtors of the region. Its relative success must be attributed in part to its strong export performance (see below) and in part to its West German connection. It is widely believed that bank credits to East Germany guaranteed by West Germany (the FRG) improved its creditworthiness and prevented a sharp liquidity squeeze because bankers believed that a West German umbrella sheltered East German debt.

Within Eastern Europe only Bulgaria and Czechoslovakia managed to

---

27. In 1982–83 two-thirds of the new credit Hungary received came from the IMF and the World Bank, and the remaining one-third came from commercial loans that would not have been available without the IMF's implicit "seal of approval" on Hungary's adjustment program. See Sherman Robinson, Laura Tyson, and Leyla Woods, "Conditionality and Adjustment in Eastern Europe" (Paper presented at the Conference on the Soviet Union and Eastern Europe in the World Economy, Kennan Institute, 1984).

avoid a severe financial crisis in 1981–82. In part this reflected the fact that they entered the 1979–84 period with debt burdens lower than those of the other countries. In addition, Bulgaria had begun to realize a trade surplus with the West by 1978, while Czechoslovakia first registered a trade surplus in 1980. In both countries, domestic austerity measures proved adequate to the task of reducing current account deficits at the rate that external capital-market conditions required. There was an important difference between the two countries, however. In Bulgaria the trade balance with the West improved as a consequence of growth in exports to Western markets rather than as a consequence of sharp cutbacks in Western imports. Bulgaria's export success can in part be attributed to the Soviet Union's apparent willingness to supply oil in excess of Bulgaria's needs at subsidized intra-CMEA prices and to allow Bulgaria to reexport such oil to buyers outside the CMEA at higher world prices. In Czechoslovakia improvement in the Western trade deficit necessitated cutbacks in imports which had detrimental effects on domestic output levels.

The debt crisis in Latin America, which occurred about one year after the crisis in Eastern Europe and Yugoslavia, began in the second half of 1982, although severe balance-of-payments difficulties were evident throughout the region much earlier. Both Brazil and Mexico initially reacted to the second wave of trade and capital-market shocks by continuing their growth-cum-debt strategies; indeed, growth rates in both countries accelerated in 1979–80. Behind this similar response lay vastly different economic situations. Mexico, as a growing oil exporter, benefited from the 1979 increase in world oil prices. The vision of mushrooming oil revenues in the future encouraged an investment-led expansion that foreign lenders seemed delighted to finance. Mexico was a sought-after borrower and paid relatively low interest rates compared to other developing countries. Under these conditions, its debt doubled between 1978 and 1981.[28] The driving force behind this debt accumulation was internal excess demand fed by an excessively ambitious expansion of investment and public-sector spending. In addition, an increasingly overvalued exchange rate not only depressed nonoil exports but also led to massive capital flight in expectation of an inevitable devaluation of the peso. When oil prices began to drop, the confidence of both foreign lenders and Mexican authorities in Mexico's ability to service its debt collapsed, and Mexico began to negotiate a major rescheduling program and to develop a domestic austerity program.

The situation in Brazil differed sharply from that in Mexico and was more similar in its general features to that of the oil-importing countries of Eastern Europe and Yugoslavia. As early as 1978, Brazil was in a precarious financial

28. For a complete and elucidating discussion of the evolution of the debt crisis in both Mexico and Brazil between 1979 and 1984, see Albert Fishlow, "Latin American Adjustment to the Oil Shocks of 1973 and 1979," in J. Hartlyn and S. Morley, eds., *Latin American Political Economy: Financial Crisis and Political Change* (Boulder: Westview, forthcoming).

situation, forced to use a major portion of new external finance simply to
meet its servicing obligations on existing debt. In this respect, the Brazilian
situation resembled the Polish one. By 1978 Poland was also using new
credit mainly to cover servicing, leaving considerably less to finance net
imports, which had been declining since 1976. Rising interest rates sharply
increased Brazil's servicing requirements, and the rise in oil prices sharply
increased its oil import bill. Initially, the Brazilians failed to respond to these
negative external developments and continued to pursue their debt-cum-
growth strategy. Internal politics played a role in the continuation of this
progrowth strategy, as indicated by the replacement of a planning minister
who attempted to moderate expansionary policies. By the end of 1980, however, the necessity and wisdom of austerity were recognized, and deflationary
measures began to be applied with force in 1981. The measures, however,
proved too little and too late relative to the magnitude of the crisis, and
Brazil too was forced to opt for rescheduling and harsher austerity in 1982.

5. Economic performance under austerity

Irrespective of underlying differences in structure and development strategy
and in the political and economic reasons that led to similar growth-cum-
debt choices in the 1970s, by the early 1980s all of the East European
countries, Yugoslavia, Brazil, and Mexico were forced to adopt austerity
programs to cut aggregate domestic demand. This similar response notwithstanding, important differences existed among the measures that individual countries took. Austerity measures differed in both timing and severity,
both of which were significantly influenced by the size of the debt overhang
and the constraints that external lenders imposed. Thus, Poland, Mexico,
and Brazil—whose debt-service and debt-export ratios were highest—and,
to a lesser extent, Hungary and Yugoslavia required the deepest cuts in
domestic demand. Of course, the pace of austerity and adjustment was in
part an internal choice, as Romania illustrated by opting for deeper cuts in
domestic demand and faster improvement in its trade deficit than external
capital constraints required.

   Austerity measures also differed in kind among individual countries, reflecting both the policy instruments appropriate to different economic and
political structures and the political choices about the distribution of the
austerity burden across various domestic programs and income groups. In
general, the underlying economic structure and political control in Eastern
Europe allowed the state to use direct administrative means to influence
both the aggregate level of domestic demand and its distribution. This meant
that deflation could be realized more quickly and sustained for a longer
period of time and that the state could realize its distributional objectives
more closely than was true for Yugoslavia, Brazil, and Mexico. Poland, of

course, is a glaring exception within Eastern Europe, and its experience demonstrates that the administrative controls of the CPE work effectively only when there is the requisite political unity and strength at the top.

In Brazil and Mexico greater differentiation between state and economy necessitated greater reliance on indirect price and financial regulators to control economic behavior than in Eastern Europe. In addition, political tensions aggravated by deteriorating economic performance and populist pressures undermined the ability of governments to adhere strictly to austerity programs over prolonged periods. Such pressures also interfered with the formation of a political consensus about the appropriate distribution of the austerity burden and meant that the political strengths of competing social and economic groups influenced the actual distribution.

Overall, the political constraints on the formation and implementation of austerity measures were more severe in Brazil than in Mexico. After the presidential election in the summer of 1982, the ruling Popular Revolutionary party in Mexico was able to push through an austerity program that resulted in a dramatic decline in real wages by 24.3 percent in 1983 and another 7.5 percent in 1984.[29] The fact that the new administration was not forced to introduce an indexation scheme to protect workers' incomes from accelerating inflation was a sign of its ability to contain the populist political pressures associated with deteriorating economic performance. In Brazil, on the other hand, the transition from military to civilian rule increased both the number of channels and the incentives for expression of competing interests. As a result, political pressures on the new government emanating from dissatisfaction with the costs of austerity were substantial and constrained its ability to adhere to an austerity policy. In Brazil and, to a lesser extent, in Mexico accelerating inflation was a reflection in part of the state's inability to resolve distributional conflicts and of the efforts of different groups to try to protect their interests through the wage-price mechanism. Under these circumstances, the different abilities of groups to protect themselves from the ravages of unanticipated inflation became an important determinant of how the burden of austerity was shared.

The Yugoslav case falls somewhere between the cases of Eastern Europe and those of Latin America in terms of both the kinds of instruments used to achieve austerity and the extent to which political conflicts diminished their effectiveness. Despite decades of decentralization and reform, the direct administrative controls available to the Yugoslav state resembled those of the planned economies in Eastern Europe more than those of the market economies of Latin America. In particular, the lines of authority between state actors and enterprises were stronger and more direct in Yugoslavia than in Brazil and Mexico, especially in the area of resource allocation. Only

---

29. These figures are taken from Wharton Econometric Forecasting Associates, *Diemex-Wharton: Mexican Economic Outlook*, May 1985, Appendix, Table 1.

in the state enterprise sector did the Brazilian and Mexican situations closely resemble the Yugoslav one. On the other hand, unresolved and worsening regional tensions in Yugoslavia, like populist political pressures in Mexico and Brazil, weakened the ability of political leaders to formulate and implement a coherent adjustment strategy, to sustain it over time, and to avoid the inflationary consequences of struggles over the distribution of its burden.

Not only did the instruments and objectives guiding adjustment differ among states, but the actual consequences of adjustment also differed. Differences existed in macroeconomic performance, indicated by differences in output growth rates, inflation rates, and unemployment rates; in the incidence of austerity across components of spending and groups of spenders; and in the effects of austerity on trade deficits, current account deficits, and debt levels. Finally, and perhaps most significant for the future, whether and how underlying structures and development strategies were adjusted to abet the austerity process and to ameliorate its adverse economic effects also differed.

a. Output losses and austerity

In principle, austerity—whether forced or voluntary—involved only a reduction in either the level or the growth of domestic demand. It did not require a reduction in either or both the level or rate of growth of domestic output; indeed, any such reduction could be viewed as waste, imposing an unnecessary burden on domestic demand. In practice, however, either a fall in domestic output or at the very least a fall in its rate of growth always accompanied austerity. This was true even in the short-lived voluntary deflations that occurred in East Asia in the mid-1970s and early 1980s.

The explanation for this phenomenon—an explanation with some validity for all of the countries examined in this essay—is that in the short run there were real limitations on an economy's flexibility. Most important, there were limitations on the ability to shift from imported inputs to domestic ones; on the ability to economize on the use of a critical input such as oil when it suddenly became more expensive; on the ability to shift resources from the production of goods for the home market to the production of goods for foreign markets; and on the ability to shift sales from one foreign market to another.

A country's structure and economic strategy were the major determinants of the extent of such sources of inflexibility. In this respect, the countries of Eastern Europe, Brazil, Mexico, and Yugoslavia are quite distinct from those of East Asia. For reasons of both structure and development strategy, the former group of countries had considerably less flexibility than had the latter. In the former group, long histories of import substitution meant that imports had been pared down to productive inputs for which there were only limited domestic substitutes. Almost all of Eastern Europe's imports from the West were of this nature, except for food imports. Accordingly, reductions in either the level or growth of Western imports accompanying austerity required reductions in either the level or growth of domestic output at least until substitutes could be developed in the Eastern bloc or supplies enlarged. The situation was similar in Yugoslavia and in Brazil where increasingly stringent import controls during the 1970s limited imports mainly to raw material and capital inputs. The Mexican case, though similar, was less dramatic because Mexico did not rely on oil imports and because a significant amount of import liberalization had occurred during the 1979–82 boom.

In East Asia, too, imports were predominantly productive inputs, many of which were not readily producible on domestic markets. An important difference in East Asia, however, was that its outward-oriented development strategy provided an export base that made export expansion rather than import contraction an effective strategy for adjustment even in the short run. In contrast, in Eastern Europe and, to a lesser extent, Latin America a long history of inward-looking industrial and investment choices impeded the mobilization of exports to reduce trade deficits and led to greater reliance on import cutbacks. In Eastern Europe, except Hungary and East Germany, during the first three years of austerity (1980–83), dollar export revenues in convertible-currency markets fell. During this period imports from convertible-currency markets fell sharply in dollar terms in all countries except East Germany and Bulgaria.[30] In contrast to the East European experience, during the first three years of austerity in Latin America (1982–84), export revenues increased in both Brazil and Mexico. In both countries, however, imports in nominal terms declined even more sharply than exports increased and bore the disproportionate share of the adjustment in the trade deficit.[31] In contrast, during the 1979–82 adjustment period in Korea, the growth in export revenues was sufficient to allow continued growth in nominal imports even as the trade deficit improved.[32]

30. To an important extent, the slow growth or declines in the nominal dollar values of convertible-currency imports and exports throughout Eastern Europe during the period are attributable to the appreciation of the dollar, which depressed the dollar value of trade denominated in other convertible currencies. As an illustration, the nominal dollar value of Hungary's exports to nonsocialist markets increased by about 4% between 1980 and 1983, while the real volume of these exports increased by about 21%. These figures are calculated from data in United Nations, Economic Commission for Europe, *Economic Bulletin* for Europe 37 (December 1985), chap. 4.

31. Between 1980 and 1984 nominal merchandise imports declined by 36.6% in Brazil and 56.2% in Mexico, while nominal merchandise exports rose by 13.7% in Brazil and 23.4% in Mexico. These figures are based on preliminary estimates of import and export changes in Morgan Guaranty Trust Company of New York, *World Financial Markets*, October–November 1984, Tables 3 and 4. Since the bulk of Brazil's and Mexico's trade was denominated in dollars, the appreciation of the dollar relative to other convertible currencies during this period did not depress the nominal dollar values of their imports and exports. Consequently, changes in dollar trade flows in Latin America are a better indication of changes in real trade flows than they are in Eastern Europe.

32. Between 1979 and 1982 merchandise export revenue increased by 42.1%, while merchandise imports increased by 23.1% in Korea. These figures are based on World Bank data presented in *World Tables*, 3d ed.

Structure, like development strategy, enhanced the flexibility of the East Asian NICs and undermined that of the other countries. The sensitivity of both state and private decision makers in the East Asian NICs to changing prices and international market conditions tended to minimize the output costs of temporary deflation. Higher world prices of inputs were quickly translated into higher domestic prices, and profit-sensitive producers responded by quick adjustments in input use. Declining sales prospects in one market, whether foreign or domestic, led to a rapid search for others. As a result, an increase in exports rather than a loss in domestic production tended to offset a decline in domestic demand resulting from deflationary measures at home.

The situation was dramatically different in the countries of Eastern Europe where a combination of the failure of domestic prices to adjust automatically to world prices and soft budget constraints eliminated the incentive of producers to change their behavior to conform to changes in world-market conditions. In the absence of active policy responses, there was simply no incentive to adjust flexibly, for example, by economizing on products such as oil that had become more expensive or by switching sales to foreign markets when austerity reduced sales prospects on domestic markets. Given the low degree of differentiation between state and economy and the high degree of centralization in economic decision making, responses of this type required a degree of flexibility inconsistent with the style of repetitive, bureaucratic decision making in these systems.

The economies of Latin America fall somewhere between the structural inflexibilities of the East European economies and the structural flexibilities of the East Asian ones. At least within the private segments of the Latin American economies, changing prices and changing sales prospects could be expected to induce flexible adaptive responses. Under these circumstances, the absence of such responses and resulting output losses can often be traced to policy errors—such as recurrent overvaluation of the exchange-rate and tax-subsidy schemes that distorted the price signals guiding private actors.[33] This perspective informs the IMF's view that combining austerity measures with measures to "get the prices right" would considerably reduce the output losses associated with such measures. In contrast, given the structure of the East European economies, getting the prices right would do little without a base of radical institutional change. A similar observation applies to the state enterprise sector in the Latin American economies where relatively soft budget constraints weakened sensitivity to price-profitability signals.

The behavior of the output growth rates presented in Table 2 is consistent with the view that differences in the degree of flexibility attributable to under-

---

33. Cases in point are Brazil's policies to restrain the domestic price of oil as world prices skyrocketed in the late 1970s and Mexico's failure to devalue in 1980–81, despite the growing differential between its inflation rate and the rates of its trading partners.

lying differences in structure and development strategy were an important determinant of the output costs of austerity.[34] In the East Asian NICs periods of voluntary deflation to achieve balance-of-payments objectives in the mid-1970s and early 1980s were short-lived. By 1976–77 growth rates had recovered from slowdowns in 1974–75, and by 1983–84 they had recovered from slowdowns in 1980–82 to become among the highest in the world. Overall, during the 1980–84 period real output levels continued to increase rapidly in these countries, despite the dramatic slowdown in the world economy. This performance is especially remarkable given the openness and size of these countries which made them especially vulnerable to adverse trade shocks.

In Eastern Europe the output costs of austerity were much more pronounced and long-lived. The gradual strenthening of voluntary austerity measures during the 1976–1980 period reduced growth rates in all countries below their 1971–75 levels. Continued austerity, tightened by the 1981–82 liquidity squeeze, produced even more dramatic declines in growth rates in 1981–83. By 1984 growth rates recovered but remained below 1976–80 levels in Bulgaria, Czechoslovakia, and Hungary. In Poland the 1984 growth rate was sharply higher than the 1976–80 and 1981–84 level, but because of the dramatic fall in output between 1981 and 1983, output in 1984 was more than 7 percent below its 1980 level. In addition, no sustainable improvement in Poland's external situation accompanied the revival in its growth rate in 1984. Only in East Germany and Romania did 1984 growth rates rise to 1976–80 levels, and the Romanian numbers must be viewed with great suspicion. What is more remarkable, among all the growth rates of the countries considered here, including the East Asian NICs, only East Germany's returned to its 1971–75 level.[35]

34. It is important to emphasize that because of differences in the concepts and measurement techniques underlying estimates of output, comparisons of growth rates between the countries of Eastern Europe and the other countries I examine can be seriously misleading. Growth rates can be compared among countries within Eastern Europe and among the Latin American and East Asian NICs, but comparisons between the two groups of countries are ill-advised. Growth estimates for Yugoslavia are probably more comparable to those of Eastern Europe than to those of Latin America and East Asia. The usual caveat about the reliability of Romanian statistics applies to comparisons among the East European countries.

35. CIA estimates of output levels in Eastern Europe based on standard GNP accounting concepts and corrected for some suspected biases in official East European data do not support this conclusion. According to these estimates, growth performance in Eastern Europe during the period under consideration is as follows:

	1971–75	1976–80	1981–84	1984
Bulgaria	4.7	0.9	2.2	2.5
Czechoslovakia	3.4	2.1	1.2	2.0
GDR	3.5	2.3	2.2	2.5
Hungary	3.3	2.1	0.4	0.5
Romania	6.7	4.0	1.9	3.5
Poland	6.5	0.7	−0.3	3.0

Sources. The 1971–83 figures are based on figures contained in CIA, Directorate of Intelligence, *Handbook of Economic Statistics, 1984* (Washington, D.C., September 1984). Figures for 1984 are based on Vañous's estimates in Vañous, "Diverging Trends in CMEA Economies in 1984," Table 2.

TABLE 2. *The effects of austerity on growth and output performance*

	Average Annual Rate of Growth[a]			
	1971–75	*1976–80*	*1981–84*	*1984*
Newly Industrializing Countries				
Mexico	6.5	6.7	1.5	3.5
Brazil	10.4	6.7	0.0	4.4
Korea	9.5	7.8	7.5	7.9
Taiwan	8.9	10.3	5.7	7.0
Singapore	9.6	8.7	8.1	8.2
Yugoslavia[c]	5.9	5.6	0.7	2.0
East European Countries[d]				
Bulgaria	7.8	6.1	4.2	4.6
Czechoslovakia	5.7	3.7	1.4	2.8
GDR	5.4	4.1	4.3	5.5
Hungary	6.2	3.2	2.0	2.9
Romania	11.2	7.3	2.8	7.7
Poland	9.8	1.3	−3.8	5.1

	Real Output in 1984 as a Percentage of Real Output in 1980
Newly Industrializing Countries	
Mexico	97.5[e]
Brazil	100.5
Korea	124.7
Taiwan	124.8
Singapore	136.5
Yugoslavia	102.6
East European Countries	
Bulgaria[d]	118.0
Czechoslovakia	105.6
GDR	118.5
Hungary	108.6
Romania	116.7[f]
Poland	92.7

a. Simple average of annual growth rates during each period.

b. Output figures are based on World Bank estimates of real gross domestic product (GDP) presented in World Bank, *World Tables*, 3d ed. An update of these estimates was provided to me by the World Bank.

c. Output figures are based on figures for real gross material product contained in official Yugoslav statistical sources.

d. Output figures are based on real net material product produced and are derived from official country statistics reproduced in Jan Vaňous, "Diverging Trends in CMEA Countries in 1984," Wharton Econometric Forecasting Associates, *Centrally Planned Economies: Current Analysis*, 27 March 1985, Table 6.

e. Because austerity did not begin in Mexico until 1981, this figure compares 1984 output to 1981 output.

f. Most observers believe this figure overestimates real output in 1984 compared to 1980.

Given irrationalities in the allocation of import cutbacks and the nature of Western imports throughout Eastern Europe, it is not surprising to find that output losses—as measured by the extent of the deceleration or fall in output—were largest in those East European countries that suffered the largest deceleration or decline in Western imports, namely Poland and Romania.[36] In contrast, the strong performance of output growth in East Germany must be attributed in part to its strong export growth, which precluded sharp cutbacks in Western imports.[37]

In Brazil and Mexico the output costs of enforced austerity during the 1981–84 period were also substantial and related clearly to disruptions in production caused by dramatic import reductions.[38] As in Poland the output level in Mexico did not return to its pre-austerity level by 1984, while in Brazil austerity resulted in output stagnation during the 1980–84 period (see Table 2). In both Latin American countries, as in Poland, given outstanding debt-service burdens the growth recovery in 1984 was not sustainable over the longer run without more debt relief. In Yugoslavia the output costs of austerity took the form of a sharp reduction in growth rates in the 1981–84 period, with only a slight recovery in 1984 but no sustained decline in output levels. Yugoslavia, however, like Poland, Brazil, and Mexico, continued to confront an onerous debt burden that hampered its prospects for future growth.

Undoubtedly, the severity of the output costs of austerity in Poland, Mexico,

36. In real terms, nonsocialist convertible-currency imports declined by approximately 52% between 1980 and 1983 in Poland and then stagnated in 1984. In Romania nonsocialist convertible-currency imports fell in real terms by approximately 43% between 1980 and 1983. In contrast, real nonsocialist convertible-currency imports fell by approximately 5% in the GDR between 1980 and 1982 and then rose sharply to about 14% above 1980 levels by 1984. The only other East European country with comparable real import growth was Bulgaria. These estimates are based on nominal imports presented in Vaňous, "Diverging Trends in CMEA Economies in 1984," Table 10, and estimates of import and export prices for Eastern Europe's convertible-currency trade presented in United Nations, Economic Commission for Europe, *Economic Survey of Europe in 1984–1985* (New York: United Nations, 1985), chap. 5, Table 5.3.3.

37. Import cutbacks from the West tend to overstate overall import cutbacks in East European countries, because a significant fraction of their imports comes from bloc sources. Given the complementary nature of bloc and Western imports, the possibilities for decreases in the latter without incurring a loss of output were limited in the short run. Nonetheless, import increases from bloc sources cushioned the losses in output that would have occurred if total imports had fallen to the extent Western imports fell. Only in Poland and Romania was the cutback in overall imports comparable to the cutback in Western imports. According to U.N. estimates, total real imports in Eastern Europe in 1983 as a percentage of total real imports in 1980 were as follows: Bulgaria, 119%; Czechoslovakia, 98%; GDR, 99%; Hungary, 104%; Poland, 75%; and Romania, 77%. Ibid., Appendix Table 8.15.

38. Between 1981 and 1983, in Mexico real merchandise imports fell by 63% and even after a modest recovery in 1984 reached only 44% of their 1981 levels. In Brazil real merchandise imports fell by 13% in 1981 and then by 21% between 1982 and 1983. These figures are based on updates of the World Bank, *World Tables*, 3d ed. Not all of the decline in imports is attributable to reduction in domestic demand and austerity. For example, in Brazil the realization of import-substitution projects in energy contributed to a drop in oil imports which was helped by declining world oil prices after 1982.

and Brazil was the result of factors other than import cutbacks and the structural and policy barriers to flexibility noted here. In Poland the severity of such costs resulted from deep and unresolved political cleavages in all aspects of economic life, ranging from the daily efforts of individual workers to the methods for allocating import cutbacks across competing projects. In Brazil and Mexico it must be attributed at least in part to the short-run dramatic improvements in the trade balance which capital-market constraints required. The shorter the time period required for such improvements, the greater the output losses because economic flexibility is much more limited in the short run than in the long run. In this respect, the adjustment costs in Eastern Europe, except Poland, were less severe in part because adjustment efforts had begun earlier and were spread out over a longer period of time.

A final reason why output losses tended to be more severe in Latin America was the more limited ability of the state to control the level of domestic demand. Only one component of domestic demand, namely government spending (including spending by the state enterprise sector), was under the direct administrative control of the state. The other two components of aggregate demand—consumption and the even more volatile investment— were largely guided by the interests of private actors which the state could influence only imprecisely through a variety of policy instruments that changed the signals to which these actors responded. Under the extreme changes in economic conditions that accompanied the debt crisis, these policy instruments often proved little more effective than pushing on a string. Under these circumstances, the possibility of "overkill" in austerity was a real one; that is, an austerity program designed to reduce domestic demand only enough to meet the trade target consonant with external capital-market conditions might in fact reduce domestic demand by much more, with consequent losses of output in demand-driven economies.

b. The distribution of the burden of austerity

Because austerity required a reduction in domestic demand, states faced critical choices about the distribution of that reduction across categories of domestic demand and across social groups. The resulting choices depended on policy objectives but were constrained by existing structures that limited state control over distributional outcomes.

There is one important similarity in the distributional outcomes of austerity measures among the debtor countries discussed here. As a result of similar policy choices realized through different policy instruments, investment spending bore a disproportionate share of the cutback in domestic demand. As the figures in Table 3 illustrate, the decline in investment spending was much more precipitous than the decline in total domestic demand, as a result of which investment rates fell sharply in all of the countries.[39] By 1984 investment rates were dramatically lower in all debtor countries than they had been during the 1976–80 period, except in Korea where the investment rate after a relatively small and brief drop in 1981–82 recovered to 96 percent of its average 1976–79 level by 1984.

There are several reasons why states opted to impose a disproportionate share of the austerity burden on investment spending, although their relative importance varies among them. First, as a matter of policy, political leaders chose to protect consumption levels from deep, sustained reductions in order to avoid the overt and covert political dissatisfaction and social malaise that probably would have ensued. Since private consumption in all countries was by far the largest component of domestic spending, this choice put a very heavy burden on investment, the much smaller but second largest component of such spending. Large cuts in investment rates were matched by increases in the share of total consumption spending (both private and public) in domestic demand. Despite these increases, however, declines in the levels of such spending produced at least temporary declines in real consumption levels in Czechoslovakia, Romania, Poland, Yugoslavia, Brazil, Mexico, and Korea. As Table 4 indicates, such declines were especially deep and sustained in Poland where real consumption is estimated to have fallen by as much as 7 to 10 percent between 1980 and 1984; in Yugoslavia where real consumption fell by about 3 percent during the same period; and in Mexico where real consumption fell by 4 percent between 1981 (the onset of austerity) and 1984. In contrast, by 1984 real consumption levels had surpassed 1980 levels in the remaining countries, with the largest increases occurring in Bulgaria, East Germany, and Korea.

With annual population growth rates of approximately 2.4 percent in Brazil and 3.0 percent in Mexico, stagnation or declines in consumption levels implied a sharp drop in real consumption per capita—about 8 percent in Brazil between 1980 and 1984 and 12 percent in Mexico between 1981 and 1984. In contrast, population growth rates in Eastern Europe and Yugoslavia were considerably lower, ranging from −0.2 percent in East Germany to 0.9 percent in Poland, Romania, and Yugoslavia.[40] Clearly, if official numbers are to be believed, only in Poland was the decline in per capita real consumption (about 10% between 1980 and 1984) similar in magnitude to that in Mexico and Brazil.[41]

39. In both Eastern Europe and Brazil the decline in investment rates continued a trend that began in 1976. In Eastern Europe this trend was the result of the voluntary adjustment efforts during the 1976–80 plan period.
40. The population growth rate estimates are based on data appearing in World Bank, *World Development Report* (New York: Oxford University Press, 1984).
41. There is considerable skepticism about the reliability of Romanian consumption figures. Anecdotal information based on various reports of shortages of consumer goods in 1981–82 suggests that consumption levels may have fallen significantly in those years. In addition, as the essay by Thomas Baylis in this volume indicates, consumption levels in the GDR may have declined temporarily in 1982.

TABLE 3. *The effects of austerity on investment rates*

	Investment Rate (%)[a]					1984 Rate as a Percentage of 1976–80 Rate
	1976–80	*1981*	*1982*	*1983*	*1985*	
Newly Industrializing Countries[b]						
Mexico	22.0	30.0	21.0	17.9	17.4	71.6
Brazil	24.5	23.5	22.3	19.0	18.0	73.5
Korea	33.5[c]	29.4	29.3	30.4	31.7	96.5
Yugoslavia[d]	33.5	28.2	26.5	24.1	21.4	63.9
East European Countries[e]						
Bulgaria	35.4	35.7	35.4	34.6	33.1	93.5
Czechoslovakia	33.7	31.6	30.8	30.3	29.8	88.4
GDR	30.7	28.6	26.4	25.3	24.0	78.2
Hungary	37.2	33.7	32.3	31.0	28.2	75.8
Romania[f]	41.1	39.2	36.9	36.4	35.9	87.4
Poland	30.7	24.8	23.1	23.8	24.5	79.8

a. Because of differences in concepts and measurement techniques, rates are not comparable between the NICs and the East European countries. Figures for Yugoslavia are comparable to those of Eastern Europe.

b. Investment rates are measured as the share of real gross domestic investment in real GDP. Rates are calculated from World Bank real gross investment and real GDP estimates presented in World Bank, *World Tables*, 3d ed. An update of these estimates for 1981–84 was provided to me by the World Bank.

c. This is the 1976–79 average investment rate in Korea. In 1980 the rate fell to 30.7% in reaction to austerity measures in that year.

d. Yugoslavia's investment rate is measured as the share of real gross fixed investment in real gross material product produced. Figures taken from official Yugoslav statistics. The figure for 1984 is preliminary.

e. Investment rates are measured as the share of gross fixed capital formation as a percentage of net material product produced. Rates are taken from United Nations, Economic Commission for Europe, *Economic Survey of Europe in 1984–1985* (New York: United Nations, 1985), Table 4.4.2.

f. The usual caveat about Romanian statistics applies.

TABLE 4. *The effects of austerity on real consumption levels*

		1984 Real Consumption Level[a] *as a Percentage of Pre-Austerity Level*	
Newly Industrializing Countries[b]			
Mexico[c]		96 (98)[d]	
Brazil[e]		101 (101)[d]	
Korea[f]		121 (121)[d]	
Yugoslavia[g]		96 (95)	
East European Countries			
Bulgaria	116[h]	117	108[j]
Czechoslovakia	107	103	105
GDR	109	109	106
Hungary	106	105	103
Poland	93	90	99
Romania	106	104	103

a. Because of differences in concepts and measurement techniques, these figures are not comparable between the NICs and the East European countries, although they are representative of differences within groups. The estimate for Yugoslavia is best compared to estimates for Eastern Europe.

b. The results for the NICs are based on World Bank estimates of real private consumption in World Bank, *World Tables*, 3d ed. An update of these estimates for 1981–84 was provided to me by the World Bank.

c. Pre-austerity in Mexico is defined by the level of real consumption realized in 1981.

d. The figure in parentheses includes both private and government consumption spending, whereas the adjacent figure includes only private consumption spending.

e. Pre-austerity in Brazil is defined by the level of real consumption realized in 1980.

f. Pre-austerity in Korea is defined by the level of real consumption realized in 1979.

g. Pre-austerity in Yugoslavia is defined by the level of real consumption realized in 1980. The figure in parentheses includes both personal and collective consumption spending. The figures are based on real gross material product accounts from official Yugoslav sources.

h. This column of figures for Eastern Europe shows the total real consumption fund (private and collective consumption) in 1984 as a percentage of the 1980 level. Figures based on data in Vañous, "Diverging Trends in CMEA Economies in 1984," Table 1.

i. This column of figures for Eastern Europe shows the volume of retail trade in 1984 as a percentage of the 1980 level. Figures are based on data in United Nations, *Economic Survey of Europe in 1984–85*, Appendix Table B.4.

j. This column of figures for Eastern Europe shows 1984 real private consumption as a percentage of the 1980 level. Figures are calculated from estimates of real consumption levels calculated by the Research Project on National Income in East Central Europe. See Thad P. Alton et al., *Eastern Europe: Domestic Final Uses of Gross Product, 1970 and 1974–1984*, Occasional Paper no. 87, Research Project on National Income in East Central Europe (New York: L. W. International Financial Research, 1985).

A second reason for the reliance on investment cuts rather than consumption cuts was that existing structures gave states more direct and rapid administrative control over investment. Throughout Eastern Europe and even in more decentralized, differentiated Yugoslavia, investment decisions were largely administrative in nature, involving direct lines of control between the planning authorities, the national banks, and where relevant the ministries and the enterprises. Although competition among these authorities and the ever-present investment hunger of enterprises often produced excessive investment relative to plan targets, once states recognized the need for austerity, the existing administrative chain of command became an effective mechanism for direct control over both the level and the composition of investment. In contrast, administrative controls over consumption tended to be less precise, working mainly through wage regulations that could be circumvented by enterprises and in some countries through price increases whose effect on consumption was uncertain since it depended on how households adjusted their saving and spending behavior.[42]

In Mexico and Brazil, because a significant share of decisions about investment was private and influenced by expectations of risk and profitability, the state had less precise control over both the level and composition of investment spending than in the East European setting. The relative openness of Mexico's capital market, which allowed private actors to choose between investment at home and investment abroad, undermined the state's ability to control domestic investment spending. Capital flight of an estimated $15 billion in 1982 alone—compared to a current account deficit of $4.9 billion in the same year—indicates the magnitude of domestic private investment that may have been lost. It also indicates the extent to which the actions of private individuals taken to shelter their capital in anticipation of austerity sharply aggravated the debt crisis confronting the state.

On the other hand, the large fraction of investment spending in Brazil and Mexico for which public or state-owned enterprises were responsible enhanced state control. By the early 1980s nearly half of all investment in both countries was under direct state control. Outside of Eastern Europe, few other states directly controlled such a large share of investment resources.[43] Both sharp reductions in public-sector investment engineered by the state and sharp reductions in private investment owing to stricter credit policies and adverse expectations lay behind decreases in investment spending.

A final reason for the disproportionate impact of austerity on investment was the effort by state authorities to minimize short-term output losses associated with import cuts. In order to maintain the flow of imports of raw

42. In the case of Yugoslavia, control over consumption was made even more difficult by large holdings of foreign exchange in the household sector, the domestic purchasing power of which jumped dramatically as a result of large depreciations in the dinar.

43. See Peter Knight, *Economic Stabilization and Medium-Term Development Strategy in Brazil*, Discussion Paper (Washington, D.C.: World Bank, 1985).

materials and other inputs required for immediate production, states squeezed imports of capital goods required for investment projects and future productive capabilities disproportionately. Although a rational policy from a short-term perspective, this response was more questionable from a long-term point of view.

Regarding consumption, the means available to countries to control both the level of overall consumption spending and its distribution among different groups differed considerably. To some extent these differences reflected active policy choices, but once again structural constraints on what was feasible affected how states acted. Of particular importance was the extent to which the state could exercise control over the course of nominal incomes, especially money wages.

In Romania, Czechoslovakia, East Germany, and Bulgaria this control was relatively strong and could be used to influence both the level and incidence of consumption cuts. In these economies, the authorities relied mainly on money wage restraint, along with a combination of selective price increases and occasional rationing of specific goods—by informal or formal means—to control consumption; thus inflation rates remained low. In Hungary, where state control over nominal wages was also comparatively strong, the authorities opted for a combination of nominal wage restraint and rising consumer prices to cut consumption and determine its incidence. This choice was consistent with a long-term goal of economic reform, namely cutting subsidies on consumer goods.

In Poland the use of price increases to check consumer spending was fraught with political risk, as the periodic explosions of worker unrest following such increases indicated. Despite this risk, the extent of excess demand on consumer markets was so strong that once the Jaruzelski regime had stabilized, it introduced major increases in consumer prices: these jumped 110 percent in 1982. Thereafter, stricter nominal wage control abetted austerity in consumption, but shortages of many basic consumer goods persisted, and prices continued to increase, albeit at a much slower pace, attesting to the depth of the underlying macroeconomic disequilibrium.

In Brazil, Mexico, and Yugoslavia the state did not exercise strong control over nominal wages except within the government sector itself. Moreover, because of the strength of unresolved conflicts about the appropriate distribution of the austerity burden and the political threats implicit in such conflicts, the authorities were either unwilling or unable to use income controls to limit spending. In these circumstances, the behavior of real wages—the single most important determinant of consumption spending—was mainly the result of the uncontrolled interaction of nominal wage growth and inflation, and given the history of inflationary expectations and the unpredictable links between inflation and currency depreciations, inflation was both unpredictable and difficult to control in the short run. In these countries, the struggle over the burden of austerity predictably caused inflation to accelerate as groups sought to protect their living standards by raising nominal wages and prices.

Overall, the East European countries and to a lesser extent Yugoslavia exercised more control over the distribution of the austerity burden across firms, households, and individuals than did Brazil or Mexico. This was largely the result of structural differences: in Eastern Europe and Yugoslavia the state used a variety of microeconomic means, including wage controls, price controls, and enterprise-specific allocation of capital and foreign exchange to achieve both macroeconomic and distributional objectives. Such controls grew out of a long tradition of state involvement in the economy for the explicit purpose of realizing "fairness" in the distribution of income. In Brazil and Mexico, in contrast, market forces had played and continued to play the dominant role in determining the distribution of income both among firms and among individuals. The ability and willingness of the state to pursue "fairness" or "equity" in distribution were limited in both countries, as the dramatic inequalities in income distribution and the existence of a large underclass living at or near subsistence indicate.[44]

This argument is not to suggest that the East European states had complete control or that the Latin American states had no control over distributional outcomes. The difference is one of degree of control. Even within Eastern Europe, there were differences in the extent of such control, differences that the importance of second-economy—private legal and illegal—activities significantly influenced. For example, in Hungary anecdotal and sample evidence suggests that about three-fourths of Hungarian families earn extra incomes from the second economy, and these incomes amount to almost one-half of wages paid by the socialist sector.[45] The flow of income through second-economy channels of such magnitude can undermine the effects of state control over relative incomes in official channels. Nonetheless, by controlling wages and employment levels in the socialist sector, the East European states were willing and able to provide a socialist safety net that limited the tendencies toward greater income differentiation which austerity policies produced in Latin America.[46]

44. According to Knight, as late as 1980 the basic needs of perhaps one-third of the Brazilian population were still not being met. Ibid., p. 5.

45. These estimates are based on work on the second economy in Hungary by Istvan Gabor. His findings also suggest that at least one-fifth of total output in Hungary is produced in second-economy channels. See Gabor, "The Second Economy in Socialism: General Lessons from the Hungarian Experience," in Edgar L. Feige, ed., *The Unobserved Economy* (Cambridge: Cambridge University Press, forthcoming).

46. In part, the socialist safety net operated automatically through the labor market. In Eastern Europe and Yugoslavia layoffs are essentially precluded except in the relatively small private sectors, so no loss of jobs accompanied slowdowns or reductions in output. In this way, social-sector employment acted as part of the socialist safety net and made possible a more even distribution of the burden of real income loss among workers. In contrast, in Latin America, because most employment and unemployment decisions were private, the state exercised only limited control over the distribution of the decline in real incomes between those lucky enough to retain employment and those who lost their jobs or failed to find employment as a result of austerity.

c. External economic performance under austerity

In Eastern Europe austerity measures produced dramatic improvements in convertible-currency trade balances and, beginning in 1982, growing current account surpluses in all countries except Poland. These surpluses, along with large changes in the exchange rate, led to dramatic declines in gross debt measured in dollars.[47] Foreign-exchange reserves of convertible currency also rose sharply, as a result of which levels of net debt (gross debt minus reserves) fell even more sharply: by 62 percent in Bulgaria, 70 percent in Czechoslovakia, 36 percent in East Germany, 22 percent in Hungary, and 55 percent in Romania between 1981 and 1984.[48] The decline in debt levels produced a decline in debt-export ratios as well. In addition, the debt-service ratios declined to levels that were relatively low compared to the levels realized in the late 1970s or early 1980s. Despite this progress, even in 1984 debt-service requirements amounted to more than one-third of convertible-currency export revenues in both East Germany and Hungary. In East Germany, however, export revenues were still sufficient to purchase 10 percent more convertible-currency imports in dollar terms than had been purchased in 1980. In contrast, slower export growth combined with heavy debt-service requirements resulted in about a 16 percent reduction in nominal nonsocialist imports in Hungary between 1980 and 1984.[49]

By 1983–84 the success of austerity policies in Eastern Europe meant that for all practical purposes the debt crisis was over, except in Poland. Reserves had risen to levels required for liquidity for trade-related purposes, and private channels of medium- and long-term lending had reopened on a voluntary basis for all countries except Poland and Romania, which had arrears on previously contracted debt.

If the debt crisis was largely resolved in most of Eastern Europe, it remained serious and unresolved in Poland, Brazil, Mexico, and Yugoslavia. As the data in Table 1 indicate, debt-export ratios in these economies remained alarmingly high and debt-service burdens remained substantial. Because of outstanding payment arrears and formal or informal rescheduling, additional medium- and long-term finance supplied on a voluntary basis by Western

47. The appreciation of the dollar relative to other Western currencies during the 1982–84 period caused the dollar value of East European liabilities denominated in Western currencies to decline. Since 40–50% of the hard-currency debt of a typical East European country was denominated in currencies other than the dollar, the impact of changes in exchange rates on the size of the debt at times exceeded the impact of current account surpluses. Since the developing countries held their debt mainly in dollars, the appreciation did not result in a comparably large decline in their debt.

48. These figures are taken from Vañous, "Diverging Trends in CMEA Countries in 1984."

49. In real terms, imports from nonsocialist sources actually increased by about 2.4% between 1980 and 1984 in Hungary. Using Hungarian import prices to deflate nominal convertible-currency imports in East Germany suggests that in real terms imports from nonsocialist sources may have increased by nearly 34% between 1980 and 1984 in East Germany. See United Nations, Economic Commission for Europe, *Economic Bulletin for Europe* 37 (December 1985), chap. 4.

banks was unavailable. Prospects for meeting current and future repayment obligations without continued austerity were dim, suggesting further tradeoffs between external adjustment and improvements in domestic living standards. Since these countries had already suffered substantial declines in per capita consumption during the 1980–84 period, lowering living standards further was bound to be politically risky and socially straining.

In Poland debt levels increased between 1981 and 1984, despite changes in the exchange rate which significantly reduced the dollar value of outstanding debt. In addition, even with the unilateral Polish suspension of servicing payments on debt owed to Western governments and even with the rescheduling of principal and some interest owed to Western banks, debt-service requirements continued to eat up the lion's share of Poland's export earnings in Western markets. Consequently, the dollar value of convertible-currency imports that Poland was able to sustain in 1984 was only 73 percent of its 1981 level and only 46 percent of its 1980 level. As noted earlier, the compression in imports contributed to the sustained fall in output over the 1980–84 period, and this in turn contributed to Poland's inability to expand exports. Without the infusion of new credit and a major rescheduling of private and public debt, it is hard to imagine how Poland can get out of this vicious circle in the next several years, even with a major reform to improve economic efficiency, a development that is unlikely under current political conditions.

In Brazil and Mexico export revenues grew at a rapid rate during the first two years of austerity, boosted to a large extent by rapid demand growth in the United States in 1984. The expansion in export revenues allowed for some recovery in nominal import levels, but because of the heavy burden of debt service, imports remained sharply below pre-austerity levels, amounting to 76 percent of their 1981 level in Brazil and to only 45 percent of their 1981 level in Mexico. Meanwhile gross and net debt levels continued to mount in both countries.

Results for the first half of 1985 indicate that the export growth of 1984 is not likely to be repeated, in large part because the slowing U.S. economy is no longer able to absorb Latin American imports at the 1984 rate. As a consequence, both Brazil and Mexico will probably encounter further difficulties in meeting servicing commitments, requiring further rounds of rescheduling.[50] In these countries as in Poland the debt crisis remains unresolved, and in the absence of substantial amounts of new financing, the servicing of existing debt will continue to limit growth and development prospects over the next several years.

A similar conclusion also applies to Yugoslavia. Yugoslavia's gross and

50. In October 1985 Mexico's major creditors agreed to postpone nearly $1 billion in loan repayments due from Mexico in order to avert an outright default. *New York Times*, 2 October 1985.

net debt levels began to decline in 1983, but the decline was much less dramatic than in the other countries of Eastern Europe. In 1984 Yugoslavia's debt-export ratio (in convertible currency) was comparable to that of Brazil and Mexico and among the highest in the world. Even with reschedulings in 1983 and 1984, the debt-service ratio remained high, amounting to about 35 percent of merchandise exports in 1983.[51] Moreover, despite impressive gains in convertible-currency export revenues—which were about 17 percent above their 1980 level by 1984—convertible-currency imports remained strictly controlled and were only about 69 percent of their 1980 level at the end of 1984.[52] Its strict adherence to IMF austerity conditions since the end of 1980 notwithstanding, Yugoslavia has been unable to attract new credit on a voluntary basis, and additional reschedulings may be required in the future.

Korea's external performance contrasts starkly with the external performance of Poland, Brazil, Mexico, and Yugoslavia during the 1981–84 period. Like Poland, Brazil, and Mexico, Korea continued to build up its level of gross debt through 1984. In Korea, however, the debt-export ratio and debt-service ratio remained dramatically lower than those realized in Brazil, Mexico, and Poland. In Korea, without any rescheduling, debt-service requirements amounted to only 14 percent of export revenues in 1983. With reschedulings that sharply reduced these requirements, the comparable 1983 figures for Brazil and Mexico were 54 percent and 38 percent, respectively. Interest payments alone absorbed more than one-third of merchandise export revenues in Brazil and Mexico and about 45 percent of such revenues in Poland in 1983, while accounting for only about 14 percent of such revenues in Korea in that year.

In part, Korea's performance can be attributed to the fact that public debt with lower interest rates accounted for a much larger share of total debt— nearly 50 percent in 1981—than it did in the other countries.[53] To an important extent, however, Korea's large and growing export base was the linchpin of its external performance. Continued growth in export revenues covered debt-service requirements, a healthy level of foreign-exchange reserves, and the continued import growth required to sustain domestic ex-

51. If the debt-service ratio is calculated by comparing servicing requirements to revenues from both merchandise and nonfactor service exports, the ratio for Yugoslavia was only about 25% in 1983.

52. Because of the use of statistical cross-exchange rates rather than world-market cross-exchange rates in official Yugoslav trade statistics, these changes in dollar export and dollar import values must be interpreted cautiously. For more on the possible distortions resulting from this procedure, see Jan Vaňous, "Yugoslav Foreign Trade Performance and Payments Situation in 1984," Wharton Econometric Forecasting Associates, *Centrally Planned Economies: Current Analysis*, 30 April 1985.

53. In the other three largest, non-OPEC debtor countries—Brazil, Mexico, and Argentina— only about 25% of total debt was from public sources. OECD, *External Debt of Developing Countries 1983 Survey* (Paris: OECD, 1984), p. 43.

pansion at a rapid rate.[54] This performance is even more remarkable in light of the fact that Korea was one of the four largest non-OPEC debtors in the world—along with Mexico, Brazil, and Argentina—as well as one of the countries with the highest level of floating-interest-rate debt during the 1981–84 period.

Because of the glaring contrast between the dramatic declines in debt levels throughout Eastern Europe and the continued buildup in debt in the other debtor countries examined here, it is tempting to interpret efforts to reduce debt in Eastern Europe as evidence that East European states have decided to reduce integration with the West because of their disappointment with the results of greater openness in the 1970s. From this perspective, rapid external adjustment might be interpreted as the cost of greater policy-making autonomy in the future and as a sign of a turn inward and eastward in trade and financial relations. This interpretation seems to be somewhat appropriate for Bulgaria, Czechoslovakia, and Romania. Both Bulgaria and Czechoslovakia declined to take on new medium- and long-term debt in 1983–84, although they were viewed as creditworthy by Western banks. Romania adjusted at a rate widely deemed to be excessive relative to that required by external lenders and expressed active disinterest in borrowing further from both the IMF and the International Bank for Reconstruction and Development (IBRD) in 1983 and 1984.

In contrast, the decline in debt levels in East Germany and Hungary seems to have been a reflection of a long-term decision to expand ties with the West. Their buildup of reserves and reductions in debt made these countries increasingly attractive to Western lenders, and by 1983–84 they were borrowing actively on medium- and long-term private capital markets at rates at or near pre-austerity levels. In addition, Hungary was receiving additional substantial credits from both the IMF and IBRD, hardly a sign of closure to international capital markets.

Finally, just as a rundown in debt need not indicate a desire for greater closure from world trade and financial markets, so continued accumulation of debt need not indicate a desire for greater openness. Given their precarious economic situations and the debt-service burden they face, Poland, Brazil, Mexico, and Yugoslavia confront severe constraints on the pace at which they can reduce debt levels without generating unacceptably high political risks. Continued reliance on external finance has been the price of maintaining internal political stability.

6. The debt crisis and prospects for the future

Despite differences in underlying objectives and structure, the states that opted to borrow heavily in the 1970s all confronted the need for austerity

---

54. Korea was also helped by the shift in the terms of trade against net commodity exporters and in favor of net commodity importers during the 1983–84 period. Brazil and Mexico were hurt by this shift, and the falling price of oil cut into Mexico's export revenues.

in the 1980s. This was as true for Korea, where austerity was voluntary and short-lived, as it was true for Brazil, Mexico, Yugoslavia, and the East European countries, where external constraints necessitated sustained austerity measures. The major distinction that emerges among the group of countries examined here is that which exists between those that chose not to build up debt in the 1970s—namely Singapore and Taiwan—and those that did.

Among the group of countries that chose the borrowing strategy in the 1970s, there were important differences in the costs and effectiveness of austerity measures adopted in the 1980s. Both the extent of the adjustment required—that is, the size of the improvement in external performance required by external capital-market constraints during a given period of time—and the policy instruments available to realize the adjustment explain these differences during the 1981–84 period. These policy instruments, in turn, were the product of a given politico-economic structure, and the legacies of past development strategies significantly influenced their effectiveness.

In the short run, in all of the countries examined here austerity involved temporary policy responses to a change in economic priorities that new external conditions dictated, rather than fundamental changes in these priorities and in the underlying economic structure and strategy constructed to realize them. As austerity wore on, as its domestic economic and political costs mounted, and as expectations that it would persist for the foreseeable future strengthened, state leaders were forced to consider such fundamental changes more seriously. Such was not the case in Korea, however, where continued export growth and a severe but temporary deflation averted a debt crisis, promoted the continued provision of external finance to support rapid growth, and seemed to confirm the strength of Korea's unique economic structure and development strategy.[55] In the other debtor countries, in contrast, domestic interest and political groups and public and private external creditors in both the East and the West increasingly called into question the wisdom of past choices.

It is still too early to determine whether the reassessment of structure and development strategy touched off by the debt crisis in Latin America will have any fundamental effects over the long run. A common ingredient in the rescheduling discussions in both Mexico and Brazil has been an emphasis on the need for greater outward orientation or export promotion in development strategy, the need to reduce the share of state investment and state industry in the economy, and the need to correct various price distortions to bring domestic and world prices closer together. This focus in part reflects

55. Because of the continued buildup of debt during the 1981–84 period, Korea may find itself in economic difficulty in the future if world trade slows appreciably or if protectionist measures sharply reduce its export prospects, especially in such critical products as textiles. In this sense Korea has continued to pursue a very risky debt-cum-growth strategy that could encounter difficulties very suddenly. Growing awareness of this risk made this strategy and the issue of debt a major political controversy in Korea in 1985.

the views of the IMF and the Western banks, and it is hard to judge the strength of support for such views by the country leaderships. In Brazil, of course, political uncertainty stemming from the recent change in leadership clouds the picture still further. Finally, in both countries, in the absence of an increase in external financing, the constraints of austerity will limit the scope for meaningful changes in both strategy and structure. It is hard to imagine a meaningful policy of greater decentralization in the use of capital or foreign exchange when external constraints necessitate strict control over investment and imports. Foreign-exchange constraints on import liberalization and capital constraints on new export-promoting industrial investment undermine any move toward more outward orientation.

The situation in Yugoslavia is similar to that in Latin America. Under pressure by the IMF, the Yugoslavs have introduced a variety of policy measures, such as substantially higher interest rates and a major real devaluation, that could signal a long-term development strategy that is both more outward-oriented and that reduces the state's role in the allocation of resources. Indeed, a more market-oriented structure and strategy of this type were formally proposed by a special government commission and officially ratified by the government in 1983. Clear indications, however, point to sharp disagreements among different interest groups, most often divided along regional lines, about the wisdom of such changes; and so far lack of compliance has postponed or undermined many of the policy measures proposed to realize them. In the absence of a strong, unified national leadership, fundamental modifications of economic structure and strategy are unlikely in the next few years. Furthermore, as in Brazil and Mexico, continued scarcity of foreign exchange and austerity will impede the realization of such modifications, even if a political consensus supporting them does emerge.

In the countries of Eastern Europe there are signs that the experience of austerity is promoting a rethinking of development strategy and, in some countries, a renewed interest in reform of the economic structure as well. In all of the countries of the region, austerity in domestic demand rather than expansion in domestic supply affected improvements in the external economic situation during the 1981–84 period. Because of the dramatic reduction in investment rates and growing constraints on labor supplies attributable to demographic changes, future growth depends critically on an expansion of supply, and this in turn depends critically on more efficient use of resources. Without changes in economic structure, the prospects for such improvements are poor. The administrative instruments of central planning have proven themselves to be powerful tools for the compression of demand, but they have also proven themselves to be poorly designed for the promotion of supply except via the rapid mobilization of capital and labor resources, a choice constrained by current and future scarcities.

In addition to changes in economic structure, future economic performance in Eastern Europe will also depend on changes in economic strategy. More efficient use of resources will require not only different economic incentives but also different and better technology, much of it currently available only from the West. Imports of Western technology, however, have contracted sharply as a result of import cutbacks and declines in investment austerity, implying that the East-West technology gap has widened during the last several years. Given the accelerating pace of technological change, the costs of restricting technology imports will become even greater in the future, especially in the areas of electronics and computers where the East-West gap is especially dramatic.

Because of their experiences of the last decade, neither international bankers nor East European leaders are likely to attempt to close the technology gap by imports of Western technology financed by imports of Western finance, their strategy in the 1970s. Such a strategy resulted in an asymmetric openness: imports and debt increased more rapidly than exports. The future will require greater symmetry. If imports from the West are to recover from their current depressed levels, then development strategies must be modified to foster exports to the West, which will finance a larger fraction of import needs.

An alternative, but in the long run much less promising, strategy is a strategy of greater inward orientation toward Eastern-bloc markets. Such a strategy can only serve to widen the technology gap within the bloc and thereby frustrate the Soviet Union's efforts to upgrade the quality of imports of industrial goods from its bloc partners and to keep up with Western military technology. Indeed, new Soviet pressures on Eastern Europe for higher-quality industrial goods in exchange for oil and raw materials strengthen the pressures for both changes in structure and greater openness to the West as an avenue for technological upgrading over the longer run.[56]

To date, the evidence on recent changes in both strategy and structure in Eastern Europe is mixed. Both East Germany and Hungary seem to be pursuing a more outward-oriented strategy toward the West, as suggested by their renewed borrowing on Western financial markets and by their efforts to resolve the debt crisis by expanding Western exports more than by contracting Western imports. Both countries have also introduced special policies to promote exports to the West, and export performance has been elevated to a major indicator of enterprise success and reward. Both of these countries are the most developed in Eastern Europe—indeed, East Germany has significantly increased its lead over the rest of the bloc over the last five years[57]— and stand to lose the most from continued closure to Western technology.

56. In the short run, Soviet pressures on its East European trading partners to increase their exports of hard goods to the Soviet Union are likely to impede greater openness to the West among bloc countries by diverting exports from Western markets to bloc markets.

57. Between 1980 and 1984 the GDR increased its lead in per capita GNP over every other East European country. In 1984 the GNP per capita in Czechoslovakia, the second most developed country in the bloc, was only 84% of the GDR level, and in Romania, the least developed country in the bloc, only 53% of the GDR level. See Vaňous, "Diverging Trends in CMEA Economies in 1984," Table 7.

In contrast, Bulgaria, Czechoslovakia, and Romania seem to be opting for greater autonomy from Western trade and capital markets and orienting trade more toward the bloc.[58] This policy, while attractive from a short-run perspective, is likely to prove costly in the longer run, particularly for Czechoslovakia, which will only continue its precipitous decline as an industrial and technological competitor both inside and outside the bloc. Since bloc trade among the East European countries remains small compared to trade between these countries and the Soviet Union, without a radical change in trade flows and increased specialization within the bloc, the ability of Hungary and East Germany to provide high-technology imports in lieu of Western supplies to Czechoslovakia, Bulgaria, and Romania will remain limited.

In terms of structural change Hungary appears to have gone the furthest in recent years, reaffirming its commitment to strengthening market forces and reducing administrative intervention in economic decisions. At least on paper, the structural changes introduced in Hungary have been more far-reaching than those introduced elsewhere in Eastern Europe, including Poland, Bulgaria, and East Germany.[59] In Hungary these changes call for the continued dismantling of central control over the economy, whereas elsewhere in Eastern Europe such changes are designed ultimately to strengthen and improve such control. If East Germany persists in its strategy of greater openness to the West, pressures for more meaningful structural changes will mount, since centralized administrative modes of decision making are ill-suited to competition on Western markets and to the effective use of Western technology.

Finally, in Poland where the political consequences of borrowing and failed adjustment in the 1970s have been profound, where the output losses from austerity are among the largest in the world, and where the personal political and economic costs of austerity for the population have been dramatically high, there has been little evidence of major changes in either structure or strategy. Although the leadership has talked of meaningful economic reform, actual changes have been limited to measures designed to improve the central planning system, not to weaken it in favor of market forces.[60] Depressed

58. It is hard to determine the extent to which Romania is opting simply for greater inward orientation or autarchy, even at the expense of growth, or for greater bloc integration. In the early 1980s Romania was pushing for tighter trade links with the bloc, but the failure to win Soviet agreement to its request for subsidized oil imports tempered enthusiasm for this strategy. Little evidence to date supports the notion that Romania is willing to give up its national development objectives or autonomy to realize the possible benefits from greater specialization within the bloc.

59. In Hungary the ambitious reform blueprint introduced in 1985 has yet to be implemented to any large extent. Continued austerity conditions will undoubtedly slow the pace of its implementation.

60. The Jaruzelski leadership has declared itself in favor of the economic reform plans drawn up in Poland before the imposition of martial law. These plans call for the introduction of a Hungarian-type economic reform that would give greater decision-making authority to the enterprises. In keeping with this objective, the gigantic associations of enterprises have been abolished, and authority has been passed down to the enterprises in the expectation that they will exercise this authority when quantitative central plans are eliminated. To date, however, central planning has remained the dominant tool for economic management and enterprise discretion has remained limited.

levels of investment and hard-currency imports almost preclude the possibility of a real change in development strategy. Finally, it is unlikely that the current Polish leadership views a significant change in either structure or strategy as a primary objective. Instead, the paramount policy objective probably remains the stabilization of the political situation and the consolidation of power, an objective that meaningful reforms would threaten. Overall, the Polish experience of both the 1970s and 1980s clearly illustrates the primacy of politics over both structure and development strategy in determining how individual economies respond to and perform under changing external conditions.

Postscript

Several months after this chapter was completed, the United Nations Economic Commission for Europe issued new data on the trade flows of the East European countries through the end of 1984. These new statistics allow one to distinguish between changes in the dollar values and real volumes of such flows and shed additional light on the role of import cutbacks and export growth in the adjustment strategies of individual East European countries.[61]

The new information confirms the importance of sustained slowdowns or cutbacks of imports from nonsocialist sources in all of the countries of the region except Bulgaria and the GDR. By 1984 real nonsocialist imports were sharply below 1980 levels in Romania, Poland, and to a lesser extent Czechoslovakia, and were only about 3 percent above their 1980 level in Hungary. In contrast, real nonsocialist imports continued to increase, in Bulgaria to nearly 50 percent above their 1980 level by 1984, in the GDR to nearly 34 percent above their 1980 level by 1984 after a temporary decline in 1981–82.

On the export side the new information suggests that export expansion, promoted by vigorous export campaigns and related administrative means, was a more important component of adjustment than is widely believed. Real exports to nonsocialist markets increased in all East European countries except Poland during 1980–84. Growth was especially rapid in the GDR, followed by Romania, Hungary, and Bulgaria. Only in Poland did nonsocialist exports decline sharply, attesting to supply bottlenecks in the economy, especially in the critical coal sector.

---

61. Estimates are based on UN data on current dollar values of trade flows for each country. To get estimates of real trade flows, dollar values were deflated by Hungarian foreign trade price indexes. Clearly, the procedure introduces errors into the figures, which are approximations. See United Nations, *Economic Commission for Europe* 37, 34 (December 1985).

Despite impressive export growth in some countries, overall export performance in Eastern Europe showed several signs of weakness. In three countries—Bulgaria, the GDR, and Hungary—a rapid expansion in energy exports in 1982 and 1983 was a major factor in export growth. These three countries are net importers of energy, so it seems likely that their oil exports to the West resulted from the re-export of Soviet and OPEC deliveries. Exports of machinery and equipment to Western markets increased in real terms in Czechoslovakia, the GDR, Hungary, and Romania between 1980 and 1984. But Eastern Europe's share in Western markets for machinery and equipment continued to follow a long-term decline dating from the mid-1970s. Finally, despite major export campaigns, Eastern Europe's share in total world exports increased only marginally through 1984 and failed to regain its 1975 level.[62]

62. Using UN data, Csaba calculates that Eastern Europe's share of world export markets declined from a postwar peak of 6.1% in 1965 to 5.1% in 1975 and 4.65% in 1983, up slightly from 4.1% in 1981. Lazlo Csaba, "CMEA in a Changing World," Institute for the World Economy (Budapest, 1984).

CMEA: effective but cumbersome political economy Michael Marrese

This essay addresses five questions. First, what are the preferences upon which the Council for Mutual Economic Assistance (CMEA) is constructed?[1] The most influential preferences are Soviet: an affinity for central planning, ambition to behave as a superpower, and the desire to maintain a strong defense. With respect to these preferences, the CMEA has provided the Soviet Union with an effective but cumbersome politico-economic policy-making apparatus that is becoming less effective and more cumbersome over time.

Long-term East European preferences for a secure supply of fuels and raw materials from the Soviet Union and for improved terms of trade vis-à-vis the Soviet Union have heavily influenced the choice of intra-CMEA price-formation formulas. However, these price-formation formulas have produced only a vague understanding of "prices in real terms." More important, East European leaders have influenced the character of the CMEA by articulating the short-term pressures they face and then bargaining to exchange "allegiance" to the Soviet Union for economic subsidization of trade. Allegiance is measured both by the economic, ideological, political, and strategic non-market benefits (defined in section 6) that an East European country supplies

The initial version of this essay was prepared for the Conference on Foreign Economic Strategies of Eastern Europe, University of California, Berkeley, 1–2 February 1985. Subsequent versions benefited from the critical remarks of conference participants, especially the extensive and intriguing comments of Ellen Comisso. I am also grateful for assistance from Bela Balassa, Marjorie Castle, Benjamin Cohen, Keith Crane, Peter Katzenstein, Ronald Linden, Paul Marer, Perry Patterson, Kristopher Schmidt, Daniel Shiman, Laura Tyson, and several knowledgeable referees. The remaining errors are my responsibility.

1. Principally because of the Soviet Union's desire to promote economic and political integration among the socialist planned economies of Eastern Europe, the CMEA was established in January 1949 with the Soviet Union, Bulgaria, Czechoslovakia, Hungary, Poland, and Romania as its original members. East Germany (the GDR) joined in 1950, Mongolia in 1962, and Vietnam in 1978. The CMEA was not a serious policy-making arena until the latter part of the 1950s. In this essay, "CMEA" refers to the seven European members—the Soviet Union, Bulgaria, Czechoslovakia, the GDR, Hungary, Poland, and Romania.

International Organization 40, 2, Spring 1986   0020-8183 $5.00
© 1986 by the Massachusetts Institute of Technology and the World Peace Foundation

to the Soviet Union and by the domestic stability of that East European country. The Soviet Union may have been able to use other means to extract some of these nonmarket benefits from East European countries but freely chose to utilize subsidization. Moreover, if an East European country becomes unstable, then that country clearly becomes much less valuable to the Soviet Union from economic, ideological, political, and military points of view. The economic subsidization received from the Soviet Union has allowed East European countries to postpone potentially destabilizing reforms or policy changes and thus helps to solidify the positions of East European leaders.

Second, how are CMEA characteristics related to these preferences? Soviet–East European negotiations concerning trade and technology occur in bilateral forums and sharply differentiate economic relationships between the Soviet Union and each individual East European country. (Quantitative measures of these relationships appear throughout this essay.) The bilateral character of negotiations follows from a need to reconcile the long-term political preferences of Soviet leaders with the short-term pressures facing East European leaders. Since each East European country has different attributes that interest the Soviet Union (the only superpower in the CMEA), and each East European country faces unique pressures, bilateral bargaining is a sensible outcome.

Third, what are the static and dynamic economic costs and benefits to CMEA member countries? All of them experience static and dynamic costs as a result of CMEA prices that differ from world-market prices, inadequate incentives to innovate and to share technology, protection from world-market competition, and many trade-inhibiting CMEA institutional characteristics such as the inconvertibility of the transferable ruble. In addition, the Soviet Union accepts the static cost of implicit trade subsidization of Eastern Europe, which of course, is a static benefit for Eastern Europe.

Fourth, why have costs for all member countries risen over time? Implicit subsidization has increased steadily in real terms because: (a) world-market price shocks and East European borrowing from the West in the 1970s (coupled with unfortunate investment decisions) increased the risk of economic and political instability in Eastern Europe; (b) the world-market price shocks were unanticipated and therefore produced sizable unanticipated subsidies; (c) the flow of East European nonmarket benefits to the Soviet Union may have increased; and (d) East Europeans may have improved their bilateral bargaining skills over time. The dynamic costs have risen because the obstacles to increased trade and technology transfer within the CMEA have been more detrimental during the recent period of very rapid technological innovation and specialization in the rest of the world.

Fifth, how is intra-CMEA trade likely to change during the next decade? If certain hypothetical changes in long-term Soviet political preferences occur, the most probable scenario for future CMEA interaction is increasingly differentiated Soviet bilateralism with individual East European countries.

Although these five questions represent a broad spectrum of analysis, their analysis has been conducted under severe limitations. (These limitations are discussed in the Appendix.) Here it is important to identify those aspects of the CMEA that have been reasonably investigated in the literature and those that are based on speculation. For instance, statements concerning the preferences, goals, and status of member countries are based on careful analysis. Yet statements concerning the relative influence that member countries have over CMEA policies and institutions are based on speculation, as are statements about the actual proceedings of bilateral bargaining. Likewise, analysis of CMEA institutional characteristics, trade flows, terms of trade, implicit subsidization, and overall efficiency is solid, but answers to why certain trends have emerged and may emerge in the future remain speculative. In the tradition of the available literature, this essay speculates about the actual bargaining process but focuses primarily on the inputs and outputs of bilateral bargaining, along with the implications of such observable behavior.

Another caveat applies to the body of work underlying this essay, namely research carried out by Jan Vaňous and Michael Marrese. According to Marrese and Vaňous, the Soviet Union subsidizes East European countries by being primarily a net exporter to CMEA countries of fuel and nonfuel raw materials at CMEA foreign-trade prices (*ftps*) that are below corresponding world-market prices (*wmps*) and by being a net importer of manufactured goods at *ftps* that are above corresponding *wmps*. The Soviet Union engages in annual bilateral bargaining over the composition of trade to enable some countries to receive greater implicit subsidies from trade with the Soviet Union than do others. Moreover, the differential subsidies are related to the nomarket benefits provided by each country and to each country's domestic stability, as well as to the costs of obtaining nonmarket benefits via the stick rather than the carrot.

The Marrese-Vaňous view, emphasizing the political calculus of the carrot and the stick, stands in sharp contrast to three earlier perspectives in the literature: (1) the naive perspective (defined in detail in section 6), which portrays the CMEA as the focal point of socialist solidarity and unselfish mutual cooperation; (2) the cold war perspective, valid from 1945 to 1955, which depicts the Soviet Union as the dominant power in the region, exploiting Eastern Europe in all dimensions, including trade; and (3) the customs union approach, based on strictly economic reasoning and presented most thoroughly by Franklyn Holzman, which argues that the CMEA promotes trade among its members and restricts trade with nonmembers. If the CMEA is a customs union, it is not surprising that CMEA *ftps* differ from corresponding *wmps* because the resource endowments of CMEA countries differ from the resource endowments of the rest of the world. Moreover, it is theoretically possible (under conditions that I reject; see section 6 for details) that though terms of trade for the Soviet Union within the CMEA are disadvantageous relative to its terms of trade on the world market, all CMEA countries could be better off by participating in the CMEA rather than by trading as individual countries on the world market.[2]

The final warning refers to assumptions that Soviet behavior differs substantially from East European behavior. That the Soviet Union has made decisions based on the long-run political preferences mentioned above and on a profound understanding of the static and dynamic lessons of international political economy is a premise of this essay.

One such static lesson is that trade based on comparative advantage leads to a higher level of real national income. This increase in national income can be used to pursue any national goal: hospital, road, or missile. The Soviet Union has applied this lesson to trade with, among others, the West, Romania, and Yugoslavia. Another static lesson is that preferential trade treatment may be given to a country in exchange for nonmarket military, political, ideological, and economic favors. The Soviet Union has applied this second lesson to trade with, among others, Bulgaria, Czechoslovakia, East Germany (the GDR), Hungary, and Poland.

Albert Hirschman designated the first static lesson "the supply" effect and the second lesson "the influence effect," whereas in Marrese and Vaňous's terminology they are referred to as "conventional" and "unconventional" gains from trade.[3]

The relevant dynamic lesson focuses on the substantial costs that are incurred if an already established institutional and production structure is altered. For example, country B's trade dependence on country A is defined as B's dependence on the particular markets, demand patterns, and prices offered by A. An increase in B's trade dependence on A is related to the extent that A either bribes or forces B to alter its institutional and production structure to meet those needs of A which do not conform to world-market standards. In the 1950s the Soviet Union strove to mold East European economies into cheap sources of inputs for Soviet industry and to transform East European nations into strong Soviet allies. As the 1950s progressed, it became clear that the Soviet goal of rendering East European economies completely dependent on the Soviet economy at terms very favorable to the Soviet Union directly conflicted with the Soviet goal of transforming East European nations into allies. The Soviet Union soon realized that the allegiance of East European countries could no longer be secured effectively via

2. For the original work on this subject, see Franklyn D. Holzman, "Soviet Foreign Trade Pricing and the Question of Discrimination: A 'Customs Union' Approach," *Review of Economics and Statistics* 44 (May 1962), pp. 134–47; Holzman, "More on Soviet Bloc Trade Discrimination," *Soviet Studies* 17, 1 (July 1965), pp. 44–65. For a comparison of the customs union approach and the Marrese-Vaňous approach, see Josef C. Brada, "Soviet Subsidization of Eastern Europe: The Primacy of Economics over Politics?" *Journal of Comparative Economics* 9 (March 1985), pp. 80–92.

3. Albert O. Hirschman, *National Power and the Structure of Foreign Trade* (Berkeley: University of California Press, 1945), pp. 3–34; Michael Marrese and Jan Vaňous, "Unconventional Gains from Trade," *Journal of Comparative Economics* 7 (December 1983), pp. 382–99.

the stick and resorted to a new policy that employed a combination of the carrot (trade subsidization) and the stick (the threat of armed intervention). Since the 1950s the Soviet Union has attempted to increase Eastern Europe's trade dependence by instituting intra-CMEA product specialization, joint investment programs, and proposals for transnational planning.

East European behavior contrasts sharply with Soviet behavior because East European countries have made decisions about trade and technology which reflect short-run economic pressures more strongly than long-run political preferences. Two reasons stand out. First, because East European economies are more dependent on trade than is the Soviet economy, they have suffered more severely from external shocks. Second, the Soviet Union is the dominant long-term policy maker of the CMEA. East European countries may have some influence over certain characteristics of joint projects and over whether to participate or not, but they have virtually no influence over which joint projects will be selected. More generally, when preparing for bilateral trade negotiations with the Soviet Union, East European leaders weigh the costs and benefits of more preferential trade with the Soviet Union versus more trade with the West.

More precisely, the costs to an East European country of more preferential trade with the Soviet Union are increased trade dependence on the Soviet Union and diminished national sovereignty. Loss of national sovereignty includes the loss of an independent foreign policy, subordination of the nation's armed forces to the Soviet high command, acceptance of limitations on domestic political institutions and policies, and restrictions on the design and operation of the economy. The costs of more trade with the West are short-term economic losses in the form of initially less favorable terms of trade with the West, the start-up costs of penetrating Western markets with relatively unknown products, and short-term transition costs of competing on world markets which could include bankruptcy and unemployment.

With respect to benefits, more preferential trade with the Soviet Union translates into some combination of implicit subsidies, bilateral deficits in ruble trade, and bilateral surpluses in dollar trade. Such economic subsidization (coupled perhaps with the threat of Soviet military intervention) may temporarily solidify the positions of East European leaders. The benefits of more trade with the West include increased exposure to the competitive pressures of the world market, which could lead to increased efficiency and access to new technology and managerial techniques. A long time lag, during which the transition costs of bankruptcy and unemployment would fall most heavily on the political leaders in power, would precede receipt of such benefits.

1. Assumptions about Soviet political preferences

The view of international political economy described above presumes that the country seeking additional power rationally evaluates the perceived benefits against the expected costs. Proponents of this view assume that a country's domestic policies are distinct from its international policies. Such a separation rarely exists anywhere, certainly not in the Soviet Union. Thus a narrower conception of rationality, loosely called *effectiveness*, proves a more appropriate norm by which to judge the CMEA from the Soviet perspective. Effectiveness describes the extent to which the CMEA appears successfully to fulfill the Soviet political preferences mentioned below. These political preferences define Soviet political preeminence within the CMEA in the sense that East European opposition to them has not significantly altered their character.

Central planning. The Soviet Union has a strong preference for an environment within the CMEA that conforms to the needs of Soviet-type central planning.

Superpower ambitions. The Soviet Union, as the only superpower in the region, attempts to control the region's foreign policies toward the rest of the world.

Defense. The Soviet Union places a high value on Eastern Europe's strategic importance to the defense of Soviet territory.

The preference for central planning encompasses the notion that CMEA trade, industrial cooperation, and specialization have been designed to respect two features of the Soviet economy: taut material balance planning and the protection of the domestic economy from external shocks. The Soviet Union utilizes tautness in place of competitive market forces to stimulate rapid economic growth and engages in material balance planning because it is understood and can be controlled by high-level government decision makers. Moreover, the protection of the domestic economy from foreign market conditions via long-term trade agreements is a direct consequence of Soviet ideological aversion to the chaos of the market. A quantity-oriented economy, such as the Soviet Union's, is not designed to respond to market fluctuations. Thus, the Soviet Union strongly prefers CMEA practices that are responsive to the needs of a taut, highly centralized, quantity-oriented Soviet economy.

The Soviet Union's utilization of the CMEA to further its superpower ambitions can be inferred from the Soviet practice of treating its CMEA partners differently depending, among other things, on each partner's willingness to follow Soviet foreign-policy leadership.[4] Evidence of differential treatment includes the uneven distribution of implicit Soviet trade subsidies (see section 5), Soviet surpluses in ruble trade, intra-CMEA trade in convertible currencies, and bilateral Soviet–East European cooperation agreements.

4. See Michael Marrese and Jan Vaňous, *Soviet Subsidization of Trade with Eastern Europe— A Soviet Perspective* (Berkeley: Institute of International Studies, University of California, 1983), pp. 68–86; Marrese and Vaňous, "Soviet Trade Relations with Eastern Europe, 1970–84" (Revised version of the paper presented to the Conference on the Soviet Union and Eastern Europe in the World Economy, Washington, D.C., 18–19 October 1984), pp. 24–37.

The Soviet preference for comprehensive defensive protection means that despite major changes in military technology since 1945, the Soviet Union perceives Eastern Europe as crucial to its defense. Thus, one important objective of Soviet policy is a strong Warsaw Pact (WP) alliance. In turn, the strength of the WP depends on the economic, political, and social stability of East European nations, and on the amount of resources, preparedness, and enthusiasm which East European populations and leaderships devote to the WP. (See section 5 for a description of Soviet bilateral bargaining with an East European country in order to secure unconventional gains from trade—for example, a strong WP.)

It is precisely because the CMEA reflects these Soviet preferences that Soviet policies are not consistent with traditional trade theory, which, as we will see, advocates the maximization of conventional gains from trade via strict adherence to the principles of comparative advantage. The CMEA is primarily a forum for bilateral Soviet–East European bargaining over the economic, foreign-policy, and defense needs of member countries. Soviet bargaining strength is related to its economic, political, and military preeminence. Each East European country's bargaining strength rests with its geopolitical characteristics, level of economic development, allegiance to the Soviet Union, domestic stability, and options with the West.

2. Background

Even though the CMEA was established in 1949 to promote economic and political integration among socialist planned economies, the massive net resource transfer from Eastern Europe to the Soviet Union during 1945–55 pointed to Soviet economic exploitation of Eastern Europe. The Soviet Union secured East European transfers via a variety of techniques: dismantling East European industrial installations and shipping them to the Soviet Union; demanding deliveries of commodities to the Soviet Union for reparation; conducting trade at prices very favorable to the Soviet Union; locating joint stock companies in Eastern Europe but organizing them to maximize Soviet interests to the detriment of local interests; and enforcing East European provision of supplies to Soviet troops stationed in Eastern Europe.[5] Paul Marer estimated that from 1945 to Stalin's death in 1953, an unrequited flow of resources from Eastern Europe to the Soviet Union accompanied Soviet political domination of the region. The size of this flow was approximately equal to the resources transferred from the United States to Western Europe under the Marshall Plan.[6]

5. See Paul Marer, "Soviet Economic Policy in Eastern Europe," in Joint Economic Committee, *Reorientation and Commercial Relations of the Economies of Eastern Europe* (Washington, D.C.: GPO, 1974), pp. 135–63.
6. Ibid., p. 136.

Two features of Soviet behavior toward Eastern Europe during 1945–58 are especially noteworthy. Soviet economic exploitation was directed not only at its former enemy countries (the GDR, Hungary, and Romania) but also at its former allies (Czechoslovakia, Poland, and Yugoslavia). In addition, Soviet aid to Eastern Europe during this time was in direct response to actual or potential East European domestic instability. The Soviets provided loans immediately after World War II to relieve specific troubled situations, offered loans in 1947–48 as compensation for nonparticipation in the Marshall Plan, extended loans and other concessions to East Germany in 1953 in response to the Berlin riots of that year, and implemented a comprehensive, large-scale aid program during 1956–58 in reaction to the Polish and Hungarian revolutions of 1956.[7]

The pattern of transfers and the two above-mentioned features suggest that neither altruistic socialist solidarity nor a vengeful desire to punish its former enemies guided Soviet behavior. Two goals clearly influenced Soviet actions: to mold East European economies into cheap sources of inputs for Soviet industry and to transform East European nations into strong Soviet allies. As the 1950s progressed, it became clear that the goal of rendering East European economies completely dependent on the Soviet economy at terms very favorable to the Soviet Union directly conflicted with the goal of transforming East European nations into allies.

Also at this time CMEA countries perceived that the opportunities for extensive growth within the CMEA based on large annual increases in the flows of labor and capital were diminishing and that intensive growth based on productivity increases was becoming more important. Intra-CMEA specialization in production, exchange of information regarding managerial techniques and reward schemes, technological transfer, and joint research and development (R&D) efforts were identified as potential sources of productivity growth. However, effective utilization of these sources could occur only as a result of CMEA policies that were much less one-sided than those of the early 1950s.

3. CMEA characteristics

This section investigates eleven important characteristics of CMEA institutions. The first four of these are closely associated with the Soviet preference for central planning. The fifth and sixth characteristics are consequences of the first four. All remaining characteristics are related to the predominant form of CMEA economic interaction, namely the bilateral relationships between the Soviet Union and each East European country. Such bilateral relationships allow the Soviet Union to bargain regularly and covertly with

7. Ibid., p. 143.

East European countries in order to obtain nonmarket benefits that support Soviet superpower ambitions and defense concerns.

First, intra-CMEA trade is organized on a governmental level. Such an arrangement respects the Soviet preference for centralized control. Export and import flows are negotiated in interstate government agreements and are not based on contracts between enterprises. The five-year agreements contain obligatory quantitative quotas for the large-volume, high-value commodities and aggregate value quotas for such categories of commodities as machinery and equipment, fuels, nonfood raw materials, food and raw materials for food, and industrial consumer goods. Detailed specifications (and for that matter the degree of detail) for the products included in the quantitative and value quotas are established bilaterally. At annual bilateral negotiations policy makers adjust the five-year agreements in light of unexpected events and put into operation commitments made on an aggregate level. During the annual negotiations, quotas can be changed and commodities not previously mentioned can be added to the agreements.[8]

Second, the majority of transactions in intra-CMEA trade are settled according to transferable rubles (TRs), an accounting unit that is not convertible into any of the international "hard" currencies.[9] Thus a surplus of TRs cannot be used to purchase goods on Western markets. Inconvertibility is necessary if Soviet prices are to differ from *wmps*, because it lessens the probability that a CMEA country can take advantage of the differences in relative prices between the CMEA market and the world market. Convertibility and differential relative prices imply the opportunity for arbitrage. If, for example, the TR is convertible and personal computers are inexpensive with respect to a given exchange rate between dollars and TRs on the world market and expensive on the CMEA market, a CMEA country could import personal computers from the world market and profitably export them to the CMEA market. Such potential for arbitrage would force relative domestic prices within the CMEA to move much closer to relative *wmps*. It is also true that convertibility would probably lessen the planners' control over the distribution of goods produced, because planners would not have control over the purchases of Westerners.

Third, the TR is also inconvertible within the CMEA. This means that a country with a surplus of TRs accumulated in one bilateral inter-CMEA relationship cannot use the surplus to purchase any commodity it wishes from another CMEA member with which it runs a deficit.[10] The rationale

---

8. Bela Csikos-Nagy, *Socialist Economic Policy* (Budapest: Akadémiai Kiadó, 1973), p. 219.

9. For details on the extent of trade conducted in convertible currencies, see Kalman Pecsi, *The Future of Socialist Economic Integration* (Armonk, N.Y.: M. E. Sharpe, 1981), pp. 122–48; Jan Vaňous and Michael Marrese, *Soviet-East European Trade Relations: Recent Patterns and Likely Future Developments*, Study prepared for the U.S. Department of State, no. 174-320182 (Washington, D.C.: Wharton Econometric Forecasting Associates, 1984), pp. 181–94.

10. László Csaba, "The Transferable Rouble and Convertibility in the CMEA," in C. T. Saunders, ed., *Regional Integration in East and West* (London: Macmillan, 1983), p. 237.

for this policy is that if a country could use its trade surplus to purchase any commodity from the deficit country, then the deficit country could face greater uncertainty over which commodities would be available for domestic use. In a taut, centrally planned economy, unexpected shortages of some commodities cause serious disruptions in the entire economy.

Fourth, relative CMEA *ftps* bear little resemblance to corresponding *wmps*. To understand the reasons for this, remember that relative domestic prices among all CMEA members, except perhaps Hungary, tend to deviate significantly from their counterparts on the world market. In addition, relative domestic prices vary widely among CMEA countries. In part because of the diversity among domestic prices, CMEA prices, according to the CMEA Price Clause adopted in Bucharest in 1958 and amended in 1975, are supposed to be based on some lagged average of *wmps*. Since 1976 the reference period for prices in any given year has been the preceding five years. If a commodity has been traded on the world market during the preceding five years (as is often the case for fuels, raw materials, and certain food items), then application of the CMEA Price Clause is relatively straightforward. However, prices for commodities that are not traded on the world market (industrial consumer goods, and machinery and equipment) rely on a complicated series of bilaterally negotiated proxies: a concrete world market is selected, one that would have been used in the absence of the CMEA; a representative product is then chosen, one of similar product characteristics and quality; and finally, adjustments may be made to reflect transportation costs, a macroeconomic concern for CMEA price stability, short-term CMEA aims such as product specialization or technological transfer, the type of currency utilized, and the partners involved.

For those commodities that do not have a clearly definable counterpart on the world market, CMEA price formation involves a bilateral bargaining process in which the price for a machinery import may be set "high" relative to its corresponding *wmp* in exchange for a "high" price for an industrial consumer good export. Thus such an intra-CMEA *ftp* may bear little resemblance to the lagged average of *wmps* of a similar commodity.

These remarks concerning CMEA price formation deal with the *ftps* utilized in ruble trade. However, hard-currency transactions based on prevailing *wmps* are also found in the CMEA. For example, Soviet trade with Eastern Europe, transacted in hard currency and based on prevailing *wmps*, grew steadily from 1970 to its peak in 1981 and has tapered off since then.

Fifth, intra-CMEA bilateral negotiations focus on the overall pattern of prices and quantities. In effect, one country barters its commodities for another country's commodities. Such bilateral barter is a direct consequence of trade based on government negotiations, inconvertibility, and prices that deviate significantly from *wmps*.

Sixth, for CMEA countries foreign trade has been significantly less than is typical in market economies at similar levels of economic development.[11] In short, the aforementioned characteristics have been obstacles to economic integration.

When judged with reference to the criteria operating in a market environment Comecon integration appears as a passive and wasteful process: participation in the grouping has led to losses due to undertrading with non-members which are only partially made good by intra-group trade (leaving aside the losses from sub-optimal specialization on account of the lack of a rational intra-Comecon price system). On the other hand when judged by the criteria dominating the study of economics in most of Eastern Europe the verdict would be radically different. Undertrading would be regarded as a positive measure ensuring that domestic production planning is isolated from disruptive effects of the capitalist markets; the disproportionate trade with member countries would be interpreted as a sign of active integration designed to reap the natural advantages stemming from trading with countries having the same socio-political systems.[12]

Seventh, bilateral balancing of trade has been an important fact concerning ruble trade between any two East European countries. Currency inconvertibility and the uncertainty that a surplus country faces with respect to what and when it will receive payment from the deficit country are the reasons for this relatively strict bilateral balancing. However, bilateral balancing has not characterized trade between Eastern Europe and the Soviet Union. Since the mid-1970s the Soviet Union has had a persistent surplus in ruble trade with Eastern Europe (see Table 1).

Soviet surpluses in ruble trade generally have been considered advantageous to Eastern Europe for two reasons: the Soviet Union may not demand complete repayment, and the associated interest rate of 2 percent has been much lower than world-market interest rates. Soviet hard-currency trade deficits also have been considered advantageous to Eastern Europe because Eastern Europe's domestic cost of earning a dollar of foreign exchange has been less in the Soviet market than in Western markets. This discrepancy is a result of the lower costs Eastern Europe pays for market penetration, advertisement, and product distribution in the Soviet Union.

Estimates of Soviet hard-currency trade with Eastern Europe for 1970–84 show that the Soviet Union experienced a stream of hard-currency trade deficits with Hungary, a mixed pattern of hard-currency trade balances with Romania, and virtually no hard-currency trade imbalances with the rest of

11. For the original work on this subject, see F. L. Pryor, *The Communist Foreign Trade System—The Other Common Market* (London: Allen & Unwin, 1963). For a summary of all studies of this nature, see Vladimir Sobell, *The Red Market: Industrial Co-operation and Specialization in Comecon* (Aldershot, England: Glower, 1984), p. 3. Also see László Csaba, "The Role of CMEA in the World Economy in the 1980s," *Aces Bulletin* 26 (Summer–Fall 1984), p. 2.

12. Sobell, *The Red Market*, p. 3.

TABLE 1. *Soviet ruble trade with Eastern Europe (in millions of rubles)*

Year	Bulgaria	Czechoslovakia	GDR	Hungary	Poland	Romania	Total
1970	−128.4	−27.8	181.2	46.6	80.0	−29.3	122.2
1971	−100.7	13.4	−11.6	118.6	64.9	−82.5	2.0
1972	−102.4	−118.4	−363.9	−38.8	−188.9	−112.1	−924.6
1973	−93.2	−51.7	−252.5	−31.7	−110.3	−92.1	−631.5
1974	52.9	−7.3	13.9	90.1	92.8	−33.8	208.6
1975	128.3	127.7	337.2	158.9	41.1	−134.1	659.2
1976	87.9	97.7	438.6	107.2	265.2	−59.5	937.2
1977	164.2	243.5	594.8	144.6	323.8	−87.0	1,383.9
1978	146.9	−56.6	270.9	−69.1	−150.4	−11.2	130.5
1979	138.9	179.5	299.5	336.5	102.0	63.0	1,119.4
1980	221.3	112.2	546.8	466.9	809.6	−9.4	2,147.5
1981	677.6	277.5	371.5	411.1	1,710.5	84.6	3,532.8
1982	596.5	315.6	643.4	428.6	715.9	−107.9	2,592.1
1983	457.5	451.2	202.1	380.0	487.6	−34.1	1,944.3
1984[a]	530.0	600.0	−170.0	400.0	600.0	80.0	2,040.0

a. Estimate based on data for the first six months of 1984.
Note. Trade balance = exports − imports.
Source. Vaňous and Marrese, *Soviet-East European Trade Relations*, Appendix B.

Eastern Europe.[13] This evidence and the results from Table 1 indicate that Soviet trade imbalances have benefited all CMEA countries except Romania. Given that such imbalances do not characterize bilateral trade relations between any two East European countries, these results demonstrate the Soviet ability to discriminate bilaterally in a way that provides differential benefits to its trading partners. Soviet assistance in the form of trade imbalances became more noticeable beginning in 1975, when CMEA *ftps* began to reflect the changes in relative *wmps* caused by the 1973 oil-price shock. While Soviet deficits in ruble trade and surpluses in dollar trade clearly allowed the recipient countries to adjust more slowly to deteriorating terms of trade (thereby lowering the probability of East European instability), it also may be true that the Soviet Union bargained for increased nonmarket benefits such as support for Soviet foreign policies.

Eighth, intra-CMEA trade transacted in TRs between any two East European countries has exhibited balanced trade in "hard" goods (fuels, nonfood raw materials, and to a lesser degree food and raw materials for food) and balanced trade in "soft" goods (machinery and equipment and industrial consumer goods). The principal reason for this behavior is the intra-CMEA *ftps* of soft goods are high relative to corresponding *wmps*, whereas intra-

13. Vaňous and Marrese, *Soviet-East European Trade Relations*, Appendix B.

CMEA *ftps* of hard goods are low. The overvaluation of CMEA soft goods relates to their lower quality relative to goods available on West European markets. The term *quality* encompasses the reliability, service, and design of a commodity, and any accompanying technical assistance it may require.

The Soviet Union, however, does not follow the pattern of balancing trade in hard goods and in soft goods. The Soviet Union has been primarily a net exporter of fuel and nonfuel raw materials at prices below corresponding *wmps* and a net importer of manufactured goods at prices above corresponding *wmps*. Hence, the Soviet Union has experienced an opportunity loss in trading with CMEA countries at intra-CMEA *ftps* rather than with the West at *wmps*. Marrese and Vaňous refer to these losses as implicit subsidies (see section 6). Table 2 depicts their most recent estimates of implicit Soviet trade subsidies to Eastern Europe, measured in nominal terms. The distribution of subsidies among CMEA countries, measured in constant 1984 dollars (see Table 3), illustrates that the Soviet Union has utilized bilateral trade agreements to provide differential implicit subsidization, perhaps to secure unconventional gains from trade. (An in-depth interpretation of Tables 2 and 3, a presentation of the Marrese-Vaňous methodology on which these tables are based, and a summary of some of the controversy that surrounds their work appear in the Appendix.)

Ninth, production specialization among CMEA members has emphasized the permanent division of the development and production of commodities among countries in order to take advantage of economies of scale and to avoid duplication of R&D efforts.[14] Governmental involvement, initiated by CMEA organizations or bilateral technical and scientific cooperation committees, rather than interenterprise communication, has been the primary force behind production specialization.

Two practices, both related to the predominance of agreements being negotiated on the governmental level, have limited production integration within the CMEA: specialization has been primarily in finished products; hence specialization in components and subassemblies has been neglected; and research activities have been physically and organizationally separated from production.

Tenth, scientific and technical cooperation within the CMEA has not developed anywhere near its full potential because of inadequate incentives for such cooperation.[15] It is still a common practice, as articulated by the Sofia Principle, for licenses and documentation to be exchanged for only the actual printing costs. Such an arrangement ignores two needs: to share R&D expenses and to counteract the reluctance of the originator of the innovation to transfer technological knowledge because of a fear of creating potential

14. Remarks concerning production specialization summarize Pecsi, *The Future*, pp. 10–16, 37–39. He also provides supporting quantitative evidence.
15. For greater detail on scientific and technical cooperation see ibid., pp. 41–43. See also Sobell, *The Red Market*, pp. 211–24.

TABLE 2. *Implicit Soviet trade subsidies to Eastern Europe*

	In millions of TRs			$/TR conversion rate		In millions of $				
	X (1)	M (2)	TB (3)	X (4)	M (5)	X (6)	M (7)	TB (8)	Adj (9)	Sub (10)
					Baseline calculation					
1970	6,063	5,940	122	0.87	0.71	5,302	4,191	1,111	71	1,040
1971	6,195	6,193	2	0.87	0.72	5,465	4,482	982	−9	992
1972	6,703	7,627	−925	0.87	0.76	5,860	5,781	79	−693	772
1973	7,342	7,973	−631	1.12	0.90	8,225	7,190	1,035	−569	1,604
1974	8,643	8,434	209	1.83	1.10	15,823	9,265	6,558	219	6,339
1975	11,770	11,111	659	1.42	0.96	16,655	10,706	5,949	620	5,329
1976	12,992	12,055	937	1.32	0.89	17,172	10,769	6,403	833	5,570
1977	15,054	13,670	1,384	1.32	0.93	19,825	12,685	7,140	1,282	5,858
1978	14,765	14,634	131	1.27	0.93	21,338	15,457	5,881	120	5,761
1979	18,293	17,174	1,119	1.52	1.00	27,838	17,137	10,701	1,138	9,563
1980	20,621	18,474	2,148	1.91	1.04	39,414	19,130	20,283	2,204	18,079
1981	23,664	20,131	3,533	1.72	0.93	40,714	18,777	21,937	3,200	18,737
1982	26,176	23,584	2,592	1.42	0.86	37,235	20,216	17,019	2,242	14,777
1983	28,922	26,977	1,944	1.15	0.77	33,168	20,792	12,367	1,516	10,860
1984	32,010	30,000	2,010	1.03	0.70	33,153	21,026	12,026	1,427	10,700
				Calculation with high $/TR conversion rates for manufactured goods						
1970	6,063	5,940	122	0.94	0.84	5,725	5,006	718	101	617
1971	6,195	6,193	2	0.94	0.86	6,119	5,600	520	4	515
1972	6,703	7,627	−925	0.95	0.91	4,388	4,961	−574	−835	262
1973	7,342	7,973	−631	1.22	1.10	8,938	8,734	204	−687	891
1974	8,643	8,434	209	1.94	1.31	16,774	11,078	5,697	269	5,428
1975	11,770	11,111	659	1.51	1.16	17,758	12,866	4,892	771	4,121
1976	12,992	12,055	937	1.41	1.08	18,357	13,037	5,320	1,026	4,294
1977	15,054	13,670	1,384	1.41	1.13	21,263	15,427	5,835	1,587	4,248
1978	14,765	14,634	131	1.38	1.15	23,065	19,114	3,950	146	3,804
1979	18,293	17,174	1,119	1.43	1.22	29,768	21,024	8,744	1,398	7,346
1980	20,621	18,474	2,148	2.01	1.27	41,413	23,419	17,995	2,717	15,277
1981	23,664	20,131	3,533	1.80	1.15	42,521	23,053	19,468	3,932	15,536
1982	26,176	23,584	2,592	1.49	1.05	38,895	24,856	14,039	2,763	11,276
1983	28,922	26,977	1,944	1.20	0.95	34,802	25,619	9,183	1,860	7,323
1984	32,010	30,000	2,010	1.09	0.87	34,798	26,001	8,797	1,743	7,053

Calculation with low $/TR conversion rates for manufactured goods

1970	6,063	5,940	122	0.82	0.60	4,984	3,579	1,405	48	1,357
1971	6,195	6,193	2	0.82	0.62	5,324	3,994	1,330	−19	1,349
1972	6,703	7,627	−925	0.82	0.64	5,464	4,895	569	−586	1,155
1973	7,342	7,973	−631	1.05	0.76	7,690	6,031	1,659	−480	2,138
1974	8,643	8,434	209	1.75	0.94	15,110	7,906	7,204	182	7,022
1975	11,770	11,111	659	1.34	0.82	15,828	9,087	6,741	506	6,235
1976	12,992	12,055	937	1.25	0.75	16,283	9,068	7,216	688	6,528
1977	15,054	13,670	1,384	1.25	0.78	18,747	10,628	8,119	1,053	7,066
1978	14,765	14,634	131	1.20	0.76	20,043	12,714	7,329	100	7,228
1979	18,293	17,174	1,119	1.44	0.83	26,391	14,222	12,169	943	11,225
1980	20,621	18,474	2,148	1.84	0.86	37,914	15,914	22,000	1,820	20,180
1981	23,664	20,131	3,533	1.66	0.77	39,359	15,570	23,789	2,651	21,137
1982	26,176	23,584	2,952	1.37	0.71	35,991	16,736	19,255	1,851	17,403
1983	28,922	26,977	1,944	1.10	0.64	31,943	17,172	14,771	1,258	13,513
1984	32,010	30,000	2,010	1.00	0.58	31,919	17,294	14,625	1,189	13,436

Note. X = exports; M = imports; TB = trade balance; Adj = dollar value of the ruble trade balance; Sub = implicit subsidy. The above figures do not total exactly because of rounding.
Source. Marrese and Vaňous, "Soviet Trade Relations," p. 17.

Michael Marrese

TABLE 3. *Implicit subsidies (in millions of 1984 dollars) in Soviet trade with CMEA countries*

	Bulgaria	Czechoslovakia	GDR	Hungary	Poland	Romania	Total
			Baseline calculation				
1970	−9	541	1,165	264	454	176	2,589
1971	−26	606	1,108	261	448	102	2,499
1972	−110	380	959	114	367	70	1,780
1973	250	592	1,284	351	566	28	3,071
1974	1,352	1,669	2,673	1,090	1,340	59	8,183
1975	1,030	1,361	1,820	649	1,341	12	6,213
1976	1,008	1,605	2,223	672	1,350	82	6,941
1977	1,022	1,634	2,300	542	1,307	96	6,901
1978	1,185	1,494	2,099	598	946	154	6,476
1979	1,655	1,915	2,605	989	1,705	169	9,037
1980	2,700	3,399	3,958	1,654	2,974	303	14,987
1981	2,782	3,534	4,059	1,653	3,234	289	15,552
1982	2,324	2,917	3,455	1,524	2,611	277	13,107
1983	1,658	2,374	2,677	1,115	2,019	322	10,165
1984	1,744	2,425	2,758	1,246	2,148	379	10,700
		Calculation with high $/TR conversion rates for manufactured goods					
1970	−32	255	780	83	257	195	1,537
1971	−33	314	680	55	190	91	1,298
1972	−145	52	590	−117	148	75	603
1973	185	253	827	117	308	17	1,707
1974	1,275	1,416	2,283	880	1,101	52	7,007
1975	953	1,024	1,317	423	1,065	23	4,805
1976	895	1,229	1,692	399	1,051	84	5,350
1977	860	1,203	1,695	230	899	117	5,004
1978	983	1,008	1,416	229	483	156	4,276
1979	1,411	1,461	1,953	669	1,274	174	6,942
1980	2,417	2,931	3,248	1,289	2,477	303	12,665
1981	2,449	2,944	3,285	1,226	2,722	269	12,895
1982	1,928	2,206	2,499	1,063	2,035	272	10,002
1983	1,256	1,562	1,641	632	1,470	294	6,854
1984	1,314	1,513	1,643	697	1,542	344	7,053
		Calculation with low $/TR conversion rates for manufactured goods					
1970	8	755	1,453	399	601	162	3,379
1971	−21	825	1,428	416	641	111	3,400
1972	−83	626	1,236	287	531	67	2,663
1973	298	846	1,627	527	759	37	4,094
1974	1,410	1,859	2,965	1,248	1,519	65	9,065
1975	1,087	1,614	2,197	819	1,549	4	7,270
1976	1,093	1,888	2,622	876	1,574	81	8,134
1977	1,143	1,956	2,754	776	1,614	80	8,323
1978	1,337	1,858	2,611	874	1,294	151	8,125
1979	1,838	2,254	3,094	1,229	2,029	164	10,608
1980	2,912	3,749	4,490	1,928	3,348	302	16,730
1981	3,032	3,977	4,639	1,974	3,619	304	17,544
1982	2,621	3,451	4,172	1,870	3,043	280	15,437
1983	1,960	2,983	3,453	1,477	2,432	342	12,648
1984	2,066	3,109	3,595	1,658	2,602	405	13,435

Source. Marrese and Vaňous, "Soviet Trade Relations," p. 26.

competitors. The fear of potential competition has proven to be especially problematic between East European countries in the fields of telecommunications, precision engineering, pharmaceuticals, and medical instrumentation. Soviet enterprises, not noted for their strength in these fields, have not felt the same threat and therefore the exchange of technical know-how has been biased toward bilateral movement between the Soviet Union and individual East European countries. Since the partial abandonment of the Sofia Principle in the late 1960s and early 1970s, bilateral agreements between the Soviet Union and individual East European countries and some multilateral agreements have been negotiated which specify appropriate transfer prices for technological documentation and cost-sharing arrangements for joint research. However, bilateral agreements continue to be rare among East European countries.

Eleventh, long-term target development programs and many CMEA joint investment projects evolved as a direct response to the upheaval in CMEA growth plans that followed the 1973 oil-price shock.[16] Until 1973 CMEA growth was predicated on the exchange of low-priced Soviet fuels and raw materials for East European manufactured goods. After 1973 that growth strategy presented the Soviet Union with much higher opportunity losses because the *wmps* of fuels had risen and because East European manufactured goods, designed for an era of low-cost fuels, were increasingly outdated. Hence, uncertainty abounded concerning the price at which supplies of fuels and raw materials would continue to be available. The target development programs and joint investment projects were conceived as a way to guarantee supplies of a wide range of crucial products. Target programs for 1976–80 were initiated mainly for fuels and raw materials. In addition, eight out of the ten planned projects were built in the Soviet Union. Thus far, target development programs and joint investment projects have emerged as responses to crises rather than as effective tools of long-range planning. East European countries regard these measures with a certain skepticism in part because a high proportion of investment for these projects ended up in the Soviet Union. At the same time, the Soviet Union became disillusioned by this paradox — it was receiving long-term investment credits for Eastern Europe's contribution to the joint investment projects yet, simultaneously, was granting long-term commercial credits for its trade surpluses.[17]

Evidence of disenchantment with the multilateral target development programs includes the absence of any new multilateral projects for 1981–85. Instead the current Five-Year Plan emphasizes the completion of existing multilateral projects and bilateral agreements between the Soviet Union and individual East European countries in manufacturing sectors.

16. J. M. van Brabant, "The Global Economic Recession and Socialist Economic Integration in the 1980s," *Osteuropa-Wirtschaft* 29, 3 (1984), pp. 206–8; Pecsi, *The Future*, pp. 65–81.
17. Marie Lavigne, "The Evolution of CMEA Institutions and Policies and the Need for Structural Adjustment" (Paper presented at the Conference on the Soviet Union and Eastern Europe in the World Economy, Washington, D.C., 18–19 October 1984), p. 23.

The final three characteristics mentioned above indicate that product specialization, technology transfer, and CMEA joint investment projects have been more prominent in bilateral Soviet–East European relations than either in a multilateral framework or between East European countries.

4. Soviet behavior since the mid-1970s

This section analyzes four examples of Soviet behavior: the 1974 change in the Bucharest Price Clause, Soviet ruble trade credits to Eastern Europe, Soviet exports of oil, and Soviet preferences regarding future CMEA interaction as revealed by the 1984 CMEA Summit. This section attempts to show that: Soviet aid extended to Eastern Europe has been the outcome of a bargaining process in which the Soviet Union has been aware of the relevant benefits and costs; the Soviet Union distributed economic assistance in a sharply differentiated manner that is generally consistent with its superpower ambitions and defense concerns; and the Soviet Union, via increased use of bilateralism, intends to put selectively more pressure on East European countries and, in effect, either receive more nonmarket benefits for its subsidies or reduce the level of subsidization.

Let us begin with the Soviet reaction to the first oil-price shock. According to the Bucharest Price Clause, 1971–75 intra-CMEA *ftps* were supposed to be guided by average *wmps* for 1965–69. The Soviet Union initiated the earlier-than-scheduled restructuring of *ftps* because the 1973 and 1974 oil-price increases on the world market implied that the Soviet Union was forgoing much higher hard-currency earnings when it supplied oil to Eastern Europe at *ftps* far below *wmps*. Marrese and Vaňous interpret this restructuring and subsequent negotiations over the CMEA price formula as evidence of Soviet sensitivity toward the opportunities available on world markets.

> During negotiations over the choice of the price-formation formula for intra-CMEA trade, Soviet representatives have tended to focus on *wmp* ratios, not on domestic Soviet cost ratios. In 1974 the Soviets proposed several options for the formula to be introduced in 1975: (1) the current *wmp* base (more of a trial balloon than a serious suggestion); (2) a three-year moving average of past *wmp*'s; (3) an array of criteria in which formulas for hard goods would be based on a shorter lagged moving average of *wmp*'s than those for soft goods. The formula introduced in January 1975, basing intra-CMEA *ftp*'s on a lagged five-year moving average of *wmp*'s (except for oil and a few other commodities for which prices in 1975 were based on a lagged average of *wmp*'s for 1972–74, in 1976 on *wmp*'s for 1972–75, and from 1977 on the basis of five-year moving averages of *wmp*'s), was the result of a major *compromise* in which the Soviet Union agreed to make concessions from its initial proposal. Early in 1981 the Soviets again tried to modify the

CMEA price formula, strongly pushing for a reduction of the five-year moving average to a three-year moving average.[18]

The 1975 change in the CMEA price formula was truly a compromise. On one hand, Eastern Europe suffered a much greater deterioration in its terms of trade with the Soviet Union during 1975–84 than it would have under the Bucharest Price Clause. On the other hand, Soviet trade offered Eastern Europe protection from the even greater deterioration of terms of trade that would have resulted if trade had been conducted according to *wmps* (see the estimates of implicit subsidies in Tables 2 and 3).

At the same time, the Soviet Union was keenly aware of the effect that the change in the CMEA price formula would have on East European terms of trade. Thus in 1974 the Soviet Union indicated that it would extend ten-year loans on generous terms to Eastern Europe.[19] The Soviet Union granted all CMEA countries except Romania substantial ruble trade credits during 1975–84 (see Table 1). Although there is insufficient information available to determine what portion of these trade surpluses were loans and what portion were related to debt repayment or payment for unreported invisible transactions, it is generally believed that a large portion consisted of loans at favorable interest rates.

Although it is impossible to draw definitive conclusions from the distribution of imbalances of ruble trade found in Table 1, the distribution is consistent with a number of observations concerning Soviet efforts to maintain political and social stability in Eastern Europe and a strong WP alliance. From 1975 (the first year of the new CMEA pricing formula) to 1979 (the final year before Polish hard-currency debt problems and domestic instability severely altered intra-CMEA trade bargaining), East Germany had by far the largest deficit in ruble trade with the Soviet Union, followed by a tie for second between Hungary and Bulgaria, and then Czechoslovakia and Poland. East Germany may have relied on its position as the most strategic CMEA nation and its role as the socialist competitor with West Germany to obtain Soviet ruble trade credits to dampen its deterioration in terms of trade. Further speculation suggests that Hungary, Bulgaria, and Czechoslovakia may also have presented their cases to the Soviet Union in similar attempts to soften deteriorating terms of trade.

Poland's situation is clearer because Poland pleaded for economic assistance from Moscow in 1976 to quell severe domestic instability. The unrest of Polish consumers in 1975 and early 1976 over chronic meat shortages plus the widespread violence of workers protesting of the large price hikes of June 1976 prompted a "swift" Soviet reaction to Poland's request.[20]

18. Marrese and Vaňous, *Soviet Subsidization*, p. 66.
19. See Martin J. Kohn, "Soviet-East European Economic Relations, 1975–78," in Joint Economic Committee, *Soviet Economy in a Time of Change*, vol. 1 (Washington, D.C.: GPO, 1979), pp. 250–53.
20. Gary R. Teske, "Poland's Trade with the Industrialized West: Performance, Problems and Prospects," in Joint Economic Committee, *East European Economic Assessment*, pt. 1, *Country Studies 1980* (Washington, D.C.: GPO, 1981), p. 81.

Moscow responded to Polish pleas with a substantial aid package that included a 1 billion ruble loan (which allowed Poland to run a trade deficit with the U.S.S.R.), above plan shipments of raw materials, consumer goods, and a resumption of grain deliveries. . . . In addition, the Soviets agreed to boost annual crude oil shipments from 11 million tons to 13 million tons in 1977–80 and may have agreed to increase deliveries of raw materials, such as iron ore, that Poland buys from the West for hard currency.[21]

However, this swift reaction may have been more propaganda than substance. Marrese and Vaňous estimate that Soviet trade subsidies actually declined in 1977 and 1978 (see Table 3). Moreover, although Poland enjoyed a 323.8 million ruble trade deficit with the Soviet Union in 1977, the situation in 1978 shows a 150.4 million ruble trade surplus (see Table 1). More generally, Soviet economic assistance did not prevent widespread domestic unrest in Poland; rather, the large increases in ruble trade credits and in trade subsidies came after the domestic crisis had erupted. Given the Soviet Union's observation of events in Poland and the statements of Polish leaders about the severity of the situation, the Marrese-Vaňous view of Soviet behavior does not explain Soviet policies toward Poland very well. This view of Soviet behavior makes much more sense for Romania, however. Romania, the only country not willing to follow the Soviet lead in foreign policy and a minimal participant in the WP alliance, experienced a surplus in ruble trade surplus vis-à-vis the Soviet Union, in direct contrast to the situation of other countries.[22]

From Tables 1, 2, and 3 it is clear that the Soviet Union is able to implement differentiated policies toward East European countries within the institutional confines of the CMEA. However, those tables represent the interaction of the quantities and CMEA *ftps* agreed upon in bilateral trade agreements and actual *wmps*, which may differ from the *wmps* the Soviet Union anticipated would prevail.

The pattern of Soviet oil exports to the CMEA illuminates Soviet intentions concerning the distribution of implicit subsidies.[23] The Soviet Union has been selling relatively underpriced oil for TRs to Bulgaria, Czechoslovakia, East Germany, Hungary, and Poland. Romania has repeatedly tried to secure some preferentially priced Soviet oil since 1973–74. Romania became a net importer of oil in 1975, yet the Soviets have steadfastly refused to sell preferentially priced oil to Romania and at most have consented to barter, for example, 2.7 million metric tons (mmt) in 1981 of crude oil valued in hard currency at *wmps* for Romanian exports of food and certain raw materials also valued in hard currency at *wmps*. The connection between Ceaușescu's independent foreign policy and Soviet unwillingness to provide Romania

---

21. Ibid.
22. Marrese and Vaňous, *Soviet Subsidization*, p. 69.
23. This discussion summarizes Marrese and Vaňous, "Soviet Trade Relations," pp. 36–37.

with the trade advantages offered to other East European countries seems highly plausible.

The most recent example of this connection occurred in 1984. Romania received from the Soviet Union 1.5 mmt of crude oil, 300 million cubic meters of natural gas, and 2 mmt of processed oil. These deliveries were not included in the annual trade protocol, therefore Romania did not receive the preferential terms that have been applied to other CMEA members. Rather, Romania paid in terms of hard currency plus food and raw materials valued in hard currency at *wmps*.[24] The widespread speculation surrounding these negotiations indicated that Romania would have boycotted the 1984 Summer Olympics in Los Angeles if the Soviet Union had exported oil to Romania on preferential terms.[25]

Poland, a long-time major net importer of raw materials from the Soviet Union, began to be a major net importer of fuels starting in 1975. Polish net fuel imports from the Soviet Union in current prices were 0.3 billion rubles in 1975, 1.0 billion rubles in 1979, and 2.3 billion rubles in 1983.[26] However, Polish domestic fuel supplies and Polish fuel imports from the Soviet Union were not able to cover domestic needs. For example, during 1978–80 Poland annually imported about 1.8 mmt of oil on a net basis from nonsocialist countries. The Soviet Union was simply unwilling to export additional fuel to Poland at preferential prices. Moreover, after the full eruption of the Polish economic crisis in 1980, the Soviets reportedly promised the Poles that they would make up the 2 mmt loss of crude oil imports from the Middle East associated with the Polish shortage of hard currency. They did not keep their promise. Subsequently, they promised to exempt the Poles from the 10 percent cut in oil deliveries in 1982 that applied to the rest of Eastern Europe (except Romania). Yet, official Polish statistics show that by 1983 combined Soviet deliveries of crude oil and refined oil products were more than 7 percent below the 1981 level. The failure by the Soviets to keep their promises may be related to the "failure" of the Jaruzelski regime to satisfy Soviet preferences concerning domestic Polish policies.

Bulgaria stands in dramatic contrast to both Romania and Poland. During 1979–82 Bulgaria received oil imports from the Soviet Union that more than met domestic needs and allowed Bulgaria to reexport annually an average of 2.4 mmt of Soviet oil in crude or refined form. Thus, Bulgaria earned huge arbitrage profits by buying Soviet oil at preferential prices for rubles and reselling it at prevailing *wmps* for hard currency. It is more difficult to speculate about Bulgaria than about other CMEA members. On one hand, Bulgaria has been both naturally friendly to the Soviet Union and domestically stable, so Soviet trade subsidization seems to contradict the Marrese-Vaňous

24. *East-West* (fortnightly bulletin), no. 339, 22 May 1984, p. 7.
25. Keith Crane, *The Creditworthiness of Eastern Europe in the 1980s* (Santa Monica: Rand, 1985), p. 8.
26. Vaňous and Marrese, *Soviet-East European Trade Relations*, p. 91.

view. On the other hand, the Soviets may have been rewarding Bulgaria's willingness to follow their suggestion of specialization in agro-industry and electronics in the 1970s. Bulgaria is the CMEA country that has tailored its production and trade structure most clearly to meet the needs of the Soviet economy. This logic supports the Marrese-Vaňous view, as does the much more inconclusive rumor that the activity of the Bulgarian secret police increased in direct response to Soviet preferences and as a direct result of Soviet trade subsidization.

Thus the Soviets have manipulated the quantities of their energy exports in order to reward a particular country when desirable. In addition, they can reward a country by permitting it to pay for Soviet exports by increasing the share of manufactured goods in Soviet imports from that country. For example, in 1983 the share of manufactured commodities in Soviet imports from individual East European countries (in ruble trade only) was as follows: East Germany, 88 percent; Czechoslovakia, 86 percent; Hungary and Poland, 74 percent; and Bulgaria and Romania, 72 percent. These shares are the subject of Soviet bilateral negotiations with each country, and changes in them can have an effect on each country's overall terms of trade with the Soviet Union.

The most recent illustration of energy policy within the CMEA comes from the CMEA Summit of June 1984.[27] The following section from the "Statement on the Main Directions of Further Developing and Deepening the Economic, Scientific and Technical Cooperation of the CMEA Member Countries," a communiqué released after the summit, contains the official CMEA position on the supply of energy and raw materials.

> To create economic conditions ensuring the implementation and continuation of deliveries from the Soviet Union of a number of types of raw materials and energy carriers to satisfy the import requirements in volumes determined on the basis of the coordination of plans and long-term accords, the interested CMEA member-countries shall gradually and consistently develop within the framework of an agreed-upon economic policy their structure of production and export and carry out the necessary measures for this in the field of capital investments, reconstruction and rationalization of their industry with the aim of supplying the Soviet Union with the products it needs, in particular foodstuffs and industrial consumer goods, some types of construction materials, machines and equipment of a high quality and of the world technical level.
>
> Mutually acceptable decisions on these questions shall be worked out with due consideration for the objective economic conditions of the USSR and other CMEA member-countries as well as the structure of production and mutual trade turnover of these countries. This shall en-

27. The basis for the analysis of the CMEA Summit is Vaňous and Marrese, *Soviet-East European Trade Relations*, pp. 87–98.

sure a mutually advantageous compensation of expenditures and open up the possibility of further deepening a stable long-term specialization of production within the framework of the socialist community.

It was found expedient to make a change in the structure of energy production and to expand cooperation in the field of the predominant development of atomic power generation and the fuller utilization of all types of energy carriers, including new non-traditional sources of energy. The CMEA member-countries shall jointly work out programmes to build atomic power stations and atomic heat-supply stations up to the year 2000.[28]

The Soviet commitment to maintain deliveries of energy and key raw materials to Eastern Europe is thus conditional. Moreover, the Soviets seem to have abandoned a multilateral approach to easing shortages of energy and raw materials among CMEA countries. It appears that the Soviets intend to negotiate bilaterally with individual East European countries and adjust their long-term supply commitments with respect to energy and raw materials, depending on the relative attractiveness of the exports that each country offers. Those countries more forthcoming with food, industrial consumer goods, or high-quality, sophisticated machinery will find it easier to secure adequate supplies of Soviet energy and raw materials.

The second paragraph quoted above affirms the Soviet's intention of bringing "objective economic conditions of the Soviet Union" to bear on its energy and raw material supply commitments to Eastern Europe. This may mean that either a shortfall in production of energy or raw materials in the Soviet Union because of production difficulties or an adverse movement of prices on the world market could be used to justify a sudden reduction in deliveries of these commodities to CMEA countries. On the other hand, the Soviet Union can alter its supply policies by taking into account objective economic conditions in other countries—for example, by squeezing supplies to those countries doing relatively well (the GDR, Bulgaria) and boosting supplies to those doing relatively poorly (Poland). The present system of bilateral trade allows the Soviet Union to opt for any of these policies.

Meanwhile, the Soviet Union expects Eastern Europe to increase its deliveries to the Soviets of food products; industrial consumer goods; and certain types of construction materials and machinery and equipment that meet world-market technological standards. Each of these three expectations is highly problematic. First, the increase in supply of food presupposes increases in East European food production. However, except perhaps in Hungary and Bulgaria, agriculture is relatively weak in East European economies. Second, the increase in the supply of industrial consumer goods will require a costly and time-consuming expansion of production capacities. Third, the

28. "Statement on the Main Directions of Further Developing and Deepening the Economic, Scientific and Technical Cooperation of the CMEA Member-Countries," CMEA communiqué, June 1985, p. 3.

improvement in the quality and technological sophistication of East European machinery and equipment may require additional capital imports from the West plus the adoption of Western managerial techniques, quality control procedures, and, perhaps, increased work incentives.

5. East European behavior since the mid-1970s

As is true for the Soviets, the East European conception of the CMEA encompasses *both* political and economic factors. Moreover, support among CMEA members for the current institutional character of the CMEA (and therefore implicit willingness to accept its static and dynamic economic disadvantages) varies depending on the relative importance each country places on political goals versus economic goals.

Many Western specialists in trade assert that because the CMEA is economically inferior for all members (compared to alternative market-type trading arrangements), tremendous pressure for reform must exist. The case that the CMEA is economically inferior for all members is very strong. The characteristics discussed in section 3 provide clear evidence of the economic disadvantages for the Soviet Union. Implicit subsidies, ruble trade deficits, and dollar trade surpluses—all advantageous to Eastern Europe from a static viewpoint—somewhat cloud the East European picture. However, from a dynamic perspective, Eastern Europe's trading relationship with the Soviet Union has had long-term detrimental consequences for the production structure of Eastern Europe. For example, the East Europeans in the 1950s altered their economics to conform to the traditional Stalinist mode. In addition, East Europeans contend that gearing their marketing strategies to the Soviet Union in the 1960s and 1970s was responsible for three tendencies that inhibited efficiency: poor incentives to produce high-quality manufactured goods; weakened pressure to innovate along the line dictated by relative *wmps*; and a reduced need to adjust relative domestic prices to relative *wmps*.[29]

That the CMEA reduces the efficiency of its members is true; yet this does not necessarily lead to a uniform attitude toward reform of the CMEA. For instance, East European support for reform of the CMEA depends on the extent to which the political fortunes of the leaders of individual countries transcend the present CMEA trading arrangements, including the static advantages of preferential trade treatment. Thus the preferences of political leaders, which often differ substantially from those of the populations they represent, are key determinants of the complicated nature of bilateral bargaining between the Soviet Union and any given East European country. On one hand, Soviet leaders are more interested in maintaining an international

29. Marrese and Vaňous, *Soviet Subsidization*, p. 5.

socialist empire than is the Soviet population. On the other hand, the support that East European leaders receive from Soviet leaders—all forms of preferential trade treatment, the threatened intervention of WP troops, and so on—allows certain East European leaders either to retain power (most recently, Czechoslovakia, the GDR, and Poland) or to bypass the short-term consequences of immediate, complete adjustment to negative terms of trade that develop on the world market (Hungary and Bulgaria).

These differences in preferences are responsible for the covert nature of the bilateral bargaining in which the Soviet Union exchanges preferential trade treatment for unconventional gains from trade. The Soviet political leadership does not want its population to be fully aware that Eastern Europe is being subsidized for three reasons. First, Soviet propaganda proclaims the strength of international socialist cooperation. Accordingly, it should be unnecessary to compensate Eastern Europe for its "friendship"; this should be forthcoming freely because of identical beliefs and values. Second, the Soviet people might be angered if they realized that East European standards of living, already higher than the Soviet standard, are being further bolstered as a result of implicit trade subsidization. Third, even if the Soviet political leadership were to explain to the Soviet population that it is necessary to grant economic aid to Eastern Europe as a reward for providing various services, the Soviet population and the Soviet political and military leadership do not share the same taste for maintaining an empire. At the same time, East European political leaders do not want their populations to know that national sovereignty is being "sold" in return for implicit subsidization by the Soviets to help stabilize their economies.

Finally the annual bilateral trade negotiations offer possibilities for bargaining, the scope of which directly reflects the current concerns of political leaders.[30] Even though prices in TRs are supposed to correspond to a five-year moving average of *wmps*, "the actual fixing of concrete contract prices evolves in a process of negotiation between the trading partners where the position of political and economic strength is at least as important for the outcome as the price basis established according to the principles adopted at the IXth meeting of the CMEA."[31]

In general the difficulties of bilateral bargaining stem from the presence of a range of mutually beneficial outcomes, but the agreed-upon division of the benefits depends on the bargaining process itself. Since the mid-1970s, the Soviet Union has tended to bargain for reductions in preferential trade treatment, for expansion of CMEA joint investment programs designed to extract fuels and raw materials from the Soviet Union, and for a range of nonmarket benefits. The Soviets' primary threat is the reduction of trade

---

30. For evidence of this see Marrese and Vaňous, *Soviet Subsidization*, pp. 77–80.
31. Friedrich Levcik, "Czechoslovakia: Economic Performance in the Post-Reform Period and Prospects for the 1980s," in Joint Economic Committee, *East European Economic Assessment*, pt. 1, *Country Studies 1980* (Washington, D.C.: GPO, 1981), p. 413.

subsidization. Simultaneously, each East European country has bargained for at least several of the following: an assured long-term supply of fuels and raw materials from the Soviet Union, purchasable with TRs and at favorable *ftps*; implicit loans in the form of trade deficits; convertible currency for exports of nonfuel and "hard" goods (for example, Hungarian exports of wheat and meat); and an expansion of exports of manufactured goods to the Soviet Union. Each East European nation can threaten to withhold non-market benefits; the strength of its position depends on the strength of its economy and its possibilities for interaction with the West. An East European nation's bargaining position becomes stronger when either it is willing to provide additional nonmarket benefits or the existing nonmarket benefits have become more valuable to the Soviet Union; the health of the economy is so poor that domestic political and social stability is in danger; or its options with the West become more attractive.

Although a comprehensive analysis of East European behavior during bilateral negotiations with the Soviet Union has never been published and is beyond the scope of this essay, an examination of the trends in implicit subsidization (one of the primary end-products of bilateral negotiations) reveals several interesting developments. For example, Soviet implicit trade subsidies to Eastern Europe for 1980–84 grew 81.4 percent in real terms relative to the corresponding magnitude for 1975–79 (see Table 3). The six reasons that Marrese and Vaňous offer for greater Soviet willingness to subsidize Eastern Europe in order to secure unconventional gains from trade provide a rationale for this real growth.[32] First, the steady increase in tension between the Soviet Union and the United States led to the growing Soviet appreciation of and reliance upon the military, political, ideological, and economic advantages of maintaining a strong alliance with Eastern Europe. Second, changes in Soviet and Western defense doctrines made it more likely that any future conflict in Europe would depend on conventional rather than nuclear forces. Third, as a result of the change in the relative costs of arms in recent years, procurement of "allegiance" via trade subsidization may have become a less costly input into the Soviet defense production function than additional purchases of arms. Fourth, Soviet hegemony over Eastern Europe weakened during the late 1970s and early 1980s, as evidenced by events in Poland, Hungary, and East Germany. To counter the West's attractive credits, available technology, and offer of improved trade relations, the Soviets may have felt the need to increase the scale of preferential trade treatment. Fifth, Soviet propaganda about the dangers of nuclear warfare backfired as East European populations began actively to support neutralism. Thus support for Soviet defense decisions became more costly for East European leaders, who may have demanded greater compensation. Sixth, East

32. For details concerning each of these six points, see Marrese and Vaňous, "Soviet Trade Relations," pp. 38–40.

European leaders may simply have argued that increased preferential trade was imperative to prevent the spread of domestic instability prevalent in Poland.

In addition, implicit subsidies to individual countries have grown at different rates. Comparing the figures for 1980–84 in Table 3 to those for 1975–79, we find that Bulgarian growth was 10.6 percent faster than growth for all Eastern Europe; Czechoslovakian, 1.8 percent faster; Hungarian, 33.5 percent faster; Polish, 17.1 percent faster; and Romanian, 275.9 percent faster. Only East Germany grew more slowly than average—34.8 percent more slowly than Eastern Europe. We can assume that the behavior of Bulgaria, Czechoslovakia, Hungary, and Poland reflects a uniform (but unknown) relationship with the above-mentioned six points, because their growth rates for 1980–84 relative to 1975–79 fall within a relatively narrow range: 82.9 percent to 108.5 percent; hence only East Germany and Romania require our attention.

In absolute terms, East Germany has received the largest amount of implicit subsidies from the Soviet Union (see Table 3). In addition, its economic performance during 1979–84 was by far the strongest in Eastern Europe. The Soviet Union may have increased subsidies to East Germany at a relatively slow rate because East Germany was already being rewarded well for the nonmarket benefits it provided the Soviet Union and because its domestic situation was stable.

It is interesting to speculate that the large cutbacks in real Soviet implicit trade subsidies to East Germany which began in 1982 and East Germany's lack of international creditworthiness from 1980 onward (owing to its own hard-currency debts and the problems in Poland) encouraged it to move closer to West Germany. Apparently the bank credits to East Germany which West Germany guaranteed, one billion West German marks in 1983 and 950 million West German marks in 1984, improved East Germany's international creditworthiness and "access to other Western credits because of the conviction that its debts are now sheltered by a West German 'umbrella.' "[33] These loans and other financial advantages offered by West Germany seem to have been part of an exchange; for its part East Germany eased the conditions for travel and contact between East and West Germany and in 1984 extended official permission for about 40,000 East Germans to emigrate legally to West Germany.[34]

In absolute terms, Romania has received the smallest amount of implicit subsidies (see Table 3). In fact, Romania paid modest implicit trade taxes to the Soviet Union during 1960–69 but received minor implicit subsidies during the 1970s.[35] Subsidies to Romania, though still low, jumped in 1980 and stayed at approximately that level during 1981–84.

33. Thomas A. Baylis, "Explaining the DDR's Economic Strategy" (Paper prepared for the Conference on Foreign Economic Strategies of Eastern Europe, University of California, Berkeley, 1–2 February 1985), p. 26.
34. Ibid., pp. 35–36.
35. Marrese and Vaňous, *Soviet Subsidization*, p. 114.

There is some basis for speculation that Romania's economic problems prompted a move toward better relations with the Soviet Union. The timing of economic difficulties coincides with such speculation. "It was really only the second oil price shock (1979) which produced adjustment policies in Romania. This increase in oil prices occurred simultaneously with the depletion of Romania's two key domestic resources: energy, especially petroleum, and labor. Having failed to adjust earlier, large-scale energy-intensive industry—and indeed the economy as a whole—found itself dependent to a much greater degree on foreign sources of fuel, manufactured goods and increasingly, financing."[36]

Romania's foreign-trade response to this economic crisis is also consistent with the above-mentioned speculation.

Romanian trade overall began to shift from West to East. In two years (1980–82) Romanian imports from OECD countries were cut in half; by 1983 Romania was the least active importer of Western goods. As exports to the capitalist states remained stable—though lower—the hard currency trade surplus grew. At the same time, the Romanians began making overtures to the Soviet Union and its CMEA partners indicating their desire to "improve cooperation" in the areas of raw material and energy trade. Romania's purchases of Soviet oil—at world market prices in hard currency—cost them some $700 million in 1981. Though the Romanians' desire for more favorable terms was rejected, trade with CMEA nevertheless increased. CMEA trade, which had accounted for 33% of Romanian total trade turnover in 1980, accounted for 53% in 1983.[37]

During this period of increased CMEA trade, Romanian exports of investment machinery to the Soviet Union proved to be the source of the rapid rise in implicit subsidies. During 1980–84 these exports grew by 129.1 percent when compared to the corresponding total for 1975–79; whereas total Romanian exports to the Soviet Union for 1980–84 grew by only 78.4 percent relative to the corresponding total for 1975–79.[38]

It may be that in return for increased exports of investment machinery to the Soviet Union, Romania did not strongly protest the Soviet invasion of Afghanistan in late 1979, voiced no direct criticism of WP discussions of the Polish situation in 1980–81 (even took part in one such meeting in December 1980), and renewed its participation (albeit on a minimal level) in WP military exercises after abstaining from 1976 to 1979.[39] However, other actions by Romania, including the continuation of close ties with China,

36. Ronald H. Linden, "Socialist Patrimonialism and the Global Economy, the Case of Romania" (Paper prepared for the Conference on Foreign Economic Strategies of Eastern Europe, University of California, Berkeley, 1–2 February 1985), p. 14.
37. Ibid., p. 22.
38. Vaňous and Marrese, *Soviet-East European Trade Relations*, p. 193.
39. Linden, "Socialist Patrimonialism," pp. 21, 23.

support for Eurocommunists in the face of Soviet opposition, and adherence to its distinctive foreign policy,[40] indicate that Romania's rapprochement with the Soviet Union was very limited.

6. CMEA interaction: three perspectives

There are three (overlapping) views on CMEA interaction: the naive perspective, represented by official pronouncements of CMEA organizations; the enlightened perspective, represented by the work of Kalman Pecsi; and the pragmatic perspective, following from the work of Marrese and Vaňous.

Crucial aspects of the naive perspective include the claim that major conflict is absent among CMEA countries because of socialist solidarity, a rejection of the principle of comparative advantage because of the market chaos it would create, and a belief in economic integration based on mutual profitability and coordination of economic plans. Several statements from the June 1984 CMEA communiqué articulate this view:

> The experience and practice of the CMEA member-countries convincingly demonstrate the fundamental advantages over capitalism that are inherent in socialism, such as social and national equality, planned development of the economy, ideological unity of society, confidence in the morrow, constant concern for man and the all-round development of the individual. . . .
> The economic and social progress of the CMEA member-countries is in sharp contrast with the crisis situation in capitalist countries. Principles of socialist internationalism, respect for state sovereignty, independence and national interests, non-interference in internal affairs of countries, full equality, mutual advantage and comradely mutual assistance . . . have been established in relations between them, are being implemented and will be consistently implemented. A considerable contribution to the deepening of the all-round interaction of the fraternal states, to the strengthening of their unity and cohesion is made by each CMEA member-country, especially the Soviet Union.[41]

Pecsi best represents the enlightened perspective because he offers a comprehensive evaluation of the current situation and then presents a format for reform of the CMEA. Table 4 contains some of the dimensions of this evaluation and illustrates the following inaccuracies in the naive perspective: conflicts between the interests of the Soviet Union and the interests of Eastern Europe occur far more frequently than do situations of mutual profitability—compare the frequency of conflictual situations represented by $(-, +)$ and $(+, -)$ with that of complementary situations represented by $(+, +)$ and $(-, -)$—and, from a strictly economic perspective, the current CMEA struc-

40. Ibid., p. 24.
41. CMEA communiqué, June 1985, p. 1.

TABLE 4. *Distribution of economic advantages and disadvantages between the Soviet Union and Eastern Europe at the end of the 1970s*

			Eastern Europe	Soviet Union
I.		Quantifiable Economic Effects		
	A.	Trends in Terms of Trade		
		1. Energy and raw materials	−	+
		2. Agricultural goods	+	−
		3. Manufactured goods	−	−
	B.	CMEA Price Formula		
		1. Energy	+	−
		2. Agricultural goods	+	−
		3. Manufactured goods	+	+
	C.	Credit Relations		
		1. Inflationary erosion of CMEA bank credits and bilateral trade credits	+	−
		2. Investment credits	−	+
	D.	TR/$ Exchange Rate		
		1. Energy prices	+	−
		2. Prices of other commodities	−	+
	E.	Trade in Convertible Currencies		
		1. Direct trade	+	+
		2. Convertible-currency content of exports	−	+
		3. Reexported energy-intensive products	+	−
	F.	Noncommercial Transactions		
		1. Tourism	−	+
		2. Transportation and other services	−	+
		3. Wages and other contributions to joint investment programs	−	+
	G.	Incorrect decisions with regard to capacity utilization and determination of the pattern of investments	−	−
II.		Unquantifiable Economic Effects		
	A.	Opportunity Costs of Commodity Trade		
		1. Soviet exports vs. East European imports	+	−
		2. Soviet imports vs. East European exports	−	+
	B.	Quality of Commodities Traded		
		1. Energy, raw materials, and food	+	+
		2. Manufactured goods	−	−
	C.	Reliability of Trade in Commodities		
		1. Meeting delivery deadlines and utilization of contingencies in the face of missed deadlines	−	−
		2. Transportation and delivery difficulties	−	−
		3. Uneven distribution of deliveries	−	−
	D.	Political and Strategic Dimensions to Trade		
		1. Energy and raw materials	+	−
		2. Agricultural goods	−	+
		3. Manufactured goods	−	−
	E.	Cooperation in Production Relative to the Potential for Such Cooperation		
		1. Macro-level specialization and cooperation	−	−
		2. Enterprise-level specialization and cooperation	−	−
		3. Erroneous decisions in structural policy	−	−
		4. Technological gap vis-à-vis the West	−	−
	F.	Dynamic Effects		
		1. Incentive to switch to an intensive growth path	−	−
		2. Reaction to price shocks on the world market	−	−
		3. Commercial, financial and technological exchange with foreign countries	−	−

Note. Advantages: +. Disadvantages: −.
Source. My interpretation and reformulation of Table 6 from Kalman Pecsi, "The Realization of the Principle of Mutual Interests in CMEA Member-Countries' Trade between Themselves and the Influence of Economic Growth in Eastern Europe during the Eighties" (Paper presented to the Eighth U.S.-Hungarian Economic Roundtable, Budapest, 30 November–3 December 1983).

ture is, on aggregate, disadvantageous to both the Soviet Union and Eastern Europe.

One consequence of Pecsi's arguments is that the customs union rationale for Soviet participation in the CMEA, which is based on strictly economic grounds, appears to be erroneous. Although a truly accurate understanding of the static and dynamic benefits and costs of the CMEA as a customs union requires an in-depth comparison of either the "pre-CMEA" tariff-trade-production structure of the Soviet Union or some hypothetical tariff-trade-production structure with the tariff-trade-production structure of the Soviet Union since the CMEA's inception, some brief observations are in order.

Trade creation (a beneficial effect) and trade diversion (a potentially detrimental effect) are measures of the static impact of the formation of a customs union.[42] Trade creation could be very significant, if before integration the actual output patterns of the integrating economies were rather similar as a result of protective tariffs. With the elimination of these protective tariffs, it may prove rational for integrating economies to specialize within the customs union along the lines of comparative advantage. If such specialization occurs, trade between member countries will increase.

Trade diversion is detrimental if the increased trade among member countries siphons trade away from the world's low-cost producers (who are not members of the customs union) toward relatively high-cost producers who are members of the customs union (yet low-cost producers within the customs union). Clearly, if member countries of a customs union are among the most efficient producers in the world, the detrimental consequences of trade diversion are minor.

Dynamic gains related to the formation of a customs union include economies of scale, the stimulus of competition, and incentives for greater investment.

Now let us apply these concepts to Soviet participation in the CMEA. Because the Soviet Union is a large net importer of manufactured goods from Eastern Europe, according to Pecsi, the static economic rationale for Soviet participation is weak. It is true that substantial trade creation has occurred between the Soviet Union and Eastern Europe and that both sides have benefited from conventional gains from trade. However, the detrimental effects of trade diversion may well outweigh the benefits of trade creation, because East European countries are not among the world's low-cost producers of manufactured goods. Moreover, as Pecsi points out, the quality of CMEA manufactured goods is poor (see Table 4).

The dynamic picture is even more discouraging. Pecsi notes that incorrect

42. For a nontechnical discussion of the static and dynamic aspects of a customs union, see R. E. Caves and R. W. Jones, *World Trade and Payments* (Boston: Little, Brown, 1977), pp. 235–41; C. P. Kindleberger and P. H. Lindert, *International Economics* (Homewood, Ill.: Irwin, 1978), pp. 172–82.

investment decision making, faulty policies with regard to capacity utilization, insufficient specialization, lagging technological cooperation and exchange, and poor incentives to increase productivity characterize the CMEA (again, see Table 4). A dynamic economic rationale for membership in such a customs union is nonexistent either for the Soviet Union or for Eastern Europe.

Table 4 is also the basis of Pecsi's overall argument. Production integration in the form of plan coordination, specialization, and industrial cooperation has been the basis of the CMEA's extensive growth thus far. However, the CMEA has neglected integration based on market forces. Pecsi claims that a more comprehensive economic integration can occur through communication among enterprises that respond to market signals and planned financial incentives. Such market integration would imply direct contact between enterprises and would lead to, among other things, greater specialization in the production of subassemblies and parts, more effective transfer of technical know-how, and more serious efforts to share R&D information and costs.[43]

The pragmatic perspective of Marrese and Vaňous is founded upon Soviet preeminence within the CMEA and pays particularly close attention to the bilateral relationships between the Soviet Union and individual East European countries. It is also pragmatic because of its focus on the Soviet political leadership's use of economic leverage to affect Eastern Europe's strategic, economic, political, and ideological impact on the Soviet Union (and hence on the probability of the Soviet political leadership retaining its power).

Marrese and Vaňous note that the Soviet Union subsidizes East European countries by being primarily a net exporter of fuel and nonfood raw materials at prices below corresponding *wmps* and by being a net importer of manufactured goods at prices above corresponding *wmps*.[44] The Soviet Union trades with Eastern Europe at such disadvantageous terms of trade in order to secure the allegiance of the political leaders of individual East European countries.

The term *allegiance* includes a range of unconventional gains from trade (nonmarket benefits) accruing to the Soviet Union in the form of military, strategic, political, ideological, and special economic benefits. Allegiance of East European countries increases overall Soviet security and substitutes for Soviet military manpower and hardware. Because the Soviet Union is the dominant power within the CMEA, it is perceived to produce security services both by conventional means, that is, through labor and military hardware, and by securing allegiance through preferential trade treatment of its East European neighbors.

Soviet subsidization of East European economies through preferential trade treatment should be viewed as an extremely cumbersome form of resource transfer. *Cumbersome* because the Soviets can determine only two out of

43. Pecsi, *The Future*, p. 12.
44. For more details, see Marrese and Vaňous, "Soviet Trade Relations," pp. 2–12.

the three dimensions of the implicit transfer, namely, the quantities and *ftps* of their intra-CMEA exports and imports. However, the Soviets have no control over *wmps*. Thus the Soviets face two problems: quantities traded according to preferential prices are set before *wmps* are known with certainty (a feature of all forward contracts), and the intra-CMEA price-formation formula introduces some degree of rigidity (however, the Soviets have deviated from the dictates of the formula on numerous occasions in order to improve the terms of trade for specific East European countries). Consequently, unexpected fluctuations in *wmps* may produce either more or less subsidization than was intended. In other words, estimates of implicit Soviet subsidies consist of "anticipated" and "unanticipated" components, which Marrese and Vaňous estimate. They show that anticipated subsidies have exhibited reasonably stable growth over time and interpret this trend to mean that the Soviet Union perceives an increase in value in the mix of nonmarket benefits supplied to it by Eastern Europe.

The Marrese-Vaňous hypothesis is difficult to validate because little is known about the detailed nature of bilateral bargaining. However, the early work by Marrese and Vaňous uncovered indirect evidence for the high correlation between the magnitudes of subsidies distributed to individual CMEA countries for the period 1960–78 (see Tables 5 and 6). In Table 5 they rank from high to low the unconventional gains from trade provided to the Soviet Union: East Germany, Czechoslovakia, Bulgaria, Hungary, Poland, and Romania (virtually no benefits). The ranking in Table 6 according to the total dollar value of subsidies for 1960–78 yields East Germany, Czechoslovakia, Poland, Hungary, and Romania; whereas the ranking according to per capita dollar value of subsidies yields East Germany, Czechoslovakia, Hungary, Bulgaria, Poland, and Romania.[45]

The distribution of implicit subsidies for 1970–84 can be obtained from Table 3 by totaling the annual figures. The ranking according to the cumulative dollar value of subsidies is East Germany, Czechoslovakia, Poland, Bulgaria, Hungary, and Romania; whereas the ranking according to per capita dollar value of subsidies is East Germany, Bulgaria, Czechoslovakia, Hungary, Poland, and Romania.

Other indirect evidence supporting the Marrese-Vaňous hypothesis has been cited earlier, namely, the pattern of Soviet oil exports and the growth of subsidies during 1980–84 as compared to 1975–79.

Clearly caution should be taken in attributing any meaning to annual shifts in subsidization because of the presence of substantial amounts of unanticipated subsidies.

Finally, Marrese and Vaňous contend that the Soviet Union is likely to

---

45. The total dollar ranking focuses on the nonmarket benefits received and neglects considerations of East European domestic stability. The per capita ranking is a rough means of including some consideration of domestic stability.

TABLE 5. *Unconventional gains from trade provided to the Soviet Union by CMEA member countries, 1960–75*

Type of Unconventional Gain Provided	Ranking of Provider[a]				
	Bulgaria	Czechoslovakia	GDR	Hungary	Poland
Strategic					
Location	5	2	1	4	3
Availability of military bases	5	2	1	4	3
Stationing of Soviet troops	N/A[b]	2	1	3	4
Proxy intervention	N/A	2	1	N/A	N/A
Effectiveness as ally against NATO invasion	5	3	2	4	1
Domestic stability	1	4	1	3	5
Overall strategic ranking	5	2	1	4	3
Political					
Assistance in maintaining Soviet Union's dominance in WTO	1	4	2	3	5
Allegiance in international forums	1	1	1	1	1
Government and media support	1	3	2	4	5
Support of population	1	N/A	N/A	N/A	N/A
Overall political ranking	1	4	2	3	5
Ideological					
Agreement with Soviet view of CMEA cooperation	1	2	2	2	2
Successful centralization of decision making	3	2	1	4	5
State sector's role in agriculture	1	3	3	2	5
Control over domestic dissent and diversity of opinion		4	2	3	5
Overall ideological ranking	1	3	2	4	5
Economic					
Provision of needed goods	3	2	1	3	5
Enhancement of CMEA's economic stability	1	1	1	1	5
Overall economic ranking	3	2	1	3	5
Overall ranking	3	2	1	4	5

a. Rankings are in descending order of importance: 1 = highest.
b. N/A = not applicable.
Source. Marrese and Vaňous, *Soviet Subsidization*, p. 72.

TABLE 6. *Rankings of CMEA member countries according to nonmarket benefits provided to the Soviet Union and three measures of implicit subsidization*

Area of Ranking	Rankings[a]					
	Bulgaria	Czechoslovakia	GDR	Hungary	Poland	Romania
Nonmarket benefits	*Implicit subsidies, 1960–78*					
By dollar value	5	2	1	4	3	6
Per capita dollar value	4	2	1	3	5	6
Per dollar of Soviet exports[b]	5	3	1	2	4	6
	Implicit subsidies, 1974–78					
By dollar value	4	2	1	5	3	6
Per capita dollar value	1	3	2	4	5	6
Per dollar of Soviet exports[b]	3	2	1	4	5	6

a. Rankings are in descending order of importance: 1 = highest.
b. Average of corresponding annual figures; based on dollar values of Soviet exports.
Source. Marrese and Vaňous, *Soviet Subsidization*, p. 85.

continue implicit trade subsidization as long as there are conflicts between empire-building Soviet leaders and ordinary Soviet citizens with more basic concerns. The magnitude of such subsidization should fluctuate with the strategic, economic, political, and ideological value that Eastern Europe provides to the Soviet Union and with the general politico-economic stability of Eastern Europe.

It is useful to contrast the abilities of these three perspectives to explain some dimensions of CMEA interaction. The naive perspective assumes that because countries are socialist, conflicts among them will be reduced to a minimum. Hence the material incentives for more effective product specialization and technological transfer receive insufficient attention. In addition, because the naive perspective fails to incorporate the Soviet Union's strong superpower ambitions, it overlooks the Soviet Union's attraction to bilateral policy instruments that allow for differential treatment of individual CMEA countries.

The enlightened perspective comprehensively evaluates the current situation of the CMEA and recommends specific reforms. However, its forward-looking recommendations for reform ignore Soviet political preferences and Soviet behavior since World War II.

In arguing for the establishment of regulated socialist competition within the CMEA, the enlightened perspective focuses solely on economic consequences and ignores the political and strategic externalities that are so important to the Soviet Union. More specifically, it analyzes the benefits and costs of bilateral negotiations on a governmental level only with respect to economic consequences, although the majority of CMEA political leaders still rely on such negotiations to help stabilize their economies in the short run, in the face of crises. Hence the enlightened perspective may be better for the populations of the CMEA in the long run but is not attractive to many CMEA political leaders in the short run.

The pragmatic perspective accounts for both the differences in preferences between political leaders and populations and the preeminence of the Soviet Union within the CMEA. Hence it overcomes some of the shortcomings of the other two perspectives. However, because it is based on static analysis of the CMEA at various points in time, it neglects to evaluate dynamic economic consequences in a sufficiently comprehensive manner.

7. An integration of ideas

As a prelude to speculation about the future, a summary of the general ideas presented here appears as answers to three simple questions. First, what is the CMEA? The CMEA is primarily a forum for bilateral bargaining between the Soviet Union and each of the CMEA countries over mutual economic, foreign-policy, and defense needs. The bilateral negotiations take place in an atmosphere of tremendous concern for Soviet political preferences and for the economic-political stability of East European countries.

Second, why is the CMEA so different from the European Economic Community? For the most part, the CMEA has ignored many of the advantages of multilateral trade and technological interaction. In addition, the CMEA's use of relative prices that differ from *wmps* has led to widespread inefficiency and has discouraged innovation.

Third, why has there been so much constancy within the CMEA? From the Soviet perspective, political preferences have not changed; therefore the bilateral, government-negotiated (as opposed to enterprise-negotiated) style has retained much of its attractiveness. Although participation in the CMEA may have high long-term costs for East European leaders, the prospect of bearing the short-term costs of sharply reducing ties with the Soviet Union has proven to be even more distasteful.

With regard to the future, the naive perspective argues that ideological aversion to widespread utilization of the market mechanism within the CMEA is still strong. Accordingly, the principle of comparative advantage is not likely to reign supreme in the near future. However, the enlightened perspective contains convincing evidence that the CMEA's failure to adopt more market-oriented procedures is becoming increasingly costly, hence economic pressure for reform is building. The pragmatic perspective emphasizes the political rationale for bilateral negotiations on a government level, namely, the desire among political leaders of the CMEA to maintain power.

Given that the CMEA has been effective from the Soviet point of view because it has satisfied Soviet political preferences and from the East European point of view because it has helped leaders maintain their positions, is it reasonable to expect the CMEA to remain in its present form during the next ten years? No, the pressure for reform seems to be becoming too strong for maintenance of the status quo. Implicit subsidies are increasing in real terms; there are inadequate incentives to stimulate productivity growth; the current institutional characteristics of the CMEA stifle cooperation in product specialization and exchange of technological information; and growth rates in CMEA countries have dropped precipitously.

By eliminating any one of the three Soviet political preferences, a new CMEA would emerge. Suppose the attraction to central planning fades away and a major decentralizing reform of the Soviet economy is introduced. Such reform would permit the CMEA to be restructured more along the lines of the European Common Market. Bilateral negotiations to secure nonmarket benefits could still be arranged, but in this case the purchase of nonmarket benefits would replace implicit subsidization and other forms of preferential trade treatment.

Suppose the Soviet Union renounces its superpower ambitions but retains central planning and its perception that Eastern Europe plays a vital role in the defense of the Soviet Union. Pacification of both Western and Eastern Europe would be one potential outcome. Eastern Europe could modernize with the help of Western Europe, and the Soviet Union could trade with either Western or Eastern Europe according to the principle of comparative advantage.

Suppose the Soviet Union concludes either that the nonmarket benefits which Eastern Europe provides have been overrated or that the costs of using a stick to acquire nonmarket benefits have decreased relative to the costs of using a carrot. The Soviet empire would then rely on force rather than subsidization to maintain its hold over Eastern Europe. The Soviet Union could cut back on preferential trade treatment on a step-by-step, case-by-case basis and tailor any remaining trade subsidization to obtain only the more valuable nonmarket benefits. This seems to be the most likely direction for CMEA development because it follows the spirit of intensification of bilateral commitments that the Soviet Union articulated at the 1984 CMEA Summit.

Appendix: statistical methodology

Marrese and Vaňous's conception of implicit trade subsidies is based on statistically determined estimates of subsidies and their interpretation of the resulting estimates.

This appendix presents their notion of implicit subsidies and estimation methodology; see section 6 for their interpretation.

The Marrese-Vaňous method revalues Soviet ruble exports to and imports from six East European countries (originally transacted at intra-CMEA *ftps*) according to dollar *wmps*. This revaluation is done separately for exports and imports and for each of six commodity categories—investment machinery, arms, fuels, nonfood raw materials, food and raw materials for food, and industrial consumer goods. In particular, for each series of bilateral commodity trade flows a corresponding series of dollar/ruble conversion coefficients has to be constructed to reflect the relationship between intra-CMEA ruble *ftps* and dollar *wmps* (East-West trade dollar prices). Marrese and Vaňous collected the available pairs of intra-CMEA ruble *ftps* and dollar *wmps* (East-West trade prices) and produced dollar/ruble conversion coefficients for fuels, nonfood raw materials, and food. For investment machinery and industrial consumer goods trade flows, only benchmark estimates of conversion coefficients— mostly for 1982—could be obtained; they derived a time series of conversion coefficients by comparing the developments in intra-CMEA ruble *ftps* (based on official Hungarian and Polish dollar/nonsocialist trade price indexes). In particular, faster (slower) growth of dollar prices than of ruble prices implies an increase (decline) in the dollar/ruble conversion rate. Finally, for trade in arms, the dollar/ruble conversion rates represent an educated guess, namely, that the appropriate bilateral dollar/ruble conversion rates for arms are double the corresponding bilateral rates for trade in investment machinery. Much higher dollar/ruble conversion rates are appropriate for trade in arms because the quality of arms manufactured within the CMEA is much higher than the quality of investment machinery relative to world-market standards. One reason for the quality differential is that arms manufacturers have had access to better inputs, including a more highly paid labor force, than have manufacturers of investment machinery.

Once Soviet ruble commodity trade flows at intra-CMEA *ftps* are converted into dollars at *wmps*, the rest of the subsidy calculation is simple. If Soviet ruble trade with a particular East European country is balanced, the implicit trade subsidy measured in dollar terms simply equals the surplus of dollar trade calculated as the difference between the dollar value of total Soviet exports and the dollar value of total Soviet imports. However, if the Soviet balance of ruble trade with the country is other than zero, then the implicit subsidy simply equals the balance of dollar trade minus the dollar equivalent of the balance of ruble trade. In order to convert the balance of ruble trade into dollar terms, a realistic or settlement dollar/ruble exchange rate is needed. For this purpose Marrese and Vaňous use the average dollar/ruble conversion rate for all Soviet imports from a particular country. In other words, they assume that the realistic dollar value of any Soviet surplus of ruble trade with a given East European country is the dollar value of a typical basket of East European goods that will be delivered in the future when the Soviet ruble trade credit to that country is repaid through delivery of these goods.

Table 2 illustrates this methodology. Column 1 (2), containing the ruble value of Soviet intra-CMEA exports (imports), is multiplied by column 4 (5), which contains a weighted average of Soviet intra-CMEA export (import) conversion rates for the six above-mentioned categories of commodities, to yield column 6 (7), the dollar value of Soviet intra-CMEA exports (imports). The dollar value of the Soviet intra-CMEA trade balance appears in column 8 and is calculated by subtracting column

7 from column 6. Column 10, containing the estimate of implicit subsidies from the Soviet Union to six East European nations, is derived by subtracting column 9 (the adjustment for unbalanced ruble trade) from column 8.

Three sets of estimates of these subsidies over time appear in Table 2—a baseline estimate, an estimate based on high dollar/ruble conversion rates for manufactured goods (investment machinery and equipment, arms, and industrial consumer goods), and an estimate based on low dollar/ruble conversion rates for manufactured goods. The purpose of presenting three sets of estimates rather than one is to illustrate the sensitivity of these estimates to changes in assumptions about the conversion rates for manufactured goods, which involve considerable uncertainty.

The baseline estimates of subsidies, considered by Marrese and Vaňous to be "most reliable," are based on empirically derived conversion rates for manufactured goods. The calculation based on high conversion rates for manufactured goods simply reflects an across-the-board 33% increase in all conversion coefficients for the three types of manufactures for all years. Thus it incorporates a higher evaluation of the quality of CMEA-manufactured goods than Marrese and Vaňous estimate empirically. The 33% increase leads to estimates of derived conversion rates for investment machinery and consumer goods which experts generally agree are high upper bounds. For instance, using the 33% increase, the estimated conversion rates for East German exports of consumer goods to the Soviet Union are 1.37 in 1978, 1.47 in 1979, 1.52 in 1980, 1.36 in 1981, and 1.25 in 1982. Compare these figures to the official dollar/ruble exchange rates, which are generally considered to be highly overvalued: 1.47 in 1978, 1.52 in 1979, 1.54 in 1980, 1.39 in 1981, and 1.38 in 1982.[46] Finally, the calculation based on low conversion coefficients for manufactured goods reflects an across-the-board 25% reduction in these coefficients; it therefore includes a lower quality evaluation than Marrese and Vaňous estimate empirically.

When implicit subsidies are expressed in real terms as seen in Table 3, an upward trend holds until 1981; sharp declines follow in 1982 and 1983. This pattern is misleading because of the presence of unanticipated subsidization, as a result of the unexpected increase in the 1979 *wmps* of oil. By breaking down subsidies expressed in real terms into anticipated and unanticipated components, Marrese and Vaňous show that the anticipated components grew steadily over time.[47]

Marrese and Vaňous have engaged in a debate with Marer over the validity of the subsidy estimates. Marer's position is based on several criticisms of the Marrese-Vaňous approach and his lonely insistence that the official Soviet dollar/ruble exchange rate is more appropriate for subsidy calculations than is the realistic rate on which Marrese and Vaňous rely. Marer's main criticisms are as follows:

> Three sets of factors account for the large discounts on East-bloc exports of manufactures to the West. One is the poor quality of the East's products. A second is the systematic shortcomings of Eastern export pricing: exporting on the basis of plan directives, which reduces the flexibility required to obtain the best price; preference for barter and compensation deals inconvenient for the Western partner, who therefore pays a low price for such products; and hard-currency balance-of-payments pressures, which often force Eastern countries to make drastic price concessions. The third set of reasons for Eastern export price

46. Vaňous and Marrese, *Soviet-East European Trade Relations*, pp. 162, 206.
47. Marrese and Vaňous, "Soviet Trade Relations," pp. 3–9.

discounts is Western discrimination—whether in the form of high-tariff or non-tariff barriers to CMEA goods.

Since Marrese and Vanous argue that a portion of Soviet subsidy arises because the Soviet Union pays more for imports from Eastern Europe than it would have to pay if the same goods were purchased from the West, the correct dollar opportunity cost is not East-to-West export but East-from-West import prices. If the Soviet Union imported the same manufactured goods from the West, it would not be able to obtain as large discounts as when the East exports to the West because the second and third sets of discount factors would be absent. In missing this point and assuming that they can substitute East European export prices for Soviet import prices to value Soviet purchases from Eastern Europe, Marrese and Vanous introduce a significant upward bias into their calculation.

There is an even more fundamental criticism of their subsidy computations. Just because an East European machine or consumer product is not of the latest Western design—that it is not equipped with the ultimate series of gadgets, does not have all the assortment, packaging, and other convenience features that characterize the most modern Western products—does not mean that the Soviet importer of these goods provides a subsidy to Eastern Europe equivalent to the Western quality discount. There must be many instances where the East European products are as, or even more, suitable to Soviet conditions than the most modern Western counterparts.[48]

The essence of Marer's first argument is that because of West European trade discrimination against CMEA-manufactured goods, the correct dollar opportunity cost for manufactured goods is based on East-for-West import prices, not East-to-West export prices. Marer's claim is weak for several reasons. First, the CMEA generally does not import the same type of manufactured goods from Western Europe that it produces domestically. For example, automobiles are both imported from Western Europe and produced in the CMEA, but the quality differential is so great that a dollar unit value based on East-from-West import prices is not comparable to a ruble unit value based on intra-CMEA trade. The CMEA simply does not import from Western Europe the types of automobiles that it produces. However, East-to-West export prices can produce a reasonable comparison of a dollar unit value with a ruble unit value because Western Europe imports automobiles that are produced and traded within the CMEA.

Second, Marer offers neither evidence that such trade discrimination occurs nor, of course, estimates of the quantitative impact of trade discrimination. In addition, he fails to mention a factor that may more than offset any upward bias imposed by Western trade discrimination, namely, that East European nations tend to export, for any particular commodity title for a manufactured good, a higher quality composition of products to Western Europe than to the Soviet Union. In their most recent empirical work, Marrese and Vaňous analyze commodities and partner Western markets in an effort to minimize the presence of both the upward bias (trade discrimination) and the downward bias (higher quality goods going to Western Europe). This compromises their baseline estimate.[49] For those who strongly believe that the

48. Paul Marer, "The Political Economy of Soviet Relations with Eastern Europe," in Sarah Meiklejohn Terry, ed., *Soviet Policy in Eastern Europe* (New Haven: Yale University Press, 1984), p. 177.
49. Vaňous and Marrese, *Soviet-East European Trade Relations*, pp. 166–80.

upward bias dominates, Marrese and Vaňous offer estimates with high dollar/ruble conversion rates for manufactures; for those who strongly believe that the downward bias dominates, they offer estimates with low dollar/ruble conversion rates for manufactures.

It is reasonable to ask why Marer does not simply use the Marrese-Vaňous estimates based on high conversion rates. Marer rejects all such estimates because they are based on a "realistic or settlement" dollar/ruble exchange rate that Marrese and Vaňous estimate. Marer, on the other hand, advocates the use of the official Soviet dollar/ruble exchange rate in the subsidy calculation. Marrese and Vaňous strongly disagree with his selection because the official exchange rate is strictly an accounting device that has no decision-making or policy role on the enterprise, ministerial, national, or CMEA level. A lengthy and detailed account of the debate between Marer and Marrese-Vaňous appears elsewhere.[50]

50. Marrese and Vaňous, "Soviet Trade Relations," pp. 16–23; Marrese and Vaňous, *Soviet Subsidization*, pp. 103–16.

The historical evolution of Eastern Europe as a region   Iván T. Berend

What is Eastern Europe? Many observers now argue that such a question can be answered only in political terms. Eastern Europe for them is identical with the Soviet bloc. Its boundaries were settled at Yalta when Stalin, Roosevelt, and Churchill drew a line on the map along the river Elbe. There and then Germany, and indeed all of Europe, was divided into two, East and West. Eastern Europe now means a different political system, a different economic system, different conditions of life. But what makes the difference? Is the meaning of Eastern Europe determined by the military alliance of the Warsaw Treaty or the economic organization of the Council for Mutual Economic Assistance (CMEA)—does its definition truly depend on the relationships between the small countries of the region and the neighboring superpower, the Soviet Union?

Events since 1945 have certainly helped to shape the physiognomy of the area. I shall argue, however, that Eastern Europe has evolved not in four decades but over the centuries. Similar economic, social, and political structures have established in the course of European history a distinct region of the immense area from the Elbe and Saale rivers as far as the Urals, from the Black Sea to the Adriatic. With the passage of the centuries the boundaries of the region have moved, of course, shifting now eastward, now westward; but the area has never had an equivalent of the Great Wall of China to freeze its boundaries in some kind of permanence.

Within the region as a whole, with all the many common characteristics that have developed over a long history, there are, however, marked economic, social, and cultural differences as well. We have to distinguish among various subregions. One is (in the narrow geophysical sense) Russian East Europe. The Balkan subregion is also distinctive, its separate identity based primarily

Because of the survey nature of this essay, a bibliography was deemed to be more useful than footnotes to readers. The most important studies relating to this essay appear at the end of the text.

International Organization 40, 2, Spring 1986   0020-8183 $5.00

on an Ottoman occupation that lasted half a millennium and on an unsuccessful reaction to the challenge posed in the 19th century by the Industrial
Revolution. The third historical subregion is the area I shall call Central
East Europe, its backbone the peoples of the Carpathian Basin and the Polish
plain. Finally, one can distinguish a western zone of the region: in medieval
times the territories of Austria, Bohemia, and Germany shared similar experiences on the road to development, later they encountered the same
hindrances to national development, and in the 19th century all three struggled
to catch up economically with the most advanced regions of Europe. Given
these common conditions, social development in this western subregion has
preserved kindred traits.

These different and distinctive subregions tend to produce somewhat different solutions to the common tasks of economic and social development.
Local traditions also involve the application of different methods and institutions. Far from having disappeared, therefore, intraregional differences
have resisted attempts, such as those of the 1950s and 1960s, to ignore or
uproot them.

Initial differences

Locally distinctive features of society and economy are not discrete "objects"
but a complex of layers built up during the great transformation periods of
the world system. Eastern Europe was already displaying specific traits as
early as the very beginnings of medieval European development, in the 5th
to 8th centuries. Those local traits would mark later processes far more
profoundly than would the political division of East and West. And it is
important to note that local identity was established not in trauma, not in
the drama of unprecedented and unexpected catastrophe, but in the long
accumulation of regionally specific experience.

The differences that separate Eastern Europe from the rest of the continent
have their source in divergent trends within early feudalism. The immense
area between the Elbe and the Urals was populated by peoples of Slavic,
Finno-Ugric, and Turkic origin. From the 7th century onward Europe was
divided in two: a coherent Roman-Germanic world in the West and a separate
Byzantine-Islamic world in the East. Settlement patterns and ethnic conditions
in the East were still in a state of flux, however, when their equivalents in
the West had already been determined.

Europe east of the Elbe-Saale line is both a meeting ground for and a
peculiar combination of the West with Asia. Eastern Europe itself mirrored
developments in the continent as a whole, breaking into two parts, one with
a Latin and Western orientation and the other with a Greek and Eastern
orientation. All Europe would be joined in a Christian cultural community
only later, in the second half of the 10th century, when the Poles, the Hun-

garians, and the Russians founded Christian states. Subsequent centuries did not, however, witness the establishment in the East of feudalism in the Western sense of the word, for a social and institutional system based on private law was beyond the reach of Roman legal tradition. To the East *regnum* became *patrimonium*, and the entire nobility became subjects in the sense of public law. The forms of feudalism might have been established there, but the substance of feudalism was never integrated into the social fabric of East European life.

The Western, "classical" model of feudalism, as Marc Bloch points out, was characterized by a harmonious and proportionate amalgamation of Roman (classical) and Germanic (barbaric) elements. In the East such an amalgamation of elements proved impossible. In the northern part of the region Asiatic (barbaric) elements became dominant; in the south Byzantium integrated such elements with its own understanding of the classical in a system typified by "defensive rigidity." Meanwhile, Western Europe came into being within the well-defined boundaries of the Carolingian Empire; its eastern frontier was the Elbe, Saale, and Leitha rivers. This Roman Catholic–feudal society began to monopolize the idea of Europe toward the end of Charlemagne's reign, around 800 A.D. By the 11th to 13th centuries, however, the frontier of Western Europe had shifted considerably to the east, as far as the lower Danube, the eastern Carpathians, and the forest belt that separated Polish from Russian territory. Europe, a merely geophysical formation, became synonymous with Roman Catholicism, a cultural and what we might even term a "structural" identity.

It was at this shifting frontier, from the White Sea to the Black Sea, from the Polish plain to the Urals, that the Russian state hammered in the dawn of modern times. Aiming to incorporate the area into the concept of Russia, Russian activities shaped a homogeneous Eastern Europe. Crucial in this process was about 200 years of Mongol occupation, starting in the 13th century. The Asian nomadic world drove a wedge into the body of Europe as far as Hungary; later, in the twilight of the Middle Ages, an Osmanli Turkish advance from the southwest also reached Hungary; both reduced the areas concerned to a borderland. Direct contacts with Asia, in Russian territory and in the Balkans, impeded the fuller unfolding of the Western version of feudal development and helped to stiffen the Greek Orthodox, East European archetype of feudalism. In the intermediate region of Central East Europe—the Carpathian Basin and the Polish lowlands—structures of the Western type (sharply distinct from autochthonous East European structures) developed rapidly. The change from the western edge of geographical Eastern Europe into the eastern fringe of "Western Europe" (structurally west, that is) was characterized first and foremost by an extraordinarily concentrated and rapid period of development.

The historiography of countries in the region frequently refers, despite this late start, to trends practically identical to those in the West and resembling them in structure. It tends to recognize "deviations" from the Western model, along the lines of the East European style of development, as beginning only at the start of the 16th century or thereabouts. Despite nearly 500 years' delay, a "compressed" or "concentrated" rapid feudal development ensued in several countries of the region. It was a qualitative catching up and was basically problematical because its lesser duration made it more difficult to consolidate and elaborate feudal structures.

> Social structural elements that developed organically in the west in several stages, over almost 500 years [9th–13th centuries], through the dismantling of parts of previous achievements and the rearranging of the main elements at every stage, appeared in the eastern zone, including Hungary, in a concentrated form and parallel with one another in little more than one and a half centuries. It is hardly surprising that the forms they took were in some places inorganically truncated or raw, in others still unarticulated, rough, or mixed, and in yet others demonstrating here and there various archaic features or differing from their pattern in their proportion to one another. (Szücs 1983, p. 153)

All this gave the western region of Eastern Europe its Janus-faced quality: Western-type structural elements took root, but the root stock was never more than superficial. Even in Hungary, for example, feudal allegiance appeared only in the rudimentary form of "familiarity"; such allegiance lacked the institutionality and constancy of its Western counterpart and thus never became a true obstacle to the unity of central state power. Indeed, one principal characteristic of feudalism in the West is said to be that, with the disintegration of central executive power, the feudal system replaced the state with social relations, so to speak. The administrative, military, judicial, and other functions of the state, once divorced from sovereign power, were divided stepwise in a feudal society based on private law. It was in this milieu that the basic idea of the social contract, later destined to be so important, was conceived. Ideological and political, spiritual and profane spheres separated, and the continued "detotalization" of power through urbanization ultimately resulted in a Western society that could not be integrated from "above." In the West, as a consequence, integration started to act from "below."

Given its lack of a genuine and deep-rooted social fabric, the area annexed to Carolingian Europe between the 11th and 13th centuries cannot be regarded as structurally part of Western Europe. The idea of "Central East Europe" captures that whole area as early as the Middle Ages: Western models and norms applied from the very outset but did so with modifications perceptible in practically all parts of the structure of the East European environment. In this case, however, Russian East Europe and Polish-Hungarian Central East Europe, both essentially different from Western Europe, also fundamentally resembled each other. Prior to the 11th century both areas were clearly excluded from the Roman Catholic–feudal West just as after the 15th and 16th centuries they would lean eastward. The sharp line of demarcation between the economic and social structures that divided Europe in two after approximately the year 1500 (the far more spacious eastern half would become the territory of the "second serfdom") ran with astonishing precision along the Elbe-Leitha frontier of about the year 800 A.D.

Nor, despite all the essential differences, did Russian East Europe travel an entirely dissimilar road. The state of Kiev, having absorbed Norman and Byzantine influences and converted to Christianity (even if it became not Roman Catholic but Greek Orthodox), was comparable to the Hungarian state, their social structures showing obvious analogies. From the 13th century onward, however, Asian influences interrupted the unfolding of a late antique–barbarian symbiosis (a late repetition of the Roman-Frankish formula) and put new obstacles in the way of catching up. Russian development, even if it did so belatedly, followed the East European version of feudalism — indeed, it followed the classical form of East European autochthonous development. Feudal dues were appropriated there indirectly (that is, not directly by right of the feudal lord), a situation essentially identical with the Central East European (Bohemian, Hungarian, Polish) system of "services." Similarities can also be observed in the land-tenure system.

Despite its increasingly independent imperial, civilizational, and "world economic" potentials, the Russian state remained for a long time outside the modern world system that was beginning to take shape. The Tartar conquest and the lasting rule of the Golden Horde was the main and obvious reason for this delay. The agrarian price revolution of 16th-century Europe did not affect Russian territory; the religious revolution of the Reformation also avoided it. But Tartar invasion alone cannot explain the differences, which are also connected with structural defects inherent in the Byzantine origins of Russian society and culture. From the 18th century, however, the isolation of Russia first weakened and then ended, and by the turn of the 19th century the Russian Empire had become a peripheral part of the European world economy. The earlier separation and the later reintegration of the area naturally induced marked differences from developments in the West. In comparison with the economic, social, and political systems of the Western type, moreover, those differences seem in general to become more pronounced as one travels further to the East.

Such observations eventually serve to heighten the significance of the Elbe-Saale line of demarcation. East of this line one can distinguish different variants, or subtypes, of a general East European type that differs profoundly from the Western model of social development.

It is at least as important to distinguish the essential differences within the vast area from the Elbe to the Urals as it is to recognize developmental affinities there. Russian East Europe and the Balkans differ from Central East Europe substantially; at the same time these subregions display similarities in economic, social, and political development which must be kept in mind if one is to understand the history of the region. If these similarities are ignored, it becomes virtually impossible, for example, to understand the spread of the pan-Slavic or the pan-German idea or to identify common solutions to historical problems. It would be virtually impossible to understand how Germany, which had been catching up with the economically advanced countries since before unification, relapsed with the historical shocks of World War I and the Great Depression to seek a typically backwardness-prompted solution based on similarities of social development and on the spiritual, attitudinal, and ideological communities that ensue from those similarities. Equally incomprehensible would be the adoption after World War II, in the countries of the region, of Stalin's model of industrialization. Notwithstanding the many and important differences, therefore, I consider the similarities valid across the entire region of Eastern Europe to be determinative. It is not so much medieval processes as the "deviation" since the 15th century and the general similarities of 19th-century reactions to the Industrial Revolution that bring me to this conclusion.

The significance of the 16th-17th century change

Practically all historians see an incontestable change at about the turn of the 15th to the 16th century, a serious decline in the development of Eastern Europe. As regards the Kingdom of Hungary (including what is now the northwestern part of Yugoslavia) many think they find an explanation in the tragedy of 1526–41, in the Turkish occupation of the country.

That tragedy broke the natural processes of catching up, and decline became very noticeable. "The people who by the opening years of the 16th century," as one Hungarian historian writes, "had advanced to the early stages of capitalism fell back within a single decade to the level of their nomadic ancestors." The Turkish era thus interrupted the course of development. In the 17th century, according to G. Szekfü, "conditions in Hungary *for the first time* take a course different from that in the west." In the case of Hungary these interruptions are practically self-evident, and I do not question the impact of tragedies already detailed by various historians. When, however, one takes into account developments in neighboring countries and, more important, makes a thorough international comparison, it is obvious that changes cannot be attributed solely to such local causes as military defeats, the collapse of centralized states, and foreign occupation. While Western Europe was evolving capitalist conditions, the region east of the Elbe sharply deviated from that experience. Self-managing latifundia, relying on socage, were established: serfs were again bound to the soil as they had been at the time of early feudalism, and feudal dues paid in crops and labor, the "second serfdom," gradually replaced the customary money rent. This change began at about the end of the 15th century simultaneously in the territories of eastern Germany (Prussia, Brandenburg, Mecklenburg), Poland, Hungary, and Russia. The two halves of Europe, east and west, clearly split. Though evidently influenced by local circumstances, in part by attacks from outside, the phenomenon to the east of the Elbe had a universality indicative of more general interconnections. As many analysts have noted, in the case of the Balkans, for example, Turkish dominion (which there lasted longest and had the most serious effects) cannot be blamed exclusively for the backwardness of the region; the initial setback actually predated the Ottoman occupation. The same situation holds for the interconnection of Russian development and Tartar conquest.

The new backwardness of Eastern Europe was indisputably connected with the transformation of the world economic system. Medieval "world trade" traditionally concentrated on luxury articles; as it yielded its place to the modern exchange of the goods of mass consumption, world trade saw a substantial change in routes. The traditional Levantine route, leading from the Near East across the eastern Mediterranean Basin and Eastern Europe, was superseded by the trade routes of the Atlantic littoral—from the Baltic ports to Gibraltar and through to the western Mediterranean—as well as by overland trade routes between Western and Eastern Europe. The transport of bulk foodstuffs also began, from Eastern Europe to the Baltic.

This interpretation puts the deviations of Eastern Europe's agrarian development from the Western model in the context of the modern world system. Its proponents thus avoid the earlier "disaster explanations." The division of labor that took place in the modern world economy then forming reduced the countries of Eastern Europe to the role of suppliers of cereals and livestock. This relegation was obviously not unrelated to geographical factors. Geographical discoveries and new, transatlantic shipping lanes not only put the countries of the Atlantic coast at the center of the new international commerce but also offered them special opportunities for the primitive accumulation of money capital. The inflow of precious metals and the related agrarian price revolution underlay internal structural changes and also linked the third factor of the modern world economy, namely the creation of the modern colonial system, to economic and social processes.

The countries of Western Europe came to play a dominant role in the world system. The countries of the Atlantic littoral reacted to these changes, however, in radically different ways. Thus outside challenges created only conditions and possibilities, and what was of decisive significance in the seizing or missing of those opportunities was what we might call the domestic responsive readiness of particular countries and regions. The consequence in Eastern Europe was to stress socioeconomic features that had existed at the birth of feudalism and had survived into the Middle Ages despite adjustment to the West. Stagnant urban development and too large an aristocracy hindered the peasantry from becoming a bourgeoisie (the nobility was 1% of the population in Western societies, 4–10% in Hungary and Poland).

More generally, features of social structure common to the nations of the outermost fringes of Europe now came to play a decisive role in the "position taking" made possible by world economic transformation. The stiffening of the social structure and a new system of bondage (*Leibeigenschaft*) set back the peasants who earlier had been confirmed in their freedoms, and it made impossible the emergence of middle classes from the mass of society. Nor could some contradictory combination of historical processes compensate for these developments. The peasants, for example, were able rather vigorously to defend their institutional freedoms, and ambitions and wishes given expression in law did not become concrete realities of life. "Liquidated" economic, social, and political phenomena survived legal abolition and suppression with an often extraordinary persistence. The organization of society may have inspired the belief that there was no fundamental law other than the ruler's will. But ukases often got stuck in what was now an autotelic apparatus. However frequently edicts were issued, the scribe still coolly marked them "execution impossible," and the provincial clerk on receiving aggressive and unrealistic instructions from higher quarters became accustomed to ignoring them. Such conditions opened peculiar historical "side doors"; natural processes became deformed by the need to take detours in order to forge ahead. The blocking of the peasantry's rise to the bourgeoisie under stiffening feudal conditions, for example, led to an overgrown nobility. It was still possible to rise in society, but the specific environment usually required the purchase of noble rank. The privileges of nobility thus became a strange sort of security for the embourgeoisement of peasant and urban masses.

As a result, East European development became not only more complicated and contradictory but also more receptive to other influences, even though developmental regularities prevailed. (As always in history, however, these "regularities" imply only an abstraction, an accentuation of principal tendencies, and never the many-colored reality of life. Yet we can no more query the validity of abstractions than refute the validity of physical laws. We can hardly deny the physical distinction between elastic and inelastic substances, for example, but this distinction is just as much an abstraction as the historical distinction between east and west in Europe. Elastic rubber only stretches so far; it then becomes inelastic and snaps. Inelastic wood, up to a critical stress point, bends very elastically under pressure.) The noblemen massed behind the shield of noble privileges—a dominant tendency in Eastern Europe—secluded themselves from what smacked of the bourgeois. The Hungarian landlord who was still carrying on trade in the 16th century gradually abandoned it in the 17th, and by the 18th he despised such activities as incompatible with his gentlemanly status. In the middle spheres of society, isolated from below and excluded from above, alien strata gained ground and established for themselves a bourgeois existence. In sum the countries of Eastern Europe had only a subordinate, peripheral position in the new world economic system. Having deviated from the ascent to capitalism, they underwent the bitterness of refeudalization and were stranded in the quagmire of a centuries-long, stagnant, and painfully slow "late feudalism."

All these processes were interlinked with the specific development of states and nations, and consequently the unfavorable change in economic and social development made its effects felt at the political level. What followed from the structure of the second serfdom resembled what in the early medieval period had followed from the first: economic exploitation and extra-economic (politico-legal) compulsion again combined at the level of the village, of the landlord's domain. The consolidation of decentralized rule by the nobility, the stiffening of feudal institutions, the survival of seigneurial and regional organs of coercion—in these and other ways state structure suited the formation of the second serfdom as against the centralization of political power. Only in the Polish-Lithuanian state of the 16th and 17th centuries did this happen consistently, and the Polish *Rzeczpospolita*, the republic of the feudal nobility sometimes known as the "democracy of nobility," was the sole pure example of this political process. But similar tendencies also appeared in the Hapsburg Empire. The feudal *Ständestaat* gained a strong foothold in the Electorate of Brandenburg and in the eastern German provinces, too. By the early years of the 17th century, therefore, feudalism seemed to have triumphed in this part of Europe.

To this rejuvenated feudalism, however, the growing military power of absolute states to the west and north was not merely a potential threat but an immediate danger. The invading armies of Sweden at the height of its glory advanced in successive waves, launching attacks on Brandenburg and the Hapsburg, Polish, and Russian states. By the 1640s they had already occupied a large portion of Moravia and encamped at Prague. In the next decade they took possession of Warsaw and Kraków as well. The Swedish deluge swept away the *Rzeczpospolita*, showing that the democracy of nobility was not a viable formation, and in the course of the 17th century the superior might and outward pressure of the northern and western absolute monarchies gave force to aspirations in the East for a similar absolutism that would suppress internal autonomies. This tendency was to be seen in Brandenburg/ Prussia, the Hapsburg monarchy, and Russia. It is indicative that 1653, the year when Friedrich Wilhelm concluded his social contract with the Junkers, was also the year in which the last Zemski Sobor assembled in Russia: the change from the feudal representative state to the absolute monarchy was rapid. Poland, on the other hand, stubbornly retained its loose, feudal state structure. It not only declined as a nation but actually lost its independent statehood.

But newly established absolutisms were embedded in differing economic and social environments, thereby differing widely in structural terms from Western models. In societal terms they were linked to the system of the second serfdom; historically, they were built on the precedent that, contrary to Western feudal practice, "étatized" society rather than "socializing" state functions. This combination of circumstances ultimately created a firm basis for the establishment of an outwardly defensive, strong, and rigidly autotelic central power. In contrast to the absolute monarchies of Western Europe these state formations did not pave the way for capitalist development. Rather, they became bases for a rigid form of feudalism, virtually incapable of adapting to new circumstances and often pursuing aggressive expansion as a counterpoise to their internal uncertainties.

Even more significant, however, the central state power established in the face of an external threat was in Eastern Europe not identical with the nation. To the west the boundaries of the modern state and the nation coincided during centuries of capitalist bourgeois development. In Eastern Europe, on the contrary, painful and tremendous historical shocks—the breakup of Germany, the formation of Hapsburg, Ottoman, and Russian empires—caused the boundaries of nations and states to separate. National existence and the territorial status of the nation, moreover, were left permanently undecided. The end to the independence of the Bohemian, Polish, and Hungarian states, the repeated partition of Poland, and long-lasting Turkish dominion over the Balkans clearly demonstrated this undecidedness, which became the starting point for the "political hysterics" of the nations of Eastern Europe.

The absolute states of Eastern Europe, mostly established within a multinational framework (because central power and the nation separated from each other), could never be really successful. The state made the feudal nobility representative of the national cause, thereby strengthening it. Despite all these deadlocked political and social processes, however, agricultural commodity production made great progress. As Imanuel Wallerstein argues, the refeudalizing of Eastern Europe became part of the multisectoral modern world economy that was then developing. Faced with the challenge of the new world economy, the feudal absolute monarchy—which was less Janus-faced than its Western variant—finally became an efficient force for structural reforms that, initiated and implemented from above, had also marked the first feudalism in Eastern Europe.

From the mid-18th century the states of the East had to respond to the challenge of the recent and tremendous transformation of the West, which called into being a system of enlightened absolutisms. This characteristically East European type of state subsequently tried to make good the weaknesses inherent in its socioeconomic and national development. In the absence of bourgeois development, and under the inspiration of enlightened absolutisms, entrepreneurs began to emerge in modest numbers from social strata that had embarked upon the road to assimilation. The peasant land communities that had stoutly endured backwardness and oppression by landlord and state were communal self-governments. Even these peasant communities, and the self-government of noblemen so characteristic of aristocratic societies (and so regressive from the Western perspective of bourgeois development), had the potential to act as starting points for new developmental processes, some of them spurred by nationalist aspirations.

The Western challenge of the "double revolution"

In the "long 19th century" the industrialized, bourgeois democracies took shape under the impact of what Eric Hobsbawm has termed Western Europe's "double revolution," the Industrial Revolution in England and the socio-political revolution in France. They developed extremely rapidly and, during the first half of the century, continually widened the gap between West and East. The difference in levels of development is captured by capita gross national product, which changed from a ratio of 1:2 to 1:3 in the span of five decades.

This great transformation of the world system again posed multiple challenges to Eastern Europe, which was once again set back. At the same time, however, the industrializing West opened its markets to a growing amount of food and raw materials. Immense additional markets stimulated the modernization of East European agriculture, for the traditional system had mostly relied on inefficient serf labor. It was, of course, the ruling elite of landlords that most interested itself in change. The challenge, however, pervaded the whole of sociopolitical life. First, the exploitation of new export markets required the removal of such rigid obstacles as the privileges of nobility and the bonds of serfdom. The Western institutions that supported the capitalist economy also needed to be captured. Second, the ideas of the French Revolution and the attractions of the British industrial economy posed a profound threat to society, providing another reason to reform sclerotic feudal systems and accommodate them to the West. Last but not least, Western progress upset the established military-political balance of forces. The traditional great-power status of nations now falling behind was endangered. They faced the possibility of being reduced to vulnerability and even subordination.

The first Eastern reply to this Western challenge was the historical reflex of the region, a series of reforms introduced from above by the state: Stein's and Hardenburg's reforms in Prussia, the emancipation of the serfs in Russia, the Austro-Hungarian Compromise that ended revolution by appeasement and reforms, as well as Stolypin's innovations in Russia intended to advance the reform of 1861. But such replies were by no means formulated within narrowly national bounds. Indicative of a wider context were the construction of a continental railroad network using Western capital; the expansion of free trade; the establishment of an international monetary system, the gold standard; the creation of a modern banking system that closely resembled the intensive Western financing of the consolidation of the economy and of modern statehood; the development of extractive industries with foreign capital; and the extension not only of traditional external trade, which increased in volume several times over, but also of ever stronger financial and credit relations.

With the success or the failure of reactions to this global challenge, regional boundaries once again began to shift. The western zone of Eastern Europe, the German states and the western half of the Dual Monarchy, matched other European zones of backwardness, mainly Scandinavia, in successfully and completely catching up with the West. The Balkan countries, along with other lagging states (mainly the former great powers of the Iberian Peninsula) not only fell further behind "Europe" but plunged, occasionally through direct financial control, even more deeply into defenselessness. Countries between these extremes, such as Hungary, the Kingdom of Poland, and Russia, resembled Italy in replying half-successfully to the challenge.

Despite all the progress made, even in the unsuccessful Balkans, quantitative growth was on the whole located within the traditional structural framework. Although the partially successful countries had achieved essential transformations, including the building of a modern infrastructure and a threefold increase in agricultural production, even they could not overcome the backwardness inherent in their agrarian-peasant structures. Increased agrarian exports, moreover, helped establish new industries—occasionally export-oriented ones—and the internal accumulation of capital was growing in importance. The spectacular success of economic catchup was Germany, which actually took a continental lead in productivity. Success, however, brought its own problems: it eliminated earlier economic backwardness and the other harmful effects of a delayed start, but it widened the gap between an increasingly modern economic system and a rather rigid sociopolitical structure. The traditional ruling elite (landowning and military-bureaucratic) had outlived its time but retained political power and decisive social influence. Both the elite and the autocratic political system, the rule of militaristic absolutism, came to seem ever more flagrant anachronisms.

Capitalist development continued in spite of more or less significant impediments and the economy was updated, sharpening the conflict that focused around the lagging sociopolitical transformation of Eastern Europe. At the head of capitalist transformation marched the landowning aristocracy and the bureaucratic-military elite characteristic of the area from Germany to the Balkans, a peculiar *Ersatzklasse* (substitute class) that had risen because of the weakness of burghers and the new bourgeoisie, or because of their absence. The rise of the *Ersatzklasse* had been the greater because structural reforms were imposed from above, under the guidance of the state, just as the state had given legislative backing to railroad construction and industrialization, and guarantees to foreign capital.

The traditional ruling elite, supported by the system of large estates, thus preserved its power. Earlier the gentry (that is, the lower nobility), having lost their privileges and most of their estates, captured the offices of the state, the municipalities, and the army. This military-official gentry gained considerable strength and hindered the peasantry from rising in the social scale. Some peasants had small plots of land, but most of them were emancipated without land, and even the narrow segments of richer peasants remained strangely "outside society." In preponderantly peasant countries there were no peasant parties, and schools and offices were closed to the pleasantry—this was so even in the Balkans, where the landowning elite had fled with the passing of Turkish rule. The system of large estates was ended, and power in these "mutilated societies" passed into the hands of a new, national ruling elite—but it was an elite that sprang from urban merchants and civilian and military officers eager to get rich quick, very rarely from the ranks of wealthier peasants. During the 19th century foreign merchants and other middle-class immigrants became the vanguard of capitalist enterprise (especially in Polish, Romanian, and Hungarian territories). One-third to one-half of shopkeepers and skilled handicraft workers came from their ranks; some, by means of capital accumulated through intermediate trade in farm produce, even rose to important positions in the newly founded banks and in large-scale industry. They were also significant in the nascent working class, for big industry could not satisfy demand for skilled workers locally and had to recruit laborers from abroad.

These societies developed a peculiar dualism. Within the ruling elite a new bourgeois stratum, mostly of German-Jewish bankers and industrialists, supplemented the traditional political leadership of the big landowners, just as the gentry middle classes were joined by groups of foreign origin, modern bourgeois and petit-bourgeois elements that emerged as a consequence of capitalist development. This duality also characterized the newly rising intelligentsia: side by side with intellectuals recruited from among the former nobility and gentry and working in the intellectual professions of the civil service (judges, lawyers, teachers) were "self-employed intellectuals," a considerable number of them from the fast-assimilating Jewish middle class.

These societies were consequently faced with serious unsolved problems: the gentry question, the peasant question, and the "Jewish question." In this respect the imitative strategy of catchup that Eastern Europe deemed an unequivocal requirement in the century before 1914 produced a crisis regardless of its success or failure. This inevitability of crisis resulted in no small measure from the discouraging effects of failure and partial success, often from the impossibility of making any progress at all. Even when economic conditions were favorable, national development, impeded by earlier problems, could not always profit.

National awakening, delayed by outside hindrances, first and emphatically manifested itself in the form of cultural and linguistic aspirations. It was impossible to satisfy such aspirations and simultaneously satisfy the rugged conditions of catchup. The earlier problems of national development had, moreover, accustomed the elite of these nations to building upon demands instead of reality, upon claims instead of performance, and to ignoring simple cause and effect. Intense, and intensely deceptive, experiences had influenced many generations. The communal shocks of national grievance aroused mass passions and rendered the masses susceptible to half-truths and lies that gave some vent to their feelings. Such problems were exacerbated by the' lessening self-confidence of the advanced capitalist and parliamentary democracies of the West. The Hungarian poet Batsányi at the end of the 18th century and the politician-reformer Count Széchenyi in the first half of the 19th had automatically imitated French and English examples. Their successors looked westward to countries now wracked with doubts about values that the era of liberalism had regarded as natural.

All these questions assumed particular importance in the aftermath of World War I. Eastern Europe developed new patterns of reaction, prompted by backwardness and its belated start, by the hindrances and problems of economic, social, and national development, by the presence of numerous and only partly assimilated ethnic and national-religious minorities. It was in this precise region, in the early years of the 20th century, that Rosa Luxemburg and V. I. Lenin coupled international Marxism with the challenge of backwardness. The socialist revolutionary movement was spreading in Eastern Europe, and the region saw the experiments of the revolution (Germany, Hungary, Bulgaria) as well as its first bridgehead (the Soviet Union). Marxist theory further evolved in Eastern Europe, and the socialist model that was taking shape there would ultimately try a novel way to break out of backwardness, to industrialize, and to secure the necessary sources of domestic accumulation to do so.

The failure of revolutionary experiments and the isolation of the socialist revolution in Russian East Europe brought alternatives to the fore in the region. Some small countries thought they could find a remedy for all their crucial socioeconomic problems in their belated national revolutions. National independence they linked with "economic nationalism," stressing import substitution from the early 1920s onward. These new governments wanted independence from foreign imports and so increased their industrial tariffs and introduced the first stage of import substitution (concentrated on consumer goods). The more industrialized countries of the region (Austria, Czechoslovakia, Germany) reacted with agricultural protectionism and themselves became more self-sufficient. Autarchy became ever more dominant in the Eastern Europe of the 1930s.

Basic trends may have been rather similar, but there were marked differences in economic and political performance. Poland, Austria, and Hungary were among the economically less successful countries of Europe, while Czechoslovakia caught up with Western Europe and transformed itself into a democratic state. The Balkan countries, though they followed an obsolete development policy of autarchy, achieved more rapid industrial growth. Independent of this economic change (though, in some cases, in connection with it) some of these countries proclaimed war on the Western values of the French Enlightenment and British liberalism. Theirs was the spirit not of a social revolution and repudiating capitalism but of right-wing radicalism and mystic racial-national ideologies. As countries were driven even further to the periphery, furious domestic opposition to the paths being followed caused the ascendancy of irrational ideas. This irrationalism was not, however, a simple unreasonableness. In it, rather, we can see a characteristically peripheral ideology. The sense of failure to catch up was in part similar to the frustration of Germany, an economic leader that still could not join the club of colonial powers and was later rebuffed when it tried to force its way in. Failure naturally inspired rejection of the rationality of the rules of the game which the dominant powers had established. New, "irrational" rules tailored to peripheral strengths might secure advantage in the competition, and in this sense savage irrationalism was all too rational. Ruthless dictatorships, Nazi-type regimes, royal autocracies, and frenzied nationalist pseudofascisms consumed the entire region from Germany to the Balkans.

The decades after World War II

The current dividing line between Eastern and Western Europe re-creates the Carolingian boundary between East and West of about the year 800 A.D. Socioeconomic development after the turn of the 15th to the 16th century reinforced this division of the continent along the Elbe-Leitha line, and this is, with astounding precision, where Germany is divided at the present time.

Eastern Europe was the principal arena of World War II, and in several countries of the region the victory of the Soviet Union brought to power the socialist model that had failed to establish itself after World War I. After 1945 the dependent and underdeveloped countries of Asia and Africa, those peripheries of the world order, unleashed their revolt against subjection, and the centuries-old colonial system, partly because of the opportunities offered by a newly bipolar world, collapsed in about two decades. As the world system changed, so the countries of Eastern Europe also embarked upon transformation. The spur for transformation came mainly from outside.

Internal economic and social contradictions and distortions and archaic systems of political oppression, however, generated demands from the masses for internal changes, making structural reforms possible (if, as tradition warranted, initiated from above). In the early postwar years these demands were in part oriented westward. Peasant and other democratic parties acted as advocates for long-needed democratic reforms. The system of large estates was shattered. Autocratic states collapsed "automatically," as it were, with the fall of Nazi and pseudofascist regimes, and more than one country held its first truly democratic elections immediately after the war.

As a result of power relations within the world system, however, in 1947 and 1948, for the first time in a millennium, Western solutions did not prevail; a specifically East European socialist model came to fruition. The socialist answer followed the 19th-century strategy of imitation of the West and the interwar repudiation of Western rationality by "irrational" right-wing dictatorships. Formulated in the historical processes of Eastern Europe, this model rejected Western capitalism. Soviet socialism had been molded in a concrete historical environment, on the basis of Russian precedents and specific postrevolutionary conditions. It was not only considered ideologically obligatory for a long time (deviations, even though only partial, were branded "revisionist" and viewed as an attempt to return to capitalism), but its one-sided dominance—which the Soviet government self-critically condemned toward the end of October 1956—also posed a considerable handicap to relations between states. Despite these distortions, the model was not only forced upon countries in the region, it was voluntarily copied from Yugoslavia to the People's Republic of China and Latin America. It furnished the great hope of catching up with the West and even surpassing it. As Stalin himself had proclaimed in 1931, Soviet socialism in one decade looked to compensate for the century of more by which Russian industry lagged behind the West; nearly three decades later Khrushchev set a twenty-year schedule for over-taking the most advanced countries of the West in production, productivity, and standard of living. Widely differing responses thus concealed one common aim: to catch up.

The ensuing rearrangement was on a massive scale, and the Soviet model, copied in a uniform and orthodox manner, rendered Europe east of the Elbe more homogeneous than it had ever been before. The role of the state in socialist transformation became practically absolute. The state could thus ensure the conditions that would allow formerly agrarian countries to ac-celerate their one-sided industrialization, which changed both the internal economic structures of the countries of the region and the place they occupied in the international division of labor. The conscious application of socialist ideology eliminated the traditional rural-peasant character of society, or at least began to eliminate it. Socialism broke the extremely hierarchical character of earlier social structures, often by drastic means. Social restratification affected on average about one-fifth to one-quarter of the population: the majority of the middle strata, as well as the former power elite, sank in the social scale, and new intellectual strata rose from the people to positions of leadership.

National economies were deliberately guided down the same road, societies were organized to the same pattern within the framework of similar political organizations, states for the first time in history united in a single system of political-military alliance under Soviet leadership. Political Eastern Europe had, for the most part, become identical with historical Eastern Europe.

The leitmotif of the postwar transformation was forced industrialization, which dramatically changed economic structure: all of the East European countries became industrialized. One-half to two-thirds of the gross national product is now generated by industry—on average, compared to prewar conditions, at least a tenfold to fifteenfold increase in industrial production. Rural population dropped from 40–60 percent to 15–30 percent of national totals. The breakthrough of industrialization characterized structural modernization in the region.

At this point, however, we have to stress the abstract character of our description of this process. If Eastern Europe is becoming from several perspectives more united than ever, the reality of attitudes and activities—in spite of identical institutional systems and remarkably similar social structures—still displays manifold deviations from outward regularity (as I have already pointed out in respect of the 16th to 18th centuries). The antecedents of economic and social development varied in spite of similarities, levels of development on occasion differed to a considerable extent, and these earlier differences in political institutions and in culture eventually paved the way for diverse solutions and policies. Now, for example, the economies of Eastern Europe function in three distinct ways: the "classical" Soviet model is itself starting to transform, but Yugoslavia developed a rather different, self-managed market economy, and Hungary (as a result of three major waves of economic reform starting in 1957, 1968, and the late 1970s) has developed a reformed system that combines elements of central planning and market profit. An export orientation is also beginning to replace "classical" import substitution in some countries. The countries of Eastern Europe now clearly exhibit the considerable dissimilarities of subregions defined by internal developmental differences, dissimilarities that can be seen on the street, in characteristic forms of behavior, and in economic and social structures.

The historical tide of the past one-third of a century, regardless of how one judges it politically, has deposited new layers over formations of structural similarity that have accumulated for a millennium. And with this realization we can revert to the question with which we started, for the history of the region (*when* kindred features took shape) is indistinguishable from the establishment of the geographical boundaries of the region (*which* territories are characterized by these kindred features). The two questions cannot be separated. The Eastern Europe of today is characterized by considerable transformations achieved in the past thirty-five years or so in practically all of the countries of the region, and it is also characterized by similarities among countries built upon long-lasting historical antecedents and by the duality of underlying differences and deviations.

Eastern Europe developed as a historical region in the course of a thousand years of history. "The past," as Thomas Mann stressed, "is existing, always existing, in the present," and historical continuity in a way determined changes, responses to new challenges. Nevertheless, history always offers alternatives; adjustment to major transformations, at the dramatic turning points of history, is an open set of possibilities. This was and is manifest in the frequently changing boundaries of Eastern Europe, which shift eastward and westward with time, and in subregional differences of adjustment to world socioeconomic challenges: success, partial success, and failure.

Bibliography

Berend, I. T., and Ránki, G. *Economic Development of East-Central Europe in the 19th and 20th Centuries*. New York, 1974.

Bibó, I. *A keleteurópai kisállamok nyomorusága* [The Misery of the Small States of Eastern Europe]. Budapest, 1946.

Bidlo, J. "Was ist die osteuropäische Geschichte?" *Slawische Rundschau* (1933), pp. 361–70.

Dvornik, F. *The Making of Central and Eastern Europe*. London, 1949.

Halecki, O. *The Limits and Divisions of European History*. Longon, 1950.

Hobsbawm, Eric. *The Age of Revolution, 1789–1848*. Cleveland, 1962.

Jászi, O. *The Dissolution of the Hapsburg Monarchy*. Chicago, 1929.

Makkai, L. *Feudalizmus és az eredeti jellegzetességek Európában* [Feudalism and the Genuine Characteristics in Europe]. Budapest, 1976.

Niederhauser, E. "Zur Frage der osteuropäischen Entwicklung," *Studia Slavica* (1958), pp. 359–71.

Pach, P. S. "East Central Europe and World Trade at the Dawn of Modern Times," *Acta Historica* (1981), pp. 281–316.

Perényi, J. "L'Est européen dans une synthése d'histoire universelle," *Nouvelles Études Historiques* 2 (1965), pp. 379–405.

Seton-Watson, R. W. *The Southern Slav Question and the Habsburg Monarchy*. London, 1911.

Seton-Watson, R. W. *The Rise of Nationality in the Balkans*. London, 1917.

Stadtmuller, G. *Geschichte Südosteuropas*. Munich, 1950.

Szakály, Ferenc, et al. "Études Historiques Hongroises," in *Hungary and Eastern Europe: Research Report*, vol. 2, pp. 613–805. Budapest, 1980.

Szücs, J. "The Historical Regions of Europe," *Acta Historica* 29, nos. 2–4 (1983).

Taylor, A. J. P. *The Habsburg Monarchy 1809–1918*. London, 1957.

Teleki, P. *The Evolution of Hungary and Its Place in European History*. New York, 1923.

Wallerstein, I. W. *The Modern World-System. Capitalist Agriculture and the Origins of the European World-Economy in the Sixteenth Century*. New York, 1974.

Socialist patrimonialism and the global economy: the case of Romania
Ronald H. Linden

Discussions of Eastern Europe seem inevitably to include the phrase "except for Romania." The subject posed by this volume, the relationship between external economic disturbance and internal power, requires a similar differentiation. Romania's involvement with the noncommunist international economy began earlier (the mid-1960s) and was more rapid and extensive than that of the other East European states. The foreign policy that supported and accompanied this involvement differed substantially from that of its allies. During the 1970s international economic forces buffeted Romania as they had most other East European countries. In Romania, as in others, adjustment was delayed. But when a response did come it proved more vigorous and involved more punishing consequences for the population than anywhere else in the region save Poland.

The explanation for these divergences lies in another: the evolution of the Romanian governing regime not toward a collegial system of powerful counterbalancing elites but toward a system in which the power distribution at the top was highly unequal, in which one person and the group most closely associated with him were able to determine, without significant opposition, both the direction and intensity of the country's policies.

Contrary to suggestions in much of the development literature and contrary to the experience in Hungary or Poland, economic modernization in Romania did not produce a pluralistic distribution of power in either the Romanian Communist party (RCP) or the state. Instead, Romania's rapid economic development enabled the party leader to increase his power. By the time objective conditions began to indicate the need for change, the system had

I gratefully acknowledge the support of the National Council for Soviet and East European Research and from the University Center for International Studies and the Russian and East European Studies Program of the University of Pittsburgh for this research. I am indebted also to Ellen Comisso, Peter Gourevitch, Peter Katzenstein, Paul Marer, Laura Tyson, and Thomas Wolf who read and commented on earlier versions of this paper, as well as the reviewers. If any mistakes remain after all these people read it, it must be their fault.

International Organization 40, 2, Spring 1986   0020-8183 $5.00
© 1986 by the Massachusetts Institute of Technology and the World Peace Foundation

lost the capacity to translate such a need into the political influence required to shift direction. Change was delayed. Ultimately, the nature and pace of the country's belated economic demarche—shifting of investment, sharp restriction of consumption, cutting of ties with the West, increased interest in trade and cooperation with the Council for Mutual Economic Assistance (CMEA)—were the product of the ideology and power of the country's dominant individual and a governing system that lacked political counterweights to moderate his policies.

Can Romania under the rule of Nicolae Ceaușescu be accurately characterized as a "socialist patrimonial state"? To recall Weber, a patrimonial state is characterized by highly centralized power flowing from the personal authority of the ruler and, to some extent, the ruler's family. The patrimonial ruler dominates the administrative structure, defines the parameters of political authority and enforces his will in various ways over other individuals and over society as a whole. Office-holders (the political elite) derive their position and power from their personal relationship with the leader, who uses punishment and reward to maintain their loyalty and relative weakness.[1] In Weber's terms, the patrimonial leader is himself limited and guided by his obeisance to tradition. The strong presence of tradition, plus the personal, discretionary nature of the patrimonial administrative structure—as opposed to one that is rational, legal, and specialized—seems to preclude the characterization of a modern, bureaucratic state (like Romania) as patrimonial.

Simon Schwartzman has nonetheless found useful ways of adopting Weber's concept of patrimonialism to modern states, namely those in Latin America. He suggests that in a modern state raison d'etat, acting as the "substantive" (as opposed to formal) rationality, replaces tradition as the guiding force of the patrimonial regime and forms the basis for the creation of complex, bureaucratic structure. In Schwartzman's words, "The domination of a central government only ruled by its 'raison d'etat' and a passive and instrumental 'propertyless' mass is the definition of a modern, patrimonial, bureaucratic regime."[2]

In Romania in the 1970s we can see both the discretionary personal power of the ruler (Ceaușescu) that Weber stressed and the state-determined rationality (national Marxism-Leninism) Schwartzman suggests. This state was then faced with a series of economic disruptions. The analysis presented here will explore how Romania's socialist patrimonialism produced the country's particular response and whether this system of rule was itself affected by the external economic shocks.

1. Max Weber, *Economy and Society* (New York: Bedminster, 1968), pp. 1006–69.

2. Simon Schwartzman, "Back to Weber: Corporatism and Patrimonialism in the Seventies," in James M. Malloy, ed., *Authoritarianism and Corporatism in Latin America* (Pittsburgh: University of Pittsburgh Press, 1977), pp. 89–106; quote is from p. 98.

Political and economic structure and dynamics

Ceauşescu assumed control in 1965 of a governing system in which the party dominated other institutions and the party leader and his closest associates dominated the party itself. Ceauşescu's predecessor, Gheorghe Gheorghiu-Dej, had in his time succeeded in weakening or eliminating potential rivals, thus preventing the emergence of the kind of collective, challengeable leadership that characterized the Soviet Union at the time.[3] Domination of government and state structures increased during the first decade of Ceauşescu's rule to the point where national bodies such as the Grand National Assembly (GNA) and local organs such as the people's councils became essentially symbolic and representational bodies, with little political responsibility or authority. Substantial personnel overlap between party and state bodies ensured both control of government by the RCP and control of regions by the central administration. Administrative reforms in local government in 1968 and Ceauşescu's personal appointment of regional party first secretaries, who were simultaneously people's council presidents,[4] strengthened the power of party administrators. In 1972 party economic secretaries were simultaneously appointed vice-chairmen of the people's councils. In some sectors the merging of party and state bodies was formalized at the highest level, for example, the creation in 1974 of the Supreme Council of Economic and Social Development. Through the decade, party dominance of the governmental system and its constituent bodies grew. Non-RCP bodies had marginal policy-making power, and party and state organs became increasingly unified.[5]

The major challenge at this point to the new leader's ability to attain personal predominance was the presence of the old leader's colleagues. Hence the party itself also went through a similar process of change and concentration of power at the top. In 1965 Ceauşescu established a Political Executive Committee with fifteen full and ten candidate members, designed essentially to circumvent and subordinate the existing Presidium and Central Committee. By the Tenth Party Congress (1969) Ceauşescu had effectively muted, weakened, or excluded what opposition there might have been from the old Gheorghiu-Dej regime or among the new cadres. In 1974 an even smaller Permanent Bureau was created, composed of the five people closest to Ceau-

3. For a discussion of the Gheorghiu-Dej period, including its characterization as patrimonial, see Kenneth Jowitt, *Revolutionary Breakthroughs and National Development: The Case of Romania, 1944–1965* (Berkeley: University of California Press, 1971), especially pp. 191–96.
4. See Mary Ellen Fischer, "Political Leadership and Personnel Policy in Romania," in Steven Rosefielde, *World Communism at the Crossroads* (Boston: Martinus Nijhoff, 1980), pp. 222–27. For a discussion of the network of Romanian local government, see Daniel Nelson, *Democratic Centralism in Romania: A Study of Local Communist Politics* (Boulder: East European Monographs, 1980; distributed by Columbia University Press, New York), pp. 26–50.
5. See Andreas Tsantis and Roy Pepper, *Romania: The Industrialization of an Agrarian Economy under Socialist Planning* (Washington: International Bank for Reconstruction and Development, 1979), p. 40; hereafter cited as World Bank, *Romania*.

şescu. Originally conceived of as a subunit of the party Executive Committee, the Permanent Bureau grew to fifteen by 1979. This body facilitated Ceauşescu's personal control over the party and thereby over national policy, while speeding the elevation of loyal (or related) cadres to the highest levels.[6] The Executive Committee also grew, but, like the Central Committee and the party itself, it became essentially the ratifier and instrument of Ceauşescu's wishes. Although the RCP expanded and added more workers, its "leading role" in society, like the leading role of its Central Committee, became nearly as symbolic and formal as that of the government and state in relation to the party.

In Ceauşescu's first decade of rule he added to his title of party general secretary (changed at the Ninth Congress in 1965), that of chairman of the Council of State, president of the republic (an office created for him), chairman of the National Defense Council (another joint party-state body), and supreme commander of the armed forces. During this period, the symbolic elevation of Ceauşescu himself also began, from a position of *primus inter pares* to that of an exalted, omniscient leader of party, state, and people. This was indicated by the growing deference toward and adulation of Ceauşescu, his initiatives, ideas, and plans. "By the mid-1970s," Mary Ellen Fischer writes, "no Romanian official could deliver a report or write an article without referring to President Ceauşescu's political inspiration and guidance."[7]

In contrast, for example, to Yugoslavia, where the political and economic center had to contend with increasingly powerful regional forces, the governing dynamics in Romania at the middle of the 1970s were unquestionably top-to-bottom and center-to-periphery. A relatively closed top party leadership, essentially those around Ceauşescu, determined both the country's overall direction and the parameters of its day-to-day activities, and implemented its decisions through the party to the government and through both to the society at large.

6. On the evolution of the Bureau, see Fischer, "Political Leadership," pp. 221–22. Members of Ceauşescu's family in important positions include: Elena (wife), member of RCP Political Executive Committee and Permanent Bureau, chairman of Commission on Cadres, first deputy prime minister, chairman of National Council on Science and Technology; Nicu (son), first secretary of Union of Communist Youth and (automatically) minister of youth, member of executive bureau of National Council of Socialist Democracy and Unity Front, member of National Council of Working People; Ilie (brother), lieutenant general, deputy minister of defense and head of Higher Political Council of Romanian army; Nicolae (brother), lieutenant general, position in Ministry of Interior; Ioan (brother), vice-chairman of State Planning Commission and vice-chairman of Council on Forestry; Manea Manescu (brother-in-law), member of Political Executive Committee, vice-chairman of State Council and of Supreme Council for Economic and Social Development, prime minister from 1974 to 1979; Gheorge Petrescu (brother-in-law), deputy prime minister, chairman of section for transportation and communication of Supreme Council for Economic and Social Development. See Radio Free Europe Research, 5 February 1980, 7 June 1983, and 20 January 1984; hereafter cited as RFER. See also *New York Times*, 27 November 1979, p. 2.

7. Mary Ellen Fischer, "Idol or Leader? The Origins and Future of the Ceauşescu Cult," in Daniel Nelson, ed., *Romania in the 1980s* (Boulder: Westview, 1981), p. 118.

Spurred by the events in Czechoslovakia in 1968 and Poland in 1970, the regime dutifully went through the motions of "reforming" national political institutions such as the GNA and the Socialist Unity Front. But these modifications entailed no yielding of real authority; combined with the growing practice of merging party and state personnel and institutions, they were designed in fact to increase rather than decrease Ceaușescu's control of the party and especially of its executive organs.[8] Although there is evidence that local leaders in both state and party roles held different views on the country's needs and even contested some aspects of these reforms,[9] Ceaușescu's tight hold over party cadres—a hold increased by repeated "rotation" of these cadres—ensured that by mid-decade the essential components of a highly centralized patrimonial state were in place.

State-society dynamics during that time reflect the party's appetite for total control and, as noted below, the desire to mobilize Romanian society for the purpose of socialist economic development. Organs formally intended to represent social needs to the top, for example, trade unions, workers' and people's councils, acted instead as "transmission belts" for the government's mobilization plans. Similarly, the appropriate direction of and limits to minority, cultural, and political expression were explicated in detail and subordinated to the RCP's need for mobilization and development. On an index of "subsystem autonomy or liberalization," developed by Jan Triska and Paul Johnson, Romania ranked the lowest in Eastern Europe except for Albania.[10]

The economy at the beginning of the decade was similarly structured. Cadres, directives, and a minimally reformed system of central planning ensured the domination of the Communist party. Enterprise and worker autonomy were severely limited, despite the formal establishment and trumpeting of a system of "industrial centrals" (in 1969)[11] and workers' councils (in 1971).[12] In both the industrial and agricultural sectors private enterprise was also minimal, represented by individual artisans and small private plots. Plans, quotas, and central control of prices, wages, and credit—rather than

8. Fischer discusses the reforms in "Participatory Reforms," pp. 217–30; see also Kenneth Jowitt, "Political Innovation in Rumania," *Survey* 20 (Autumn 1974), pp. 132–51.

9. See Nelson, *Democratic Centralism*, pp. 51ff.; Jowitt, "Political Innovation," pp. 138–39; Alan H. Smith, "Romanian Economic Reforms," in NATO, Economic and Information Directorates, *Economic Reforms in Eastern Europe and Prospects for the 1980s* (Elmsford, N.Y.: Pergamon, 1981), pp. 37–38.

10. See Jan Triska and Paul Johnson, *Political Development and Political Change in Eastern Europe: A Comparative Study* (Denver: University of Denver, Monograph Series in World Affairs, 1975), pp. 11–16.

11. See Michael Garmarinikow, "Balance Sheet on Economic Reforms," in Joint Economic Committee, *Reorientation and Commercial Relations of the Economies of Eastern Europe*, 93d Cong., 2d sess., 1974, p. 208.

12. Daniel Nelson, "Workers in a Workers' State," in Nelson, ed., *Romania in the 1980s* (Boulder: Westview, 1981), p. 177.

market forces—determined the cost and supply of factors and commodities, the direction of the economy, and the population's standard of living.[13]

Economic policies during this period reflected the party's program of rapid and broad development. Targets were set high and often revised upward; and goals of the Five Year Plan were subject to campaigns for fulfillment in four-and-a-half years. Economic growth, especially in industry, was the most rapid in the region. For the 1970–75 period, net material product grew by more than 11 percent per year; 14 percent per year in industry and 11 percent per year in transportation and communication.[14] Investment growth was similarly high (averaging over 11% annually for 1971–75 and exceeding 15% in 1975). Industry took the lion's share of investment (57.2%) to the disadvantage and neglect of agriculture (16.1%). Consequently, agricultural growth was quite uneven, averaging half the growth rate of industry.

For its rapid expansion the Romanian economy at first relied primarily on its own resources. Industry's demand for workers was satisfied by drawing from the agricultural labor force. Forestry and agriculture's share of the labor force fell from 49 percent in 1970 to 34 percent in 1975.[15] The financial demands were met by restricting consumption; in the years from 1971 to 1975, for example, the government allocated only 8.4 percent of all funds invested in industry to the production of consumer goods.[16] External borrowing was modest. In 1976 Romania's gross debt ($2.9 billion) and debt-to-export ratio (18%) were the lowest in Eastern Europe, excluding Czechoslovakia.[17] From 1972 to 1975 the ratio of increase in debt to that in gross national product (GNP) was 10 percent, also the lowest except for Czechoslovakia.[18] The country supplied most of its own energy. Energy imports in 1975 constituted 15 percent of Romania's energy consumption, the lowest in Eastern Europe, and Romania was by far the largest net exporter of oil

13. See World Bank, *Romania*, pp. 34–73.

14. Thad P. Alton, "Comparative Structure and Growth of Economic Activity in Eastern Europe," in Joint Economic Committee, *East European Economies Post-Helsinki*, 95th Cong., 1st sess., 1977, p. 239. Calculated as GNP, the respective rates are 6.2%, 9.4%, and 8.6%; see Thad P. Alton et al., "Economic Growth in Eastern Europe 1965, 1970, and 1975–1980," Research Project on National Income in East Central Europe, *Occasional Papers* (New York: L. W. International Financial Research, 1981), p. 25. For a discussion of the uncertainties of Romanian national statistics, see Paul A. Marer, *Evaluation of the National Accounts, Prices, Exchange Rates and Growth Rates of the USSR, Eastern Europe and Cuba, with Alternative Estimates of Their Dollar GNPs* (Washington, D.C.: World Bank, 1985), pp. 109–110, 115–19, 127–30, 140.

15. World Bank, *Romania*, p. 139.

16. Marvin R. Jackson, "Industrialization, Trade, and Mobilization in Romania's Drive for Economic Independence," in Joint Economic Committee, *East European Economies Post-Helsinki*, 95th Cong., 1st sess., 1977, p. 914.

17. Joan Parpart Zoeter, "Eastern Europe: The Hard Currency Debt," in Joint Economic Committee, *East European Economic Assessment*, pt. 2, *Regional Assessments*, 97th Cong., 1st sess., 1981, pp. 729, 730.

18. See Paul Marer, "Economic Performance, Strategy, and Prospects in Eastern Europe," in Joint Economic Committee, *East European Economies Post-Helsinki*, 95th Cong., 1st sess., 1977, pp. 542, 543.

and natural gas in the region.[19] Industrialization did require an expanding supply of imported machinery and raw materials, both of which came in increasing amounts from capitalist countries.[20] Still, as Marvin Jackson points out, Romanian economic development during this period was essentially self-sufficient. As a share of total invested equipment, for example, imported and Western equipment declined over the period of rapic economic development.[21]

Despite the unbalanced development picture, most indicators show improvements in the standard of living during this period, though it still remained the lowest in Eastern Europe.[22] Unlike the new Gierek regime in Poland or the fearful administration of Gustav Husak in Czechoslovakia, the Romanian party leaders had no demon of social upheaval pushing them to stock the marketplace with consumer goods. The regime's firm social control, combined with slow but steady economic improvement and the non-Eastern-bloc orientation of foreign policy (discussed below), substituted for the extension of political freedom or individual enrichment as sources of regime legitimacy.

Moreover, unlike the policies of its allies which were increasingly aimed at satisfying social demands and responding to the needs articulated by representatives of particular sectors, Romania's policies were devoted to broader long-term national goals defined by Ceauşescu. Taken together these goals defined an ideology which, like the raison d'etat Schwartzman suggests and the tradition Weber stressed, operated as the major limitation on—as well as rationale for—Ceauşescu's actions.

After taking over leadership of the RCP in 1965, Ceauşescu pursued a policy promoting the "multilateral development" of Romania; that is, the achievement of a modern, multifaceted, industrially based economy, no longer confined to the second-class status of producer of primary materials. Like his predecessor Gheorghe Gheorghiu-Dej, Ceauşescu put the country on a path designed to expand the nonagricultural sector rapidly, taking advantage of natural and human resources and international opportunities.[23] The campaign for the country's multilateral development made the party the prime

19. Central Intelligence Agency, *Energy Supplies in Eastern Europe: A Statistical Compilation* (Washington, D.C.: National Technical Information Service, 1979), pp. 11, 14 (comparison excludes the Soviet Union). However, also during this period coal production fell below consumption for the first time since 1960. Ibid., p. 68.

20. See John M. Montias, "Romania's Foreign Trade: An Overview," in Joint Economic Committee, *East European Economies Post-Helsinki*, 95th Cong., 1st sess., 1977, pp. 865–85.

21. Marvin R. Jackson, "Perspectives on Romania's Economic Development in the 1980s," in Daniel Nelson, ed., *Romania in the 1980s* (Boulder: Westview, 1981), p. 271.

22. Edwin M. Snell estimates the Romanian standard of living in 1975 to be at 40–50% that of East Germany. See "East European Economies between the Soviets and the Capitalists," in Joint Economic Committee, *East European Economies Post-Helsinki*, 95th Cong., 1st sess., 1977, p. 27.

23. See Jowitt, *Revolutionary Breakthroughs*; John M. Montias, *Economic Development in Communist Rumania* (Cambridge: MIT Press, 1967); and Ronald H. Linden, *Bear and Foxes: The International Relations of the East European States* (Boulder: East European Quarterly, 1979; distributed by Columbia University Press, New York), pp. 177–203.

mover behind (and in front of) Romania's advancement into the modern world while mobilizing the population to discharge the tasks necessary to achieve this end.

The campaign also accorded with the needs of the leader and party to achieve political mobilization. For example, it fit well with the regime's use of nationalism (such as in foreign policy) to build its own legitimacy. It allowed the party to promise and for a time to point to substantial economic achievements attributable to the system (socialism) and the country (Romania). Rapid development also meshed with the regime's goal of maintaining its political monopoly by co-opting, buying off, or suppressing firmly any potential or real opponents. Boosting Romanian nationalism served to establish clear limits of behavior for the country's minorities, primarily the 2 million Hungarians.[24] Economic progress allowed for the provision of some payoffs to the party faithful and to workers, especially those in important sectors. At the Eleventh Party Congress (1974) Ceauşescu pointed to a 23 percent increase in real salaries (from 1970 to 1975). But while the minimum salary increase was 42 percent, that for a skilled worker increased 60 percent and started from a higher base.[25]

Finally, the penetrating party control over the state and economy that multilateral development necessitated further enhanced the party's social and political control. The formal upgrading of various existing institutions, the establishment of new ones, such as the workers' councils, and the institution of multicandidate elections to the GNA were intended both to improve the party's penetration of political organs and to demonstrate its genuine ties to the working class.

Despite the quadrupling of oil prices in 1973 and 1974 and the recession in the Western economies, Romania's plans for the 1976–80 period continued the trends of the previous period: high growth rates and high investment, especially in energy-intensive heavy industries—steel, chemicals, and refining—and increased foreign trade, including in petroleum. According to the plan approved at the Eleventh Congress and subsequently revised *upward*, overall growth was to increase by 11 percent per year, with a similar rate for industrial output. Labor productivity, agricultural output, investment, and foreign trade were all to grow at rates higher than the already high rates achieved during 1971–75.

But the country's vigorous growth did not continue during the second half

24. See the letter to the Central Committee by Karoly Kiraly, former alternate member of the RCP Presidium and member of the Central Committee, in the *New York Times*, 1 February 1978, p. 23. See also Manuel Lucbert, "La minorité hongroise de Transylvanie est nécontente de son sort," *Le Monde*, 5 May 1978, p. 4; Paul Lendvai, "Achilles heel of Romanian nationalism," *Financial Times*, 31 January 1978.

25. See Nicolae Ceauşescu, "Raportul Comitetului Central cu Privire la Activitatea Partidului Comunist Român în Perioada dintre Congresul al X-lea şi Congresul al XI-lea şi Sarcinile de viitor ale Partidului," in *Congresul al XI-lea Partidului Comunist Român* (Bucharest: Editura Politică, 1975), p. 56.

of the 1970s and the early 1980s. The growth of GNP, which had averaged 6.2 percent for 1971–75, declined to below 5.0 percent for 1975–80 and for 1979 and 1980 grew at 4.3 and 0.1 percent, respectively. By 1980 industrial growth had fallen to half its 1970–75 rate, while agriculture turned in consecutive disastrous years in 1979 and 1980.[26] The growth in labor productivity slowed (2.4% in 1981, as compared to the planned 7.0%).[27] Exhaustion of the country's labor pool, in terms of both its structure and absolute numbers available, made it difficult to continue to shift workers from agriculture or, indeed, to expand in any area. The growth of heavy industry and especially the huge expansion of the oil-refining sector—from 18.5 million tons annually (mta) in 1973 to 33.0 mta by 1980—had produced dramatic increases in the amounts of crude oil that Romania imported. From 5.1 million tons in 1975, Romanian imports grew to 12.5 million tons in 1979 and included for the first time Soviet oil (350,000 tons). At the same time, domestic production peaked at 14.6 million tons in 1977 and declined to 11.6 million tons by 1981.[28] Although its refining capacity did allow the country to reexport a substantial amount of that oil,[29] the amount was insufficient to cover a chronic hard-currency deficit in machinery, manufactured goods, and raw materials; nor could the weaker agricultural sector compensate. By 1978 Romania's trade deficit with developed capitalist countries exceeded $800 million, while the modest surplus run with less developed countries (LDCs) at the beginning of the 1970s had become a $660 million deficit.[30] Increasingly, the Romanians took advantage of outside sources of financing, including commercial loans and government-backed credits, as well as loans from the International Monetary Fund (IMF) and the World Bank. Though the debt-service ratio remained modest (25% in 1979), total debt grew rapidly, more than doubling in four years. By 1982 the servicing demand ($2.6 billion) proved more than the country could manage and Bucharest demanded a rescheduling from its creditors.[31]

26. Alton et al., "Economic Growth in Eastern Europe," p. 25; for detailed data on agricultural production see Thad Alton et al., "Agricultural Output, Expenses and Depreciation, Gross Product and Net Product in Eastern Europe 1965, 1970, and 1975–1980," Research Project on National Income in East Central Europe, *Occasional Papers* (New York: L. W. International Financial Research, 1981).

27. *România Liberă*, 12 February 1982, p. 1, and Agerpress, 6 October 1980 [Foreign Broadcast Information Service, 17 October 1980, p. H4]; hereafter cited as FBIS.

28. Direcţia Centrală de Statistică, *Anuarul Statistic al Republicii Socialiste România, 1980* (Bucharest: Direcţia Centrală de Statistică, 1981), p. 179, and U.S. Embassy, "Romania: Key Economic Indicators" (Mimeo, Bucharest, 1982).

29. In 1981 Romanian export of oil products earned $2.2 billion and represented 17% of the country's exports (in dollar value); see Wharton Econometric Forecasting Associates (hereafter cited as Wharton), "Romanian Foreign Trade and Balance of Payments during January–June 1982 and Outlook for the Rest of 1982," *Centrally Planned Economies: Current Analysis,* no. 89, 8 November 1982, p. 4.

30. Wharton, Centrally Planned Economies Foreign Trade Databank (Washington, D.C.: Wharton, 1982); hereafter cited as Wharton Foreign Trade Databank.

31. *Economist,* 24 April 1982; *Financial Times,* 8 December 1982, p. 14; a second agreement was also reached covering 1983 obligations. See *Financial Times,* 7 February 1983.

The uses of foreign policy

In contrast to the orthodox, centrally planned rigidities of the domestic structure, Romania's pattern of foreign relations at the beginning of the 1970s was innovative, flexible, and generally out of step with those of its allies in Eastern Europe. Romanian foreign policy played a crucial dual role for the RCP. Concomitant with its desire to make rapid progress in economic development, Romania had pursued since the early 1960s a policy of seeking economic ties with the West. At the same time, its international positions and ideological statements established and embellished a framework for such a policy which both appealed to Romanian nationalism and supported the legitimacy of the Ceauşescu regime.

The Romanian party had been directing its efforts toward rapid and broad industrialization since the days of its Second Congress (1955). While this goal occasionally coincided with Soviet notions of the "simultaneous transition" of all the East European states to socialism, by the beginning of the 1960s Nikita Khrushchev seemed more interested in specialization within the CMEA. As producers mainly of primary products, the Romanians feared that a policy of economic specialization would leave them as they were before the war: the "gas station and breadbasket" of (Eastern) Europe.

After struggling with Moscow behind the scenes for a time, Romania in 1964 publicly rejected Soviet notions of organizing the CMEA along lines of economic specialization. As Bucharest saw it, this would have clearly circumscribed Romania's international and domestic options: "Our party has very clearly expressed its point of view, declaring that, since the essence of the projected measures lies in shifting some functions of economic management from the competence of the respective state to that of superstate bodies or organisms, these measures are not in keeping with the principles that underlie the relations among the socialist countries."[32]

Bucharest backed up these assertions with a pattern of economic and political interactions quite unlike the patterns of its allies.[33] From 1960 to 1970 the Soviet–East European share of Romanian trade fell from roughly two-thirds to less than one-half.[34] Romania especially increased involvement with West Germany and in 1967 became the first state in Eastern Europe

32. "Statement on the Stand of the Rumanian Workers' Party Concerning the Problems of the International Communist and Working Class Movement" (April 1964), text in William E. Griffith, *Sino-Soviet Relations: 1964–65* (Cambridge: MIT Press, 1970), pp. 269–96, quote is from p. 282. See the discussion in Montias, *Economic Development*, pp. 187–230.

33. See Linden, *Bear and Foxes*, pp. 10–52, 177–203.

34. Trade statistics for these periods can be found in Paul Marer, *Soviet and East European Foreign Trade, 1946–1979* (Bloomington: Indiana University Press, 1972), pp. 30, 40; Montias, "Romania's Foreign Trade"; Direcţia Centrală de Statistică, *Anuarul Statistic al Republicii Socialiste România, 19–* (Bucharest: Direcţia Centrală de Statistică, annual); and Direcţia Centrală de Statistică, *Comerţul Exterior al Republicii Socialist Român, 1973* (Bucharest: Direcţia Centrală de Statistică, n.d.).

(preceding even Yugoslavia) to extend diplomatic relations to that country. It pursued economic and political contacts on a global instead of a regional scale, with the aim of supporting in principle and in concrete terms its rapid economic development.

When the CMEA's "comprehensive program" was adopted in 1971, the Romanians continued to insist on the sovereignty of national economies and the sanctity of the "interested party" approach to involvement in CMEA projects. Romania did not, for example, join the first CMEA-sponsored international industrial association, *interatominstrument*, formed in 1982.[35] In its relations with the Soviet Union and its other allies, as well as with the world at large, the Romanians asserted both national and party prerogatives. They rejected notions of "limited sovereignty"[36] and the idea that there could be a dominant "leading center" of the world communist movement.[37] Under Ceauşescu the RCP elucidated an international policy based as much on old-fashioned nationalism as on proletarian internationalism.

Many of these assertions put Romania at odds with its East European allies and with the Soviet Union, especially when its actions—for example, its extensive contacts with China—demonstrated Romanian willingness to pay more than lip service to its stated philosophy. Its participation in the Warsaw Pact (WTO) was limited, as measured by several indexes, including its nonparticipation and condemnation of WTO actions against Czechoslovakia; its extremely limited participation in WTO maneuvers and frequent nonparticipation in WTO efforts to coordinate foreign policy; and its consistently low expenditures for national defense.[38] Within the world communist movement Romania underscored its support for the autonomy of individual parties by maintaining its contacts with independent ruling parties, such as that of Yugoslavia, as well as with such anathemas to the Soviet Union as the nonruling Communist party of Italy.

Probably the most significant new aspect of Romania's international policy under Ceauşescu was the shift in Romania's self-definition from a socialist country to a "socialist developing country." In this Romania sought to dif-

35. Zbigniew Fallenbuchl, "East European Integration: COMECON," in Joint Economic Committee, *Reorientation and Commercial Relations of the Economies of Eastern Europe*, 93d Cong., 2d sess., 1974, p. 105.

36. See Ceausescu's speeches of 29 November 1968 and 7 February 1969, both in *Romania on the Way of Completing Socialist Construction*, vol. 3 (Bucharest: Meridane, 1969), pp. 682–83, and 826. See also Nicolai Ecobescu and Sergiu Celac, *Politica externă a României Socialiste* (Bucharest: Editura Politică, 1975).

37. See Ceauşescu, "Raportul," pp. 41–42; see also Jowitt, *Revolutionary Breakthroughs*, pp. 233–72.

38. For the Romanian attitude toward Czechoslovakia and other WTO-coordinated positions, see Linden, *Bear and Foxes*, pp. 53ff. For a list of WTO maneuvers, see Christopher D. Jones, *Soviet Influence in Eastern Europe* (New York: Praeger, 1981), pp. 301–8. Romanian defense expenditures as a percentage of GNP were the lowest in Eastern Europe for 1970–73; see Thad P. Alton et al., "Military Expenditures in Eastern Europe: Some Alternative Estimates," in Joint Economic Committee, *Reorientation and Commercial Relations of the Economies of Eastern Europe*, 93d Cong., 2d sess., 1974, pp. 502–3.

TABLE 1. *Interaction pattern for Romania and Czechoslovakia, 1970–71*

	Romania		Czechoslovakia	
Target	*Interaction Score (IS)*[a]	*Percentage of Total IS*	*Interaction Score (IS)*[a]	*Percentage of Total IS*
Albania	—	—	—	—
Other communist countries	36	9.4	19	5.2
China	35	9.1	3	0.8
Eastern Europe	80	20.8	143	39.5
Soviet Union	47	12.2	111	30.7
Yugoslavia	28	7.3	15	4.1
Neutral/Nonaligned	86	22.3	53	14.6
Europe	—		10	
Middle East	14		28	
Africa	59		2	
Asia	13		13	
West	57	14.8	13	3.6
Europe	49			
Middle East[b]	5		1	
Asia	3		7	
Latin America			5	
West Germany	8	2.1	5	1.4
United States	8	2.1	—	—
TOTAL	385	100[c]	362	100[c]

a. For the derivation of the Interaction Score see Appendix.
b. Iran.
c. Percentages may not total 100 due to rounding.

ferentiate itself from its more developed socialist neighbors and at the same time to receive preferential treatment from them and from noncommunist countries and organizations, for example, the European Economic Community (EEC). This redefinition, which Ceauşescu introduced in 1972,[39] gained greater significance for Romanian foreign policy later in the decade—leading, for example, to its strong support for the idea of establishing a New International Economic Order and a general "democratization" of international relations.

Romania's overall interaction patterns reflect its broadening choice of partners. As Table 1 illustrates, Romania's 1970–71 Interaction Score (measuring international visits and agreements; for derivation, see Appendix) with Western states (targets labeled West, West Germany, and United States)

39. See Ceauşescu's speech to the 1972 National Party Conference, in *Romania on the Way of Building up the Multilaterally Developed Socialist Society*, vol. 7 (Bucharest: Meridane, 1973), pp. 519–20.

TABLE 2. *Interaction pattern for Romania and Czechoslovakia, 1975–76*

Target	Romania Interaction Score (IS)[a]	Romania Percentage of Total IS	Czechoslovakia Interaction Score (IS)[a]	Czechoslovakia Percentage of Total IS
Albania	2	0.4	—	—
Other communist countries	28	5.3	60	10.2
China	22	4.2	1	0.2
Eastern Europe	88	16.6	126	21.4
Soviet Union	44	8.3	118	20.1
Yugoslavia	12	2.3	12	2.0
Neutral/Nonaligned	182	34.3	115	19.6
Europe	25		27	
Middle East	71		32	
Africa	58		31	
Asia	32		25	
Latin America	17		—	
Israel	5	0.9		
West	131	24.7	143	24.3
Europe	86		114	
Middle East[b]	15		17	
Asia	24		5	
Latin America	6		7	
West Germany	4	0.8	13	2.2
United States	17	3.2	—	—
TOTAL	530	100[c]	588	100[c]

a. For the derivation of the Interaction Score see Appendix.
b. Iran.
c. Percentages may not total 100 due to rounding.

constituted 19 percent of its total Interaction Score, while its score with neutral and nonaligned countries accounted for over 22 percent. By contrast, the figures for Czechoslovakia are 6.0 percent and 14.6 percent. By 1975–76 (Table 2) Romanian interaction levels with neutral and nonaligned countries exceeded those for the Soviet Union and Eastern Europe combined (which declined), while those with Western target groups increased (28.7% total). Thus Ceaușescu's redefinition of Romania as a developing country was made a diplomatic reality at the expense of Romania's WTO allies, not its involvement with the West. While Czechoslovakia's interactions with the West also increased by 1975–76, the Soviet–East European share of its Interaction Score remained substantially higher. Romania also broadened the range of its interactions within the neutral and nonaligned group, increasing levels of involvement with the Middle East (the highest of the neutral, nonaligned targets in 1975–76) and with Asian and European neutral and nonaligned states.

Romania's economic interactions reflected its growing involvement with nonsocialist partners and included several "firsts" for East European states. It began participating in the General Agreement on Tariffs and Trade (GATT) in 1971, joined the IMF and World Bank in 1972, and in 1973 became the first CMEA country to receive generalized trade preferences from the EEC. In 1971 it became the first state in the region to allow joint ventures to operate within its borders. Between 1970 and 1974 Romanian exports to and imports from developed capitalist countries more than tripled in value, while the respective increases with CMEA countries were 57 and 43 percent. Machinery, raw materials, and semimanufactured products made up the bulk of the Western imports (95%) and constituted from 45 to 46 percent of Romania's imports of these goods. By 1974 Romania's trade with the developed capitalist countries surpassed that with CMEA states.[40] Also during the early 1970s Romania's exports to LDCs grew from 12.3 percent of its total to 23.0 percent and its imports from them increased from 7.5 percent to 15.9 percent.[41]

In addition to supporting its international search for the wherewithal to pursue rapid, broad economic development, Romania's foreign policy served an important domestic purpose. By establishing a unique Romanian posture on the international level and staking out distinctively non-Soviet positions, the RCP in general and Ceauşescu in particular used foreign policy as an instrument of legitimation. Romania's foreign policy established a link between regime and populace which could not be ensured in other ways, such as through individual economic prosperity—still a long-run proposition—or a genuine opening up of political or economic processes—a choice the government perceived as having more dangers than rewards.

Romania's assertion of differing and occasionally controversial foreign-policy positions, from the regime's point of view, placed it securely within the country's long historical tradition of diplomatic ingenuity. It also protected its prerogatives against encroachment by friends as well as enemies and allowed Ceauşescu to achieve, at relatively low cost, a visibility for himself and the country disproportionate to its size and influence. Taking a position in support of full national sovereignty, for example, allowed Ceauşescu simultaneously to oppose the bifurcation of Europe into military blocs, to assert the role and rights of the smaller, less developed states, to serve in principle and in practice the needs of Romanian economic development, to reject Soviet interference in Romania's internal affairs, and to strike a states-

40. Data in Montias, "Romania's Foreign Trade," pp. 872, 882–85.
41. Data from Marvin R. Jackson, "Romania's Economy at the End of the 1970s: Turning the Corner on Intensive Development," in Joint Economic Committee, *East European Economic Assessment*, pt. 1, *Country Studies, 1980*, 97th Cong., 1st sess., 1981, p. 272; years compared are 1970 and 1975.

manlike posture that appealed both to Western countries and to his own countrymen.

The early and mid-1970s produced no dramatic conflicts with Moscow, as the invasion of Czechoslovakia had. But the flourishing of detente and concurrent East-West economic contacts and the favorable economic environment of the period proved propitious for the Romanian international strategy—for a while. Only after—in fact, substantially after—this environment deteriorated did some aspects of Romania's foreign-policy change as part of the country's overall adjustment to international economic disruption.

The pattern of Romania's reaction

Romania's response to the first oil shock did not differ markedly from those of other East European states: despite its extensive involvement with the noncommunist world economy, it made minimal adjustments. The country's overall economic situation, comparatively more favorable than that of its allies, made this possible; the leadership structure and the ideology of the leader himself made it likely. When the regime finally did shift its domestic and international policies, its actions were all the more dramatic and severe because of that structure and that ideology.

In the mid-1970s Romanian economic growth continued to be robust, oil imports continued to grow, and investment remained very high. This was possible, in part, because of economic factors that were to change by the end of the decade. For example, while Romania was the leading CMEA importer of OPEC oil, neither the amount nor the uses to which it was put were significant enough to resonate through the economy. In 1974 Romania was able to supply 86 percent of its needs from domestic energy resources (compared to an average of 56% for the other East European states).[42] Domestic production of all energy supplies was still growing, as was the regime's ability to draw from the agricultural labor force to support industrial development. While the Western recession certainly hurt Romanian exports, dropping the developed capitalist countries' share from 39 percent in 1974 to 28 percent in 1977, the regime's active cultivation of friends and markets among the LDCs took up a large part of that slack. The LDC's share of Romanian exports grew from 17.6 percent in 1974 to 24.2 percent in 1977.

Romania's trade deficit with the West, though substantial and growing, was less than one-fourth that of Poland and was mitigated by Romania's ability to negotiate preferential treatment with the EEC and favorable loan terms with the IMF and World Bank. The country's debt of $2.9 billion

42. Figure for Romania is from Jackson, "Industrialization, Trade and Mobilization," p. 922; for the other states (figures are 1975) see CIA, *Energy Supplies*, p. 11. Excluding Poland, the figure for the other East European states is 50%.

(1976) was not troubling, whether measured on a per capita basis or in comparison to the country's resources or vigorously growing economy. In addition, of course, the jump in petroleum and other commodity prices in the mid-1970s benefited Romania because of the structure of its trade, which included the reexport of processed petroleum products.[43]

Most crucially, the regime's nearly total control over the accumulation and disposition of the country's natural and earned resources allowed it to continue to force high levels of investment into industry and to restrict individual consumption. Unlike Poland, Romania's Western strategy did not have as a component the rapid increase of consumer satisfaction in order to purchase social peace and political acquiescence. These were ensured through the carrot of Romanian nationalism and the stick of harsh suppression.

By the time of the second oil shock, however, key domestic circumstances had changed, making it less possible to avoid reacting. First, Romanian oil production had peaked, necessitating greater dependence on OPEC-supplied oil; until 1979 Romania bought no Soviet oil. Second, exploitation of the country's human resources was also reaching its limit. The shift of agricultural labor into industry had essentially been completed by 1978.[44] In addition, the slackening growth of the whole labor force was becoming a problem.

The Romanian economy was also beset by many of the problems that affected the other East European states—problems which could be overlooked in times of easy credit and abundant energy at low prices but which made the country more vulnerable to serious disruption than it might have appeared. These included artificial full employment, unrealistically low factor prices necessitating state subsidies, rigid bureaucratic central state control, and a lack of incentive for enterprises to improve efficiency or take initiatives. In Romania years of unbalanced investment in industry to the neglect of agriculture compounded such problems. Thus, when the country needed to increase food production to cover increasing external costs, the capacity was not there. At the same time, the huge investments in petrochemical refining made Romania a kind of "Rotterdam of the East" at a time when more sensitive economies were scaling back on their use of imported petroleum. This left the energy sector unable to return the investment and soon substantially idle.

Finally, the Ceauşescu regime's first serious labor strike brought into question the regime's ability to push the work force to ever higher levels of production. In August 1977 mine workers in the coal-producing Jiu Valley went on strike, closed the mines, and occupied party headquarters. Among their demands were better working conditions and an improved supply of

43. Marer, "Economic Performance, Strategy and Prospects," pp. 540–44; Jackson, "Romania's Economy," p. 287.
44. See data in Jackson, "Perspectives on Romania's Economic Development," pp. 256–57.

consumer goods. When several levels of party officialdom failed to resolve the issue, Ceauşescu went to the area himself where, during an angry meeting, he promised various reforms.[45]

In response to the strike the regime did improve some of the immediate conditions, but it also dismissed the leaders of the strike. Coming roughly one year after the food price riots in Poland, the Jiu Valley action seems to have spurred the regime to put forth at least the semblance of a mechanism to increase worker involvement in, if not control over, enterprise direction. In 1978, with substantial fanfare, workers' self-management was introduced as part of a broad economic reform. The powers of the existing workers' councils were strengthened, and through their assemblies workers were to gain a greater say in enterprise financing and planning and in the distribution of the profits of enterprises. At the same time, the New Economic Mechanism (NEM) itself was introduced, designed to improve economic performance through a system of financial incentives and penalties. For example, the NEM increased the maximum amount of funds an enterprise could dispose of on its own under optimal conditions.[46] Formal participation in the government was also expanded: in 1979 the number of GNA elections in which more than one candidate stood for election was increased.

But the granting of greater formal responsibility in the government and economy was effectively circumvented by an increase in direct party influence either through cadres, directives, or both. The workers' self-management system, like the earlier reorganization of "industrial centrals," increased rather than decreased party involvement in enterprise management. For example, beginning in 1978 workers' councils, the vehicles for self-management, were headed by the party first secretary for the enterprise. And legal restrictions limited the representation of workers on the councils to minority levels. As Alan Smith describes workers' self-management in Romania, "the combination of the principle [self-management] with the single-national plan . . . indicated that it should not in any way be confused with Yugoslav-type self-management."[47] Multicandidate elections for the essentially powerless GNA held even less significance, and in any case the party retained control over nomination procedures.[48]

The Twelfth Party Congress in 1979 continued the introduction of formal reforms. Here Ceauşescu suggested that each county should be responsible for its own provisioning (*autoprovizionarea*); the appropriate laws were enacted in late 1981.[49] But the introduction of *autoprovizionarea* was not ac-

45. *New York Times*, 27 November 1977, pp. 1, 3; RFER, 12 August 1977, 26 October 1977.
46. Smith, "Romanian Economic Reforms," pp. 48–52.
47. Ibid., p. 51; see also the discussion in Nelson, "Workers in a Workers' State," pp. 174–91.
48. See Mary Ellen Fischer, "Nicolae Ceauşescu and the Romanian Political Leadership: Nationalization and Personalization of Power," Edwin M. Moseley Faculty Research Lecture, Skidmore College, 1982, p. 34.
49. *România Liberă*, 30 October 1981, p. 2; *Scînteia*, 3 December 1981, pp. 1, 2.

companied by devolution of authority over securing or allocating resources — powers that would have enabled counties to fulfill their new responsibilities. Moreover, the party's first secretary for the county was also the head of the county people's council, ensuring continued central control.

Both the system of self-provisioning and workers' self-management in fact became added tools with which to achieve mobilization as the regime began to react to harsher economic realities. The basis of mobilization shifted during this period to emphasize the present situation — difficult but heavenly compared to the past or to the miserable situation in the capitalist countries; and the brighter future that present sacrifices would make possible.[50] In addition, the expansion of formal participation, mentioned above, and other changes, such as the increase in the number of workers in the party, were also used to compensate for and legitimate further reductions in public consumption. The New Economic Mechanism and especially the system of self-provisioning also provided a way for the central regime to deflect responsibility from itself for the country's deteriorating economic situation.[51]

In the economic realm, mobilization for growth was replaced by campaigns for efficiency, reduction in consumption of resources, personal sacrifice, and improved production of key raw materials and exportable goods. As the regime's ability to draw on a continuously growing labor force leveled off, it had to rely on such campaigns, administrative shifting of workers, some economic incentives, and the use of the army and "volunteers" to maintain production levels.

At the same time, public pronouncements took another form, one rarely seen in the early 1970s. Virtually every speech of Ceauşescu's and, in appropriate measure, of his subordinates criticized poor performance, waste of resources, lack of discipline, even corruption.[52] The aim was twofold: 1) to spur party activists to greater contributions toward meeting the country's real needs; and 2) to convince the party and the population at large that no activities such as those in Poland were necessary in Romania because the regime was responsive and responsible.

Malleable though the population was in the face of the RCP's tight control, Ceauşescu clearly feared at least the possibility of a Romanian Solidarity. Thus, while sacrifice did become the general watchword, some sectors received dispensation and even increased incentives for production: miners, and metal and oil workers received bonuses and salary increases, and farmers received

---

50. See, for example, Ceauşescu's speech at the Congress of Working People's Councils, *Scînteia*, 13 September 1980, pp. 1–2.

51. See, for example, Ceauşescu's speech at Braşov, in *România pe Drumul Construirii Societăţii Socialiste Multilateral Dezvoltate*, vol. 21 (Bucharest: Editura Politică, 1981), pp. 307–27.

52. See *Scînteia*, 17 October 1980, p. 2; Bucharest Domestic Service, 26 October 1980; *Scînteia*, 18 December 1980, pp. 1, 3. See also the Twelfth Congress speeches of Ilie Verdeţ (prime minister), Cornel Burtica (minister of foreign trade), and Paul Niculescu (minister of finance), all of whom subsequently lost their jobs, in *Scînteia*, 21–23 November 1979.

higher prices for crops and bonuses.[53] Some compensatory pay or pension increases usually accompanied price increases.[54] With these actions, the regime hoped to head off possible agitation among workers who had troubled the regime in the past, namely the miners; to improve production in crucial areas of the economy; and, especially in the case of agricultural prices, to rationalize the existing price structure.

Evidently all these measures failed to improve economic performance or party control, because in 1982 "public instructors" were appointed to oversee "political-ideological" as well as educational and cultural activity throughout the country.[55] And the regime contined to employ direct repression to ensure if not economic productivity at least political quiescence. Even before the birth of Solidarity, the Romanian government had crushed an embryonic free trade-union movement, and dissent of all types was subject to severe government action.[56] Restrictions on minorities—especially the Hungarians— by most accounts, increased.[57]

Belatedly, Romanian economic strategy also changed. The 1981–85 Five-Year Economic Plan, which had several incarnations, called for an annual growth rate in social product of just over 6 percent, and in industry of under 9 percent (the latter a downward revision from original directives). Significantly, the plan called for agricultural production to grow at 4.5–5.0 percent, a substantial improvement over previous years. Overall investment was to grow much more slowly than it had in the past (just over 5.0%) with a slight increase in agriculture's share. In addition the regime adopted a separate agricultural plan for the period, specifying among other things that the largest growth (except for agricultural services) would occur in the volume of agricultural trade (9.0%). The plan scheduled coal production to more than triple by 1985 while both natural gas and oil production were to double. The highest growth overall (except for services) was to occur in foreign trade, nearly 12 percent per year, a revision upward from plan directives. Export growth was to increase even more. This growth was to occur, however, while the country achieved a 40 percent *reduction* in the consumption of energy by 1990.[58]

53. *Scînteia*, 1 November 1980, p. 3; 19 December 1980, p. 7, and *România Liberă*, 17 December 1981, pp. 1, 2.

54. *România Liberă*, 15 February 1982, pp. 1–3.

55. *Scînteia*, 9 February 1982, p. 1.

56. RFER, 19 March 1979; see also Trond Gilberg, "Modernization, Human Rights and Nationalism: The Case of Romania," in George Klein and Milan Reban, eds., *The Politics of Ethnicity in Eastern Europe* (Boulder: *East European Quarterly*, 1981; distributed by Columbia University Press, New York), pp. 204–6.

57. In 1980 Karoly Kiraly published a second letter updating the regime's policy toward the Hungarian minority; see RFER, 22 July 1980.

58. For all figures, compare the Twelfth Party Congress directives given in *Congresul al XII-lea Partidul Comunist Român* (Bucharest: Editura Politică, 1981), pp. 690–91, with the plan as finally adopted (*România Liberă*, 2 July 1981, pp. 1–4. The congress directives did not specify an agricultural share of overall investment, but Ceauşescu's report indicated that of 1300–1350 billion lei to be invested, approximately 155 billion lei (or 11.7%) would be devoted

Domestic consumption was to be suppressed not only by reducing investment levels but also by severely restricting personal consumption and the growth of individual income. Between the Twelfth Congress (1979) and the adoption of the plan in mid-1981, the regime revised downward all indicators of personal income. Prices were increased for virtually every category of purchases; power cuts and restrictions were instituted in 1979 and 1982; and food rationing and shortages became common in 1981 and 1982.

Foreign policy remained a key element of the regime's political mobilization strategy, but for the most part the late 1970s did not produce salient issues or crises on which the regime could capitalize. Some issues, such as the dispute with the Soviet Union over the proposed increases in defense spending in late 1978 and the arms race, were exploited for domestic purposes.[59] But on the occasion of more compelling Soviet actions, such as the invasion of Afghanistan in late 1979, there was no similar display.

On the international level, Romania's adjustment predictably included a drive to increase exports and reduce imports, especially from hard-currency countries. Between 1974 and 1977 exports to the developed West had shown virtually no growth, while exports to CMEA states had grown by two-thirds. This trend was reversed during 1978–81: exports to the West grew by two-thirds but to CMEA states by only 40 percent. Imports from the West also rebounded in 1978 and 1979 but leveled off again in 1980 and fell (by 6.6%) in 1981. Romanian imports of machinery from developed capitalist countries, which had more than doubled from 1976 to 1978, fell by more than 20 percent in the next two years, and the regime also cut back imports of raw materials. Romania cut its trade deficit with the developed West roughly in half in 1979 and turned a surplus in 1980 and 1981. Trade with LDCs nearly doubled but after 1977 was substantially in deficit because of a 430 percent increase in the cost of imported fuel.[60] In 1981 the deficit with LDCs was cut; oil imports were also cut that year by 3.2 million tons, returning to the level of 1978.[61]

Romanian trade overall began to shift from West to East. In two years (1980–82) Romania halved its imports from countries of the Organization for Economic Cooperation and Development (OECD); by 1983 Romania

---

to agriculture (*Congresul al XII-lea*, pp. 36–40). The plan as adopted put the agricultural share at 12.9% (*România Liberă*, 2 July 1981, p. 3). The Twelfth Congress adopted several special programs on development to 1990, including one on energy (*Congresul al XII-lea*, pp. 767–86).

59. See *Scînteia*, 25 and 26 November 1978, and Ceauşescu's speeches of 27 and 29 November 1978 [Agerpress, same dates]. On the arms race, see Ceauşescu's message to both Soviet President Brezhnev and U.S. President Reagan urging the elimination of medium-range missiles from Europe, in *Scînteia*, 4 December 1981, p. 1, and the reports of a huge peace and disarmament rally in Bucharest, *Scînteia*, 6 December 1981, pp. 1–4.

60. Wharton Foreign Trade Data Bank, and Wharton, "Romanian External Financial Situation at the End of 1981," *Centrally Planned Economies: Current Analysis*, 1 March 1982, p. 5.

61. Wharton, "Romania's Economy at Mid-1982 and Outlook for the Rest of 1982," *Centrally Planned Economies: Current Analysis*, no. 90, November 1982, p. 3, and *Anuarul Statistic*, 1980, p. 523.

was the least active importer of Western goods. Because exports to the capitalist states remained stable during this time (though lower), the hard-currency trade surplus grew. At the same time, the Romanians began making overtures to the Soviet Union and its CMEA partners, indicating their desire to "improve cooperation" in the areas of raw material and energy trade.[62] Romania's purchases of Soviet oil—at world-market prices in hard currency—began in 1979 and were costing some $700 million a year by 1981. Though the Soviet Union rejected the Romanians' desire for more favorable terms, trade with CMEA states nevertheless increased from 33 percent of Romanian total trade turnover in 1980 to 53 percent in 1983.[63]

The reduction of economic involvement with the West extended to credit as well. By the end of 1981, gross debt had reached nearly $10.5 billion, of which $10 billion was owed in hard currency. That year Ceauşescu began to complain about "new forms of exploitation including those of financial capital," and soon after Romania indicated it would seek no new commercial loans.[64] Western commercial banks and governments were disinclined in any case to grant further loans, after the Polish events and several slow Romanian repayments. In 1982 and 1983 Romania and its creditors reached rescheduling agreements covering commercial and government loans.[65] New loans were incurred only with the IMF and World Bank.[66]

It might be expected that Romania's reduction of some of its Western economic ties and its concurrent desire to improve its position vis-à-vis the CMEA and the Soviet Union would have led it to abandon its distinctive foreign policy. But its interaction and participation patterns do not show such a shift in diplomatic activity. Romania continued broad international involvement with neutral and nonaligned countries (see Table 3). These countries accounted for over 43 percent of its Interaction Score, nearly twice the share it had in 1970. The interaction pattern also shows expanded involvement with the Middle East and Africa. Czechoslovakia also increased its attention to the neutral and nonaligned countries. But unlike Romania, this increased attention came much more at the expense of its involvement with the West than with its own allies. Comparing raw Interaction Scores for this period, we can see that Romania was roughly twice as actively involved with neutral and nonaligned countries (N/N) as was Czechoslovakia

62. See Prime Minister Ilie Verdeţ's speech at the thirty-fifth session of the CMEA Council, *România Liberă*, 7 July 1981, p. 5; see also Agerpress, 30 July 1981 [FBIS, 31 July 1981, pp. AA1–2].

63. Wharton, "Romanian Foreign Trade," p. 5; RFER, 28 September 1984.

64. See *Scînteia*, 8 July 1981 [FBIS, 13 July 1981, p. H3] and 23 September 1981 [FBIS, 24 September 1981, p. H8]. The Romanians also began promoting the idea of an international agreement to establish ceilings on interest rates, with developing countries receiving preferential rates; see Agerpress, 19 May 1982.

65. *Financial Times*, 8 December 1982, p. 14; *Wall Street Journal*, 4 January 1983, p. 33; *Financial Times*, 7 February 1983.

66. *Financial Times*, 24 June 1982; *East European Markets*, 25 January 1982, p. 2, and 31 May 1982, p. 8.

TABLE 3. *Interaction pattern for Romania and Czechoslovakia, 1980–81*

	Romania		Czechoslovakia	
Target	Interaction Score (IS)[a]	Percentage of Total IS	Interaction Score (IS)[a]	Percentage Total IS
Albania	3	0.3	–	–
Other communist countries	74	6.9	73	12.5
China	27	2.5	6	1.0
Eastern Europe	147	13.8	106	18.1
Soviet Union	81	7.6	103	17.6
Yugoslavia	18	1.7	17	2.9
Neutral/Nonaligned	468	43.9	254	43.4
Europe	62		27	
Middle East	167		72	
Africa	182		67	
Asia	47		81	
Latin America	10		7	
West	209	19.6	20	3.4
Europe	149		14	
Asia	25		6	
Latin America & Canada	35			
West Germany	13	1.2	6	1.0
United States	26	2.4		
TOTAL	1065	100[b]	585	100[b]

a. For the derivation of the Interaction Score see Appendix.
b. Percentages may not total 100 due to rounding.

(Czechoslovakia's IS for N/N = 254; Romania's IS for N/N = 468). Romania conducted a greater percentage of its trade with LDC partners than did any of its East European allies, and provided more capital assistance and committed a greater share of its overall economic assistance to the LDCs than did the other East European states.[67] In 1976 Romania obtained "guest" status at the Conference of Nonaligned States, joined the Group of Seventy-seven, and participated in the United Nations Conference on Trade and Development "side by side with other developing countries."[68]

Romanian participation in the Warsaw Pact remained limited, as evidenced

67. Roger Kanet, "Patterns of Eastern European Economic Involvement in the Third World," in Michael Radu, ed., *Eastern Europe and the Third World* (New York: Praeger, 1981), pp. 312–14, 330.
68. Ion Barac, "Romania and the Developing Countries," *Revue roumanie d'études internationales* 11, no. 1 (1977), p. 72. See also Ion Mielcioiu, "The Colombo Conference of the Heads of State of the Non-Aligned Countries, Romania's Participation," ibid., pp. 73–88.

by the 1978 dispute over contributions to the alliance and Romania's emphasis on national control of the armed forces.[69] Romanian participation in WTO exercises was minimal (no participation at all from 1976 to 1979), and its contribution, as measured by the ratio of defense spending to GNP, declined. Moreover, independent arms production and joint or licensed production agreements with France, Yugoslavia, and China indicated the regime's desire to rely on its own resources for its national defense.[70] But unlike its response to Warsaw Pact action during the Prague Spring, Romania voiced no direct criticism of pact efforts to discuss the Polish situation in 1980–81 and even participated in one such meeting in Warsaw in December 1980.

Romania's participation in the CMEA did grow during the decade; for example, Romania became a member of four out of five multilateral economic associations formed since 1973.[71] Romanian participation in the IMF and World Bank—no longer unique after Hungary joined both in 1982—also broadened with the use in 1981 of an IMF credit line of $1.5 billion and the temporary acceptance of the Fund's conditions regarding economic reform.[72] In addition Romania remained the only CMEA state with a generalized trade agreement with the EEC.

The RCP's position as an autonomous actor in the world communist movement was reaffirmed at the 1976 Berlin conference of European Communist parties and by its nonparticipation in a similar Soviet-sponsored conference in Paris in 1980.[73] Romanian contacts with non-Soviet-oriented communist states such as Yugoslavia and China were equally salient during this period, including a particularly provocative (from the Soviet point of view) visit of Hua Guofeng to Romania in 1978 and again after Tito's funeral in 1980. In addition, Romania continued to fully support Eurocommunists such as Santiago Carrillo, head of the Spanish Communist party, in the face of strong Soviet opposition.[74]

69. *Scînteia*, 25 and 26 November 1978; Agerpress, 27 and 29 November 1978.

70. William M. Reisinger, "East European Military Expenditures in the 1970s: Collective Good or Bargaining Offer," *International Organization* 37 (Winter 1983), p. 147; Alex Alexiev, *Romania and the Warsaw Pact: The Defense Policy of a Reluctant Ally*, Rand Paper Series, No. P-6270 (Santa Monica: Rand, 1979), pp. 10–12.

71. Paul Marer and John Michael Montias, "CMEA Integration: Theory and Practice," in Joint Economic Committee, *East European Economic Assessment*, pt. 2, *Regional Assessments*, 97th Cong., 1st sess., 1981, p. 152.

72. The IMF conditions reportedly involved adjustments of prices and interest rates, reduction of investment, and the release of more complete information, *Financial Times*, 23 and 24 June 1982; Romania also borrowed $32.5 million from the World Bank in fiscal 1981–82, *East European Markets*, 31 May 1982, p. 8.

73. For the Romanian statement at Berlin, see Agerpress, 29 June 1976 [FBIS, 30 June 1976, pp. CC8–17]. the Romanian point of view on the Paris conference can be seen in "Solidaritatea și unitatea tuturor forțelor democratice, progresiste—imperativ fundamental al epocii contemproane," *Era Socialistă*, 5 May 1980, pp. 1–3; cf. Pamfil Nichitelea, "Independența națională și socialismului, un tot organic," ibid., pp. 4–7. See also RFER, May 13 1980.

74. Carrillo was invited to Bucharest in August 1977 at a time when he was the subject of harsh attacks from the Communist party of the Soviet Union (RFER, 4–11 August 1977). He visited Bucharest again in August 1978 (*Scînteia*, 29 August 1978), in November 1979, for the Twelfth Party Congress (Bucharest D.S., 11 November 1979), and in April 1982 (Agerpress, 10 April 1982 [FBIS, 12 April 1982, p. H4]).

Nor did Ceauşescu abandon the key elements of his foreign-policy philosophy. The conception of Romania as a developing country remained prominent in pronouncements as did support for the economic goals of the LDCs followed by renewed opposition to nuclear arms.[75] As it had previously, Romania maintained positions on several issues which diverged from those of its allies; for example, on questions of European security and arms control, and the Middle East.[76] In 1979 Bucharest condemned the Vietnamese invasion of Cambodia in terms reminiscent of those used after the invasion of Czechoslovakia. But when China invaded Vietnam the following month, the Romanians confined themselves to a general call for peaceful settlement of international conflicts and the withdrawal of "all foreign troops within national frontiers."[77] Their reaction to the Soviet invasion of Afghanistan, though more muted, also differed from that of their allies. Bucharest reaffirmed its condemnation of policies of force or "*diktat*" and called for "the right of each nation to develop itself freely, independently, to choose independently its path of social and economic development, without any kind of interference from outside."[78] Romania did not join its allies in voting against a UN General Assembly resolution calling for the withdrawal of foreign troops from Afghanistan, though by mid-1980 it had accommodated itself to both the WTO position on Afghanistan and the Babrak Karmal regime itself.[79]

The politics of adjustment in Romania

Given that Romania faced roughly the same external shocks as did its East European allies, why did its adjustment occur the way it did? In part, the answer lies in the nature of the economic base itself, as noted above. But that alone does not explain the Romanian nonreaction-reaction pattern. After all, even though circumstances were not dire in the mid-1970s, some genuine reform actions might have been taken. Nor, as other cases in this volume illustrate, was comparatively drastic economic retrenchment the only possible response to the more serious situation that existed at the end of the decade.

The explanation for Romania's particular path to adjustment can be found in the nature of the Romanian polity, socialist patrimonialism; in Ceauşescu's

75. See Romania's statement on the desirability of a "new international security order" in *Lumea*, 23–29 April 1982, pp. 14–15, and *Lumea*, 30 April–6 May 1982, pp. 8–9.

76. See, for example, Ceauşescu's mildly favorable reaction to the Reagan "zero-option" proposals regarding European-based nuclear weapons (*Scînteia*, 22 November 1981, p. 1). Unlike its allies, Romania supported the Camp David peace framework (*Scînteia*, 22 September 1978) and the peace treaty that eventually emerged between Egypt and Israel (*Scînteia*, 15 March 1979).

77. *Scînteia*, 20 February 1979.

78. *Scînteia*, 3 January 1980, p. 1, and 4 January 1980, p. 4.

79. Michael Radu, "Romania and the Third World: The Dilemmas of a 'Free Rider'," in Michael Radu, ed., *Eastern Europe and the Third World* (New York: Praeger, 1981), pp. 246–48.

ideology, which linked multilateral development and national sovereignty; and in his method of rule, which involved manipulation of key personnel, institutions, and society. The leader and his system brought Romania to its extensive involvement with the Western capitalist world and provided the political parameters within which Romania reacted to disturbances in that world.

To begin with, there is Ceauşescu himself. As described by Fischer:

> Ceauşescu is a dedicated Marxist in that he defines civilization in terms of industrialization, specifically the rapid growth of heavy industry rather than consumer goods and services. Since a very early age, his entire life has revolved around the collective experience of revolutionary and post-revolutionary activity within the Romanian Communist Party. His only education was in the small circle of underground Marxists active in Bucharest in the 1930s, and he has lived his entire life within the borders of Romania. It is no wonder that his policies all reflect one goal: the rapid industrialization of socialist Romania. He views any reform, any organizational change, as a means toward economic development. He permits economic reform measures so long as they do not interfere with centralized planning and high rates of accumulation.[80]

Ceauşescu's Marxism-Leninism combined an orthodox commitment to rapid, broad industrial development with a nationalist orientation designed to heighten and capitalize on identification with the Romanian nation.

He was not the first Romanian, or the first East European leader, to stress national prerogatives or traditions. Under Gheorghiu-Dej, for example, the Romanians took actions designed to de-Russify and de-Slavicize Romanian culture, including changing the spelling of the name of the country (from Romînia to România). But Ceauşescu, especially because of the events in Czechoslovakia and the opportunity afforded by West German *Ostpolitik* and later detente, sought to put such actions on a broader, ideological footing, to establish that economic advancement was inextricably intertwined with national—and later, his personal—prerogatives. As with the original revolution itself, Ceauşescu pictured the process of national assertion as irreversible.

> The Marxist-Leninist analysis of the contemporary social relations can only lead to the conclusion that the revolutionary parties must do everything for the development and assertion of the nations. In the countries where the communist parties have become ruling parties, they must be the most loyal exponents of the national interests; they must work for the strong assertion of the new features of the nation, for the flourishing of the socialist nation as the basis *for a long time to come* for the development of the socialist world, for an equal cooperation between all nations.[81] (Emphasis added.)

80. Fischer, "Nicolae Ceauşescu and the Romanian Political Leadership," p. 30.
81. Ceauşescu's speech to the 1972 National Party Conference, in *Romania on the Way of Building up the Multilaterally Developed Socialist Society*, vol. 7, p. 505.

Although movement in this direction had begun before Ceaușescu, after his ascension external events made opposition to his goals more difficult. After the crushing of the Prague Spring, stressing national sovereignty was popular; and with the coming of detente, economic advancement through cooperation with the West seemed possible. However, another aspect of Ceaușescu's vision was evidently the achievement of personal power, a predilection also inherited from his predecessor, and he moved quickly to make himself more than simply *primus inter pares*.

By the time of the 1969 party congress, Ceaușescu had established himself and his own people as the dominant rulers of the party, the state, and society. He had isolated or eliminated holdovers from the previous regime and promoted his own associates into key positions. Moreover, he had skillfully employed nationalist symbols—especially foreign policy—to boost his own standing with the population. In this way by the beginning of the 1970s he had come close to achieving both the power and the authority to rule Romania by himself. The 1970s then saw an exploding campaign of glorification and adulation of Ceaușescu himself and the attribution of the country's achievements to him and his thought. Each party event and national anniversary provided an occasion to further elevate Ceaușescu above the society, the state, and the party. By the Eleventh Congress (1974) Ceaușescu's rule was limited only by his personal conception of the country's future, which dictated the creation of a broadly industrialized socialist state. His position atop the patrimonial state was ensured through tight central control; through the manipulation of national symbols; through repression, co-optation, and the extension of privilege; and through the use of personal loyalty or bloodline instead of technical or administrative skill as the key criteria for appointment.

By the time of the first external disturbances, then, the political dynamics within Ceaușescu's Romania were as distinctive from those of its allies as its pattern of foreign relations. In a system of collegial leadership, the politics of the powerful elite, who are presumably checking one another, should explain change or adjustment. In the socialist patrimonial system, however, adjustment to external shock relates directly to the impact of the shock on the leader himself and on his perceptions of the country's present and future. No adjustment followed the first oil shock largely because the disruption was not great enough to shake Ceaușescu's personal commitment to the country's rapid industrialization. The first oil-price hike did not force him to reassess this commitment since Romania was not yet fully tied into the world petroleum economy, and, moreover, the increase in petroleum prices benefited Romania's terms of trade for that commodity. Nor, as we have seen, did the resulting recession in the West require a major change in Romanian strategy because the effect was temporary, and diplomatic activity carried out in accordance with Ceaușescu's notion of Romania as a developing country had put Romania in a good position to find substitute buyers among the LDCs.

Nor was there anyone in a position to mount an opposition to continued heavy industrialization. Such a person would have had to have been within the Ceauşescu inner circle: by definition, a Ceauşescu loyalist. At lower levels, potentially influential people were kept off balance by the policy of "rotation," that is, the frequent transfer of key personnel to other duties and/or other locations outside Bucharest. This policy co-opted some potentially disgruntled people with promotions, prevented the establishment of power bases by them or others, and sometimes caused their physical removal from the capital. Ultimately, Ceauşescu came to rely increasingly on family members in key positions. All of these actions reduced even further the possibility of a faction forming around an alternative policy.

Ceauşescu was also able to forestall adjustment (i.e., to continue to build up heavy industry, to import large amounts of Western equipment, and to increase the purchase of non-Soviet petroleum) because for most of the decade his policies seemed to be working. He could point to the highest growth rates in the region and, for a while, the lack of severe disruptions in the economy such as were being felt elsewhere. This apparent success, in addition to his foreign policy, allowed Ceauşescu to monopolize the nationalist position. He represented Romania. He had guided the country to its successes and embodied its economic and diplomatic independence. Thus to oppose him entailed opposing not only apparently successful policies but also the very course on which he had placed independent socialist Romania, a course that was not unpopular in the party or, for a time, among most of the population.

And what policy alternatives could have been advanced? Genuine devolution of power to enterprises would have put the party elite's own prerogatives and position at risk, as it did in Poland, and run counter to the entire thrust of Romania's economic policies since the late 1960s. Unlike Hungary or even Poland, where at least bureaucratic battles were fought over the issue, in Romania such an alternative had no past and offered only an unsettling future.

Even more modest alternatives such as lowering investment levels or reducing the imbalance between agriculture and industry called into question the fundamental direction of the country's development. Although some people may have argued for such adjustments in the mid-1970s, until economic slowdown and stagnation occurred such suggestions seemed heretical and unnecessary.

What about closer integration with the CMEA? This alternative too would have run counter to the policies not only of the Ceauşescu era but also of the Gheorghiu-Dej era and might have been personally risky to advocate. In 1972 a member of the Higher Political Council of the armed forces, Lt. Gen. Ioan Serb, was charged with engaging in pro-Soviet activities and executed. Only Ceauşescu himself could cause such a shift to be tried, as it was in the early 1980s.

Even if someone could have argued for closer integration with the CMEA or for some other policy without being accused of being a foreign agent, another powerful factor militated against the formation of policy-oriented factions. This was the recognition in the RCP of the need for unity in order to avoid possible manipulation or domination by Moscow. One of the sources of the success that the Romanians had in pursuing their deviant foreign policy was this unity. The development of factions in the party would have weakened it and possibly allowed the kind of intrusion the RCP had been holding off since the days of Gheorghiu-Dej. And unlike in Poland or Hungary, in Romania no tradition of opposition exists. During the 1950s Gheorghiu-Dej used the de-Stalinization period to remove the last of his already weakened opponents,[82] and within four years of his ascension, Ceaușescu had done the same.

Nor was there a strong intellectual tradition of opposition in the society as a whole, as was the case elsewhere. Although reports surfaced from time to time of worker or consumer protests, potential opponents did not have a strong autonomous institution, such as the Polish Catholic church, to offer symbolic or real support for such opposition.[83] While this situation may be a function of political culture or simply geography—contrast Romania's relative isolation from intellectual and other support in the West with the proximity of Poland, Hungary, or Czechoslovakia—it adds up to the absence of alternative political forces. Combined with Ceaușescu's personal manipulation of power, personnel, and policy positions, this makes for a situation where policy-oriented faction building seems nonexistent.

Still it would be foolish to state flatly that no opposition or proto-opposition has existed in Ceaușescu's Romania. Several things suggest that at least Ceaușescu himself perceived the possibility of opposition: the 1972 "Serb affair," mentioned above; the relentless pressure on and co-optation of intellectuals and dissidents of any kind; the continual rotation, and demotion, of cadres, even those once close to him; and his increasing use of family members as their replacements. In addition various incidents suggest, however obliquely, the possibility of opponents, if not factions. In 1978 and 1980 Karoly Kiraly, a Hungarian member of the Central Committee, published letters in the West attacking the regime's policies toward the country's Hungarian minority. In 1979 a veteran party stalwart of eighty-four, Constantin Privulescu, stood up at the party congress and denounced Ceaușescu for placing himself above the country. In 1983 rumors circulated of an attempted coup by military officers. Given the military's restricted and declining budget, its relative isolation from the Warsaw Pact and its supply of sophisticated

---

82. See Stephen Fischer-Galați, *The New Rumania* (Cambridge: MIT Press, 1967), pp. 44–78.

83. On this point see Fischer, "Nicolae Ceaușescu and the Romanian Political Leadership," p. 42. In the fall of 1981 disturbances were again reported in the Jiu Valley; reportedly, when Ceaușescu tried to visit the area his helicopter was stoned (BBC, 13 November 1981; *Financial Times*, 17 November 1981).

weapons, its deprofessionalization through integration with local "patriotic guards" (militias), and its use in civilian projects, it is not impossible to imagine grievances sufficient to motivate it to move against Ceauşescu.

Other inferential evidence points to possible disagreement on issues. For example, the 1979 suggestion that counties be made responsible for their own provisioning was not enacted until late 1981, possibly as a result of both local and central opposition.[84] And it does not take a leap of faith to envision genuine grievances within the population itself against policies that have made daily life increasingly intolerable. But no evidence suggests these have found a champion yet in the party hierarchy or that this hierarchy has been willing or able to sustain opposition groups centered around alternative policies or people.

When adjustment did occur, the same factors responsible for the rapid gains in the Romanian economy were also responsible for the severity of Romania's reaction: Ceauşescu's goals and the political system he created to achieve them.

For Ceauşescu, economic development was intimately connected with national sovereignty. He insisted that the country maintain as full a range of policy options as possible, with choice determined by himself within the limits both he and the Soviet Union tacitly recognized (no withdrawal from the Warsaw Pact, no direct challenge to Soviet security interests, and so on). Whereas the Bulgarians could achieve economic development through close association with the Soviet Union, for example, and the Hungarians profit while pursuing a foreign policy that followed rather than led the pack, Romania needed to advance economic development and national sovereignty simultaneously. In the 1960s and early 1970s, the threat to economic and political sovereignty came from the economic stultification of the CMEA and, in extremis, the political repression of the Soviet Union.

In the late 1970s and early 1980s, the goals remained the same, preserving the prerogatives of Romania and Ceauşescu. But the threat this time was from the West, mainly in the form of deficit and debt. With debt came obligations that constrained the course of Romanian development, for example, toward more exports, which accorded with regime desires, but also toward more imports (in order to produce more exports), more loans to pay for imports and old loans, and, especially as a price for the latter, more penetration of the economy by external forces. In short, Ceauşescu began to see the Romanian economy becoming hostage to the very economic forces that had helped it develop. While the Romanian government denied it was "another Poland," it nevertheless could see the dangers inherent in Western bankers' increasing demands for information about and involvement in the Polish economy. Ceauşescu reacted by rejecting this "exploitation" and "in-

84. For other discussions of possible opposition, see Nelson, *Democratic Centralism*, and Jowitt, "Political Innovation."

terference," and in 1982 the regime preemptively demanded a rescheduling of Romanian debt and announced that the country would take no new commercial credits. The Romanians had already temporized so long on applying IMF conditions that the organization suspended lending. The IMF eventually resumed lending, but in 1984 the country refused to take up the first part of a standby credit in order to avoid further conditions. Avoiding the influence of creditors was also behind Ceauşescu's drive to have the country pay off its debt as quickly as possible. Between 1980 and 1984 the debt was cut from nearly $10.0 billion to $7.5 billion. Only by such drastic reductions could Ceauşescu ensure Romania's freedom of action and avoid the kind of capitalist involvement in the economy he saw happening in Poland and, later, Yugoslavia.

This policy, of course, also protected Ceauşescu's political position as director of the country's future and prevented an alternative elite from establishing a foothold. Just in case one might have coalesced, however, Ceauşescu continued to apply his methods of rule. "Rotation" of cadres became demotion. Heads and deputies in virtually every key ministry, including the prime minister and long-time Ceauşescu associate Ilie Verdeţ, lost their positions, implicitly or explicitly blamed for the country's deteriorating situation. Already weakened by a decade of often dizzying personnel changes, none of those dismissed were in a position to protect themselves, much less mount a shadow cabinet to Ceauşescu.

These moves served to compound the severity of the adjustment measures. Already few enough "influentials" remained to moderate Ceauşescu's strategy. Moreover, Ceauşescu's evident "success" in weathering the extreme difficulties of the late 1970s and early 1980s further strengthened his position. He turned the bottom line around—though at great cost to the population— thus proving the merits of his actions. He did so while avoiding encroachment on the country's economic or political sovereignty by either East or West, something Poland was unable to do.

In fact, the only factor, internal or external, which seemed for a time to have a mitigating effect on the harshness of the adjustment policies and which did produce some modification in Romania's distinctive foreign policy, was the situation in Poland. Romanian adjustment occurred simultaneously with the establishment of Solidarity and the disintegration of party power in Poland. This complicated Ceauşescu's situation by placing him on the horns of two separate dilemmas. First, the need to adjust the economy required sacrifices in a living standard which, though the lowest in Eastern Europe, had been improving. Ceauşescu needed to force these sacrifices while at the same time avoiding the kind of upheaval that had occurred in Poland. It is unlikely that an analogy between the Gdańsk shipyard workers and the Jiu Valley miners escaped Ceauşescu.

Second, on the international level, Ceauşescu's commitment to the principle of national sovereignty was being sorely tested by the Polish government's clear inability to handle its own working class. Since Ceauşescu had based so much of both his international stature and domestic legitimacy on the sanctity of national prerogatives, how could he abandon this in the Polish case? On the other hand, considering what was happening there, how could he not?

While Solidarity thrived in Poland, some "softening" of both foreign and domestic policy occurred. Ceauşescu did allow himself to comment critically on the Polish government's handling of developments there, as well as on the presence of "antisocialist elements" in Poland.[85] The Romanians did attend a Warsaw Pact meeting in December 1980 at which the key item on the agenda was Poland. But unlike its allies, the RCP continued to insist that the Poles should solve their own problems without any outside interference.[86] Still, there can be little doubt that the declaration of martial law in Poland in December 1981 brought sighs of relief as deep in Bucharest as in Moscow.

In implementing domestic economic policy the Romanian regime eased the impact of strict adjustment to external economic problems for workers in key sectors: oil, coal, metal industries. In addition, the Ceauşescu-driven campaign of criticism was clearly aimed at reminding party cadres of the dangers of separating themselves too much from the working class. "Let us see," Ceauşescu said in September 1980, "that our leadership bodies, from top to bottom, will also be the genuine representatives of the aspirations of our people, of our working class—the leading class of our socialist society." The next month the party issued a decree ordering all cadres to declare the total value of their private assets.[87] Needless to say, during this time official organs of workers' representation and management also came in for effusive praise, while society was staunchly protected against any unofficial activities.

That Romania's adjustment strategy was mitigated by events in Poland is demonstrated by the fact that beginning in 1982, that is, after the imposition of martial law in Poland, more oppressive measures were adopted, including severe food and energy rationing measures; production quotas for farmers' private plots and stocks, designed to reduce consumption to the absolute minimum and gain every last exportable good from the domestic market;[88] institution of "voluntary" purchase by workers of shares in their own enterprises, as a way of creating a new source of investment funds;[89] abandonment of minimum pay levels and the substitution of a sliding scale

85. *Scînteia*, 17 October 1980, p. 3; *Scîntea*, 22 September 1981 [FBIS, 24 September 1981, pp. H1–H3].

86. *Scînteia*, 5 November 1980, p. 6, and 26 December 1981, p. 6.

87. Bucharest Domestic Service, 26 September 1980 [FBIS, 30 September 1980, p. H6]; *România Liberă*, 18 October 1980, p. 3.

88. *Christian Science Monitor*, 10 February 1982, p. 9; *Vjesnik* (Zagreb), 2 November 1982; *Financial Times*, 7 June 1984; on quotas for private production, see *Scînteia*, 19 January 1984, pp. 2–3.

89. Reuters News Service, 3 November 1982; RFER, 12 November 1982.

designed to "more strictly tie the income of each working person to the results obtained in production."[90]

While the collapse of the Polish economy made life more difficult for Romania because of the inevitable comparisons between the two, the chilling of relations between the United States and the Soviet Union that accompanied, *inter alia*, the imposition of martial law, did return some of the gloss to Ceaușescu's distinctive foreign-policy position. On issues ranging from European security to the Olympic Games, the "new cold war" allowed him to reaffirm his stance in opposition to the renewed arms race, especially in Europe, and as the champion of the rights of smaller, less developed states threatened by the division of the world into hostile blocs.

On balance, international economic difficulties seem to have had less of an impact on the Romanian patrimonial system than that system had on the country's adjustment to those difficulties. After adjustment the Romanian regime seemed further from one of collegial leaders or offsetting power brokers than it was before. In some countries, for example Yugoslavia, the demands of adjustment seemed to affect the distribution of power among the elite, while in others, say Poland, the very ability of the elite to stay in power was called into question. In Romania the essential dynamics of the system were exaggerated rather than changed by adjustment.

That this occurred even though the direction of key policies changed—to slower growth and fewer ties with the West, for example—underscores the degree of power held by the patrimonial leader in this modern incarnation of the system. More precisely, it highlights the fact that the power of a patrimonial leader resides as much in the system itself as in the leader's particular policy or vision. Though these may be important, even crucial, to his initial achievement of power, it is the manipulation and dominance of the system which seem to ensure his survival.

The Romanian case also suggests, ironically, that a patrimonial system need not necessarily mean an economy and population driven fiercely in pursuit of the leader's vision. If the leader could shift a policy as dramatically as Ceaușescu did on international borrowing, for example, then presumably he could have implemented other alternatives. Theoretically a patrimonial leader could articulate and pursue a variety of less painful policies of development and adjustment, though some alternatives would be less likely, for example, those perceived as giving rise to a counterelite. On the other hand, the case of Poland stands as proof that the absence of a patrimonial system is itself no guarantee that a country can avoid inappropriate policies and belated and painful adjustment to external shocks.

Appendix: derivation of Interaction Scores

Interaction Scores are determined by the coding of a state's international interactions. All *bilateral* visits, exchanges, agreements, or actions, as reported in the *Daily Report*

90. *Scînteia*, 2 July 1983, pp. 1–2, and 7 September 1983, pp. 1, 5.

of the Foreign Broadcast Information Service (FBIS) for the three time periods (1970–71, 1975–76, 1980–81) were recorded, by date, duration, personnel involved, and the nature of any agreement signed. These were then coded as follows:

Event coding system

Coded Value	Type of Event
5	Establish or resume diplomatic relations; high-level visit, i.e., party leader, state government head, or foreign minister
4	Sign or renew long-term multipurpose treaty; visit of defense minister, deputy or vice premier, or deputy prime minister
3	Multipurpose trade agreement (3–5 years); extend credit; troop stationing treaty; visit of trade or aid delegation; visit of foreign trade minister or other ministers, e.g., light or heavy industry, labor, engineering, sports, etc.; visit of Planning Commission chairman; visit of deputy ministers; visit of Politburo or Presidium member
2	Multipurpose trade protocol (1–2 years); tariff agreement; license or co-production agreement; raise diplomatic legation to embassy level; visit of Planning Commission delegation, trade union national chairman, governor of national bank, or other Central Committee member; visit of military delegation, local government of national legislative assembly delegation
1	Scientific and technical exchange; cultural, consular, or visa-travel agreement; agreements on medicine, health, transportation, or repayment of debts; one-item trade contract; establish trade-promoting company, commission, or bureau; agreements on "cooperation" in fields, e.g., education, economics; extend relief aid through international agency

Events not coded: out-of-power politicians, party members or dignitaries from the West; hosting of cultural or educational fairs or conferences; youth, trade union, or writers' conferences or delegations without the national chairman of same; industrial exhibitions (though any contracts reported as a result are included); meeting of standing mixed commissions; visits to the United Nations or between minsters therein; ambassadorial audiences by the host country; visits from non-ruling Communist parties, with the exception of the Provisional Revolutionary Government of South Vietnam (or the National Liberation Front) for 1970–71, 1975–76.

Events are discrete entities, coded for their value as such. Thus, a visit by a foreign trade minister is coded as a 3, but one that culminated in a trade protocol of one year is coded as 3 plus 2 or 5.

If an event is an asymmetrical visit, e.g., deputy minister to a foreign minister, the higher-level leader determines the value of the visit.

Interaction Scores with different countries were then combined by target or partner group, as follows:

Interaction partners

Albania

People's Republic of China

Other communist countries—North Vietnam and Provisional Revolutionary Government/National Liberation Front of South Vietnam (for 1980–81, both Socialist Republic of Vietnam), North Korea, Mongolia, Cuba

USSR

East Europe—Bulgaria, Czechoslovakia, East Germany, Hungary, Poland, Romania, Yugoslavia

Neutral/Nonaligned
  for all years: Austria, Finland, Ireland, Lichtenstein, San Marino, Sweden, Switzerland
  for 1970–71:   Cambodia
  for 1970–71:   Nonaligned determined by participation in Third Conference of Nonaligned Countries, Lusaka, 1970
  for 1975–76:   Nonaligned determined by participation in Fifth Conference of Nonaligned Countries, Colombo, 1976
  for 1980–81:   Nonaligned determined by participation in Sixth Conference of Nonaligned Countries, Havana, 1979

Israel

West
  Europe: All NATO members (excluding West Germany, see below), plus Spain, Malta (1970–71 only), the Vatican, European Economic Community, Bank for International Settlements
  Middle East: Iran (for 1970–71, 1975–76 only)
  Asia: Australia, New Zealand, Philippines, Japan, Pakistan (1970–71, 1975–76 only)
  Latin America and Canada—all, excluding Nonaligned

West Germany

United States

Two independent coders recorded and coded events; both coders were unaware not only of each other's codings but also of the aims of the research. Previous research (see below) has shown the reliability of the coding system to be quite high. In this case intercoder reliability was estimated using the most stringent test: the percentage of exact matches between sample codings for the two coders. By this test intercoder reliability was assessed at 90.3%.

The data source (FBIS) did contain a bias toward received as opposed to dispatched interactions, that is, receiving visitors as opposed to sending them. While future research can correct this bias by providing for cross-checking with other sources, such events were not added in this case in order to keep data comparable. The exhaustive country-specific coverage of the source, plus the use of three separate two-year time periods, is expected to minimize distortion.

For a complete discussion of the development of Interaction Scores, see Ronald H. Linden, *Bear and Foxes: The International Relations of the East European States* (Boulder: *East European Quarterly*, 1979; distributed by Columbia University Press, New York), pp. 12–18.

Explaining the GDR's economic strategy Thomas A. Baylis

The economic policies of the German Democratic Republic (GDR), when compared to those of the other East European states considered in this volume, are distinguished by their relative orthodoxy and by their surprising success. We must search initially for the sources of both the orthodoxy and the success in the fundamental differences between the GDR and its Eastern neighbors. First, the GDR is the most prosperous and the most technologically advanced of the members of the Council for Mutual Economic Assistance (CMEA); it is predominantly a technology "supplier" to its partners rather than a "receiver."[1] Second, the economic and political fortunes of the GDR are influenced profoundly and in complex ways by the presence of its large and even more successful capitalist neighbor, the Federal Republic, which shares with the GDR a common language, a common history up until 1945, and many cultural attributes, and whose citizens maintain a web of familial connections in the GDR. Third, while all the CMEA states are heavily dependent on the Soviet Union—economically and otherwise—the GDR is the object of special Soviet attention. It is the Soviet Union's leading trading partner and supplier of machinery and other capital goods, arguably its most capable military ally as well as the westernmost outpost of the Warsaw Pact,[2] and, along with the Federal Republic, one of the foci of the Russians' historically well-grounded preoccupation with the "German question."

Decision making in the GDR is highly centralized, even by Eastern-bloc standards; it is mitigated neither by any sort of federalism or de facto territorial diffusion of power (as in Yugoslavia, the Soviet Union, or even Czechoslovakia), nor by the existence of social classes or institutions that are at all

---

1. Siegfried Schoppe, "Die intrasystemaren und die intersystemaren Technologietransfers der DDR," in Gernot Gutmann, ed., *Das Wirtschaftssystem der DDR: Wirtschaftspolitische Gestaltungsprobleme* (Stuttgart: Gustav Fischer Verlag, 1983), pp. 359–60.

2. An estimated 380,000 Soviet troops are stationed in the GDR, twice the number in Poland, Czechoslovakia, and Hungary combined. C. Bradley Scharf, *Politics and Change in East Germany* (Boulder: Westview, 1984), p. 176.

International Organization 40, 2, Spring 1986   0020-8183 $5.00

autonomous from the ruling party (such as the peasantry and the Catholic church in Poland).[3] Major—and many minor—policy decisions are made in the weekly meetings of the collective leadership body of the Socialist Unity party (SED), the Politburo, which Erich Honecker, its general secretary, leads but does not dominate. Primary responsibility for administration belongs to the SED Secretariat, all of whose members also belong to the Politburo. The political process in the GDR is veiled in even greater secrecy than it is in most other East European states, and internal conflict is correspondingly muted, but it appears that divergent policy viewpoints must be channeled to, or through, Politburo members to have an impact upon final decisions. Numerous formal and informal avenues exist through which information and influence can flow to the Politburo from economic experts, government and regional party officials, and enterprises; the specialized departments of the SED Central Committee bureaucracy are perhaps the most strategic points of contact.

I shall argue in this essay that the GDR's fundamental economic strategy since 1971, as reflected in but also modified by its response to the price shocks of 1973–74 and 1979 and their consequences, has been shaped in important measure by the pressures imposed and the opportunities offered by its complex relationship with the German Federal Republic. The pivotal influence of this relationship on the GDR's economic choices, however, must also be seen against the background of the direct and indirect constraints imposed by the GDR's status as junior partner in a military, economic, and ideological alliance with the Soviet Union, and by the terms of the still somewhat tenuous accommodation that the regime has worked out with its own citizens. Conflict and consensus building within the GDR's elite are based in part on the assessment of all these factors, and in part on divergent interests and personal alliances.[4]

All of these elements were apparent in the remarkable sequence of events which occurred between late 1983 and September 1984 when the GDR, much to the surprise of academic and journalistic observers, seemed to essay a new role for itself in East-West politics. These events culminated in the abrupt "postponement" of Honecker's planned September visit to the German Federal Republic. Relationships between the GDR and the Federal Republic had, contrary to most expectations, begun to warm after the stationing of American Pershing and cruise missiles on West German territory. By the summer, however, shrill criticisms from the Soviet, Czechoslovak, and Polish

3. A partial exception must be made for the East German Evangelical church which, while by no means the powerful force that the Catholic church is in Poland, offers an important alternative to state-sponsored organizations for young people and others in East German society.

4. This essay differs from some of the others in this volume insofar as it attributes a less prominent causal role to factional conflicts in the GDR's leadership. Reliable information on such conflicts is scarce, and in my opinion elite disagreement in the GDR tends to be an intervening variable between larger forces in the political and economic environment and specific policy decisions.

press of West German intentions and, by implication, East German gullibility had begun to undermine the developing inter-German rapprochement. The divergence between the East German and Soviet perspectives was particularly evident in the Soviet response to the announcement in late July that West German banks had agreed to extend 950 million deutsche marks in credits, guaranteed by the Federal government, to the GDR, and the simultaneous revelation of a number of East German concessions easing the conditions of East-West travel.[5] The Soviet Union remained unpersuaded that these two events were unconnected. Two days after the formal announcement of the credits, *Pravda* warned that the West German government was using "economic levers" as well as "political contacts" to undermine the stability of the East German regime as part of a larger effort to advance its revanchist claims and to promote NATO's "crusade" against socialism. On 2 August *Pravda* specifically attacked the linking of Western "demands" to the credit extension—although the GDR had in fact already agreed to these demands.[6]

The 1984 credit agreement followed a similar one for 1 billion deutsche marks brokered a year earlier by the conservative Bavarian minister-president, Franz-Josef Strauss, at a time when the GDR was facing a particularly acute liquidity squeeze; together with other developments that I shall explore below, the two agreements suggested that a significant modification in the GDR's economic strategy might be underway. While East German political rhetoric emphasized the mutual responsibility of the two Germanies for keeping open a window of detente during a period of deteriorating superpower relations, Western observers tended to stress the economic motivations behind the GDR's surprisingly bold efforts to build a "coalition of reason" with its capitalist neighbor. I shall suggest in this essay that we must view the GDR's shifting policies toward West Germany in the context of its broader economic strategy and its response to the price shocks and ensuing debt crisis. However, many of the modifications of the GDR's strategy and its rejuvenated interest in West German political and economic ties originated in earlier periods of the GDR's development, and, particularly, in the changes that accompanied Erich Honecker's assumption of the SED leadership in 1971.

This essay thus begins with a brief account of the background of the economic situation that confronted the East German leadership at the beginning of the 1970s and then outlines the economic strategy first enunciated by Honecker at the Eighth SED Congress in June 1971. Next it describes the effects on the GDR's economy of the fuel and raw materials price shocks of 1973–74 and 1979 and the Politburo's policy response to them. This response, I shall argue, consisted of a set of immediate short-term measures and three broader, long-term strategies: "socialist intensification," a turn

5. See the declaration of Minister of State Philip Jenninger, 25 July 1984, reprinted in *Deutschland Archiv* 17 (September 1984), pp. 988–90.

6. L. Bezymensky, "Under a Canopy of American Missiles," *Pravda*, 27 July 1984, p. 4; translated in *Current Digest of the Soviet Press*, 22 August 1984, p. 4.

toward "reform in small steps," and the selective expansion of the GDR's economic ties to the Federal Republic. After identifying the essential features and peculiarities of the political process in the GDR, I shall undertake to explain the political logic first of Honecker's original strategy and then of the short-term and each of the three long-term responses to the shocks. To conclude I shall offer a tentative explanation for the apparent success of the GDR's policies.

The GDR and its economy in 1970

By 1970 the German Democratic Republic had already become in economic terms the most important of the Soviet Union's East European allies. The GDR was the Soviet Union's leading trading partner, supplying it with vital capital goods in exchange for raw materials and energy, and was responsible for the largest share, after the Soviet Union, of the total internal trade volume of the CMEA. It was, with Czechoslovakia, the most industrialized of the Eastern-bloc states (some 48.9% of its work force held jobs in manufacturing and construction in 1970), and its citizens enjoyed the highest standard of living (measured by estimates of gross national product [GNP] per capita) of any communist nation except Czechoslovakia, which it was in the process of surpassing.[7] Having erected the Berlin Wall to stop skilled workers and technical personnel from emigrating to the West, it had at its disposal a skilled, highly trained, and—by Eastern-bloc standards—disciplined work force. Its leader Walter Ulbricht had reason to suggest, as he did at the end of the 1960s, that the GDR might be profitably looked upon as a model for the construction of socialism in advanced societies.[8]

Yet the GDR's economy faced serious obstacles.[8] The East German state was and is poor in natural resources. Apart from some uranium exploited jointly with the Soviet Union (which then assumes control of it, selling some of it back to the GDR), its only abundant domestic energy source is brown coal; yet, in addition to its comparatively low heating value and the severe pollution its use entails, this coal is becoming increasingly expensive to reclaim. Like most of its Eastern neighbors, the GDR has also suffered from a continuing, severe labor shortage, aggravated by the emigration to the West before August 1961 of predominantly young, male workers and technical intelligentsia. The percentage of women and older citizens in the work force

7. "On a Wrong Course," *Pravda*, 2 August 1984, p. 4; translated in *Current Digest of the Soviet Press*, 22 August 1984, pp. 4, 8. Work force data from *Statistisches Jahrbuch 1983 der Deutschen Demokratischen Republik* (Berlin: Staatsverlag der Deutschen Demokratischen Republik, 1983), pp. 16, 18; Thad Alton and his associates calculate the per capita GNP for the GDR and Czechoslovakia in 1970 as $4,776 and $5,010 respectively, and in 1982 as $6,669 and $6,082. Alton et al., *Economic Growth in Eastern Europe* (New York: L. W. International Financial Research, 1983), p. 23.
8. See the helpful discussion in Scharf, *Politics and Change*, pp. 68–77.

is among the highest in the world and cannot expand further to any significant degree. Low productivity (by Western though not by Eastern-bloc standards), neglect of the infrastructure, and, in many sectors, outmoded plant and equipment also contribute to the tautness of the economy. Furthermore, like its East European neighbors, the GDR has not been able to develop a fully satisfactory system of economic organization and management.

In 1963 the GDR was the first of the Eastern-bloc states to undertake a program of Liberman-style economic reforms—serving, it has been suggested, as an experimental laboratory of sorts for the Soviet Union, which began similar reforms two years later.[9] Initially the "New Economic System" (NES) was received enthusiastically by both elites and ordinary citizens, and appeared to stimulate a surge of economic growth. However, the SED's fear that extensive decentralization of economic decision making might weaken its political control limited the scope of the reforms almost from the outset.[10] Numerous ambiguities clouded the actual redistribution of economic authority and responsibility, and the regime proved unable or unwilling fully to implement the thoroughgoing price reform—in particular to risk introducing market elements directly into the pricing system—that would have been necessary to make any form of "indirect steering" of the economy produce the desired results.

A second stage of the reforms, undertaken in 1967 and 1968, granted enterprises and enterprise associations (VVBs) greater decision-making responsibilities but also brought the administrative designation of certain "structure-determining" sectors of the economy that were, in effect, exempted from the reforms and given special attention and disproportionate resources. GDR officials later admitted that this policy created serious "disproportions" in the economy arising from the neglect of the nonpriority sectors. Party critics also blamed the NES for permitting the "unplanned" growth of disparities in the compensation of different groups according to their position in the economic system.[11] By 1970, faced with a growing economic crisis brought on in part by severe weather conditions, the GDR's leaders must have felt that they had to choose between two options: continue to pursue the reforms, which, to have been successful, would have required dramatic additional measures with all their potential for social disruption, or abandon the reforms entirely and return to something like the earlier, centrally steered economic system in spite of its faults. Highly conscious of the fateful linkage of economic reform with political ferment in Czechoslovakia, the GDR's

9. See Gert Leptin and Manfred Melzer, *Economic Reform in East German Industry* (Oxford: Oxford University Press, 1978), chap. 1.

10. See Thomas A. Baylis, *The Technical Intelligentsia and the East German Elite* (Berkeley: University of California Press, 1974), pp. 244–47.

11. See Helga Michalsky, "Social Policy and the Transformation of Society," in Klaus von Beyme and Hartmut Zimmermann, eds., *Policymaking in the German Democratic Republic* (New York: St. Martin's, 1984), p. 245; Jürgen Strassberger, "Economic System and Economic Policy: The Challenge of the 1970s," in ibid., pp. 124–25, 127.

leadership must have felt that it could not realistically entertain the first alternative; it thus chose a variant of the second.[12]

The beginning of the 1970s was also a political and diplomatic watershed for the GDR. The *Ostpolitik* of Willi Brandt and his Social Democratic–Liberal coalition in West Germany had found a willing collaborator in the Soviet Union. The Soviet Union prodded its reluctant East German ally into abandoning some long-asserted demands, relinquishing some of its leverage over West Berlin, and opening its borders to greater Western influence, in exchange for international legitimation, in the form of membership in the United Nations and virtually universal diplomatic recognition. The *Ostpolitik* treaties, which ended West Germany's long-standing policy of seeking to keep the GDR internationally isolated, opened up new economic as well as political opportunities for the East German leadership. Although the GDR had successfully developed a substantial amount of trade with Western countries even while being denied official recognition, its new status permitted it to expand its economic dealings more openly and to utilize well-publicized state visits by high-level party and governmental officials to this end. The negative side of this bargain was the risk that the GDR's internal stability would be undermined by the massive influx of visitors from West Germany and West Berlin (which was to reach 7.8 million in 1978),[13] the expansion of inter-German telephone facilities (telephone calls from the Federal Republic and West Berlin in fact increased from 700,000 in 1970 to 18 million in 1976),[14] and other measures that might re-awaken pan-German aspirations. The almost simultaneous introduction by the GDR's leaders of a policy of *Abgrenzung* ("demarcation" or, less literally, "distancing"), which sought to insulate the GDR's citizens as much as possible from Western influence, suggests the extent of their concern over this possibility. On one level an ideological injunction, *Abgrenzung* also took concrete legal forms: sharp limitations on the work of Western correspondents in the GDR and, most notably, a prohibition of all unapproved contacts between middle- and high-level government and party officials and Western visitors (*Kontaktverbot*).

Finally, the beginning of the 1970s brought a new leader to the helm of the East German party. Walter Ulbricht, the dominant political figure of the GDR since its founding, had survived the worker uprising of June 1953 and a number of attempts by Politburo rivals to unseat him, as well as the persistent domestic discontent that finally required the construction of the Berlin Wall; but in May 1971 he was forced from office. Ulbricht's resistance

12. Manfred Melzer, "The GDR—Economic Policy Caught between Pressure for Efficiency and Lack of Ideas," in Alec Nove, Hans-Hermann Höhmann, and Gertrud Seidenstecker, eds., *The East European Economies in the 1980s* (London: Butterworth, 1982), pp. 45–49.

13. Hartmut Zimmermann, "Die DDR in den 70er Jahren," in Günter Erbe et al., *Politik, Wirtschaft und Gesellschaft in der DDR*, 2d ed. (Opladen: Westdeutscher Verlag, 1980), p. 70.

14. Michael J. Sodaro, "External Influence on Regime Legitimacy in the GDR," in Sodaro and Sharon L. Wolchik, eds., *Foreign and Domestic Policy in Eastern Europe in the 1980s* (New York: St. Martin's, 1983), p. 94.

to the concessions necessary to conclude agreement on the *Ostpolitik* treaties, his attempts in his last years to stake out a modest degree of distinctiveness in the GDR's ideological position, and the long-nourished resentment on the part of some of his Politburo colleagues of his autocratic leadership habits apparently motivated the Soviet Union to approve, if not to require, his removal.[15] We do not know whether disagreements over economic policy and/or the "growth crisis" of 1969–70 might also have contributed to his enforced retirement.

Ulbricht's lieutenant, Honecker, replaced him as first secretary. The significance of this change for economic policy and in other respects was not immediately apparent. No other major changes in the SED leadership accompanied Ulbricht's removal, and Honecker himself, while acquiescing to the *Ostpolitik* treaties, was closely identified with the policy of *Abgrenzung*. Initially assessed in the West as a loyal but rather colorless and conservative party bureaucrat, Honecker had previously headed the SED youth organization and later directed the security and party cadres sectors; he lacked experience in economic affairs and was not associated with the young economic specialists who had assumed prominent positions in the party and state in the 1960s. Under Honecker the SED quickly scuttled the ideological innovations of the late Ulbricht era and reemphasized the brotherly solidarity of the GDR with the Soviet Union—hardly a neglected theme under Ulbricht.[16] The economic reforms, though closely identified with Ulbricht, had already been abandoned at a Central Committee plenum in December 1970. As Honecker assumed office, the regime was scaling back its new Five-Year Plan in response to the production bottlenecks and consumer shortages that had resulted from the policies of the late 1960s as well as from a harsh winter and two hot, dry summers.

Honecker's economic strategy

The Eighth SED Congress in June 1971 laid down an explicit new economic strategy that emphasized the scientific-technological revolution and its prom-

---

15. Most Western accounts emphasize the external factors in explaining Ulbricht's fall. See, for example, Angela Stent, "Soviet Policy in the German Democratic Republic," in Sarah Meiklejohn Terry, ed., *Soviet Policy in Eastern Europe* (New Haven: Yale University Press, 1984), pp. 38–41; Myron Rush, *How Communist States Change Their Rulers* (Ithaca: Cornell University Press, 1974), pp. 191–219. According to one report, however, Honecker privately told GDR writers that "we overthrew [*haben gestürzt*] Ulbricht." Joachim Seyppl, *Ich bin ein kaputter Typ* (Wiesbaden: Limes Verlag, 1982), p. 16.

16. See Peter C. Ludz, *The Changing Party Elite in East Germany* (Cambridge: MIT Press, 1972), pt. 4; Rüdiger Thomas, "Materialien zu einer Ideologiegeschichte der DDR," in *Wissenschaft und Gesellschaft in der DDR* (Munich: Carl Hanser Verlag, 1971); Thomas A. Baylis, "Ideological Adaptation in Postindustrial Communism" (Revised version of paper presented at Wingspread Conference on the GDR in Comparative Perspective, Racine, Wisconsin, 14–17 April 1983).

ise of consumer goods and social benefits. Since the congress took place only a little more than one month after Honecker's accession to the party leadership, it is unlikely that much of its content can be credited to his personal initiative, but subsequent party propaganda unambiguously identifies the strategy with the period of Honecker's leadership. The two party congresses that followed the introduction of this strategy reiterated its principles, which continue rhetorically almost unchanged today.

The strategy, which should be viewed as a political as much as an economic one, is summed up in the so-called principal task (*Hauptaufgabe*) enunciated at the Eighth Congress (and virtually duplicating a similar pronouncement at the Twenty-fourth Congress of the Communist party of the Soviet Union [CPSU]): to raise the "material and cultural standard of living of the people on the basis of a rapid rate of development of Socialist production, in increasing effectiveness and scientific and technical progress, and in accelerating the rate of growth in labor productivity."[17] In other words, the SED promised to improve living standards as long as economic growth based largely on the more efficient and intensive use of existing natural and human resources justified such improvement—in short, provided that the population recognize what soon came to be called "the unity of social and economic policy."

This was the GDR's version of the "social contract" that each East European state has in some sense offered its citizens, promising material benefits and less tangible improvements in the quality of life in exchange for hard work and political loyalty. What has distinguished the GDR's social contract from that of several of its neighbors has been, first, the GDR's greater economic ability to fulfill its part of the transaction and, second, the pressure on it to do so at a fairly high level. The contract was offered, after all, to citizens who had for years been exposed to the West German media's particular vision of Western prosperity (albeit also of Western social ills), and who were now to be inundated by a flood of relatives and tourists from the West, along with their telephone calls and gift packages. Early in the Honecker period the regime sought to deliver, suitably publicized, the first installment of the promised benefits and held out the prospect of additional ones for the future, while tirelessly reminding the population of the quid pro quo: the "socialist intensification" of production.

On the level of economic planning and management the new strategy brought a return to the centralized, administrative direction of the economy. The Council of Ministers, individual ministries, and the State Planning Commission took back powers that had been delegated to the VVBs and individual enterprises under the reforms. New investments, for example, though still funded primarily from enterprise or VVB resources or from bank credits,

---

17. Erich Honecker, *Report of the Central Committee to the Eighth Congress of the SED* (Dresden: Verlag Zeit im Bild, 1971), p. 27.

now required the approval of higher authorities—in the case of amounts exceeding 50 million deutsche marks, that of the Planning Commission itself. The government froze prices at existing levels until 1975, a date it later extended to 1980. This action temporarily ended the attempt to relate prices to production costs on a continuing basis and thereby to make them effective instruments of economic steering. Enterprises were required to fulfill an increased number of plan indicators, and the once central indicator of "profit" was relegated to a secondary position. Physical planning was given renewed emphasis, and most of the reforms' "indirect steering" devices were abolished or modified, the most notable survivor being the *Produktionsfondsabgabe*, in effect a charge on capital designed to force enterprises to utilize their plant and equipment as fully as possible.[18]

What remained of the New Economic System was its verbal emphasis on the "scientific-technological revolution" (STR) and on the importance of "scientific" planning and management, though some of the more extravagant ideological fetishes of the late Ulbricht period—the fascination with cybernetics and systems theory, for example—were ridiculed.[19] The specific agenda of technological innovation attracted extraordinary ideological as well as practical attention; by the end of the decade party rhetoric had begun to emphasize industrial robots and the development of microelectronics as well as the need to shorten the time lag between technological discovery and its utilization in production. Ideologically, the SED, by continuing to stress the STR, sought to capture for itself some of the technological appeal that had initially attached to the reform program; the party attempted to identify itself as closely as possible with the process of advanced modernization.[20]

The Eighth SED Congress implemented its promise to give higher priority to improving the quantity and quality of consumer goods available to GDR citizens with some restraint. One measure of overall consumption is retail trade turnover: according to official statistics it increased by 27 percent (in current prices) between 1970 and 1975, slightly below the overall increase in national income of 30 percent but well above the Five-Year Plan's goal of 22 percent.[21] The GDR, cognizant of the 1970 riots (repeated in 1976 and 1980) in Poland, prudently chose to maintain its subsidy of basic consumer goods, rents, and public transportation, thus minimizing the effects of inflation on the consumer, though at an increasing cost to the state budget.

---

18. For details, see Ralf Rytlewski, "Phasen der Wirtschaftspolitik seit 1963," *DDR Handbuch*, 2d ed. (Cologne: Verlag Wissenschaft und Politik, 1979), pp. 806–8; Melzer, "The GDR," pp. 48ff.; Strassberger, "Economic Systems," pp. 122, 126–27; Leptin and Melzer, *Economic Reform in East German Industry*, pp. 98–160.

19. See Kurt Hager, *Die entwickelte sozialistische Gesellschaft* (Berlin: Dietz Verlag, 1972).

20. See Hartmut Zimmermann, "Politische Aspekte der Herausbildung, dem Wandel und der Verwendung des Konzepts 'Wissenschaftlich-technische Revolution' in der DDR," in the annual special issue of *Deutschland Archiv* 12 (1976), pp. 17–51; Baylis, "Ideological Adaptation," pp. 15ff.

21. Melzer, *Economic Reform in East German Industry*, p. 53.

TABLE 1. *Consumer goods per 100 households in the GDR*

Year	Automobiles	Refrigerators	Washing machines	Television sets
1960	3.2	6.1	6.2	16.7
1970	15.6	56.4	53.6	73.6
1980	38.1	108.8	84.4	105.0
1983	43.7	125.0	94.0	114.1

Source. Helmut Koziolek, "Über das Wachstum unseres Nationalreichtums," *Einheit* 39, nos. 9–10 (1984), p. 877.

Throughout the decade the proportion of GDR households owning consumer durables steadily increased. By 1983 there were more refrigerators and television sets than households in the GDR, and enough cars for 44 percent of the households (in some cases a single household had more than one of a given item). (See Table 1.) The success of efforts to improve the quality of consumer goods is more difficult to measure but has probably been significant, reflecting the need to satisfy the demands of Western markets as well as those of the East German consumer.[22]

The regime's efforts to slake the ideologically questionable thirst of GDR citizens for automobiles are a useful index of the extent of its orientation to consumer desires. Not only has the GDR steadily increased its own automobile production, but on occasion it has made dramatic purchases of Western vehicles (10,000 Volkswagens in 1977; 10,000 Mazdas in 1981; and some 6,000 Citroëns and Renaults in the same year). Imports from the Soviet Union, however, virtually halted in the 1980s, and for most models of domestic as well as foreign vehicles the waiting period is now said to exceed ten years.[23] Apart from automobiles, the GDR imports most Western consumer goods in relatively small numbers; many of these imports are sold only in *Intershops* for certificates that consumers must purchase with hard currency, or in *Exquisitladen* for elevated prices in East German marks.

The SED moved quickly under Honecker to implement the broader improvements in "social policy" promised at the Eighth Congress. Although one important improvement — voluntary supplemental retirement insurance — had already been introduced in March 1971, the first major wave of social policy measures came in 1972, with the raising of minimum wages and pensions, rent reductions, other "improvements in social provisions," birth

22. One indicator of uncertain value is the proportion of industrial goods inspected that were awarded the GDR's "Mark of Quality 'Q' " in 1982 — 29% — as opposed to the corresponding proportion in 1970 — 9%. Figures from *Statistisches Jahrbuch 1983*, p. 151.

23. See Conrad Kiechel, "East Germany Imports Western Automobiles," RAD Background Report 246, *Radio Free Europe Research*, 31 August 1981; Hans-Dieter Schulz, "Produktionsplan zum erstenmal seit 1974 erfüllt," *Deutschland Archiv* 17 (March 1984), p. 298.

grants, and assistance for working mothers. The last took the form of the celebrated "baby year," which permits a working mother to take up to a year off with compensation after the birth of her second child.[24] The centerpiece of "social policy" was the undertaking of a massive program of home construction intended to solve the GDR's severe housing shortage; some 3 million units were to be constructed or modernized by the program's completion in 1990. Similar measures have followed periodically, including wage improvements, increased vacations, and a reduced work week for those working second or third shifts.[25]

The fervent proclamations of fealty to the Soviet Union at the Eighth Congress and afterward seemed to suggest that the economic strategy entailed even closer adherence to the Soviet economic model and increasingly intimate trade ties to the Soviet bloc, including expanded cooperation within the CMEA and a more far-reaching division of labor among its member states. It is now apparent, however, that the GDR, utilizing its new international status, sought during this period to shift its trade in modest measure toward the West and thus reduce its dependence on the Soviet Union and other bloc countries. The Soviet Union's desire to strengthen its own Western trade and reduce the rate of growth of its energy and raw materials exports to other CMEA members encouraged the GDR as well as many of its neighbors in this course.[26] By 1974 the proportion of the GDR's total trade carried out with the Soviet Union had dropped from 39.1 percent (1970) to 31.4 percent (see Table 2), while the proportion of the GDR's total trade with industrialized capitalist nations had risen from 24.4 percent to 30.9 percent (based on total trade turnover in current prices)—at a time when total GDR trade was increasing much faster than its gross domestic product (GDP).[27] To be sure, part of the shift reflected greater Western inflation rather than an actual increase in the quantity of goods exchanged. After 1974, the GDR's proportion of trade with the Soviet Union began to rise once again, largely because the price of Soviet oil and other raw materials increased sharply beginning in 1975. Starting in 1977, the proportion of the GDR's trade with other CMEA nations fell steadily, a trend that continued through 1983.[28]

24. This measure, like similar ones introduced elsewhere in Eastern Europe, was also intended to raise the birth rate and ultimately ease the GDR's labor shortage.

25. See Melzer, "The GDR," p. 51; Michalsky, "Social Policy," pp. 241–42; Wolf-Rainer Leenen, "Sozialpolitik," *DDR Handbuch*, pp. 981–87.

26. Paul Marer, "East European Economics: Achievements, Problems, Prospects," in Teresa Rakowska-Harmstone, ed., *Communism in Eastern Europe*, 2d ed. (Bloomington: Indiana University Press, 1984), pp. 311–12.

27. See, however, the discussion of the severe statistical difficulties involved in assessing GDR-Western trade on the basis of the GDR's statistics in Deutsches Institut für Wirtschaftsforschung, *Handbook of the Economy of the DDR* (Westmead, England: Saxon House, 1979), pp. 238–39 (hereafter cited as *Handbook*). There are often serious discrepancies between the GDR's figures and those of its trading partners.

28. It also appears that in the course of the decade the GDR became more assertive of its own interests in the CMEA, e.g., with respect to "specialization" agreements and measures to reduce the gap between the richer and poorer CMEA states. See Hanns-Dieter Jacobsen, "Foreign Trade Relations of the DDR," in von Beyme and Zimmermann, *Policymaking in the GDR*, pp. 154–55; Scharf, *Politics and Change*, p. 178.

TABLE 2. *GDR foreign trade turnover by groups of nations (percentage of total trade)*

Year	Socialist	CMEA	CMEA excluding USSR	USSR	Developing	Capitalist
1950	72.3%	72.3%	32.6%	39.7%	0.4%	27.3%
1960	74.6	67.6	24.8	42.8	4.3	21.1
1965	73.9	69.4	26.6	42.8	4.5	21.7
1970	71.6	67.3	28.2	39.1	4.0	24.4
1971	71.6	67.2	29.1	38.1	4.1	24.3
1972	71.1	67.9	30.2	37.7	3.2	25.6
1973	68.7	66.0	31.4	34.6	3.4	27.9
1974	64.1	61.0	29.6	31.4	4.9	30.9
1975	69.7	66.2	30.5	35.7	4.4	25.9
1976	67.1	63.9	31.4	32.5	4.6	28.3
1977	71.4	67.9	32.5	35.4	4.9	23.7
1978	72.1	68.8	32.0	36.0	5.2	22.7
1979	68.8	65.8	29.7	36.1	5.2	26.0
1980	66.5	62.7	27.2	35.5	6.1	27.4
1981	66.6	63.5	26.0	37.5	4.9	28.5
1982	66.0	63.0	25.0	38.0	5.8	28.2
1983	65.2	62.5	24.6	37.9	5.4	29.4

Sources. Calculated from *Statistisches Jahrbuch 1983 der Deutschen Demokratischen Republic* (Berlin: Staatsverlag der Deutschen Demokratischen Republik, 1983), p. 236; *Statistisches Jahrbuch 1984*, p. 239.

Trade turnover figures—the only ones that the GDR publishes in any detail—understate the dramatic degree to which Western imports increased during this period (see Table 3). To pay for these imports, the regime utilized the then enthusiastic readiness of Western banks to extend credit. The GDR's net Western debt rose from an estimated $1.4 billion in 1970 to $4.8 billion in 1975; by 1980 it had reached $11.2 billion—on a per capita basis higher than Poland's even in 1980, though considerably lower as a percentage of GDP. The debt-service ratio reached an estimated 36 percent by 1980 (see Table 4). What did the GDR acquire for its unprecedented accumulation of debt to the capitalist world? The greatest increase in Western imports in the 1970s came in basic materials and intermediate products, and, probably most important, in capital goods, particularly West German machinery.[29] Imports of consumer goods, on the other hand, continued to amount to only a small proportion of Western imports, despite the emphasis of the economic strategy on raising the level of consumption.

29. *Handbook*, pp. 246–49.

TABLE 3. *GDR imports and exports, Western capitalist states*

	1965	1970	1975	1980	1981	1982	1983
	millions of valuta marks[a]						
Imports	2,681	5,464	11,442	19,194	19,754	19,054	22,790
Exports	2,665	4,203	7,892	13,777	18,073	21,762	24,471
Balance	−16	−1,261	−3,550	−5,417	−1,681	+2,708	+1,681
	exports as % of imports						
	99.4	76.9	69.0	71.8	91.5	114.2	107.4

a. 4.67 valuta marks = 1 transferable ruble, valued in turn at $1.35 in 1983.
Sources. Calculated from Deutsches Institut für Wirtschaftsforschung, *Handbook of the Economy of the DDR* (Westmead, England: Saxon House, 1979), p. 335; Heinrich Machowski, "Uncertain Outlook for East-West Trade," *DIW Economic Bulletin*, April 1984, pp. 6, 9.

TABLE 4. *Estimates of the GDR's net Western debt*[a] *(in $ billion)*

	1970	1975	1977	1978	1979	1980	1981	1982	1983
Marer	1.4	4.8				11.2	11.0	9.2	
Cornelsen			5.7	7.3	8.7	9.9	10.2	8.4	6.7
Haendcke-Hoppe								10.3	8.5
Debt-service ratio (Marer)	13%	24%				36%	35%	29%	

a. All figures include debt in inter-German trade. Cornelsen does not include an estimate of amount owed foreign creditors other than the debt to banks reported by the Bank for International Settlements. Marer's figures are those of Wharton Econometrics.
Sources. Paul Marer, "The Political Economy of Soviet Relations with Eastern Europe," in Sarah Meiklejohn Terry, ed., *Soviet Policy in Eastern Europe in the 1980s* (New Haven: Yale University Press), p. 185; Paul Marer, "East European Economics: Achievements, Problems, Prospects," in Teresa Rakowska-Harmstone, ed., *Communism in Eastern Europe*, 2d ed. (Bloomington: Indiana University Press, 1984), p. 313; Doris Cornelsen, "Successful Production Efforts: The GDR Economy in Mid-1984," *DIW Economic Bulletin*, October 1984, p. 11; Maria Haendcke-Hoppe, "Konsolidierung in der DDR Aussenwirtschaft," *Deutschland Archiv* 17 (October 1984), p. 1060.

Initially, official statistics (which we must view with some caution)[30] indicated that the new economic strategy had been impressively successful. All of the major goals of the 1971–75 Five-Year Plan were exceeded, with the exception of industrial labor productivity which nevertheless increased by 28 percent.[31] Targets for 1976–80 were set at about the same level as for 1971–76 and below the actual results attained. This time, however, actual growth was substantially less impressive (see Table 5); the 22 percent increase in produced national income (PNI) fell well below plan targets,[32] as did most other key indicators. Retail trade turnover also increased by 22 percent, thus meeting the plan target but falling short of the 1971–75 results—moreover, part of the increase was apparently due to higher prices charged for luxury goods.[33] The Soviet Union and most of the other East European states had similar weaker overall growth figures.

The GDR's response to the price shocks

Most of the East European states, though not the Soviet Union, could blame the slowing of growth rates in part on the direct and indirect effects of the price shocks of 1973 and 1979. The sudden rise in the price of oil and other raw materials in 1973–74 affected the GDR's Western purchases in those years, and in 1975 the prices the Soviet Union charged its allies, particularly for oil and natural gas, began to reflect these increases. By 1975 the GDR, which had been increasing its use of oil relative to domestically mined brown coal, relied on the Soviet Union for 27 percent of its energy, a figure that rose to 33 percent by 1980—roughly the average for East European CMEA members without Romania.[34] Overall, the discrepancy between the price increases for GDR imports and those for its exports, according to calculations from official figures, caused the GDR's terms of trade to deteriorate by 13 percent between 1972 and 1975.[35] The economic stagnation of most

30. On the problematic quality of GDR statistics, see Paul Marer, "The Political Economy of Soviet Relations with Eastern Europe," in Terry, *Soviet Policy in Eastern Europe*, p. 181; Schulz, "Produktionsplan," pp. 296–97; Schulz, "Auch Honecker sieht eine Wende," *Deutschland Archiv* 18 (February 1985), pp. 113–14; note 27 above.

31. Melzer, *Economic Reform in East German Industry*, p. 53.

32. Western economists generally regard East German (and most other East European) PNI figures as exaggerating growth rates, in part because of hidden inflation. Attempts to calculate GNP figures comparable to Western statistics suffer from serious gaps in the available data, however. See the estimates of Alton et al., *Economic Growth*, in Table 5 and the discussion in Paul Marer, *Evaluation of the National Accounts, Prices, Exchange Rates and Growth Rates of the USSR, Eastern Europe, and Cuba, with Alternative Estimates of Their Dollar GNPs* (Washington, D.C.: World Bank, 1985).

33. "DDR-Wirtschaft im Strukturwandel," *DIW Wochenbericht* 48 (5 February 1981), pp. 71, 74.

34. Jochen Bethkenhagen, "Oil and Natural Gas in CMEA Intra-bloc Trade," *DIW Economic Bulletin*, February 1984, p. 8.

35. *Handbook*, p. 237.

TABLE 5. *GDR economic growth: selected indicators (% change over previous year)*

	1966–70	1971–75	1976–80	1981	1982	1983	1984[a]
Produced National Income	5.2	5.4	4.1	4.8	2.6	4.4	5.5
Gross National Product	3.4	3.7	2.5	2.4	0.5	–	–
Gross Industrial Production	6.6	6.5	4.7	5.5	3.7	3.9	4.5
Gross Crop Production	–	–	0.5	0.9	– 1.7	0.6	14.0
Work Productivity	5.7	5.4	4.6	4.2	2.6	3.4	5.0
Investment	9.9	4.7	4.6	2.7	– 5.2	0.0	– 5.0
Retail Trade Turnover	4.8	5.4	4.1	2.5	1.0	0.7	4.1

a. Preliminary figures.
Note. Figures for 1966–70, 1971–75, and 1976–80 are yearly averages. GNP figures are Western estimates. Investment figures for 1966–70 and 1971–75 are for "gross plant investment"; later figures are for "total investment."
Sources. "Problematische Planziele der RGW-Länder," *DIW Wochenbericht* 48 (19 June 1981), pp. 282–83; Doris Cornelsen, "Consolidation at the Expense of Private Consumption," *DIW Economic Bulletin*, April 1984, p. 6; Doris Cornelsen, "Improved Supply Situation—but Decline in Investment," *DIW Economic Bulletin*, April 1985, p. 5; Thad P. Alton et al., *Economic Growth in Eastern Europe* (New York: L. W. International Financial Research, 1983), p. 19.

Western countries in the wake of the price shock also affected the markets for GDR products and contributed to its continuing trade imbalances and rising debt. The second explosion of oil and gas prices in 1979 affected the GDR in still more dramatic ways, although the CMEA's system of basing prices on the average world price over the previous five-year period again cushioned its immediate impact. As the SED Politburo recognized in its report to a Central Committee plenum: "We are dealing not merely with the further worsening of what was already a complicated situation; we are confronted by a new situation." By 1982 the GDR was reportedly paying an average of 139.44 transferable rubles (TRs) per ton of Soviet oil, ten times what it had paid in 1973.[36] In the same year the Soviet Union cut its soft-currency deliveries of oil to Eastern-bloc countries by 10 percent, a deficit the GDR made up by substituting imports from the Middle East, particularly Iraq and Iran.[37] Nevertheless, by 1982 the value of Soviet energy

36. Cited in Doris Cornelsen, Manfred Melzer, and Angela Scherzinger, "DDR-Wirtschafts-system: Reform in kleinen Schritten," *Vierteljahreshefte zur Wirtschaftsforschung*, no. 2 (1984), p. 200; Bethkenhagen, "Oil and Natural Gas," p. 6.
37. See the sudden jump in GDR trade figures for both countries in *Statistisches Jahrbuch 1983*, p. 237. GDR figures indicate that the actual drop in Soviet deliveries was only 7%; the

exports amounted to over half of *all* its exports to the GDR—a figure once again close to the CMEA average.[38]

The crisis in Poland added further pressures to those generated by the price shocks. The Poles were unable to supply the anticipated quantity of hard coal to the GDR in 1980 and especially 1981, and the GDR had to make hard-currency purchases from the West to cover the shortfall. The GDR also made a hard-currency contribution equivalent to 250 million "valuta marks" to the Poles and provided other economic assistance. In early 1982 Western banks cut off the credit spigot to the GDR as well as to other East European borrowers, and the Federal Republic threatened to reduce the "swing"—the interest-free line of credit intended to cover ostensibly temporary imbalances in inter-German trade. (The two countries subsequently agreed to reduce the "swing" from 850 million "accounting units," equal to the same number of West German deutsche marks, to 600 million by 1985. The latter figure approximates the actual GDR deficit at the time of the agreement.)[39] Meanwhile, the GDR's cumulative trade deficit with the Soviet Union had ballooned, amounting to 3.4 billion TRs between 1976 and the end of 1983. Part of the GDR's obligation to the Soviet Union may well have been in hard currencies, although we lack precise information.[40] Numerous reports suggested that Soviet pressures to reduce the deficit were mounting, preferably through the GDR's delivery of high-quality industrial and consumer goods that would otherwise be salable to the West.[41]

Broadly, the GDR's short-term response to these pressures resembled that undertaken in the other East European states, but the degree of adjustment required proved to be less wrenching than elsewhere. In the terms of the "absorption equation,"[42] the GDR had to choose some combination of a number of mostly unpleasant alternatives, each of which carried with it certain economic and/or political risks: increasing exports, decreasing imports, reducing domestic consumption, lowering government expenditures, reducing investment. The GDR turned its attention first to closing its trade gap with the West and reducing its hard-currency debt. It did so largely by increasing its exports to Western markets—by 31.2 percent in 1981, 20.4 percent in

---

discrepancy can probably be explained by hard-currency purchases. See ibid., p. 251; Maria Haendcke-Hoppe, "Konsolidierung in der DDR-Aussenwirtschaft," *Deutschland Archiv* 17 (October 1984), pp. 1061–62, 1066.

38. Bethkenhagen, "Oil and Natural Gas," p. 12.

39. Ronald D. Asmus, "New Inter-German Agreement on 'Swing' Credit Announcement," RAD Background Report 141, *Radio Free Europe Research*, 28 January 1982.

40. Heinrich Machowski and Maria Elisabeth Ruban, "The Soviet Economy 1983/1984," *DIW Economic Bulletin*, August 1984, p. 8; see Marer, "East European," pp. 309–10.

41. Fred Oldenburg, "Werden Moskaus Schatten länger?" *Deutschland Archiv* 17 (August 1984), p. 834; Siegfried Kupper, "Mühsamer Aufstieg—trüber Aussicht," *Deutschland Archiv* 17 (August 1984), pp. 846–48; "DDR und UdSSR vereinbaren neues Wirtschaftsabkommen," *Süddeutsche Zeitung*, 8 October 1984, p. 20.

42. See Laura d'Andrea Tyson, "Aggregate Economic Difficulties and Workers' Welfare," in Jan F. Triska and Charles Gati, eds., *Blue-Collar Workers in Eastern Europe* (London: Allen & Unwin, 1981), pp. 110–14.

1982, and 11.6 percent in 1983—in the face of intensified competition and the widespread Western recession.[43] The increase came disproportionately in sales to Western purchasers *outside* the Federal Republic. The GDR roughly maintained its previous level of Western imports measured in monetary value in 1981 and 1982—an impressive achievement when compared to the sharp cutbacks of other East European states—but the actual quantity of goods received dropped substantially because of high Western inflation rates. Coveted consumer items, such as tropical fruits and Italian textiles, were among the casualties, and, at least in inter-German trade, the importation of investment goods dropped in favor of materials needed for current production. In 1982 a 14.5 percent increase in West German imports compensated for a large drop in imports from other capitalist economies, a course apparently dictated by the GDR's international liquidity problems. In 1983 this pattern was partially reversed: overall Western imports grew by 20 percent, while West German imports rose by only 9 percent; in the first part of 1984 West German imports actually dropped, while other Western imports continued to grow.[44] Overall trade figures, particularly in 1983, may have been inflated to an indeterminable degree by the GDR's *Drehgeschäfte*— its purchase of certain Western goods (steel, oil) on credit for immediate resale for hard currency.[45]

The GDR also increased its export surplus with CMEA countries other than the Soviet Union, while continuing to reduce the proportion of its trade with these countries relative to its total trade. Its debt to the Soviet Union, on the other hand, increased by a billion TRs between 1980 and 1982. In 1983, the GDR reduced its annual Soviet trade deficit to 200 million TRs, and in 1984 it began for the first time to run a surplus by sharply increasing its exports and reducing its "real" imports in most categories.[46]

Predictably, the GDR's export offensive and its curtailment of imports took their toll on domestic consumption, particularly in 1982 when severe shortages were reported in different sections of the country. Official statistics indicate a nominal growth of retail trade turnover of 1 percent in 1982 and 0.7 percent in 1983 (see Table 6), but these figures do not take into account acknowledged and unacknowledged price increases. The GDR continued to subsidize the ostensibly unchanged prices of goods categorized as meeting "basic needs" (in the past alleged to cover 80% of production for domestic consumption) but openly increased prices on certain luxury items.[47] Enterprises sometimes pursued the familiar stratagem of introducing in the "basic

43. Heinrich Machowski, "Uncertain Outlook for East-West Trade," *DIW Economic Bulletin*, January 1985, p. 6. These figures appear to refer to nominal growth.
44. Ibid.; Haendcke-Hoppe, "Konsolidierung in der DDR," p. 1065.
45. Haendcke-Hoppe, "Konsolidierung in der DDR," pp. 1065, 1068.
46. Ibid., p. 1062; Doris Cornelsen, "Improved Supply Situation—but Decline in Investment," *DIW Economic Bulletin*, April 1985, p. 10.
47. See Manfred Melzer, "Wandlungen im Preissystem der DDR," in Gutmann, *Das Wirtschaftssystem der DDR*, p. 64.

TABLE 6. *Growth in planned and actual retail trade turnover in the GDR, 1981–84*

Year	Five-Year Plan	Actual
1981	4.0%	2.5%
1982	4.0	1.0
1983	3.0	0.7
1984	2.2	4.1[a]

a. Preliminary figure.

Sources. Hans-Dieter Schulz, "Produktionsplan zum erstenmal seit 1974 erfüllt," *Deutschland Archiv* 17 (March 1984), p. 297; Cornelsen, "Improved Supply Situation," p. 4.

needs" category higher-priced, "new" products that actually differed little in quality or content from those they replaced. Government expenditures did not drop; GDR figures show increases in the state budget of 4.3 percent in 1981, 8.9 percent in 1982, and 5.3 percent in 1983, with no dramatic deviations in the major spending categories listed (nominal defense and internal security spending increased by about 7% each year).[48] No new improvements in social policy, which had previously come with some regularity, were announced through 1983; however, the massive housing program was continued, albeit with a slight shift away from new construction toward the modernization of the existing stock.

The SED acknowledged absolute expenditure cuts in one category, investment. After a small increase in 1981, reported investment dropped by over 5 percent in 1982, appeared to stagnate in 1983, and dropped again in 1984.[49] This was clearly the category with the greatest short-term "give"; investment in the GDR had proceeded at a high level (about 30% of PNI) throughout the 1970s,[50] and the regime had already committed itself to reducing the rate of investment growth in the 1981–85 Five-Year Plan while trying to improve its productivity.

Long-term responses

Many of these short-term measures were just that: temporary palliatives rather than an enduring adaptation to the GDR's new international economic position. The regime's long-term response to the price shocks and credit

48. *Statistisches Jahrbuch 1984 Deutschen Demokratischen Republik* (Berlin: Staatsverlag der Deutschen Demokratischen Republik, 1984), pp. 259, 261.

49. Doris Cornelsen, "Successful Production Efforts: The GDR Economy in Mid-1984," *DIW Economic Bulletin*, October 1984, p. 5; Cornelsen, "Improved Supply Situation," p. 5.

50. Rudolf Knauff, "Die Investitionspolitik der DDR," in Gutmann, *Das Wirtschaftssystem der DDR*, p. 336; *Statistisches Jahrbuch 1984*, pp. 13–14.

squeeze is more significant but also harder to separate neatly from modifications of its 1971 strategy undertaken on other grounds. The long-term
response may be divided into three components, the first of which stood at
the center of the ten-point economic program set forth by Honecker in his
report to the SED's Tenth Congress, held in April 1981 to the accompaniment
of the growing Polish crisis. The phrase "socialist intensification" sums it
up:[51] give still more urgent priority to reducing the consumption of raw
materials, energy, and labor, while continuing to expand production. Enterprises and *Kombinate* (industrial combines) and even individual groups
of workers publicly pledged themselves to achieve specified savings on fuel
and materials while raising output; and the state plan emphasized corresponding indexes—"net production" and basic material costs per 100 marks'
worth of production. Available investment funds were concentrated heavily
on energy and energy-related projects. "Renewal, modernization, and reconstruction" and not new projects became the focus of investment, with
enterprises and *Kombinate* responsible as far as possible for fabricating their
own "means of rationalization."[52] The regime promoted the expansion of
second and third shifts in order to utilize existing plant and equipment more
fully. It announced the imposition, beginning in 1984, of a 70 percent levy
on the total payroll ("wage funds") of each *Kombinat* and enterprise in order
to force them to shed excess "reserves" of labor. The GDR institutionalized
its preoccupation with expanding export markets by making exports one of
the four principal indicators for evaluating enterprise performance in 1983.

The GDR did not publicly label the second and third components of its
long-term strategy as such; these also significantly modified its 1971 strategy
but were potentially much more volatile politically than "socialist intensification." One was to return quietly to certain institutional and motivational
devices similar to those of the abandoned reforms of the 1960s. The other
was to employ the GDR's special West German connection to improve its
economic position and its overall trade and credit standing in the West.

The GDR did not go so far as to follow the Hungarian reform course of
moving openly toward a "regulated market economy" by instituting far-
reaching measures of economic decentralization.[53] Indeed, no broad reform
discussion appeared in either the general or the specialized press, but the
state adopted a number of discrete yet significant changes in the direction
of the economy during the late 1970s and the 1980s. Taken together, they
could be said to amount to a "reform in small steps,"[54] although no one

51. Erich Honecker, "Bericht des Zentralkomitees der Sozialistischen Einheitspartei Deutsch-
lands an den X. Parteitag der SED," *Neues Deutschland*, 12 April 1981, pp. 6–7.
52. See Werner Gruhn and Günter Lauterbach, "Rationalisierungsmittelbau mit neuen Auf-
gaben," *Deutschland Archiv* 17 (November 1984), pp. 1180–83.
53. See Comisso and Marer's essay in this volume.
54. See Cornelsen, Melzer, and Scherzinger, "DDR-Wirtshaftssystem"; Karl C. Thalheim,
"Ordnungspolitische Aspekte der heutigen Wirtschaftspolitik der DDR," *Deutschland Archiv*
17 (May 1984), pp. 509–27.

acknowledged them as such publicly. Rather, officials employed such phrases as "further perfecting"—*weitere Vervollkommnung*—of the "socialist planned economy" and justified the changes as strengthening "democratic centralism."[55] In fact the GDR sought to rationalize economic decision making and to make greater use of parametric, or "indirect steering," devices and even of a modest degree of private initiative.

The reform that the GDR itself has publicized most vigorously and that has received a great deal of credit for its relative economic success in the early 1980s is the creation of giant amalgamations of industrial enterprises, the *Kombinate*. Like the VVBs of the 1960s, the *Kombinate* are supposed to combine economic and administrative functions; unlike the VVBs, they are integrated vertically as well as horizontally, bringing the producers of goods in a particular sector together with their major suppliers, research and development sections, and marketing units. Most *Kombinate* now also have their own foreign-trade divisions, although these remain subject to the regulations of the Ministry of Foreign Trade. Overall, the *Kombinate* are supposed to speed the efficient incorporation of scientific and technical innovations into production and to afford greater flexibility in response to rapidly changing foreign and domestic demand. The general directors of the *Kombinate* are said to have much greater authority over individual enterprises, for example, to shift resources and production tasks among them, than did their VVB predecessors; it is less clear how much power they enjoy relative to government ministers.[56]

The most significant of the indirect economic steering devices introduced in the 1980s are the restoration of "profit" as one of the four "chief indicators" for judging economic success, the ongoing adjustment of prices to make them more effective as incentives, the expanded use of the *Produktionsfondsabgabe*, and the introduction of the "contribution to the societal funds"—the 70 percent levy on payrolls mentioned above. The elevation of the indicator of profit—a measure taken simultaneously with the downgrading of the traditional gross output indicator, "industrial goods production"—is supposed to lead to a more efficient use of plant, materials, and labor, *and* to greater attention to marketability. To be sure, individual *Kombinate* or enterprises remain limited in the amount of profit they can retain and the uses

55. See Günter Mittag, "Theoretische Verallgemeinerung der Erfahrungen der Entwicklung der Kombinate für die Leistungssteigerung in der Volkswirtschaft, insbesondere bei der Nutzung der qualitativen Faktoren des Wachstums," *Wirtschaftswissenschaft* 32, no. 1 (1984), pp. 10, 25–26; and Mittag, "Ökonomische Strategie der Partei dient der weiteren Verwirklichung des Kurses der Hauptaufgabe," *Einheit* 39, nos. 9–10 (1984), pp. 809–10.

56. On the *Kombinate* generally, see Mittag, "Theoretische," pp. 18–25; Thalheim, "Wirtschaftpolitik der DDR," 515–26; Melzer, "The GDR," pp. 77–80; Werner Klein, "Das Kombinat—Eine organisationstheoretische Analyse," in Gutmann, *Das Wirtschaftssystem der DDR*, pp. 79–101; Leslie Holmes, "The Industrial Associations in the 1980s—Some Points for Discussion" (Paper presented at Wingspread Conference on the GDR in Comparative Perspective, Racine, Wisconsin, 14–17 April 1983); Pieter Boot, "Continuity and Change in the Planning System of the German Democratic Republic," *Soviet Studies* 35 (July 1983), pp. 331–42.

to which they can put such profit. The absence of a comprehensive price reform mitigates the value of profit as an incentive, but the government has revised some industrial prices annually since 1976 to reflect costs more closely and introduced a pricing system for new products which favors innovating firms.[57] The payroll levy—which appears to be unique in Eastern Europe—is intended to "free" unnecessary labor for assignment elsewhere and perhaps strengthen work discipline, but it is qualified by provisions for "temporary" subsidies for enterprises unable to meet it. We have no reports as yet on its effectiveness, though the regime has had to assure its nervous population that no GDR citizen will face the prospect of unemployment.[58]

The GDR has also sought to raise production and reduce costs through reforms in its agricultural sector, where performance has stagnated in recent years.[59] At the beginning of 1984 the GDR moved to bring producer prices more closely in line with costs, in effect shifting the state's food subsidy entirely to the direct support of low retail prices. Simultaneously, the state gave greater emphasis to agricultural production on private plots.[60] Since 1976 the regime has also given new support to the GDR's single remaining stronghold of private ownership, small trades (*Handwerk*), particularly repairs and services, permitting the creation of new firms and even providing an ideological justification for their continued existence under socialism.[61] Presumably the discontent of GDR consumers over the limited availability of such services was a more immediate reason for this policy.

Overall, the reforms do not constitute a comprehensive, integrated program but are rather a complex yet pragmatic, apparently ad hoc combination of direct and indirect instruments of economic management and control.[62] Many of the reforms are designed to provide incentives for the realization of the program of socialist intensification or to increase the competitiveness of GDR goods in capitalist markets. What is striking, however, are the reminders

57. Mittag, "Theoretische," pp. 28–30; Cornelsen, Melzer, and Scherzinger, "DDR-Wirtschaftssystem," p. 212.

58. See, e.g., Günter Schneider and Kurt Völker, "Wissenschaftlich-technischer Fortschritt und Arbeit im Sozialismus," *Sozialistische Arbeitswissenschaft* 28 (January–February 1984), pp. 26–38.

59. "DDR-Wirtschaft," p. 72; Doris Cornelsen, "Consolidation at the Expense of Private Consumption," *DIW Economic Bulletin*, April 1984, pp. 6, 8.

60. Doris Cornelsen, "Stabilization of Growth by Changing the Economic Mechanism," *DIW Economic Bulletin*, October 1983, p. 7; Cornelsen, "Successful Production Efforts," pp. 7–8.

61. Thalheim, "Wirtschaftpolitik der DDR," pp. 524–26; Rainer Consilius, "Die Wirtschaftsetappen in der SBZ/DDR," *Deutsche Studien* 21 (December 1983), p. 376; Irene Falconere, "Zur Rolle der Handwerker und Gewerbetreibenden im gesellschaftlichen Reproduktionsprozess der DDR unter der veränderten Reproduktionsbedingungen der 80er Jahre," *Wirtschaftswissenschaft* 30 (September 1982), pp. 1337–52.

62. Claus Biefeld, Karola Hesse, and Rolf Schüsseler call attention to the "extraordinarily difficult, but surely not insoluble problem" that "directive" regulations may hamper the effectiveness of indirect measures in their article, "Vervollkommnung der wirtschaftlichen Rechnungsführung und Entwicklung des Wirtschaftsrechts," *Staat und Recht* 33, no. 8 (1984), p. 639.

of the broader NES reforms in some of the GDR's contemporary rhetoric. Honecker's pronouncement that "what is useful for the economy as a whole must also be advantageous for the factories and the *Kombinate*" repeats almost verbatim the phrase of Liberman's which became one of the most familiar slogans of the NES period.[63]

The third and most controversial component of the GDR's long-term response to the shocks was its attempt to utilize its special economic relationship to the Federal Republic to overcome the bottlenecks of the early 1980s, to restore its Western creditworthiness, and to expand its access to Western technology.[64] The most immediately available avenue for pursuing this course was "inter-German trade" (which the Federal Republic calls "intra-German trade" and continues to distinguish from "foreign" trade). The Federal Republic (including West Berlin) has for many years been the GDR's second largest trading partner, after the Soviet Union. Inter-German trade offers the GDR special advantages: Common Market tariffs, for example, do not apply to GDR exports to West Germany,[65] and imports from and exports to the GDR are subject to a greatly reduced West German value-added tax (VAT). Until 1980 the GDR usually ran a deficit in its West German trade, which was covered in part by the interest-free "swing." Since 1980 the trade has been roughly in equilibrium; the GDR expanded its volume in this period, especially in the critical year 1982, but overall its growth was no greater than that of the GDR's trade with other capitalist nations.

The quantity of inter-German trade may be less important than what is exchanged. "FRG deliveries," as Arthur Stahnke notes, "have always most importantly included the elements required for the construction of basic industrial capacity, from coke and steel to complete plant and machinery."[66] "A large proportion" of GDR imports from the Federal Republic, experts from the German Institute for Economic Research conclude, "consists of goods which the DDR does not produce itself and cannot obtain in internal CMEA trade."[67] Steel, chemical products, and machinery are among the

63. Cited in Thalheim, "Wirtschaftpolitik der DDR," p. 514.

64. One might argue that the measures undertaken were really only "short-term" ones intended to meet the immediate emergency. The GDR continued to pursue many of them after it had restored its international credit standing, however, which suggests that such measures are more accurately characterized as part of a long-term strategy.

65. Such tariffs do, however, apply to GDR goods destined for other EEC states, even if they go via West Germany. Thus the frequent assertion that the GDR has become a "de facto member of the Common Market" (Stent, "Soviet Policy," p. 52) is incorrect. See Arthur A. Stahnke, "The Economic Dimensions and Political Context of FRG-GDR Trade," in Joint Economic Committee, *East European Economic Assessment*, pt. 1, 97th Cong., 1st sess., 1981, pp. 366–71.

66. Ibid., p. 355.

67. Doris Cornelsen, Horst Lambrecht, Manfred Melzer, and Cord Schwartau, *Die Bedeutung des Innerdeutschen Handels für die Wirtschaft der DDR* (Berlin: Duncker & Humblot, 1983), p. 179.

leading import items.[68] About 20 percent of the GDR's imports usually fall in the category of "investment goods," although this figure dropped in the 1982–84 period";[69] "high technology" imports—for example, those that might support the GDR's campaign to expand dramatically the use of microelectronics and industrial robots—do not appear to be a major component of the exchange.[70] Inter-German trade has been especially important to the GDR as a source of emergency materials and spare parts to compensate for failures of planning or shortages of hard currency; such needs "can be satisfied through intra-German trade quickly, without complications, and without long delays for transportation."[71] In the early 1980s the GDR used it in precisely this way: to replace the loss of Polish coal and to make up for the lack of other Western imports that had fallen victim to the 1982 credit squeeze. The GDR also, as noted above, purchased West German steel on credit in order to resell it immediately for hard currency.

The GDR's exploitation of its special relationship to West Germany in response to economic necessity extended beyond the framework of inter-German trade. The two government-guaranteed bank credits of 1 billion and 950 million deutsche marks respectively—particularly the first—appear to have helped reestablish the GDR's creditworthiness in the West by improving its international liquidity. The GDR is said to have used the first credit primarily to repay earlier Western short-term, high-interest loans and to raise its cash reserves in Western accounts.[72] Both credits, it should be underscored, permit the purchase of goods from Western partners other than the Federal Republic, including those, like Austria, in which NATO-imposed restrictions on technologically sophisticated exports to Eastern Europe do not directly apply.[73] More generally, Bonn's policies have probably eased

68. "Die Entwicklung des innerdeutschen Handels," news release of Federal Economics Ministry, *Deutschland Archiv* 17 (May 1984); *Statistisches Jahrbuch 1983*, p. 243; Statistisches Bundesamt, *Statistisches Jahrbuch 1984 für die Bundesrepublik Deutschland* (Stuttgart: W. Kohlhammer, 1984), p. 257.

69. "Die Entwicklung," p. 556.

70. Published trade statistics, however, neither verify nor refute American suspicions that strategically important technology "leaks" across the West German border through legal and, especially, illegal channels. See, e.g., Jack Anderson, "High-Tech Leaks," *Washington Post*, 27 January 1985, p. C7, who cites a CIA report on technology leaks from the Federal Republic to the Soviet bloc.

71. Armin Volze, "Zu den Besonderheiten der innerdeutschen Wirtschaftsbeziehungen im Ost-West Verhältnis, *Deutsche Studien* 21 (September 1983), p. 190; Schoppe, "Technologie-transfers," p. 360, argues that this is largely true of all the GDR's trade with the West.

72. *Süddeutsche Zeitung*, 9 October 1984, p. 23. The GDR's reason for seeking the second credit remains somewhat mysterious, since its debt situation had considerably improved by 1984 and its cash reserves were relatively high. The GDR borrowed another $473 million from Western banks in October and November, for equally unclear purposes. See Haendcke-Hoppe, "Konsolidierung in der DDR," pp. 1067–68; Cornelsen, "Improved Supply Situation," pp. 8–9.

73. Economist Intelligence Unit, *Quarterly Economic Review of East Germany*, no. 1 (1984), p. 17; no. 3 (1984), p. 15. Austria has now become the GDR's second largest Western source of imports. It has, however, come under growing American pressure to restrict its high-technology exports to the Eastern bloc. Machowski, "Uncertain Outlook," p. 9.

the GDR's access to other Western credits because of the conviction that a West German "umbrella" now shelters the GDR's debts.

The GDR also acquires hard currency for purchases in the West through most of the special payments made by the Federal Republic to the GDR for such services as the maintenance of the transit routes to West Berlin, visa fees for West Germans, postal services, and the liberation of political prisoners. These payments (excluding the sum for political prisoners, which is unknown), together with the "minimum currency exchange" requirement West German visitors must meet when entering the GDR and the cash gifts West Germans provide to friends and relatives there, provide the GDR with an estimated 2 billion deutsche marks annually.[74]

Much of the significance of the GDR's use of its West German connection must thus be seen in the context of its Western trade in general. Maintaining good economic relations with the Federal Republic not only provides the GDR with receptive markets for goods that might not be commercially viable in other Western countries and with privileged access to needed West German goods and credits, but it also opens up access to technology and credit elsewhere in the West. As a source of both West German and other Western technology as well as of "emergency" materials and parts, inter-German economic relations help GDR industry to be competitive in Western export markets while also satisfying growing Soviet demands for high-quality goods.

What is astonishing in retrospect is how well and how quickly the broad palette of measures that the GDR took to meet the challenge of the price and credit shocks seems to have worked. Exports increased substantially and the growth in imports was curtailed. The GDR began to run a surplus with its Western trading partners, and its debt to Western banks decreased, though probably in part because of the rise in the value of the dollar. By 1984 Western banks were again competing with one another to loan money to the GDR.[75] In 1984 the GDR also achieved a surplus in its trade with the Soviet Union—apparently the only CMEA state to do so.[76] Despite a fall to 2.5 percent growth in 1982, the GDR's PNI posted impressive annual gains (at least in the official statistics), exceeding the plan target in 1983 and 1984.[77] Moreover, this growth went hand in hand with an impressive reduction in the proportionate use of energy and raw materials. Günter Mittag,

74. Rudolf Herlt, "Das Geschäft mit dem Westen," *Die Zeit* [North American ed.], 7 July 1984, p. 4. Paul Marer gives a higher estimate of Western payments and gifts and adds to it an estimate of $500 million in "nonstandard commercial benefits," for a total of $1.5 billion (some 4.5 billion deutsche marks at current exchange rates) annually. "Economic Policies and Systems in Eastern Europe and Yugoslavia," in U.S. Congress, Joint Economic Committee, compendium of studies on the economies of Eastern Europe, forthcoming.

75. Cornelsen, "Improved Supply Situation," pp. 8–9; Frederick Kempe, "East Germans Benefit from U.S. Bank Credits," *Wall Street Journal*, 19 March 1985, p. 32.

76. Cornelsen, "Improved Supply Situation," p. 10.

77. See Table 5. The GDR achieved an impressive 5.5% increase in PNI in 1984 with the help of a 14.4% leap in gross agricultural crop production, the first substantial increase in that sector in a decade. Cornelsen, ibid., p. 7.

the SED's secretary for the economy, claimed that in 1982 "for the first time in the history of the GDR, the growth in national income was achieved with an absolute reduction of consumption [of fuels, raw materials, and other materials] in production."[78] The virtual stagnation in domestic consumption of 1982 and 1983 gave way to an officially reported 4.1 percent growth in retail trade turnover in 1984. And in mid-1984 the GDR resumed its periodic announcements of improvements in social policy: pensions were increased, and the "baby year" was extended to eighteen months for mothers of three or more children.[79]

This apparently imposing record requires some qualification. Beginning in 1982 the GDR reduced annual targets for major plan categories to a level below that necessary to achieve the original goals of the Five-Year Plan— for example, the level at which PNI growth exceeded the target in 1983 was below the level that failed to meet the 1981 target. The improvement of retail trade turnover in 1984 does not take account of price increases, either hidden or open, and the increase in pensions was more modest than in earlier years. In 1984 investment once again declined sharply,[80] suggesting that the SED had sacrificed it to the need to show concrete improvements in consumer and social benefits in order to counter new symptoms of unrest, for example, the occupation of West German embassies and missions by GDR citizens seeking to emigrate. Overall, however, it is difficult to gainsay the GDR's achievement; in a remarkably short time it appears to have absorbed the impact of the oil and other shocks and upset the pessimistic predictions of Western observers at the beginning of the 1980s.

The political process in the GDR

Before turning to a political explanation of the GDR's short- and long-term choices of economic strategy, I want to consider the processes by which and the limiting conditions under which the GDR's political decisions are made. "Politics," in the sense of the conflict among groups and individuals over the choice of public goals and policies and their implementation, whether based on personal ambitions, competing interests, or opposing ideological positions, is normally nearly invisible in the GDR. Politburo members certainly sometimes disagree over policy issues, and high-level party and gov-

78. Mittag, "Theoretische," pp. 10–11. Between 1980 and 1983 the use of "economically important fuels, raw and semi-finished materials" (not further defined) is said to have dropped 9.1%. Mittag, "Ökonomische Strategie," p. 803. For 1983 plan-fulfillment figures see "Mitteilung der Staatlichen Zentralverwaltung für Statistik über die Durchführung des Volkswirtschaftsplanes 1983," *Neues Deutschland*, 19 January 1984, pp. 3–5.

79. Cornelsen, "Successful Production Efforts," pp. 8–10; "Planstart 1985 mit Tatkraft und Optimismus," *Neues Deutschland*, 3 January 1985, p. 2.

80. Cornelsen, "Successful Production Efforts," p. 8; Cornelsen, "Improved Supply Situation," p. 8.

ernment officials, managers, and experts find ways of advocating diverse positions privately and sometimes—generally in veiled or esoteric language—publicly. But the regime's deeply rooted devotion to a conflict-free, integrative social model,[81] and its highly restrictive information policy (born especially of a fear of providing ammunition to the "class enemy" in the Federal Republic),[82] mean that evidence of policy conflict is more slender and exceptional than it is in Yugoslavia, Poland, Hungary, or even the Soviet Union.

Ellen Comisso's illuminating description of East European leadership politics, outside of "patrimonial" Romania, as a collective "politics of notables"—characterized by shifting factional alliances, mutual checking, and, ideally, an overarching framework of consensus managed by an astute *primus inter pares*[83]—applies with some qualifications to the GDR. The institutional locus of the GDR's ruling notables is the twenty-one-member SED Politburo. Günter Gaus, the first head of the Federal Republic Standing Mission in East Berlin, notes that important questions arising in negotiations with GDR officials invariably must await the Politburo's regular Tuesday meetings for resolution.[84] Insiders from various phases of the GDR's history report that Politburo meetings are long—with forty or more items normally on the agenda—and sometimes stormy. Decisions, however, are said usually to be made (as they are in Western cabinets and the Soviet Politburo) by "consensus," presumably defined by the general secretary, rather than by formal vote.[85] Politburo members appear to specialize highly both inside its meetings and outside them; each takes primary responsibility for dealing with matters in his or her area of competence, and in some measure speaks for (without in the Western sense, "representing") those working in that area. The assertion of Franz Loeser, a former SED functionary, that "each one of the Politburo members is unconditional ruler in his own sphere,"[86] is exaggerated, however. Appointment to the Politburo is believed to be through co-optation by existing members.

Gaus remarks that "I have never been able to perceive any tendencies toward faction building in the Politburo,"[87] but more temporary alliances

---

81. See Scharf, *Politics and Change*, chap. 6.

82. See, e.g., Mittag's 1968 warnings against providing the "imperialists" with economic data, cited in Hans-Dieter Schulz, "Mit alten Sorgen auf neuen Posten," *Deutschland Archiv* 9 (December 1976), p. 1244.

83. See her introduction to this volume.

84. Günter Gaus, *Wo Deutschland Liegt—eine Ortsbestimmung* (Hamburg: Hoffman & Campe, 1983), p. 110.

85. Wolfgang Leonhard, *The Kremlin since Stalin* (New York: Praeger, 1962), pp. 4–5; Fritz Schenk, *Im Vorzimmer der Diktatur* (Cologne: Kiepenheuer & Witsch, 1962), p. 244; Rüdiger Thomas, *Modell DDR: Die kalkulierte Emanzipation*, 6th ed. (Munich: Carl Hanser Verlag, 1977), pp. 32–33; Gaus, *Wo Deutschland Liegt*, p. 148.

86. Franz Loeser, "Der Rat der sozialistischen Götter," *Der Spiegel*, 6 August 1984, p. 112; see also Eckart Förtsch, *Die SED* (Stuttgart: W. Kohlhammer Verlag, 1969), p. 41.

87. Gaus, *Wo Deutschland Liegt*, p. 148; see also Thomas, *Modell DDR*, p. 33.

among its members undoubtedly arise. Politburo members represent a variety of functions, levels of education and expertise, and political generations; these divisions, however, cut across one another and are complicated by personal ties and animosities. The appointment to Politburo seats and other high places of a number of former subordinates of Honecker from his years as head of the GDR's Free German Youth suggests that a certain "patrimonial" element is not absent from SED staffing decisions.[88] There are indications, however, that not all of Honecker's former co-workers have remained his unquestioning Politburo supporters. It is plausible to assume that while Politburo alliances tend to be unstable and often transient, certain recurring issues (policies toward West Germany, security questions, economic reform) produce more consistent alignments.

The role of the *primus inter pares* in the collective leadership is, as Comisso recognizes, pivotal. The media hyperbole and symbolic trappings that accompany Honecker's simultaneous occupancy of the positions of SED general secretary, head of state, and chairman of the National Defense Council, as well as his fourteen years in office, his success in promoting to the Politburo his former colleagues and presumed adherents, and his support from the Soviet Union (see below) strengthen his position relative to that of his colleagues. Yet there is no evidence that Honecker makes important decisions, as Ulbricht sometimes did, on his own, without Politburo approval. On the other hand, the degree to which official sources have identified Honecker personally with certain policies (such as the advocacy of an inter-German "coalition of reason") and anecdotal reports on internal Politburo relations suggest that he is not just a broker and consensus builder among and above Politburo factions but when necessary an advocate and leading participant in such factions.[89]

The Politburo does not make its decisions in splendid isolation; a dense network of specialized state and party agencies and research institutions supports it. It regularly invites policy specialists to offer advice and answer questions at its meetings and sometimes creates ad hoc commissions and calls special conferences to lay the groundwork for its decisions.[90] The initiative tends to come from the top down, however; bodies below the Politburo are said to be reluctant to make more than routine decisions on their own, and enterprise, ministries, and other specialist groupings as a rule advance their own interests only in veiled form.[91] Specialized economic ministries dominate

88. Heinz Lippmann, "Die personelle Veränderungen in den Machtzentren der SED als Ausdruck kollektiver Führung," *Deutschland Archiv* 6 (December 1973), p. 1267; Lippmann, *Honecker and the New Politics of Europe* (New York: Macmillan, 1972), pp. 225–28. Honecker's wife and brother-in-law also occupy important political positions, although this particular patrimonial practice does not appear to have reached the proportions it has in Romania.

89. See Gaus, *Wo Deutschland Liegt*, pp. 147–48.

90. Gero Neugebauer, *Partei und Staatsapparat in der DDR* (Opladen: Westdeutscher Verlag, 1978), pp. 62–86.

91. See ibid., p. 58; Leslie Holmes, *The Policy Process in Communist States* (Beverly Hills: Sage, 1981), pp. 267–68.

the Council of Ministers (government); along with the State Planning Commission and key *Kombinat* directors, these ministries are responsible for second-order economic decisions and important implementation measures. But policy initiatives are more likely to come from the small bureaucratic "departments" of the SED Central Committee, many of which parallel the ministries; the departments are also the pivotal institutions for ensuring that Politburo decisions are carried out.[92] Pinpointing the role in the policy process of key party "think tanks," such as the Institute of Politics and Economics and the Academy for Society Sciences, is more difficult, but it seems to be substantial.[93]

The role of the "masses"—whether rank-and-file party members or the citizenry at large—in influencing policy decisions in the GDR is indirect but must be taken seriously into account. As Comisso argues, other party leaders would view any open attempt by a Politburo faction to mobilize popular support on its own behalf as a grave violation of party norms; nevertheless, the SED's acute sensitivity to its legitimacy appears to give the assessment of popular moods a central place in Politburo deliberations. Many formal channels for the articulation of citizen opinion are available—local government, trade unions, or National Front nominating meetings—but these are often subject to manipulation and more suitable for the expression of narrow grievances than of broader political sentiments. The regime, however, regularly polls its citizens and is sensitive to blunter indicators of mass discontent: exit permit applications, youth disturbances, lax work discipline, and absenteeism.

Despite the apparent concentration of decision-making power in the SED Politburo, policy choices do not simply reflect the preferences of the majority of that body or of the triumph of one faction over another. Even more than in most political systems, the range of realistic policy options—indeed, the very definition of the problems to be confronted and the lines along which disagreement is formulated—is in any given case apt to be rather narrow because of forces outside the control of the leadership. These include not only the expectations and demands of relevant societal elites and mass publics but also the regime's own prior history and commitments, the restrictions that the international political and economic systems impose, the pressures of allies, enemies, and other interested powers, and limits on the system's capacity for implementation. Each of these elements has played a role in circumscribing the Politburo's political choices, but I want to stress two factors that are particularly constraining for the GDR: the influence of the Soviet Union, and the complex of legitimacy problems associated with the proximity of the Federal Republic.

92. Neugebauer, *Partei und Staatsapparat*, pp. 59–60.
93. See Anita Mallinckrodt, *Wer Macht die Aussenpolitik der DDR?* (Düsseldorf: Droste Verlag, 1972), pp. 212–13; *DDR Handbuch*, pp. 34–35.

The Soviet Union is an important player in SED leadership politics as well as in the SED's policy deliberations, whether by direct intervention or through its use as a resource by competing factions and individuals. As I noted earlier, analysts have attributed Honecker's replacement of Ulbricht in 1971 to Soviet pressures—and certainly the change required Soviet approval. We do not know whether the Soviet Union directly intervenes in the selection of other Politburo members, but there seems to be no case in which a member has been chosen in opposition to Soviet wishes. We do know that many Politburo members were educated in the Soviet Union and that many have regular professional contacts with their Soviet counterparts. The configuration of functional specialization on the Soviet Politburo resembles that in the GDR body, suggesting that policy disagreements and thus factions in the latter may closely parallel—or even directly reflect—those in the former. The degree of policy leeway the Soviet Union views as appropriate for the GDR and the precision with which it specifies limits are unknown, but analysts usually assume that restrictions are somewhat greater upon the GDR than on other Eastern-bloc countries, reflecting both the Soviet Union's sensitivity to German matters and the GDR's special strategic and economic importance. The SED Politburo's awareness of its military and economic dependence on the Soviet Union and its own ideological commitments unquestionably inhibit it from departing sharply from Soviet precedents and desires. This does not mean that East German actions always slavishly imitate Soviet precedents. Two recent careful comparative studies of Soviet and East German policy making (on industrial organization and the environment) show many close resemblances, particularly on the rhetorical level, but some significant differences in the actual policies; moreover, the GDR has often implemented these policies with greater success.[94] The influence of the Soviet Union on policy making in the GDR, however, is not just a result of conscious intervention by the former or conscious imitation by the latter; unilateral Soviet decisions (on, say, energy production or arms control negotiations) can also greatly affect the environment in which the GDR formulates policy.[95]

The GDR's relationship to the Federal Republic, like its relationship to the Soviet Union, profoundly influences the regime's authority in the eyes of its own population. Each East European state has its own distinctive set of legitimacy problems; the GDR's revolve particularly around the unresolved question of national identity.[96] Since its inception the Federal Republic has been a rival and negative role model by which the GDR's regime and its

---

94. Holmes, *Policy Process*; Joan DeBardeleben, *The Environment and Marxism-Leninism* (Boulder: Westview, 1985).

95. On Soviet–East German relations in general see Melvin Croan, *East Germany: The Soviet Connection* (Beverly Hills: Sage, 1976).

96. See Gebhard Schweigler, *National Consciousness in Divided Germany* (Beverly Hills: Sage, 1975).

citizens evaluate GDR policies; it has radiated a continuing, seductive attraction for East German citizens, millions of whom fled to the West before August 1961, and hundreds of thousands of whom are currently reported to be awaiting permits to emigrate.[97] The arranged marriage, or better, dalliance, between the Federal Republic and the GDR that the Soviet Union imposed on its ally at the beginning of the 1970s brought the regime new economic and political opportunities, but for many East German leaders the fears of the possibly destabilizing consequences of the Western embrace far exceeded their appreciation of its likely benefits. These fears notwithstanding, the new relationship created a network of formal and informal inter-German ties that no East German regime can now easily dismantle.

The politics of the GDR's economic strategy

An understanding of the compelling and often conflicting influences of the Soviet Union and the Federal Republic on East German decision making is essential if we are to comprehend the political logic of the economic strategy pursued under Honecker and the GDR's response to the price shocks of the 1970s. The *Ostpolitik* decisions of the Soviet Union created much of the setting for the adoption of the strategy of 1971, and the changed relationship with West Germany, along with the GDR's attendant preoccupation with its still-tenuous legitimacy, helped to shape and then gradually to modify the content of the strategy. We must also consider, however, the additional influence of the economic reform experience of the 1960s and the changes in the party elite that accompanied it.

As we saw, by late 1970 the crisis of plan fulfillment and the shortages and bottlenecks of 1969 and 1970, joined to a more fundamental unwillingness to accept either the political or the full economic implications of reform, had led the SED finally to abandon the New Economic System. It did not, however, want to lose either the economic vitality the reforms had generated or their usefulness in strengthening acceptance of the regime, particularly among the GDR's young, well-educated, and somewhat privileged technical intelligentsia. By associating the SED with scientific and technical modernization and a more flexible and pragmatic approach to economic and political decision making, the NES had contributed to the party's self-confidence and broadened its basis of legitimacy. On one level, then, the task for the SED was to change the substance of its system of economic management while retaining the broad rhetorical appeal and some of the genuine accomplishments of the previous system.

Changes in the composition of the higher echelons of the party and state

---

97. *Süddeutsche Zeitung*, 17 October 1984, p. 4, gives an estimate of 800,000. Most other sources mention a figure of 400,000 to 500,000.

that had accompanied the reforms reinforced the need to find such an approach. Well-educated and comparatively young economic and managerial cadres now occupied many of the positions once dominated by older functionaries with limited formal education whose loyalties to German communism dated to the 1930s or before.[98] At the same time, a new generation of ideological and organizational specialists (Horst Dohlus and Werner Lamberz, Central Committee secretaries for organization and agitation respectively, are prominent examples) had also risen in the party, but they, like the economic specialists, were well-educated and politically sophisticated, and had absorbed the lesson of the NES period that political and ideological leadership required a concomitant measure of economic and technical understanding. For both groups, the abandonment of economic reform could not mean simply a reversion to "tonnage ideology" and neo-Stalinist methods of economic direction.[99]

The Politburo itself as of 1971 included members of both groups together with older party veterans who had viewed the economic reforms with reservations from the beginning; one such veteran was probably Erich Honecker.[100] Walter Halbritter's resignation as Politburo candidate in 1973 was a belated indicator of factional disagreements over reform which probably dated from the 1960s but persisted into the 1970s. Halbritter had been one of the architects of the NES. At the same time an SED regional first secretary without formal economic training, Werner Krolikowski, replaced Günter Mittag (who remained on the Politburo) as SED secretary for the economy. Willi Stoph, who had presided over the administration of the economy as chairman of the Council of Ministers in the 1960s, was elevated to the largely honorific post of chairman of the State Council. This experiment apparently misfired, and Mittag was back at his economic post by the end of 1976, just as the GDR was beginning to feel the waves from the first price shock. Simultaneously, Stoph returned to his earlier position. These changes proved to be harbingers of the first modest re-adjustments of policy in response to the changed economic environment, and perhaps of a significant shift in Honecker's own commitments.[101]

The original strategy of the Honecker period, then, responded to a combination of elements: the legacy of the reforms and the altered composition

98. David Granick argues that the GDR was "the only one of the east European countries in which politically acceptable managers who were technically inefficient have been demoted on a fairly large scale"; he specifically notes the absence of a similar policy in Romania, Czechoslovakia, and Hungary. See Granick, *Enterprise Guidance in Eastern Europe* (Princeton: Princeton University Press, 1975), pp. 213–15.

99. On all this see Baylis, *Technical Intelligentsia*, especially chap. 10.

100. Evidence on the point is sketchy, however. See Peter-Claus Burens, *Die DDR und die "Prager Frühling"* (Berlin: Duncker & Humblot, 1981), pp. 115, 121, 125–28.

101. See Fred Oldenburg, "Ost-Berlin wieder auf härterem Kurs," *Deutschland Archiv* 6 (November 1973), pp. 1121–24; Ilse Spittman, "Die NÖS-Mannschaft kehrt zurück," *Deutschland Archiv* 9 (November 1976), pp. 1121–24; Schulz, "Mit alten Sorgen," pp. 1243–45.

of the party elite; the involuntary opening to the West brought about by the East-West treaties; and the circumstances of Ulbricht's enforced retirement which required acceptance of the treaties but also close outward adherence to the economic principles laid down at the Twenty-fourth CPSU Congress and within the CMEA. The new strategy also allowed Honecker to establish his own leadership profile in the eyes of both the GDR's population and the SED elite.

Under the Honecker strategy, the recentralization of economic management proceeded simultaneously with the continuing celebration of economic modernization and of the scientific-technological revolution. A more populist appeal to working-class hegemony replaced the technocratic language of the later years of the Ulbricht era, though protestations of the technical intelligentsia's continuing importance continued, and the more concrete promises of Communist consumerism replaced the uncertain prospects of future benefits from economic reform. Party officials contrasted the growing economic difficulties of the now more accessible capitalist West to the social protection and security (*soziale Geborgenheit*) that "real socialism" could offer. The not insignificant problem of paying for these benefits was met by tying them to the improvement of productivity and the parsimonious use of resources— the "unity of social and economic policy." The new "openness" of the GDR to Western influence, though unavoidable, was celebrated as proof of the GDR's internal strength, even while the regime made strenuous efforts to contain its effects through *Abgrenzung*.

The social contract between the GDR and its citizens at the heart of this strategy depended in a number of respects on the relationship of both to the Federal Republic. The clauses of the contract which had an especially marked appeal to East Germans were those that provided for expanded opportunities for contacts with West Germans, in person and via telephone and mail; the availability of West German deutsche marks (which increasingly became the GDR's "second currency") and Western goods, as gifts from West Germans and through the *Intershops*; and access to Western "culture," in the form of rock music, blue jeans, and the like, no longer proscribed and in some cases actively promoted by the SED. The assurance that the two German states would make a serious effort to deal with their differences in a variety of areas through ongoing negotiations and, emerging more gradually, a joint German commitment to reducing international tensions—to making sure that "war does not again break out from German soil"—also seemed to become part of the contract. Over the years East Germans came to regard these improved Western links as a critical part of what was "due" them in exchange for their hard work and political quiescence. Along with a wider range of consumer goods and social benefits, they came to be regarded as socialist "entitlements," which the regime could withhold only at its peril.

For its part, the regime could only view the creeping institutionalization of its Western ties with ambivalence; leadership conflict has undoubtedly accompanied each step. On the one hand, the relatively stable relationship with the Federal Republic assured the GDR of access to needed technology and other productive inputs, and offered it financial advantages not available to its CMEA partners. In some respects it also offered the GDR means for shoring up its domestic stability, both by permitting measured concessions to its citizens' desires and by providing a safety valve for discontent—in extreme cases, allowing the regime to export its most obstinate troublemakers in exchange for hard currency.

On the other hand, the regime fully recognized that the economic generosity of the Federal Republic has its price, including escalating and not always resistible West German demands for political concessions. It also was aware that there is a close if not always demonstrable relationship between its ties to the Federal Republic and manifestations of internal unrest. The dissident writers and intellectuals of the 1970s regularly published their work in the West, and Western radio and television promptly transmitted it back to GDR listeners and viewers. East-West church connections and the examples of the West German peace movement and the Green party helped inspire the GDR's church-based, "autonomous" peace and ecology movements—which the regime could not ruthlessly suppress without appearing to abridge the "social contract." Western models and visitors have also shaped the rise of a GDR "youth culture" whose values are often at odds with officially proclaimed ones.[102] West German television advertising influences and probably heightens East German consumer demand. The presence of a West German diplomatic mission in East Berlin together with the publicity given to the Helsinki Agreement helped generate a wave of applications for exit permits. For the GDR's leaders, assessing the balance between the costs of its West German connection and the presumed economic benefits thus continues to be a rather uncertain exercise.

The politics of the response to the shocks

The dimensions of the GDR's dilemma became particularly apparent when it was forced to respond to the price shocks and ensuing debt crisis. By the mid-1970s it had begun to recognize that its worsening terms of trade with both the West and the Soviet Union necessitated some adjustments. The return of Mittag as economic secretary and Stoph as premier signaled this awareness, which was reflected in policy terms by greater emphasis on work productivity, material savings, and the use of indigenous raw materials; a stress on developing microelectronics and industrial robots; and the attempt, from 1975, to bring industrial prices more in line with costs. What the GDR

102. See Wolfgang Büscher and Peter Wensierski, *Null Bock auf DDR—Aussteigerjugend im anderen Deutschland* (Reinbek bei Hamburg: Rowohlt, 1984).

did *not* do was turn away from the West, economically or politically: the importance of Western technology for Honecker's program and the support that Western trade provided to the GDR's efforts to raise living standards were apparently too great, and the easy availability of Western credits too enticing.

It was only after the second price shock, in 1979, and especially after the mounting crisis in Poland threatened to close down its access to Western credit markets, that the GDR seems to have been fully persuaded of the seriousness of its problems and undertook rather drastic short-term measures to deal with them. The choices it made were virtually dictated by the choices it wanted at all costs to avoid. Sharply cutting domestic consumption or reducing the subsidization of consumer staples—a major government expenditure taking up 11.8 percent of the total budget in 1982[103]—was unthinkable in the light of the events in Poland. Honecker's expensive "social policy" measures were a vital part of his regime's identity and thus could not be severely cut, although the regime could not for the moment afford to expand them further. Under pressure from the Soviet Union and facing increases in NATO military budgets, the GDR apparently felt it had little choice but to increase its military expenditures.[104]

Politically, the course of least resistance was to reduce and reorient investment, which, as we saw, was quickly done. The GDR's decision to press the increase of exports rather than drastically to reduce imports indicates the significance it placed on the latter. Of course, other East European countries might well have made the same choice had they been able to economically. The GDR's most striking choice was to maintain most of its Western trade, even in the short term, which put it in the unaccustomed position of being the East European CMEA state with the highest proportion of such trade.[105] It is noteworthy that even the modest drop in consumption levels in 1982 and 1983 brought a renewed expansion of Western trade in 1983.[106]

"Socialist intensification," the first leg of the GDR's long-term response to its new economic situation, was, as far as we know, essentially uncontroversial both internally and inside the CMEA. Domestically, the benefits of fuel, material, and labor savings were scarcely disputable. Such measures also corresponded well to overall CMEA goals and coincided with the Soviet desire for its allies to reduce their dependence on Soviet raw materials. The reorientation of investment away from large-scale new projects doubtless provoked resistance in interested quarters and was also subject to challenge

103. *Statistisches Jahrbuch 1983*, p. 255.

104. Ibid., p. 257; " 'Dann kann der Erich zu Hause bleiben,' " *Der Spiegel*, 9 July 1984, p. 18.

105. Machowski, "Uncertain Outlook," p. 6.

106. See Cornelsen, "Consolidation," p. 10; *Statistisches Jahrbuch 1984*, p. 239; Machowski, "Uncertain Outlook," p. 6.

on broader economic grounds, but little public evidence on this point has surfaced.[107]

We must view the second component of the long-term strategy—the return to a process of "reform in small steps"—as an acknowledgment that the time-honored measures of ideological exhortation and mobilization and the further proliferation of plan indicators would not be sufficient to overcome the economic squeeze facing the country. Although no open "reform party" comparable to Hungary's has been visible in the SED leadership since the 1960s, it appears that the economic pragmatists surviving from the NES era and their critics have struck a compromise. Under its terms, the parametric devices and other policy changes introduced are not to be called "reforms" and are to be justified ideologically as a means for "perfecting" central planning and strengthening democratic centralism. Public discussion of such matters as the Hungarian reforms or of the advantages of International Monetary Fund membership is not tolerated. Although the directors of the *Kombinate* have been given greater authority to manipulate resources internally, they do not have a free hand over either investment or the importation of materials. The network of financial and political controls, rather than being simplified, is in some respects being made even more dense.

Whether this compromise is a stable one, or whether, alternatively, the economic specialists supporting it see it as a wedge that might open the way to a more far-reaching and comprehensive reform program can as yet be only a matter of speculation. Some GDR writers admit that directive and parametric methods of economic steering may conflict with one another,[108] and acknowledge at least implicitly the possibility that *Kombinate* and ministries may clash over their respective prerogatives[109]—suggesting that a rationale for pressing the reforms further is available if it is wanted. It also appears that the economic specialists are better positioned than at any time since the 1960s to carry their point of view in the Politburo. Two veterans of the NES era, Werner Jarowinsky and Günter Kleiber, were elevated to full Politburo membership in May 1984 after long service as nonvoting candidate members. Mittag himself has enjoyed high visibility as the SED's authoritative spokesman on domestic economic questions and as economic emissary to the Federal Republic, having met in Bonn with members of the Kohl government in April 1983 and April 1984 prior to the bank credit agreements of those years, and again in April 1985.

The economic utilization of the West German connection—the third com-

107. The influential head of the Academy of Social Sciences, Otto Reinhold, has, however, remarked that "rationalization cannot be a substitute for scientific-technological progress." Cited in Gruhn and Lauterbach, "Rationalisierungsmittelbau," p. 1182.

108. See Biefeld, Hesse, and Schüsseler, "Vervollkommnung."

109. For a plea to strengthen the position of the general directors vis-à-vis the ministries, see Roswitha Dittman and Ludwig Penig, "Die Stellung der Kombinate im staatlichen Leitungssystem," *Staat und Recht* 30, no. 12 (1981), pp. 1089–97.

ponent of the long-term response—was the most controversial. In late 1982, after the GDR had quietly approached the Bonn government about a large credit, the Berlin SED first secretary Konrad Naumann sharply attacked those in the GDR who wanted to "evade the severity of the international class struggle." Naumann, a former co-worker with and earlier a presumptive supporter of Honecker, insisted that "the political principles of the GDR are not wares to be haggled over, they cannot be bought with dollars and in others ways."[110] Because of his later attacks on the Federal Republic at a time when Honecker and other leaders had begun to talk of an inter-German community of interest,[111] Western journalists have placed him among a Politburo faction hostile to Honecker's Western policies, along with the defense and police heads Heinz Hoffmann and Erich Mielke, Premier Stoph, and possibly others.[112] This putative division within the Politburo parallels one that has appeared in the GDR's foreign-policy literature; some articles portray the Federal Republic as an independent threat to peace, others as a somewhat hesitant and potentially movable ally of Ronald Reagan's United States.[113]

The same dispute exists in the Soviet literature, and the apparent divergence between Honecker's path and the views of the Soviet leadership that took on the dramatic form of the dispute I described at the beginning of this essay may conceal a great deal of ambivalence on the Soviet side. Although disparities between East German and Soviet rhetoric date from the fall of 1983, it does not appear that Honecker set out openly to defy the Soviet Union. He reportedly had received the imprimatur first of Yuri Andropov and then of Konstantin Chernenko (with whom he conferred in June 1984 during the CMEA summit) for his approach to the Federal Republic and had not reckoned on the latter's disappearance from public view (and presumably his inability to lead the deliberations of the Soviet collective leadership) for two months. What remains extraordinary is the fact that Honecker's "misunderstanding" was not cleared up in private but required a bitter public exchange, which quickly expanded to a blocwide dispute involving the Czechs,

110. Cited in Ilse Spittman, "Der Milliardenkredit," *Deutschland Archiv* 16 (August 1983), p. 785.

111. See Konrad Naumann, "Freude über das Erreichte—kämpferisch an neue Ziele" (Speech at Seventh Central Committee Plenum), *Neues Deutschland*, 11 November 1983, p. 7.

112. Christian Schmidt-Häuer, "Der lange Papierkrieg der roten Brüder," *Die Zeit* [North American ed.], 17 August 1984, pp. 3–4; Wolfgang Seiffert, "Eine verlorene Schlacht," *Der Spiegel*, 10 September 1984, p. 20; Seyppl, "Ich bin," pp. 16, 112–13; *New York Times*, 5 September 1984, p. 8; " 'Dann kann der Erich,' " pp. 18–19. East Berlin officials ridicule such reports of leadership conflicts. "When the situation demands, we are all either hawks or doves," Politburo member Egon Krenz told West German reporter Theo Sommer ("Mit der Geschichte auf dem Buckel," *Die Zeit* [North American ed.], 10 August 1984, p. 3). In November 1985 Naumann was removed from the Politburo; in early December Hoffman died of a heart attack.

113. See Michael J. Sodaro, "In the Shadow of the Missiles: East German and Soviet Perceptions of West German Foreign Policy" (Paper presented at Wingspread Conference on the GDR in Comparative Perspective, Racine, Wisconsin, 14–17 April 1983).

Hungarians, Poles, and Bulgarians, before Honecker finally capitulated and "postponed" his visit.[114] At one point *Pravda* went as far as to attack Honecker's own phrase, "damage limitation," attributing it to the West Germans.[115]

Soviet pressures against the Honecker visit leave unresolved the question of how the CPSU leadership views the developing pattern of East German economic links to the Federal Republic and to other capitalist nations. On the one hand, a new trade and economic cooperation agreement with the Soviet Union commits the GDR to high-technology exports, further participation in Soviet investment projects, and the close coordination of industrial development until the year 2000.[116] Fulfilling these assignments will make it difficult for the GDR to maintain its present level of Western trade, much less expand it. On the other hand, the Soviet Union benefits directly or indirectly from any Western technology the GDR obtains with the help of its West German connection; indeed, many of the high-quality industrial and consumer goods the Soviet Union wants from the GDR rely on a continuing flow of Western technology and in some cases Western components. Reduced dependence of the GDR on Soviet deliveries would also free more "hard" goods for the Soviet Union to sell on the world market for hard currency. It also should be emphasized that the Federal Republic remains the Soviet Union's own leading Western trading partner and a major Soviet creditor,[117] an important fact that imposes at least some limits on the ferocity of Soviet attacks on East German–West German ties and even more on crude measures to curtail them. It may be assumed that the Soviet Union wants to have first claim on the GDR's most sophisticated exports and remains hypersensitive to signs of any substantial warming of inter-German relations; yet it sees significant advantages for itself in the GDR's Western trade. The result is probably to allow the GDR some leeway in charting its future course—as the renewed movement in inter-German relations following the naming of Mikhail Gorbachev as CPSU general secretary suggests.[118]

114. For detailed accounts, see Schmidt-Häuer, "Papierkrieg," pp. 3–4; "Moskau—Opfer des Immobilismus," *Der Spiegel*, 10 September 1984, pp. 29–32; Oldenburg, "Werden Moskaus."
115. "On a Wrong Course," pp. 4, 8.
116. "DDR and UdSSR," p. 20; according to the GDR's minister of foreign trade, Horst Sölle, "collectives from our republic are currently working on fifteen construction sites in the Soviet Union in projects which are also of great significance for the prospective securing of the energy and raw materials needs of the DDR." Cited in Michael Schmitz, "Das Beste für den grossen Bruder," *Die Zeit* [North American ed.], 25 January 1985, p. 12.
117. Thus in September 1984, shortly after the postponement of the Honecker visit, the Soviet Union signed a DM 500 million credit deal organized by a West German bank. "Economic Ties with the West," RAD Background Report 189, *Radio Free Europe Research*, 12 October 1984, p. 14.
118. See John Tagliabue, "East German Chief Will Visit Rome," *New York Times*, 6 April 1985, p. 2.

Conclusion: the sources of success

If the combination of inter-German factors, Soviet-inspired constraints, and domestic pressures helps explain the GDR's choice of economic strategy and its modifications of that strategy in the wake of the price and credit shocks of the 1970s and early 1980s, it does not explain the GDR's relative economic success. That success was already evident in the comparatively limited measures that the GDR was required to take to get its balance of payments in order and reduce its debt. East German consumers were spared the privations undergone by their Polish, Romanian, and Yugoslav counterparts. Moreover, two years after the worst of the debt squeeze, the GDR had reestablished its creditworthiness in Western eyes, achieved its highest reported growth in PNI in a decade, substantially increased its domestic trade turnover, and maintained the flow of needed Western imports.

The temptation is great to ascribe these successes to the GDR's West German connection. Is it true, as Ronald Francisco suggests, that "the West Germans increasingly provide [the GDR's] liquidity, its access to foreign markets, its technology, and its financial security"?[119] As we have seen, the Federal Republic offers a privileged market for GDR goods, is the source of subsidies on the order of two billion deutsche marks a year, serves as a guarantor of GDR creditworthiness, and by these means offers its neighbor greater access to other Western markets. The GDR's ability to utilize inter-German trade as a source of emergency inputs is particularly valuable for a socialist economy characteristically beset by bottlenecks and shortages.[120] On the other hand, West German trade by itself amounts to just 8.5 percent of the GDR's total foreign trade and includes relatively little high technology. Predominantly a technology "supplier" to other CMEA states, and the most advanced among them in this respect, the GDR must obtain as much technology as it can from the Federal Republic and other Western nations, but the level of its Western trade, as Siegfried Schoppe has concluded, has thus far been insufficient for Western technology to serve it as a truly "dynamic growth factor."[121]

Undoubtedly one reason the GDR was able to surmount the energy and credit crunch with relative ease was the strong economic position it occupied prior to the price shocks—reflected in its larger productive capacity (relative to population) and in its ability to increase its exports to the West even at a time of capitalist recession. Whatever its flaws, East German industry is

119. Ronald A. Francisco, "The German Democratic Republic: Stability and External Adaptation" (Paper presented to the National Convention of the American Association for the Advancement of Slavic Studies, Kansas City, 22–25 October 1983); Francisco cites in turn Frederick Kempe, "The Two Germanies Build a Relationship," *Wall Street Journal*, 16 September 1983, pp. 1, 10.
120. See Comisso's introduction to this volume and János Kornai, *Economics of Shortage*, 2 vols. (Amsterdam: North Holland, 1980).
121. Schoppe, "Technologietransfers," pp. 359–60.

demonstrably better equipped than its CMEA neighbors to produce goods of sufficient quality to appeal to Western markets (albeit with the help of some price cutting). Here, too, a tempting explanation also rests upon the West German connection. The GDR has a more capable economy, it might be argued, because of its years of competition with the Federal Republic. Like Avis, the GDR may have succeeded because it has been forced to "try harder."

Although this explanation has a strong intuitive appeal, the exact mechanisms that lead from the GDR's own sense of competition with the Federal Republic (*not* for the most part direct competition in the marketplace) to superior economic accomplishment are difficult to specify. There is no solid evidence that the competition itself has given the GDR technological advantages or a more intimate acquaintance with Western management techniques than the other CMEA states have enjoyed. At least until recently, Poland and Hungary have been more inclined than the GDR to agree to the sort of far-reaching joint undertakings with Western capitalist firms which might bring such benefits.

A still broader and more familiar explanation suggests that the GDR does better because its citizens are "German" or, even more, "Prussian." There is undoubtedly some truth underlying this assertion, insofar as it means that East Germany, despite all the destruction and loss of skilled personnel it suffered during and after World War II, began with a more developed and technologically sophisticated industrial base, a more skilled work force, a better educational system, and possibly a higher level of "achievement motivation" than its neighbors (with the possible exception of Czechoslovakia, which one might argue is still suffering from the trauma of the 1968 invasion). Unlike most of the other East European states, the GDR did not have to undergo the difficult transition from a primarily peasant to an industrial society under Communist rule.

We cannot neglect political factors in accounting for the GDR's success. In spite of the size of the party—more than one of every six adults in the GDR is an SED member—it has maintained strong internal discipline and has managed to keep "reformist" elements, such as those that surfaced in Czechoslovakia in the mid-1960s and Poland after the rise of Solidarity, from asserting themselves in its ranks. Neither the corruption of the Polish United Workers' party, the personalization of power in the Romanian Communist party, nor the fragmentation of the Yugoslav League of Communists have afflicted the SED. In fact, under Honecker the party has balanced repression and flexibility with notable skill, limiting severe doses of repression to exemplary cases and permitting and sometimes encouraging especially persistent opponents to depart the country.

The GDR's success casts some doubt upon the fond belief of many Western commentators that a centralized system of economic direction, however effective it might be in forcing industrial development in relatively backward societies, is a hopelessly clumsy and inefficient way of organizing a technologically sophisticated economy or satisfying the increasingly exacting demands of its consumers. The GDR remains, of course, a long way from achieving its goal of overtaking the Federal Republic in productivity and living standards. But statistically, in material terms it does not fare badly in comparison with such Western states as Britain and Italy. The structural inefficiencies of command economies are all present in the GDR, but it has done well enough in spite of them to suggest that a mixture of central direction, ideological exhortation and mobilization, indirect financial incentives for both individuals and economic entities, and Western (and perhaps Soviet) subsidies can produce a reasonably modern economy that "works."[122]

The future of Honecker's economic strategy nevertheless remains uncertain. I have suggested that in order to implement the strategy under the world economic conditions that emerged in the 1970s, the SED has been forced to make a series of almost Faustian choices between Western and especially West German economic linkages and politico-ideological purity[123]—which it values perhaps more than do most of its sister parties. These choices have left it vulnerable to political and social changes and to a degree of involvement with the Federal Republic that neither the GDR's own ideologues nor the Soviet Union can be entirely sanguine about. Because, however, they are intimately linked with the GDR's continuing search for a national identity and to the legitimacy dilemmas going along with it, the necessity for such agonizing choices is likely to persist.

122. Marrese and Vaňous have calculated that the GDR has been the greatest beneficiary of Soviet "implicit subsidies" since 1974; if they are correct, this would help explain the GDR's success. Their assertion, however, rests heavily on their controversial (and, as they admit, "uncertain") estimate of the degree to which the prices paid by the Soviet Union for East European manufactured goods allegedly exceed world market prices. See Marrese's essay in this volume.

123. Francisco, "German Democratic Republic," p. 14.

The economics and politics of reform in Hungary Ellen Comisso and Paul Marer

What distinguishes Hungary's reaction to highly unfavorable changes in the international economy from that of other participants in the Council for Mutual Economic Assistance (CMEA) is that a series of wide-ranging reforms in the economic system has accompanied austerity measures. Designed to make the economy more efficient, the reforms give prices and profits more active roles in resource allocation and enterprises more autonomy to respond to them. Thus, reform of the economic structure is a distinctive element of Hungary's foreign economic strategy in the 1980s.

Both economic and political factors led to such a response. In section 1 of this essay we shall review the evolution of the Hungarian economic system, development strategy, and performance before and after the first major economic reform in 1968. The economic need for reform stems from Hungary's status as a small country, poor in energy and raw materials, and heavily dependent on foreign trade. Since CMEA suppliers can no longer meet many of Hungary's essential import needs, the country's long-term economic prospects are tied closely to its ability to economize on imports and increase exports to non-CMEA states.

The obstacles to economic reform lie in a heritage of policy choices which ignored precisely these exigencies. Responding to domestic and CMEA supply constraints, postwar development priorities were not based on Hungary's comparative advantages in the larger international economy. Decisions to specialize made before and after 1968 undercut the systemic reforms of that

Ellen Comisso thanks the International Research and Exchange Board and the German Marshall Fund for generously funding the field research on which her contribution to this essay is based. She completed the essay while a fellow at the Center for Advanced Study in the Behavioral Sciences; the Exxon Educational Foundation provided financial support during her stay there. Paul Marer acknowledges the Mellon Summer Research Grant awarded him by Indiana University's Russian and East European Institute.

International Organization 40, 2, Spring 1986   0020-8183 $5.00

year and made Hungary exceptionally vulnerable to international economic shocks in the 1970s and 1980s. The resulting "crisis" of 1979–82 both reordered policy priorities and led to new changes in economic structure and allocation mechanisms, designed to improve the adaptability of the domestic economy to changes in the world economy.

Why Hungary made such institutional and policy choices is also a product of political factors, analyzed in section 2. Politically, the acceptability of reform in Hungary is a result of its unique national trauma, the 1956 revolt, combined with general changes in economic priorities and party-state relations that hit all CMEA states in the mid-1950s. Like leaders of other states in Eastern Europe, the post-1956 Hungarian leadership rejected the accelerated, "one-sided" industrialization strategy of the early 1950s in favor of more gradual development based on existing natural endowments and resource constraints. Like most others in Eastern Europe, Hungarian leaders also rejected one-man rule over the party in favor of collective leadership within it. Yet Hungarian collective leadership was unique in that it included advocates of the introduction of a limited market mechanism, a strategy that implied substantial modifications in the economic system. Moreover, unlike reformists elsewhere, Hungarian advocates of economic reform sought not to weaken the party but to use it to pursue their particular economic goals. That the Hungarian party continues to accommodate these reformists points up how far-reaching the lessons of 1956 have been. Their continued inclusion in top party policy-making bodies has made the bases of conflict and cohesion within the Hungarian party unique within Eastern Europe.

Although general commitment to the political norms and structures surrounding collective leadership has kept economic reform alive in Hungary, those same norms and structures make reform advocates inherently weak politically and create major obstacles to implementation of their policy preferences. Political contradictions were critical to the erosion of reformist influence in 1972–78 which led to policy choices that stopped and in some respects reversed the reform process begun in 1968. The international economic shocks of the 1970s, however, revealed contradictions between development goals and real economic capacities, causing the intraparty balance of forces to shift back in favor of reformists. In section 3 of this essay we shall examine the political and economic implications of the post-1979 institutional changes, analyzing the degree to which the politico-economic contradictions that underlay the reversal of the 1968 reform are likely to reappear in the 1980s.

1. Economic aspects of Hungarian reform

To determine the impact of external economic disturbances in the 1970s on Hungary and its subsequent response, we must distinguish between the country's economic system and its economic policies. The economic system has four main building blocks: the scope and methods of central planning and regulation, the instruments used, the economy's institutional structure, and the scope of the private sector. Hence it includes the degree of centralization and differentiation in state and economy as well as the mechanisms through which they communicate their preferences to one another.

Economic *policy*, in contrast, is the set of decisions by policy makers about the relative importance of certain economic objectives (from rates of growth of consumption and investment to the commodity and geographic composition of foreign trade) and the ways to achieve them. Policy makers may treat the economic system as given, or they may change it in order to achieve their policy objectives.

Economic policy, reform, and performance to 1978

Hungary is a small country at a medium level of development—in terms of per capita gross national product (GNP) comparable, say, to Greece or Spain—and heavily dependent on foreign trade. Its population is small and ethnically homogeneous. Although its territory is poor in the energy and raw materials required for industrial development, the Danube Basin is well suited for agriculture.

Despite these features, in the early 1950s Hungary copied the centrally planned economic system (CPE) introduced by Stalin in the Soviet Union in the 1930s, including the ruthless collectivization drive that made a shambles of Hungarian agriculture. Economic policies that emphasized investment at the expense of consumption, industry at the expense of agriculture, and heavy industry at the expense of light industry also reflected the Soviet model. Despite the lack of the required natural resources, mining and metallurgy were promoted in the hope of making Hungary a "country of iron and steel." The requirements of the CMEA determined most of Hungary's output. First and foremost among CMEA members to specify what it wished to import was the Soviet Union, which supplied growing quantities of crude oil, iron ore, and much of the equipment Hungary needed to establish its iron and steel industry.[1]

The 1956 revolt came as a tremendous shock. It caused leaders to question the accelerated and one-sided growth of heavy industry and prompted them to consider policies more suited to specific Hungarian conditions and far-

1. Accounts of the pre-1956 period include Ferenc Vali, *Rift and Revolt in Hungary* (Cambridge: Harvard University Press, 1961); Paul Zinner, *Revolution in Hungary* (New York: Columbia University Press, 1962); David Irving, *Insurrection! Budapest 1956* (Paris: Albin & Michel, 1981); and Bennet Kovrig, *Communism in Hungary* (Stanford: Hoover Institution Press, 1979). On the economic system see János Kornai, *Overcentralization in Economic Administration* (Oxford: Oxford University Press, 1959) and Bela Balassa, *The Hungarian Experience in Economic Planning* (New Haven: Yale University Press, 1959).

reaching reforms in the economic system. Nevertheless, recommendations that a party-appointed expert commission made in 1957 were shelved until interest in reform revived in the mid-1960s under more favorable politico-economic conditions.

During and after 1956, most collective farms disbanded spontaneously or lost most of their members. In 1958 efforts to recollectivize agriculture began; however, these differed greatly from the initial collectivization drives. Rather than relying on poor peasants to take the lead and provoke class war in the countryside, collectivization in 1958 aimed to attract better-off peasants in the hope that others would voluntarily follow. Voluntary contracts replaced compulsory production and delivery obligations at more favorable prices even in 1957, and peasants could choose the type of cooperative or collective they would join as well as whether or not to participate in farm management. Moreover, the government provided inputs and substantial investment resources to the new collectives, as a result of which Hungary was the only CPE in which crop output did not decline during collectivization.

Economic policy in the 1960s halted the earlier neglect of agriculture and effected a growing number of institutional changes in that sector, motivated in part by grass-roots pressures. New incentive mechanisms were introduced; private, collective, and state farm production and marketing were integrated; later, socialist agricultural units were permitted to engage in entrepreneurial ventures in industry, construction, and services.

Given the economic success of the individualized incentive mechanisms, reforms in agriculture were difficult to reverse. Each time restrictions were placed on agricultural producers, output stagnated or declined, prompting the leadership to lift the restrictions. Agriculture thus became the vanguard of Hungary's reform movement. Increased agricultural yields and output have contributed significantly to improved economic performance and allowed the sector to serve as a model and rationale for the introduction of economywide reforms in 1968.

While agriculture was slowly being transformed, in industry the traditional CPE and the policies of import substitution associated with it remained; however, planned growth rates dropped significantly from the pressurized pace characteristic of the early 1950s. Engineering and chemicals became priorities in the 1960s, reflecting efforts to integrate more closely with the CMEA. Far from reducing imports, such policies rapidly increased them; only their composition changed: from machinery and consumer goods to energy, raw materials, and semifabricates—precisely the commodities whose prices "exploded" twice in the subsequent decade.

The traditional CPE and its policies created serious difficulties even in the 1960s. Externally, constraints on the rate of growth in energy and raw materials available from the CMEA and cumulating evidence that new technology would have to be imported from the West posed problems. Internally, diminishing returns in mining and the exhaustion of labor reserves from the rural and female populations were additional barriers to further extensive growth. Not surprisingly, growth rates began to drop, and severe tensions in the balance of payments with convertible-currency areas arose, making it appear imperative to improve the efficiency of the domestic economy rather than continuing to rely on increased inputs for growth.

To do so, the leadership inaugurated comprehensive economic reforms in 1968. Although the measures comprising the New Economic Mechanism (NEM) did not seek to abandon central planning, they did reduce its scope greatly and changed its main instruments.[2]

Under the NEM, planning was to focus on macroeconomic issues, such as determining the rate of investment and general priorities governing its allocation. At the same time, targets lost their compulsory character and were allowed to be revised as needed to facilitate flexible adaptation to unforeseen events.

The NEM limited the scope of direct microeconomic planning to large investments and certain high-priority sectors (including those that fulfilled major CMEA obligations). Otherwise, the NEM replaced compulsory directives with economic "regulators"—for example, prices, exchange rates, credits, taxes—through which the center would communicate its preferences to theoretically profit-oriented enterprises.

Enterprises could thus formulate their own production, sales, financial, and investment plans in the context of the national plan and the regulators. The responsibility for many decisions regarding inputs and outputs and some decisions concerning personal compensation and investment devolved from central ministries to the enterprises.

Yet many controls remained. Firms had to allocate profits to separate funds for wages, investment, and reserves—each taxed at a different rate. Enterprises, especially large ones, could not accumulate sufficient profits to fund major investments, and credit remained a monopoly of the central bank. In addition, many firms were not allowed to discontinue production of unprofitable commodities that authorities deemed "necessary" for domestic consumption or to alter their price.

At the same time, decades of administrative "protectionism" and the already taut convertible-currency balance of payments deterred meaningful import liberalization—although its absence precludes the possibility of real competition on many product markets in a small country such as Hungary. Direct foreign-trading rights were granted to some producers, and partnership-type arrangements between some foreign trade enterprises and firms were allowed. Nevertheless, although volume of convertible-currency imports

---

2. Descriptions of the measures contained in the NEM are numerous. See István Friss, ed., *Reform of the Economic Mechanism in Hungary* (Budapest: Akadémiai Kiadó, 1969); Paul Marer, "Economic Reform in Hungary: From Central Planning to Regulated Market," in Joint Economic Committee, *East European Economies: Slow Growth in the 1980s* (Washington, D.C.: GPO, 1986).

continued to rise, their composition continued to be administratively regulated; by and large such imports consisted only of goods unavailable from domestic and CMEA sources.

Nor did the NEM create much domestic competition. Indeed, in 1968 there were only 840 industrial enterprises in all of Hungary, forcing the NEM to operate in a country with one of the world's most highly concentrated industrial structures. Easing restrictions on the economic activities of the private and cooperative sectors and allowing large agricultural producers to engage in nonagricultural pursuits somewhat reduced the problems resulting from the skewed industrial structure after 1968. Both measures improved the supply situation and created some new competitors. Nevertheless, competitive pressures on Hungarian firms remained weak, clearly diminishing the effectiveness of the economic controls the NEM had counted on to discipline enterprise choices to macroeconomic goals. As a result many administrative controls remained in place, facilitated by the continued existence of the branch and functional ministries to issue and enforce them. In the absence of competition, the prices of many products—as well as of factors of production—could not become market clearing, perpetuating an often enterprise-specific determination of the regulators (e.g., prices, taxes, wages, exchange rates). The responsibility of ministries for keeping "their" firms profitable also encouraged tailoring the application of the rules to each case rather than forcing the firms to adapt to general rules. The considerable discretionary powers retained by the branch ministries and other central authorities, in turn, often gave enterprises an incentive to accord more importance to central "expectations" than to market forces.

Thus the firms, especially the large ones, continued to depend on ministries and other central organs. Not only did ministries often initiate and partly finance major investments, but together with party bodies, they continued to exercise the functions of ownership: appointing, replacing, and rewarding managers and tightly regulating what firms could do with their after-tax profits. Hence, although the NEM involved significant economic decentralization, it failed to introduce a corresponding degree of differentiation between state and economy. Not surprisingly, this failure created pressures that counteracted decentralization itself.

Enterprise managers did, however, begin to think in economic terms and to orient output toward domestic and foreign consumers, with whom they now often had direct links. The increased importance of profits as *one* of the criteria for judging performance did make managers more sensitive to prices and improved the quality and assortment of their outputs. In addition, smaller firms in the state and especially the cooperative sectors of industry and agriculture proved particularly adept at exploiting new opportunities. Not only did they increase rapidly the production of many goods and services in short supply, but they could often reward their employees better than could the less flexible, large state enterprises.

The five years after 1968 were the NEM's "golden age." The economy grew at a good tempo, there was no open unemployment, prices were relatively stable, and the balance of payments was in equilibrium. Yet beginning in 1972 domestic and international developments converged to halt the further implementation of the NEM. Although the leadership did not formally abandon NEM principles, concentration and central and administrative intervention increased significantly during the next phase of Hungarian economic policy, the "age of illusions."

In one of the fascinating paradoxes of economic decision making, the transitory achievements of the NEM's golden age helped shape the "policies of illusion" in the 1970s. During this period, Hungarian policy makers believed that the economy could be insulated from external shocks (first illusion), that the most advisable policy was to accelerate the rate of growth (second illusion), that the best way to do it was to return to traditional CPE-type investment and trade policies (third illusion), and that it would be appropriate to halt and in some areas reverse the earlier reforms (fourth illusion).

The first set of external shocks that reinforced the tendencies of Hungarian leaders to change course was the explosion in world energy and raw material prices and the resulting Western recession. The deterioration of Hungary's terms of trade with dollar- and ruble-settlement areas reveals the impact of these shocks on Hungary (see Figure 1). With the dollar area, terms of trade deteriorated by 20 percent in 1974–75 alone, although ultimately deterioration in the ruble area was the greatest.

Hungary reacted to the shocks as did other CMEA states, insulating domestic from foreign prices completely for many commodities and partly for others. Yet the large share of energy and raw materials in total imports, the direct link between world and intra-CMEA prices after 1975, the constraints on incremental CMEA supplies of these goods, and the unavailability of advanced technology from CMEA sources prevented Hungary (then and now) from insulating its economy from the world market. (Although Hungary was not a significant net importer of non-CMEA fuel before 1973, the inability of CMEA sources to meet its increasing needs compelled it to import a rising share of energy and raw materials from the West by the end of the decade.)[3]

The second illusion was that economic growth should be accelerated. In fact, an acceleration of growth required a more than proportionate increase in convertible-currency imports. Since growth was led by investment, and exports could not keep up with growing import needs and the deterioration in the terms of trade in both directions, both convertible-currency debts and ruble debts grew rapidly.

The policy of accelerating investment growth so that the share of gross

---

3. See Alan A. Brown and Márton Tardos, "Transmission and Response to External Economic Disturbances: Hungary," in Egon Neuberger and Laura D'Andrea Tyson, eds., *The Impact of International Economic Disturbances on the Soviet Union and Eastern Europe* (Elmsford, N.Y.: Pergamon, 1980).

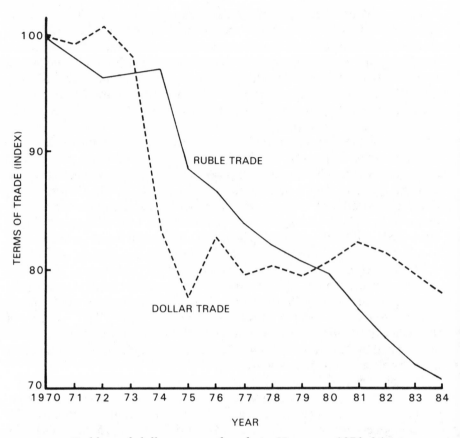

FIGURE 1. *Ruble and dollar terms of trade in Hungary, 1970–84*
(1970 = 100)
Source. Külkereskedelmi Évkönyv (Budapest: Central Statistical Office, yearly).

investment in gross domestic product (GDP) rose from 34 percent in 1970
to 41 percent (!) in 1978 was equally illusory. Such growth disproportionately
increased demand for convertible-currency imports.[4] In addition, Hungary
had initiated several large, major projects on the basis of pre-1974 prices
and demand patterns. Not only was the economic rationale for such projects
questionable, but their long gestation periods required a continual flow of
imports without being able to generate exports. And as the output of many
of these projects was designed primarily for CMEA markets, they preempted
resources that could have been used to improve the competitiveness of

4. See Edward A. Hewett, "The Hungarian Economy: Lessons of the 1970s and Prospects
for the 1980s," in Joint Economic Committee, *East European Economic Assessment*, vol. 1
(Washington, D.C.: GPO, 1981).

manufactures on the Western and the Eastern markets. Investment policy thus aggravated the hard-currency trade balance.

Fourth, manipulating prices to insulate the economy while pursuing rapid growth and investment required increased central intervention in economic decisions. The political backlash against the NEM which had formed even before the price shocks reinforced this trend. One consequence of curbing enterprise independence and restraining the activities of smaller producers was to isolate firms further from market forces, so they paid less attention to the wasteful use of materials and the international competitiveness of their products.

Deficits in convertible-currency trade made it possible for domestic absorption to exceed domestic production. During the 1970s, net real inflows from the West (imports minus exports) enabled Hungary to spend, on average, 2.2 percent more on consumption and investment (absorption) than it produced. In 1978, the convertible-currency import surplus added nearly 5 percent to production. The deficit was financed almost entirely by foreign borrowing throughout the period. During the 1970s, Hungary also ran a trade deficit with the CMEA, although its cumulative total was less than half the convertible-currency trade deficit and a significant part of it could be financed by a surplus on invisible transactions.[5]

Dollar and ruble import surpluses helped to support expansion of output, consumption, and investment until 1979. But the policies of illusion also brought large trade deficits and increased the gross convertible-currency debt from $1 billion in 1970 to $9 billion in 1980.[6]

Austerity comes to Hungary

By 1977–78 Hungarian policy makers had realized that the country would not be able to meet its debt-service obligations in a few years unless the trends were reversed. They introduced a stabilization program in 1979 which made improvements in the convertible-currency trade balance and maintenance of consumption levels the highest priorities. Major cuts in investment were to improve the convertible-currency trade balance. In addition, the reform impulse was renewed and measures linking foreign and domestic prices more closely were instituted.

The planned cut in domestic absorption, however, proved insufficient to maintain creditworthiness in the wake of new external shocks during 1979–82. Further sharp increases in world energy prices substantially worsened Hungarian terms of trade with both the Soviet Union and convertible-currency areas (see Figure 1). In addition, interest rates on external debt rose steeply

5. See World Bank, *Hungary: Economic Developments and Reform* (Washington, D.C.: World Bank, 1984), Table 3.3.
6. Ibid., Table 7.

after 1979. While Hungary's real interest rates (i.e., nominal rates adjusted for the price increases on Hungary's exports) were low or negative before 1979, they became high positive afterward.

In 1979 Hungary was already in a precarious convertible-currency situation, thanks to the policies of illusion that delayed adjustment after 1973. This precariousness aggravated the severity of the shocks of 1979–82. Other decisions concerning external finance exacerbated the difficulty Hungary had making payments. One such decision had been to borrow on the Eurocurrency markets at variable interest rates rather than to use intergovernmental loans with fixed rates. There was certainly a rationale for this decision, as the proceeds of syndicated Eurocurrency loans could be spent freely, whereas government loans are normally tied to purchases from the creditor country. Nevertheless, skyrocketing interest rates after 1979 badly hurt the balance of payments. Moreover, 45 percent of the debt was in highly volatile short-term loans and 80 percent of the total convertible-currency debt outstanding in the early 1980s had to be repaid in five years, making the debt-service ratio about 33 percent.[7]

Poland and Romania became insolvent in 1981, shattering the confidence of the Western financial community and restricting all of Eastern Europe's access to external borrowing. Hungary's financial crisis was triggered between January and March of 1982, when foreign-exchange reserves dropped from $1.7 billion to less than $.5 billion—barely sufficient to cover one month's imports—as Western, OPEC, and (reportedly) Soviet-bloc banks pulled out short-term deposits.[8] Plunged into a liquidity crisis, Hungary still did not have an adjustment program of sufficient bite in place to stabilize its debt situation within a time frame judged desirable by Western bankers.

Hungarian policy makers—by this time strongly influenced by reform advocates—viewed rescheduling as a calamity to be avoided: it would have only postponed the problem while imposing an additional financial burden, and it would have compromised the favorable perceptions of foreigners about the country's economic management. Hence, three sets of measures were taken to steer clear of rescheduling; the absence of any one of them would certainly have made it unavoidable. First, Hungary joined the International Monetary Fund (IMF) in 1982 and the World Bank during 1983–84 and obtained about $2 billion in loans from these organizations. It also mobilized the political and financial goodwill it had built up over the years in order to obtain bridge financing before IMF and World Bank loans could be arranged and became the first CMEA country to reenter private financial markets. Such goodwill was available not only because of past practices but also thanks to the other measures Hungary took at the time, namely, developing a much

7. See Paul Marer, "Hungary's Balance-of-Payments Crisis and Response, 1978–84," in *East European Economies: Slow Growth in the 1980's.*
8. See Ron Miller and Dennis Barclay, "The East European Financial Situation and Debt," in ibid.

TABLE 1. *Index of gross domestic investment and per capita real wage earnings of the population in Hungary (1978 = 100)*

Year	Gross Fixed Investment in Socialist Sector[a]	Real Earnings of the Population
1978	100.0	100.0
1979	83.3	98.4
1980	80.4	96.8
1981	78.7	98.0
1982	76.0	97.2
1983	70.4	94.0
1984	68.5	94.9

a. Total investment plus changes in stock.
Source. Statisztikai Évkönyv (Budapest: Central Statistical Office, 1984), pp. 17 and 76.

stronger stabilization program and introducing new reforms in the economic system.

Economic austerity is the centerpiece of the second set of measures. Any significant improvement in the trade balance within a relatively short period requires a program to curb domestic absorption (i.e., aggregate demand) in the economy by constraining levels of investment or consumption or both. In Hungary, as elsewhere in Eastern Europe, investment declined much more than did consumption, both for reasons of social policy and because increases in investment require especially large increases in convertible-currency imports (see Table 1).

While austerity has forced a dramatic cut in imports, it has also involved much greater emphasis on expanding exports. As a result, foreign trade with hard-currency areas, traditionally a "residual" concern in a CPE, became the main focus of macroeconomic policy and the principal determinant of the growth rate.

Since 1978 investment has been cut much more than consumption, for the reasons already mentioned. Although per capita real wages stagnated between 1977 and 1984, transfer payments, public consumption, and nonwage incomes have increased modestly.

The third set of policy measures was the introduction of new reforms in the economic system, detailed in section 3. Concrete measures taken in 1979–84 returned the economy to its NEM course of economic decentralization and set the stage for potentially major advances in the second half of the decade toward a regulated market economy.

The new reforms involve changes in the structure of economic institutions, regulatory mechanisms, and planning methods. They were enacted in an economic environment far more forbidding than the 1968–72 period. Austerity measures in 1982–84 were more severe than planned, partly hindering and partly helping the reform measures. While the deteriorating external environment prohibited significant import liberalization, it also acted to strengthen the resolve of authorities to proceed with reform. A consensus developed that since heavily trade-dependent Hungary could not look either to the CMEA or to the West to solve its problems, it had to find an economic mechanism that forced domestic firms to become more efficient and to adapt better to world and regional market conditions. We shall return to the "new" New Economic Mechanism in section 3, following an analysis of the political dynamics that produced it.

2. The politics of economic reform

The reforms adopted in Hungary after 1979 are as much a return to previous policy as a departure from it. Hence, to understand Hungary's current response to changes in the international economy, one must explain not only the decision to reform the economic system in 1980 but also the reform process itself—including its several reversals.

The acceptability of economic reform in Hungary stems from two characteristics: first, the composition of the post-1956 political elite and second, the features of the collective leadership which guide its decision making. While Hungary shares each of these characteristics with other CMEA states, the combination of the two in Hungary is a unique product of the 1956 revolt.

The leadership clustered around János Kádár in 1956 represented an amalgam of political figures, all of whom were anxious to avoid the "excesses" of the previous regime. For the economy, this anxiety translated into a rejection of the pressurized development strategy of the early 1950s in favor of a more balanced development trajectory based on specific Hungarian conditions. Whether major alterations in the centrally planned economic system should accompany new policy priorities, however, was a subject of debate—a signal that a reformist wing had emerged at the highest levels of the Hungarian Socialist Workers' party (HSWP).[9]

9. The party's analysis of the 1956 revolt reveals the coexistence of "reformist" and "conservative" tendencies at the highest levels of the HSWP. Although the capture of reform initiatives by "counterrevolutionary" forces and the stalemate it provoked in the party were criticized, neither economic reform nor even the Nagy reform program per se were condemned. Nor was the traditional CPE rejected; rather only the "excesses" and "distortions" "subjectivism" in economic decision making had imposed upon it were condemned. These, in turn, were attributed to the politics of the "cult of personality" and not the CPE itself. Consequently advocacy of both the wider use of market mechanisms or central planning became acceptable stances within the HSWP. See Kovrig, *Communism*, pp. 300–350; William Robinson, *The Pattern of Reform in Hungary* (New York: Praeger, 1973), pp. 30–50.

At the time advocates of economic reform in Hungary were far from isolated in Eastern Europe. Reform advocates had an influential position in Poland, and they soon began to rise to prominence in Czechoslovakia, too. Critical to these new alignments was the end of accelerated industrialization throughout the CMEA, a change whose roots could be traced to new Soviet emphases on the production of consumer goods and intra-CMEA specialization. Along with the "thaw" in the cold war that allowed trade with the West to resume, such developments provided opportunities East European reformists sought to capitalize upon.

In Czechoslovakia, the coalition that came to power in the aftermath of the 1968 invasion politically eliminated reformists and their policy preferences. In Poland, however, economic reform continues even today to remain an acceptable policy option. Nevertheless, the emergence of strong and aggressive nonparty forces—from workers and the church to the police—and the reliance of intraparty factions on them for support so divided the Polish communist party that it proved incapable of implementing an effective economic reform. In Hungary, by contrast, the lessons of 1956 taught both advocates and opponents of economic reform that a strong and united HSWP was the only agency capable of effecting reform. Rather than mobilize support outside the party, Hungarian reformists have sought to promote their cause within it; rather than challenging party control of state and society, Hungarian reformists have attempted to utilize such control for their own purposes. This brings us to the second aspect of the reform process in Hungary: the political norms on which it is based.

Although the Kádár leadership disagreed over the need for systemic economic reform in the aftermath of 1956 and in the end reinstituted most aspects of the traditional CPE, no such debate occurred over the need to restore and maintain political control. Yet just as the determination of the Kádár coalition to avoid "excesses" caused it to question accelerated industrialization in the economy, the same commitment led it to repudiate the "cult of personality" and the one-man rule in the state and party that had prevailed prior to 1956.

Significantly, such a repudiation did not involve changes in state structures, which remained virtually identical to those prevailing before 1956—especially once the decision to retain the CPE was made. Rather, the lessons of 1956 were political and were manifested in three distinctive commitments that the post-1956 HSWP leadership made. First, the state was brought under party control by subjecting it to "socialist legality." Second, society was brought under political control by reestablishing the mass organizations along traditional "transmission belt" lines. Finally, the HSWP was reconstituted so that it could control itself through genuine collective leadership.

Like "balanced" economic development, such commitments originated in Moscow, in the determination of the communist party of the Soviet Union (CPSU) to bring the police under party control, deter spontaneous social ferment in the wake of de-Stalinization, and prevent the rise of another Stalin within the party. Similar modifications in political processes occurred throughout Eastern Europe at the time, but in Hungary the three changes proved ideally suited to the political exigencies of the Kádár leadership. Making such commitments allowed the party not only to regain its monopoly of the means of collective action in 1956 but also to preserve it during the next thirty years, while uniting all the various tendencies within it around that goal.

The result is the political system that operates today. Its basic lines are virtually indistinguishable from those of East Germany and Czechoslovakia, but the actors within it and their policy preferences continue to reflect the specificity of the Hungarian experience and the lessons of 1956 in particular.

Adherence to socialist legality in the state, a "transmission belt" role for the mass organizations, and collective leadership in the party on the part of *all* political actors have been essential to the continued influence of reformists within the HSWP. At the same time, however, these commitments and the political structures they rest on make reformists politically weak and obstruct consistent implementation of their policy preferences.

The apparatus of rule: party and state

The establishment of socialist legality meant preventing officials within the state apparatus from using their positions to exercise power independently of the party (i.e., "bureaucratizing" the state apparatus). Before 1956, they did so frequently, and the secret policy had virtually replaced the party itself in many spheres.[10] Since 1956, however, party leaders have been politically committed to distinguishing between legal authority and political power: while exercise of the former is regulated by law and delegated to the state administration, the latter remains the monopoly of the party.

In fact, a system of checks and balances characterizes party-state relations. On one side, top party bodies define the political goals and tasks of the hierarchical and centralized state administration and approve the appointment of its leading officials. Moreover, an equally centralized party apparatus supervises the use of administrative discretion to ensure that its exercise is consistent with the party's overall political objectives. For example, enterprises cannot close obsolescent facilities or lay off workers without the approval of party leaders responsible for the political consequences of such actions.

On the other side, the competences and jurisdiction of state organizations are defined by law. As long as a state official acts within his or her legal authority, individual party leaders can intervene only with difficulty. For

10. On the police see Béla Szász, *Volunteers for the Gallows* (London: Chatto & Windus, 1971). In fact, the entire state administration was riddled with citadels of personal power often used to get rid of enemies and satisfy individual ambitions.

example, in 1981, the Ozd Steelworks applied for a low-interest loan from the State Development Bank. Despite protests of the politically influential county party organization, the Hungarian National Bank could show that it alone was legally empowered to grant the credit for which it charged the prevailing interest rate, and the enterprise was forced to accept its terms.

Hence, although state officials normally possess the authority they need to accomplish their tasks, they lack autonomous power. Indeed, the goals and tasks of a state organization are defined outside the organization itself, and its interests by and large lie in carrying them out. Bargaining between state authorities thus occurs within arenas and over issues that the party prescribes rather than those state organizations themselves propose. For example, in response to austerity measures, the steel industry and the metallurgical ministry scaled down ambitious expansion plans. Bargaining was intense, but it was over how much—not whether—to cut back and in particular how much investment (as opposed to, say, employment or wages) to reduce, quite in accord with party priorities.[11]

Typically, bargaining between state entities occurs as lobbying for "exceptions," should a strict application of rules jeopardize an organization's ability to satisfy the superiors to whom it is legally responsible. Exceptions are often granted on an individual, case-by-case basis, and claims are best advanced on the basis of a "unique" situation.[12] The logic of exceptionalism thus militates against officials forming organizational coalitions—a genuinely collective, political action—that could alter the rules themselves.

Certainly, state officials often hold strong opinions about both economic policy and the shape of the economic system. They do not express such opinions, however, in the course of exercising their legal authority but in political forums controlled by the party. In such a context, their preferences are subject to the scrutiny of other leaders who need not share their views.

Nor do the policies state functionaries advocate in their political roles necessarily express the "interests" of the organization they manage. For example, directors of enterprises in Hungary are notoriously anxious to expand their firms' assets, investment, and labor force. Seated on party committees, however, they are far from uniformly in favor of expansionary policies. Paradoxically, state officials' political/"public" preferences are their private opinions, while their individual/bureaucratic lobbying activities reflect their public responsibilities. Such behavior explains how Hungary can adopt capital allocation policies and foreign-trade strategies that run counter to the "in-

---

11. Interviews by Ellen Comisso, 1981–82, Hungary. See also "Milliárdos Fejlesztés—Gondokkal," *Figyelö*, 4 March 1979, pp. 1, 3.

12. The literature on exceptionalism in Hungary is extensive. See I. Huszár, "Reflections on the 1979 National Economic Plan (Some Experiences of 1978)," *Acta Oeconomica* 22, nos. 1–2 (1979), pp. 1–9; László Antal, *Fejlödés—Kitérövel* (Budapest: Penzügyi Kutatási Intézet, 1979); Teréz Laky, "Enterprises in Bargaining Position," *Acta Oeconomica* 22, nos. 3–4 (1979), pp. 227–46; and David Granick, *Enterprise Guidance in Eastern Europe* (Princeton: Princeton University Press, 1975), pp. 234–323.

terests" of the largest firms and strongest ministries. It also explains why widely supported policies get watered down by exceptions that even the most avid advocates of agreed-upon policies are likely to claim. Finally, and most important, it suggests that both the barriers to and the impulse for economic reform lie within the political leadership itself and *not* within a state administration that has neither the interest nor the power to act independently of it.

The determination of party leaders since 1956 to enforce "socialist legality" is designed to protect the HSWP's monopoly of power. But curbing the ability of state officials to act outside the law has also made an enormous difference in the lives of private citizens. Although individual rights are still limited, at least they are genuine. After the initial terror of 1957–58, private citizens gradually became able to live their daily lives with increasing degrees of personal security.[13] Moreover, the development of the legal private sector in the economy would have been impossible without such security.

Since state positions cannot be used to generate power independently of the party, they can be filled with apolitical technocrats who are not even party members. Indeed, this strategy is the essence of Kádár's "alliance" policy. Far from entailing coalitions with organized social *groups*, the alliance policy has simply meant that an *individual's* social origins or group ties do not bar him or her from holding a position of authority. As for groups, the party's monopoly of the means of collective action by definition precludes their autonomous organization.

Pacifying society: the mass organizations

If socialist legality eliminates the ability of state officials to challenge party hegemony, organizing the mass organizations—from the Popular Front and the trade unions to youth organizations and pensioners' clubs—as "transmission belts" makes society an equally unlikely source of challenges. Like state officials, leaders of mass organizations are approved for the offices they hold by the party, based on their previous records of activity and the party's judgment as to the "appropriateness" of their political orientation for the organization in question.[14] Thus, organizations tend to represent their leaders rather than vice versa, and the leadership itself answers to the party whose policies it implements within the respective organization. Hence, when leaders of mass organizations take political positions on issues, these seldom spring

13. Known political dissidents, however, do not find their rights so automatically protected—a sign that the "rule of law" in Hungary still does not rest so much on constitutional guarantees as on the political will of the HSWP to uphold it. See Tad Szulc, "Hungary between Two Worlds," *New Republic*, 16 October 1979, pp. 11–13.

14. "Previous activity" need not even be in the mass organization itself. The present head of the national trade union federation is the ex-minister of industry; the president of the Metalworkers' Union is the retired director of the Danube Steelworks.

from their organizations' "interests"—much less from the interests of members who have no way to keep leaders accountable. Rather, they reflect the political interests and orientation of the (party-approved) leaders themselves, and they are articulated within party bodies rather than outside them. For example, although the Popular Front now nominates candidates in parliamentary elections and unions have an important voice in enterprises, it is not because these organizations or their members "demanded" these rights. Rather, the party itself decided they should have them.

Nor can the so-called union opposition to the NEM in the 1970s be explained on the basis of either organizational or membership interests.[15] As for union organizational interests, the reform actually expanded union prerogatives in the firm. Had wage policy become more flexible, the autonomy of the national union federation would have increased, too, as it would have been able to bargain over differentials rather than simply accept the small and more or less uniform wage increases prescribed by planners attempting to control the total wage bill in the interest of price stability. Egalitarianism, however, is normally a strong ideological preference (and very much in the political interest) of the leaders favoring economic centralization who dominate the Hungarian trade union federation.

As for workers, although income levels in the cooperative and private sectors—particularly in agriculture—rose more rapidly than those in the state industrial sector after 1968, wages in the large enterprises remained relatively high, especially in industries preferred by the planners. Equally important, a substantial proportion of the Hungarian proletariat works in both the private and state sectors, and this proportion increased with the expanded opportunities the NEM provided.[16] Although such mobility benefited workers, it posed serious implications for the political clout of union leaders: should a significant segment of the labor force fall outside normal union channels, the leadership's influence in policy-making forums could be severely compromised.

Even workers employed exclusively in the socialist sector could have benefited from the expansion of the private/cooperative sector had the resulting labor shortages been exploited to raise wages in the state firms. But for the unions to have led them in this endeavor would have put them on a collision course with central authorities and the larger political leadership anxious to restrain inflationary pressures. Rather than mobilizing their following, then,

15. For such a view see Richard Portes, "Hungary: Economic Performance, Policy and Prospects," in Joint Economic Committee, *East European Economies Post-Helsinki*, 95th Cong., 1st sess., 1977, p. 786; Robinson, *Reform in Hungary*, pp. 310–45.

16. In "Hungary's Long-Term Social Evolution," *New Hungarian Quarterly* 20 (1975), p. 88, Rudolf Andorka estimates that in 1975 half of the working class lived in villages. Labor turnover rose from 20% to 25% to 41% in 1970. See Julius Rezler, "Recent Developments on the Hungarian Labor Market," *East European Quarterly* (Summer 1976), pp. 255–67; and Gábor Révész, "Enterprise and Plant Size of the Hungarian Industry," *Acta Oeconomica* 22, nos. 1–2 (1974), pp. 47–68.

union leaders pushed for an across-the-board wage increase in 1972, the maintenance of central wage controls, and measures both restricting the activities of cooperatives and taxing private incomes more stringently. In sum, the union leadership sought to *ease* the labor shortage for its own reasons rather than to take advantage of it to benefit union members.

Hence neither the persistence of nor the barriers to economic reform can be attributed to popular initiatives or support, as there are simply no political mechanisms through which "society" in Hungary can exert collective pressures.[17] To the degree that society's preferences enter the political arena, it is through individual actions outside organizational frameworks and not coordinated group efforts. Political leaders thus have a wide range of options available (e.g., they can counter high labor turnover by making it more difficult to change jobs or by instituting hiring freezes rather than by raising wages). Nevertheless, such individual actions can be successful, as agricultural policy indicates. In 1975, for example, rumors that peasant incomes would be taxed more heavily caused farm output to drop immediately, forcing Hungary to import fruits and vegetables in 1976. Not only were the rumors quickly put to rest, but a new minister of agriculture was appointed and in 1977, the Central Committee itself called for help to small farmers. The political lesson of this experience was not lost on reformers in 1979.

The organization of power: the HSWP

The bureaucratization of the state and the pacification of society meant challenges to party hegemony were unlikely to originate outside party ranks. They could, however, come from within the HSWP itself if individual leaders were able to create personal power bases and use them to pursue individual objectives independently of the will of the party organization as a whole.[18]

The extremely hierarchical distribution of power within the HSWP is one barrier to such actions. As power flows from top to bottom, those who would acquire access to it must gain support from above rather than mobilize a constituency from below. Power is thus available to lower party leaders only on conditions determined by higher party bodies and can be withdrawn if used for purposes not to the center's liking.

---

17. For example, while workers can affect their individual earnings by bargaining informally over norms, absenteeism, turnover, and the like, their impact on wage policy is slight. Problems in controlling aggregate demand in Hungary have not been caused by excessive personal incomes, which by and large have followed plan projections, but by overinvestment. See Hewett, "Hungarian Economy," p. 491.

18. On the party see Ivan Volgyes and Peter Toma, *Politics in Hungary* (San Francisco: Freeman, 1977); M. Molnar, "The Communist Party of Hungary," in Stephen Fischer-Galati, ed., *The Communist Parties of Eastern Europe* (New York: Columbia University Press, 1979); Robinson, *Reform in Hungary;* Kovrig, *Communism.* We have also relied on Jerry F. Hough, *The Soviet Prefects* (Cambridge: Harvard University Press, 1969), and the various editions of *Pártmunkások kézikönyve* put out by the Kossuth Press in Budapest.

Consequently, popular support is not a particularly valuable asset for an ambitious politician. In fact, attempts to organize nonparty groups to support individual goals would jeopardize the party's monopoly of the means of collective action; the center would likely question one's ability to "manage" the political situation; and one's influence within the party would be weaker, not stronger, as a result.

Nor does control of economic resources generate power. On the contrary, political power brings "responsibility" for the economic resources that state organizations allocate. Access to power and promotion depends on how party superiors evaluate a leader's competence in carrying out tasks—namely, aiding non-party-state and secondary associations to fulfill central priorities and ensuring that their leading personnel abide by them.

Because "responsibility" for the performance of socialist institutions is integral to party leaders' exercise of political influence, they usually favor expanding the socialist sector in their area regardless of the economic logic of or popular support for such growth. For example, rural party elites tend to be less than enthusiastic over prosperity in private agriculture: high peasant incomes may bring them local popularity, but supervision of big industrial complexes of national importance is what counts politically. Thanks to the highly centralized state administration, it is only by influencing central priorities that local leaders can influence what local institutions do. Not surprisingly, support for economic decentralization has been much weaker in regional party circles than among top-ranking elite at the center.

Similar dynamics characterize the mass organizations. What "counts" politically is not membership support but membership control and the size and strategic value of the group for which one is responsible. The reaction of trade union leaders to workers leaving the socialist sector is illustrative.

The centralized state, the "transmission belt" mass organizations, and the hierarchic distribution of power in the party all place a premium on having influence in the center and provide disincentives for leaders to exercise power unilaterally for their own goals. But as the pre-1956 experience demonstrated, institutional barriers are effective only if leaders are politically determined to maintain, support, and abide by them in practice—especially leaders at the very top of the hierarchy who do not face the structural constraints that apply to subelites.

The principles of collective leadership

Political means must control leaders when no group or organization outside the leadership itself can. "Collective leadership," an arrangement whereby political leaders control each other, emerged after 1956 as such means.

Collective leadership originated in Moscow after the death of Stalin, and the resistance of the pre-1956 Hungarian party leadership to its adoption helped produce the political crisis that precipitated the 1956 revolt. Since

1956, however, commitment to the norms of collective leadership within the HSWP has allowed the party to avoid a political stalemate despite often sharp disagreements within its ranks. That commitment is seen in the Kádár leadership's support for: (1) the "socialization" of political power; (2) tolerance of diversity within the party; (3) restrictions on political resources; and (4) decision making by consensus.

The *"socialization" of political power* means that decisions are made by collective bodies (i.e., hierarchically arranged party committees following geographic and functional lines) in which each member's power rests on the power of the collective body (and hence the party) as a whole. Furthermore, each member's political resources—from "responsibility" to control of appointments—are granted by the body to which he or she belongs and neither possessed by nor accumulated for the individual leader's own use. The price of admission to policy-making bodies is an a priori commitment to carrying out decisions regardless of one's personal views.

Political power in Hungary is thus in many respects a collective good; unless the appropriate party committee decides what is to be done, no individual member can legitimately act alone regarding questions of major importance. Individual power is thus the ability to influence collective decisions and leaders compete to wield it. Hence it is in the interest of all to strengthen the body from which each member's power and opportunity for influence derive, and in no leader's interest to make the organization (e.g., the local party apparatus, an enterprise, or a trade union) he or she "manages" on a day-to-day basis autonomous of collective party control.

Thus, the head of the Economic Department of the Central Committee, the Hungarian National Bank, or the Trade Union Federation never "controls" industry, banking, or the trade unions respectively. The Politburo and the Central Committee approve such individuals for their positions after judging them or the lines of action they propose to be appropriate. These individuals are responsible to these same party bodies for implementing the latter's decisions, and maintaining their influence on policy formulation depends on the political judgment and competence they show in doing so.

With such constraints, even opponents of policies can be put in charge of carrying them out and frequently are. For example, Lajos Méhes, the sole Politburo member said to have resisted the reorganization of the Ministry of Industry in 1980, found himself in charge of the very consolidation he had opposed. As the new minister of industry, he worked to restructure the ministry not because he agreed with the change but because maintaining his influence in the Politburo required it.

Certainly, the minister of industry, the president of the National Bank, or the head of the trade unions has a major voice and privileged position in questions of industrial policy, credit allocation, or wage regulation, respectively. Appointments are thus a critical component in the exercise of influence and are hotly debated. Reorganizations that reshuffle cadres are controversial for the same reasons. Yet even a major voice is not necessarily a determining one, especially since the body to which one is accountable is quite likely to have one's opponents as well as one's sympathizers among its members.

Given the socialization of political power, *tolerance for diversity* of views on specific issues within the party is both possible and desirable. If political leaders cannot act on their preferences without the consent of their peers or superiors in the party hierarchy, the need to control and censor their preferences at the outset is greatly reduced. The competition for influence on collective decisions stimulated by disagreement also motivates leaders to control each other's implementation of policy. Not only is competent execution of current decisions critical for the exercise of future influence, but rivals have an incentive to attack leaders who act unilaterally or subvert policies because their own power is threatened when collective decisions are not carried out. Political checks and balances within the HSWP itself thus supplement the institutional controls of the party-state relationship.

Diversity within the HSWP originates in disagreements at the very top of the party hierarchy over policy issues. There it remains within bounds and is articulated by leaders who accept that the power of the party and the political elite as a whole ultimately determine who wins and who loses. Acceptance of that principle characterizes both of the informal "wings" that have emerged on economic policy questions. At the same time, the fact that one of those wings is committed to a reform of the economic system distinguishes the diversity on economic issues in Hungary from the lines of cleavage in other CMEA parties, and explains the emergence and persistence of debate over economic reform within the HSWP.

Although "liberal" and "conservative" stances on issues (trade orientation, price determination, investment allocation, etc.) can be identified, the HSWP bans factionalism every bit as strictly as do other Marxist-Leninist parties. Hence specific leaders rarely develop a consistent set of preferences: "liberals" in trade or financial questions may well join "conservatives" in wage or industrial policy debates and vice versa. In addition, since leaders are accountable to the party rather than to concrete social or organizational interests, they have few external pressures on them to take consistent positions. The importance of competently implementing policies that vary with the balance of forces also deters them from assuming too distinct a political profile. Yet precisely because tendencies do not have a stable composition, they cannot be eliminated: opponents on one issue are frequently allies on another, and the defeat of a liberal or conservative stance on one issue is no guarantee that liberal or conservative positions will not reappear with new protagonists on other issues.

Restrictions on political resources is the third characteristic of collective leadership. "Political resources" can be thought of as sources of support valuable to political leaders advancing claims on collective choice. In pluralist systems, both the assortment and value of political resources are quite different from those in single-party Leninist ones.

In competitive political systems, mobilizing a constituency constitutes a claim on power, and political entrepreneurs have incentives to expand the political public as they search out supporters. Constituency size and breadth, access to funds, unilateral control of an organization, and the ability to disseminate information are thus critical to advancing a cause. Since individuals operating outside formal political channels can create such resources, their allocation cannot be controlled by a central organization, either.[19]

In Hungary, however, individuals who mobilize a constituency threaten the party's monopoly on collective action; given the socialization of political power, it is in no leader's interest to do this. Instead, a leader may acquire influence on collective choice by seeking support from above (including other communist parties), attaining responsibility for an organization or region (especially one whose activities affect national priorities), and obtaining (as exclusive as possible) access to information. Significantly, the party center can control the allocation of such assets, and their use is governed by the institutional and political checks and balances to which all political actors are subject. Exercising influence thus gives leaders an incentive to *reduce* the relevant public; in effect, the very conditions that preserve limited pluralism in the party work to prevent the emergence of real pluralism in society.

Because all political actors have a common interest in preserving the party and its monopoly on the means of collective action, decisions on even quite controversial questions can be made by consensus. That is, political leaders who support one policy option justify it in terms of the demands and criteria that their opponents embrace, demonstrating that the proposed action is in the collective political interest of the decision-making body and the elite as a whole.

Examples of *consensual decision making* abound in cases of microeconomic industrial policy as well as on broader macroeconomic and institutional questions.[20] The political genius of János Kádár has been precisely to select and frame issues to be decided in such a way that a common denominator can arise on even hotly debated questions and to articulate it in a way all can accept. Like a true legislative leader, Kádár acts as an "agent with multiple principals," and steers between building winning coalitions and keeping peace in the family. Thus, he "seeks out those issues that unite his principals, and failing that, he keeps his head down and casts about for structural or procedural

19. For example, the rise of a Jimmy Carter or a Green party started with the creation of an independent organization, funded initially by personal contributions from candidates and activists. A popular constituency was formed and enlarged as information was disseminated by both the independent organizations and the national media.

20. Examples include the decision to complete the Danube Steelworks, recollectivizing agriculture, the enterprise-ministry reorganization of 1963–64, and the textile modernization program. See, for example, Iván T. Berend, "Continuity and Changes of Industrialization in Hungary after the Turn of 1956–7," *Acta Oeconomica* 27, nos. 3–4 (1981), pp. 221–51.

devices to at least make himself acceptable." Maintaining his *primus inter pares* position and building consensus in the HSWP requires using the "tools of leadership influence" well known by, say, the U.S. Speaker of the House: "legislative rescheduling, committee assignments, patronage, services for members, etc."[21] Like Sam Rayburn, Kádár rarely initiates legislation — but no "bill" passes the HSWP over his opposition. Nor is it accidental that "conservatives" find themselves farmed out to the trade unions while "liberals" dominate financial institutions. And just as Henry Clay introduced standing committees into the U.S. Congress to mitigate the tensions of his coalition, Kádár can be thought of as the father of the expert commission in Hungary.

Collective leadership and economic reform

The process of economic reform in Hungary illustrates the political dynamics of collective leadership since 1956.[22] At that time, launching a broad economic reform was politically feasible only if a strong party could direct the effort. Rebuilding the HSWP, however, meant recruiting loyal members wherever they could be found and rewarding those who had stayed with the regime in its moments of deep crisis. In principle the party was open to reformists, but in practice it was cadres who had disliked Nagy's "new course" policies, fought against the 1956 revolt, and strongly opposed any concessions to the "counterrevolution" who returned in full force. A major economic reform would, therefore, have been so politically divisive that it was not in the political interest of even its supporters to insist on its implementation — an important reason why the sweeping economic reforms, proposed in mid-1957 by a party commission, were tabled. In addition, new CMEA arrangements that stressed specialization within the traditional CPE framework held out the possibility of both a rapid economic recovery and reinforcement to a still weak political center. Hence reform proposals were quietly laid to rest by common agreement.

The return to a CPE in Hungary did not, however, signal the expulsion of reformists from the party or even from leadership posts, as it had in Czechoslovakia after 1968. For one thing, an internecine struggle within the Hungarian elite in 1956–57 over economic issues would have been self-defeating for both sides because it would have jeopardized the sine qua non of *any* economic policy: the restoration of party hegemony. Hence it was

21. Quotations are from Kenneth Shepsle and Brian Humes, "Legislative Leadership: Organizational Entrepreneurs as Agents" (Paper presented at the Conference on Adaptive Institutions, Stanford University, 8–9 November 1984).
22. On early reform proposals see Berend, "Continuity and Changes"; László Antal, "Historical Development of the Hungarian System of Economic Control and Management," *Acta Oeconomica* 27, nos. 3–4 (1981), pp. 251–67; László Számuely, "The First Wave of the Mechanism Debate in Hungary (1954–1957)," *Acta Oeconomica* 29, nos. 1–2 (1982), pp. 1–24.

not in the interest of even those opposed to reform to eliminate its advocates. Moreover, reformists were as devoted to restoring party control as were the most ardent conservatives: a strong HSWP was as necessary to the introduction of economic reform as it was to the maintenance of central planning. Finally, faced with the task of rebuilding a party that had dissolved during 1956, the leadership could hardly be too fussy about opinions when simple loyalty was in such short supply.

Yet if maintaining central control over the economy and society meant abandoning reform in 1957, it was also an important factor in the introduction of reform in 1968. By that time, the economic barriers to further "extensive" development supported the argument of reformists that communicating central priorities to economic units through general economic parameters rather than by detailed instructions could make the economy more responsive to central objectives. On such grounds, economic reform could be conditionally supported even by those quite hostile to market mechanisms.

Thus, while the economic objective of the NEM was to improve efficiency and performance, its political rationale was improving central control and coordination of economic behavior. Consequently, when reform measures seemed to impede central control of the economy and to jeopardize the attainment of central policy objectives they were expected to facilitate, the NEM began to be reversed—despite (and partly because of) the good economic performance of the golden age.

The political backlash against the NEM reached its apogee in the policies of illusion of 1972–78. It had already gained considerable steam by 1972 (well before the oil shocks), and grew out of contradictions in the same institutional and political arrangements that had brought reformists to power in the 1960s.

The first contradiction was in the use of centralized political power to introduce economic decentralization. Institutionally, the centralized state administration and hierarchical distribution of power in the HSWP meant that the NEM could be introduced only at central initiative. Politically, it was precisely the strength of reformists at the top of the party hierarchy that had kept the reform option alive and initiated the NEM itself. But having captured the center, reformists had little interest in political decentralization. On the one hand, weakening the top of the HSWP would have undermined its ability to oversee and coordinate the implementation of the new measures. On the other, since support for economic reform was weaker (although far from nonexistent) in local and regional party organs, decentralization would have thrown political resources into the hands of opponents.

Regional fears over the potential impact of economic reform did lead to a party reform in 1966. Giving county party organs a voice in managerial appointments and greater responsibility in the local economy, the reform kept power concentrated in the hands of national party leaders but gave regional elites greater opportunities to influence its use. As such, it countered opposition to the NEM in the provinces and reinforced the reformist hold on the party center.[23] By 1972, however, intraparty alignments had changed substantially.

Since exercising power continued to mean having influence in the center, regional elites had little to gain from proposals to break up large enterprises into smaller units. Quite the contrary: they continued to fix their sights on acquiring responsibility for large firms or their subsidiaries and for operations that hooked into key central projects, as these were the surest methods of increasing their influence on the determination of national priorities. Hence, if the economic incentives created by the NEM militated in favor of smaller firms and competition, the political incentives perpetuated by the centralized power structure worked in precisely the opposite direction. They impeded attempts to deconcentrate the industrial structure in 1968 and were a major force behind the Hungarian merger movement of the 1970s that even further reduced the number of enterprises and cooperatives. Likewise, the manifold pressures to expand enterprises helped produce the investment surge of 1971. Caught by surprise, reformists at the center undercut their own position by curtailing the availability of credit and foreign exchange, actions that necessarily recentralized investment decisions and circumscribed enterprise autonomy.

The second contradiction eroding the reformist position lay in the NEM's attempt to stimulate entrepreneurial initiative through politically determined and administratively enforced rules.[24] Institutionally, again, this was the *only* way in which reform could be introduced; firms would engage in entrepreneurial behavior only if "told" to do so by authorities in the bureaucratic state structure. Economically, the use of rules rather than market forces was justified even to reformists by the high level of monopoly on the domestic market. Politically, rules could reflect the political consensus underlying the adoption of the NEM, a consensus over means and mechanisms which often veiled nagging conflicts over goals and priorities (e.g., preventing economic dislocation versus adapting to the international market).

23. The reform did not give county party organizations greater autonomy to formulate their own objectives in their regions. Nor did it give them resources for such purposes: no fiscal decentralization accompanied the change. Local revenues continued to depend on centrally set formulas and not on the income generated within the local economy. What regional elites gained was increased influence over the activities and management of firms headquartered in their area. See Robinson, *Reform in Hungary*, pp. 91 and 195–205.

24. The literature on the administrative and practical contradictions of the NEM is vast. See János Kornai, *Economics of Shortages*, vol. 2 (Amsterdam: North Holland, 1981); Tamás Bauer, "The Contradictory Position of the Enterprise under the New Hungarian Economic Mechanism," *Eastern European Economics* 15 (Fall 1976), pp. 3–24; Márton Tardos, "Enterprise Independence and Central Control," *Eastern European Economics* 15 (Fall 1976), pp. 24–45; Andrea Deák, "On the Possibility of Enterprise Decisions on Investment," *Eastern European Economics* 14 (Winter 1975–76), pp. 14–25. Case studies appear in Márton Tardos, ed., *Vállalati Magatartás— Vállalati Környezet* (Budapest: Közgazdasági és Jogi Könyvkiadó, 1980), and Granick, *Enterprise Guidance*.

Hence a market did not come into being in the socialist sector; rather, administratively adjusted economic regulators "simulated" its operations. As a result firms exposed to market forces often found regulations (on wages, employment, supply obligations, etc.) that impeded adaptations to market forces. This, in addition to the desires of many firms to avoid altogether the adverse consequences of market forces, evoked a stream of petitions for exemptions and exceptions. At the other end of the spectrum, firms insulated from market forces (e.g., because their prices or supply obligations were fixed) could also experience low profits, leading to additional appeals for special considerations and concessions. Meanwhile, the same lack of competition which necessitated state regulation meant economic criteria were unavailable to guide it; not surprisingly, political considerations remained important.

The paradox of the "unhappy monopolist" is illustrative. It was most pronounced in the largest firms, whose size and monopoly position made them the most strictly regulated. Many, for example, were the sole source of supply for vital commodities at prices fixed by central authorities. Since they could neither discontinue producing such items nor raise prices, the only avenue open—given the stress on profitability—was to lobby for subventions or seek additional capital either to produce such goods more cheaply or to expand more profitable lines. Likewise, if workers (and more important, cadres) could neither be fired nor transferred, the only solution was to add additional employees. In effect, insofar as firms faced fixed regulations, the only way to introduce flexibility into their operations was to increase "slack" within the organization. And since the size and importance of the industrial operations that political leaders answered for were so important for the exercise of political influence, it was very much in the interest of party leaders connected with the firms to support such expansion, no matter how sympathetic they were in principle to the NEM. Nor could reformists at the center offer much resistance, given that their own retention of political influence was contingent on the survival and prosperity of the state sector. As one exception rapidly led to another, principles and practice became increasingly separated.

The third contradiction reformists confronted was the disjuncture between political power and economic performance. Politically, the NEM had been adopted to strengthen the socialist sector by making it more efficient and competitive on domestic and international markets. This was to be done— and could only be done—by keeping state firms subject to the political and institutional checks and balances that applied to all public organizations. Only the content of some of the checks changed, from direct instructions to economic regulators.

Consequently, a plethora of regulations continued to constrain managerial action in the state sector. Even enterprises wishing to take on the competition did so with one hand tied behind their back. Not surprisingly, the NEM's golden age saw the less regulated and thus more flexible and entrepreneurial private and cooperative sectors of the economy growing stronger at what often appeared to be the expense of their socialist competitors; the less regulated industries proved especially able to attract and reward skilled labor. On the one hand, this situation made the NEM vulnerable to attack on the very grounds that had led to its adoption; rather than strengthening the center's (and the party's) control of resources, it was stimulating precisely the sectors in which central and party control were weakest. On the other, the sectors and groups benefiting the most from the reform were politically powerless once the NEM came under attack.

International factors and the reform process

Further weakening the reform momentum was the deterioration in the terms of trade following the 1973 energy shocks and recession in the West. These difficulties played into the hands of those favoring a more centralized model of economic decision making by making insulation of domestic prices from world-market prices a politically appealing alternative to all sides. Even for reformists the immediate effects of transferring these shocks to the domestic economy would have been as politically damaging as insulating the economy was politically compromising. Belief (in Hungary as elsewhere) that the price shocks would be temporary facilitated the decision. Meanwhile, foreign credit opportunities supplied a means to cover increasing and more expensive imports without imposing major sacrifices.

But the policies of illusion were shaped as much by Hungary's position in the CMEA as by developments in the larger international economy. Responding to CMEA specialization programs of the 1960s and 1970s, Hungary had narrowed its product lines and oriented exports principally to the CMEA while relying on relatively cheap CMEA energy and raw materials. Thus both before and after the NEM, production decisions in a large segment of the economy were guided by CMEA obligations. Yet the economics of CMEA trade (the bulk of it with the Soviet Union) exerted strong pressures for economic centralization and administrative control. For example, after 1968 authorities had to ensure via taxes and subsidies that enterprise dealings on CMEA markets were neither excessively nor insufficiently profitable. Such practices ran directly counter to the basic principle of the NEM: to allow increased differentiation in enterprise profitability and to let profits guide output decisions. Nevertheless, the economic benefits of purchasing supplies within the Eastern bloc (especially in the mid-1970s) and the difficulty of reorienting trade to the West prohibited alternative arrangements. Meanwhile, firms producing for the CMEA found their product structures and internal organizations inappropriate for trading on Western markets, where technical specifications, lot sizes, production rhythms, delivery times, and price relations differed.[25]

25. See Paul Marer, *East-West Technology Transfer: A Study of Hungary, 1968–1984* (Paris:

While integration in the CMEA hampered efforts to expand convertible-currency exports, it stimulated demand for these imports, because many of the inputs for Hungary's CMEA exports were available only from Western sources. The central development programs (CDPs) approved during 1968–73 and implemented during 1968–78 best illustrate the interaction between CMEA exports, convertible-currency imports, and recentralization in the domestic economy.

CDPs involved large projects (to manufacture buses, process aluminum, develop computers and petrochemicals, and modernize the textile industry) whose implementation typically cut across branches and preempted huge investment resources for five to fifteen years. The sheer scale of such commitments prescribed the central allocation of investments, and program implementation and coordination required state direction, often involving day-to-day intervention by the industrial ministries in enterprise decisions. Designed to expand CMEA exports, the ability of the CDPs to generate hard-currency earnings was predictably weak. Nevertheless, a significant share of the technology and the inputs they employed came from the West.[26]

Because the CDPs typically involved extensive cooperation with the Soviet Union (as either a consumer of outputs or a supplier of inputs), they illustrate how Soviet trade policy influences Hungarian economic decisions. For example, Soviet supplies at attractive prices and Soviet demand for large lots of manufactures made big, concentrated industries appear economically viable, even though smaller and more decentralized enterprises adapted best to NEM incentives. Likewise, temporary Soviet willingness to supply needed materials at favorable prices along with high demand for Hungarian exports made rapid economic expansion seem attractive. Yet rapid expansion helped to create the shortages and tensions in the economy which forced central authorities to revert to direct intervention in resource allocation. Ironically, Soviet "generosity" in aiding Hungarian adjustment in the 1970s itself created pressures for that adjustment to take nonmarket forms.

Finally, there is the direct political influence of international actors, especially that of the Soviet Union, on Hungary's reform process. Leaders of the HSWP learned all too well in 1956 that the forces favoring an "independent" Hungary hardly favored an independent Hungary controlled by a communist party. Hence, maintaining a strong Soviet presence and close ties to the Soviet Union has remained in the interest of the HSWP itself. Kádár was far from engaging in idle flattery when he declared that "there never has been, and there never will be, an anti-Soviet Communist."[27]

OECD, 1986), and Márton Tardos, "Importing Western Technology into Hungary," in M. Bornstein, Z. Gitelman, and W. Zimmerman, eds., *East-West Relations and the Future of Eastern Europe* (London: Allen & Unwin, 1981), pp. 221–42.

26. For more detail see Marer, *East-West Technology Transfer.*

27. Cited by Toma and Volgyes, *Politics in Hungary,* p. 32.

Although the terms of ties with the Soviet Union may be debated, it is not in any leader's interest to reject them. Moreover, maintaining the ties makes Soviet preferences an important political consideration in Hungarian party debates. In 1966, when the party initiated the discussions leading to the NEM, Soviet interest in economic reform worked to favor the HSWP's liberals. Following the invasion of Czechoslovakia, however, the Soviet political climate shifted in important ways.[28] The result was not that the CPSU openly opposed economic reform in Hungary but simply that reform sympathizers within it were no longer in a position to aid allies in the East European parties. Consequently, to the degree Soviet support was available as a political resource to be deployed within the HSWP, it tended to be more accessible to opponents of the NEM.

By 1974, then, the political climate in Hungary differed a great deal from the one in which the NEM was introduced. The energy shocks and the Western recession, the inability of the CMEA to alter trade and currency arrangements in ways that would have relieved external pressures for economic centralization, the availability of Western credit, and economic cooperation with the Soviet Union reinforced the domestic developments already eroding the position of reformists within the HSWP. The new basis of party consensus was far less sympathetic to market experimentation; its outcome was the policies of illusion.

Yet if the reform coalition dissolved in practice, tolerance for diversity kept it alive in principle. Even Rezső Nyers, the architect of the NEM, kept his seat on the Central Committee after his expulsion from the Politburo. Hence, when domestic and international conditions changed again at the end of the 1970s, reform could once again appear on the political agenda. The increasingly costly convertible-currency inputs embodied in exports to the CMEA, the unavailability of raw materials and energy from CMEA sources in sufficient quantity and quality, the apparent inability of Hungary sufficiently to enlarge export capacities for Western markets, and the need for a stabilization program reducing growth, investment, and subsidies helped deprive reform opponents of the key political resources that had kept their coalition together. Moreover, only reform advocates offered any real program that could arguably shore up the center's ability to impose discipline on the economy. Nevertheless, it took the crisis of 1979–82 to get that program adopted.

3. The "new" NEM and politics in Hungary

The changes introduced since 1979 suggest that reform advocates learned their political lessons well in the 1970s. From a political angle, recent changes appear to be more difficult to reverse than the NEM proved itself to be.

28. See Karen Dawisha, "The 1968 Invasion of Czechoslovakia: Causes, Consequences, and Lessons for the Future," in Dawisha and Philip Hanson, eds., *Soviet-East European Dilemmas* (New York: Holmes & Meier, 1981), pp. 9–26.

First, in 1980 three industrial ministries were consolidated into a single Ministry of Industry to reduce the size of the bureaucracy that thrives on the detailed supervising of firms. At the same time, new methods of appointing enterprise managers were introduced, and new ways were found to link domestic prices to foreign prices and wages to the enterprise profitability. Many large firms and trusts were broken up into smaller units; by 1983 about 300 new enterprises were created in this way, hardly an insignificant number given that there were only 702 state enterprises in all of Hungary when the process began in 1979. In addition, new measures facilitated the establishment of new small and medium-sized ventures in both state and cooperative sectors; traditionally, such firms have been subject to far less central supervision than large ones. Recent legislation, to be implemented during 1985–87, has also prescribed that firms with less than 300 employees will be self-managed; many medium-sized firms will be controlled by representatives elected both by workers and employees and by management.[29]

Economically, such measures are designed to reduce day-to-day administrative intervention in enterprise decisions, allow firms to adapt more flexibly to domestic and international market forces, and encourage competition. Yet these measures may easily fall by the wayside without the political context of this decentralization. This can be best understood by comparing the present situation with that prevailing at the time the NEM was introduced. Let us recall that the initial impact of the 1966 party reform had been to encourage regional leaders to bring central resources to their areas. By 1980, however, substantial industry was already located outside traditional urban centers. Meanwhile, local party organs had begun to play a much greater role in the local and national economies, reinforced by the endemic labor shortages only the regional party was capable of managing. In Győr County, for example, the number of economic indicators the party kept track of increased tenfold in the 1970s.[30]

If attracting large enterprises to their area was in the interest of regional elites in 1968, by 1980 it was often in their interest to loosen the ties between local subsidiaries and headquarters. Should a local plant in an area become an independent firm, not only would a whole new management be appointed but responsibility for the appointments and the firm would be entrusted to the region where it was headquartered. Moreover, managing local shortages was easier if local employers did not depend on orders from a distant company headquarters. Even party leaders opposed to reform in the abstract could now acquire a concrete political interest in decentralization—quite the opposite of the situation in the late 1960s and early 1970s.

A second set of measures expanded the scope and eased restrictions on

29. For details of the recent reforms see Marer, "Economic Reform in Hungary."
30. Interviews conducted by Ellen Comisso, 1983, Hungary. See K. Fazekas et al., "Kereseti és Bérviszonyaink," *MTA Közgazdaságtudományi Intézet Közleményei* 29 (Budapest: MTA Közgazdaságtudományi Intézet, 1983).

the legalized private sector in 1982. For example, individuals may now form independent contract work associations (ICWAs) to manufacture or provide services for enterprises, cooperatives, budgetary organizations, or the population. This measure seeks to create a complementary relationship between the socialist, cooperative, and private sectors—somewhat like that which prevails in agriculture—based more on specialization and comparative advantage than on direct competition. For example, a socialist firm losing money on some operations (e.g., small restaurants) may now lease such facilities to private entrepreneurs or ICWAs, turning a loss into a rental income. Private competitors, rather than threatening socialist firms economically, in such cases may aid them.

Likewise, firms that previously had to confine purchases of services, equipment, and goods to suppliers from the socialist sector may now contract with private and cooperative associations for such inputs. To the degree this protects firms from the shortages, late deliveries, and other dysfunctions of the sellers' market of the socialist sector, it helps them respond to pressures for greater efficiency.

Economically, such measures are designed to increase the quality and diversity of goods available; enhance competition between and within the private, cooperative, and socialist firms; and make it easier for socialist firms to abandon unprofitable activities. If such arrangements benefit the state firms economically, the political consequences could be to turn defenders of the socialist sector into de facto supporters of private entrepreneurship, too.

The new enterprise contract work associations (ECWAs), operating since 1982, also illustrate these paradoxical political relations. Representing an attempt to adapt the arrangements to provide incentives that prevail in agriculture to industry, ECWAs are groups of workers who contract with their own firm to carry out tasks the enterprise cannot otherwise perform, using enterprise facilities and inputs the firm provides. By October 1983 close to 100,000 workers were involved in ECWAs.

ECWAs represent a partial lifting of strict wage regulations in a controlled setting. That is, ECWAs are permitted only when they clearly produce additional output. Moreover, since they represent voluntary associations of small groups of workers whose remuneration is tied closely to performance, ECWAs typically are composed of the firm's best workers. If restrictions on general wage increases were lifted, there is no assurance that, under the prevailing economic mechanism, pressures for higher wages could be contained or offset by a proportionate increase in output.

ECWAs provide management with a politically approved and entirely legal means of getting around the barriers to allocating labor efficiently in the firm created by labor shortages, wage regulations, and legally protected employee rights. While workers must stay at their assigned posts during regular work hours, they can now be shifted to more productive activities by "contract" after work. Further, if good workers cannot be rewarded within the official wage system, they can be rewarded under ECWA contracts. And since workers can earn more "on contract" than by working overtime, they are willing to cooperate and are less likely to find jobs outside the socialist sector appealing. Finally, the earning opportunities ECWAs afford make it easier for the government to raise prices of consumer goods without cutting the real incomes and purchasing power of employees in the socialist sector.

Ironically, the sectors in which ECWAs may be the most useful are the heavy industries hit the hardest by the limits on investment and imports which austerity has brought. Firms in these sectors are also those that count the most politically and whose economic viability has had to be protected at the expense of economic reform in the past.[31]

Party and union functionaries in the firms also have a political interest in establishing ECWAs. While the fears of union leaders that members would exit into the nonsocialist sector were a key factor in their opposition to the NEM, ECWAs help keep up incomes in the socialist sector. Hence it is in the interest of union leaders to push their formation—despite traditional antagonism to private activities and market mechanisms.

Finally, ECWAs provide workers with an autonomous organization. Legally, of course, ECWAs have purely economic functions, but they also constitute a structure workers can use to bargain directly with management in the present and resist attempts to tax or abolish them in the future. Just as peasants were able to overturn proposed taxes in the 1970s, workers may now have a legitimate vehicle to exert claims on industry. Thus it is doubly ironic that the forces most active in the reversal of the NEM in the past are likely to advance the formation of ECWAs in the present.

Beginning in 1980, the center took other measures to increase competition in the foreign-trade field, namely, the selective elimination of foreign-trade monopolies in some industrial sectors and the extension of foreign-trading rights to dozens of additional firms. However, austerity measures have prevented the import liberalization that is a necessary condition of any real competition in the domestic economy. Small new financial institutions were created to provide limited competition on the domestic capital market, and discussions began that aimed at decentralizing the Hungarian National Bank into a central bank and an independent commercial banking network. In addition, measures were taken to encourage foreign investment: particularly important were the steps Hungary took toward currency convertibility (i.e., unification of the commercial and tourist exchange rates) as part of its decision to join the IMF and the World Bank in 1982.

Viewed from the perspective of the other CMEA countries, Hungary's recent and prospective future reforms represent very impressive changes and

31. For example, a director of the Danube Steelworks has achieved some renown for being the local expert on the organization of ECWAs and small entrepreneurship. In serious trouble after the collapse of the world steel market, the enterprise found ECWAs to be an essential mechanism for integrating forward and moving labor out of less profitable basic steel operations.

make the country appear to be "on the move" again. But the same measures are far less impressive contrasted with reasonably efficient market economies. In any event, Hungary still has a long way to travel on the reform path before its economic system becomes an efficient "centrally regulated market economy."[32]

The political implications of the "new" new economic mechanism are perhaps best described as the first steps toward a limited "debureaucratization" of the state: the leadership has taken some important steps to lay a foundation for organizations in the socialist sector to acquire real interests as opposed to simply wishing to satisfy the next highest level of command. Such possibilities can be seen in the measures encouraging electoral choice for delegates to Parliament, the introduction of self-management in medium-sized firms (which gives them a means and an incentive to protect their autonomy), the attempts to interest enterprises in general economic policy (as opposed to exceptionalism and bureaucratic dealings) by organizing them through the Chamber of Commerce and in ECWAs. Some fiscal decentralization appears to be the next logical step, as it would give local governments a genuine interest in the performance of enterprises in the area.

Debureaucratizing the state is a far cry from diminishing party hegemony. It merely allows a measure of simulated pluralism to accompany the simulated market. In effect, groups organized under party auspices via the state apparatus may now have an opportunity to influence proposals the party puts before them. But debureaucratization can have a major impact on the balance of forces within the party itself, because for the first time reformists may be able to avail themselves of political support outside the HSWP.

Whether such support will actually materialize is far from certain. Enterprises may now be encouraged to form coalitions and exert influence on overall economic policy, but they may well find it more advisable to stay neutral and limit themselves to lobbying for exceptions in bureaucratic corridors. Similarly, decentralization may be popular among Hungary's powerful county party leaders, but it is far from equivalent to support for the market. In fact, to the degree enterprises are available for political mobilization, firms may well be used against allocating resources on economic grounds, especially if regional leaders simply fill in the space now being vacated by the industrial ministries.[33] ECWAs can also easily be transformed from vehicles for raising labor productivity into instruments for keeping wages up to deter labor from seeking more productive outlets. Moreover, if they produce inequalities that appear simply to reflect managerial favoritism, workers may turn against them altogether. In fact, because in recent years incomes in the rapidly growing "pure" private sectors have been increasing steadily while in the

---

32. For a more detailed analysis see Marer, "Economic Reform in Hungary."
33. See E. Szalai, "The New Stage of the Reform Process in Hungary and the Large Enterprises," *Acta Oeconomica* 29, no. 102 (1982), pp. 41–42.

"pure" socialist sectors they have been stagnating, strong political forces opposing the reform have been emerging in the 1980s.

The newly self-managed firms might also be expected to guard their independence. Yet if enterprise, party, and union organizations co-opt worker representation, the self-management bodies will reflect larger party and union priorities rather than those of the enterprise labor force. Needless to say, the former are far less likely to place a premium on enterprise autonomy.

Further, whether a complementary or conflictual relationship evolves between the private, cooperative, and socialist sectors remains to be seen. Should outright competition become the norm, the prosperity and expansion of ventures outside the socialist sector will hardly constitute a political resource for reformists. Likewise, to the degree competition from the more flexible private sector creates problems for state firms, political figures connected to them are unlikely to favor the continuing expansion of the private sector.

Finally, international developments will continue to be decisive for Hungary's internal political and economic evolution. Future changes in the Kremlin will continue to have major ramifications for the alignment of political forces in Budapest. So, too, will internal developments within the other East European countries and progress on CMEA integration. Currently stressing the "deepening" of integration along traditional "plan coordination" lines, the CMEA hardly appears supportive of domestic reform in Hungary.

If Hungarian firms are unable to increase their convertible-currency exports for systemic reasons or because of Western protectionism, recession, or a further deterioration in East-West relations, there will be strong pressures to reorient trade toward the CMEA, in addition to the recentralizing measures that will follow. Even if Hungary does continue to expand its exports and surmount the present crisis, strong redistributional pressures may resurface once austerity measures are relaxed. Indeed, such recentralizing pressures are already making themselves felt, as evidenced in the debates preceding the 1985 HSWP congress, in the changes in the HSWP leadership made on that occasion, and in a February 1985 decision to impose a 10 percent surcharge on ECWAs. Such developments are a graphic reminder that as much in the 1980s as after 1968, the process of economic reform in Hungary is neither concluded nor unidirectional. Nevertheless, many of the reforms Hungary has introduced appear unlikely to be reversed even if reformists should again find their political influence eroded. To have made these changes under adverse political and economic circumstances at home and abroad is no small accomplishment; whether or not further systemic changes will follow remains a question.

Economic adjustment and political forces: Poland since 1970 Kazimierz Poznański

The consequences of the crisis that shook Poland in 1979 differ from those that other East European countries have faced. The economic crisis has been more severe in Poland than in any other Eastern-bloc country, and it is going on its sixth consecutive year, whereas some of the other East European countries have restored economic stability and are showing modest growth. Why were the difficulties facing Poland so much more severe than those elsewhere in Eastern Europe?

Admittedly, the expansionary policy Edward Gierek selected in 1971 — different more in degree than in kind from the expansionary policies of many other leaders in Eastern Europe — would have caused Poland serious economic difficulties had there been no intervening factors. However, it was Poland's inability to institute an adjustment policy which worsened the crisis far beyond what one would have predicted on the basis of Gierek's policy alone, and this is exactly what made Poland's the worst crisis in Eastern Europe.

Moreover, it is argued that unresolved political tensions have prevented the regime from introducing an adequate rescue package at critical times. The Polish experience as well as the experiences of other East European countries show that the economies in the region are equipped with remarkably powerful stabilizing mechanisms that help them restore macroeconomic equilibrium quickly (though at a large cost). But these mechanisms work only under conditions of political stability which allow the regimes to enforce unpopular measures without undermining their ability to govern the economy. Poland is the only country that did not meet this requirement during most of the adjustment period.

Proof that Poland has not enjoyed the kind of political stability common among East European countries after 1976 is not difficult to find. Poland

This essay was written during my stay as a 1984–85 National Fellow at the Hoover Institution, Stanford University. I am very grateful to Laura Tyson and Stanisław Gomułka for their comments, and to Ellen Comisso for her detailed and thorough review.

International Organization 40, 2, Spring 1986   0020-8183 $5.00
© 1986 by the Massachusetts Institute of Technology and the World Peace Foundation

has been the only country in Eastern Europe to experience both widespread and prolonged disturbances involving a majority of industrial workers. Likewise, only Poland had a rapid succession of changes in the composition of party leadership during 1980–81, a period that culminated in an overall change from civilian to military rule (for all practical purposes a sign that the political system itself had collapsed). Moreover, the stalemate in political life continues: signs of the party's recuperation from the damages incurred are limited, and evidence suggests that the forces of social opposition, though weakened by the declaration of martial law, continue to resist repressive measures.

I shall discuss three factors contributing to these unusual tensions in the 1970s: first, an exceptional lack of unity and/or division within the leadership which tend to intensify during periods of economic difficulty and/or political challenges to the regime; second, the growth of autonomous and increasingly well-organized social groups outside party control (i.e., Catholic clergy, industrial workers, and intellectuals) to a degree unknown in other East European countries; third, external political pressures that interfered with internal developments to a larger degree than in the rest of the Eastern bloc, mainly as a result of Poland's critical role in both Soviet and Western geopolitical strategies.

On many occasions the interaction of these three sources of political tension exacerbated one another, particularly during the period of open activity by the independent union Solidarity. Intraparty conflicts prompted some factions to coerce certain social groups into joining those conflicts, thus strengthening independent political forces and placing additional pressure on the party. The overall effect was often to strengthen foreign pressures, thus making it more difficult for the regime to come to terms with internal social opposition and narrowing the number of alternatives acceptable to organized labor and other sources of opposition.

1. Gierek's expansionary program of 1971-75

a. Major economic policy changes

When Gierek took over as first secretary of the Polish United Workers' party (PUWP) at the end of 1970, Polish industry was stagnating and losing its technological edge in the world economy. Moreover, years of deflationary income policies had had a detrimental impact on labor productivity and discipline among workers. Gierek's first response was to take limited corrective measures, mostly in agriculture. They were followed by a set of far more radical moves that laid the foundations for the economic expansion of 1971–75.[1]

---

1. S. Gomułka, *Growth, Innovation and Reform in Eastern Europe* (Brighton: Wheatsheaf, 1985), chap. 12.

High investment. The outstanding feature of the new economic policy was a decision to accelerate investment in an unprecedented buildup of production capacities. By 1975 the volume of investment exceeded the 1970 level by 133 percent. The share of investment in the gross national product (GNP) soared above 25 percent (e.g., 29.0% in 1975 versus an average of 19.4% for 1965–69),[2] a stronger level than that in any other East European country at the time. Even Romania, despite its aggressive growth policy, reported an increase in total investment of about 72 percent. Only in Hungary did the share of investment in GNP approach that of Poland, but even there the increase in the level of total spending was not so abrupt as in Poland.[3]

Gierek's decision radically to speed up the investment program was motivated in part by the logic of central planning under which industrial units—from enterprises to ministries—continually seek to push investment as high as possible. In the past, however, national leaders responsible for the economy as a whole have had an interest in restraining such built-in "expansionary drives" and "investment hunger" on the part of the individual industrial units, insofar as the national economy faced "hard" budget constraints (e.g., shortages of hard currency to pay for foreign equipment, limited physical capacity of the construction industry). In Gierek's case, no such incentives to restrain investment existed.

Instead, by acceding to administrative pressures Gierek was buying support from important political actors in the state bureaucracy.[4] In fact, Gierek's assumption of the post of first secretary in Poland was heralded by the elevation into high-ranking positions of a large number of cadres with strong industrial backgrounds who showed much less concern for overall economic balances than had the previous leadership elites.

Expansionary income policy. Another important policy change was a decision to accelerate sharply the growth of real income, which during the period 1966–70 had grown more slowly than elsewhere in Eastern Europe. This target had to be achieved with relatively stable prices, a constraint that industrial workers almost forced upon Gierek. Ironically, although the price rise Władysław Gomułka imposed in 1970 was a primary factor in Gierek's rise to power, Gierek initially resisted workers' demands to roll back the price increases. However, faced with massive strikes in Łódź in February

2. *Statistical Yearbook CMEA* (Moscow: CMEA, 1984).
3. E. Comisso and P. Marer, "Explaining Economic Strategy in Hungary" (Paper presented at the Conference on Foreign Economic Strategies of Eastern Europe, Berkeley, California, 1–2 February 1985). Significantly, Hungary and Romania also faced serious economic difficulties at the end of the decade as a result of such aggressive investment policies. Unlike in Poland, however, domestic and external political barriers did not undermine regime adjustment strategy.
4. W. Brus, "Economics and Politics: The Fatal Link," in A. Brumberg, ed., *Poland: Genesis of a Revolution* (New York: Random, 1982). Almost none of the top leaders under Gierek possessed the same qualities as the old "watchdogs" of balanced plans under Bolesław Bierut (e.g, Minc and Szyr), or Władysław Gomułka (e.g., Jędrychowski and Jaszczuk).

1971, he restored the previous prices and promised not to raise them for the next five years.

Unexpectedly, the actual growth in incomes greatly exceeded initial plans to increase consumption. In 1971–75 nominal wages were allowed to increase by an average of 9.6 percent yearly, more than three times the original plan figure (see Table 1). The annual rate of growth of real wages was around 6.8 percent, several times higher than the level permitted under Władysław Gomułka. The latter rate was more than twice the rates in the two other East European countries that had adopted models of "consumer socialism," namely East Germany and Hungary. These wage increases resulted from the unexpectedly high rate of growth in revenues of industrial associations and from the centrally instituted reforms in wage schemes of particular trades as well as from the retirement system.

Gierek's willingness to provide for a rapid expansion of income contrasted with the behavior of his predecessor. Gomułka had also sought to gain popularity by accelerating income growth and allocating more resources to industries that produced consumer goods, yet his favorable income policy was short-lived. As soon as his leadership became established and settled other conflicting pressures, it withdrew its commitment to promoting consumption. However, in Gierek's case, the decision to allow consumption to grow was (or was perceived to be) a long-term commitment forced on him in part by the high level of political leverage that workers had achieved at that time.

The new political philosophy of the recently arrived ruling elite also favored such concessions. This rather unorthodox approach called upon the party to "earn" its authority not only through indoctrination and threats but also by responding to the needs of people (i.e., consumer aspirations). Like the investment policy, then, Gierek's wage and price policy adjusted economic plans in order to capture the support of what were important strategic political actors, in this case the industrial workers.

Shifting toward the West. Such rapid jumps in investment and consumption required financial assistance from the West. Poland also needed credits from the West to provide the booming economy with the modern technology not available in the Soviet Union. Gierek—unlike his predecessor—did not hesitate to open the economy to outside contacts. This openness coincided with the ongoing effort by Western countries to stimulate sales of products in Eastern Europe and the Soviet Union by liberalizing restrictions on technology and offering generous credits. Both measures radically intensified after the 1973 oil-price shock.

The regime took full advantage of existing external opportunities. By 1971 Poland still showed a positive balance of trade with Western countries, though later it entered into large deficits. The single most dramatic change, which took place in 1973, reflected a sudden increase in the accessibility of Western

TABLE 1. *Basic economic indicators, 1970–80 (annual growth, in percentages)*

	1970	1971	1972	1973	1974	1975	1976	1977	1978	1979	1980
GNP	5.2	8.1	10.6	10.8	10.4	9.0	6.8	5.8	3.0	−2.3	−6.0
Industrial output	8.1	7.9	10.7	11.2	11.4	10.9	9.3	6.9	4.9	2.7	−0.2
Agricultural output	2.2	3.6	8.4	7.3	1.6	−2.1	−1.1	1.4	4.1	−1.5	−9.6
Investment	4.1	7.4	23.0	25.4	22.3	10.7	1.0	3.1	2.1	−7.9	−10.5
Investment/GNP ratio	20.5	20.6	23.3	25.9	28.3	29.0	27.0	27.1	25.9	22.7	17.3
Employment	0.6	1.9	2.6	1.9	1.8	0.6	0.0	0.6	3.0	0.5	0.6
Labor productivity	5.5	5.7	5.6	8.5	9.5	10.0	8.8	6.2	2.7	−2.0	−1.0
Nominal wage	2.8	5.3	4.7	9.1	14.3	13.6	8.8	7.1	5.6	9.1	12.8
Cost of living	1.2	−0.2	0.0	2.6	6.8	3.0	4.7	4.9	8.7	6.7	9.1
Real wage	1.6	5.5	4.7	6.3	7.0	10.3	3.9	2.1	−2.9	2.2	4.0
Real wage productivity ratio	—	0.96	0.84	0.68	0.70	1.03	0.43	0.33	−1.12	—	—

Source. Rocznik Statystyczny, Komunikat GUS (Warsaw: GUS, various years).

credits. Accordingly, the net debt to the West increased rapidly from an easily manageable sum of $1.2 billion in 1971 to $7.6 billion in 1975 (see Table 2). Although other East European countries adopted similar borrowing strategies—and with clear encouragement from the Soviet Union—none pursued borrowing as aggressively and as early as Poland.

One of the internal reasons underlying this more aggressive Polish borrowing policy was Gierek's desire to emancipate himself somewhat from the political control of the Soviet Union by developing economic contacts with Western countries. Unlike many other leaders in Eastern Europe, Gierek had not been simply mandated by the Soviet Union; rather he was elected by the PUWP. By successfully constructing a coalition to undermine his predecessor Gomułka, Gierek acquired the domestic base necessary to pursue a somewhat independent political line that appealed to traditionally strong nationalist currents within the Polish party.

A number of external factors, both economic and political, made Poland particularly attractive to Western investors as well. For example, Poland's large deposits of sulfur, copper, and coal—especially valuable after the 1973 energy crisis—put it in a unique situation for an East European country in that it did not have to rely so heavily on goods that were difficult to sell on Western markets, namely manufactures, in order to cover its credits. In addition the West has traditionally favored Poland economically, hoping to exploit the strong sympathies among Poles for Western culture and nationalism in order to weaken Soviet control over Eastern Europe.

b. Systemic reforms and continuity

Gierek turned to economic reforms in part to fulfill his commitment to trimming Poland's unwieldy bureaucracy, widely criticized by workers, state officials, and even the party itself. In addition, his expansion program looked to systemic reform to strengthen incentives for the productive use of resources and exports. By 1972 a broad package of systemic changes in the economy was ready, and by 1973 a small part of industry had adopted some but not all of the recommended changes. The rest of industry was scheduled to convert to the new economic system during 1974–75.[5]

Gierek's intentions notwithstanding, the reforms were not only very limited but also lacked much coherence. In fact the actual modifications amounted to only one important organizational change, namely amalgamating enterprises into associations and converting them into "account units" with greater authority over wages, investment, and production decisions. In theory such new autonomy required accompanying measures to prevent monopolistic abuses: either the strengthening of direct supervision from the ministries or

5. See G. Blazyca, "Industrial Structure and Economic Problems of Industry in a Centrally Planned Economy: The Polish Case," *Journal of Industrial Economics*, no. 28 (1980).

TABLE 2. *Polish trade with Western countries, 1971–84 (in billions of dollars)*

	1971	1972	1973	1974	1975	1976	1977	1978	1979	1980	1981	1982	1983	1984
Total exports	2.3	2.6	3.4	5.1	5.7	6.1	6.8	7.4	8.4	10.1	—	—	—	—
Total imports	2.0	2.7	4.8	7.2	8.7	8.9	8.6	8.9	10.3	10.8	—	—	—	—
Trade balance	0.3	−0.1	−1.4	−2.1	−3.0	−2.8	−1.8	−1.5	−1.9	−0.7	—	—	—	—
Net foreign debt	1.2	1.5	2.8	4.8	7.6	11.2	14.3	16.9	20.7	23.5	25.5	25.4	26.4	26.8
Debt service	0.4	0.4	0.5	1.0	1.5	2.1	3.1	4.5	6.3	8.4	10.9	—	—	—
Debt-service/export ratio	12.4%	15.4%	14.7%	19.5%	26.3%	34.4%	45.6%	60.8%	75.0%	83.2%	—	—	—	—

Sources. A. Lubowski, "Gdzie sie podzialy te miliardy," *Zycie Gospodzrcze,* no. 18 (May 1981); *Komunikat GUS, Wiadomòsci Statystyczne,* no. 2 (1985).

the introduction of real competition from abroad. In practice the regime took neither measure.

Associations (also called "large economic organizations") in practice provided managers with increased opportunities to exploit the potential for monopolistic practices. Not only were price controls loosened (e.g., by allowing managers freely to set prices for new products), but wage regulations were softened. In theory the economy looked more like a market economy, but in practice the scheme merely introduced more chaos into the operation of the economy and weakened incentives for efficiency. At the same time, the increased power of industrial associations provided additional momentum to the expansionary drive of Gierek's political leadership.

The reform package in agriculture was no more innovative. Initially, agricultural reform meant more favorable economic policies toward private farms, but in 1972 the regime returned to Poland's previous policy of collectivization. Under this policy the vehicle for change was to be a large state-owned farm, a strategy very much in line with the earlier concentration of agricultural activities in Bulgaria and elsewhere in Eastern Europe and the Soviet Union. This new faith in gigantic agricultural units was, at the same time, in the spirit of parallel reforms in Polish industry.[6]

The regime's explanation for the economic rationale behind this move emphasized Poland's urgent need to modernize agricultural production, which was dominated by small private farms with little specialization and poor mechanical equipment. Though not without chances for success in the long run, this policy ran the immediate risk of undermining overall agricultural productivity in the short run by diverting economic resources to a nonprivate sector whose state farms and cooperatives showed only one-half of the productivity that private farms achieved.

The political mechanism underlying this policy shift in agriculture was representative of the Polish leadership, which constantly faced a tradeoff between economic rationality (i.e., the needs of the agricultural sector) and ideological obligations. Paradoxically, the very good performance of private farms in 1971–73 made it easier for the regime to return to collectivization.[7] In this regard, the cause for the policy change appears to have been less Gierek's own initiative than a result of the pressures of agricultural lobbyists reinforced by encouragement from the Soviet Union, which had been traditionally wary about the political risk of a large private sector in agriculture. Thus in agriculture, too, the need to cement a political coalition had a critical impact on economic decisions.

c. New political style

Intraparty relationships. One of the major political problems facing Gierek after he assumed the highest post in the party was to make it work effectively

6. Z. Fallenbuchl, *Polityka Gospodarcze PRL* (London: Odnowa, 1980).
7. Brus, "Economics and Politics."

again and work in his way. One of the challenges that Gierek inherited was a highly divided party apparatus. By the end of 1971 he had removed not only most of the top members of Gomułka's team but also his temporary allies against Gomułka, namely, the faction that grew up around Mieczysław Moczar. Unlike previous cleanups in the Polish party and unlike the purge in Czechoslovakia in 1968, Gierek's purge was not total. Nor did Gierek try to build the kind of "coalition leadership" that characterized the Soviet party under Leonid Brezhnev. Instead he decided to integrate the party around his personal leadership with the help of "exchange relations" (power or bonuses for support) rather than with ideological and police intimidation.

Gierek's other important move within the party was to replace low-skilled cadres with young and well-trained apparatchiks. As a result, the party leadership in Poland became the youngest (the average age of the PUWP Central Committee members was close to forty) and the best educated (almost 80% of the members of the Politburo claimed to have university degrees) among Eastern-bloc countries. Predictably, such changes had far-reaching implications for party behavior.

The new generation of apparatchiks was made up of people who, much like Gierek himself, did not care much for ideological purity. To most of them the party career was like a job for which they expected to be properly rewarded. Accordingly, the ideology of the party became a kind of window dressing needed to preserve an image of continuity and to please more orthodox parties in the region, and it continued to serve as the one "language" commonly understood by all apparatchiks. As a result, the party came closer to resembling the society, but at the same time one of its integrating forces was weakened: the sense of common political mission.

Party-state relations. Gierek's leadership also effected important changes in the organization of both the state administration and the party. Theoretically, the underlying purpose of the changes was to reduce bureaucracy by eliminating overlapping responsibilities of the state and party apparatuses. In addition, administrative reforms sought to strengthen the central party leadership's control of local units. The most essential of these reforms occurred in 1973–75, when a three-tiered regional administrative system running from provinces to counties to townships was collapsed into two tiers. Townships grew and provinces (*wojewodztwo*) doubled in number. The party organization changed accordingly, and the state administration acquired some of its functions.

These reforms helped the central party authorities to subordinate the lower-level political ranks more effectively, but at the same time the party as a whole lost much of its previously firm control over the state administration as a result of the elimination of midlevel units (i.e., county committees). At this level the party had traditionally enjoyed a particularly strong position vis-à-vis the state administration (owing to its knowledge of local problems and wider political responsibility). By eliminating these units, the party lost the arm that had been most effective, among other things, in disciplining enterprise managers, who now became almost solely responsible to the powerful associations.

Several changes in planning procedures weakened the party's control over the administration. The Planning Commission, hitherto strongly under the control of the party leadership, lost some of its authority to the ministries. While such moves whetted the expansionary ambition of the state administration, they also weakened the ability of the central party leadership— practically the only institution concerned with macroeconomic balances— to prevent the economy from drifting into extreme disequilibrium.

Party workers and the church. Gomułka's brutally repressive reaction to the 1970 strikes not only outraged workers but also alienated them from the party. To improve its image the Gierek regime pursued frequent, direct contact with workers (conducting on-site visits to factories and public discussion of state decisions, devising new rules for handling citizen complaints, and polling public opinion regularly—all from the repertoire of "corporatist techniques")[8]—but without, however, acceding to their demands for independent representation on the plant level.

Gierek also did not consider legalizing strikes, despite initial promises to this effect. Yet neither did he turn to repressive measures to discourage protest. Rather he opted for an unusual (by East European and Soviet standards) policy of letting strikes happen and countering with economic concessions (i.e., wages). That the regime did not consider strikes an unacceptable embarrassment but rather a fact of life was another expression of its own peculiar "crisis-oriented" mentality.

In addition, to help his political image Gierek also adopted another innovative policy, namely, "borrowing" some legitimacy from the Catholic church and using cooperative relations with the clergy to counterbalance intraparty opposition.[9] It was an ingenious move, since Gomułka had successive confrontations with the church. Gierek began by granting long-awaited concessions to the church: permits for new building construction, better access to the media, and a higher quota for candidates to the priesthood, among others.

In fact Gierek had little choice but to come to terms with the church, which at this point had a solid political base among Poles and hence an increasing ability to pursue an independent line. Much of this newly acquired strength came from the clergy's successful attempt to expand the traditional base of support for the church—private farmers—to include workers. Their efforts succeeded in part as a result of a more progressive agenda that focused

8. J. Staniszkis, *Self-Limiting Revolution* (Princeton: Princeton University Press, 1983).
9. Ibid.

on the primary importance of work, human dignity, and individual rights. This change also helped the clergy to attract intellectuals anxious to find an organization outside the party itself through which to exercise influence.

To conclude, in political terms Gierek's expansionary program of "renewal" attempted to create a new political equilibrium that would synthesize and reorient conflicting forces in the PUWP, state administration, and society. For the party's traditionalists Gierek offered an ambitious investment program, a return to collectivization in agriculture, and the rejection of genuine market-based reforms. For the upward-moving generation of industrial bureaucrats and state administrators he provided increased access to sophisticated technology. For workers there were wage increases and "dialogues" within each firm. For the church there was an atmosphere of acceptance and reconciliation, and for intellectuals there was increased respect in the form of requests for consultation and promises of political relaxation. If conflicts among these forces subsequently undermined Gierek's leadership, their initial accord was critical to its establishment.

In economic terms Gierek's new policies helped to revitalize the economy. With an annual average rate of growth in GNP close to 9.4 percent in 1971–75 (see Table 1), Poland outperformed all other centrally planned economies with the possible exception of Romania. Together with the large range of semiliberalization measures, this performance made Gierek popular outside the party while strengthening his control within it. Gierek's domestic policies and unprecedented activism in the international arena gave him a good reputation among Western leaders, particularly those in Europe; and his continued loyalty to the socialist alliance and political triumph over the more extreme nationalist elements in the Polish party led by Moczar gave the Soviet Union cause for satisfaction as well.

2. The incomplete adjustment of 1976–79

To ensure continued economic growth after 1975 the leadership had to make some policy adjustments. When the oil-price shocks and prolonged recession on Western markets began to affect Poland around 1975, Gierek had to find a solution to an increasing shortage of hard currency. The least difficult adjustment was to allow the economy to continue its boom with the help of Western credits. Recently many economists have argued that this is exactly the strategy Gierek decided on and constitutes proof of his alleged lack of realism. However, the post-1975 record proves this view to be far from correct.

Neither the package of economic measures introduced in 1976, referred to by the regime as an "economic maneuver," nor the following steps constitute evidence of Gierek's immobilism. In fact the regime in Poland seemed to be if not the first, one of the first, in Eastern Europe to revise its economic program in response to the crisis; moreover, Gierek pursued his adjustment policy quite aggressively even as other East European states were encountering similar internal adversity.

a. Response to external adversity

Cutting down investment. Both the rising price of oil—imported in large quantities in return for hard currency—and the weak demand for Polish goods on Western markets hampered Poland's ability to import capital goods, hence the regime had to consider curtailing investment programs. Some scaling down of investment outlays was also needed to correct the growing imbalance between investment requirements and domestic construction capabilities. Accordingly the 1976–80 plan called for cutting the average annual rate of growth in investment to 8 percent. The actual rate turned out even lower than the planned one (i.e., around 2.0% annually in 1976–78 and then −7.9% in 1979). In contrast, other East European countries (with the possible exception of Bulgaria) invested heavily up to 1978; for example, Hungary reported an average growth rate of 8 percent during 1976–78.[10]

These cuts went hand in hand with several systemic measures aimed at reducing the power that mammoth industrial associations, joined by their respective ministries, were able to bring to bear on investment choices in the early years of Gierek's tenure. For example, the 1973 reforms were dismantled, marking a return to the highly centralized system of the past. However, most of the investment funds previously controlled by the associations were frozen, and so-called wild investment (i.e., not accepted in the central plans) was scrutinized more severely.

Were these cuts sufficient? Many economists argue that they were not, since the measures taken only slowed down the *expansion* of investment, leaving its share in the GNP very high (in 1978 it was one point below the 1976 level but still around 25%). Conclusive evidence is lacking, however, for any deeper cuts in investment would probably have caused more harm than good, freezing projects and closing factories that were supposed to provide material supplies for them.

Wage and price policy. Any reduction of demand for hard currency also required some reduction in domestic consumption. Though necessary, such a move naturally ran the risk of provoking renewed labor protests. The regime had therefore to select with care a strategy for curbing consumption. Three nonexclusive policy options presented themselves: raise inflation, decrease nominal wage increases, and finally, slow employment growth (or even allow for open unemployment).

10. *Statistical Yearbook CMEA* (Moscow: CMEA, 1981) and national statistics for Hungary.

The regime obviously preferred to try to achieve as much as possible by curtailing nominal wages, and in fact the recentralization of 1977 was partly designed to help the regime enforce such restrictions. But workers strongly resisted these. As many as several hundred strikes reportedly took place in 1976–79. In most cases the workers won wage concessions, for the regime continued to prefer "corporatist" measures to police ones. This willingness to accommodate protesters undermined the regime's effort to reduce nominal wage increases, and the annual rate of growth in nominal wages in 1976–79 was 7.4 percent, only slightly less than in 1971–75 when the regime did not try to block wage increases (see Table 1).

Thus the regime had no other choice but to resort to a less favorable option, namely, price increases. In 1976 Gierek was no longer bound by the earlier promise to keep food prices frozen; as a result he had some basis for hoping that open price rises would not impair his credibility. However, when increases in food prices were announced in July 1976, strikes broke out in several old industrial centers (e.g., Ursus, Random), forcing Gierek to roll back the new prices. The regime responded with more aggressive hidden price increases, as a result of which the cost of living indicator rose in 1976–79 by 6 percent on an annual basis, almost three times the 1971–75 rate of increase (Table 1).

Despite these political obstacles, Gierek's policy achieved a limited success, at least from a purely economic perspective. Through inflation and nominal wage limits, the regime succeeded in bringing the rate of growth of real wages during 1976–79 to 1.3 percent a year (with a drop of 2.9% in 1978), far below the rates permitted in 1971–75 and in contrast with the rest of Eastern Europe, where the slowdown in real wages did not come until 1980. This wage decrease brought some relief to the heavily disturbed economy but not enough to allow for substantial cuts in grain imports.[11] Clearly, a further series of restrictions on consumption was needed.

Agricultural dismay. The reduction of grain imports—these imports absorbed almost one-fifth of the money that the regime borrowed from Western banks through 1976—could not have been accomplished only by slowing consumption; improvement in the agricultural sector was needed as well. Even with the large import of grain (used mostly for meat production), agriculture performed very poorly, reporting substantial declines in grain production and meat supplies in both 1975 and 1976 (see Table 1). The poor performance could be attributed largely to the unfavorable policies toward private farming, particularly the difficulties private farmers had purchasing imported grain (provided mostly to state and cooperative farms) and the losses of income due to price mismanagement.

11. W. Charemza, "The Centrally Plannned Economy in the International Crisis, Poland 1974–1980" (Paper delivered at the Centre for Russian and East European Studies, Birmingham, England, 1984).

Only in 1977 did the regime decide to try to revitalize private farming. Among other things, Gierek eased procedures for land purchase, enacted measures to prevent further outmigration, and raised some key commodity prices in order to make private farming profitable again. However, acceding to pressures from the "collective farming" lobby, Gierek continued to allocate most of the productive supplies (including Western grain) to the less efficient nonprivate sectors.[12]

Consequently the total output of agricultural products grew at an insignificant rate from 1977 to 1979. Although increases in the number of livestock forced Poland to escalate grain imports, there was insufficient meat to satisfy domestic demand. Hence, the regime was forced for the first time to import large amounts of meat in return for hard currency. Contrary to many other areas of the economy, the adjustment in agriculture did not produce any significant improvements and was in fact a major failure, the otherwise well-directed adjustment of 1976–79 notwithstanding.

Energy conservation. To reduce pressure on foreign currency, the regime had to consider some energy conservation measures. First, it had to deal with the expanding costs of oil imports, fueled by both the post-1973 price increases and the sudden increase in domestic demand (related to the mass motorization program, among others).[13] In addition, domestic consumption of coal had to be reduced, because Polish coal exports have been traditionally a major source of hard-currency earnings.

Many economists, R. Portes among them,[14] currently studying the Polish crisis argue that the impact of rising oil prices would have been lessened if Gierek's regime had not put so many resources into high energy-intensive projects. Even if this claim is true, we should keep in mind that Poland did not possess an East European monopoly on energy-intensive investment

12. Z. Fallenbuchl, "The Polish Economy in the 1970's," in Joint Economic Committee, *East European Economies, Post-Helsinki*, 97th Cong., 1st sess., 1977.

13. Under Gierek Poland not only was relatively more dependent on hard-currency oil imports than were many other East European countries, but its purchases were also cleared mostly with Western countries, whereas other East European countries dealt mostly with the developing nations, particularly Libya and Middle Eastern oil-producing countries. The latter transactions were certainly easier to finance, because many of them were cleared by Eastern Europe with military deliveries. For instance, in 1978, Poland imported 3.6 million tons of hard-currency oil, while Czechoslovakia imported 1.3 million tons. In per capita terms these imports were very similar, but the share of hard-currency imports in Poland's total oil imports was twice as high as that for Czechoslovakia. More than two-thirds of Polish hard-currency imports came from the West, whereas the West provided only one-third of the Czechoslovakian imports. In addition, almost no Polish imports of crude oil were shipped to the West, while almost half of Czechoslovakian hard-currency imports were reexported for hard currency (i.e., practically all oil imports from the developing nations). See Wharton Econometric Forecasting Associates, "Soviet and East European Trade and Financial Relations with the Middle East," *Centrally Planned Economies: Current Analysis*, 11 October 1983.

14. R. Portes, *The Polish Crisis: Western Policy Options* (London: Royal Institute of International Affairs, 1981).

choices at that time. Thus, although investment in energy-intensive steel production quintupled in Poland from 1970 to 1975, Romania also doubled its capital outlays in steel over that period, and Czechoslovakia followed a similar path, despite only a modest overall expansion of its industrial sector. Likewise, the East European countries put enormous effort into producing modern petrochemicals, with Hungary—almost completely dependent on foreign sources of fuels—outdoing them all.

To save on fuel the regime raised energy prices sharply for enterprises, but given the cost insensitivity of firms, such measures had only a minimal effect.[15] Predictably, more direct measures, including direct restrictions on supplies, followed soon after. In addition, the regime slowed down production in a few fuel-intensive sectors, including petrochemicals, where some projects were simply never completed (although petrochemicals continued to grow at high rates in Hungary). Prices for consumers (e.g., of gasoline) were increased around that time too.

All these measures helped Poland to reduce imports of fuels. Although its last increase in quantities of imported oil took place in 1976, most of Eastern Europe continued to buy additional oil for another few years (e.g., Romania increased the quantity of its imports by more than half and East Germany by one-quarter in 1976–79). However, because the prices for oil continued to rise in both the world market and in the Soviet Union, import payments increased. With only modest expansion of hard coal exports, Poland became unable to pay for its oil imports. As a result, in 1979 Poland became a net importer of fuels for the first time in the postwar era, necessitating even further cuts in energy consumption.

Foreign trade. To facilitate efforts to achieve a balance of trade and stabilize the growing foreign debt (see Table 2), the regime returned to pre-1973 detailed plan targets in their most opaque version. In accord with this policy, exports to Western countries grew on average around 4 percent in constant prices from 1976 to 1979, a rather disappointing figure (for instance, Hungarian exports to the West grew annually by 9% in that period). In constant prices, imports from Western markets increased for the last time in 1976, after which they declined at a yearly rate of 6 percent during 1977–79. None of the other East European countries began as early as Poland to cut imports from the West so deeply (e.g., Hungarian purchases grew by roughly 12% annually in 1976–78).

Even with these import cuts—probably excessive at this point in time[16]— Poland continued to run a trade deficit with the Western economies until 1979, though the size of the deficit declined rapidly (e.g., the deficit amounted

15. J. Kornai, *Economics of Shortage* (Amsterdam: North Holland, 1980).
16. G. Fink, *Economic Effects of the Polish Crisis on Other CMEA Countries* (Vienna: Institute of Comparative Economic Studies, 1983).

to 40% of Polish imports in 1976 but to only 21% in 1979). Debt-service payments were mounting at the same time, as payments of the principal and interest charges accumulated rapidly. Because more credits had to be raised in order to cover the trade deficit and to meet payments, Poland's net debt reached $20.7 billion in 1979, almost three times the 1975 level (see Table 2). This amount, however, was still comparable to debts reported by most other East European countries (e.g., from 1976 to 1979 Hungarian debt more than tripled, going from $2.1 to $7.3 billion).[17]

Some economists argue that Poland's poor trade performance was mainly a result of bad investment choices, including excessive dispersion of capital means, which did not create enough export potential to back up its credit-based program.[18] However, a careful study of trade data reveals that, the manner of investment notwithstanding, Poland was able to replace a number of traditional exports with more sophisticated products (e.g., cars and trucks, consumer electronics, construction machinery). To allow a necessary concentration of investment, some industrial sectors, including a large sector of machine-tool building, were not designed to produce goods that would expand the export market. With this new export potential, Polish sales of manufactures from Western markets grew faster than in most other East European countries, and Poland was paid the highest prices as well (with the exception of Hungary).[19]

Yet by far a more important factor was the strong demand for exportable goods on the domestic market, a demand that came from both the powerful associations and the workers. The demand was particularly strong for products built with the most recent imports of Western technology—exactly those the regime wanted to use for export promotion to the West. If these domestic pressures had relaxed, the amount of goods available for exports on Western markets would have increased greatly. Political factors, however, prevented this from happening.

b. Beginning of a political crisis

Gierek's early program was predicated on economic expansion. But with the adjustment policy of 1976–79, fewer and fewer goods were available to "pay" for necessary political support. Gierek did not, however, decide to change his style of leadership, returning, for example, to old-fashioned repression. Instead, he continued to rely on support he was no longer able to afford; not surprisingly, it was increasingly less available. As a result, the

17. L. Tyson, *Economic Adjustment in Eastern Europe: Hungary and Romania* (Santa Monica: Rand, 1984).
18. J. M. Montias, "Poland: Roots of the Economic Crisis," Working Paper no. 848, Institute for Social and Policy Studies, Yale University, New Haven, Conn., March–April 1982.
19. K. Poznański, "State Policy towards Technology Transfer in Poland during the 1970's," *Research Policy* (forthcoming).

political system became less stable, as evidenced by the regime's declining popularity.

Disobedience and dissent. The political costs of the 1976 struggle over wage and price policies included growing frustration among workers. That the regime purposely avoided using force and instead retreated from its position on price reform did not earn Gierek the popularity one might expect. Rather, it caused protesters to think that the regime was weak and, in effect, encouraged workers to be more militant. Their criticism of industrial managers and the local party apparatus became more vocal, and their readiness to back up their complaints with strikes and work stoppages increased.

The 1976 confrontation also triggered a buildup of various nonparty opposition forces among intellectuals. The scale of this movement, clearly unprecedented in Eastern Europe, as well as its tactics were ultimately a crucial factor in the political evolution of Poland. Before 1970 opposition among Polish intellectuals—the so-called revisionist group associated with Włodzimierz Brus and Leszek Kołakowski, for example—had attempted to reform the political system by appealing to the party. After 1970, intellectuals directed their efforts toward the workers. Initially, these efforts took the form of financial and legal assistance to harassed strike leaders, but later they were aimed at encouraging political activism among workers, in particular, those mobilized around the cause of "free" unions. Some members of the clergy joined intellectuals in this effort as well.

Another major strategy that the opposition pursued was the formation of an underground press. Illegal publications (including books) were not new to Poland, but the number of titles and their circulation had been insignificant. As a result of the increased visibility and popularity of the independent press, it began to pose a real threat to the state monopoly of mass media. Though the regime had the capacity to penetrate and crack down on the illegal press, its harassment of those involved was limited, and it made no attempt to punish the readers, a course of action that contrasted sharply with actions taken under similar circumstances by other East European countries and by the Soviet Union.

Intraparty conflicts. Gierek's "repressive tolerance" toward social opposition seemed a sensible instrument for reducing domestic tensions while helping Poland to arrange better deals with Western creditors. Yet this policy produced a growing dissatisfaction among some party members. To many of the apparatchiks Gierek's policy was an unacceptable display of "softness" which could backfire later, causing more political damage than a temporary loss of popularity among the population. In fact, much of the brutality during the poststrike repression stemmed from efforts made by some party members (including those in the police) to discredit Gierek while disciplining workers.[20]

20. Staniszkis, *Self-Limiting Revolution.*

The policy of extended borrowing in addition to Gierek's active political contacts with Western countries also cost him support within the party. Gierek's opponents objected to Poland's increasing dependence on Western financing on political grounds, claiming that it was giving Western leaders too much leverage over the party. In addition, they felt that this shift toward Western economies undermined traditional ties with the Soviet Union which they saw as crucial for the political survival of the Communist leadership in general and many of Gierek's intraparty opponents in particular.

A growing number of Soviet leaders shared this perception of Gierek's policies. The Soviet regime gradually lost much of its initial enthusiasm for Poland's efforts to build up Western ties as it became clear that many of Gierek's specific choices ran directly counter to Soviet priorities. From the Soviet point of view, Gierek's strategy appeared detrimental to long-lasting cooperation agreements (e.g., regarding the tractor industry), or to sales opportunities for Soviet goods (e.g., color televisions), or to certain joint efforts sponsored by the Soviet leaders (e.g., the regional program for computers, known as RIAD).

The most significant criticism of economic policies came from an intraparty faction led by Politburo member Stefan Olszowski, who staged a letter-writing campaign among several local party chiefs in 1979 expressing their opposition to Gierek and then arranged a series of attacks on his policies at an important party meeting the same year. That Olszowski's faction also encouraged criticism from outside the party was shown by the publication in 1979 of a report critical of Gierek by a group of reformist Marxist intellectuals.

In summary, the adjustment of 1976–79 slowed the growth rate of consumption and cuts in investment, causing the growth rate of the GNP first to decline and then in 1979 to become negative (see Table 1). But at the same time the regime succeeded in reducing the size of the trade deficit with Western countries, a necessary step toward stabilizing the rapidly increasing foreign debt. The regime also reduced the gap between demand and supply for many commodities on the domestic market. These are the usual economic tradeoffs: more radical improvements in domestic and external equilibrias would have been possible only at the expense of overall growth.

Politically, these measures eroded the synthesis of political forces which Gierek had created through his expansionary policies of the early 1970s. Rather than each sector of society—workers, intellectuals, party hard-liners, technocrats, reform advocates, and so on—finding itself the beneficiary of an individual "deal" that Gierek engineered, all sectors found themselves the victim of sacrifices each suspected its traditional opponents of having imposed. In effect, the political consequence of austerity was to inspire groups both inside and outside the party to seek to shift the burdens of adjustment onto one another. Doing so would eventually create a major confrontation among them which Gierek's leadership, increasingly compromised by the deteriorating economic situation, proved powerless to prevent.

3. Political stalemate and economic crisis: 1980-81

While the regime was completing the 1976–79 adjustment, the most difficult period was waiting in the wings. Debt-service payments were about to peak, as credits borrowed earlier reached maturity. In addition, the economy had to cope with the second wave of oil-price shocks in 1979. To raise money for the debt payments under these circumstances, the regime had to introduce measures sharper than previous ones. Not only were further cuts in the absolute size of investment unavoidable, but a temporary freeze on or drop in consumption proved necessary. These measures notwithstanding, credits were still needed to achieve a viable financial solution.

For Gierek's austerity package to succeed fully, two political conditions had to be met. First, internal political stability was needed to ensure that an austerity program would not provoke workers to walk out—as they had on several occasions in the past—thus undermining the foreign-trade effort by causing losses in production. Second, continued good relations with foreign economic partners, particularly Western creditors, were critical. Much of the ease with which Poland obtained credit, as mentioned, was owing to particular political interests that Western governments had in the country—interests reflected in Poland's large shares of government-guaranteed credits—and these interests had to be preserved if the necessary credits were to be available.[21]

However, when Gierek moved ahead with the austerity plan in the mid-1980s, it became clear that his regime could meet neither of these two political requirements. Domestic disturbances erupted, accompanied by a dramatic worsening of political relations with Poland's major foreign partners. These political developments undermined not only Gierek's austerity measures of 1980 but also later measures. As a result, instead of enduring a few "lean" years and thereby solving the financial problem, Poland ended up in an extended economic crisis and even deeper financial difficulties, which have not abated to date.

21. Only the Soviet Union has been receiving larger shares than Poland of its Western credits from government-guaranteed sources in the region. For instance, in 1970 these sources provided 61% of Soviet credit, and 63% of Polish credit, but only 7% of East German and 28% of Czech credit. In 1980 the respective shares were: the Soviet Union, 50%; Poland, 25%; East Germany, 22%; Czechoslovakia, 11%. To give another example, in 1981 59% of Poland's gross debt was accumulated in guaranteed credits, whereas in Romania this share amounted to 22%. See Wharton Econometric Forecasting Associates, "Lending to the Eastern Bloc by Western Governments," *Centrally Planned Economies: Current Analysis*, 25 May 1982, p. 2.

a. Open economic crisis

Loss of control. Many economists argue that the reduction in GNP by 2.3 percent in 1979 marked the beginning of an extended period of declining basic economic indicators. But the truth is that in the first half of 1980 the economy showed a sharp recovery (e.g., a 9% rate of growth in industrial output, in constant prices). However, this strong growth could not be continued, because the damage to food production from widespread spring floods, the worst ever reported in the postwar years, halted this strong growth. As a result the economy did show another negative rate of growth for 1980 as a whole.

The extent of this recovery depended to a large degree on the regime's ability to curtail real wages, particularly given the (expected) decline in domestic supplies of food. After an extensive "demobilization campaign" that presented the people with a gloomy picture of the economy, the regime raised the prices of all basic consumer goods in July 1980. Despite the regime's promises of financial compensation, workers responded to the move with widespread domestic disturbances that caused the whole austerity attempt to fail. Accounting for the compensations that the workers won, the growth rate of real wages for 1980, 4 percent, dealt a decisive blow to the ongoing recovery.

More important, these strikes gave birth to the free (as opposed to official, party-controlled) trade unions, whose power greatly reduced the regime's ability to pursue further austerity measures. For example, when Gierek's successor Stanisław Kania tried to restore the domestic market balance by increasing the rate of inflation, workers proved powerful enough to seek and achieve wage increases that more than kept pace with the escalation of prices. Thus, in 1981 real wages grew again, this time by 1.5 percent, leaving the internal market even more unbalanced than before Kania began his efforts (see Table 3).

This use of strikes to gain leverage for bargaining purposes also caused serious damage to production; moreover, workers won the additional concession of a shorter work week. Although the impact of strikes and the reduced work week varied by sector, output losses in many sectors were significant. Coal production, a major source of convertible currency, was probably slowed the most. The estimated loss of hard-currency revenues during these two critical years was around $1.8 billion, close to 10–15 percent of Poland's debt-service payments to Western countries for that period.[22]

Credit squeeze. Both the uncontrollable pressures to increase wages and the total chaos this caused to domestic production had a chilling effect on Western creditors. Although in 1980, according to Polish sources, the country

---

22. Fink, *Economic Effects of the Polish Crisis.*

TABLE 3. *Basic economic indicators, 1980–84 (annual growth, in percentages)*

	1980	1981	1982	1983	1984
GNP	−6.0	−12.0	−5.5	4.5	5.0
Industrial product					
total	−0.2	−11.0	−2.0	−	−
sales	−	−12.6	−2.0	6.7	5.3
Agricultural product					
total	−9.6	4.1	−4.5	3.6	5.7
crops	−15.2	20.3	−3.3	6.0	7.6
animals	−3.3	−12.5	−5.8	1.0	3.6
Investment	−10.5	−25.0	−19.0	4.8	10.0
Investment/GNP ratio	17.3	20.0	17.9	−	−
Employment	−0.6	0.3	−4.0	−0.2	0.5
Labor productivity	−1.0	−12.2	4.0	8.0	5.9
Nominal wage	12.8	25.8	51.0	25.4	19.6
Cost of living	9.1	24.3	101.5	23.0	16.0
Real wage	4.0	1.5	−25.0	1.8	−
Real wage/productivity ratio	−	−	−	0.22	−

Sources. E. Zaleski, "La crise economique polonaise et son impact sur le C.A.C.M. 1984" (Mimeo), and *Rocznik Statystyczny, Komunikat GUS* (Warsaw: GUS, various years).

was still able to obtain $8.8 billion of medium- and long-term credits from Western countries (an amount close to what Poland had been borrowing annually from the West in the few years preceding), by 1981 Poland could obtain only $4.9 billion in medium- and long-term credits,[23] reflecting the decline of new credits.

Whereas in 1979 the Polish loan was largely oversubscribed by Western banks, by 1980 it was governments, not banks, that took the lead, a sign that the banks were getting more and more uneasy about Poland's economic condition. By 1981 Western banks had started to panic and suddenly withdrew their short-term deposits; similar moves by East European countries followed. Western governments tried to come up with assistance, providing around $1.4 billion. But with the large outflow of money to the banks Poland received only a net of $200 million for the whole year.[24]

23. J. Mościcki, "Po umowie paryskiej," *Zycie Gospodarcze*, no. 30 (1985). See also S. Roczkowski, "Debt Rescheduling: Benefits and Costs for Debtors and Creditors," in C. T. Saunders, ed., *East-West Trade and Finance in the World Economy* (New York: St. Martin's, 1985).

24. E. A. Goldstein, "Soviet Economic Assistance to Poland, 1980–1981," in Joint Economic Committee, *Soviet Economy in the 1980's: Problems and Prospects*, 97th Cong., 2d sess., 1982, pp. 567–69.

Because the 1981 inflow of credits was not enough to cover the outstanding debt payments for that year, Kania's regime had to open talks on rescheduling its debts. Talks were concluded after more than six months with an agreement that permitted Poland to postpone $2.4 billion in payments due that year. However, Poland needed something more than a quick-fix rescheduling package. No long-run plan for solving financial difficulties was worked out, and the agreement provided for no fresh credits. This situation differed greatly from most other large rescheduling deals, such as the one by Yugoslavia in 1981 or Brazil in 1982.[25]

The major reason for these short-sighted solutions was that the Western banks were left almost entirely on their own when it came to making rescheduling arrangements. Strong involvement by governments was necessary to put negotiations in a proper perspective. Western governments did not provide this kind of leadership since no clear, unified political strategy toward the Polish crisis had been worked out, largely because they were very uncertain about the outcome of ongoing political struggles between the free unions and the party. Alternatively, an international institution such as the World Bank or the IMF could have provided this kind of guidance, but Poland was not a member of any such agency at that time. Moreover, in distinct contrast to Hungary,[26] Poland was denied membership in the IMF by a U.S. veto.

Poland turned to the Soviet Union for assistance and found that country willing to provide help but only on a temporary basis and to an inadequate degree.[27] Significantly, the Soviet Union did not provide Poland with additional material resources to offset the losses in Western supplies but merely kept up current deliveries. In fact, despite the extremely serious political and economic situation, the Soviet Union generally treated Poland the way it treated other East European allies, though their economies were stronger and their societies stable.[28] Such treatment was ironic, for the Soviet Union

25. For details on Yugoslavia's rescheduling agreement see P. Marer, "East-West Commercial Relations and Prospects for East Europe and Yugoslavia" (Paper presented at Allied Social Science Association Annual Meeting, Dallas, 29 December 1984). For details on Brazil's rescheduling agreement see W. Cline, "Progress on International Debt," *New York Times*, 15 April 1985.

26. During 1982–84 Hungary obtained $1 billion in medium-term loans from the IMF. The World Bank arranged the long-term credit of $400 million. The World Bank also helped Hungary to negotiate $800 million in long-term loans from private bank sources. With other credits— including some from governmental souces—Hungary received a total of $4.1 billion in these three years. *Polityka* [Warsaw], 6 April 1985.

27. Fink, *Economic Effects of the Polish Crisis*. In 1980–81 the total assistance amounted to $3 to $4 billion, which included $1 billion in hard-currency credits and a nonrepayable grant of $500 million. The rest consisted of trade deficits not cleared by Poland, which had no direct impact on its ability to service the debt to Western countries. Eastern Europe did not provide any substantial help (the only important exception was a small emergency shipment of goods by East Germany); in fact, East European countries put additional pressure on Poland by reducing exports in order to cut their recent trade surpluses.

28. E. Hewett, "Soviet Current Account Surplus with Eastern Europe" (Mimeo, Brookings Institution, Washington, D.C., 1985).

was certainly capable of discriminating among its East European allies. Bulgaria, for example, received additional quantities of oil to reexport in return for hard currency in 1979. Poland, however, did not merit such "special" treatment.[29]

Further decline. With a failing austerity plan and no hope for financial assistance from the West or material aid from the East, Kania's regime spent almost all of 1981 cutting both Western imports and investment outlays. These cuts were heavier than any previous ones. A relatively modest drop in Western imports of 8.2 percent in 1980 was followed by as much as a 34.6 percent decline in 1981 (both measurements in constant prices). Sharp squeezes on imports not only drastically reduced the number of new projects but also froze or terminated many ongoing ones. Altogether, investment outlays dropped by 10.5 percent in 1980 and by 25.0 percent in 1981, a decline the size of which Poland had never before experienced.[30]

To minimize the negative impact of both reduced imports and lower investment, the regime had to revise its planning priorities quickly and act accordingly. This did not happen, however, because too much energy went into political struggles with the several million members of the free trade unions. In addition, the lower officials in the state bureaucracy, confused by the new configuration of political power, preferred to do nothing rather than follow their orders and upset the workers or give in to the pressures by the workers and displease the supervisors.[31] Consequently, the cuts were pursued without a clear list of priorities and in a disorderly manner, thus aggravating existing shortages.

Free trade unions and some political radicals within the party pressed the regime to arrest the chaos by instituting a complex reform of the bureaucratic economic system. But, like all major economic issues at that time, the issue became highly politicized. An ambitious program had been designed in mid-1981 along the lines of the highly praised Hungarian system of 1968. Whether this kind of system could have worked under the existing economic conditions is unclear; but the workability of the program was not yet an issue. The politically crucial question, namely that of who would appoint managers, totally divided the party and the free trade unions, which effectively blocked the reform program for months.

The difficult year of 1980, which saw a 6 percent drop in the GNP, was followed by the disastrous year of 1981, when GNP declined by 12 percent.

---

29. M. Marrese, "Hungarian Agriculture: Drive in a Proper Direction" (Mimeo, Northwestern University, Evanston, Ill., 1983). Also, while Poland cleared all its trade with the Soviet Union in nontransferable rubles, Hungary also ran dollar accounts with the Soviet Union. In 1980 these accounts provided Hungary with a surplus of about $500 million, a sum close to the Hungarian trade deficit with Western countries in that year.

30. S. Gomułka, *Growth, Innovation, and Reform*, chap. 13.

31. Ibid.

At this point about 40–50 percent of industrial capacity became idle, primarily in the manufacturing sector. With these losses in output, total exports declined by 19 percent, and an even sharper drop in exports to Western countries occurred: −22.1 percent in 1981. The Western debt increased by another several billion dollars, reaching almost \$25.5 billion by the end of 1981.[32] Although these indicators clearly showed that the economy had collapsed, the regime still had not developed either a solid program or the authority necessary to launch a package of anticrisis measures.[33]

b. Continuation of a political stalemate

The collapse of Poland's economy had much to do with economic forces such as overinvestment and wage escalation, to name two. However, an analysis of the political situation that emerged in the 1980s is critical to understanding the serious economic deterioration of 1980–81 and the inability of the party and the government to take the steps to correct it. Poland's highly unstable political situation made it impossible for the regime to move ahead with measures that could have minimized inevitable losses in production and related deterioration in domestic and external imbalances.

Limited political conflict. When faced with workers' protests, Gierek decided to rely again on his previously successful tactic of negotiated settlement in order to keep the confrontation focused on purely economic issues. Nevertheless, it became impossible to prevent workers from making political demands as well.[34] The establishment of separate striking committees set some communication guidelines that forced the party to talk about political issues with representatives of the organized workers. In September 1980, the regime agreed to the workers' most critical and controversial demand, the establishment of free trade unions (i.e., Solidarity, led by Lech Wałesa).

At the time, the incorporation of independent unions into the political system of Poland seemed feasible. In the first months of the existence of these unions, workers insisted on a nonpolitical formula, viewing their unions as "veto committees" that would leave actual decision making to the party.[35] Although there was a risk that independent unions could turn into a political body, properly executed reform could well have prevented and/or deterred any deleterious consequences. Moreover, that the party continued to function

32. For more details see E. Zaleski, *Kryzys Gospodarki Polskiej: Przyczyny i Srodki Zaradcze* (London: Instytut Romana Dmowskiego, 1983).

33. D. Nuti, "The Polish Crisis: Economic Factors and Constraints," in *The Socialist Register* (London: Merlin, 1981). Also D. Kemme, "The Polish Crisis: An Economic Overview," in J. Bielasiak and M. Simon, eds., *Polish Politics: Edge of the Abyss* (New York: Praeger, 1982).

34. Staniszkis, *Self-Limiting Revolution.*

35. This nonrevolutionary and nonpolitical attitude was characteristic of the prewar history of the labor movement in Poland, as R. Blobaum points out in "The Traditions of Workers' Protest in Poland" (Mimeo, Cornell University, Ithaca, N.Y., 1983).

for a while meant the regime was still in a position to "deal" with workers rather than to seek a confrontation.

In addition, at this point the church was helping to stabilize the conflict. The clergy clearly sympathized with the workers, particularly because the free unions strongly pressed for more religious freedom. However, their support was not unqualified, because the desire of the church to preserve the basically hierarchical character of society meant that many of its interests were far from identical to those of the workers.

Of course, the Soviet Union opposed any move by the party to allow even limited independent representation for workers on ideological and political grounds. Nevertheless, had the party quickly produced a workable package of reforms and stood firm, the regime might have been able to withstand Soviet pressures, much as it did in 1956 when decollectivization was put through. But unlike in 1956, the party in 1980–81 faced widespread social opposition and proved unable to successfully manipulate workers.[36]

Moreover, the party did not consolidate around new leadership as it did in 1956 but experienced heated internal struggles. The initial clashes occurred between the Gierek team and the fast-growing opposition headed by Olszowski and backed by Moczar. The opposition succeeded and Gierek lost his post in December 1980. But Kania succeeded Gierek, largely because of the support of Wojciech Jaruzelski, chief of the army and Politburo member (apparently Cardinal Wyszyński openly opposed Olszowski's candidacy). These intraparty struggles continued even after Kania's appointment, thus making it impossible for a compromise to achieve sufficient support within the party.

Crisis escalation. The intraparty fight had a decisive impact on further political developments.[37] In particular, the inability of the party to develop a reform package forced the free unions to resort to various tactics, with strikes proving to be the strongest weapon. In addition, the anticorruption campaign that the intraparty opposition had launched to dislodge Gierek (a campaign that included many false stories), backfired insofar as it merely undermined the popularity of the PUWP. As a result, the free trade union Solidarity—now several million members strong—started to radicalize, and its base of support became more diverse as well. Soon the union split into a number of political factions, with a cautious wing, led by Wałesa and close to the church, seeking a compromise with the party on one side of this spectrum, and militant groups pushing for a full-scale confrontation with the party and an end to the Soviet domination on the other (the most prominent militant figure was Andrzej Gwiazda).

The radicalization of Solidarity worked, in turn, to catalyze the further

36. Staniszkis, *Self-Limiting Revolution.*
37. This view is shared by A. Johnson, *Poland in Crisis* (Santa Monica: Rand, 1982). See also J. Curry, *The Polish Crisis of 1980 and the Politics of Survival* (Santa Monica: Rand, 1980).

polarization of the party. Many apparatchiks, particularly those at the lowest levels, got involved in a grass-roots movement calling for establishment of contact among low-level party members (hence bypassing the traditional vertical command system) and for gradual replacement of their bosses through democratic elections. The conservatives responded to the aggressiveness of unions and to the radical reformists within the party with even louder calls for a blunt response to both challenges. In addition, reactionary groups advocating police repression and a return to Stalinist-type propaganda emerged; such groups were responsible for beating Solidarity activists in Bydgoszcz, in March 1981.

This polarization of the party turned out to be self-destructive. A growing number of its members began to see the party as politically bankrupt, and large-scale desertions followed. During the first three months after the registration of the free unions, the party membership did not change much, dropping by 50,000 or so during September–December 1980. Later, however, the number of dropouts began to skyrocket. By December 1981, the membership had declined 17 percent, from 3.2 million registered in July 1980 to around 2.7 million.[38]

As the party weakened, the center of power shifted toward the state administration, led by Prime Minister Jaruzelski since February 1981. Jaruzelski was joined by other members of the military who took over several key administrative posts, indicating that the party had decided to pass or was forced to resign its authority to both the administration and the army. As the only working institution of the political establishment (except for the police), the army was seen as best prepared both to protect the party from total collapse and to deal with economic issues. The role of the military had increased steadily since February 1981, as evidenced by Jaruzelski's election to the position of secretary general of the party in September 1981.

The change in the party leadership related directly to the occurrence of the first national meeting of Solidarity. The meeting indicated that radical elements in the free unions would soon dominate the movement. Wałesa, symbol of workers' resistance and a moderate, was elected chairman of Solidarity by only a small margin. Radicals called for free elections to Parliament (a politically taboo request during the union's first months). Moreover, many low-level union activists worked to remove party representatives from industrial factories and local offices. The party reacted with a tougher political line, and almost no room remained for negotiations in the months to come.

Foreign political interferences. To make matters worse, external political interventions accompanied these escalating domestic tensions, as Poland's domestic disturbances invited Soviet interference. From the very beginning

---

38. From R. Staar, *Communist Regimes in Eastern Europe* (Stanford: Hoover Institution Press, 1983).

the Soviet leaders sought to disband independent unions; yet at the same time, they were anxious for Poland to find an internal solution to the problem which would not involve direct military involvement by their forces.

The Soviet party embarked on an indirect approach to achieve these ends. Their techniques included a blocwide campaign of accusations against Solidarity, frequent reprimands—private and public—to Polish leaders when they suggested making concesssions, occasional economic threats, and, of course, the ever-present threat of direct military intervention.

Political pressures came from Western countries as well. By and large, Western governments reacted to the crisis in Poland with open sympathy for Solidarity but supported a compromise solution that would be acceptable to both the party and organized labor. Political realism prevented these governments from hoping for a collapse of the communist system in Poland, because they correctly assumed that Soviet leaders would not allow this to happen under any circumstances. However, it was clear at that time that many Western politicians were eager to see some liberalization of Poland's economic and political policies.

Completely new to the picture were Western unions, which became one of the most determined political supporters of Solidarity in the West. However, Western unions did not call for a "class war" between the workers and the party in Poland but rather for providing organized labor with the package of rights their members had traditionally enjoyed.

While Soviet pressures were upsetting a balance within the free union by provoking radicals, in its own way the support that a number of Western countries provided bolstered the spirits of militant activists as well. At the same time, within the party Western involvement strengthened moderates while Soviet pressures helped the conservatives, thus preventing a shift toward either of these sides. Such external pressures constrained the options available to both the regime and the social opposition, thus increasing the explosiveness of the domestic political situation.

In summary, the 1980 austerity program, introduced after a few years of measures curtailing consumption, was absolutely necessary to control the growing foreign debt, but it did not work. Instead, it provoked mass unrest that the regime found—for the first time in the postwar period—impossible to dispel quickly. Given the lack of "negotiating" procedures and the strong external pressures, the conflicting forces—the party and the workers—were unable to reach a compromise. Instead, they provoked each other to take such increasingly extreme postures that a radical solution became unavoidable. These political developments diverted Poland from pursuing the kind of economic adjustment that occurred elsewhere in Eastern Europe. The inevitable deep reduction in production proved impossible to stop promptly. Thus, the stage was set for the next phase, martial law.

4. The imposition of martial law: 1982 to the present

a. Jaruzelski's program

Although economic concerns were not the major reason for imposing martial law in December 1981, the move allowed the Jaruzelski regime to regain some control of the economy. Military rule was instituted to crush the free unions, but as a result the regime finally gained the power needed to impose an austerity program. In February 1982, prices of all consumer goods increased 300 to 400 percent, raising the cost of living index by 100.5 percent in that year. Even with the wage compensations that followed, the real wage dropped by 25 percent as a result of the price reform,[39] a cut unknown to other East European countries (excluding Romania) at that time.

Having arrested the domestic disturbances, Jaruzelski moved to restore order to the planning machinery and end the chaos in production. He intended to achieve these goals by incorporating the so-called strategic plans into existing decision making, with as much as 30–40 percent of all materials being distributed through these plans. In addition, the regime replaced the majority of industrial managers and other state officials with people (many of them military) whom the party perceived as more reliable. Jaruzelski also decided to go ahead with plans for economic reform drawn up before the imposition of martial law, which resembled those of Hungary. He formally abolished the gigantic associations, reduced the power of ministries, and gave extensive authority to the enterprises, with the understanding that they would fully enjoy the new freedoms after the ultimate elimination of the strategic plans.[40]

These new planning arrangements have allowed the regime to refocus production efforts on a very limited number of targets. In particular, the mining industry has priority because it is a critical source of hard-currency revenues for Poland. Miners have been among the major recipients of wage raises (next to the police and military forces), and the industry has the highest priority for material supplies. With these advantages, the hard coal industry started to recover in 1982: its output reached 189 million tons compared to 163 million tons in 1981. By 1984 coal production had almost reached the precrisis level—200 million tons as reported in 1979. The production of sulfur, primarily intended for foreign markets, increased too and by 1985 was almost back to its 1979 peak.

Paradoxically, although the regime has both implemented a drastic austerity program and restored production, Western creditors have not reopened financial lines to Poland. Initially, the West intended to punish the regime for the brutal suppression of the free trade unions by banning governmental credits and refusing to negotiate the rescheduling of both private and gov-

39. Zaleski, *Kryzys Gospodarki Polskiej.*
40. S. Gomułka and J. Rostowski, *Growth, Innovation, and Reform,* chap. 14.

ernment-backed debts. Since then talks on both types of debt have been resumed, in 1983 with the banks and in 1985 with the governments. However, Poland has not managed to join either the IMF or the World Bank, and no fresh credits of significant size have arrived since (though the United States withdrew its veto of Poland's application for membership in the IMF in late 1984).[41]

Moreover, although the Soviet Union certainly played a major role in Jaruzelski's decision to impose martial law and destroy the free unions, it has not given any significant economic assistance to the regime. Neither the Soviets nor the other East European countries have supplied any new hard-currency credits to help debt repayments since 1981. The regime also has not received additional supplies of Soviet oil to substitute for dollar deliveries that were cut from 500 million tons in 1980 to 3.5 million tons in 1981. This happened despite Soviet promises of these supplies. In addition the pressure on Poland to eliminate its outstanding trade deficits with the Soviet Union (and Eastern Europe) has, if anything, intensified under the new Soviet leadership.

b. *Illusion of recovery*

Jaruzelski's policies have produced certain improvements in the economy. Industrial production had picked up by the end of 1982, though overall for the year a -2.0 percent rate of change was reported. But in 1983, industrial output grew by 6.7 percent, in 1984, 5.3 percent (see Table 3). Agricultural production increased as well, with respect to both grain and livestock. As a result, after reaching an all-time low in 1982, GNP has been increasing modestly ever since: 4.5 percent in 1983, and an estimated 5 percent in 1984.[42]

Nevertheless, the recovery is at best disappointing,[43] particularly given the very low level of production reached in 1982. With 50–60 percent of existing production capacity for that year, the economy had the potential for much higher increases, with little or no investment required. Roughly 20–30 percent of capacity is still idle in most industries, and this situation may last for a

41. The amount of Western credits that Poland received has declined further since the 1981 squeeze. Medium- and long-term credits reached $1.2 billion in 1982, $6 million in 1983, and hit bottom in 1984, with $2 million in Western credits reported (see Mościcki, "Po umowie paryskiej"). On European borrowing see A. Lenz, *Controlling International Debt: Implications for East-West Trade*, report prepared for the Office of Trade and Investment Analysis, U.S. Department of Commerce (Washington, D.C.: GPO, 1983).

42. E. Zaleski, "The Polish Economic Crisis and Its Impact on the CMEA" (Mimeo, Centre International de la Recherche Scientifique, Paris, 1985).

43. Z. Fallenbuchl, "The Polish Economy under Martial Law," *Soviet Studies* 36, no. 4 (October 1984), provides a large number of relevant statistics. According to him, "There is a serious danger that the stabilization of the economy will take place at a very low level of per capita income and consumption, and will be followed by a prolonged period of stagnation," a view I share.

while. And if growth rates like those reported lately stay the norm, the GNP will not approach the 1978 level any earlier than 1990. This means that Poland will require altogether about twelve years to get out of this crisis, by no means a common length of time in the context of Poland's industrial history.

A positive economic sign has been an upward turn in investment. In 1982 a 19 percent decline in real investment was reported, whereas in 1983 investment increased by around 4.8 percent, and in 1984 by 10 percent. However, most of the problems plaguing investment processes before the onset of martial law have not vanished. The investment cycle (i.e., gestation period) has in fact become longer by almost a year, so that on the average it takes almost fifty months for a project to be completed. The amount of resources frozen in uncompleted projects increased by another 600 billion zloty during 1983–84. By the end of 1984 it amounted to the total of 1.6 trillion zloty, or almost one and a half times the value of new investment spending in that year.

With such a slow investment upturn, industry is fast becoming technologically obsolete. Machinery in the industry was on average about 60 percent depreciated in 1982. This decapitalization process affects some of the key sectors of industry, including automobile production, where equipment is seventeen years old, and allegedly only an injection of at least $1.5 billion in new machinery can prevent an irreversible collapse. (This is an industry that was furnished with advanced machinery under Gierek and became one of the success stories in the export promotion in those years; however, it has lost most of its market gains since then.)

Poland's low investment outlays also prevent it from resuming its previously active imports of disembodied Western technology. In 1973–75 some fifty to sixty license agreements were signed annually, but none have been signed since 1980,[44] so that the total number of licenses in use has been cut in half (it is now below the 1970 level of 140 licenses). As a result of the trade disturbances with Western economies, Poland also has had to give up many of its cooperation agreements, another potentially important source of technological assistance.

As proof of the success of his policies, Jaruzelski points to the reduction in shortages on the domestic consumer market and the lowering of inflation since the aforementioned doubling of prices in 1982. However, Poland's market remains the most unbalanced among the East European countries (except perhaps for Romania), and its dramatically expanded black market — or, more neutrally, "second economy"—continues to play a more important role than elsewhere in the region. Inflation is still very high by East European standards. The rate of inflation was roughly 15 percent in 1984, and with

44. Poznański, "State Policy towards Technology Transfer."

a 20 percent increase in nominal wages last year, this rate is going to be in the double digits again.

More important, this wage and price spiral is gradually dissolving the impact of the 1982 austerity measures. For the economy to produce a trade surplus sufficient to halt the debt increase, consumption should remain on the 1982 low level for a minimum of several years. Jaruzelski's regime, like that of his predecessors, is giving in to popular pressures, so that in 1983–84 the level of total real consumption (excluding services) reportedly increased by a cumulative rate of 10.5 percent. In per capita terms this rate was around 7.0 percent (so that the real consumption per capita is only about 7.5 percent below the 1978 precrisis level).

Certainly, Poland's transformation of its trade deficits with Western countries into surpluses has been a positive change. In fact, Poland reported in 1980 that trade with the West was almost balanced, and the situation remained the same in 1981. In 1982 the economy produced a surplus close to $500 million, an amount that rose to $1.5 billion in both 1983 and 1984. However, this surplus was achieved mainly through very low imports combined with a rapid increase in the exports of raw materials and food. Nonetheless, exports to Western markets are still below the 1979 level, and sales of manufacturing goods have declined continuously since 1980 (the same trend holds for most of the other East European countries).[45]

This improvement in the balance of trade with the Western countries notwithstanding, Poland has been unable to begin paying back the bulk of its debt. The trade surplus earned so far is only sufficient to allow Poland to resume servicing some of its debt, though payments represent only a fraction of what Poland would have had to pay without the rescheduling agreements. According to J. Vaňous,[46] in 1984 the Polish balance of current accounts was probably negative, with about $200 million in payments due not being met. Clearly, in sharp contrast with other East European countries, Poland has yet to get its foreign debt under firm control. (Hungary reduced its debt to Western countries by almost $1 billion in 1982–84.)[47] And it is not going to get such control soon.[48]

45. J. Poznańska, "Foreign Trade Adjustment of Indebted Countries in Eastern Europe, Latin America and Far East" (Mimeo, Skidmore College, Saratoga Springs, N.Y., 1985).

46. J. Vaňous, "Polish Foreign Trade Performance during the First Nine Months of 1984," Wharton Econometric Forecasting Associates, *Centrally Planned Economies: Current Analysis*, January 1985.

47. Reportedly, Poland will be able to allocate $2.2 billion to finance its $2.7 billion in debt service in 1985, meaning that the balance of current accounts is going to be negative this year as well (Mościcki, "Po umowie paryskiej"). The increasing Polish debt stays in contrast with debts of other East European countries and the Soviet Union. Reportedly, the whole region reduced its net debt to Western countries from $75.1 billion by the end of 1982 to $65.1 billion by the end of June 1984. Between June 1983 and June 1984, the debt of Bulgaria declined from $1.3 to $1.0 billion; in Czechoslovakia from 2.5 to 2.0; in East Germany, from 8.8 to 7.3; in Hungary, from 7.0 to 6.8; and in Romania, from 8.4 to 7.8. Meanwhile, Polish debt grew from $25.2 to $25.3 billion (these data differ from those provided in Mościcki's article but still show a trend in the same, upward direction).

48. See for instance debt projections for Poland by K. Crane, *The Credit-Worthiness of Eastern Europe in the 1980s*, R-3201-USDP (Santa Monica: Rand, 1985).

Yet these trends do not point to the ultimate success of Jaruzelski's policy, and there is little hope that his reform program will contain any dramatic changes. Central, detailed directives—once limited to the special programs—dominate decision making again. Reportedly, in most of the provinces the central authorities set yearly targets for employment by enterprises, a practice unknown even during most of Gierek's period. Industrial associations, threatened by the 1982 reform, have regained most of their power over enterprises (mostly because the former allocate most of the scarce raw materials and parts). The power of ministries, which are staffed with the least qualified cadres ever, is also becoming overwhelming.

c. *Military takeover and after*

These economic developments are a result of the political evolution of Jaruzelski's regime since he imposed martial law in December 1981.[49] His goal was to create conditions for the regime to topple the leadership of Solidarity and then dissolve organized labor, thus laying foundations for the return of the party as Poland's leading political force. Doing so also required temporarily reducing the party's own authority, a move that some interpreted mistakenly as evidence of conflicting political ambitions between the military and the apparatchiks. On the contrary, open confrontation with organized labor left the party so weak that the regime was forced to repeat the kind of fundamental work it did in the first postwar years. Then the party had also found itself without a solid political basis in the midst of a hostile population and had had to assign an important political role to the military (the Soviet army, then stationed in Poland in large numbers, had a role in instituting the communist system as well).

Initially, Jaruzelski's tactics included police repression and an ideological campaign to discredit organized labor. In addition, Jaruzelski sought to distance himself from the compromised party, as the arrest of several relatively high party officials from Gierek's team (including Gierek himself) shows, while reaching out to other social groups through the creation of new "Popular Front" type organizations (similar to those installed right after World War II). However, unlike in the early postwar years when the party had a program that finally attracted different sections of the society (e.g., urban jobs for millions of peasants, promise of full employment for industrial workers), in the 1980s the party had little along these lines to offer.

The regime has also found it difficult to rely on force because of pressures from Western countries. The United States and members of the Common Market condemned the crackdown on Solidarity and imposed a large number of economic sanctions against both Poland and the Soviets. In fact, some sanctions were also introduced to hurt other East European countries (e.g.,

49. Staniszkis, *Self-Limiting Revolution.*

the reclassification of special credits to higher-interest groups). Jaruzelski's regime could not afford such sanctions for a long period, given pressures from the Eastern bloc. Besides, the regime needed some relaxation of the sanctions in order to gain some legitimacy.

While Western pressures were mounting, the Soviets were hardly in a position to request decisive moves from Jaruzelski. For one thing, they did not have much choice at the time but to deal with Jaruzelski, a centrist within the party, since the conservatives were not strong enough to take control. On the one hand, most party activists did not show much support for the conservatives, fearing that their hard line would ruin what chances remained for them to regain social acceptance by the party. On the other, during the few months preceding martial law, Jaruzelski had already consolidated his power by putting a number of his people in key positions. Soviet support, if a real fact, was not sufficient to put the conservatives in control of the party.

Though not in control of the party, conservatives have tried to press Jaruzelski to take harder stands anyway, mainly by exercising control over the media and by resorting to provocative acts, the killing of the Catholic priest Stanisław Popiełuszko by the police being perhaps the most well-known example. Nevertheless, such actions proved counterproductive to the hard-liners' cause, since they strengthened the social opposition and enabled Jaruzelski to take some moves (e.g., the policemen involved in the killing of Popiełuszko were tried in an open court and received harsh sentences) that served further to discredit the intraparty opposition while—coincidentally—appearing to be concessions and gestures that would reduce remaining political tensions in society.

The regime appears to have settled for another, significantly harsher, version of "repressive tolerance." In April 1983, martial law was lifted, though most of its extraordinary regulations were incorporated into the civil and criminal codes. However, the number of jailed Solidarity members has declined since then. Although they are harassed, the active members of the illegal Solidarity continue their political activities, risking physical abuse and occasionally murder by the police. The regime did not try to attack the clergy during the period of martial law, and it has only slightly changed its policy since, even though a large number of priests openly advocate the idea of Solidarity, and churches provide shelter for its banned activities.

In summary, the military regime seems temporarily to have diffused political tensions and "deescalated" the cycle. The party remains highly divided, the opposition continues to be very active, and the external political pressures have not ceased despite four years of military rule. No political program with potential for integrating the society around common goals—such as Gierek experimented with—has been produced or is likely to be produced under the current regime. Thus, the political cycle will begin to escalate again, should this fragile balance be upset.

In economic terms, military rule has not provided a framework for genuine recovery. Poland is enduring another period of immobilization and hence is unable to take advantage of many important policy alternatives. The austerity program is falling apart under continuous wage pressures from the workers. Intraparty traditionalists are sabotaging badly needed systemic reforms. No working mechanism for promoting exports to hard-currency markets has been developed so far, so that severe import restrictions serve as the major source of improvements in the balance of payments. The picture of the economy under Jaruzelski's rule is not altogether different from that which existed before the transfer of power to the military.

Conclusion

Poland's story since 1970 is of a centralized, one-party country whose political institutions have first resulted in an overtly unbalanced growth program and then prevented its leadership from undertaking the necessary adjustment measures. Because of the political environment, the leadership has had to settle for inferior policies or to refrain from doing anything. In the absence of strong leadership, the economy underwent a devastating crisis, hit bottom somewhere in 1982, and is now experiencing an elusive recovery that will probably lead not to another period of rapid growth but to stagnation.

The lesson from Poland's recent past is that the current political system does not provide a forum for negotiating conflicting interests, whether those interests are inside the party or outside it. The lack of such political procedures does not hamper the effective functioning of most countries with effectively suppressed group interests—most of the East European countries and the Soviet Union in particular. Yet the extent of the conflicting interests in Poland—the actual rejection of communist ideology by a majority of workers and their commitment to Catholicism instead—and the fact that the PUWP is a deeply divided party still in search of some kind of identity make Poland's economic crisis a unique case.

Attack on protectionism in the Soviet Union? A comment Jerry F. Hough

Unlike the other countries in what we tend to call "the Soviet bloc," the Soviet Union benefited financially from the oil crises of the 1970s, for it was a major petroleum and natural gas exporter. The oil crises also benefited the Soviet Union indirectly as a number of radical Third World oil producers acquired money to buy more Soviet arms. Moreover, the windfall increase in petroleum prices was supplemented by a similar windfall increase in the price of the other major Soviet export product, gold. The subsidies that the Soviet Union provided to Eastern Europe did not entail any sacrifice of resources that had been previously committed but required only that it forgo even greater gains. The politics underlying the Soviet decisions were the politics underlying the rapid expansion of export earnings.

The East European countries had exposed themselves to the Western economy in varying ways and varying degrees, and they had been "burned." Poland, for example, had exploded, and the Soviet leaders could thank their good fortune that they had not been forced to send in their own troops in order to preserve the system. The natural conclusion for the Soviets to draw from the East European experience was that Eastern Europe had made a mistake, that it should redirect its economic ties more toward the Soviet Union, and that the Soviet Union should learn from the experience and not expose itself to the world economy in the same way. That the Soviet experience with importing technology was not working well reinforced these lessons. Because of the windfall export prices, the Soviet Union had been able to import larger than anticipated quantities of technology without incurring a major foreign debt. Yet the results were not encouraging: Soviet output grew at an average rate of 5.3 percent a year in the late 1960s before the import policy was instituted, but the annual average rate fell to 3.7 percent in the first half of the 1970s and to 2.6 percent after 1976.

Nevertheless, the policy of importing technology had itself been a response to economic difficulties. The complaints about the dysfunctional consequences

International Organization 40, 2, Spring 1986   0020-8183 $5.00
© 1986 by the Massachusetts Institute of Technology and the World Peace Foundation

of Soviet incentive and planning systems which appeared in the Soviet press in the mid-1950s differ little from recent complaints—or from those made in the 1960s and 1970s. When Nikita Khrushchev abolished the industrial ministries in 1957 and established regional economic councils (*sovnarkhozy*), he was attempting to solve real problems, and the drastic nature of the solution taken testified to the seriousness of the problems. By the early 1960s it had become clear that administrative reorganization itself would not do the job. If the Brezhnev solution of technology imports proved unsatisfactory, the alternative of returning to the problems and solutions of the past is scarcely appealing.

This comment explores the issues concerning Eastern Europe which the Brezhnev leadership faced in the 1970s and the early 1980s and looks at the policies it chose. It also examines the dilemmas that the current leadership faces as it tries to incorporate lessons from the past into its own policy, and speculates about the foreign-policy implications of possible outcomes.

Dilemmas of the Brezhnev leadership

The difficulties that Eastern Europe faced in the 1970s confronted the Soviet leaders with various issues, at the center of which was the maintenance of the empire. In fact, for Leonid Brezhnev and the inner core of the Politburo of the time, this was undoubtedly the only issue. Brezhnev seemed to understand the need for economic reform in the Soviet Union, but the Czech experience and the overthrow of Władysław Gomułka (in addition to Edward Gierek's fate after the rise of Solidarity in Poland) taught him that reform could unleash forces or create resentments that posed real dangers for a leader's political security. Brezhnev knew that he would not live past the mid-1980s, and in terms of his own political security, it was not rational for him to take the risks of reform. He certainly did not do so.

In maintaining its control over Eastern Europe throughout the 1970s, the Soviet Union faced tremendous dilemmas. The Soviet leaders obviously preferred to keep a tight rein on Eastern Europe, not least because they feared that internal deviation from the Soviet model might legitimate similar tendencies within the Soviet Union. Yet, if East European experimentation proved successful, Soviet leaders could use the results in their own country. In 1981 Brezhnev himself pointed to agriculture in Hungary, rationalization of industry in East Germany, social security in Czechoslovakia, and agro-industrial cooperation in Bulgaria as socialist examples from which the Soviet Union could profit. His audience applauded.[1] Even more important, the Soviet Union had come to the realization that East European stability de-

---

1. *XXVI s"ezd Kommunisticheskoi partii Sovetskogo Soiuza [23 fevralia–3 marta 1981 goda], Stenograficheskii otchet* (Moscow: Politizdat, 1981), vol. 1, p. 24.

pended on some identification of these regimes with local nationalism and that this in turn depended on some independence from—and even defiance of—the Soviet Union. Moreover, the Soviet Union had to reduce its objections to East German contact with West Germany—indeed, to push the old East German leadership into more contact with West Germany—as the price for detente with West Germany.

In the economic realm the dilemmas were no less severe. On the one hand, the Soviet Union had always encouraged greater integration of the East European countries into Comecon, and many in the Soviet Union had feared that greater economic relations between Eastern Europe and the West would lead the former to depend politically on the latter. If, for example, Poland had suppressed the growing dissident and free trade union movments in the second half of the 1970s, the Carter administration might well have cut off agricultural credits on human rights grounds, a factor that may have played an important role in Gierek's "liberal" policies.

On the other hand, the Soviet Union was not happy about the quality of the manufactured goods that Eastern Europe was sending it. If Gierek's strategy of importing Western machinery and Western raw materials worked, then presumably Poland would have better goods to send the Soviet Union. If East European manufacturers were forced to raise the standards of their production to world levels as they competed with foreign manufacturers, this would redound to the Soviet benefit as well. And, of course, looking at the high percentage of Yugoslav and Romanian trade going to the Comecon countries, one could scarcely conclude that trade with the East necessarily meant foreign-policy subservience to the Soviet Union.

Once the increase in oil prices occurred, another dilemma arose. As the major petroleum supplier to Eastern Europe, the Soviet Union obviously stood to benefit from the increase and could demand a much larger quantity of manufactured goods in return for its oil. If, however, the strain of supplying more goods to the Soviet Union resulted in lower standards of living in East European countries, the possibility of unrest and riots clearly intensified. On the one hand, it scarcely made sense to extract a few extra rubles and then be forced to launch an extremely costly invasion to maintain control. On the other hand, the Soviet leaders did not like being subjected to blackmail every time an issue arose with an East European country and being told that they had to yield or risk revolt.

In practice, the Soviet Union had an easy compromise available. Indeed, it would have required an active effort to avoid compromise. Comecom priced petroleum according to a formula that was based on a five-year average. As long as prices were rising, the five-year average remained below the current market price. Even if prices leveled off, it would take five years for the Comecon price to catch up with the market. Thus, Eastern Europe did not have to bear the full brunt of the oil-price increase immediately but could adjust slowly.

The decision to maintain the pricing formula even in the new five-year plans beginning in 1976 and 1981 was not an inherently difficult one. It was a subsidy that put no serious burden on the Soviet Union. No one in the Soviet Union had to give up budgets or programs that they had already been granted; the subsidy simply meant that the increase in oil profits would be somewhat less and that Eastern Europe would have to provide fewer goods than they otherwise would have in exchange for petroleum—but still many more than before the oil crisis.

The Soviet Union was less tolerant in the debt crisis. Hard information is difficult to obtain, but the Soviet Union did apparently forgo payment on some of its own loans, especially from Poland. Nevertheless, to the consternation and apparent surprise of the foreign bankers, the Soviet Union provided little help to Poland to meet its obligations to them. It did little to prevent Poland from falling into a deep depression during the Solidarity period and did relatively little to assist the recovery.

After the crisis in Poland was resolved, the Soviet Union naturally argued that the socialist countries should never again become so overcommitted to foreign banks for loans; however, there was little new in this position. The borrowing behavior of the Soviet Union in the 1970s had been cautious, and it had already warned East Europeans against excesses. Moreover, one did not have to be a conservative Communist hegemonic power to warn against overcommitment to foreign banks in the early 1980s: the foreign bankers were saying that themselves. The Soviet Union certainly did not insist that foreign borrowing end altogether. Even when it successfully applied pressure to prevent Erich Honecker from going to West Germany in 1984, it permitted him to accept a loan engineered by the hard-liner, Franz-Josef Strauss.

Gorbachev's choices

Men of the Brezhnev generation did not have to worry about the long-range implications of East European difficulties. They knew that they would not live long enough to be forced to face them. Mikhail Gorbachev, by contrast, has a very different time horizon, for he will be only sixty-nine in the year 2000. If he hopes to survive in office until that time, he must confront the economic difficulties that have been recognized for three decades before they begin to cause political problems. He undoubtedly dreams of triumphantly ushering in the 21st century as the leader who reversed Russia's decline of recent years and set the stage for a successful new century.

Gorbachev has already indicated that he has a clear sense of the nature of the problem. He has warned that if the Soviet Union does not raise its technology to world levels, it will not remain a major power in the 21st century. The foreign-policy and military consequences of the Soviet Union's technological backwardness have already been enormous.[2] Gorbachev is also quite right in saying that this backwardness has consequences for political stability. If more countries, such as South Korea, Taiwan, and Brazil, develop the ability to export technology, and the Soviet Union remains the last Third World country to do so, the impact on the legitimacy of the ideology and the link between the Communist party of the Soviet Union with nationalism could threaten the survival of the system itself.

But how should the Soviet Union solve the problem of technological backwardness? Unfortunately, in the United States we often attempt to answer this question without a comparative perspective, and consequently we have little sense of Soviet options or Gorbachev's likely choices.

First, we take Soviet technological backwardness so for granted that we cannot conceive of the Soviet Union as a technological near-equal and as an exporter of high-quality, high-technology manufactured goods. How can the Soviet export high-technology goods, we ask, when its manufactured goods are so inferior? We accept Brezhnev's assumption (or at least hope) that the Soviet Union's only option is to import Western technology, and at heart we assume that this solution will merely slow the decline of the Soviet Union.

Yet, when we look at the East Asian newly industrializing countries (NICs), we do not see countries that began to export once they had reached world levels of technological sophistication. In 1955 John Foster Dulles stated that one thing the United States never had to worry about was Japanese acquisition of the ability to challenge it in high-technology exports. In the mid-1960s South Korea and Taiwan had sleepy economies. They began an export strategy not because they were advanced, but because they saw it as a way to become advanced. They began with less sophisticated exports, they competed with low prices, and they assumed that as their manufacturers were exposed to foreign competition on foreign markets, the quality of the goods would improve. And, indeed, they were right.

Why in principle could the Soviet Union not follow the same strategy? Indeed, as the Soviet leaders look at the success stories in the Pacific Basin, why should it not adopt a similar strategy? Obviously, for political reasons it does not have the access to American markets which the Pacific Basin countries have, and competition through favorable pricing will initially produce charges of dumping in the West as well. However, the Third World is a natural market in which the Soviet Union can begin to compete with Western manufacturers, as long as in the beginning it orients its policy more toward the large, moderate countries than toward the small, radical ones.

A second obstacle to our understanding of Gorbachev's options is that we view the aim of Brezhnev's policy during the 1970s as one of integrating

---

2. See the discussion in Jerry F. Hough, "Gorbachev's Strategy," *Foreign Affairs* 64 (Fall 1985), pp. 39–40.

the Soviet Union into the world economy. Even scholars speak about "the decision to terminate regional economic autarchy," about the movement going "a long way toward reversing the historic East-West economic isolation," and about "the greater Soviet recognition of the existence of only one world economy."[3] As a consequence, we see the Soviet choice as lying between continuing to open its economy toward the West and returning to autarchy, and the Soviet problem as one of accumulating sufficient foreign currency to import massive amounts of technology.

In actuality, however, Brezhnev adopted the conservative alternative in the 1970s. The excessive accumulation of debt in Eastern Europe aside, the East European and especially the Soviet economies remained quite isolated from the world economy. The percentage of gross national product generated by foreign trade increased, but the Soviet manufacturers remained completely protected from foreign competition both at home and abroad. For that reason, the Soviet Union received few of the benefits associated with integration into the world economy. In fact, little integration occurred; hence a third alternative to autarchy and to the Brezhnev policy is a genuine opening to the world economy which begins to attack protectionism.

This analysis is not a common one in the literature, for most scholars and commentators take the Western economic system for granted and have difficulty understanding the Soviet system in Western terms. Words such as *protectionism* are applied to practices—tariffs and quotas, for example—which governments take to thwart the natural working of the existing market-based economic system. Because the Soviet Union does not have a market economy or even a convertible currency, foreign trade is not regulated through tariffs and the like but is conducted through direct negotiations with the Ministry of Foreign Trade. Because the Soviet Union does not use the traditional techniques of protectionism, it is not seen as protectionist.

Yet, the Soviet Union has a level of protectionism that is far beyond that known even in such highly "protectionist" societies as the Japanese. At least in Japan, some imported goods enter the country and compete with domestic manufacturers. More important, domestic manufacturers are interested in the exportation of their goods, and sometimes governments force them in this direction. Thus, they must compete with Western manufacturers on foreign markets. And if Toyota is forced to produce a car that sells well in California, it will also produce a good car for the domestic market. In the Soviet Union the incentive system and state policy work very differently.

The issue of the Soviet relationship to the world economy was decided in the Soviet Union in the early 1920s. After the Civil War, the Soviet Union had repudiated the tzarist debt, expropriated private property (including that

---

3. Valerie Bunce, "The Empire Strikes Back," *International Organization* 39 (Winter 1985), p. 34. David Ost, "Socialist World Market as Striving for Ascent?" in Edward Friedman, ed., *Ascent and Decline in the World System* (Beverly Hills: Sage, 1982), p. 246.

of foreigners) without compensation, and at the same time nationalized foreign trade under a People's Commissariat (Ministry) of Foreign Trade. In the early 1920s, as the Soviet Union moved toward the New Economic Policy (NEP) that relaxed some of the economic policies of the Civil War period, foreign economic policy was reconsidered. At the 1922 International Economic Conference in Genoa, Lloyd George offered a compromise on the debt as a way of reintegrating the Soviet Union into the world economy; a number of high-level Soviet officials advocated acceptance of the idea and pushed for a more decentralized system of foreign trade controlled by more traditional mechanisms such as tariffs.[4]

Lenin's rejection of the advice of his top officials at Genoa to accept Lloyd George's offer was almost hysterical,[5] and his views carried the day.[6] These were expressed in a letter he wrote in 1922 explicitly calling for a protectionism that went beyond tariffs:

Our border is maintained not so much by customs or border guards as by the monopoly of foreign trade. This Bukharin does not see—and this is his most striking mistake— . . . that no tariff policy can be effective in the epoch of imperialism and of the monstrous difference between poor countries and improbably wealthy ones. Bukharin several times refers to tariff protection, not seeing that any of the rich industrial countries can completely break this protection. It is enough for it to introduce an export subsidy for the importation into Russia of those goods that are covered by our tariff protection. Any industrial country has more than enough money for this, and, as a result, any industrial country will surely break our indigenous industry. . . . Russia can be made an industrial power not by any tariff policy, but exclusively by a monopoly of foreign trade. Any other protectionism is in contemporary conditions completely fictitious—a paper protectionism . . . We should struggle against this with all our might.[7]

---

4. As two highly respected Western economists later wrote in 1924, the Soviet Union faced a real dilemma. On the one hand, the debt service was so high that "a thriving agricultural, commercial, and industrial Russia would be quite out of the question" if an effort were made to pay it. On the other hand, when the regime repudiated the debts and nationalized foreign property without compensation, it "uprooted so far as Russia was concerned the whole economic system based on private contract and by rejecting the very foundations upon which international credit and commercial intercourse among civilized nations is built, isolated Russia from the rest of the world." The obvious solution was for Russia to recognize the legality of the debts and compensation, but for the West to accept arrangements by which they would not be paid in full. Leo Pavlovsky and Harold G. Moutton, *Russian Debts and Russian Reconstruction* (New York: McGraw-Hill, 1924), pp. 4–5, 55, 162, and 167.

5. A. O. Chubarian, *V. I. Lenin i formirovanie sovetskoi vneshnei politiki* (Moscow: Nauka, 1972), pp. 261–81, esp. pp. 272–73.

6. See the discussion in Richard B. Day, *Leon Trotsky and the Politics of Economic Isolation* (Cambridge: Cambridge University Press, 1973), pp. 73–76, and V. S. Pozdniakov, *Gosudarstvennaia monopoliia vneshnei torgovlia v SSSR* (Moscow: Mezhdunarodnye otnosheniia, 1969), pp. 26–35.

7. V. I. Lenin, "O monopolii vneshnei torgovli," in V. I. Lenin, *Polnoe sobranie sochinenii* (Moscow: Politizdat, 1978), vol. 45, pp. 220–23.

This policy was continued by Lenin's successors, and it was further institutionalized and strengthened once central planning was established in the 1930s. As the economy was completely nationalized, the system of planning and incentives which was established that rewards managers on the basis of the fulfillment or lack thereof of a predetermined plan centered on gross output. They are assigned suppliers and customers, and the higher the level of supplies in the plan, the easier it is to fulfill plan targets. Supplies are free for the managers, who have every incentive to inflate their requests for supplies (including imports) and little incentive to reject anything they are allocated. Hence demand, especially for goods intended for other factories, is virtually infinite. Moreover, of course, the managers have incentives to push for simply designed products that do not change, for this simplifies the fulfillment of the production targets.[8]

The consequences of this incentive system are an even stronger protectionism than that which the monopoly of foreign trade itself implies. Because of the near-infinite demand for machinery, the importation of foreign technology does not cause local manufacturers to lose business, and hence the local manufacturers do not have to improve their product to compete with the imports. Likewise, since supplies are free, managers have little cause to limit their demand for imported goods, whose costs the state itself must bear.

In addition, the nature of the incentive system leads manufacturers to try to avoid exports at all costs. The higher quality and technological level required for the foreign market would make gross production plans harder to fulfill. Variations in foreign demand, unless completely absorbed by the Ministry of Foreign Trade, would introduce variability into the plan or into plan fulfillment if foreign sales were to become a key indicator for judging managers.

The so-called opening of the Soviet Union to the outside world which was undertaken in the late 1960s and early 1970s did almost nothing to change the incentive system under which the managers and ministries operated. The industrialists remained protected from foreign competition by a sellers' market that provided almost guaranteed sales even if goods produced were well below world standards. The reasons for Brezhnev's decision are unclear. The man was, in principle, inherently cautious and probably opposed any fundamental change. Yet, the fear that an attack on the job security, subsidized prices, and egalitarian wages enjoyed by the workers might produce unrest was surely also a factor. Protectionism for the managers also meant protectionism for the workers, and this social policy was a key part of the Soviet formula of political stability.

8. These issues are discussed in some of the essays in Egon Neuberger and Laura D'Andrea Tyson, eds., *The Impact of International Economic Disturbances on the Soviet Union and Eastern Europe: Transmission and Response* (Elmsford, N.Y.: Pergamon Press, 1980).

The fundamental problem for Gorbachev is that another part of the Soviet formula for political stability has been the government's tie with Russian patriotism. The stability of communist countries that have such a tie compared with those (such as Poland) that do not have it suggests that it is an absolutely crucial component. The Communists promised not only equality with the West and the consolidation of national defense but also the creation of a superior society. Unfortunately from the Soviet point of view, autarchy and isolation from the world, especially when coupled with nationalization (which created natural monopolies in industries organized under single ministries), produced backwardness rather than leadership, especially as Russia began moving from the smokestack stage of industrialization to the electronic-computer stage. The predictions of free-trade textbooks about the consequences of protectionism proved correct.

For this reason, Gobachev's choices are much more limited than it may appear on the surface. He may hope that a continuation of the Brezhnev's foreign economic policy, coupled with greater discipline, a more rapid turnover in personnel, and a higher rate of investment, will suffice to solve the Soviet problems. And, indeed, over the next five to ten years, such a strategy might well increase the growth rate from 2.5 percent to 3.0 or 3.5 percent a year and bring about a slow improvement in technology.

Gorbachev, however, has been making much more sweeping promises: an annual 4.5 percent increase in national income until the end of the century, the maintenance of petroleum production at present levels (and in the first half of 1985 it was only 96% of the level of the first half of 1984), the achievement of world levels of technology and superiority in computers in the Soviet Union, and a "historic transformation of the economic system." Again and again, he has insisted that deeds must correspond to words. If he thinks that increased discipline and a little worker enthusiasm will achieve this, Gorbachev is a fool. And if he is raising expectations for no reason, risking disillusionment when slow progress would give him a five- to ten-year honeymoon, he is a total fool. Assuming that he is politically astute—and he has given every indication of being so—we can hypothesize that he is setting the goals so high because he plans a major reform and wants to use the gap between the goals and their fulfillment that will inevitably occur a few years from now as his weapon in overcoming conservative opposition.

To achieve drastic change, Gorbachev must begin taking steps to integrate the Soviet Union more fully in the world economy. The subjecting of Soviet manufacturers to foreign competition in the domestic market—or at least the domestic market for capital goods—presupposes fundamental changes in the economic system and is not likely to be realized on a large scale in the near future.[9] A change in the incentive system used to encourage or

9. Consumer demand is not infinite, and manufacturers producing for the consumer do face the danger of losing markets and not fulfilling their plans. For this reason, an intelligent Soviet strategy would be to concentrate more on imports in the consumer sector than they have done in the past.

require exports is somewhat simpler and is likely to come first. Joint production wth foreign firms is already being proposed to the Japanese, and foreign investment in he Soviet Union, with joint ownership, seems highly probable, especially in more isolated sectors such as petroleum exploration and extraction.

Speculation that Gorbachev will follow such a policy remains deductive, for he has not spelled out how he plans to achieve his goals. The case rests first on the assumptions that finding a solution to the technological problem is indispensable for political stability, that Gorbachev clearly recognizes this, and that he has few alternatives if he is serious about reaching his goals. It rests, second, on evidence from published Soviet debates about the Third World. The vast majority of Soviet economists simply take for granted (and say it in print) that the Soviet economic model is not the best for economic growth in the Third World.[10] Instead, they assert, growth is facilitated by integration into the world economy, foreign investment, and the preservation of a private sector along with a nationalized one. In the words of one leading Soviet economist writing about the Third World,

> A course toward a closed economy or, in other words, toward economic autarchy is, as history shows, a course without a future. It is a path leading to a dead end. . . . The higher the level of participation in the system of the international division of labor, the higher the tempos of economic growth. . . . Extreme protectionism, carried out over an unjustifiably long period, is fraught with negative consequences (the preservation and extension of backward, noncompetitive, inefficient production with high costs of production, low productivity of labor, and low quality of production).[11]

Such analysis obviously is meant to apply to the Soviet Union as well. Indeed, every reader in the Soviet Union knows that the "as history shows" of the first sentence refers to the history of the Soviet Union. Since the Soviet scholars writing in these terms are policy scholars whose promotion depends on the acceptability of their published and classified work to higher officials, it is difficult to believe they would express themselves so openly if they did not feel that their views were acceptable to the coming generation of leaders.

Foreign-policy implications of Gorbachev's choices

The degree to which domestic policy and foreign policy are related in any country is always a controversial question for scholars, and it is particularly

10. The evolution of the Soviet debates is discussed in Jerry F. Hough, *The Struggle for the Third World: Soviet Debates and American Options* (Washington, D.C.: Brookings Institution, 1986).

11. A. I. Dinkevich, "O strategii ekonomicheskogo razvitiia osvobodivshikhsia stran," in Dinkevich, ed., *Razvivaiushchiesia strany: nakoplenie i ekonomicheskii rost* (Moscow: Nauka, 1977), pp. 8, 12.

so in the Soviet case. Gorbachev, however, has pointed quite explicitly to such a link. He deliberately ended his interview with *Time Magazine* with a personal statement, a "few words that are important in understanding what we have been talking about all along." He stated that "foreign policy is a continuation of domestic policy" and then asked his readers (Soviet as well as foreign, for the interview was also reprinted in the Soviet media) "to ponder one thing. If we in the Soviet Union are setting ourselves such truly grandiose plans in the domestic sphere, then what are the external conditions that we need to be able to fulfill these domestic plans?"[12] He repeated the same point in even stronger language on his trip to France.

Gorbachev did not answer his own question in the *Time* interview. "I leave the answer to that question with you" was the enigmatic last sentence in both the American and Russian versions of the interview. Americans have thought wishfully that he was saying that the Soviet Union has to have good relations with the United States in order to cut Soviet military spending. This wishful thinking is based on several decades of experience with a general secretary and a foreign minister who did not want economic reform and who found a bipolar foreign policy fit very well with that domestic policy. A leader who wants economic reform—and especially one who is thinking of greater integration into the world economy—has or will have very different foreign-policy imperatives.

First, of course, large-scale increases in investment and production of consumer goods (both of which are promised) are incompatible with a major increase in military spending. In fact, they require a decrease in military spending. However, arms control is not a prerequisite for such a development. The major defense costs are produced by the number of troops and the size of conventional procurements. Changes in these spheres require agreements with China and Western Europe, not the United States. Strategic expenditures will reflect how the Soviet Union responds to the American buildup. The most intelligent response is a slow and inexpensive deployment of the mobile SS-25 in order to reduce the vulnerability of the Soviet land forces to an American first strike. Such a move would require no agreement with anyone.

Second, any movement toward an export strategy will require a substantial shift in emphasis in Soviet Third World policy. The United States will not deliberately provide a market for the Soviet Union as it did for its Pacific Basin allies. Instead, as the Soviet Union attempts to break into markets with manufactured goods, it will have to make price concessions to compensate for quality, which, in turn, will stimulate charges of dumping in the Western countries.

The Third World is where the Soviets ought to begin competing with Western manufacturers, but underlying such a move must be a far stronger emphasis on state relations than the promotion of revolution requires. Radical

12. *Time Magazine*, 9 September 1985, p. 29.

revolutions are occurring only in preindustrial countries, and by definition such countries have little money with which to buy manufactured goods. The focus of an export-oriented policy should be the moderated or right-wing regimes that are typically found in industrializing Third World countries. Support for revolutionary movements that are trying to overthrow such regimes is not going to achieve good relations with them.

Already such a change in policy has been implemented. Before Gorbachev's election, Soviet relations with moderate countries such as Kenya, Egypt, and Jordan were improving. Since then, the Soviets have established relations with Oman, launched sports diplomacy with Saudi Arabia, and put out many feelers to Israel. At Chernenko's funeral, Gorbachev met with Mrs. Marcos and assured her that the Soviet Union would not support the rebels in the Philippines. Subsequently, the Soviet Union awarded President Marcos a medal for his role as former ambassador and, incredibly, was slow to abandon him and recognize the impending victory of Corazon Aquino.

Third, an export strategy would almost certainly be associated with the toleration or even encouragement of much closer economic ties between Eastern Europe and the outside world. At the simplest level, it would be very difficult to prevent the East European leaders from following the path of the Soviet Union. More important, however, if the Soviet Union wants high-quality goods from Eastern Europe—and it certainly does—then it has an interest in exposing East European manufacturers to world competition in order to raise the quality of their products. East Germany produces the most advanced goods in the communist world, and its access to the West German market is surely a major reason for this. Gorbachev has spoken warmly about the East German experience.

Many Americans would like to believe that an improved relationship with the United States is also indispensable for Gorbachev's policy. The likelihood of such a link is, however, dubious, for it would give the Reagan administration veto power over Soviet domestic plans which the administration could use to set impossibly high conditions for an improvement in Soviet-American relations. No superpower is going to give the leaders of its main enemy the ability to determine its internal evolution.

What many Soviets have come to realize is that improved Soviet-American relations are not essential for domestic reform and may even be counter-productive. An emphasis on the long-term American danger, coupled with substantial concessions to Europe and Japan, permits a Soviet leader to justify taking the politically dangerous course of opening to the West as attacking the American position. The Strategic Defense Initiative (SDI) is particularly valuable to a Soviet reformer. It poses no short-term danger and hence does not legitimate pressure by Soviet conservatives to increase military expenditures. Yet, it is a potentially enormous long-term danger that can be met only by improving Soviet computer and other technological capabilities. It legitimates the radical reform necessary to effect such improvement.

In other respects, too, the logic of economic reform leads in the direction of a more multipolar policy. Or perhaps it would be better for the United States to treat the bipolar policy as unnatural, a policy that was maintained because of an anachronistic Soviet fear of German and Japanese military power and a desire to control it with American power, and because of what the Soviet newsman Alexander Bovin called "a healthy ideological instinct."[13] A multipolar policy in an age of minimal military danger might break down an "evil empire" view of capitalism and lead East European countries to press for a more differentiated policy.

Of course, in international economic relations the world has already become multipolar. Western Europe, which bowed to U.S. pressure to allow the installation of the Pershing missiles, went ahead with the construction of the natural gas pipeline to the Soviet Union which the United States opposed. Argentina sold the Soviet Union grain during the U.S. embargo, even though it participated in U.S. covert actions in Central America and boycotted the Moscow Olympics. The major American military buildup of the last eight years hardly translates into Japanese willingness to do what the United States wants in the economic realm. Rather, it is more accurate to say that there was a tradeoff between military power and economic independence—that the Japanese bought the right to behave somewhat outrageously in the foreign economic sphere by behaving very subserviently in the strategic one.

For their part, East European countries also took a series of economic actions—for example, Poland assumed an extremely high level of foreign debt—that the Soviet Union obviously did not desire. They also made a number of domestic political concessions—most notable, in the case of East Germany—that the Soviets feared were linked to their desire for Western credits.

The question is whether a Soviet policy of opening further to the West and of concentrating far more attention on powers other than the United States will lead to a politically more multipolar world. Or, because that is almost inevitable, perhaps we should ask what political multipolarity means in the framework of a world in which there are only two major nuclear powers, both of which are able to destroy each other.

What it has meant thus far in the Soviet Union is a Gorbachev effort to de-ideologize foreign policy. He has spoken the language of national interest and praised the "great Palmerston" who said that nations do not have eternal friends or eternal enemies (for which read West Germany and Japan) but eternal interests. He said that President Reagan was "banal," "irresponsible," and "politically dangerous" to treat Third World issues in East-West terms.[14]

---

13. " 'Tsentry sily'—doktrina i real'nost," *Rabochii klass i sovremennyi mir*, no. 2 (1985), p. 80. Bovin also seemed to taunt Gromyko by noting that a multipolar policy also "complicates the work of the diplomats." Ibid., p. 82.

14. *Pravda*, 22 November 1985.

Soviet conservatives know that Marxism-Leninism did the same thing and that the general secretary is revising their ideology in his attack on Reagan.

In part what it means is that military power will probably have less and less importance in the nuclear age. The Gromyko-Reagan generation was already in its late twenties at the beginning of World War II, in its mid-thirties when atomic bombs were exploded, and in its mid-forties before intercontinental missiles were developed. They have found it difficult to unlearn the thinking that was relevant to World War II and the diplomacy leading up to it. They have found it very difficult to think seriously about propositions such as that allies may threaten security in the nuclear age rather than contribute to it.[15]

The older Soviet leaders have found it difficult to assimilate the fact that the Soviet Union no longer has any real need for a military buffer zone in Eastern Europe. For several centuries the plains of Poland were the major avenue of invasion and one used several times. In a nuclear age, Germany cannot think of invasion, and the "path of invasion" of missiles that is now dangerous to the Soviet Union is not through the Poles but over the Pole. No buffer zone will protect against that danger. The older Soviet leaders have found it hard to understand that only four East European countries have posed no real problem for them in recent years—Albania, Austria, Finland, and Yugoslavia—and they have given even fewer signs that they have thought about how the other East European countries could be turned into neighbors that cause so little worry or expense.

For their part, the older American leaders—and perhaps many in the Soviet Union—have no sense that the Soviet Union is uninterested in pursuing a military victory over Western Europe. Such movements as Solidarity are far more dangerous to the Soviet Union than are Pershing Two missiles in West Germany. A Soviet victory in West Germany would mean a united communist Germany that might become as independent as China, a communist regime in Italy that would be worse than Solidarity, and the end of any justification for the stationing of Soviet troops in Eastern Europe. In addition, communist economies in Western Europe would not be able to provide the Soviet Union with the quality of technology currently provided by West European capitalist economies.

As these realities of Eastern and Western Europe become absorbed, as it becomes even clearer that military power that will not be used confers no political power, the huge military forces facing each other across the "iron curtain" are almost surely going to be gradually reduced in size and scope. Zbigniew Brzezinski is undoubtedly correct to anticipate an increasing reintegration of Western and Eastern Europe as the century begins to wind down,[16] but it is difficult to believe that this development will stop at the

15. Robert W. Tucker, "The Nuclear Debate," *Foreign Affairs* 63 (Fall 1984), p. 30.
16. Zbigniew Brzezinski, "The Future of Yalta," *Foreign Affairs* 63 (Winter 1984–85), pp. 279–302.

Polish-Soviet border. Recently the Soviet Union permitted East Germany to build a television cable to bring West German television to Dresden—the one area in East Germany which cannot already receive such programs freely. It is a decision that is indicative of the future.

Vadim Zagladin, the first deputy head of the international department of the Central Committee, wrote several years ago that the dominant economic trend was in the direction of the internationalization of the world economy, and that this would require a new kind of international relations.[17] This was policy advocacy, not a statement of policy, but it was also a prediction that is likely to come true. As the bipolarism that marked the postwar world begins to dissolve, the world will finally leave the postwar era.

Soviet theorists such as Zagladin are already involved in the effort to rethink a new international relations. It should become a key element on the agenda of U.S. political scientists as well. As international economic relations become the increasingly crucial component in international relations, theorists of international political economics should be at the forefront of this reconceptualization.

17. V. Zagladin, "Marxism-leninism o roli rabochego klassa v mezhdunarodnykh otnosheniiakh," *Rabochii klass i sovremennyi mir*, no. 4 (1964), pp. 16–17.

Orthodoxy and solidarity: competing claims and international adjustment in Yugoslavia
Susan L. Woodward

Yugoslavia, like many newly industrializing countries (NICs), experienced a serious deterioration in its external trade account and sharp rises in domestic prices as a result of the changes in the world economy in the 1970s and 1980s. By the 1980s, low and then stagnant growth, high unemployment, and accelerating inflation plagued the Yugoslav economy. Throughout the period policy makers faced a conflict between the need to protect the country's balance of payments and their preference for an economic policy of high growth, full employment, and egalitarian distribution.

The ability of the Yugoslav government to adjust to the inflationary spiral of international trade in the 1970s and the sustained recession after 1980 as well as to contain the domestic conflict generated by stagflation was hampered, furthermore, by domestic political developments. These included the aftermath of a constitutional crisis over economic policy in 1967–72 and the growing incapacitation and then death in May 1980 of Marshal Tito, Yugoslavia's leader for the entire postwar period.

Given the change that characterized both international and domestic conditions in the 1970s and 1980s, what is striking about the Yugoslav policy response is its continuity with the past. This continuity can be seen in four elements. First, monetary policy continued to bear the dual burden of macroeconomic management in Yugoslavia—both to increase employment by stimulating economic growth and to curb inflation and reduce balance-of-payments deficits by restricting demand. The expansionary preferences of

This essay is based in part on research conducted in Yugoslavia in the fall of 1982 under fellowships from the International Research and Exchanges Board and the U.S. Department of Education Fulbright-Hays Program, whose assistance I gratefully acknowledge. In addition to the many generous Yugoslavs who have shared their knowledge and wisdom over the years, I thank Ellen Comisso, Anne Henderson, Miljenko Horvat, Miles Kahler, Louka Katseli, Deborah Milenkovitch, Steven Rosenstone, Laura Tyson, and the review committee for this volume for their valuable assistance, and in particular David Cameron for his careful reading of the present version.

International Organization 40, 2, Spring 1986   0020-8183 $5.00

policy makers were frequently overridden by orthodox policies of deflation and devaluation as monetary authorities gave priority to reducing an external deficit. As it did before 1973, macroeconomic policy oscillated between contraction and expansion, depending on the external current account, and, as a result, intensified the domestic effects of world economic cycles.

Continuity was also apparent in the supplementary measures that the federal cabinet employed to adjust to external conditions and still pursue its developmental and socialist goals. As in the past, such policies included trade negotiations to ensure crucial imports and to redirect export markets from the advanced industrial countries in recession to member countries of the Council for Mutual Economic Assistance (CMEA) and the Third World, liberalized rules on foreign investment, temporary controls on prices and imports, and, above all, foreign borrowing. The government also tried to promote both exports and import substitution, to sponsor voluntary incomes policies to control both price and wage inflation without abandoning egalitarian principles, and to institute a system of contracting among firms to counter the differential effects of stagflation on firms, regions, and consumers with solidaristic redistribution and risk sharing.

Third, continuing a familiar pattern, policy makers reversed the orientation of the country's structural adjustment policies when international conditions changed in the 1980s. Beginning in 1980–81, the abrupt cutoff of loans from foreign commercial banks, the size of Yugoslavia's external debt, and stiff conditionality terms for International Monetary Fund (IMF) credits forced policy makers to abandon those policies of the 1970s which aimed to satisfy competing domestic as well as foreign economic and political demands. In response, authorities imposed a program of prolonged austerity to cut demand; rescheduled the debt; and initiated a policy to promote exports, international competitiveness, and economic liberalization and reform as the motor of domestic growth—in outline, at least, a return to their economic reform of the 1960s and its supporters.

The fourth and final element of this pattern of continuity is the extensive institutional change that accompanies foreign economic adjustment in Yugoslavia. To implement their policies of adjustment in the 1970s, authorities altered mechanisms of financial allocation, the organization of the banking system and of decision making on redistributive policy, rights of political representation in economic policy groups, voting rules, authoritative governmental institutions, and the scope both of central decision making in the economy and of the party's appointment power. When the adjustment policy was reversed in the 1980s, they began yet again to discuss constitutional reform.

The Yugoslav response to the external economy, compared to responses of other developing countries, reveals similarities with both the NICs and East European countries. Macroeconomic stabilization policy—and the instruments to effect it—resembled the policies of many NICs. The movement for liberalization of structural adjustment policies in the 1980s also occurred in many open, market economies in Europe and the Third World. At the same time, the pattern of association between international conditions and movements to reform both institutions of economic decision making and mechanisms of growth was similar to that found in Eastern Europe—in the current period, Hungary, East Germany, and to a certain extent Poland and Bulgaria.

How can this Yugoslav response best be explained? Most analysts, following the current emphasis on structural or institutional factors to explain policy variation, point to domestic political characteristics. Some argue that the Yugoslav state—both government and ruling party—is too decentralized to act otherwise. That is, the central government is too weak to impose other policies, such as the centrally directed use of foreign resources in Colombia, South Korea, or Hungary, the countercyclical fiscal policies of Austria, or the austerity policies of Chile. Because political leaders have local and regional power bases, they argue, central economic policies reflect particular regional economic interests, and leaders can obstruct the implementation of policies they oppose. Others argue that the system of social ownership and of populist distributional goals encourages the government to intervene administratively in the economy and to offer enterprises aid in ways that prevent effective participation in the world economy and lead to domestic crises that require harsh measures. These are partial explanations at best, however, and they do not account for variation in the extent and nature of centralization and governmental economic activity in Yugoslavia during the postwar period. Nor do they explain why the Yugoslav state has these traits.

The explanation offered here of the Yugoslav response to the external economy is that the political order in Yugoslavia rests on *two* foundations, one international and the other domestic, that together constrain policy makers' choices of foreign economic policy. This dual foundation is the outcome of the strategy chosen in the formative period of 1943–49 to develop the economy as rapidly as possible in a way that would also secure the domestic position of the new leadership against both foreign and domestic challenges. The strategy had two components—a particular relation with the world economy and a particular relation between political authorities and the economy— that have structured the arena within which policies have evolved ever since. Hence the repetition of certain policy patterns over the postwar period.

This development strategy sought to achieve the dominant goals of the new ruling coalition—to create the material basis for a long-term solution to the national question (the short-term solution having been constituted in the choice of a federal system); to further its socialist goals, above all the rapid improvement of the standard of living of the working population; and to remove the vulnerabilities of Yugoslavia's international strategic position which Nazi economic policies and the war had made transparently clear. The fates of these goals—international and domestic, political and economic—

on which the party based its future authority were thereby conjoined and in turn made dependent on the outcome of the development strategy itself. Consequently, both world and domestic economic conditions are tightly linked, and domestic conflicts over policies toward the external economy are interwoven with conflicts over domestic development and socialist goals.

Three characteristics of the Yugoslav policy process shape the particular policies that result. First, the options within the foreign economic relations of the development strategy establish the lines along which conflict over economic policy and its resolution can occur. Second, the ruling party is a coalition of groups that disagree on these policy options and whose foreign economic interests conflict; at the same time, the political norm underlying social peace in Yugoslavia is that all such interests must be accommodated. Some compromise must be found. Third, because the lines along which policy-making and administrative bodies are organized do not coincide with the distribution of economic power and of foreign-trade interests, no single interest or political alliance consistently defines policy outcomes.

To accommodate conflicting interests and competing claims to economic resources, the party leadership has sought to avoid zero-sum conflicts and irreconcilable debates by repeatedly turning to foreign resources and to promises of economic growth through trade, on the one hand, and by granting financial autonomy to firms and subordinate governments at home, on the other. However, the first tactic reinforces the influence of trends in the world economy on domestic economic and political fortunes and the difficulty of separating domestic economic policies and political debates from policies of foreign adjustment. At the same time, both tactics limit the subsequent policies that can be employed to manage the consequences of international economic fluctuations. In effect, openness to the international economy—in particular, the form such openness takes in Yugoslavia—is as critical to the party's governing strategy as it is to the strategy for economic development. At the same time, such openness has conferred differential benefits on regions, localities, firms, and individuals, and has required frequent adjustments in the economic policy-making apparatus of the state. What begins as a remedy for some internal conflicts then becomes a source of others. Hence institutions and practices of political control also vary directly with the scope for maneuver which comes from outside.

This essay describes the policy responses of Yugoslav decision makers to changes in the world economy in the 1970s and 1980s and explains those policies in terms of Yugoslavia's strategy toward the world economy, the resulting pattern of domestic interests in foreign policy, and the role of the Yugoslav state in the economy, including the distribution of rights to participate in economic policy making among social groups. I shall first elaborate on these explanatory factors.

Yugoslavia in the world economy

The main goals of economic strategy in Yugoslavia over the last four decades have been (1) to develop the domestic economy as rapidly as possible, (2) to use open participation in the international economy to promote that development, and (3) to transform the country's foreign-trade profile into that of an advanced industrial economy and thus to reduce the foreign economic and political vulnerability of its prewar profile:[1] trading primary commodities for processed and capital goods, Yugoslavia had become ever more dependent on foreign capital and markets. The development strategy adopted as early as 1949 has always distinguished the Yugoslav party from others in Eastern Europe, although Poland, Hungary, and Romania each in their own way came to share Yugoslavia's interest in Western trade and aid, and to adopt some of the reforms that integration into the world market required.

A key element of the Yugoslav approach has been the use of external capital resources (with exceptions for foreign investment) to supplement domestic resources and accumulation. As President Tito once remarked, "the more aid, the faster socialism will grow in our country."[2] The approach also relies on active international diplomacy and relatively balanced relations with both superpowers to increase economic flexibility and to keep foreign economic and political powers from interfering in domestic affairs.[3]

Although this strategy has freed the postwar government from some of the constraints of economic underdevelopment, it limits policy makers in other ways. For example, the strategy places a high premium on the rational,

1. A good source for the original assumptions of the development strategy is Nikola Čobeljić, *Politika i Metodi Privrednog Razvoja Jugoslavije (1947–1956)* (Belgrade: Nolit, 1959).
2. J. B. Tito, *Govori i Članci*, vol. 6, p. 131, as cited in Duško Duisin, "The Impact of United States Assistance on Yugoslav Policy, 1949–1959" (Master's thesis, Columbia University, 1959).
3. R. F. Miller refers to this strategy as "maximum international exposure and involvement" in *External Factors in Yugoslav Political Development*, Occasional Paper No. 14 (Canberra: Australian National University, Department of Political Science, Research School of Social Sciences, 1977). The necessity of a reasoned international strategy if rulers were to be able to pursue domestic goals, particularly socialist ones, was a central question in debates among intellectuals on how to overcome the "ideology of smallness" (Krleža) and the fate of "non-historic nations" during the 1930s, in socialist debates on foreign trade in the 1890s, 1920s, and 1947–49, and in the lesson of Hitler's eastern policy. The general argument relating ruling strategies to external pressures in Eastern Europe has been made most persuasively by Perry Anderson in *Lineages of the Absolutist State* (London: Verso, 1974); note his distinction between the Central European and Byzantine-Balkan patterns, patterns that divide Yugoslavia through the center. Joseph Rothschild provides interwar parallels in *East Central Europe between the Two World Wars* (Seattle: University of Washington Press, 1974), pp. 200–280. Czechoslovakia attempted the Yugoslav strategy in 1947–48 and perhaps again in the 1960s. Romania, until Ceaușescu endeavored to emulate the Yugoslavs, and Bulgaria, which since 1980 has also hinted of change, followed instead a patron-client strategy, according to Kenneth Jowitt in his *The Leninist Response to National Dependency* (Berkeley: Institute of International Studies, University of California, 1978). The Albanian strategy, alternating patron-client relations with isolationist autarchy, is well known, as is the Hungarian exchange, necessary perhaps because of that country's size and insufficient resource base and experience of the Soviet invasion of 1956, which remains politically loyal to the Soviet Union in order to gain internal flexibility.

best use of foreign resources so that they may contribute simultaneously to development, a particular trade profile, the revenues from exports needed to pay for imports and loans, and political independence. Investment policies always combine export promotion and import substitution. Above all, policy makers must be particularly attentive to their balance of payments. Although they expect persistent deficits and foreign debt as an inevitable consequence of the early stages of development, they have been adamant against defaulting on foreign loans.[4] Moreover, pursuit of this strategy has required an entrepreneurial and skillful foreign-policy leadership, a strong territorial defense, and a vigilance about the political consequences of international agreements that make it difficult to separate debates on foreign economic policy from questions of political allegiance and national security.[5]

By the early 1970s the Yugoslav economy had become more trade-oriented than the economies of many NICs, if one judges by the proportion of its gross national product (GNP) involved in trade (between one-third and one-half of the total volume of trade) or by the directness with which international prices were transmitted to the domestic economy.[6] According to one authority, exports in 1972 generated direct and indirect employment for the equivalent of 14 percent of the resident active labor force and for 40 percent of workers in industrial employment in the socialist sector.[7] The economy is particularly dependent on imports for basic production and consumption needs, including food during years of bad harvest.[8] It is a major recipient of World Bank development assistance for domestic infrastructure. In sharp contrast, for example, to leaders in East Germany or Czechoslovakia, Yugoslav leaders have also maintained close credit relations with the IMF since 1949.

4. This stance is supported by most producers, because of the extensive dependence of production on imports and by the general public, because of a deep cultural predisposition toward reciprocity in exchange which requires the repayment of financial obligations on both moral and pragmatic grounds.

5. As a result, for example, purchases of military equipment are limited by a one-third rule: one-third each from NATO, the Soviet bloc, and domestic sources. Defense needs require production capacity that many have considered uneconomical, for example, the iron and steel capacity developed in the early 1950s.

6. It is these transmission mechanisms that make the Yugoslav economy particularly open, rather than the proportion of trade in social product alone (according to which, for example, Hungary is considered "more open" by Egon Neuberger and Laura D'Andrea Tyson, "The Transmission of International Economic Disturbances: An Overview," in Neuberger and Tyson, eds., *The Impact of International Economic Disturbances on the Soviet Union and Eastern Europe: Transmission and Response* [Elmsford, N.Y.: Pergamon Press, 1980], pp. 7–8).

7. Laura D'Andrea Tyson and Gabriel Eichler, "Continuity and Change in the Yugoslav Economy in the 1970's and 1980's," in Joint Economic Committee, *East European Economic Assessment*, pt. 1, *Country Studies* (Washington, D.C.: GPO, 1980), p. 175.

8. National Bank of Yugoslavia, *The Economic Scene in Yugoslavia, 1980–82* (Belgrade, April 1982); Organization for Economic Cooperation and Development (OECD), Annual Economic Surveys, *Yugoslavia* (Paris: OECD, yearly); see also Charles R. Chittle, *Industrialization and Manufactured Export Expansion in a Worker-Managed Economy: the Yugoslav Experience* (Tübingen: Mohr, 1979), chap. 5; Martin Schrenk et al., *Yugoslavia: Self-management Socialism, Challenges of Development* (Washington, D.C.: International Bank for Reconstruction and Development, 1979), pp. 176, 214–17; Tyson and Eichler, "Continuity and Change."

Despite intentions to reduce external vulnerability, the Yugoslav economy is extremely sensitive to conditions in the world economy. Oskar Kovač argues, for example, that the use of foreign finance in Yugoslavia has always been determined by supply.[9] Laura Tyson and Egon Neuberger have calculated that "a 1.0 percentage point decline in average growth rates in Western Europe produces a 1.0 to 1.6 percentage point decline in Yugoslav exports."[10] Economic policy makers gain some maneuverability from their nonalignment policy. When their preferred Western markets become protectionist, for example, they can shift exports eastward as an associate member of the CMEA. They maintain many bilateral clearing agreements of economic cooperation in the Third World.[11] Associate status with the Organization for Economic Cooperation and Development (OECD) and preferential trade agreements with the European Economic Community (EEC) give them access to Eurodollar markets. Yugoslavia receives long-term public credits from countries in competing blocs, such as Kuwait, West Germany, and the Soviet Union. And it has learned to expect emergency assistance from the United States and its allies because of Yugoslavia's military defense of the status quo in the Balkans.

It is far less easy for Yugoslavia to redirect import sources, however, given its reliance on Western credits and technology, and the orientation of much of its export industry toward processing and assembly. As a result, serious imbalances in the commodity composition and terms of trade among Yugoslavia's trading areas exacerbate problems in the balance of payments. The country's trade with OECD countries remains characteristic of that of a less developed country—it imports capital goods and intermediate materials in exchange for raw materials, agricultural products, and subcontracted processed goods (e.g., textiles)—whereas in its trade with CMEA and developing countries it exchanges manufactured goods for imports of fuels and other raw materials. In the 1970s, 75–89 percent of its deficit on both trade and capital accounts was with the OECD.[12]

In fact, earnings from merchandise exports have never been sufficient to cover imports, leaving the burden of often more than half the trade deficit to earnings on factor services—above all, remittances from workers temporarily working in northern Europe—but also to tourism and transport services. Not only has the trade account shown a deficit throughout the postwar period, the current account has also shown a deficit in all but six

9. Oskar Kovač, *Platnobilansna Politika Jugoslavije* (Belgrade: Institut Ekonomskih Nauka, 1973).

10. Cited in Laura D'Andrea Tyson, *The Yugoslav Economic System and Its Performance in the 1970s* (Berkeley: Institute of International Studies, University of California, 1980), p. 92n.

11. In 1971 Yugoslavia maintained such agreements with CMEA countries, Greece, Spain, Turkey, Israel, Algeria, Tunisia, Mali, Ghana, Guinea, Afghanistan, Cambodia, India, Egypt, Cuba, and Brazil.

12. Tyson, *The Yugoslav Economic System*, p. 87.

of the last thirty-seven years.[13] Borrowing to supplement foreign reserves and to finance imports and development projects brought Yugoslavia's total debt to $2.195 billion by the end of the 1960s, nearly half of which had come due by 1972 on the eve of the oil-price rise.[14] On the eve of the world debt crisis, in December 1981, its foreign debt had reached $19.2 billion.[15]

Domestic interests and alliances in relation to foreign economic policy

No economic policy is neutral in its effects on social groups, of course, but Yugoslavia's choice of foreign strategy for development purposes had the effect of creating natural alliances around foreign economic policy which did not conform to the alliances of political organization in Yugoslavia after World War II. For historical reasons as well, political disputes over foreign economic policy always arouse strong emotions.

This "setting," given political meaning by economic policy, has three elements. The first is the ancient distinction in the Balkans between what might be termed inward- and outward-oriented regions. People situated in river valleys, on borderland plains, and on the seacoast have participated in international trade for centuries, whereas the hinterlands remained mountainous retreats for refugees, bandits, and transhumant herders.[16] The second element arises from the overlay of developmental disparities and productive specialization along territorial lines as a result of partitioning by competing empires. Thus, outward-oriented regions in the more developed northwest and less advanced southeast may disagree on development policy while sharing an interest in commercial and export policy that can ally them against those areas long exploited for mineral wealth or those restricted to self-sufficiency as a military border between empires. Because the theater of World War II was located predominantly in the poor interior, and because policy makers in the defense-conscious 1947–53 period located capital in-

13. The current account ran a surplus only in 1954, 1956, 1965, 1972, 1973, 1976. According to the OECD, Yugoslav export market shares have been declining since the early 1960s. The deterioration in its trade account began in the mid-1960s, but this had been masked by growing net invisible earnings which then began to decline with the impact of the oil-price rises on world transportation and on the West European economy. See OECD, *Yugoslavia*.

14. Michèle Ledić provides data on the Yugoslav debt in "Debt Analysis and Debt-Related Issues: the Case of Yugoslavia," *Economic Analysis and Workers' Management* 18, no. 1 (1984), pp. 35–64.

15. National Bank of Yugoslavia, *The Economic Scene*.

16. This distinction even shows up in voting patterns in the interwar period. See Lenard Cohen and Paul Warwick, *Political Cohesion in a Fragile Mosaic: The Yugoslav Experience* (Boulder: Westview, 1983), pp. 27–50. Useful sources on regional economic patterns are John R. Lampe and Marvin R. Jackson, *Balkan Economic History, 1550–1950: From Imperial Borderlands to Developing Nations* (Bloomington: Indiana University Press, 1982), and F. E. Ian Hamilton, *Yugoslavia: Patterns of Economic Activity* (New York: Praeger, 1968).

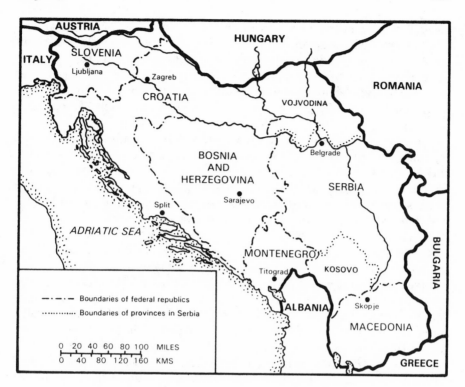

The Socialist Federal Republic of Yugoslavia

dustries in the hinterland (e.g., Bosnia, parts of Croatia and Serbia) and away from unprotected borders (e.g., the plains of Vojvodina and Macedonia), the pattern continued to be reproduced under the new regime (see map).

But inclinations are not etched in the land forever; infrastructural and industrial investments may remove these regionally inherited limits. Thus, the third element of this setting arises from the nature of current foreign-trade and developmental policies: whether they are complementary or, instead, reinforce past disparities and orientations.

These policies depend on the political organization of economic interests and on who makes policy. Political power resides with the Yugoslav Communist party (called the League of Communists, or LCY). The party sets the political agenda and initiates policy discussions, controls the boundaries of legitimate political expression and organization, and approves appointments to all authoritative positions in society—candidates for parliamentary seats, members of the cabinet, Federal Councils, the state Presidency, and federal administration, and directors of economic and social organizations. The party is a coalition of different orientations on both foreign-trade and development policy, however. It drew much of its early following from areas directly affected by foreign-trade crises, whereas during wartime its members came largely from the interior where Partisan army units were concentrated. Major purges of the party (after the Cominform dispute of 1948 and the Ranković resignation of 1966) disproportionately reduced the latter contingent, but membership campaigns in times of political and economic crisis have restored it. And as Yugoslavia's single party, the LCY claims to represent all progressive interests.

Both the party and the government are federal organizations.[17] Yet the republics and provinces (the latter are two autonomous regions—Kosovo and Vojvodina—within the republic of Serbia) are also heterogeneous co-alitions of economic interests, although Slovenia and, perhaps, Kosovo, may be considered exceptions. Although the party has organizations in workplaces with interests in economic policy (e.g., enterprises, research institutes), and although central authorities prior to 1950 maintained direct administrative links with enterprises and local administrators through a system similar to the tutorial system practiced in Eastern Europe, political struggles have been resolved over time in favor of territorially organized hierarchies and the administrative authority of governments at the republic level.[18] Economic coalitions that cross republican lines cannot be institutionalized politically, moveover, because their formation would encounter the prohibition against organized factions in this (still in principle at least) Leninist party.

If there is any pattern at all, then, politically conservative politicians tend to come from interior, poorer regions that are more protectionist and must rely on political instruments to compensate for poorer economic resources.[19] Economic liberals, on the other hand, are based in outward-oriented areas (especially cities) and particularly in technologically advanced firms and export sectors that, while not entirely absent in the south, tend to concentrate in the wealthier northern regions. This correspondence does not always hold, however, and neither political liberals nor economic radicals are so easy to place.

In Eastern Europe both foreign interference in domestic affairs and the

17. The creation and evolution of the Yugoslav federal system up to the 1970s are exhaustively discussed by Frits W. Hondius, *The Yugoslav Community of Nations* (The Hague: Mouton, 1968). According to the pact of 1943 (the AVNOJ declaration—the Anti-Fascist National Liberation Council of Yugoslavia, the provisional wartime Partisan government), the postwar Yugoslav government was established as a "voluntary union of separate peoples" along historically defined cultural-political regions.

18. The many stages of this evolution have made bedfellows of people from both sides of a policy fence, often with unintended consequences. See Hondius, *The Yugoslav Community*, and April Carter, *Democratic Reform in Yugoslavia: The Changing Role of the Party* (Princeton: Princeton University Press, 1982).

19. By *conservative* I intend the English meaning based on power—establishment and privilege—rather than the French meaning based on class—from right to left—because Yugoslav political conservatives are loyalists to party and the structural status quo. Political labels are not always helpful, however, for the party is Communist, ostensibly representing labor and the left, and its economic views tend to vary with context, constituency, and issue.

recourse to foreign resources and alliances by competing domestic political factions are time-honored traditions. In Yugoslavia these issues also arouse strong emotions because the central government must gain and hold the allegiance of separate peoples and numerous national minorities within one political community. Economic policies that emphasize foreign or domestic markets can raise doubts about the ability of a group or region to prosper and feed into long-standing uncertainties about cultural and political loyalties and about a people's reasons for membership in a Yugoslav state. Regional leaders, who represent the federal units and participate in policy making because of the devolution of financial and administrative authority to the republican governments, always view foreign economic policy from a dual perspective—their economic position relative to other regions and relative to international competition. In addition, the many-sided struggle among groups and individuals over foreign economic policy within a single-party system means that policy alliances are not only informal but also unstable and that policy choices always represent a compromise among objectives rather than a coherent platform favoring one economic program.

Interaction among foreign trade and developmental strategy, economic and political regional legacies toward the international economy, and the structure of political organization thus create numerous conflicts within the political leadership. For example, attempts to implement an export-oriented policy pit representatives of commercial power and of export producers against Partisan veterans and representatives of the poorer interior.[20] If foreign economic policies appear to conflict with policies for domestic development, as in deflationary policies or cuts in funds for redistribution, then political leaders from more developed northern regions are likely to confront leaders from less developed regions in the south. But the economic heterogeneity of most regions means that the interests of liberals are not (as some argue) identical with those of political leaders from wealthier regions, as the current stance of Croatian leaders illustrates (see below). Frequent divisions also occur within regional leaderships over exchange-rate, price, tax, and agricultural policies, and over balance-of-payments adjustment policies that demand contraction of investment priorities for foreign-trade purposes, and

20. The parliamentary elections of 1967, which took place in the midst of the economic reforms of the 1960s, are illustrative. Liberal reformers anxious to remove veterans from positions of power to make way both for the younger generation and for individuals more sympathetic to their economic policies pointed to a number of contests in Serbia, where Partisan generals unseated the official candidates, as evidence of Rankovićite (i.e., secret police, centralist, anti-reform) opposition. In one of these contests, the official candidate was the federal secretary for trade. The general who won campaigned by disparaging his opponent's war record and his policy of allowing the import of cheap apples to the detriment of local fruit growers, and by promising locals he would win their struggle for a railway line. Carter, *Democratic Reform*, p. 147.

that affect current regional specializations and inequalities.[21] Moreover, the liberal coalition divides sharply when popular dissent protests the unemployment and inequality that the foreign economic policies of liberal reforms engender. However, the most ferocious battles are fought over the central distribution of foreign developmental assistance for infrastructure and over the system that allocates foreign exchange, because of the simultaneous developmental and foreign-trade implications of transportation networks and the pervasive import dependence.

The economic role of the Yugoslav state

In the course of settling upon its international strategy, the party leadership also made a number of decisions regarding the structure of the Yugoslav economy and the relation between political authorities and economic actors. These decisions severely limited both the capacity of the central government to influence economic activity and the forms that influence could take. For example, it was decided that the predominant instrument of domestic accumulation would be autonomous producers operating on a market rather than central planning. Social control of the economy would be secured by labor-managed firms and by restrictions on capital ownership, capital markets, and other forms of economic power independent of social-sector control (either producers or governments). Administrative authority over the economy, both to implement central decisions and to stimulate structural economic change, was delegated to republican and local governments in order to allow flexibility in the face of different conditions and to retain the allegiance of regional authorities by reducing central power. Finally, the state abandoned its control over foreign trade to autonomous enterprises, its role now reduced to regulating an essentially liberal trade regime.

As a result, the economic system in theory resembles the model of Ricardian and Owenite socialists in which labor-managed cooperatives are the basic units of production and consumption, the rights to allocate surplus belong to those who create it, and growth is facilitated by exchange and by international specialization.[22] The role of the government in this Yugoslav model

21. Unemployment currently ranges from under 2% in Slovenia to 21% in Macedonia and 30% in Kosovo, and policy makers are familiar with evidence from earlier recessions (such as that which followed the economic reforms of the mid-1960s), namely, that the structural effects of contraction are far deeper and have more long-term consequences in the poorer regions than in the northwest. For an analysis of this effect see Pavle Sicherl, *A Dynamic Analysis of Regional Disparities in Yugoslavia*, Income Distribution and Employment Programme, working paper 84 (Geneva: ILO, 1980).

22. Given the domestic coalition that formed the Yugoslav Communist party, the neopopulist aspects of this strategy are not surprising. A particularly clear statement of neopopulist assumptions and the East European branch of that movement can be found in Gavin Kitching, *Development and Underdevelopment in Historical Perspective: Populism, Nationalism, and Industrialization* (London: Methuen, 1982), pp. 19–61.

is confined to sponsoring social agreements among producers to redistribute financial resources, both to protect the values of social "solidarity" (e.g., the right to a living, equal reward for equal labor input, and assistance from those temporarily advantaged by the market to those whose survival is threatened) and to ensure stable conditions of accumulation. The antistatist legacy that the Yugoslav political economic system shares with classical liberalism is apparent in the institutional assumptions of the system's main architect, Edvard Kardelj, who expected a "pluralism of self-managing interests"—the individual pursuit of self-interest by socialist persons in socially owned units, together with institutions to prevent concentrations of political or economic power—to lead to social well-being through the market and worker cooperation.

The Yugoslav government performs its economic functions in essentially five ways: it may offer firms material incentives (tax relief, subsidies, cheap credit) to invest in certain activities or in other firms; it may raise monies through bond sales or taxation to finance specific public goods; it may regulate monetary and credit conditions; it may deposit revenues in interest-bearing accounts of banks which, in turn, are loaned to enterprises for capital investment or to localities for public services, and it may use taxation to create social funds to equalize individual incomes or governmental budgets. Each governmental level is financially autonomous, preferably self-sufficient, and in all cases required to balance its budget quarterly. Fiscal policy is used primarily to balance budgets; monetary and credit policy is the main tool to influence the behavior of firms.[23]

The tensions in this system are predictable. Enterprises fight to retain as much of their revenue as possible and to prevent governmental interference in their activities, while governments increase taxation to cover expenditures and seek to reach collective goals without violating enterprise self-management. To manage this conflict, rights to participate in distributive decisions have been granted to those who provide resources, a kind of "no taxation without representation" principle weighted according to contribution. For

---

23. A number of Yugoslav economists argue that not only are governmental actions countercyclical but, worse, they exacerbate recessions: the constitutional requirement that budgets balance and the restrictions on capital markets mean governments and enterprises compete for the same funds; in a recession, governments increase taxes, and rather than reduce employment, labor-managed firms under strict rules against firing workers cover costs by raising prices. To counter the inflation, the National Bank tightens money and imposes a number of constraints to increase "financial discipline." Such measures only deepen the recession and the downward spiral until the level of enterprise indebtedness forces the government to seek credit from the National Bank in order to pay its bills. This increase in the money supply then fuels expansion, including imports, and the balance-of-payments deficit, which usually induced the recession in the first place through the monetarist policy response, re-creates the cycle. For a clear discussion, see Branko Horvat, *The Yugoslav Economic System: The First Labor-Managed Economy in the Making* (White Plains, N.Y.: International Arts and Sciences Press, 1976), pp. 206–51. For critiques of the ineffective system of public finance and the contradictory roles of monetary policy, see various years of OECD, *Yugoslavia*.

example, enterprises send delegates to local assemblies that deliberate on the provision of social services financed by enterprise funds; commercial bank credit policy is determined by assemblies of shareholders (i.e., large enterprises and governments); and the Federal Fund to Finance More Rapid Development in the Less Developed Republics and Autonomous Provinces (the Federal Fund) and the National Bank are both managed by representatives from each republican and provincial government.

Where the conflict is not between enterprises and governments but among producers themselves, as in the persistent conflicts over access to foreign exchange, there has been no stable resolution, only a constant process of pressuring the government to define and enforce "rights." In the case central to this essay, for example, three alternatives for distributing foreign exchange and therefore "import rights" recur: (1) a foreign-exchange market, preferred by final exporters,[24] wealthier firms, and parties whose claim on social resources is small (individuals, research institutes); (2) bilateral contracting to negotiate the exchange of goods or services for hard currency, preferred by producers of raw materials and intermediate goods, by firms that sell only on the domestic market, and generally by firms with fewer assets; and (3) governmental redistribution at the federal or regional level, often preferred by regional leaders pressured by firms to solve problems that result from the scarcity of foreign exchange. Perhaps because such conflicts are frequently irreconcilable, the tendency over time has been to try to remove the government (particularly the federal government) from the deliberative and redistributive processes altogether, confining its role to maintaining the conditions necessary to either a contracting or a market system, that is, reverting to the classical "liberal" principles of the government's economic role in the Yugoslav socialist model.

The formal institutions of economic policy making also aim to prevent the concentration of political power or the institutionalized advantage of one political interest within the party against another. Decisions are made in collective councils by people who are chosen to ensure representation of political "virtue" (the party), personal prominence (including experts), organized social and economic interests (producer groups, social institutions, governments), and nationality (usually the federal units), and who accept collective responsibility for the outcome.[25] All appointive positions in the government must "take into account" a person's national identity, aiming for proportional representation. All persons in authority, except the secretary

---

24. In 1983 more than 3,000 basic organizations of associated labor (BOALs) were engaged in exporting, but 110 held 72% of the trade.

25. Four councils govern at the federal level: the presidencies of both party and state, with representatives of each republic and province and of the federal government as co-equal powers, and a rotating chair; the cabinet, elected by the Parliament, which joins department heads with representatives of the republics and provinces; and a privy council (Council of the Federation) of notables. Government departments are managed by councils of civil servants, experts, and representatives of organized interests, and chaired by the cabinet secretary.

for defense, must rotate to another function after a maximum of two terms.[26] At the same time, however, the executive branch dominates all economic policy making, and the principles of rotation and the party's appointive power have resulted in a circulation of elites among these executive positions.

Unlike East European countries where Leninist parties also rule and where administrative reforms have tended to reinforce the links between central ministries and firms and to reduce the economic power of local and regional authorities, in Yugoslavia territorial units of party and government coordinate all organized interests horizontally, and formal lines of administrative authority between the central bureaucracy and local governments and enterprises have been eliminated.[27] Because party cadre policy is (as of 1969) under republican jurisdiction, people who represented organized interests and made policy in the 1970s and 1980s were always regional delegates as well. Federal economic policy, in other words, is made by political leaders who are simultaneously responsible for the economic activity of firms, the budgetary resources of the regional or local governments they represent, the living standards of their constituents, and public order in their territory. In addition, the doctrine of voluntary consent to decisions among political equals, which is built into the foundations of the political order—federalism, self-management, socialism, and democratic centralism—makes policy making into a process of achieving agreement among strategic groups, that is, the party leadership, sources of finance, and administrators, particularly in enterprises and local and regional governments. The convention in all such consultations, and, by the mid-1970s, the constitutional rule in Parliament (the Federal Assembly), is that decisions be made unanimously.

To obtain agreement, the cabinet (the Federal Executive Council, or FEC)

26. The rotation principle has had a complicated and tortuous history, beginning with its introduction in the 1963 Constitution and continuing to the Tito Initiative of 1978–79, which required yearly rotation of the chair of the party Presidency. To follow some of the many changes, see Steven L. Burg, *Conflict and Cohesion in Socialist Yugoslavia: Political Decision Making since 1966* (Princeton: Princeton University Press, 1983). For a wealth of information on governmental institutions and their many alterations, see Burg and Hondius, *The Yugoslav Community.*

27. This process took two decades and may be assuming yet a third arrangement. The strength of territorial powers originates in the military organization and wartime political strategy of the party, as in China. Vertical integration does occur functionally but usually when individual firms expand to create their own inputs or create new product lines with the waste products of their main line—hence one of the reasons for industrial oligopolies according to Stephen Sacks (personal communication, 1985) and a contributing factor to the power of some enterprises. In many ways, the system is much more like the small, open, social democracies of Western Europe with which Yugoslavia shares a system of corporate pluralism and simultaneous goals of free trade and social welfare; however, Yugoslavia is a developing country, on the periphery of West European trade alliances, and does not choose among economic policies according to a multiparty, numerical democracy. The comparison with Norway, according to Stein Rokkan's description of this conflict between corporate and numerical pluralism and its national-international linkages, is illuminating; see his "Norway: Numerical Democracy and Corporate Pluralism," in Robert Dahl, ed., *Political Oppositions in Western Democracies* (New Haven: Yale University Press, 1966), pp. 70–115.

follows a two-step procedure. First, to "harmonize the positions of interested parties," as the process of executive-initiated, corporatist negotiation is conceived, the FEC consults and bargains with central and regional party leaders, executive councils of regional governments, and economic authorities, such as the governors of the National Bank, the Federal Chamber of the Economy (an association of representatives from enterprises), and the trade union. This may be informal—between the FEC and regional governments, for example—or formal, in expanded sessions of the FEC, in its coordinating commissions, in the offices of the federal administration, and in the federal councils.[28] Experts in research institutes may be asked for opinions or for studies demonstrating the viability of a particular measure, and party leaders will organize discussions among members and at public gatherings to inform, invite suggestions on drafted legislation, and mobilize support. The second step is to obtain approval from elected assemblies of political and governmental representatives: the Socialist Alliance,[29] the party's Central Committee, and the bicameral federal Parliament—in which local and republic interests are represented.

The result of this system has been to link economic and political power, disperse it among a multitude of actors, and create a competition among powers to specify the rights and agents of "society." Over time, political conflicts have been resolved by further liberalizing the role of government in the economy, thereby making it more difficult for the government to realize its responsibility for solidarity, be it obligations to guarantee bank credits (domestic or foreign), reduce unemployment and inequality, find ways to share the responsibility for economic losses, or prevent bankruptcies. In other words, although the federal government's economic powers are analogous to those of a liberal state, its responsibilities are distinctly socialist. The paradoxical result is a central government that is committed to a passive policy stance but continues to play a significant economic role. It assumes responsibility for maintaining foreign solvency, guaranteeing foreign loan payments, engineering institutional reforms in the face of changing economic conditions, and setting priorities to guide microeconomic investment decisions.

Despite continuous negotiation over social plans and annual economic resolutions, most central policies are short term, ad hoc, and temporary interventions to correct what are viewed as aberrations in an otherwise normal market. Even when policy makers agree that a problem is structural and requires long-term policy rather than palliatives, they are limited by their lack of control over investment and of a central mechanism to command or to predict the outcome of an economic policy or to internalize externalities.

28. For the details on the process, see Burg, *Conflict and Cohesion.*
29. The Socialist Alliance of Working People of Yugoslavia, the former Popular Front mass organization, now organizes elections, political debate, and similar mass political activities.

Temporary controls accompany orthodox macroeconomic policies, and many of the socialist responsibilities are transferred to local and regional governments.

The formal structure of the Yugoslav state leads many to argue that real power lies with regional leaderships and that economic policy is a product of their mutual bargaining. But because no single region is dominant and because policy alliances are unstable, the leverage of those who guard the bases of the party's (and thus leaders') power is actually increased. By preserving the LCY's international reputation and its rules of domestic exclusion, the central leaders can distinguish clearly between decisions over which they have absolute prerogative and those they are willing to leave to local self-sufficiency or interregional bargaining. In this way they have attempted to resolve the conflict between the need for action on some matters and the many incompatible interests that must be accommodated.

This division of labor leaves up to the federal leadership decisions on international agreements and their terms, and the policies necessary to maintain balance-of-payments equilibrium and monetary stability. Monetary policy is made by the governors of the National Bank, customs policy by the secretary of foreign trade, price policy by the director of the Federal Price Office; budgetary decisions and international financial negotiations are primarily the responsibility of the secretary of finance, and so forth. The prime minister or vice-president for economic affairs of the FEC takes these to the Federal Chamber for ratification.[30]

Meanwhile, the party leadership watches both international and domestic events with an eye to their effect on national autonomy and to potentially destabilizing political behavior. Because the leadership reflects the coalition of interests and political approaches within the party, however, leaders will not be likely to agree unless confronted with a clear threat to the preconditions of their own power. Only then would they interfere with the normal course of economic decision making by changing policy direction or deciding that action on a particular problem is necessary. Such consensus can be reached under the compulsion of external necessity, for example, the threat by foreign lenders to discontinue credit unless certain conditions are met. Domestically, heads of the international security forces (the army or police) might argue persuasively that popular demonstrations against economic policies have begun to overreach their ability to maintain order; or a majority in the leadership may decide that interregional factionalism threatens the foundations of their collective rule.

In the past, President Tito's willingness to assert his charismatic authority (the personal loyalty of other top leaders), backed by his threat of a purge,

---

30. For example, although the Federal Chamber is composed of delegates from local communities, according to Burg, *Conflict and Cohesion*, they tend to consult the finance secretary of their republic for advice on legislation before them.

facilitated the resolution of policy in such cases. By dividing the ruling group into loyal and heretic, and even making a progress among local cadres for support, he could isolate potential opponents, force their resignation into private life, and prevent the formation of alliances against him and whatever policy he had chosen to support. Because Tito also used this authority to maintain his own position, challenging anyone who appeared to him disloyal or arrogant to obey or resign, he could influence the balance of political power on economic policy. However, this resource, to which leader and citizen alike tried to appeal, reinforced his power because he used it sparingly.

When economic policy requires domestic resources or implementation, the FEC will turn instead to the process of domestic bargaining and consultation, often playing only the role of broker among regional governments or producer groups. If export revenues must be raised, for example, the FEC will consult the Committee on Foreign Economic Relations of the Federal Chamber of the Economy (the seat of exporters and foreign-trade firms) to work out acceptable incentives. If price guidelines are not being followed, it will mobilize party and trade union cadre. Where social or economic policy requires a distribution of burdens or funds among regions—for example, regional responsibility for balance-of-payments adjustment and austerity cuts—the FEC negotiates with regional governments and their parliamentary delegations.

The policies chosen in such cases always reflect two factors: (1) the positions of those who hold the balance of economic power in the situation, and (2) the necessity of formulating a compromise that compensates the losers. The first occurs because the power, wealth, and reputation of leaders, as well as their ability to fulfill administrative responsibilities, depend above all on the economic resources of local enterprises, banks, and budgets. Whether interested in their own position or in the welfare of their constituents, regional representatives must lobby for policy outcomes that favor the wealth and wealth-making capacity of firms in their region and against policy outcomes that could harm their region's economy.[31] The advantage in this bargaining is held understandably by those from regions with the economic capacity to ride out policies that may not be in their interest or even to make a threat to secede plausible.[32] Advice from economists from wealthier regions and with Western contacts tends to have the most persuasive force. Furthermore, both market pressures and socialist goals have led to concentrated economic power, particularly in industrial conglomerates and foreign-trade enterprises. As a result, the incorporation into policy bargaining of associations repre-

31. This lobbying does not necessarily mean strengthening regionally based economies or promoting nationalistic or sectionalistic policies, as some claim.

32. Slovenia has used this threat several times—during the dispute over the allocation of World Bank funds for highway construction, the so-called road crisis in the 1960s, and the debate on foreign-exchange controls in the 1980s—and Croatia used it as a weapon during the late 1960s.

senting producer groups in which such firms dominate gives a distinct leg-islative advantage to those with greatest market power and those whose contribution to accumulation and to exports is greatest.[33] In contrast, regions in need of budgetary supplements from federal funds or with fewer alternative investment resources have less influence on rules specifying principles of distribution and must argue more for compensatory funds. Because economic actors in search of policies or administrative exceptions in their favor also focus their efforts where they are likely to have the most influence, this balance is cumulative. For example, the directors of industrial conglomerates call Belgrade officials frequently, but poorer firms must often resort instead to local influence.

Compromise is necessary, on the other hand, because it is also in the interest of all political leaders to resolve their conflicts, even if only tem-porarily, so as to preserve political stability and the party's authority. Fur-thermore, because the distribution of political power does not, except perhaps in the case of Slovenia, correspond to the distribution of economic power and economic policy interests, no regional representative stands in just one policy camp. That the instruments of the state are primarily financial magnifies the value of economic growth and of external sources of capital—in both cases permitting change in distributional proportions independent of political agreement and accommodating both regions whose own resources are in-sufficient to execute a policy and regions whose tax base and administrative control would be reduced by redistribution.[34]

Pressures to agree, the resulting vagueness of legislation, conflicts between market signals and the values of solidarity and socialist principles, the nu-merous obligations of territorial leaders, and so forth, all make implementation of policy difficult. The judiciary is federalized and, like civil law courts, depends on clear agreement in the government and party for its rulings. Administration of economic policy is decentralized, the responsibility of the republic and commune in which sympathies are likely to be closer to those being governed. There are few effective sanctions against noncompliant eco-nomic behavior because of the rights of self-management and the range of conditions under which solidarity is considered appropriate. Underlying all economic policy making, therefore, is a conflict over the proper methods of

33. On the very high industrial concentration of the economy, see Stephen R. Sacks, *Entry of New Competitors in Yugoslav Market Socialism* (Berkeley: Institute of International Studies, University of California, 1973). Legislation was enacted between 1967 and 1974 to break up large enterprises and industrial conglomerates into smaller, autonomous divisions (BOALs) and to regulate their interactions by negotiated transfer prices and internal banks. On this division-alization, see the important study by Stephen R. Sacks, *Self-Management and Efficiency: Large Corporations in Yugoslavia* (London: Allen & Unwin, 1983), where he also suggests parallels with Japanese *zaibatsu* and some large American firms (e.g., General Motors).

34. The negotiations over aid to Montenegro after the April 1979 earthquake illustrate the tradeoffs and bargaining, including promises that foreign credits be secured in exchange for lower domestic transfers, between regions and the FEC. See Burg, *Conflict and Cohesion*, pp. 294–95.

enforcement—both who the enforcers should be and what the criteria of enforcement should be.

Thus, for example, market- and export-oriented reforms are accompanied by changes in banking and labor legislation in order to strengthen instruments of financial discipline and by changes in appointment policies in order to restrain the influence of both party and governmental personnel on economic decisions. Rising levels of unemployment, production bottlenecks, capital shortage, high inflation, or overall recession may lead to short-term interventions by authorities, some of which may be contradictory; for example, central policy makers may try to recentralize in order to coordinate difficulties and resolve external problems at the same time that regional and local politicians seek greater authority over their own turf.

Whatever the enforcement institutions of the moment, the burden of policy implementation ultimately falls on party leaders whose interest in maintaining political order and its underlying structure of political power means ensuring that governmental policies are obeyed. Conflicts over policy can thus extend to the role of the party itself and challenge its claim to speak for the community as a whole: some use the occasion to challenge the legitimacy of its authority over economic policy, others to debate the proper methods of its governance. Whereas some think the party should be the guardian of social justice and a counterbalance to economic power, others believe it should refrain from making operational decisions and guarantee only procedures for equal rights and political participation. At the same time, in its necessarily ad hoc role as troubleshooter, the party's actions can be easily seen as "interference" when not desired, but as "aid and duty" when they are.[35] Nor has the Kardeljian system ever been completely accepted. There remains an underlying tension, inside the party and outside it, between its supporters and those who believe in the rule of *čvrsta ruka* (a firm hand).

The ability of the central leadership to command the loyalty of its members, including the heads of the instruments of coercion—the army, the public prosecutor's office, and the police—is indeed crucial, because this makes it possible to enforce its control over the boundaries of legitimate political expression and organization. Although the *nomenklatura* system is less developed and formal than in other East European countries, the party's appointment power and threat of a personnel purge, however distant, are its ultimate weapons. With these it can create uncertainty for individuals who seek power and position within society and thus control their actions through anticipatory behavior. Short of this, party leaders frequently resort to Leninist tactics: campaigns to mobilize cadre, to persuade the population of the ne-

35. For an industrial example, see Ellen Comisso, *Workers' Control under Plan and Market: Implications of Yugoslav Self-Management* (New Haven: Yale University Press, 1979); for an example in the schools, see Susan L. Woodward, "Training for Self-Management: Patterns of Authority and Participation in Yugoslav Secondary Schools" (Ph.D. diss., Princeton University, 1974).

cessity for sacrifice and unity to achieve some objective, and to signal the end of debate and the start of implementation.[36]

In sum, what are the basic characteristics of the Yugoslav political economy which shape policy makers' responses to changes in the external economic environment? First, foreign capital resources have been crucial to Yugoslavia's strategy for achieving domestic economic growth and structural change and to the ability of the ruling LCY to accommodate domestic conflicts. Second, domestic financial resources belong to producers operating autonomously in an internationally open, regulated market economy. The extent to which those resources can be mobilized for social needs depends on both the productivity of the firm and the ability of government and party representatives to secure enterprise agreement to policies of redistribution. Third, the League's constituency includes both wealthy and poor firms; developed and underdeveloped regions; export-oriented and domestic market producers; economic liberals who favor using the instruments of the market, minimal government, and openness; and economic socialists and often political conservatives persuaded of the need for social or governmental institutions to address policies directly to redistributive equity, unemployment, and underdevelopment. Fourth, policy choices reflect shifting coalitions of authoritative individuals, because no formal alliances are possible within the party and because the formal lines of decision making and administrative authority in the government do not coincide with stable positions on foreign economic policy. At the same time, once a policy is decided, the League does not permit any organized challenge, whereas there are many ways, and indeed pressures, to evade implementation.

The LCY aims to accommodate the many members of its coalition within an economic system that puts their economic interests in conflict. Toward this end it has sought primarily to increase the financial resources necessary to economic activity and social goals, and to prevent the dominance, even temporary, of one group over another. As a result, economic policy making is bound by two constraints: (1) an externally controlled budget constraint—the balance of payments, the hardness of which has depended mainly on the availability and terms of foreign financing; and (2) an internal political constraint—namely, commitment to the principles of self-management, or the autonomy of firms, which includes voluntary investment and wage and price decisions, and successive devolution and limitation of governmental authority over the economy.

36. It is often said that the party suffers from the same consequences of federalization as do other institutions in Yugoslavia, that as a result there is no such thing as a single League of Communists. With regard to tactics and policy issues, this is certainly the case, although the lines of cleavage are by no means only regional. To the extent that political and economic leaders derive their power from the party, however, they are unified against all their competing interests and against outsiders by a common interest, namely, preserving the bases of the party's power and obeying the decisions of the party leadership. Although chosen by regional parties, party leaders hold the interests of party and country, as they choose to define them, first and foremost.

Foreign economic policy in Yugoslavia

How external economic conditions affect the domestic economy shapes the options of economic policy in Yugoslavia and the policy preferences of representatives of social and economic groups. The description of foreign economic policy in Yugoslavia after 1973 can therefore be divided into two distinct periods—that which followed the oil-price shock of 1973 and lasted until the end of the decade, and that which accompanied the onset of world recession in 1980–83 and the emergence of the worldwide debt crisis of the 1980s.

The 1970s

The decade of the 1970s had two main characteristics for Yugoslav policy makers. First, Yugoslavia experienced, as did other open, developing economies, growing unpredictability and recession in world trade; for example, rising import prices for petroleum-related goods caused supply shocks, the country's terms of trade deteriorated, and export revenues were sharply reduced. The recession in OECD economies cut demand not only for Yugoslavia's tradable goods, such as shipbuilding, tobacco, and nonferrous metals, but also for the invisible goods so important to its trade balance—temporary labor, transport services, and tourism. Protectionist barriers from the EEC against Yugoslavia's textiles, steel, and beef made the situation worse. Although the plentiful and cheap supplies of foreign commercial capital after 1973 alleviated the policy constraints during the 1960s due to reduced Western lending, the ease with which credits could replace export revenues made Yugoslavia increasingly vulnerable to the actions of foreign banks: for example, the temporary ban on further borrowing from Euromarket lenders in 1975 and the soaring interest rates and short maturities after 1978.

Second, Yugoslav policy makers were operating in a political environment shaped by reaction to the consequences of a severe recession in 1965–67. During the 1960s the policy response to the payments deficit, declining growth, and rising inflation had been shaped by a coalition of economic and political reformers favoring the rights of enterprises to control their earnings, openness to international price competition, preferences for export producers in the allocation of investment funds, and a largely unmanaged domestic market. At the same time, the constitutional changes to accommodate these reforms led to widespread political debate. The economic consequences of reform brought about social unrest over growing unemployment, income differentials due to market position, disadvantaged industrial sectors (such as coal production), regional disparities in the FEC's allocation of World Bank loans, and the rights to foreign exchange. By the end of 1971, when mass demonstrations and open factionalism among regional leaders seemed to threaten political order, the central and regional party leaders decided to act. In the following year the League purged several regional and local leaderships, began a campaign to remove many enterprise directors, rejected the principle of an unregulated market, and pledged to restore the attention of policy makers to unemployment and distributional equity.[37]

Despite the apparent shift in the domestic balance of power in favor of federal leaders committed to an economic policy of reducing unemployment, policy makers responded to the balance-of-payments deficits and inflation of 1973–79 as they had in the past. Monetary authorities imposed classic adjustment policies—tight money conditions, restrictions on government expenditures and on enterprise funds for collective welfare goods, cash reserve requirements on enterprises, passive exchange-rate adjustments, and steep devaluation.[38] The FEC imposed a range of temporary controls on prices, imports, foreign exchange (linking import rights to export earnings), and investment in order to reduce inflation and, particularly, to achieve rapid cuts in imports. Subsidies were granted to stimulate export sales. When current account surpluses were obtained (in 1973 and 1976), the government removed the controls and expanded the money supply and credit to counter the bottlenecks in supply created by import controls and the recessionary effects on production and employment. This "stop-go" approach, a longstanding Yugoslav policy, is common among many other trade-oriented countries where the concern of financial authorities about the external balance overrides their concern about maintaining full domestic employment (including the British, after whom the policy is named). The oil-price rise happened to occur, however, at the beginning of an expansionary phase designed to restore growth which followed three years of contraction in 1971–73 (and one year after a policy shift from a fixed to a managed, flexible exchange-rate regime). This bad luck was repeated in 1977–79 when the second oil-price rise also coincided with an expansionary policy and thus renewed demand for imports.

In addition to macroeconomic adjustments, and particularly after 1975, federal leaders sought to ease the deficit with new sources of foreign capital and long-term preferential trade agreements. For example, they negotiated a state-level agreement with Iraq to provide suppliers' credits for the purchase of oil in 1976 and 1977, which, together with long-term contracts for Soviet oil, enabled the country to delay steeper cuts in oil consumption and petroleum

37. On the events of the 1960s and their close, see Carter, *Democratic Reform in Yugoslavia*; Burg, *Conflict and Cohesion*; and Dennison Rusinow, *The Yugoslav Experiment, 1948–1974* (Berkeley: University of California Press, 1977).

38. The exchange-rate devaluation was far steeper than necessary, according to Laura Tyson and Egon Neuberger. Exchange-rate policy is complicated in Yugoslavia by the frequently opposing directions of the U.S dollar and the deutsche mark. The dinar is pegged to both: the dollar dominates its trade account, the deutsche mark its invisibles account. See Tyson and Neuberger, "The Transmission of International Disturbances to Yugoslavia," in Neuberger and Tyson, eds., *The Impact*, pp. 214–21.

products.[39] In December 1976 the government concluded an agreement to expand relations with the EEC in an attempt to avoid another costly shock (such as the EEC's ban on Yugoslav beef imports in 1974–75) and began talks with the European Free Trade Association in 1979. President Tito conducted diplomatic visits in support of economic relations during 1977–79 to Egypt, Libya, China, France, and Britain as well as to Moscow and Washington. In 1975 and 1978 exports barred from Western markets were sold to CMEA countries, especially the Soviet Union. Over the 1974–79 period exports to developing countries rose, and trade with the CMEA was increasingly negotiated in convertible currencies.[40] At the same time, both the federal government and business banks took full advantage of increased international lending.[41] American and European banking consortia financed a series of joint ventures, particularly in energy and petrochemicals.[42]

39. Economists have analyzed the Yugoslav adjustment (or nonadjustment) to the oil-price rise endlessly without reaching agreement. John Burkett, citing a report by Wharton Econometric Forecasting Associates (1983), notes that "Yugoslavia's ratio of energy consumption to net material product (NMP) remained almost unchanged between 1960 and 1982 and that its NMP elasticity of energy demand was close to unity for 1974–82 . . . that Yugoslavia's record of energy conservation compares unfavorably to that of the centrally planned economies and still more unfavorably to that of industrial capitalist economies . . . [and] Yugoslavia is 'one of the most energy intensive economies in the world (in terms of energy requirements per $1 billion of GNP).' " He goes on to suggest that where soft budget constraints (which reduce a firm's need to respond to price signals) are produced by policy designed to redistribute income (as in Yugoslavia), then the response will be even slower than for policy designed to stimulate output (as in the CMEA); see his analysis in "Search, Selection, and Shortage in an Industry Composed of Labor-managed Firms" (Unpublished paper, Department of Economics, University of Rhode Island, May 1984). In addition, conservation and rationing in response to price increases presume the availability of short-term substitutes that simply did not exist. INA-(Industrija Nafte) Zagreb began in the late 1950s to encourage the substitution of oil for other forms of domestic energy. By the late 1960s, after a wholesale move to convert from wood and coal to oil in home heating and to close coal mines, demand was driven almost entirely by supply. INA formed a joint venture with Dow Chemical Company in 1978 to increase foreign-exchange earnings; the government selected petrochemicals as an export branch; and the use of tractors for cultivation increased dramatically after the restrictions on their purchase by private farmers were lifted under the outward strategy of the 1960s. These moves are thus parts of the story. So, too, is the monetarist response to inflation and deficits. Because INA purchases oil with foreign exchange and sells predominantly on the domestic market, it was hurt by the exchange-rate policy, and because its subsidiaries that sell exports in petrochemicals were subjected to nontariff barriers in the 1970s, debt mounted. In addition, energy policy is a republican responsibility. The push to export, rising energy prices, and differential distribution of energy resources among regions for energy led each republic to seek to become a self-sufficient energy producer, leading to vast overcapacity in oil refining. Nuclear power plants were planned, but the construction costs and the difficulties of the joint venture with Westinghouse to build one such plant, Krško, proved major obstacles to the construction of the others.

40. Exports to the CMEA averaged 43% of the Yugoslav total in 1974–78 (up from 35.6% in 1971–73), while exports to OECD fell from an average of 55.2% in 1971–73 to 40.5% in 1974–78. Tyson, *The Yugoslav Economic System*, pp. 88–91.

41. Long- and medium-term credits amounted to $500–600 million in 1974; in 1976 net official and Euromarket borrowing reached $1 billion; in 1977 and 1978 alone more than $750 million in World Bank loans was obtained for development projects in agriculture and transportation. The Yugoslavs were the first outside the EEC to receive European Investment Bank loans. Loans from Kuwait, Germany, and Japan supplemented further credit from the IMF and the U.S. Export-Import Bank.

42. Petrol Ljubljana, for example, financed a natural gas pipeline in the Eurodollar market

Whereas the behavior of firms and authorities responsible for macroeconomic and foreign policy in the 1970s appears to have been almost automatic, a result of learned behavior from persistent balance-of-payments deficits and unpredictable international conditions, more obviously political choices, such as among conflicting domestic economic policies and redistribution, were far less easy. During 1967–71 firms and regions had exchanged charges of unfair deals. While wealthier regions had protested the foreign-exchange retention quotas of the National Bank and the allocation of foreign loans, poorer ones cited growing inequalities in intraregional economic growth and incomes. Similarly, dissent was common among domestic producers who lost out in the competition for supplies and foreign exchange with export producers and among students facing growing unemployment.

The compromise of 1974, which was institutionalized in a new constitution and in its economic counterpart, the Law on Associated Labor of 1976, gave economic actors greater control over their own turf and then required them to negotiate agreements with other actors on issues of allocation. That is, it further reduced the authority of the federal government, increased republican authority, and shared the remaining central authority among regional representatives armed with the protection of a political veto over federal policy. Firms were subdivided into smaller decision-making units (BOALs), and the system already employed in the provision of social services—negotiated agreements and contracts among interested parties—was extended to apply to BOALs, firms, or firms and representatives of other social interests, such as consumers or the government. This strategy was intended to permit the coordinating tasks of government, namely, to improve the functioning of the market and to ensure equitable outcomes by sharing information, risks, and resources, to continue without undermining the promised autonomy of firms and republics. In form, therefore, the new institutions reasserted the principles of the system: continuing the evolution of the economic system along its liberal, voluntarist, and federal lines and supplementing the market with social agreements among producers for solidarity. The outcome, however, was that the operation of the domestic economy and the conditions of the world economy together made it increasingly difficult to use market mechanisms and voluntary agreements to achieve Yugoslavia's foreign-trade, developmental, and socialist goals whose legitimacy had been reasserted in the compromise. Recourse to ad hoc controls, party intervention, and governmental regulation of the economy became increasingly common as the decade wore on.

---

through Bankers' Trust International, and INA agreed to build a petrochemical-processing plant (Dina on Krk) with the participation of Dow Chemical. However, Dow Chemical pulled out of three such joint ventures (in Yugoslavia, South Korea, and Saudi Arabia) in 1982, when Dina was still under construction, because its revised predictions about world economic activity led it to expect surplus capacity and therefore losses. The pipeline stands empty today because of disagreements among regional governments over who will pay for the fuel that must remain in the pipeline for it to function.

The history of legislation on the most divisive issue, the allocation of foreign exchange and of liability for the repayment of foreign loans, aptly illustrates the new system. First, the foreign-exchange holdings of the National Bank were transferred to regional banks, and thereby to enterprises within the region which actually earned the exchange, and an internal foreign-exchange market. Because this transfer favored final producers and firms specializing in foreign trade and created production-damaging supply bottlenecks, enterprises in a production chain were required to include in their contracts the rights of each BOAL to the foreign exchange eventually earned. Second, communities of interest for foreign economic relations (CIFERs) were created at the regional and federal level in order to improve trade performance.[43] Given control over the use of the customs revenues that formerly supplemented the federal budget, representatives of foreign trade and manufacturing firms to the CIFERs were expected to coordinate foreign marketing, discuss export policy, and negotiate contracts to distribute foreign exchange between them. Third, administrative responsibility for the balance of payments was transferred to republican governments. These regional balance-of-payments accounts and the proportions of foreign borrowing to which each had a "right" were negotiated and then set down in the operational documents of the 1976–80 Social Plan. Finally, business banks were also permitted to borrow abroad. Thus, when stabilization policies imposed credit and import restrictions at home, banks could seek foreign credits to continue to meet the investment and import needs of their enterprise depositors. At the same time, complaints from Euromarket lenders at the resulting unregulated explosion of requests for small loans strengthened pressures to reform the banking system.[44] Nonetheless, heeding the advice of the governors of the National Bank, the federal cabinet responded to declining foreign reserves and pressures for debt repayment by giving free rein (in the shape of the Law on Foreign Exchange, 1977) to enterprises in foreign-capital markets for fear of the conflicts that central allocation might provoke. By 1979, fearing the consequences from both international and domestic critics of growing indebtedness, an exasperated Prime Minister Veselin Djuranović made the publication of debt figures illegal.

Between 1976 and 1978 central authorities also changed foreign-trade legislation to attract more foreign investment and to encourage joint ventures. The government significantly reduced previous limits on foreign investors designed to protect domestic producers in favor of exporters who argued that cooperation with foreign firms could make them more competitive internationally by increasing their access to both foreign marketing networks and

43. Patterned after those for education, roads, etc.
44. Donald W. Green, "Comment," in Tyson and Neuberger, eds., *The Impact of International Economic Disturbances*, pp. 248–49. Debates over proposals for the banking reform also paralleled the political factions of the period; see Shirley Jean Gedeon, "Yugoslav Monetary Theory and Its Implication for Self-Management" (Ph.D. diss., University of Massachusetts, 1982).

more advanced technology. The major new Foreign Trade Act, written between mid-1976 and mid-1978, liberalized a range of foreign-trade activities, including the right of foreign firms and banks with business in Yugoslavia to set up local representation and ending the import-licensing system. At the same time the effects of the temporary controls often countered efforts to achieve external balance by liberalization. In other words, as with monetary policy, maintaining an external balance took priority, but efforts to increase the flow of finances addressed the conflicts among domestic producers.

The effect of domestic inflation on export competitiveness also led authorities to introduce a system of contractual incomes policies on top of deflationary policies and price controls.[45] In place of federal price ceilings, enterprises and local and regional governments were expected to negotiate social compacts on prices, taxes, and consumption. These were to serve as price guidelines, subject to governmental review, for enterprise negotiations with consumers and other enterprises. (Because personal incomes are a proportion of enterprise income, such guidelines would theoretically also limit labor costs and consumer demand.) Exceptions were permitted, however, to protect the tourist industry (e.g., lower gasoline prices for foreigners) and where rising costs were a result of import prices.

Growing unemployment fed the syndicalist impulse buried within self-management: to protect the jobs of workers already employed but reduce the obstacles to accumulation (and therefore to workers' incomes) from inefficient employment. Enterprises were given control over labor relations, including the right to dismiss "disorderly and lazy workers" (ostensibly, such control was intended to reduce absenteeism and increase productivity, but often it was used to fire low-skilled labor). To reduce frictional and structural unemployment, enterprises were urged to anticipate future employment needs and contract with local schools and students. A major educational reform accompanied this solution. Local governments also negotiated social compacts on employment with firms, which amounted in many cases to less than subtle pressures to hire. New legislation permitted individuals to loan private resources to a firm in exchange for employment or to form private cooperatives as long as these did not compete with firms in the social sector. In 1978, finally, the government expanded the meager program of unemployment compensation.

Although the social plan lists only nonbinding preferences for growth rates and their components and for the sectoral investment priorities to guide credit policy, it is the main avenue for policy makers to influence longer-

45. Import prices were responsible for between one-fourth and one-half of the rise in inflation, which averaged 22% in the early 1970s, moderated momentarily, and shot up to 40% in 1979 and continued to rise. See OECD, *Yugoslavia.* The distortions from the monetary policy led as well to a growth in registered claims between enterprises well above the rate of inflation as firms adjusted to the credit squeeze, and measures to equalize income in fact led to factor indexation.

term structural adjustment and for regional leaders to discuss foreign-trade policy. The negotiations for the 1976–80 social plan took place in 1975—a year of world recession, an EEC ban on Yugoslav beef, soaring import prices, and a Euromarket credit squeeze. Negotiators represented leaders who were convinced that the policy of export-oriented investment and price increases to cut import demand had not been successful. The plan was adopted more than a year late as a result of conflicts among regional leaders over investment priorities, regional development policy, and the regional allocation of international loan monies and of foreign exchange. Among the goals of the plan, correcting the balance-of-payments deficit, particularly the structural imbalance from import dependence, took first place. The list of investment priorities, as always,[46] was a mix of export promotion (shipbuilding, agro-industry, tourism, nonferrous metals) and of import substitution (basic chemicals, ferrous metals, equipment, synthetic rubber, infrastructure, electric power, coal, petroleum and gas). Although the emphasis shifted to import substitution, many of those industries are also significant export producers (chemicals, ferrous metals, energy), and the emphasis on producers of domestically available substitutes for raw material imports whose world prices were rising suggests that the investment priorities were intended not to protect domestic producers but to satisfy exporters' needs.[47] Despite the stated goals of the 1974 compromise, the employment problem was largely unaddressed. Meanwhile, the potential impact of the investment priorities for the balance of foreign-trade power among the regions, at a time when the export market shares of manufactured goods to the OECD were already declining, was a matter of growing concern for some leaders.[48]

The usual problems of policy implementation in Yugoslavia when consensus is lacking were complicated by two additional factors. The restoration of political order after 1972 and the compromise of 1974 had been won at the expense of an increasingly powerful, if divided, reform coalition. In addition to the purges of 1972, therefore, the party reasserted its appointment power. Moral-political commissions were established in educational insti-

46. Schrenk et al., *Yugoslavia*, p. 209; Chittle, *Industrialization*, p. 106.

47. It is not wholly accurate, therefore, to identify this social plan as one of import substitution and employment growth. Nor is the plan protectionist. It did appear to resurrect the less developed areas to the position of suppliers of raw materials to exporters, while the operation of market forces continued the almost total domination of both import and export trade by Croatia, Slovenia, Serbia, and Vojvodina. On the unusual interpretations of comparative advantage by Yugoslav policy makers, see Tyson and Eichler, "Continuity and Change," p. 154, and on their concept of dynamic comparative advantage, see Diane Flaherty, "Economic Reform and Foreign Trade in Yugoslavia," *Cambridge Journal of Economics* 6 (July 1982), pp. 105–43.

48. On trade changes, see "The Relative Performance of South European Exports of Manufactures to OECD Countries in the 1970's: An Analysis of Demand Factors and Competitiveness," *Economic Bulletin for Europe* 34 (1982), pp. 503–61. The effect of OECD protectionism against steel, textiles, and shipbuilding caused significant problems for Bosnia and Croatia, for example, while the rising value of domestic raw materials and energy caused a number of concerns, including the outcome for any shifts in the distribution of economic power among regions.

tutions to facilitate party approval of appointments. *Nomenklatura* was resurrected. In 1975 a party campaign to renew discipline and reinvigorate its membership included changes in cadre policy, pressures on youth, the army, and people in decision-making positions to join the party, a major conference in Sarajevo on democratic centralism, and blatant police harassment of potential mass leaders. Behind the scenes there was substantial jockeying for power, but it was veiled by self-censorship, attacks on university professors and writers, and "between the lines" polemics.

The second problem concerned the policies themselves. Together, the confusing signals from the international system, the piecemeal response of central policy, the new institutions that, if anything, were bound to lead to greater confusion, and growing scarcities of foreign exchange and imported production materials created more rather than fewer conflicts. For example, the premise underlying macroeconomic adjustment policies—that firms would, or could, adjust rapidly to increases in input prices by cutting demand—conflicted with the conditions under which firms operate, including the lack of substitutes and the restrictions (moral and legal) on layoffs. Firms also anticipated contractionary policies by taking advantage of expansionary policies to overpurchase imports and responded to import controls by reclassifying goods. The policy commitment to greater distributional equality was undermined by the transfer of increasing responsibility for consumption to individual purchases on the market simultaneously with policies to reduce aggregate domestic demand. Inequalities in standards of living among the population increased instead according to the market position of their particular workplaces; their ability to obtain nonmarket sources of food through family ties in rural areas; their success in obtaining a socially owned apartment; and particularly, their foreign-exchange assets and their regional residence. Growing scarcities increased oligopolistic tendencies among firms and upset the balance that the 1974 Constitution had intended between republican control over economic resources in their territory and the political veto of republican representatives over central policies. Republican governments put up protectionist barriers around their region, negotiated bilateral agreements with other republics, and sought to become self-sufficient in necessary supplies, such as energy. Finally, the contracting process increased delays. Decentralization of foreign borrowing allowed firms and republics to free-ride on the federal government's guarantee of repayment. And in directing investment resources, the priorities of the plan did not always supplant economic power.

Rather than retire further from economic decision making, both governments and party organizations found it necessary to become more assertive.[49] Barter, pressures on firms from local party organizations to increase em-

---

49. This was done both with and without invitation. Some observers insist that the intention all along was to strengthen governmental economic activity.

ployment, exemptions from regional legislatures to export producers on regulations against firing labor, administrative allocation of foreign exchange, and other methods contravened the voluntary premise upon which the new institutions had been built and increased both inequalities and inefficiencies.

To resolve some delays and disagreements, federal leaders even altered rules for formulating central policy and obtaining consensus. Reflecting an effort to strengthen the federal executive's ability to cope with economic trends, the Council of the Federation was brought out of mothballs, subdivided,[50] and promoted as a place where issues that cut across regions and policy domains could be discussed prior to public debate. The public stature of these personages was, in turn, supposed to lend greater authority to federal economic policy against the many who were withholding compliance on the grounds that policy represented particularistic interests. In order to obtain agreement on a stabilization policy and regional shares of responsibility for the balance-of-payments deficit in 1979, the FEC began to apply its constitutional prerogative of a "temporary measure."[51] As regional governments and the FEC battled over international adjustment, the organization of parliamentary delegations also shifted: in 1980, the de facto division of delegates to the Federal Chamber into regional blocs was formally accepted, while the Chamber of Republics and Provinces voted to reject the principle of imperative mandate that had bound delegates to the detailed instructions of their republican assemblies.[52]

The 1980s and the debt crisis

By 1978, early 1979, the second major increase in oil prices (including for Soviet oil), coupled with a dramatic downward spiral of the prices of most primary commodities, fueled a record trade deficit in Yugoslavia. Consequently, foreign indebtedness increased dramatically to cover the balance-of-payments deficit. The government returned to contractionary policies in mid-1979 to curb the steep rise in prices. To replenish foreign reserves, it took a $340 million credit from the IMF in May and by the end of the year, requested an IMF compensatory loan facility on the grounds that the poor harvest that year, the earthquake in Dalmatian tourist areas, and the decline

50. The Council of the Federation was created by the 1963 Constitution as an advisory body to the head of state. It was subdivided into two councils—one for the economy and one for the socio-political system—in 1973, a year before Ceauşescu created the Supreme Council of Economic and Social Development, then into four in 1974—international relations and constitutional order attached to the Presidency; social order and economic development and policy attached to the FEC—and in 1979, renamed the Federal Social Councils when the Council for Constitutional Order (internal security) was absorbed by the Presidency. On its role in the 1970s, see Burg, *Conflict and Cohesion*, pp. 242–300.

51. A temporary measure, requested by the FEC, requires the Parliament to vote by delegates rather than blocs; a two-thirds majority authorizes the measure for a year until agreement is forged. See ibid., pp. 291ff.

52. Ibid.

in workers' remittances were beyond its control. It then began negotiations with the Fund to obtain a three-year standby credit. These negotiations coincided with the interest-rate shocks of the spring of 1980, drawn-out negotiations with a recalcitrant EEC over a renewal of its trade agreement, another poor harvest, and in May 1980, the death of President Tito and the election of a new government.[53]

Furthermore, between December 1980 and December 1982, in response to the Soviet invasion of Afghanistan and the Polish crisis, Western banks virtually stopped new lending to Eastern Europe, which in their eyes included Yugoslavia.[54] The onset of the 1980–83 world recession decreased the net contribution of worker remittances to the balance of payments to only 25 percent of the trade deficit by 1981. The sharp rise in interest rates for the dollar occurred when Yugoslav borrowing from commercial banks had jumped from 10–15 percent of the total to 58 percent. The impact on the Yugoslav economy could be read in any indicator: inflation rising 50 percent a year and more after 1980, unemployment above 14 percent, negative growth rates for the gross domestic product, and capacity utilization in industry below 70 percent. Problems unimagined for thirty years became commonplace, such as capital flight of enterprises' hard-currency earnings to foreign banks, long lines for scarce consumer goods affected by the import cuts (coffee, detergent, gasoline, heating fuel, and medicines), and discounts to those able to pay in foreign currency.

Taking as her mandate the party leadership's decision to restore foreign confidence, the new prime minister, Milka Planinc, accepted the Parliament's nomination on condition that she be allowed to appoint 50 percent of her ministers without regard for the nationality quotas that govern all federal positions. Over the next five years, a prolonged period of recessionary "stabilization" policies to meet the conditionality terms of the three-year standby agreement negotiated with the IMF and efforts to cut imports to the bone were either decreed by the FEC or railroaded through a contentious Parliament.

The decision to confront the level of foreign indebtedness, the balance-of-payments deficit, and domestic inflation thus began in familiar ways— IMF assistance to gain time and leverage with creditors, orthodox deflation, and additional import controls. However, the worsening of international conditions had clearly eroded the political strength of those supporting the structural adjustment policies of 1973–79. Between May 1980 and May 1981, the central leaders of the party (the party and state Presidencies), under the authoritative auspices of the Federal Social Councils, decided to call an

---

53. There is perhaps some irony in the fact that the IMF and the International Bank for Reconstruction and Development (IBRD) held their annual meeting in 1979 in Yugoslavia.

54. Bank loans outstanding to the region dropped $7.0 billion to $63.1 billion in those two years. Peter Montagnon, "Eastern Europe: Is It Coming back to the Market?" *The Banker*, October 1983, pp. 41–44.

ad hoc commission of party and government leaders to formulate a long-term program for structural adjustment of the domestic economy to the new world conditions. As in 1961, the choice of the chair (the Slovene representative to the state Presidency, Sergej Kraigher, who had held many governmental economic posts, was known for his liberal economic views, and had kept a low profile in regional offices after 1972) indicated, first, that a change of policy had already been decided and, second, that the conditions for obtaining new foreign credits and achieving external balance took priority over the potential political consequences of the recession. The balance of power among policy makers had shifted to external creditors and domestic economic liberals.[55]

At the same time, after caustic debate the leadership decided to seek new financing and foreign assistance in rescheduling the debt. The result was substantial long-term loans in 1981 and 1982; a $2 billion loan package organized by the U.S. State Department among fifteen Western countries, the IMF and the World Bank, 600 commercial banks, and the Bank of International Settlements in January 1983; and a second IMF standby arrangement in April 1984. During 1982 political leaders began to prepare the population for hardship and to wage the political fight over the policy change by referring openly to the repayment difficulties as a "crisis."

Economic policy for 1982–85 began with an austerity policy to reduce the balance-of-payments deficit and eventually pay off the foreign debt by cutting domestic absorption. Food subsidies were eliminated in 1981. Prices for energy, food, and transport were raised by one-third in 1983. All new investment for social services, infrastructure, and other governmental projects was banned. The FEC froze prices on and off over most of the period and established targets for prices and incomes in the interim. A policy of positive real interest rates was adopted in 1982 (the National Bank discount rate reached 22% by the end of 1983), and the dinar lost 90 percent of its 1979 value by 1985 as a result of two devaluations and the decision to allow the dinar to float. In addition, the government imposed restrictions on all imports unrelated to production, such as consumer goods and scientific journals, praised all efforts at import substitution with domestic materials, and in 1982–84 reluctantly permitted republican governments to issue ration coupons to consumers of meat, coffee, cooking oil, gasoline and heating fuel, electricity, sugar, and detergent. The FEC also used a range of tactics to boost exports—easy credit, exceptions to the exchange rate, fiscal incentives, and media campaigns.

To repay the debt, the FEC also chose to increase its control over sources of foreign exchange within the country. For example, to stop the massive

---

55. Vice-premier for economic affairs in the Planinc cabinet, Zvone Dragan, was quoted widely in the Western press during 1980 in support of an economic policy identical to the one that the Kraigher Commission eventually proposed.

outflow from consumers' shopping excursions abroad but avoid either alienating citizens or initiating a run on private savings accounts, in 1982 it imposed temporary financial restrictions on foreign travel, set up random police checks along highways for violations of customs regulations, and cracked down on black-market speculation. All banks were required to give priority to debt repayment over new borrowing, a rule that the FEC enforced with new sanctions. Regional governments were required to project their import needs quarterly or have the FEC do it for them; and banks, CIFERs, and enterprises that took on new obligations before old ones were paid were threatened with interest penalties and a loss of foreign-exchange rights. Because it was still illegal to reveal debt figures, the government hired a British accounting firm in 1982 (and paid in convertible currency) to establish, for the IMF, the actual level of foreign borrowing. After several efforts to negotiate an acceptable system for allocating foreign exchange, full control was returned to the National Bank in July 1983. This included the authority to prevent any regional affiliate from disbursing foreign-exchange holdings to its depositors in the event debt was outstanding, regardless of where in the country it had been incurred.

At the same time, the government began a process of reform to resolve what the Kraigher Commission (the Commission for Problems of Economic Stabilization) and its supporters identified as the source of the economy's difficulties—the economic inefficiency and arbitrary governmental and party intervention in firm decision making promoted by the policies of the 1970s. During 1982 the commission produced a set of "premises" and, subsequently, fifteen working papers designed to transform these principles into action.[56] After a year of publicity and harmonization, in July 1983 the FEC presented the "stabilization" or "long-term" program to a stormy session of the Federal Assembly to obtain the approval necessary to the conditions of the IMF loan, and above all to make it appear that the policies were internally generated rather than externally dictated, thereby winning leaders' support.[57]

The core of the commission's reform is a restrengthened market meant to replace the government and the contracting system. It entailed five changes:

---

56. The staff and its director were also drawn from economists and politicians known for their liberal views and preference for the market economy. The long-term program is contained in Komisija Saveznih Društvenih Savjeta za Probleme Ekonomske Stabilizacije, *Polazne Osnove Dugoročnog Programa Ekonomske Stabilizacije* (Sarajevo: Izdavačka Delatnost, 1982); an extensive discussion of the program can be found in World Bank, *Yugoslavia: Adjustment Policies and Development Perspectives* (Washington: IBRD, 1983); for an analysis, see John P. Burkett, "Stabilization Measures in Yugoslavia: An Assessment of the Proposals of Yugoslavia's Commission for Problems of Economic Stabilization," in Joint Economic Committee, *East European Economies: Slow Growth in the 1980's* (Washington, D.C.: GPO, 1986).

57. The Federal Assembly debated three days and two nights before it adopted the stabilization program. One night was spent waiting for the Slovene delegation to consult its base in Ljubljana before conceding to an article authorizing the National Bank to prohibit any payment to a business bank with outstanding foreign obligations, that is, before agreeing to the rule of solidarity on foreign debt repayment should it be necessary.

using world-market prices and competition to guide production decisions; instituting measures to break down regional and local barriers to labor and capital product mobility on the domestic market; providing greater autonomy to enterprises by permitting them to retain their earnings and to respond to market signals; using financial sanctions to discipline inefficient producers (implying an end to government protection of failing firms, redirection of investment for regional development, and subsidies to maintain cross-regional wage levels); and increasing the use of private resources to reduce the slack in services and employment.

In effect, these changes extend the orthodox approach toward foreign liquidity to the problems of domestic inflation and unemployment. The commission's program is also a return to the reform strategy of the 1960s and to the goal of eliminating the differences between Yugoslavia and OECD countries in labor productivity, economic efficiency, and competitiveness. The export profile that should result, according to the program, includes technologically sophisticated processed goods, particularly metal products and chemicals; tourism; and domestic raw materials and food; in addition to production techniques suited to the country's raw materials and labor surplus.[58]

To achieve these ends, the reform program advocates a "realistic" exchange rate, phased liberalization of imports, a national foreign-exchange market, economic incentives to export production, and joint-venture legislation (enacted in 1985) to enable older industries in the north to restructure with new technology. To promote regional development, the commission suggested that the Federal Fund (always a target of liberal reformers) be transformed from a vehicle of fiscal redistribution supplementing the resources of budgets in the less developed regions to a vehicle that would stimulate the growth of real capital and labor markets among regions. The program's solution to unemployment in the southern regions appears to lie in lower labor costs and a dual economy for export specialization.

A key aspect of the program is the elimination of the possibilities for financial laxness on the part of enterprises and banks. The program offers two solutions. The first would reduce the economic authority of regional and local party and government leaders. This should result from such policies as the uniform and market criteria for pricing utilities and directing economic resources, the transfer to private resources of some of the tasks of local governments (housing, social services) and the election of clients to the local boards that administer such services, the addition of delegates from enterprises to the Federal Fund, and recentralization of the accounting system for foreign borrowing. This effort to diminish their authority is also clear in the shift of responsibility for implementing the policies from regional and local govern-

---

58. As Burkett argues, this appears to be a reversal of the Heckscher-Ohlin prescription; see his "Stabilization Measures," p. 22.

ments to financial and economic experts, illustrated by the enhanced authority of the Social Accounting Service (an office of the National Bank and its regional affiliates) and the effort to increase the number of trained economists employed by enterprises. Also, the commission recommends that incomes policies—self-management agreements to tie incomes to productivity under the reform—be supervised by a firm's trade union branch rather than by government agencies.

The second solution would try to free economic decision makers from social and political pressures by extensive revision of banking and labor legislation and then to increase their economic incentives.[59] Thus, producers' prices would be freed from the contracting system. Any loss of enterprise revenue as a result of price controls to ensure minimal living standards would be compensated. Tax reform would cut tax levels from 35 to 30 percent, replace obligatory enterprise contributions to local governments and to social funds for income transfers to fulfill the principle of solidarity with taxation on incomes and property, and excuse unprofitable firms from taxes and depreciation while they reorganize. Lagging investment in housing, social welfare, infrastructure, agriculture, and trades would be stimulated by private resources: private investment and independent, small businesses (particularly to encourage the repatriation and productive use of the earnings of returning migrants as well as their employment), changes in landholding limits, user fees, and higher retail prices.

Thus, while macroeconomic stabilization policies reflected the orthodox response of monetary authorities and the FEC to deficits on the balance of payments from 1949 onward, the Kraigher Commission on policies of structural adjustment recommended a process of liberalization and export orientation similar to the economic reforms of the 1960s. Like those of the 1960s, the shifts in policy orientation in the 1980s sought to limit the opportunities for political intervention in economic decisions and thus to replace the regulatory and administrative apparatus of the previous period with new institutional actors. Because the policy also implied that solidarity as a value would no longer inform policy, it seemed likely that political reforms would be required as a substitute for financial compensation.

Conclusion

The response of Yugoslav policy makers to the world recession and debt crisis of 1980–83 introduced no change in their long-standing approach to

59. On the legislation to increase financial discipline, see Peter Knight, *Financial Discipline and Structural Adjustment in Yugoslavia: Rehabilitation and Bankruptcy of Loss-Making Enterprises*, Staff Working Paper no. 705 (Washington, D.C.: World Bank, 1984). The laws are: the Law on Rehabilitation and Liquidation of Organizations of Associated Labor; the Law on Securing Working Capital; the Law on Securing Payments among Users of Social Resources;

balance-of-payments adjustment: monetarist orthodoxy combined with administrative controls and renewed foreign borrowing while the deflationary medicine was being swallowed. The reform program that the Kraigher Commission had recommended, on the other hand, clearly reversed the policies of 1974–79 on the role of foreign trade in the strategy for economic growth, mechanisms of internal allocation, and redistributive goals. The implications of this shift for both economic advantage and political power have led to sharp disagreements within ruling circles. References to the "paper unity" of their unanimous adoption of the reform package suggest agreement on the principles of repaying the foreign debt and increasing exports but *not* on the methods of achieving those goals.[60] Two questions thus arise. Why was this choice made over others? What effect are the politics of austerity and reform likely to have on the new policies and their implementation?

This essay argues that Yugoslav foreign economic policy can best be explained by the dual base—domestic and external—on which the power of its political leadership rests. That base was formed by the development strategy chosen in the late 1940s and, in particular, by its influence on the form of Yugoslav relations with the world economy, on the limited economic role of the state, and on the bargaining among domestic interests over economic policy. In contrast to the policy shift of the early 1970s, when the domestic bases of the party's power appeared threatened, the reversal of the early 1980s was a response to the external bases of that power: namely, the conditions underlying Yugoslavia's special position in the international arena which allows it to maneuver among competing blocs and gain more than its size would predict, and its economic capacity to support a political balance among competing interests at home.

The choice of policies suggests strongly, in other words, that the ruling elite in Yugoslavia views any action that would alter either its development strategy or its special relations with the world economy as threatening.[61] Despite the objections of many leaders to rescheduling the debt, despite

---

the Law on the Social Accounting Service; a law to tie payments out of joint reserve funds to movements in the retail price index; and a law limiting increases in personal income to workers in loss-making or illiquid work organizations to 50% of that in the average minimum wage in the republic or province.

60. Gojko Marinković, "Šesnaest plenuma—jedna nit," *Danas* 162 (26 March 1985), pp. 7–9. Participants in the Central Committee discussions refer often to the parallels between the tone of these meetings and the tone of meetings leading up to "Karadjordjevo," the meeting of the party leadership in December 1971, when the Croatian leadership was asked to resign for allowing economic disagreements to manifest themselves in political nationalism, a meeting that signaled the end of the trade strategy of the 1960s. The regional disagreements were also manifest in the spring 1985 debate over the different versions of the same stories on the stabilization policy appearing in the regional editions of the LCY newspaper, *Komunist*.

61. Political integration, important in countries' responses to world economic recession, takes different forms in Eastern Europe: a single leader in Romania; a unity coalition in East Germany; the military in Poland; and the temporary success of one faction in Hungary and Yugoslavia (see the essays by Ronald Linden, Thomas Baylis, and Ellen Comisso and Paul Marer in this volume).

threats by members of the government during 1982–85 to turn eastward if the West continued to be unsupportive, and despite the sharp conflicts at high govenment and party levels over policies required by international financial authorities, rescheduling did take place. Also, the prime minister visited Washington in April 1985, and the IMF's policies toward interest rates, the exchange rate, a foreign-exchange market, and restrictions on aggregate demand (including reductions in personal income and required pay cuts in enterprises showing losses) prevailed. The renewal of these policies and the decision to speed up their implementation in 1983–84 were in response to IMF criticism made after its August 1982 visit that spending cuts, interest rates, and the pace of devaluation had not been satisfactory. The return of control over foreign-exchange allocation to the National Bank (against which the Slovene government held the Federal Assembly deadlocked for a night) came after "pressure from Western creditors to put some centralized order into its loose system."[62] The structural changes in foreign-trade policy to reduce the trade deficit were those proposed by the World Bank mission.[63]

A second reason for this policy choice is that the changes in the economic role of the government which other strategies would have required were clearly unacceptable to those chosen by the party leadership to formulate the new policy. Opting for liberalization, competing interests have agreed to disagree on specific policies and beneficiaries in order to protect the current distribution of authority over economic decision making. In contrast, planning; a coherent and directive industrial policy; a national, enforceable incomes policy; or even a countercyclical monetary and fiscal policy would require changes in the actual functions of the government's economic authority, in the rights of both enterprises and subordinate governments, and in the consensual basis of economic policy making which would also undercut the bases of economic and political power in Yugoslavia. That this is not simply an issue of centralization alone is clear from the fact that significant opposition failed to prevent the renewed authority of the National Bank—certainly a form of centralization—or the policies of a uniform, flexible exchange rate,[64] a realistic positive interest rate, and customs liberalization—all centrally defined methods of fiscal redistribution and investment policy.

Third, to the extent that there was any bargaining among domestic interests over the policy details at this stage, the advantage in Yugoslavia in what is perceived as a crisis of accumulation (trade revenues, inflation, and economic growth) lies with those who have greater market power—especially foreign trade and export firms. This bargaining strength may explain why the export profile that is being promoted reflects the current regional and sectoral dis-

---

62. Cited in David Buchan, "Rescheduling the Problem Debts," *The Banker*, October 1983, pp. 47–49.
    63. See the World Bank, *Yugoslavia: Adjustment Policies*, especially pp. 94–96.
    64. The Croatian political leadership fought unsuccessfully for a dual exchange rate; the policy of exchange-rate depreciation met significant protest.

tribution of export industries as well as the growing fears of Slovenia and many export firms that they were falling behind technologically during the 1970s. The position of reformers on redistributive issues, moreover, reflects their predominance from areas with lower unemployment and higher per capita living standards and private assets, including foreign-currency holdings.

The coalition of necessity among economic liberals, political liberals, and political conservatives who adopted the program for reform is vulnerable on a number of points. The first is the choice of new policies available should economic revival not be forthcoming. The second is the politics of austerity: the social disorder, efforts at survival, or even sabotage by the disadvantaged. The third is the politics of reform: the form of solidarity—the compensating compromise—on which political equilibrium comes to rest. This raises a second question: will the reform program be implemented or will the domestic bases of the party's power also become threatened and lead to another policy reversal?

The economic policies to address the debt produced a current account surplus in 1983 and by 1985 had reduced the deficit. Activity in foreign capital markets in 1985 indicated restored confidence, as Yugoslavia compared favorably to Latin American debtors. But exports fell in 1985, and the government and most firms had stopped borrowing. Domestic inflation continued to rise: producer prices (often significantly lower than retail prices) rose 76.9 percent between May 1984 and May 1985. Investment, particularly expenditure by governmental and social funds, had been sharply cut, threatening the economy with long-term structural damage.

The austerity policies have two consequences: they affect those with lesser assets disproportionately, and they contradict the moral economy of solidarity—the norms developed to ensure against the vulnerabilities to economic cycles. By the end of 1984, average income had fallen to 70 percent of the officially defined minimum for a family of four, and surveys reported a decline in living standards every year after 1980 for 80–86 percent of the population. Despite an increase in moonlighting, the savings of 80 percent of Yugoslav households were depleted and essentials were being cut. Almost a million people were unemployed.[65]

The survival tactics of these individuals—greater absenteeism to work second jobs, theft, barter, the exchange of produce for favors, and pressures to employ relatives—inevitably undermine the new economic policy. Politicians in poorer towns and regions most affected by the recession, faced with fewer resources to fulfill their responsibility for unemployment and local services, rely on nonmarket mechanisms: collegial reciprocity, personal connections, forced mergers of failing enterprises with profitable ones in the

65. Djuro Zagorac, "Čega se boji onaj koji radi," *Danas* (9 April 1985), pp. 21–22, and Josip Županov, "Gradjani se tresu, država je stabilna," *Intervju*, 4 January 1985, pp. 12–14. Of the 970,000 registered unemployed in mid-1984, only 50,000 received unemployment compensation, which was then on average 20% of the average wage.

same locality to spread resources and risks, and the security police. The need for political resources gives an additional impetus to efforts by party cadre to retain control, as is demonstrated by their apparent resistance on ideological grounds to increasing the scope for private resources, the spate of political trials, and the election of a predominantly conservative slate to the state Presidency in May 1984.[66]

Furthermore, both politicians and private citizens search for scapegoats and ways to differentiate in the distribution of scarce resources, such as jobs, among citizens with equal rights. The most likely result of this scapegoating in Yugoslavia is always a rise in nationalist antagonisms. Tensions were most pronounced in Kosovo, the poorest region in Yugoslavia, where student demonstrations and Albanian nationalist meetings began in the spring of 1981. Demanding changes in investment policy toward Kosovo and republic status, the protesters were answered by military occupation. Nationalist incidents, religious revival, and antifeminist backlash surfaced during the period of 1981–84.[67]

The government has nothing to offer in exchange for austerity, however, other than promises of future results. To persuade the public of the necessity of temporary sacrifices, the leadership chose a predictable but risky strategy. The decision to concede publicly the existence of a crisis began as an attempt to demonstrate the government's impotence in the face of a general international crisis and thereby rally support around the goal of defending Yugoslav independence. To explain the need to intensify austerity, the government shifted its argument. Because their difficulties were not independent of the international crisis, they argued, Yugoslavs had to assume responsibility for creating the crisis. Leaders had not implemented the wisest of policies, but citizens had also lived for a long time beyond their means. This attitude of mea culpa and democratic appeal seemed to gain the leadership the popular support it needed.[68] It did not, however, reduce the opposition of strategic

66. It is also not surprising that the Slovenes tried to institute competitive elections for the state Presidency, announcing three candidates, and that no other republic followed suit. The Slovenes consequently withdrew their initiative and sent a political conservative.

67. Nationalist incidents were reported in Montenegro in 1981; in Croatia frequently between November 1982 and May 1984; in Slovenia (over language) from January 1982 to February 1983; in Serbia, especially in response to the Kosovo troubles, since 1981; in Vojvodina and in Macedonia in 1983. On the antifeminist backlash see Slavenka Drakulić-Ilić, *Smrtni Grijesi Feminizma: Ogledi o Mudologiji* (Zagreb: Znanje, 1984). A catalogue of nationalist and religious manifestations can be found in the *South Slav Journal*. The growth in religious activities, as in many other parts of the world, is striking: 50,000 people gathered at the Marija Bistrica shrine on Assumption Day in 1982; several new, lavish mosques have been built for Moslems settled in northern cities; and meditation cults, such as that of Raja Yoga, have sprung up among the young in Bosnia. Conflicts between orthodoxy and the party have also increased; for example, in Bosnia a priest was sentenced for the content of his sermon, and in April 1985 the archbishop of the Serbian Orthodox Church refused to meet with the minister for relations with religious communities for the first time in postwar history.

68. Josip Županov, "Gradjani," calls this political quiescence the "Yugoslav miracle," although he goes on to suggest that the explanation lies in the lack of institutional vehicles for aggregating interests; the result is a fragmentation of action into informal networks, local solutions, and passive rebellion—substandard work, theft, nonpayment of bills, sick leave, and so forth.

groups, whose members included professionals entrusted to enforce the new policies and certain regional politicians. Furthermore, the invitation to participate in the search for remedies and therefore to examine causes of the crisis encouraged dissenters.

Finally, the long-term prospects for reform depend on the political equilibrium that the leadership can manufacture. In similar situations in the past, two forces have fashioned this equilibrium. Kardelj drafted new constitutions in order to institutionalize the liberal position on economic policy and, simultaneously, to create forms of representation and decision making which lessen the power of the opposition; these also prevented the accumulation of political grievances that might have threatened the system itself (e.g., a mass movement, a conflict between ethnic communities, or "dangerous alliances"—to use Kardelj's apt phrase—of rich against poor, north against south). Tito's political purges removed intransigents and halted any escalating conflicts that appeared to exceed the party's capacity to retain its power.

Between 1982 and 1985, there were increasing calls for political reform and debates on the "true meaning of AVNOJ"—the 1943 pact laying the federal and single-party foundations of the state. A proposal by a leading Belgrade politician to revise economic policy making along lines more functional than territorial was trounced at the Twelfth Party Congress in 1982, but the leadership did establish two ad hoc commissions—one on implementation of the reform, and one on constitutional reform. The second is responsible to the Federal Social Council on constitutional issues as well as to the party leadership and is chaired by a university professor of political science who is also an old-guard Partisan, a Central Committee member, a Serb, and a Supreme Court justice. Its early reports contained only a series of compromises, however.

To date the dual weapons of recession and political trial have effectively prevented mass political activity, but the party leadership remains internally divided. There have been unprecedented challenges between the Central Committee and the Presidency of the League, as well as open duels between republican politicians.[69] Disagreement within the Parliament has forced the government to resort increasingly to temporary measures to enact legislation. In December 1984 the finance minister was fired for obstructing a political compromise in the new law allocating rights to foreign exchange. The compromise was between the National Bank and enterprises, and between the conditions of the IMF program and the recommendations of the consortium

69. See note 66. The conflict between technocratic reformers without a political base in alliance with international authorities and politician-technocrats, familiar in many Latin American countries, can be seen in the published exchange of letters between two economists with different perspectives who specialize in monetary problems: Aleksander Bajt and Ivo Perišin. The latter (also a Central Committee member) charges the former with encouraging the IMF to be strict in order to push Yugoslavia over the brink of reform; see *NIN* 1784 (10 March 1985) and *Danas* 163 (2 April 1985), pp. 10–11.

of commercial banks and Western governments established to coordinate Yugoslav debt rescheduling.

If there is to be a new political compromise, it will have to meet a number of difficult conditions. First, it must satisfy the leaderships of both Croatia and Serbia, the two largest regions in which more than two-thirds of the population reside. Current Croatian leaders are the victors of a purge in 1971–72 against leaders of the reforms of the 1960s who thought Croatia would benefit by the country's assumption of an international posture and viewed the other regions as a drain on Croatia's growth potential; moreover, the current leaders predominate from poorer, inward-oriented regions in Croatia, such as Istria and the Dalmatian hinterland.[70] The near-bankruptcy of Croatia's largest bank in 1982 and the republic's need for central assistance in these matters probably reinforced the current opposition of the Croatian leaders to enlarging the scope of the market and to outwardness.[71] The current Serbian leadership favors the market and exports but is leaning against political reform because of changes in the balance of power among its producers and because of two formative purges—of economists opposed to the 1965 reform on the grounds that it dismantled federal development planning and of the governmental leadership in 1972 for supporting liberal reform of the party and challenging Tito personally. The influence of Slovenia will, as always, be significant because of its economic strength and ability to join several political alliances.

Second, any new compromise must find a way to compensate the less developed regions for their lowered economic status in the reform's foreign-trade and development policies. Third, the compromise would have to combine some of the institutional changes of the economic reformers with the continuing dominance of political conservatives because of the political lessons both groups learned in the 1960s and the difficult international conditions of the 1980s. In any case, if there is an agreement, it will be a collective agreement to sacrifice particular interests to the bases of party rule in general. The outcome in both economic policy and institutional reform should reveal much about the competing claims to authority as well as competing hypotheses about the distribution of power in Yugoslav society.

70. The prime minister was also a member of this team, however, which supports the argument that roles can determine policy more than regional representation can, at least in the federal government.

71. The threat of bankruptcy resulted from the dominance among the banks' depositors of the country's main oil producer and from several export-related investment failures, namely, the joint-venture petrochemical plant, Dina on Krk, and the aluminum-processing plant of Obrovac.

The southern European NICs
P. Nikiforos Diamandouros

To interpret the responses of Greece, Portugal, and Spain to changes in the international political economy over the past decade, I would like to borrow eclectically from the conceptual frameworks developed by both Ellen Comisso and Peter Katzenstein. From the former, I take the stress on the centrality of politics and choice and the notion that state structures create the *possibility* for a course of action without determining the action itself. From the latter, I retain the general proposition that during periods of hegemonic decline those possibilities for choice widen and include the option of changing state structure itself. To these I would add that the nature of options, the flexibility of response they imply, and the realm of choice itself depend heavily on the level of development of a particular state and civil society as well as on their relationship with one another. The more negative and less reinforcing the relationship, the more the respective needs of civil society and state will conflict. The greater the conflict, the more circumscribed the range of options available to political actors. In the case of the southern European newly industrializing countries (NICs), the changing articulation between civil society and the state and the external pressures influencing it inform both the evolution of domestic structures and the policy choices of elites within them.

The responses of the southern European states to the international economic disturbances of the 1970s and 1980s were formulated during a time of transition to and consolidation of competitive politics, that is, amidst structural change in the states themselves. To understand how such structural change was possible, it is necessary to bear in mind that although Greece, Portugal, and Spain were all late industrializers, their economies were integrated in the international market as early as the second half of the 19th century. This integration, in combination with the long urban tradition present in these countries, heightened the urban-rural cleavage in their societies and produced a social structure that is significantly different from both that which prevailed in Western Europe and that which until recently survived in Eastern Europe.

International Organization 40, 2, Spring 1986   0020-8183 $5.00

Though more urbanized than Eastern Europe, southern Europe was less urbanized than Western Europe. The inverse relationship prevailed in the rural sector, where, in addition, landlessness and minifundism existed side by side until the very recent past.

An additional, crucial characteristic of these social formations is the presence of an overinflated, cumbersome, and weak state that, whether directly through the public sector or indirectly through the ever-expanding network of publicly controlled enterprises, has traditionally played a central role in their economy. In addition to providing resources for development, the state has also acted as an employer and a source of income for a large number of citizens. A final factor responsible for the almost century-long state of suspended animation in which southern European development seemed to be held was the emergence throughout the region of large, petit-bourgeois strata, whether of the artisanal variety (which, again, had a long and honorable tradition in the area), or of state-dependent sectors, often referred to in the literature as "state bourgeoisies," which even today constitute a very significant part of the population in these countries.

Thus, the state structure that had evolved by the end of World War II was a highly contradictory one. The state itself was highly centralized; yet civil society remained heterogeneous and fragmented. Although low differentiation characterized the state's relationship with certain economic sectors, great distance prevailed between it and others, including agriculture. Despite dependence on more advanced states for resources and defense, autarchic aspirations guided the development of the state sector in all three countries, while both Portugal and Spain exerted efforts to hold onto the remains of empire. Thus, although civil societies in the southern European countries were sufficiently developed to make open and nonauthoritarian alternatives possible—a critical feature differentiating them from both Eastern Europe and East Asia—nevertheless, not until very recently were such alternatives capable of prevailing.

Indeed, it is hardly surprising that authoritarian rule seemed to the political elite a means of preventing the above-mentioned contradictions from pulling state and society apart. In sharp reversal of the sequence observed in the advanced industrial West, the liberalization of the political system and the introduction of parliamentary institutions in southern Europe occurred before industrialization and were not accompanied by the intense social struggles that in the West lessened the social distance separating the working classes from the bourgeoisie and made possible their eventual incorporation in the political system. In southern Europe, on the contrary, a weak bourgeoisie was able to exclude the working classes from autonomous participation in the political system until well into the present century. The resulting legitimacy crisis affected the systems of both liberal political democracy and capitalism, dividing these countries between parliamentary and antiparliamentary forces, capitalist and anticapitalist forces, promarket and statist forces. No single force was powerful enough to prevail upon the others and achieve a political and cultural hegemony that would allow for a peaceful resolution to the crisis. It was these cleavages and the sharply competing, often mutually exclusive, social visions to which they gave rise which accounted for the long history of alternation between competitive politics and authoritarian rule in the region.

Ironically, the preconditions for overcoming this impasse among domestic structures and for putting an end to the vicious circle of democratic breakdowns and authoritarian takeovers seem to have been laid during the latest period of long authoritarian rule which lasted from the interwar period to the mid-1970s, without interruption in the case of the Iberian countries, and with intervals of foreign occupation (1941–44), civil war (1946–49), and "restricted" democracy (1949–67) in Greece. The dramatic social and economic transformation of these societies during the past three decades, brought about by unprecedentedly high rates of growth, and the rapid, though sharply uneven, development of their productive structures seem to have significantly attenuated the intensity of some major cleavages that have long impeded social reconciliation and to have eliminated, or at least marginalized and neutralized, some of the most extreme antisystem forces.[1] In the 1970s, a combination of war and institutional exhaustion (Portugal), physical death of a leader (Spain), and foreign-policy adventurism (Greece) brought down the authoritarian regimes in the region. As a result, the coalition of forces willing to commit themselves to the rules of political democracy seemed sufficiently strengthened to stand a good chance of seeing its social vision prevail and of rendering its authoritarian alternative permanently marginal. Reinforcing this trend during the past decade has been the smooth alternation in governmental incumbency, which brought parties of the democratic left to power in all three countries, as well as the willingness—especially pronounced in Spain, the most developed of the three—of major social and political forces to moderate their demands and to enter into explicit or implicit pacts designed to contain potential dangers to the maintenance of the democratic order.

There was also an important regional dimension both to the creation of such a structural impasse and to its overcoming. Southern European fortunes have long been linked to those of its northern counterpart. Even in the 19th century, the intense struggles that so profoundly marked the region's history revolved around and reflected the major political and social debates centering on liberalism, constitutionalism, parliamentarism, and, more generally, reform which dominated the broader European scene during that period.

1. On postwar economic change in the southern European NICs, see Allan Williams, ed., *Southern Europe Transformed: Political and Economic Change in Greece, Italy, Portugal and Spain* (London: Harper & Row, 1984), and Loukas Tsoukalis, *The European Community and Its Mediterranean Enlargement* (London: Allen & Unwin, 1981), which is the best source on EC relations with the southern European NICs.

In this century, too, developments in the advanced industrial north have influenced the domestic balance of forces within the European south. The general disillusionment in Europe with the manifest inability of liberal institutions to cope with the dislocations unleashed by World War I and the subsequent economic crisis combined with the emergence of fascism as an apparently legitimate, dynamic alternative to the liberal democratic model to produce an international climate conducive to authoritarian experiments. As a result, antiliberal, antiparliamentary forces bent on exclusionist strategies of governance were able to seize power in southern Europe. Isolationism, protectionism, and general introvertedness, hallmarks of the international system during the interwar period, unquestionably enhanced their prospects for survival.

Conversely, the complete collapse and utter delegitimation of fascism during and after World War II produced a regional European climate that was decidedly hostile to authoritarian rule. Although a combination of U.S. hegemony, anticommunism, and, more generally, cold war tensions made it possible to include authoritarian Portugal and quasi-authoritarian Greece, but not Spain, in the North Atlantic Treaty Organization (NATO), the southern European regimes were poignantly excluded from all major European organizations exhibiting sensitivity over the presence or absence of competitive politics in their member countries. From 1967 to 1974, Greece's association agreement with the European Economic Community (EEC) was frozen, loans from the European Investment Bank were held up, and the regime had to walk out of the Council of Europe to avoid a formal expulsion. In short, during the postwar period the European regional environment presented southern European governments with no viable alternative to political democracy. The net result of these developments was an increasing congruence between regional and domestic structures that favored abandonment of authoritarian rule and, to use Comisso's language, defined the possibilities within which social and political forces inclined toward political democracy could act to attain their objectives.

The 1973 oil crisis and strategic considerations that subsequently arose provided an additional dimension that ultimately proved favorable to the forces of change in the region. Heightened awareness that the crisis had increased the strategic importance of the Mediterranean and had made security of access to oil a top priority precipitated a reevaluation among major international actors of their attitudes toward the southern European authoritarian regimes. According to one recent study, "[v]ery soon after October 1973, three governments at least (those of the USA, the UK and West Germany) realised the importance of maintaining pro-western stability in Southern Europe at a time when economically this had become more difficult to achieve . . . for countries which had based their industrialisation strategies on abundant and cheap energy . . . [and] were among the most energy-dependent . . . in the OECD." On the one hand, the assassination of Spain's designated heir apparent and the worsening of the Basque problem called into question Spain's ability to manage an orderly succession to the ailing Franco; on the other, Portugal was mired in a colonial war that was severely straining its resources. Not surprisingly, in the United States and Western Europe "[t]houghts turned to the question of how to facilitate an orderly transition to democracy, not leaving any void that could be exploited by the Soviet Union."[2]

Thus, at the beginning of the international dislocations associated with the oil crises of the mid- and late 1970s, when the capacity of the hegemonic power to regulate the system was rapidly declining, the possibilities open to domestic forces favoring political democracy had increased considerably in southern Europe. Favorable conditions on the regional, European level enhanced these opportunities. As Comisso correctly reminds us, however, these developments served only to expand the range of options and to provide actors with greater flexibility. They did not by themselves prescribe specific courses of action. Nevertheless, the role of politics was commensurately broadened during this period of uncertainty and flux.

Two major, related observations can be made about the southern European NICs' responses to the major events of the previous decade. One is the extent to which the trends described above continued and intensified during the critical period of regime transition, especially once authoritarian rule had formally ended, thus making the need to ensure the survival of the successor democratic regimes paramount.[3] The second observation highlights the fact that, because of the overriding significance of the various political problems associated with the southern European NICs' transition to political democracy, formulating a response to the economic dislocations that the oil crises caused was accorded a low priority, and the region delayed taking concerted action. This was especially true of the first oil crisis, which to a large degree coincided with regime changes in both Portugal and Greece.

The political classes managing the transitions to democracy in southern Europe were preoccupied with ensuring the viability of the new regimes. To this end, they employed a variety of strategies both domestic and international. Domestically, their energies were directed toward securing agreement on the rules of the transition among social and political forces supporting or at least tolerating the new regimes and, as time went on, the nascent political systems over which they presided. Although such priorities inevitably meant that strategies for resolving the economic problems associated with the oil crisis were relegated to the back burner, all three new regimes had the option of

2. Both quotations are from the valuable article by Alfred Tovias, "The International Context of Democratic Transition," in Geoffrey Pridham, ed., *The New Mediterranean Democracies: Regime Transition in Spain, Greece and Portugal* (London: Frank Cass, 1984), p. 160.
3. On the transitions in southern Europe, in general, see P. Nikiforos Diamandouros et al., *A Bibliographical Essay on Southern Europe and Its Recent Transition to Political Democracy* (Florence: European University Institute, 1986).

undertaking a series of foreign-policy initiatives that, by turning weakness into strength, would strengthen them internally.

Put somewhat differently, the southern European NICs were able to postpone their day of reckoning with the economic problems resulting from the oil crisis by capitalizing on international and, especially, regional willingness to provide them with political, economic, and ideological support in order to promote stability in what was then known as "the soft underbelly of Europe" and to contain the danger of an authoritarian involution.[4]

The case of Portugal undoubtedly offers the most striking example of such support. The weakest of the three countries economically, its weakness was exacerbated by a massive wave of repatriation from its former colonies at the very moment when the country's economy was severely jolted by the loss of those colonies and by the oil-price shock. Portugal also desired to contain the danger from the left and to neutralize the ascending fortunes of the decidedly pro-Soviet Communist party, its civilian and military allies, and collaborators. Through a variety of initiatives and channels, international actors (the United States, the International Monetary Fund [IMF], the Socialist International) and, especially, European states (West Germany, in particular), organizations (the EEC, the European Investment Bank), political parties, trade unions, and other structures extended critically needed financial and political support to the government of Mario Soares and his Socialist party which represented the largest force committed to political democracy in the country. Soares banked heavily on this European support in seeking to secure a solid electoral base for his government. Even before formally applying for membership in the EEC in 1977, he prominently played the "European card," repeatedly linking the "democratic option" with Europe and, in the 1976 electoral campaign, using "*Europa conosco*" (Europe is with us) as one of his major slogans. Financially, too, if the country's large gold reserves initially served to postpone the need for adjustment, in the long run international and European support proved vital in helping Portugal overcome two major balance-of-payments crises and avoid further dislocation to its fragile economy.

A similar scenario, albeit with certain variations that were mainly a result of its slightly stronger economic situation, prevailed in Greece. There, too, the new government of Constantine Karamanlis and his conservative New Democracy party sought to turn weakness into strength by taking full advantage of the "European option" to enhance the chances of democratic consolidation in that country. At the same time, such a policy and especially the urgency with which it was adopted reflected the new government's pressing need to distance itself from the United States at a moment when the latter's friendly relations with the colonels' regime and its perceived tilt toward Turkey in the 1974 Cyprus crisis had generated a powerful wave of anti-

4. See Tsoukalis, *European Community*, pp. 242–56.

Americanism in Greece. Stressing the European over the Atlantic connection (Greece withdrew from the military structure of NATO in protest over NATO's behavior in the Cyprus crisis) was, under the circumstances, the only viable option open to the new government which was congruent with its paramount objective of consolidating political democracy in Greece.

While these purely political considerations prevented more narrow economic concerns linked to the oil shocks from reaching the top of the government's agenda, it is also true that, initially at least, Greece was spared the full impact of the crisis because of growing exports to the Middle East and, especially, its traditionally strong invisible earnings derived from tourism, emigrant remittances, and shipping. These three sources of foreign exchange, though obviously affected somewhat by the downturn in the world economy, continued to provide Greece with sufficient flexibility to mitigate some of the more potentially troublesome aspects of the crisis.

Possessing by far the largest and the strongest economy of the three southern European NICs, Spain was best positioned to postpone responding to the oil crisis and to concentrate instead on the more pressing needs of the transition to democratic politics. In contrast to Portugal and Greece, the end of the authoritarian regime in Spain did not come about as a result of a major crisis (colonial war and military intervention in Portugal, threat of war and general mobilization in Greece) that could then serve as a symbolic *terminus a quo* from which to launch its democratic successor. As a result, the Spanish transition was protracted and extremely delicate, and therefore absorbed the attention and energies of the Spanish political class for almost four years; not until late 1977 did economic problems receive the attention they deserved.

The most striking characteristic of how the new Spanish regime handled political and economic crises was its adoption of a style of resolving problems which sought explicit and implicit agreement from strategically located actors in order to construct as broad a consensus as possible on a series of critical issues. This system of *pactismo* distinguished Spain from both Portugal and Greece. On the one hand, its emergence reflected the precariousness of the transition, the continuing strength of the right, the knowledge that the army would be certain to react in the event of any serious disruption of order, and the consequent need to bring about regime change through a scrupulously *legal* self-transformation. On the other, it was an indication of the degree of articulation attained by civil society and state in Spain which enabled domestic structures to act concertedly in pursuit of such a delicate strategy.

The principle of *pactismo*, used so successfully to generate the political pacts that ensured Spain's smooth and self-legitimating transition to democracy, was also applied to the economic field. In late 1977, through a series of social pacts that came to be known as the Moncloa Agreements, state, business, and trade unions acted together to contain the deteriorating economic scene and to bring about a sorely needed social peace. The ability of the Spanish domestic structures to engage in such inclusive, corporatist arrangements points to the increased capacity of its political and economic system. Many elements of this system resemble those of the advanced industrial north far more than those of the other southern European NICs, not to mention those of the East Asian or East European countries.

If *pactismo* differentiated Spain from the other southern European NICs, Spain's attempt to strengthen its emergent political democracy by drawing upon the widespread international and regional support for the new regime was quite similar. Transformed and rendered more competitive by the rapid industrialization of the previous quarter-century, Spanish business interests supported the country's application for EEC membership in 1977 and shared in the widespread willingness to participate in what was termed the "European adventure." More generally, between 1976 and 1979, Spain cast aside a long tradition of externally imposed isolation and self-generated withdrawal from world affairs and sought to integrate itself more firmly in the international community by joining a series of international and regional organizations, from the Council of Europe to the Inter-American Development Bank.

Ironically, however, the very strength of its more industrialized economy, which had initially allowed Spain to postpone its response to the first oil crisis, became a liability during the second crisis in 1979–80 (before the full impact of the Moncloa Agreements had taken effect). Under the strain of the new oil shock produced by the Iranian Revolution and the Iran-Iraq war, industrial production fell sharply and the Spanish economy experienced a severe recession that quickly translated into among the highest levels of unemployment and inflation in Europe. Responding promptly, the Spanish government renewed the corporatist arrangements mentioned above and instituted a series of other measures designed to prevent the economic crisis from further straining a political system already severely tested by the rise of violence associated with Basque nationalism and, especially, by the failed 1981 coup.

Internationally, the decision of the governing Unión de Centro Democrático (UCD) to seek NATO membership reflected the belief that the chance for modernization and for a broader outlook might provide the country's armed forces with a new sense of purpose and ultimately contribute to the further stabilization and consolidation of the new regime. The socialists' apparent willingness to stay within NATO once they came to power further attests to the significance they, too, came to attach to the long-term domestic benefits to be derived from integrating the military into international structures.

In Portugal and Greece, too, the second oil crisis produced severe shocks. The response, however, was different in each country. Portugal's reaction to the new strains on its balance of payments brought about by the fall in industrial production as well as in its invisible earnings, especially emigrant remittances, was to intensify its efforts to enter the European Community (EC) and to rely more on the European financial community than on the IMF for support in overcoming its problems. Although this did not prevent further recourse to IMF medicine in late 1983, it suggests the political significance Portugal attached to regional European structures and to the benefits to be derived from further integration in them.

In Greece, the effects of the second crisis were already apparent in 1980–81; these were exacerbated by heavy borrowing abroad and the inflationary policies pursued by the New Democracy forces in a vain attempt to buy time and stem the decline of their electoral support. The coming to power of the Greek socialists (PASOK) in late 1981 did not improve the situation. Initially, in fact, it made it worse: PASOK's misconceived policy of reflation and continued borrowing abroad exacerbated the crisis, which did not show signs of abating until late 1983. Thus, 1984 was the first year since 1979 in which the Greek economy registered some significant growth. Like Portugal, Greece failed to institute anything approaching corporatist measures in order to ensure social peace and contain the damage to the economy. Although calls for such measures were voiced in 1984, mainly from the direction of the hard-hit Federation of Greek Industries, the major reasons for avoiding such actions seem to have been structural as well as political. Structurally, the weakness of peak associations rendered such a policy difficult to effect and unlikely to succeed. Politically, PASOK's coming to power sharply exacerbated the left-right cleavage in Greek politics, making such a corporatist policy all the less feasible. Hence, rather than adopting a corporatist response to an external challenge, the government chose to let the state absorb the damage the shocks caused private industry by gaining control of failing firms. Such a strategy was appealing to leftist elements within PASOK; similarly, the latter's presence on the political scene made cooperation unattractive to private industry.

At the same time, the need to avoid further domestic divisions and the sharp deterioration of relations with Turkey at a time when that country's significance for the NATO alliance had considerably increased seem to account for PASOK's decision, once in power, to maintain the country's membership in both the EC and NATO rather than to withdraw from them as had been its preelectoral promise. Undoubtedly the economic gains derived from remaining in the EC and seeking to renegotiate the terms of membership were handsome: not only did such a course blunt the full effect of the crisis on the agricultural sector, which received important subsidies from the Community, but it also provided PASOK with significant political capital that contributed to its reelection in mid-1985. In turn, the unexpectedly large margin of this victory and, more generally, the further consolidation of competitive politics in the country generated the requisite political strength which enabled the government to embark on sorely needed but unpopular economic restructuring policies and, apparently, to contain most of their negative political repercussions.

On the whole, then, the southern European NICs seem to have responded to the crises of the 1970s and early 1980s with remarkable success, given that structural changes in the international economic environment coincided with regime changes in all three countries. Allowing for slight variations that reflected each country's domestic balance of forces and its position in the international division of labor, the common strategy each country followed was to concentrate on the political aspects of the transition to and consolidation of political democracy, and to postpone for as long as possible its response to the problems and dislocations that the two oil crises produced. The success with which these countries pursued that strategy reflected the increased room for maneuver available to domestic structures at that juncture, as well as their willingness to exercise options and act to ensure the survival and viability of the new democratic regimes they were heading.

At one level, this room for maneuvering was largely due to the existence of an international and, especially, regional environment that for both strategic and ideological reasons favored the reemergence of democratic regimes in the region. In this, the contrast with Eastern Europe could not be more striking. Domestically, too, the strengthening of civil society structures, created over a quarter-century of rapid industrial growth, contributed greatly to the increased political capacity of these states to lessen the intensity of social and political cleavages and to contain potentially destabilizing forces. That strengthening of civil society had economic ramifications as well. Indeed, the ability of this particular group of NICs to weather the economic dislocations of the oil crises more easily than might have been expected and successfully to contain their potential for adverse political impact was closely related to the central role the public and publicly controlled sector played in the operation of both state and economy. Put somewhat differently, increasing recourse to the mechanisms of a robust and growing informal economy combined with the well-known capacity of the public and semipublic sectors to contain unemployment to provide these countries with critically needed additional flexibility in both an economic and a political sense.[5] Again, the contrast with the highly centralized, shortage-driven economies of the CMEA suggests not merely the resilience of the structures of the southern European NICs but a certain resourcefulness in the face of adversity closely related to both the position of these countries in the international political economy and to the ability of elites committed to competitive politics to turn it to political advantage.

5. See, for example, R. Hudson and J. R. Lewis, "Capital Accumulation: The Industrialization of Southern Europe?" in Williams, *Southern Europe Transformed*, pp. 179–207. On the informal economy see the unpublished paper by Lauren A. Benton, "The 'Informalization' of Spanish Industry: The Role of Unregulated Labor in Industrial Development" (Mimeo, John Hopkins University, 1986).

The nonsocialist NICs: East Asia
Chalmers Johnson

Ellen Comisso and her colleagues are interested in the differences among all nations in their strategic economic responses to the petroleum price hikes of the 1970s—and, by extension, in why some states consistently outperform others in economic adjustment and growth. In particular, Comisso wants to know why the centrally planned economies (CPEs) of Eastern Europe reacted differently from one another to the shocks of the 1970s and yet, as a group, consistently performed less well than some reference groups, notably the East Asian NICs (newly industrialized countries). At the heart of Comisso's and the other authors' concerns are the notions of state "structure" and "process," particularly as derived from Peter Katzenstein and the other contemporary comparative political economists, since on structural grounds the East European CPEs appear similar to the quasi-corporatist or "bureaucratic authoritarian" NICs elsewhere in the world. They differ primarily in terms of performance—or so it seems. Why? Are structure and process the right variables, and if they are, have they been correctly conceptualized?

Based on the work of all the contributors, including her own, Comisso concludes that structure is the right place to look for explanations of variation in individual country behavior vis-à-vis the other East European CPEs and of all East European CPEs vis-à-vis the rest of the world. Nonetheless, for the concept of structure to be applied in the East European region, it must be modified from that conceived by Katzenstein. (Needless to say, the variable structure in the analysis of social systems is never self-actuating. Structure merely creates incentives and disincentives for various possible courses of action. Even the structure that is most propitious for some desired outcome requires that actors perceive their opportunities and act on them in formulating their policies. Thus, in Comisso's work as well as in Katzenstein's, the concept of structure is close to Karl Popper's idea of institutions: "Institutions are like fortresses. They must be well designed and properly manned.")[1]

1. Karl Popper, *The Poverty of Historicism* (New York: Harper Torchbooks, 1964), p. 66.
International Organization 40, 2, Spring 1986   0020-8183 $5.00
© 1986 by the Massachusetts Institute of Technology and the World Peace Foundation

Comisso begins by considering and rejecting four well-established theories that purport to explain the economic behavior of the East European socialist countries. These are: the ruling-class paradigm developed by Milovan Djilas, the Soviet hegemony paradigm, the group-politics paradigm, and the bureaucratic-politics paradigm. Comisso finds that these views are either too crude and undifferentiated to explain the variations that interest her or unsubstantiated by the data on political and economic behavior. She is utterly persuasive in her analysis on this score.

The author thus returns to Katzenstein but now determined to modify his concept of structure and make it applicable to Eastern Europe (a region the author acknowledges that Katzenstein did *not* have in mind when he advanced his constructs). Comisso's first two elements of structure are from Katzenstein: (1) the degree of centralization of decision making in the state and the economy—a measure that is uniformly high in all the East European CPEs; and (2) the degree to which assets are either state or privately owned—a measure that is uniformly statist in all the East European CPEs. To these elements of structure the author adds two more of her own: (1) limited sovereignty, meaning the structure of relations between a given East European party and the Communist party of the Soviet Union; and (2) the structure of the single, hegemonic party organized on Leninist lines that occurs in all the East European CPEs but with significant variations, as, for example, in Poland during the 1980s.

Supplementing this fourfold conception of structure, the author further posits and elaborates two broad types of political processes that are typical of and adapted to this structure. These two processes are important in explaining variations among outputs from the common structure. They are "patrimonialism," either of the charismatic or the personality-cult varieties, and "collegiality," either of the aristocratic or the oligarchic varieties. Although these two processes differ significantly, the author nonetheless notes that "in both patrimonial and collegial systems, the party enjoys a monopoly of the means of collective action; and power within it flows from top to bottom." As we shall see, this latter element may be more important than any differences between patrimonialism and collegiality.

This four-point construct of structure and two-point construct of process is, in essence, Comisso's theory, which she employs to explain variations in economic performance among the East European CPEs and between the East European CPEs and the rest of the world. I think it is a good one, very well presented. It does, however, raise the question of why superficially similar systems—for example, the republics of Korea (South) and China (on Taiwan)—consistently outperform the East European CPEs in terms of growth, external debt burdens, change of industrial structure, or almost any measure one would care to choose. What is it in their structures that can account for the differences, particularly when it is recalled that the Kuomintang (National People's party), the politically hegemonic party that reigns over

Taiwan, was reorganized in 1924 along explicitly Leninist lines? This is a difficult question. Given the ideological influences on politico-economic theorizing, it may be easier to explain why the East European CPEs are doing so poorly than to explain why the East Asian NICs (Hong Kong, Singapore, Taiwan, and South Korea) are doing so well. Let us nonetheless survey even if superficially some of the structural theories of East Asian NIC success.

Just as Comisso had to raise and reject four predominant theories before introducing her own, those of us in the East Asian field have one particular theory that we must acknowledge and then knock down. This is the theory, advanced by such luminaries as Milton Friedman and generally supported by professional economists in English-speaking countries, that all the governments of Japan and its successor NICs do is to "get the prices right." Actually, they do much more than that. As Gordon White of the Institute of Development Studies, Sussex, and Robert Wade of the World Bank put it, "The empirical evidence at least allows us to make the negative argument that Taiwan and South Korea cannot be used to support the generalized case that if only the government of a developing country 'gets the prices right,' then that country too can expect the marvellous growth of Taiwan and South Korea. The governments of these countries have done much more than get the prices right (plus of course provide infrastructure and maintain a macro balance). Without these other things, getting prices right may have no more effect than pushing a piece of string."[2]

All of the East Asian high-growth systems have been characterized by soft or quasi-authoritarian political structures (de facto one-party systems in Japan and Taiwan, colonialism in Hong Kong, and patrimonialism of the charismatic and military varieties, respectively, in Singapore and Korea) and guided market economies. They also have been or are the fastest growing industrial economies ever recorded. In recent years this combination of authoritarian politics and capitalist economics has exerted a profound magnetic pull on mainland China, which until very recently retained all the basic elements of Soviet-type central planning—that is, direct politico-administrative regulation of both macro- and microeconomic processes of production, distribution, exchange, and accumulation. The People's Republic of China of late seems to have rejected for its economy both Leninism and Anglo-American capitalism in favor of an approximation of the classic Japanese and contemporary Korean and Taiwanese models—or at any rate that is the trend within China under Deng Xiaoping. It is interesting to note that much of the current discussion of economic policy in China is couched in terms of alleged Hungarian theory or practice. As a Chinese economist in Beijing (who must remain nameless for obvious reasons) commented to me recently, "We write many articles about the Hungarian economy, but as you read them, you

2. Gordon White and Robert Wade, "Developmental States in East Asia," *IDS Sussex Bulletin* 15 (April 1984), p. 3.

should understand that Hungary is a euphemism for the Republic of Korea. We are not really all that interested in Hungary." It is, of course, less ideologically dangerous to talk about Chinese economic reform in putative Hungarian terms.

What, then, are the most important characteristics of the political structures and processes of the East Asian NICs? Numerous different formulations exist, all of them controversial.[3] For present purposes, perhaps the best way to begin is by using Comisso's formulation for the East European CPEs. Thus, on the Katzenstein/Comisso centralization parameter, we find in the East Asian NICs high degrees of centralization but with one critical structural innovation at the center: in all of them there is a more or less open division of labor between reigning and ruling. The formal (extrinsic) political leaders reign, holding off interest-group pressures that would undermine economic growth and performing safety-valve functions, while a technocratic, economically rational bureaucracy (intrinsic elite) actually rules. The authority of these bureaucracies is primarily meritocratic, and their recruitment and replacement are serviced by a fundamental commitment to heavy and continuing investment in education for everyone. This is one of the most marked differences between the NICs and mainland China (there are more universities in Taiwan with 18 million people than in mainland China with 1 billion people). The bureaucrats in the East Asian NICs also formulate and execute policies that are economically rational in the sense of Friedrich List's definition of political economy: "that science which limits its teaching to the inquiry how a given nation can obtain (under the existing conditions of the world) prosperity, civilization, and power, by means of agriculture, industry, and commerce."[4]

The second Katzenstein/Comisso structural feature is the extent of the private ownership of assets. Here all the East Asian NICs differ radically from the East European CPEs. In each of the Asian high-growth systems the private ownership of property is a fundamental right, defensible in law, and inheritable; such privately owned property can also be easily transferred in well-established markets. However, this does not mean that private ownership in East Asia is necessarily the same as it is in the Anglo-American democracies. This is perhaps seen most clearly in that typical institution of advanced capitalism, the limited partnership, or, above all, the incorporated joint stock company. The differences in the structure and functioning of joint

3. See, *inter alia*, Chalmers Johnson, "Political Institutions and Economic Performance: The Government-Business Relationship in Japan, South Korea, and Taiwan" (Berkeley: Institute of East Asian Studies, University of California, 1985); Chalmers Johnson, "*La Serenissima* of the East," *Asian and African Studies* (Journal of the Israel Oriental Society) 18 (March 1984), pp. 57–73; T. J. Pempel, *Policy and Politics in Japan: Creative Conservatism* (Philadelphia: Temple University Press, 1982); and James C. Abegglen, *The Strategy of Japanese Business* (Cambridge, Mass.: Ballinger, 1984).

4. Friedrich List, *The National System of Political Economy* (1885; reprint, New York: Augustus Kelley, 1966), p. 119.

stock companies among the capitalist nations are legal, not economic, but these legal differences have profound economic consequences. What I am thinking of here is the *zaibatsu* (in Japan) and the *chaebol* (in Korea) as instruments of rapid economic development in countries with little accumulated capital. Zaibatsu corporations (Mitsui, Mitsubishi, Sumitomo in Japan; Hyundai, Samsung, Daewoo in Korea) are nonfunctionally integrated conglomerates that use the profits from secure industries to finance new, riskier industries.

In the governments of the East Asian NICs, as well as in their private sectors, we find a more-or-less open (or more-or-less covert) division of labor between social goal setting and social goal execution. The developmental goals of the state are subcontracted to the zaibatsu for execution, with the understanding—utterly baffling to a Leninist—that any profit that results will remain private property. Zaibatsu corporations differ from Anglo-American corporations in that the separation of ownership and management is even more complete in East Asia, meaning that the concerns of management are focused much more clearly on long-term development and competition with other zaibatsu (and other nations) than on the rights of stockholders. Korea seems to have improved on the essentially Japanese prototype by preventing its zaibatsu from controlling their own banks, which attenuates the private concentrations of power which were so disruptive in prewar Japan. This East Asian pattern of public goal setting and private goal execution constitutes a form of "serious socialism" which is unknown in either the socialist East or the capitalist West—except in allegedly exceptional sectors such as the so-called military-industrial complex of the United States.

There *is* a higher degree of public ownership of assets in East Asian capitalism than in the North American variety (although, of course, an almost infinitely lower degree than in the CPEs). Even so, this public ownership usually takes the form of public corporations, a highly developed structure in East Asia, rather than direct administration by the central government. The trend, moreover, is toward privatization of even these public assets, a trend that was greatly accelerated by the shocks of the 1970s.

With regard to the second Katzenstein/Comisso structural feature, White and Wade remind us, "The action of developmental states should not be seen merely in terms of a state 'intervening' in an economy, which is in some sense alien or discrete. The relationship between state and economy is more organic and multifaceted and the state's impact on economic changes depends heavily on its broader, 'non-economic' social and political influences."[5] Perhaps nothing illustrates this feature more clearly than the reduced role in the East Asian NICs for economists in policy-making positions. They are of course present in the government and in the private sector as statisticians and analysts, but they are rarely given executive positions. Top bureaucrats

5. White and Wade, "Developmental States," p. 3.

and chief executive officers of private enterprises are most commonly educated in schools of public law (in the continental European sense) or engineering.

Let us turn to Comisso's additions to Katzenstein. Her first element is limited sovereignty. In the East Asian context, the equivalent to this element of structure would be the international relations of the NICs, particularly their ties to the United States. There are several points to be made. Japan, Korea, and Taiwan all have complex relations with the United States, including during the late 1940s, the 1950s, and the early 1960s extensive foreign aid, American-directed or -sponsored land reform in each of them, technology transfers from the United States at close to concessionary prices, direct investment by American-based multinational corporations in their economies, and virtually unlimited access to the American market for their exports. But most of these structural features were also available to any noncommunist nation and particularly to any American ally (e.g., Italy or Spain).

On the other hand, such features as American aid become important in the economic performances of the NICs primarily in their being cut off: it was the ending of U.S. aid in the mid-1960s to Korea and Taiwan that launched them on their high-speed growth patterns. Until this occurred Korea and Taiwan were among the world's worst examples of dictatorial maldeveloped (not underdeveloped) regimes whose viability depended almost entirely on the American taxpayer. By analogy, it would seem that if the Soviet Union wanted to stimulate the economic development of the East European nations, it should cut off economic aid to them while simultaneously completely opening its domestic market to their exports.

On the military dimension of "limited sovereignty," the Japanese have profited from their so-called free ride on U.S. defense expenditures; but this appears not to be of critical significance. Korea and Taiwan, which both have heavy defense expenditures, are matching or exceeding Japan's growth rates. Moreover, the United States has actually broken diplomatic relations with Taiwan and acquiesced with (in my opinion, unseemly) enthusiasm in Britain's negotiations over Hong Kong—negotiations that will return Hong Kong to mainland China on China's terms. This is not to say that Taiwan and Hong Kong are no longer viable, only that the American version of "limited sovereignty" seems rather harsher in some important ways than the limited sovereignty the Soviet Union imposes on Eastern Europe.

The critical elements in the East Asian NICs' positions in the world, it seems to me, are the following: (1) In none of them are their political structures securely legitimated; hence economic performance tends to legitimate their politics. (2) Each of them has experienced genuine security threats (Japan's defeat in the Pacific War, the Kuomintang's defeat in the Chinese civil war, the division of Korea during the Korean War, Hong Kong's dependence on China's toleration, and Singapore's origins as the most impressive child of the Malayan Emergency and the breakup of the Malay Federation). These

histories have helped to make each of them "serious nations." (3) Each of
the East Asian NICs has had the experience of genuine marginality in the
sense that it must make itself economically valuable to one or another of
the powers or face the threat of being sacrificed. The people of Hong Kong
recognized this most clearly; they expressed it as the doctrine of "sweet
peaches," meaning that they must continually produce sweet peaches desirable
to their neighbors and investors—rather in the way that Scheherazade saved
her life by continously inventing new tales to interest the sultan. Hong Kong,
as we now know, finally ran out of peaches.[6] Even Japan, with its population
half that of the United States in an area the size of Montana and with no
natural resources, has a pervasive sense of vulnerability in its relations with
the rest of the world.

These elements of insecurity are important in that they tend to elevate
genuine economic rationality in policy making to a much higher level than
in either Western capitalist or Leninist systems. Economic rationality—the
determination to allocate resources in an economically optimal manner regardless of any other considerations (e.g., building a road through a graveyard,
or a neighborhood, if it is the most direct route)—is actually a fairly rare
element in governmental economic policy making. It was quite rare in the
Kuomintang China of the 1930s and 1940s or in Syngman Rhee's Korea of
the 1950s, and it is fairly rare in the welfare and regulatory states of Western
Europe and North America. Its role in East Asia can be seen in the rapidity
with which all these systems during 1973–74 implemented policies of energy
conservation, petroleum stockpiling, diversification of suppliers, and investment in alternate energy sources, as well as undertaking basic shifts of
industrial structure away from capital and energy intensity toward knowledge-
intensive high-technology industries.

Comisso's second supplement to Katzenstein's conception of structure is
the single, hegemonic party organized on Leninist lines. As we have already
seen, quasi-authoritarian (camouflaged authoritarian, in the case of Japan)
regimes exist in East Asia, but they perform very different functions from
those in Leninist systems. In East Asia the politicians reign in order to
provide space for the technocratic bureaucrats to rule. Reigning is a very
specific activity: it involves creating genuine political stability, correcting
excesses committed by the bureaucracy, promoting entrepreneurship, and
avoiding the usual consequences of state intervention in economic affairs—
namely, bureaucratism, corruption, and a misallocation of resources.

In East Asia, just as in Leninist systems, whenever the politicians have
tried both to reign and to rule, economic disaster has followed (e.g., wartime
Japan, civil war China, and Korea after the 1979 assassination of President
Park Chung Hee). The role of the single party or its equivalent in the East

---

6. See Chalmers Johnson, "The Mousetrapping of Hong Kong: A Game in Which Nobody
Wins," *Asian Survey* 24 (September 1984), pp. 887–909.

Asian NICs today represents a long and tortuous learning process; the political elites have learned that they need the market and the price mechanism as much as local entrepreneurs need the risk-reducing policies of the state. Above all, they have learned the limits of political intervention: that it should be used to build rather than displace markets; and in the case of economically nonstrategic sectors, that it is best to establish disincentives for them and then ignore them.

The differences between the East European CPEs and the East Asian NICs on this score are profound. Authoritarianism in Eastern Europe is an end in itself, reflecting the history and international dependency of the area. In East Asia soft authoritarianism is only instrumental to an economic end. Where authoritarianism goes beyond this purely instrumental role, as in Korea and Taiwan, it is deeply resented and a source of political instability. In light of the experience of the East Asian NICs, the Leninist party—wherever it occurs—must be considered a serious, even crippling economic burden, one that China is in the process of trying to overcome; but this does not mean that it should be replaced by a minimalist or a pluralist state. What is needed is a capitalist developmental state—or, at any rate, that is the structural lesson taught by the East Asian NICs.

Turning to the dimension of political process, we find that the East Asian NICs display a wider range of possibilities than Comisso's patrimonialism and collegiality. The norm in East Asia is very high degrees of education, national mobilization, and nationalism among all adults, combined with exceptionally egalitarian distribution of the wealth created by high-speed growth. This egalitarianism was advanced in all those systems with an agricultural sector through land reform and is maintained by more-or-less explicit state policies of redistribution. To the extent that such policies are not forthcoming or are undercut by private interests (e.g., by differential rewards for mainlanders and native Taiwanese in Taiwan and by the growing power of zaibatsu in Korea), this becomes a major threat to the entire developmental effort. In all the East Asian systems gains in productivity are routinely translated into wage increases, but in none of them is organized labor allowed a voice in politics.

The egalitarianism of these systems, combined with genuine devolution of economic decision making to group- and family-based enterprises, produces intense group and bureaucratic competition internally and intense national solidarity externally. Generally speaking, Japan has been the most astute operator of the political system of the developmental state. Japan's great achievement has been single-party rule since 1948, but with a single party that has developed the means to change the head of state in a processual, relatively transparent manner, something that it does with great frequency. Singapore has yet to change its head of state; Korea does so only through military coups d'état; Hong Kong has dispensed with the state in favor of an administration (and as a result shows the slowest adjustment ability); and

Taiwan has thus far relied on the primitive method of lineal descent from father to son. All of these systems tend to legitimate their political leaders by means of economic performance and by giving all adults a material stake in the system, and not through ideology or political philosophy.

In conclusion, it is perhaps worth noting that Japan is the case around which the East Asian NICs have modeled their own developmental efforts; and over the past century Japan has experimented with virtually every known type of political economy, from laissez-faire to hard totalitarianism, before it perfected its post-World War II high-growth system. The East Asian NICs are in many respects improving on the Japanese system, particularly in their greater internationalism and lesser paranoia about foreigners participating in their systems, but Japan was still the pioneer.

Abstracted from history and changing environmental circumstances, the Japanese-type capitalist developmental state has four fundamental structural features.[7] These are: (1) stable rule by a political-bureaucratic elite that does not accede to political demands that would undermine economic growth or security; (2) cooperation between public and private sectors under the overall guidance of a pilot planning agency; (3) heavy and continuing investment in education for everyone, combined with policies to ensure the equitable distribution of national income; and (4) a government that understands the need to use and respect methods of intervention based on the price mechanism.

Each of these elements exists in the Japanese, Korean, and Taiwanese systems, although with differing weights, patterns of historical evolution, and tradeoffs arising from stressing one more than the others. These so-called capitalist developmental states have put together the political economy of capitalism in ways unprecedented in the Anglo-American West and with quite different tradeoffs (greater capacity for adjustment to economic change, for example, but less political participation). In a sense, however, these nations part company from the capitalist world in that they incorporate higher degrees of social goal setting than capitalist theory suggests is desirable. At the same time they manage to avoid the known consequences of socialism (above all, the maldistribution of resources). Thus, it is possible to argue that the East Asian NICs are serious socialists, whereas the East European Marxist-Leninists are not socialists at all or, at the very least, are not serious about their socialism. The East Asian NICs appear to have combined the most important features of capitalism and socialism: entrepreneurship and social goal setting.

7. See Chalmers Johnson, *MITI and the Japanese Miracle* (Stanford: Stanford University Press, 1982); and James C. Hsiung, ed., *The Taiwan Experience, 1950–1980* (New York: Praeger, 1981), pp. 9–18.

The East European debt crisis in the Latin American mirror Albert Fishlow

In these brief remarks addressed to the Latin American response to changing international conditions in the 1970s and 1980s, I shall focus on three issues: the relationship between the choice of debt as a policy instrument and state "structure," at least as loosely defined; the special problems posed by the debt option that most Latin American countries pursue; and the characteristics of enforced domestic adjustment to the absence of capital inflows beginning in 1982.[1]

Despite very obvious differences, the Latin American experience is relevant to the experience of Eastern Europe. Both regions share a common development strategy. Import substitution was not invented in Latin America after World War II; it had emerged much earlier, and naturally, among East European states as a response to their industrial backwardness relative to Western neighbors. On an intellectual level, the very similar protectionist rationale of Michail Manoïlesco and other Romanian authors predates the writings of Raul Prebisch and his Latin American followers. Not surprisingly, then, the two regions share a wholehearted commitment to industrialization and production targets, sometimes even at the expense of efficiency. In part as consequence, they also share internal structural inflexibilities that limit the speed with which resources can be reallocated and that reduce the efficacy of market signals; indeed, most East European countries have consciously ignored the latter in favor of physical planning. Related to this inflexibility is a limited degree of production directed to export but a heavy dependence on imports. It is no accident that external debt became both a preferred instrument and a source of difficulty for many countries in these two widely separated parts of the world.

1. Some of these points are treated more extensively in two papers: "Revisiting the Great Debt Crisis of 1982," in K. Kim and D. Ruccio, eds., *Debt and Development in Latin America* (Notre Dame: Notre Dame University Press, 1985), and "Latin American Adjustment to the Oil Shocks of 1973 and 1979," in J. Hartlyn and S. Morley, eds., *Latin American Political Economy: Financial Crisis and Political Change* (Boulder: Westview, forthcoming).

International Organization 40, 2, Spring 1986   0020-8183 $5.00

Much of the discussion of East European adjustment policies in this volume emphasizes their root in political circumstances. This theme also holds for Latin America. The common use of debt finance by Latin American countries with rather different state structures nonetheless reflects different politics as well as economic conditions. This point is fundamental to disaggregating what is usually seen as a regionwide debt crisis.

To facilitate comparisons, it is helpful to categorize the different economic agendas Latin American states pursued during the 1970s in three distinct groups.

One group was populist, not in the electoral sense but so named for its bias toward public overexpenditure in pursuit of growth-cum-redistribution, together with an orientation of production toward the internal market. Mexico's archetypal populist agenda was "affordable" in part because of the beneficial consequences of rising oil prices.

A second group was system-preserving authoritarianism. It was characterized by extensive and technocratic state direction of the economy; a large and expanding set of public enterprises extending to many sectors, particularly the most dynamic; and commitment to economic growth as a means for legitimating continuing political control. Brazil stands as the classic case: its economic success, growing public sector, and political stability permitted modest but not far-reaching change until severe adjustment was required after 1982.

The third was system-changing authoritarianism. It took its name from its explicit commitment to a new, market-oriented society and rationalized the imposition of repression with the need for fundamental change. The examples are Argentina and Chile, each of which relied on an unfettered price system to evoke a privately determined, optimal allocation of resources, and used the external market as the measure of which prices were right.

Latin American countries had three alternative responses to the first oil crisis in 1973. They could increase exports to cover the higher costs not only of oil but also of other imports. Or they could reduce real demand to correspond to the loss of income imposed by deterioration in the terms of trade. Finally, they could use external debt to ratify the disequilibrium in the balance of payments. (Note that even Mexico in 1973 was an oil importer on a modest scale and was adversely affected by the rise in price of manufactured imports.)

For those countries pursuing an agenda of system-preserving authoritarianism, only one alternative was successful. A decline in income was ruled out as not only politically intolerable but also of dubious efficacy. Given structural rigidities, the effect of income reduction would be to cause declining output rather than the reallocation of resources. A massive commitment to exports was also unappealing. Despite the greater degree of trade openness which characterized the late 1960s in many such countries, the conversion to faith in external markets was incomplete. It was one thing to be propelled by rapid growth in world trade and favorable prices, another to make one's way in a world economy beset by recession. The debt strategy left the production and expenditure structure substantially unchanged, lessening the abruptness and postponing the pain of required adjustment. System preservation, paradoxically perhaps, lent itself to short-term planning horizons.

For Mexico, soon favored by high-priced oil exports, and for Argentina and Chile, whose international monetarist models were predicated on a high degree of international integration rather than insulation, the explanations for debt differ. Mexico's debt converted oil reserves into ready cash to satisfy the increasing pressures for employment opportunities and rural programs. Capital inflows transformed the wealth in the ground into immediate purchasing power, averting the need for an exploitation of the resources too rapid for nationalist tastes. The new capital markets designed to recycle petrodollars did not discriminate against oil producers; on the contrary, they were preferred risks and were given favored terms. Mexican populism, especially after 1977, was satisfied by rising imports financed by debt.

For Argentina and Chile in the latter half of the 1970s, debt served still another purpose. Access to international capital was not only part of an ideological commitment to free markets and equalization of interest rates, but capital inflows also provided necessary foreign exchange to underwrite exchange rates that were deliberately overvalued in order to decelerate inflation. Central to international monetarism is a faith in the competitive capacity of potential imports to regulate domestic inflation. A country borrows to import cheaply and alter internal inflationary expectations. Such debt was not predominantly directed into public outlays or investment; private arrangements promised more accurate assessment of market risk, and individual preferences determined the correct level of capital formation (as well as the extent of foreign resources that would even stay in the country—a particular problem for Argentina).

The common Latin American reliance on debt thus conceals important variations in the source of the balance-of-payments gap it was intended to cover. The different politics characteristic of these three different economic models did matter, but, more important, external debt was a single instrument that could serve very different objectives. That is not surprising. After all, debt is, if only temporarily, something for nothing. Credit permits one to live beyond one's means; both populism and a drive for capital accumulation equally welcome and depend upon that opportunity.

Indebtedness, however, is not without its subsequent difficulties. That is my second point: the special problems of external indebtedness in the conditions of the 1970s and 1980s. One is the changed character of international finance, and an attendant increased uncertainty and vulnerability of debtors. Another is the greater instability in international economic performance and consequent cyclical impact upon the debtors. A third problem is the absence of an effective debt regime.

By its nature, a debt strategy is an uncertain strategy because it is a commitment predicated upon successful returns in the future upon the resources borrowed and applied today. Since repayment must be made through exports, gains are sensitive to the market conditions they will eventually encounter. The innovation of the Euromarket—tying interest rates on loans to the borrowing rate of the bank suppliers of credit (London Inter-bank Offered Rate)—compounded this inherent uncertainty. Cheap money could not be locked in. With interest rates adjustable every six months, the money borrowed in the mid-1970s was hostage to the fortune of international financial markets. Of what value were six-month price signals when investment decisions had a horizon of decades and more for infrastructure projects? Maturity structures were likewise mismatched: loans extended only for six to eight years, sometimes less, and required frequent rollover of principal.

This characteristic, joined with high nominal interest rates emanating from high inflation, yielded a high ratio of gross flows relative to more modest net resource transfer. Put another way, the debt-service ratio became much higher than had been the historical norm or the postwar rule of thumb. Capital supply was subject to correspondingly greater risk, since commercial bank evaluations were sensitive to upward changes in the ratio.

As a result of wide fluctuations in the commodity terms of trade, interest rates, and conditions of capital supply, debtors at first greatly benefited and then lost. After the oil-price shock in 1973, relative prices of other commodities rose and moderated the initial impact through the boost to export revenues. Low and even negative real rates of interest encouraged borrowing and limited return outflows. And lenders provided additional resources with great enthusiasm and even abandon; so long as oil exporters were content to earn negative rates, banks were happy to pass the money on for a modest additional premium.

Alas, beginning in 1978, the terms of trade began a sharp decline. The adverse impact on export earnings of the post-1980 recession helped to do in the Latin American debtor countries, those both harmed and helped by the rise in the oil price. Despite increases in export volume, weaker prices negated the extra effort. At the same time in 1981 and 1982 high positive real rates of interest exacted an even greater toll on the balance of payments. Lenders reacted to their overextended position and sought to pull back, first reducing maturities and increasing premiums, and then refusing to lend. They had seen the same situation, on a smaller scale, in Eastern Europe.

This shock of zero capital supply, on top of the recessionary shock to export earnings and the interest-rate shock, was the final blow and ushered in the debt crisis. The essence of debt is that it is most available to those who need it least. When countries required additional balance-of-payments support, they exposed themselves as less creditworthy than they had seemed, thus reducing their chances of receiving credit. The liquidity squeeze became progressively worse in 1981–82 until the dramatic Mexican collapse in August 1982.

At that time the International Monetary Fund (IMF) countered the now overt crisis with an imaginative and novel response: to compensate for the inadequacy of the private market in dealing with debtors, banks were required to sustain "involuntary" lending as the price of parallel IMF finance. Countries would not have to default but could adjust their way back to creditworthiness, leaving the assets of the banks intact by ensuring continuing interest payments. Indeed, with the additional risk premiums and rescheduling fees, "involuntary" lending actually improved the immediate profitability of bank lending.

Yet this debt regime, for all its accomplishments in averting financial apocalypse, is fatally flawed. It is biased in favor of transferring most of the burden of adjustment to the debtor countries. They are required to pay if not principal, then interest at market rates. The discipline is supposed to be salutary: in the IMF framework domestic economic recovery corresponds positively to the adjustment effort required to mobilize the needed export surpluses. The reality, however, is that the attendant large resource transfers have handicapped, not improved, performance. Lack of foreign exchange and the application of savings to external payments constrain growth. Countries have done much better on their balance of payments than by other criteria.

Relief is not forthcoming. The only way net outflows can be smaller for the heaviest debtors is for significant new, voluntary lending to offset the required interest outflows. But voluntary lending is held back pending demonstrated domestic recovery. Involuntary lending is by its very nature too minimal and inadequate to permit appropriate adjustment. At best it reinforces attention to immediate balance-of-payments targets at the expense of domestic capital formation and the potential supply of future exports. Debtors are deprived of the credit they need to facilitate their adjustment to adverse international economic circumstances.

It is a self-fulfilling and tragic prophecy: credit is limited because of lack of creditworthiness, which reflects the difficulty of adjusting without adequate credit. The IMF can elicit minimal finance from the banks because it is a worthwhile price to pay for continuing and greater return interest payments. But it can provide little more on its own. Nor has lending by the World Bank kept pace. With severe restraints imposed on the public sector, it is not surprising that debtor countries have no eligible projects.

Thus countries confront greater austerity and are advised to rely on the improbable prospect of renewed voluntary lending from banks that would prefer to expand elsewhere. They are also counseled to prove their creditworthiness by attracting back capital that has left the country and by direct investment. Neither course can be expected to succeed in depressed conditions, no matter how generous the terms. Nominally a case-by-case approach, the debt regime in reality does not discriminate among countries: all are asked to pay independently of their circumstances.

All countries faced such new borrowing and adjustment rules, but they had greater effect upon the Latin American countries because of their proportionately larger debt exposure. True to its caricature as a region of *mañana*, Latin America, despite its political diversity, almost universally gambled on debt as a solution and lost. After the post-1979 oil-price shocks, rising interest rates and recession in industrialized countries led to a new deterioration in the balance of payments, and there was no repetition of the earlier cheap and abundant international finance. In the inevitable adjustment, income declined in order to reduce imports. Between 1981 and 1983, imports fell by some 40 percent, permitting at least interest payments to be sustained while postponing principal. Countries in the region were forced to live enough within their means to meet resource outflows on an order of $30 billion annually in 1983 and 1984.

Not only real disposable income but also output declined. Lack of available imports hampered industrial production and contributed to excess capacity. Tight monetary and fiscal policy raised interest rates, discouraging private investment and even borrowing for working capital. Nothing comparable has happened since the Great Depression, as country after country compressed real wages through devaluations in an effort to stimulate exports, hoping to create employment opportunities as well as to alleviate the balance-of-payments situation. Mexico and Brazil succeeded in obtaining large trade surpluses in 1984 in this way, but they did not repeat this success in 1985. The dramatic increase of 27 percent in U.S. imports has not been replicated, because U.S. growth and the unusually large 1984 import elasticity have both declined. The rest of the industrialized world has not picked up the slack. For the smaller countries, 1984 was not a good year, as commodity prices resumed their decline. And in Brazil and Mexico, stirrings of the internal market began to reduce export supply based on excess capacity rather than new investment.

On one level, this Latin American adjustment experience is a story of inevitable accommodation at high cost to deteriorating external conditions. It has similarities to the experience of East European borrowers as a result of the lessening liquidity that was already evident in 1981. The smaller the debt burden, the easier it was to adjust to the new and more adverse international economy. For the large debtors in both regions, the greatest effects were on the level of investment, pointing up the contradiction between rapid short-run adaptation and successful, investment-intensive, medium-run reallocation of resources to more export and import-competing activities. But more of the burden seems to fall on labor income and employment in Latin America than in the socialist countries. A more careful comparison is needed which isolates how much can be ascribed to the larger Latin American balance-of-payments disequilibrium and how much to the Latin American reliance on indirect market signals rather than controls to influence micro-economic decisions.

Yet to blame matters exclusively on the adverse evolution of the world economy misses an important part of the story. After all, the East Asian economies, poor in resources and integrated into the same world economy, took the two oil shocks in stride, even though their economies, too, slowed in 1985. Seen from this perspective, the debt problem might have surfaced sooner or later in both Latin America and Eastern Europe because of the asymmetric quality of their external orientation. Countries in these regions integrated into the world economy much more completely on capital account than on trade account. They accumulated debt on a scale that was incompatible with their internally oriented production structures and that would not have automatically led to the sustained growth of exports which was the only way to service it. System-preserving authoritarian regimes—prevalent in Eastern Europe, albeit in somewhat different guise—are not committed to large-scale structural change but are more cautious in their response. Populist regimes are committed to the internal market and sustaining consumption levels. And the Latin American system-changing authoritarianism was committed to a macroeconomic policy rather than a development strategy.

The contrast with East Asia is stark. There system-changing authoritarianism started out with substantive objectives, not procedural commitments to price signals. Countries actively pursued openness but dominantly on the trade side, and very much more from the export side of the ledger. Capital accounts remained under close scrutiny and control. Taiwan and Singapore avoided large indebtedness, with the former, in particular, accepting an immediate reduction in national income as a new starting point for renewed growth. Korea did borrow more to finance increasing investment in new sectors, but it started with large public liabilities at low-interest cost and with rapidly growing exports that continue to leave its relative interest payments a much lower proportion of its foreign-exchange earnings. These economies possess the internal flexibility that enables them to forgo the seduction of externally financed adjustment in favor of domestic realignment at modest costs in temporary unemployment and excess capacity.

If what happened to Latin America and Eastern Europe was perhaps equally inevitable, and if the cost in both cases seems large relative to the initial shock, one important difference is worth noting. That is the differential commitment to preserving integration into the international economic and financial system in the two regions. For Latin America, remaining in the system is very important; for Eastern Europe, it is not, despite Hungary's decision to join the IMF and the World Bank, and Yugoslav efforts to obtain more commercial bank financing (with official U.S. support).

When Mexico teetered on the brink of a unilateral moratorium in 1982, the potential effects on the world financial system and the subsequent repercussions on Mexico were a very important part of the context. Argentina's reiteration of its commitment to pay its obligations, even though roughly half of its debt has no counterpart in domestic real assets because of capital flight, reflects its acceptance of private property rights. Brazil continues to service its interest obligations, despite internal political opposition, not only because of the trade linkage but also because of the importance it places on access to technological change through ongoing relationships with foreign private enterprises inherent in a capitalist model of development.

For these countries, the ties with the North are fundamental. For those of the East, the links with the West are marginal. Trade linkages did not alter fundamentally in the 1970s; only a new set of capital flows appeared. It is no accident then that intraregional trade seems to have operated to cushion the impact of the debt crisis with rather different effect in the two regions. In Eastern Europe the Council for Mutual Economic Assistance (CMEA) partially offset declines in Western imports to some countries. But in Latin America trade among the countries fell off more than proportionately and added to export revenue losses rather than to import levels. Attempts to promote regionwide import substitution and balanced trade expansion to expand the supply of industrial products have come to naught.

It is also true that the debt of the East European countries declines absolutely, while that of Latin America increases, albeit at a slow rate. The experiment with debt strategy having failed, there is less taste in Eastern Europe for exploring modification of debt-service terms rather than for reducing integration into capital markets. There is no East European counterpart to the multiyear renegotiations with commitment to continuing IMF monitoring which have become prominent in some of the Latin American cases. Domestic economic strategy reduces Western reliance. Export growth to Western markets may still be desirable for some countries, but the lure of a return to voluntary lending is largely irrelevant.

The Latin American countries have also learned from their unfortunate experience. Few will rush into such unwise reliance on external credits again. The danger is that the rejection of external dependence will spill over to lack of enthusiasm for expanded trade, even when exports can be beneficial and a source of greater autonomy. Mismanagement of the economy by military governments has contributed to their replacement by civilian successors. Popular pressure is rising to increase domestic expenditure rather than output for the foreign market. Moreover, the Chilean and Argentine experiments with openness and system change have been widely discredited. In addition mounting protectionism in the industrialized countries and in the United States in particular casts a pall of new uncertainty over the evolution of world trade.

There is some merit to this caution for still another reason. One of the lessons from East Asia is that it is far easier to compensate for the volatility of the international economy if the domestic economy is flexible enough to adapt rapidly. On the whole the Latin American (and the East European) countries lack flexibility. Significant progress in this direction is likely to depend more upon resumption of sustained economic expansion than upon continued imposition of austerity. To try to teach the Latin American (or the East European) countries that only export growth can be a vehicle for overall growth is to put matters in the wrong sequence. Restoring conditions favorable for economic growth through more abundant external finance and higher levels of investment has to come first.

Finally one should not ignore another East Asian lesson, especially during the current chorus of appeals for Latin American countries to cut back the public sector. That lesson concerns the constructive role of state intervention. In the last analysis successful performance of East Asian states rather than the free market helps to explain the dramatic economic results of the previous two decades. Those who counsel the countries of Latin America or Eastern Europe to adopt some of the specific East Asian exchange-rate or trade policies frequently pay inadequate attention to the underlying state structure and state purpose that make them so effective. Economic development strategies do not export as turnkey technologies. Rather, they must be rooted in sociopolitical (and economic) reality even while seeking to change it.

State structures and political processes outside the CMEA: a comparison   Ellen Comisso

As the analyses of Susan Woodward, Nikiforos Diamandouros, Chalmers Johnson, and Albert Fishlow make clear, state structures among non-CMEA NICs varied widely. Nevertheless, all differed fundamentally from the state structures in the CMEA.

Section 1 of this essay argues that those differences were as much in kind as in degree. Consequently, even nominally similar strategy choices made by Eastern Europe and the NICs were actually the product of different causes, shaped by different objectives, accomplished with different instruments, and followed by different international and domestic consequences. Likewise, despite nominally similar political processes, elites proposed substantively different visions of social order and deployed distinctly different political resources to capture power to pursue them. As a result, even when strategy choices were similar, their political consequences could be dissimilar.

At the same time, as section 2 of this essay shows, although the *substance* of structure and strategy in Eastern Europe and the NICs was different, the *relationship* between structure and strategy was similar. As in Eastern Europe, state structures in the NICs defined problems, possibilities, and political resources. Strategy, however, was the outcome of differentiated political processes in which elites mobilized allies at home and abroad to forward solutions to the issues and opportunities that state structure created.

I. State structure inside the CMEA and among the NICs

Similarities in policy responses and political processes

In several important respects, the responses of both East European states and Third World NICs to international economic disturbances in the 1970s

I wrote the original draft of this essay during 1984–85 while a fellow at the Center for Advanced Study in the Behavioral Sciences, Stanford, California. I am grateful for the financial support provided by the Exxon Educational Foundation during my stay there. In addition, I

International Organization 40, 2, Spring 1986   0020-8183 $5.00

and 1980s paralleled each other. First, both groups reacted initially to the oil-price shocks of 1973–74 by continuing their previous development strategies. Indeed, the continuities in domestic policy choices in these two very different areas, before and after 1973, despite the dramatic changes in the international economy brought about by higher energy prices, are striking.

Thus, inside the Council for Mutual Economic Assistance (CMEA) states proceeded with the energy-intensive projects based on 1973 prices they had begun or planned at the start of the decade, while the wave of interest in systemic economic reform that had already begun to ebb merely receded further. Outside the CMEA the continuities in development strategies seemed most obvious in states that sought to insulate their economies from international economic fluctuations, such as Yugoslavia, Mexico, and Brazil. Yet continuity was equally pronounced in their more "open" counterparts. According to Johnson, the East Asian NICs embarked on state-led export development in the 1960s, well before the oil-price shocks that simply gave a new impetus to pursuing it. In the Mediterranean Basin, as Diamandouros describes, the economic impact of the energy crisis was overshadowed altogether by the concurrent transition to civilian rule and the introduction of competitive politics. Even in what Fishlow terms the "system-changing" authoritarian regimes of Latin America, such as Chile and Argentina, the commitment of ruling elites to openness in the international system and monetarism in the domestic economy was typically motivated by domestic considerations that were quite independent of the energy price hike and often predated them.

Second, the vast majority of states in both Eastern Europe and the Third World NICs considered in this volume participated in the expansion-austerity cycle of the 1970s and 1980s. Continuing preexisting development strategies after 1973 led many in both groups to borrow rather heavily on international capital markets at what proved temporarily to be highly favorable interest rates. Consequently, the second increase in oil prices, which occurred in 1979 and was followed shortly by a rapid rise in interest rates and renewed Western recession, acted to test the "robustness" of the development model—and often of the political elites associated with it—both inside and outside the CMEA. Moreover, to the degree debtor states lacked the economic reserves or flexibility to meet that test, they found themselves forced by the pressures of international creditors to modify their development strategies, often at a high cost to the domestic standard of living.

The third parallel between Eastern Europe and non-CMEA NICs concerns not so much their economic behavior during the period in question but the nature of the political system that informed the strategy choices each selected. States in both groups were situated within regional economies dominated

would like to express my great appreciation to Peter Katzenstein and Peter Gourevitch for the discussions that led me to write this piece; Laura Tyson's comments and suggestions also proved extremely helpful.

by regional politico-economic powers. Equally if not more important, with the exception of the Mediterranean Basin, the authoritarian governments in Eastern Europe had counterparts in the Third World NICs. As in Eastern Europe, authoritarianism in the NICs tended to take the form of "rule by the Few" (e.g., Taiwan's "reigning but not ruling" Kuomintang, Brazil's military junta, Yugoslavia's "collective presidency"), although—as in Romania—it could also appear as "rule by the One," be it for a sporadic interlude (as in South Korea in 1980–81) or for a more prolonged period (as in the Philippines). As in Eastern Europe, too, authoritarianism in Third World NICs could exclude popular forces from political life or it could take a distinctly "populist" overtone. Whereas the former was the case in countries such as Korea, Brazil, and Chile (and East Germany, Czechoslovakia, and, for the most part, Hungary in the CMEA), the latter was characteristic in Mexico and Yugoslavia (and, to a substantial degree, Poland). Nevertheless, as we shall see below, although the combination of populism and heavy borrowing proved explosive in the East European context after 1979, it proved to be an important source of political resiliency in the non-CMEA states.

Development strategies inside the CMEA and among the NICs

Underlying these broad similarities are fundamental differences that separate the CMEA experience with international economic disturbances from that of non-CMEA NICs. Although both sets of countries continued existing development strategies after the first round of energy price increases, the development models themselves were distinctly unique, derived as they were from the structure of the states and economies in which they occurred.

The limitations and possibilities that domestic structures implied for economic strategy choices are perhaps most pronounced when we compare the import-biased, shortage economies of CMEA countries with their export-oriented counterparts in East Asia. Certainly, the features of domestic structure that Johnson describes in the latter did not by themselves produce export-led development. In fact, the same structures of centralized and authoritarian rule which elites deployed to produce an "economic miracle" in the 1970s and 1980s allowed Korea and Taiwan to rank "among the world's worst examples of dictatorially maldeveloped . . . regimes whose viability rested almost entirely on the American taxpayer" until the mid-1960s.[1]

Nevertheless, state structures in East Asia did make export-led development possible once the withdrawal of American aid gave political elites an incentive to select it as an alternative strategy for retaining control of their territories and populations. Thus, the decision of East Asian NICs to opt for rapid growth based on comparative advantage in a competitive international econ-

---

1. See Chalmers Johnson's comment in this volume.

omy certainly signified an important change in *policies* and the uses to which they put state structures. It did not, however, entail radical alterations in the highly centralized bureaucratic state, the degree of differentiation between it and an economy with an already substantial private sector, or the distinctly authoritarian and exclusive forms of rule which characterized the area. Nor did it involve an abrupt exit from the Western sphere of influence in the Pacific. Indeed, far from being an attempt to end the "penetrated sovereignty" that dependence on more powerful Western states entailed, export-led development oriented to the markets of those very same powers was designed to increase the strategic value of East Asia to erstwhile Western allies after the latter unilaterally had altered their terms of external support. Thus, an altered development strategy appealed to authoritarian elites in East Asia precisely because it promised to preserve the existing state structure and their power within it, despite international conditions of increased economic and political vulnerability.

Inside the CMEA, in contrast, state structures created very different possibilities for economic choice. There, opting for export-led development—and in particular, export-led development geared to capturing non-CMEA/Soviet markets—would have required not only a change in economic policies but a wholesale transformation of the basic structures of the state and economy as well.[2] Moreover, altering the economy from one in which domestic and CMEA shortages were the motor of growth to one in which demand and the international opportunity structure governed expansion and contraction would have meant changing the role of the ruling party, access to political resources within it, and both the trade and party/political arrangements that characterized the socialist alliance. Indeed, the actions East European elites would have had to take to pursue export-oriented development of the East Asian type probably would have eroded the very domestic and international power bases necessary to enact and implement the appropriate policies. In short, whereas export-led growth was an economically desirable structural possibility offering large political payoffs in East Asia, it required structural change that was fraught with political risk in Eastern Europe. Not surprisingly, the respective paths of development of these regions reflected these contrasting exigencies.

By and large the decision to preserve existing state structures in the CMEA eliminated the possibility of opting for an export-led development strategy. Once that choice was made, import substitution in Eastern Europe then stemmed from the structural features of the state and economy itself. Such features made economic actors responsive to the qualitative and quantitative cues emitted from the political center and highly insensitive to domestic and international prices, demand, and economic opportunities and costs. Con-

---

2. For an elaboration of these structural features, see Ellen Comisso, "Introduction: State Structures, Political Processes, and Collective Choice in CMEA States," in this volume.

sequently, further discretionary policy decisions of central authorities—from refusing to import goods when domestic substitutes were available to inducing firms to export in order to cover import needs—were required to counteract the structural biases of CMEA economies toward imports and away from exports which the absence of price sensitivity among economy actors created.

In Latin America, in contrast, import substitution evolved as a political response to the *presence* of price sensitivity among economic actors, suggesting that in many ways, political and economic dynamics in that region were fundamentally different from those observed among CMEA states. That is, import substitution in Latin America shares a critical similarity with export-led development in East Asia: both resulted from the discretionary decisions of political leaders about desirable policy alternatives and not from structural features of the economy itself, as in Eastern Europe. In fact, domestic structures in Brazil and South Korea, for example, or in Mexico and Taiwan have marked parallels; it was the objectives of political leaders, the economic opportunities that size and natural endowments offered for domestic development, and the uses to which state structures were consequently put which were different. Accordingly, political elites in Mexico and Brazil could seek to accomplish their goals through the manipulation of prices, tariffs, and exchange rates and through monetary and fiscal policy, rather than through the physical controls and administrative instructions that characterized the CMEA.

The forgoing suggests that had political elites in Latin America embraced an alternative set of goals, domestic economic activity might well have been oriented more toward international markets without altering basic economic or political structures or even the close ties of the state to industry, as would have been necessary in Eastern Europe. For example, let us consider the source of what Fishlow terms the "structural rigidities" that characterized state-owned industries in Latin America and Eastern Europe and what measures states in each area would have had to take to remove them.

In this regard, the "soft" budget constraints of nationalized enterprises in Mexico or Brazil flowed from the discretionary, voluntary political decisions of leaders who wished to develop (or nationalize) a particular industry or firm. Consequently, they awarded it a privileged position on the domestic market. In this sense, the soft budget constraints that state-owned firms in Latin America faced were fundamentally similar to the soft budget constraints that any large oligopolistic or monopolistic enterprise in a market economy confronts, that is, they diminished the importance of profitability, efficiency, and competitiveness in order to allow enterprise management to pursue a number of other goals.

Accordingly, those soft budget constraints could have been removed or "hardened" in the particular firms to which they applied without requiring an overall change in the structure and allocation mechanisms of the economy itself. For example, had the Brazilian government attempted to sell nationalized assets to private bidders or permitted a petrochemicals complex to go bankrupt, the result might well have been serious economic dislocations and significant political fallout. Yet despite the costs such an action would have entailed, it would not have altered the role of prices in the economy at large.

In contrast, the hardening of soft budget constraints in Eastern Europe would have necessitated precisely such an overall transformation. Thus, in East Germany, for example, the prevalence of soft budget constraints in socialized firms was the result of a discretionary decision by political leaders only in the sense that the decision to establish a centrally planned economy was discretionary. Once that structure was operating, however, leaders could not lift soft budget constraints for any group of firms without removing them on *all* firms, in effect altering the structure of the economy itself. In this sense, even development strategies with the same name inside and outside the CMEA were fundamentally different in kind.

The expansion-austerity cycle

CMEA states resembled the NICs not only in their decisions to continue previous development strategies in the wake of the price explosion of 1973–74 but also in their use of debt as a way to finance continued expansion. And like debtor states among the NICs, CMEA states were forced to implement policies of austerity following the second round of international economic shocks at the turn of the decade.

Significantly, too, the decision to borrow heavily from Western sources in the mid-1970s was a discretionary political act as much on the part of CMEA states as among Third World NICs, and there were exceptions to the rule (Czechoslovakia in Eastern Europe, Taiwan and Singapore among the NICs) everywhere. And although austerity came sooner to Eastern Europe, it was due less to the structural characteristics of its economies or the greater foresight of its leaders than to exogenous factors: namely, the Polish events caused international capital markets to close significantly earlier to East European borrowers (even including Yugoslavia) than to states outside the region.

At the same time, however, although their unique state structures did not prevent CMEA states from participating in the expansion-austerity cycle of the 1970s and 1980s, they did make the causes, consequences, and the experience of expansion and austerity qualitatively different inside and outside the CMEA—both politically and economically. Such qualitative differences emerge even if we compare the experiences of a nominally socialist NIC such as Yugoslavia with nominally reformed CMEA states such as Hungary and Poland during the period in question.

In Yugoslavia socialism was an integral part of a strategy for building an autonomous nation-state,[3] and Yugoslav leaders rejected at an early date the politically penetrated sovereignty that membership in the Soviet bloc entailed. Although expulsion from the socialist camp left Yugoslavia exposed to international fluctuations over which it had little control, the country was subsequently able to take advantage of opportunities provided by both East and West. One such opportunity, access to aid and loans from Western sources, caused Yugoslav postwar borrowing practices to evolve quite differently from those of its CMEA counterparts. In CMEA states foreign trade was a residual activity, and hard-currency deficits traditionally served as a stopgap means of covering temporary export shortfalls. Borrowing from Western sources to finance technology transfers began only in the 1970s; in his analysis of the Polish case, Poznański describes just how radical a departure from previous practices the use of Western capital was. In Yugoslavia, however, the use of external resources for purposes of domestic development had always played a role in its industrialization strategy. Indeed, as Woodward points out, the debts Yugoslavia incurred in the 1970s marked a quantitative but not a qualitative change in traditional borrowing patterns. Thus, differences in state structures meant that the possibilities and problems which Yugoslavia encountered in the international system differed considerably from those facing CMEA states.

Domestically, creating an autonomous nation-state meant forming a political community that included all Yugoslav citizens rather than one confined to the members of a Leninist party. Decentralization of state authority and economic activity facilitated the task of molding the nation-state to reflect the aspirations and acquire the loyalties of a heterogeneous, parochial, and conflict-prone population. Citizen loyalties could form in the course of involvement in new state institutions: the more people worked in self-managed firms, sent their children to public schools, and received medical care from socialized hospitals, the more the nation-state in which these institutions were embedded would become a part of their daily life. At the same time, since claims of the larger national community—whether for higher wages,

3. By "nation-state" or "state," I mean what is called in Yugoslavia the "socio-political community" (*društveno-političkā zajednica*). I do not mean *država*, which in this analysis corresponds to my use of the term "state administration." I use the term "nation-state" to mean the form sovereign politico-territorial organization tends to take in the 20th century (as opposed, for example, to empires or city-states); a nation-state can thus comprise several distinct nationalities, all of which carry passports bearing the name of a single national government. In addition, when I use the term "state organization" or "institution," I mean any public body established under law. State organizations in Yugoslavia are normally "self-managed" in one way or another (the major exception is the armed forces), although their functions differ. Some are directly engaged in economic or productive activity: these are "enterprises." Others perform regulatory functions (local, republic, and national governments). A third type supplies social services (schools, hospitals, etc.), while still others are largely concerned with financial transactions (banks). All, however, are public bodies and thus state institutions. The mass organizations (such as the trade unions or even the LCY), in contrast, are secondary associations whose purposes are self-defined rather than legally prescribed and whose membership is voluntary rather than legally regulated.

instruction in the native tongue, or vaccination against polio—were made through participation in state institutions, differentiation between state and economy was rather low.

Politically, one consequence of high decentralization and low differentiation was that state and economic organizations in Yugoslavia were endowed with autonomy and real power in addition to legal authority. Unlike, say, Hungarian enterprise directors, Yugoslav managers had real constituencies in the firms which they could mobilize through the workers' councils that looked to them for leadership. Such constituencies could be used to make demands on other state organizations, resist regulations they imposed, and influence the League of Communist's (LCY's) own definition of priorities. Similar possibilities were available to local governments and other institutions as the web of self-management extended itself throughout the country. Hence bargaining among leaders with their own political resources and distinct constituencies became the modus operandi of Yugoslav political life. In contrast, the appearance of such a pattern of political interaction in Poland precipitated the collapse of the political system itself.

Although the activities of state/economic organizations could reflect the preferences of their specific constituencies, it was the LCY's task selectively to articulate and mobilize these preferences. The influence it retained over the election of leaders in state and mass organizations allowed it both to mediate conflicting demands and to prevent "antisocialist" claims from being voiced in the first place. Yet because the state/economic organizations it was supposed to influence had their own autonomous power bases, the party's role came increasingly to consist of aggregating and articulating the claims such organizations put forth. Not surprisingly, competition for resources among nonparty institutions—much of it organized on a regional basis— reproduced itself as increased division within the LCY, making it extremely difficult for either higher party or government bodies to arrive at a uniform and coherent policy stance. Moreover, power was hardly the collective monopoly of a Leninist party, as in Hungary; rather, it was scattered among a panoply of state institutions and mass organizations with conflicting interests which the LCY had to "convince" to follow its lead. Failure to do so—an outcome virtually inconceivable in Hungary but frequent in Yugoslavia— could severely compromise policy implementation. And precisely because its ability to make and enforce global policy was so much weaker than that of the Hungarian party, the LCY's reliance on short-term, Leninist campaign tactics was correspondingly greater.

Economically, the immediate consequence of decentralization was to make economic actors in Yugoslavia far more sensitive to demand than were their counterparts in the CMEA. Whereas Hungarian and Polish firms typically competed for supplies, Yugoslav firms competed for markets. Hence both Yugoslav "protectionism" and methods of macroeconomic management were always closer to their Latin American variants than to those of CMEA states, and especially so after 1965. Yet low differentiation between state and economy not only made those methods less effective, it also caused broader political and regulatory bodies to be extremely responsive to the particular claims and requirements of microeconomic actors. Thus, where CMEA states deployed physical import controls to counter the expansion drives of firms hungry for inputs regardless of their costs, in Yugoslavia barriers to foreign and internal trade were a response to the pressures of enterprises for protection on the domestic market as well as a response to balance-of-payments difficulties.

Meanwhile, the lack of differentiation between state and economy endowed both economic organizations (e.g., enterprises and banks) and political institutions with an expansion drive every bit as strong as that of their CMEA counterparts. Yet the lack of centralization in the Yugoslav state and economy made the politico-economic consequences of low differentiation rather different. In Hungary "responsibility" for large, monopolistic enterprises gave political leaders greater influence in determining central priorities while subjecting firms to increased central and administrative control. In Yugoslavia, however, enterprises and regional governments were political powers in their own right, and expanding their resource base increased their ability to resist external controls—be they from the national government or market forces—in order to pursue their own purposes. Hence, whereas the robust growth of the 1970s created centralizing pressures in CMEA economies, in Yugoslavia economic expansion increased tendencies toward fragmentation without enlarging the ability of the market to order them.

Predictably, Yugoslav adjustment to international economic disturbances in both the 1970s and the 1980s was shaped by the determination of elites in political and economic organizations to shield constituencies from their negative effects. Borrowing afforded one means of protection in the 1970s, but again, thanks to Yugoslavia's distinctive state structure, both its economic uses and political functions were quite different from those within the CMEA. In Yugoslavia borrowing was a way to fuel demand to avoid both a recesssion and the "tax" that higher world energy prices would otherwise have imposed. In the CMEA relatively less expensive Soviet energy supplies initially muted the tax of higher world prices, and borrowing was a means to guarantee the supplies needed for a politically determined industrial expansion. Politically, in Yugoslavia the inflow of resources from abroad helped facilitate the logrolling and pork-barrel practices necessary to maintain a political consensus in which, to use Woodward's characterization, even losers receive compensation. In Hungary the decision to employ external resources to accelerate investment and embark on projects that were uneconomical in light of the price shocks of 1973 was a factor enabling antimarket forces within the Hungarian party to oust their reformist opponents from key leadership positions.

Significantly, much of the debt Yugoslavia accumulated in the 1970s was not even incurred by the national government but, rather, by enterprises (or, after 1974, a vast number of financially independent enterprise divisions) and regional banks acting on their own initiative. Thus, it reinforced the "pluralism of self-managing interests" that the 1974 Constitution institutionalized, increasing the obstacles to formulating a uniform national economic policy and decreasing the ability of central authorities to exert financial (and even political) discipline on the provinces. In Hungary, in contrast, firms could not even control their own hard-currency earnings much less independently· borrow abroad, and the "policies of illusion" fueled by capital imports led to such increased central intervention in enterprise decisions and concentration among the firms that the 1968 reform was, for the most part, reversed in all but principle by 1979.

The central governments in Yugoslavia and Hungary were thus in very different positions at the time of the second oil-price shock and the rapid rise in interest rates that occurred after 1980. However, both countries (and after 1982, even Poland to some extent) chose to combine austerity with institutional reform and direct reforms toward modifying the one structural feature they shared: the lack of differentiation between state and economy. Thus, in both Hungary and Yugoslavia reform consisted of attempts to impose hard budget constraints on economic actors. Yet differences in other dimensions of state structure meant that the means of achieving reform and the consequences of implementing it were as different as the obstacles confronting reform in each state.

For example, in Hungary imposing hard budget constraints meant decentralizing economic activity: breaking up large firms, giving economic units more autonomy over their own decisions, deconcentrating authority in the National Bank, widening the scope of the private sector. In Yugoslavia, in contrast, efforts to impose financial discipline on economic units meant transferring regulatory authority from regional units to the federal government, recentralizing the banking system, and diminishing the ability of enterprise divisions to pursue their own objectives.

Likewise, both the economic and political obstacles to reform in Hungary and Yugoslavia differed, internationally as well as domestically. For example, Hungarian ties to the CMEA in many ways militated against forcing enterprises to make decisions solely in response to international market conditions; similarly, balance-of-payments problems stood in the way of the import liberalization that could counteract the highly monopolistic domestic industrial structure. In Yugoslavia it was not a need to straddle two very different markets that prevented the center from imposing uniform market conditions on enterprises but the resistance of regional elites whose assent was required to implement central decisions. And, insofar as administratively imposed import quotas could reflect the political balance of forces between regions and industries and a flexible exchange rate would not, Yugoslavia resisted using the latter as an import control device until the International Monetary

Fund (IMF) forced its adoption. Significantly, physical import controls have persisted in Hungary even after the reforms of the 1980s—but in Hungary's case their longevity has been a result not of regional resistance but of the continued lack of price sensitivity among economic actors.

Finally, the consequences of austerity were very different in Hungary and Yugoslavia, and only in part because the debt burden was relatively heavier in the latter. Again, Yugoslavia looked much more like other Third World NICs than like the rest of Eastern Europe. In Hungary and most other CMEA states real income levels remained relatively constant, no significant unemployment resulted, and prices moved upward only as a result of explicit central decisions. In Yugoslavia austerity was accompanied by a significant drop in the standard of living, rapid inflation, a radical currency devaluation, and deterioration of an already serious unemployment situation. Moreover, whereas the costs of austerity were borne relatively equally by regions and industries in Hungary, quite the contrary was the case in Yugoslavia; there prices played a far more active role in defining winners and losers. Finally, although austerity in Poland and (at least in principle) in Hungary could be accompanied by reorienting trade eastward, had Yugoslavia chosen to become a full participant in the CMEA, the ensuing transformation of the structure of the economy would have been similar in scale to the one CMEA states would have had to make to pursue export-oriented development.

Political processes inside the CMEA and among the NICs

If our comparison of the economic phenomenon of "import substitution" shows its actual content to be different in the CMEA and Latin America thanks to the distinctive state structures within which it appeared, our analysis of Yugoslavia and Hungary indicates that a political process uniformly labeled "collective leadership" also played itself out differently, depending on the structure of the state and economy surrounding it. Collective leadership in Hungary was based on a distinct separation of political power and legal authority; in Yugoslavia it was founded on their fusion. In Hungary "collectivizing" political power in the party gave individual leaders a disincentive to mobilize a constituency, especially a nonparty one. In Yugoslavia the ability of leaders to accumulate and control their own political resources meant that to maintain influence on collective decision-making bodies in party and state alike, leaders had to claim to speak for a specific (and preferably regional) interest. In Hungary political support from high levels brought responsibility for economic activity; in Yugoslavia grass-roots organizations and elites could capture economic resources and translate them into increased political clout in central policy-making bodies. Thus, leaders in Hungary, none of whom had an individual power base, had an incentive to reach a consensus based on the ability of a *primus inter pares* to synthesize conflicting preferences and to see that policy implementation reflected that stance. In

Yugoslavia, in contrast, decisions could be reached only after elaborate bargaining among leaders, each of whom had an incentive to veto a consensus or jeopardize the implementation of decisions that did not take adequate account of his or her particular claims or constituency.

Hence state structures in the CMEA and the NICs not only helped define the problems that reached their respective political agendas and the possibilities for resolving them; they also affected the kind and potential of the political resources on which elites could draw in forwarding alternative solutions to them. As a result, not only were the politics of authoritarianism— whether rule by the Few or by the One—different inside the CMEA and among the NICs, but the factors affecting the survival of heavily indebted authoritarian regimes in each group differed as well.

Among the NICs, Brazil on the one hand and Mexico and Yugoslavia on the other all had varieties of authoritarian rule in the 1970s, and all experienced serious debt problems in the 1980s. In Brazil, however, "bureaucratic authoritarianism" saw technocratic elites in the military and the state administration coercively exclude popular forces from political life in order radically to restructure traditional economic sectors and to pursue policies of "modern," "efficient" growth in heavier, more advanced economic branches. In Mexico and Yugoslavia, in contrast, a distinctly populist orientation among ruling elites accompanied the absence of competitive politics and elimination of the opposition's ability to challenge the dominant political party.

Hence, in Mexico and Yugoslavia borrowing abroad allowed leaders to utilize public expenditures to redistribute income and insulate the domestic population from international inflation. In Brazil debt served to expand the importance of "incumbents of technocratic roles" in the state and economy by building a network of large public and mixed-ownership enterprises in more technologically advanced sectors of the economy, regardless of distributionary consequences.[4] In effect, where government economic policy under bureaucratic authoritarianism grew out of the absence of ties between politico-economic elites and nontechnocratic sectors of the population, in the populist NICs economic policy not only grew out of the presence of such links but itself served as a means of forging them.

In Brazil the need to make economic choices between "inefficient," tra-

---

4. According to Guillermo O'Donnell, technocratic elites are those occupying "positions in a social structure which require applications of modern technology as an important part of their daily routine. . . . This category is constituted by individuals applying modern technology, and not by those concerned mainly with the expansion of scientific technological knowledge." See O'Donnell, *Modernization and Bureaucratic Authoritarianism* (Berkeley: Institute of International Studies, University of California, 1979), p. 30. Furthermore, leaders of organizations of wage and salary earners and civilian political leaders in general are not "incumbents of technocratic roles: their activities do not usually require extensive education and routine application of modern technology. Technocratic roles . . . develop around the managing of such activities as non-artisan industry, planning, government, the military, and communications and control." Ibid., p. 31.

ditional sectors and the new, "efficient," technocratic industries solidified a coalition of military elites and economic planners in the state administration, reinforcing the vision of social order they shared with each other and with foreign "incumbents of technocratic roles" based in corporate centers abroad. The arrival of austerity and the need to reorient economic activity toward the highly competitive conditions of the international marketplace, however, split the ruling coalition. That is, once the choices were among the "efficient" industries themselves, dissent arose within the ruling group over who would bear the costs. Reluctance on the part of external economic allies to pick up the tab and the absence of domestic political reserves upon which members of the elite could draw to force them to do so complicated the situation.

Splits in the ruling coalition and politicization of bureaucratic elites in Brazil thus provided an opening for political leaders with a very different vision of political order. Their bases of appeal were several: an elected government might drive a harder bargain with foreign creditors, because it was less dependent on them to stay in power and could more credibly threaten to mobilize popular forces against them; in addition, it could appeal to advanced capitalist countries to open their markets to Brazilian goods on the basis of the pluralist sympathies leaders in those states traditionally entertained. Thus, if isolation from popular forces was a source of strength for bureaucratic-authoritarian elites in times of prosperity, it proved an Achilles' heel in times of severe austerity.

In Mexico and Yugoslavia, in contrast, leaders confronting the international challenges of the 1980s already had substantial bases of domestic support on which they could rely. Indeed, in Yugoslavia the very loyalty that a state-building strategy based on import substitution in the economy had created initially allowed leaders to enlist popular support for adaptation to the requirements of foreign banks and external actors—despite the absence of a charismatic leader to help the process along. And in Mexico the political fallout from the heavy burden of austerity which the regime imposed on the population was channeled into an anticorruption campaign, allowing changes in leading personnel to accomplish what only a change in the regime could do in Brazil. Thus, although Yugoslav and Mexican development strategies were unable to create an economy able to withstand or easily adapt to international economic shocks, they were remarkably efficacious in producing a political system that could.

Significantly, the relationship between authoritarianism, populist economic policies, debt, and regime stability in CMEA states was exactly the reverse of that in the NICs. In Hungary, East Germany, and Romania, highly centralized Leninist parties (or their single leaders) successfully monopolized the means of collective action, preventing the formation of any independent group or popular interest. In these cases, expansion was a product of the aspirations of dominant factions (or, in the Romanian case, of a single individual) in the ruling elite rather than a way of increasing the power of the population over economic life. As we saw in the Hungarian case, the labor shortages that rapid growth created gave party leaders, not workers, more discretion over the allocation of labor while awarding central planners, not independent trade unions, greater control over its price. Nor was expansion primarily a device for eliciting support from the domestic population; yet to the degree expansion involved increased participation in CMEA projects, it served to firm up foreign (i.e., Soviet) support for the regimes in question. Continuation of the political status quo thus accompanied the arrival of austerity. On the one hand, the need for severe measures reinforced the ability of the hegemonic party (or individual) to reorient economic life in line with its own priorities. On the other, the economic difficulties that such a reorientation inevitably entailed solidified the Soviet Union's political commitment to stand by its East European allies. Like the populist NICs, the authoritarian states in the CMEA in which rule by the One or the Few had barred the organization of independent, popular groups could greet the 1980s with changes in economic priorities and personnel but not with systemic convulsions.

Poland, however, was different. There Gierek's import-led development strategy of the 1970s was, in a very real sense, a CMEA variant on the kind of populism Yugoslavia and Mexico practiced. In Poland resources were used to buy support from strategic groups with their own distinct interests, both inside and outside the Polish party itself. Nevertheless, within the context of a political structure that lacked mechanisms for mediating conflicting claims, populism did less to integrate groups into the political system than to build up potential sources of regime opposition. Thus, although populism was often a source of political strength in the NICs, in Poland it played a pivotal role in causing Gierek's downfall. In effect, once austerity deprived the regime of resources with which to purchase support, previously supportive groups quickly turned hostile. And where pluralizing elites in Brazil could expect foreign support from Western governments, in Poland support from the Soviet Union came only with the restoration of nonpopulist, exclusive authoritarianism.

Authoritarianism based on exclusion collapsed under the pressures of indebtedness and austerity in many NICs. It survived, however, with only minor modifications in the CMEA; and where populist policies cemented regime support that could be drawn upon in a period of economic difficulty in the NICs, they brought on a crisis of legitimacy in the CMEA. Again, this pattern suggests that politically as well as economically, state structures were different in kind as well as degree inside and outside the CMEA, making the dynamics of political choice and the meaning of economic strategy different in each.[5]

5. Hence it is hardly surprising that attempts to apply models of policy-making processes drawn from Western states proved highly distorting in the context of CMEA politics. See Comisso, "Introduction," pp. 203–6.

2. Structure and strategy outside the CMEA

State structure thus created very different possibilities for economic policy choices inside and outside the CMEA. No state outside the CMEA faced the constraints of politically penetrated sovereignty that membership in the socialist alliance placed on its ability to compete in the larger international system. No state outside the CMEA confronted the kind of hierarchical subordination between state authorities and economic actors that provided the latter with disincentives to respond to the horizontal stimuli of the market. No state outside the CMEA had such elaborate networks of checks and controls on enterprise initiative, and no state outside the CMEA was governed by a hegemonic, centralized Leninist party able to define and evaluate economic performance in terms of its own goals rather than by standard microeconomic efficiency indicators.

Consequently, both microeconomic and macroeconomic agents in the NICs felt international economic disturbances as price changes rather than as shortage tensions. Managing shortages was the key problem political leaders in CMEA states confronted; determining the degree to which and the way in which international price shocks would be transmitted to the domestic economy was the central concern of Third World NICs. And while policy makers in Eastern Europe were preoccupied with assigning and coordinating tasks among microeconomic units, their counterparts in the NICs faced the task of anticipating economic and political responses of microlevel actors to fiscal and monetary measures.

Nevertheless, state structure was as much an underdetermining factor in strategy choices in the NICs as it was in Eastern Europe. On the one hand, NICs with very different state structures chose rather similar strategies; on the other, states with similar structures could opt for highly contrasting strategies. As in the CMEA, tools and materials in the NICs made strategy choices possible, but as in Eastern Europe, tools and materials alone did not construct a strategy. Rather, how political leaders used the possibilities and political resources that state structures created depended on the vision of social order they propounded and on the degree to which international economic changes could be employed to capture power to pursue it. Thus, although the substance of structure and strategy in the NICs was different in kind from its CMEA variants, the relationship between the two was quite similar.

For example, states in both the Mediterranean Basin and in East Asia sought to integrate domestic economic activities into a wider international marketplace in the 1970s and 1980s; nevertheless, the state structures they employed for such efforts were very different.

In southern Europe international economic shocks created opportunities for pluralistic political elites to accelerate political changes already underway. As Diamandouros suggests, it was not the oil-price shocks but the political disintegration of *ancien regimes*—be it from Franco's death in Spain, the inability of an unpopular junta to protect national interests on Cyprus in Greece, or a long and debilitating colonial war in Portugal—that provided the occasion for a regime change. At the same time, however, the way in which elected, civilian elites responded to economic difficulties was shaped by their determination to avoid a return to the authoritarianism of the past.

Their strategy was typically to postpone the day of reckoning with higher energy prices while building up a network of domestic support that would eventually provide tools for nonauthoritarian modes of economic management. It was combined with a strong commitment to pursuing trade policies that both kept domestic markets open to foreign competition and encouraged domestic producers to seek European markets for their goods.

Two factors were particularly critical in the ability of pluralist elites to manage the difficult political and economic transition. First, domestic groups were well aware that their own political influence and organizational autonomy were contingent on a permanent regime change. Consequently, it was in the interest of organized groups to support newly elected leaders, even when specific policies were not to their liking; strong resistance, in effect, might simply reopen the door to an authoritarian solution that would wipe out the substantial political gains that organizations and groups had already made. In Spain, for example, the societal corporatist arrangements that evolved by the 1980s were a reaction to vulnerability as much to a domestic challenge as to an international one. And in Greece, right-wing opposition to Papandreou's left-wing leanings was more likely to fragment than to unite around a return to an old regime no one wanted.

Second, the years political leaders committed to pluralism had spent in exile had allowed them to forge strong ties to parties and leaders in West European states. They thus had international support as well. On the one hand, such support proved extremely helpful when it came to drawing on the financial reserves of the IMF and Western banks to help mitigate the impact of higher energy costs on the domestic economy. On the other, pluralizing elites could hold out the promise of membership in the European Economic Community (EEC) to constituencies anxious to join for political and economic reasons. Not only was EEC membership an offer authoritarian elites could hardly make, but it was a promise very much in the interest of more liberal counterelites to redeem, as it strengthened both their foreign and domestic support bases. Accordingly, it was very much in their political interest to choose economic policies, adjustment strategies, and foreign political alignments that would facilitate EEC entrance, even when such choices meant imposing sacrifices on the parts of their constituencies. At the same time, adroit manipulation of the threat from the right in negotiations with regional and transnational bodies allowed such leaders to limit the extent of the sacrifices. Hence in the Mediterranean Basin, the domestic purposes embraced by pluralizing elites and the resources available for capturing power converged to make structural change in the state and an open development strategy highly desirable and complementary political choices.

In East Asia, however, pursuing an outward-oriented economic strategy reinforced the hold of authoritarian elites on state power, whether it took the form of a military-bureaucratic authoritarianism, as in South Korea, or that of a more benign paternalism, as in Taiwan or Singapore. Hence, although the East Asian NICs shared a development strategy based on openness to the international economy and support for the attempts of private and public industries to compete on the markets of more advanced capitalist states with the Mediterranean Basin, both the state structure and the political process that led to such a choice were very different.

As we have seen, it was not the structure of centralized and authoritarian rule itself but rather the determination of ruling elites to preserve it that created export-led development in East Asia. Consequently, their domestic allies were not the autonomously organized popular groups on which pluralizing elites in the Mediterranean Basin relied, but economic technocrats in the state administration and the private business community. Significantly, neither group aspired to share power with ruling elites based in authoritarian parties, military machines, or colonial administrations. On the contrary, as Johnson notes, they were happy to leave government to the politicians and the military as long as political pressures were kept out of the economizing process.

Further, elites based in private and public economic organizations shared an important community of interest with political leaders, and one that was distinctly different from the community of interest elites in southern Europe forged with a much broader constituency. If political elites in East Asia regarded economic development as vital for their ability to maintain domestic order and international security, economic leaders there saw political stability as a necessary condition of economic growth. For both, keeping the cost of labor low and its suppliers docile and disciplined was vital for their objectives.

In contrast to the Mediterranean Basin, where newly elected leaders seriously considered the possibility of withdrawing from the Atlantic alliance, in East Asia ruling coalitions were strongly anticommunist and placed a premium on maintaining close ties with the United States, Britain, and Japan. None of their members placed a particularly high value on integrating popular elements into the political system. Indeed, it was precisely the exclusion of broader social forces from government which allowed elites to pursue an economic strategy that relied on inexpensive and disciplined labor to adjust to the burdens entailed in meeting the opportunities and demands of foreign markets.

It was in this context that the oil shocks of 1973 occurred, and in an area totally dependent on imported energy, they were no small shock indeed. Predictably, the response was to intensify the export drive to cover skyrocketing import costs, a response that both solidified the narrow alliance on which export-led development was based and strengthened its hold on political power. The broader population had few economic or political means to protest any undesirable distributionary consequences this strategy entailed, and indeed, the energy crisis provided an opportunity for mass organizations controlled by the ruling coalition to launch drives for greater efforts to counter international hardship.

Whereas Singapore and Taiwan used deflationary policies rather than borrowing to adjust to the oil shocks, Korea used the opportunities provided by its more central position in the Pacific defense network and the generous credit markets prevalent at that time, to leap into large, technologically advanced industries like petrochemicals, steel, and shipbuilding. Although the development of such industries made the arrival of austerity in the 1980s problematic in Korea, the same political conditions that had originally produced export-led development also made adapting to austerity politically manageable.

Unlike the European situation, political oppositions in East Asia lacked strong ties to political leaders in the United States, Britain, or Japan. They could scarcely offer a better "deal" than the current government was getting from external political and economic actors, and to the degree they raised questions about the role of their states in the American defense effort, the deal might have been considerably worse. Government opponents could hardly provide domestic business with access to wider markets than it already enjoyed, while their promises to expand the participation of popular elements in government meant jeopardizing the politically insulated position business currently claimed. Nor was opposition influence able to penetrate state corporatist mass organizations, and the presence of a significant refugee element in the population dimmed the attractiveness of leftist appeals. In short, if alliances between an economically powerful but politically passive business sector and elites without commitments to domestic groups made export-led development possible in East Asia, they also worked to obstruct political alternatives to the ruling coalition behind it.

Not only did NICs with highly divergent state structures and political processes make relatively similar strategy choices, but states that began with very similar domestic structures and political processes often chose extremely distinctive development strategies. Again, this pattern suggests that divergencies in foreign economic strategy were not due simply to divergencies in domestic structures but to differences in the purposes that elites embraced and in their ability to capture power to pursue them.

For example, the bureaucratic-authoritarian regimes of Latin America shared structural similarities with each other as well as with the East Asian NICs. In all, technocratic elites in highly centralized states with mixed economies coercively excluded popular forces from the political arena in order to pursue a social vision based on "growth in GNP; growth in the efficient sectors of the economy, where most of these [technocratic] elites are located;

low level of social unrest . . . ; low rate of inflation; favorable external balance of payments and movement of international exchange."[6]

Nevertheless, if exclusion of popular forces was the norm, strategy varied, reflecting the vision of social order that rulers embraced and the means they were prepared to take to pursue it. Elite objectives were thus critical to the distinction Fishlow makes between "system-changing" and "system-preserving" authoritarianism. In Chile and Argentina elites were determined to create an open and competitive economy in which the invisible hand of the market would replace the politico-administrative arm of the state. Such a commitment departed radically from previous development strategies. Politically, it called for establishing a direct relationship between a laissez-faire state and the individual citizen, unmediated by the plethora of secondary associations that had represented group interests in previous regimes. Not only were labor unions and political parties repressed, but middle-class, professional, and business associations were also deprived of their earlier regulatory and representative functions. As a result, a narrow alliance of military elites and economic experts closely tied to domestic and international financial institutions could free themselves from domestic political constraints to pursue a monetarist version of capitalist development.[7] If it was a policy commitment favored in financial circles abroad, it produced disaster for industry at home.

Economically, monetarism prescribed opening the economy to international competition by eliminating tariff barriers and allowing exchange rates to fluctuate. Unlike the East Asian NICs, however, neither Chile nor Argentina accompanied openness to the international economy with an active, state-led industrial policy. On the contrary, both countries sought to divest the state of the substantial regulatory role it had traditionally played by cutting social welfare expenditures, discontinuing or sharply limiting direct state investment, and in many areas auctioning off state-owned industries to private bidders. Defense, of course, remained a legitimate function of a laissez-faire state and critical to the ability of elites to pursue the policies consistent with maintaining it. Hence military demands for arms, personnel, and salaries could be satisfied within the framework of the basic philosophy.

Meanwhile, inflation became the central concern of economic policy, replacing the earlier emphasis on economic growth. Politically, the new ruling coalitions fought inflation by eliminating the groups whose claims on the state elites held responsible for substantial government deficits in the past. Economically, anti-inflation measures consisted of restricting the money supply and raising interest rates. Thus, at precisely the moment domestic industry was expected to meet increased competition from abroad, it found capital

6. O'Donnell, *Modernization*, p. 102.
7. See David Pion-Berlin, "Ideas as Predictors: A Comparative Study of Coercion in Peru and Argentina" (Ph.D. diss., School of International Studies, University of Denver, 1984).

extremely scarce and expensive at home. Nor did multinational corporations (MNCs) have much cause to open new plants. On the one hand, they no longer needed to jump tariff barriers to reach the domestic market; on the other, a laissez-faire state unwilling to make compromises with partial interests was as unresponsive to their particularistic demands as to the pleas of domestic business.

Not surprisingly, a flood of imports and a flight of capital abroad accompanied monetarism in Chile and Argentina. The oil-price shocks exacerbated the situation, producing new deflationary monetary measures that deterred all investment, including investment for export purposes. Borrowing thus became the way of covering disequilibria in the balance of payments. Meanwhile, military expenditures continued to rise, reflecting the fact that the ruling coalition's monetarist adjustment made coercive exclusion of groups a continued political necessity. In Chile such "investments" continue to bring political payoffs to a military government determined to resist civilian incursions on its prerogatives. But where the military's ability to use coercion was jeopardized—as in Argentina following the Falklands fiasco—military rule and monetarism fell together.

In Brazil the situation unfolded very differently, despite the very similar state structure from which it started. There, technocratic elites were committed to growth and modernization and not to stable prices per se. If the political consequences of this strategy entailed excluding popular forces from politics, it did not call for the abolition of secondary associations altogether. On the contrary, it merely prescribed their regulation and control through an elaborate network of regime-controlled corporatist organizations.[8]

In the economy the state neither surrendered its role as an active force in industrial development nor simply opened the domestic market to international competition. Rather, the "old" protectionism shielding high-cost, labor-intensive sectors gave way to a new one designed to foster the growth of "efficient" economic sectors—namely, those composed of highly capital-intensive firms that employed relatively advanced technology and highly skilled labor, a significant share of whose capital was owned by MNCs based abroad. These MNCs also controlled the rate and choice of the technology they chose to transfer to Latin American affiliates. The "new" protectionism was not unintentional: both the military's ability to maintain order and economic technocrats' commitment to supply specific firms with privileged access to a large domestic market were precisely what made Brazil such an attractive site for foreign investment. Such firms could have considerable export potential as well, to the degree their product specializations fit into a broader multinational strategy in which the output of Latin American

8. See Philippe Schmitter, "The 'Portugalization' of Brazil?" in Alfred Stepan, ed., *Authoritarian Brazil* (New Haven: Yale University Press, 1973), pp. 179–233.

subsidiaries did not compete with the more advanced products or on the regional markets that MNCs reserved for other branch operations.[9]

The very success of Brazil's "efficient," domestically oriented development strategy made accelerating it with the increased availability of capital in 1974 highly appealing to technocratic elites—especially since the alternative was slowing down the rate of growth in favored sectors. Borrowing was heavy and stopped only when capital markets closed to Latin America as a whole in 1982. Like Korea, Brazil plowed much of the capital into industries— including the development of off-shore oil reserves—that found themselves hard hit when international markets contracted just at the time the loans incurred to create them came due. Unlike Korea, however, many of the new Brazilian industries had been built to satisfy domestic demand and substitute for the imports that tariff walls and currency controls had made artificially expensive. Efforts to reorient them to export markets began rather late and were hampered both by the structural rigidities that continued to plague the state firms and by the fact that MNCs often found it more profitable to contract their Brazilian facilities altogether than to put them in competition with MNC-controlled operations based in other countries.

Hence, whereas intensified export efforts solidified ruling coalitions in East Asia, the arrival of austerity and the need to reorient industrial activity outward caused them to split in Brazil. The result, as we have seen, was to accelerate opening the political stage to leaders with a very different vision of social order, leaders who often arose out of the very corporatist mass organizations and regional industrial centers that the regime itself had so diligently created. Although Argentina's transition to civilian rule was preceded by a crisis that revealed the military's inability to deploy force effectively, significantly, such was not the case in Brazil. There, the problem was not so much the junta's inability to use coercion but the fact that coercion itself could not restore dynamic growth. The prime barrier to growth was the international credit situation, a problem civilian elites in Brazil promised to deal with far more effectively. Again the Brazilian situation contrasted with that in Argentina, where the return of elected government coincided with a repudiation of the very monetarist policies that international financial organizations were now requiring of all debtor states. Ironically, although the ability and willingness of civilian elites to make commitments to domestic groups may well impede formulation of a strategy that can satisfy domestic constituencies and international creditors in the 1980s in Argentina, such characteristics may facilitate adjustment to austerity in Brazil.

Similar state structures thus accommodated a great variety of development strategies and economic policies not only in Eastern Europe but also in East Asia and Latin America. Although Brazil, Chile, and Argentina certainly had the possibility of selecting export-oriented development models similar

9. See Peter Evans, *Dependent Development* (Princeton: Princeton University Press, 1979).

to those in East Asia, ruling coalitions chose to capitalize on domestic and international politico-economic power configurations in ways that led to very different policy choices. Moreover, in cases such as Chile's and, to a lesser degree, Argentina's, the decision to replace the previous development strategy with monetarist policies led to major changes in state structure itself: not only was the state sharply differentiated from the economy, but the coalition between domestic business and government was abruptly and one-sidedly terminated.

Both within the CMEA and among the NICs, then, economic strategy was certainly related to state structure, but it hardly followed it. Reflecting nation-specific connections between historically contingent exigencies of power and purpose fought out in political processes, strategic policy choices proved capable of both altering state structures and reproducing them. Although institutional arrangements provide means for implementing policies and mechanisms for making them, institutions do not act by themselves in making the choices; although they order political incentives and resources, they cannot mobilize them. Politics, inside the CMEA and outside it, reflect our freedom and capacity to make collective choices, not the forces of necessity prescribing them for us. Politics are a sphere of strategic action, not of predetermined behavior, and even socialism turns out to be much more the governing of men than the administration of things. Political processes clearly have their rules and their limits, yet they are also capable of producing outcomes that are creative, unpredictable, and often extraordinarily open.

Library of Congress Cataloging-in-Publication Data

Power, purpose, and collective choice.

  (Cornell studies in political economy)
  Published also as v. 40, no. 2 of the journal International organization.
  1. Communist countries—Economic policy. 2. Communist countries—Economic
conditions. 3. Europe, Eastern—Economic conditions—1945–   . I. Comisso, Ellen
Turkish. II.Tyson, Laura D'Andrea, 1947–   . III. Series.
HC704.P666   1986   338.947   86-47639
ISBN 0-8014-1981-6 (alk. paper)
ISBN 0-8014-9435-4 (pbk. : alk. paper)